Construction Materials

Their nature and behaviour

Edited by

J.M. Illston

Consultant and Professor Emeritus,
University of Hertfordshire

London · Glasgow · New York · Tokyo · Melbourne · Madras

Published by E & FN Spon, an imprint of Chapman & Hall, 2–6 Boundary Row, London SE1 8HN

Chapman & Hall, 2–6 Boundary Row, London SE1 8HN, UK

Blackie Academic & Professional, Wester Cleddens Road, Bishopbriggs, Glasgow G64 2NZ, UK

Chapman & Hall Inc., One Penn Plaza, 41st Floor, New York NY10119, USA

Chapman & Hall Japan, Thomson Publishing Japan, Hirakawacho Nemoto Building, 6F, 1-7-11 Hirakawa-cho, Chiyoda-ku, Tokyo 102, Japan

Chapman & Hall Australia, Thomas Nelson Australia, 102 Dodds Street, South Melbourne, Victoria 3205, Australia

Chapman & Hall India, R. Seshadri, 32 Second Main Road, CIT East, Madras 600 035, India

First published as Concrete, Timber and Metals 1979
Reprinted 1981, 1987, 1990
Second edition 1994

Typeset in 10½/12½pt Sabon by Best-set Typesetter Ltd., Hong Kong

Printed in England by Clays Ltd, St Ives plc

ISBN 0 419 15470 1

A catalogue record for this book is available from the British Library

Library of Congress Cataloging-in-Publication data available

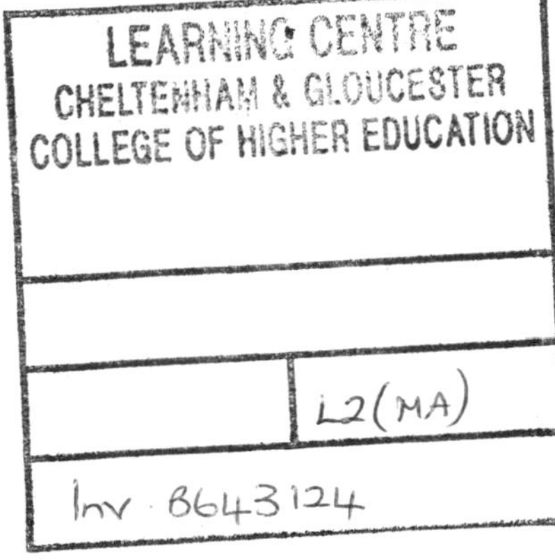

Printed on permanent acid-free text paper, manufactured in accordance with the proposed ANSI/NISO Z 39.48-199X and ANSI Z 39.48-1984

Contents

List of contributors xiii
Acknowledgements xvi
Preface J.M. Illston xvii

Part One Fundamentals W.D. Biggs 1
Introduction 3

1 **States of matter** 5
1.1 Fluids 5
1.2 Solids 8
1.3 Intermediate behaviour 11

2 **Energy** 14
2.1 Mixing 14
2.2 Entropy 15
2.3 Free energy 16

3 **Structure of the atom** 17
3.1 Ionic bonding 17
3.2 Covalent bonding 19
3.3 Metallic bonding 21
3.4 Van der Waals bonds 22

4 **Elasticity and plasticity** 25
4.1 Linear elasticity 25
4.2 Consequences of the theory 26
4.3 Long-range elasticity 27
4.4 Viscoelasticity 28
4.5 Plasticity 31

5 **Surfaces** 33
5.1 Surface energy 33
5.2 Water of crystallization 34
5.3 Wetting 34
5.4 Adhesives 35
5.5 Adsorption 37

6 Fracture 39
6.1 Theoretical strength 39
6.2 Microcrack theory 39
6.3 The Griffith criterion 40
6.4 Fracture mechanics 42
Reference 43

7 Electrical and thermal conductivity 44

Further reading 47

Part Two Metals and Alloys W.D. Biggs 49
Introduction 51

8 Physical metallurgy 53
8.1 Grain structure 53
8.2 Atomic structure of metals 53
8.3 Solutions and compounds 58

9 Mechanical properties of metals 59
9.1 Stress–strain behaviour 59
9.2 Tensile strength 60
9.3 Ductility 60
9.4 Plasticity 62
9.5 Dislocation energy 63
9.6 Strengthening of metals 63
9.7 Plastic design 66

10 Mechanical metallurgy 67
10.1 Castings 67
10.2 Hot working 67
10.3 Cold working 67
10.4 Joining 68

11 Oxidation and corrosion 70
11.1 Dry oxidation 70
11.2 Wet corrosion 70
11.3 Control of corrosion 73
11.4 Protection against corrosion 73

12 Metals, their differences and uses 76
12.1 The extraction of iron 76
12.2 Cast irons 76
12.3 Steel 77
12.4 Aluminium and alloys 81
12.5 Copper and alloys 83
12.6 Design for minimum weight 83

Further reading 85

Part Three Concrete P.L. Domone 87
Introduction 89

13 Constituent materials of concrete 91
- 13.1 Portland cements 91
- 13.2 Admixtures 103
- 13.3 Cement replacement materials 108
- 13.4 Aggregates 112
- 13.5 References 115

14 Fresh and early age properties of concrete 117
- 14.1 Fresh properties 117
- 14.2 Behaviour after placing 122
- 14.3 Strength gain and temperature effects 124
- 14.4 References 128

15 Deformation of concrete 129
- 15.1 Drying shrinkage 129
- 15.2 Carbonation shrinkage 137
- 15.3 Thermal expansion 139
- 15.4 Stress–strain behaviour 140
- 15.5 Creep 147
- 15.6 References 153

16 Strength and failure of concrete 155
- 16.1 Strength tests 156
- 16.2 Factors influencing strength 160
- 16.3 Cracking and fracture in concrete 163
- 16.4 Strength under multiaxial loading 165
- 16.5 References 167

17 Durability of concrete 169
- 17.1 Transport mechanisms through concrete 169
- 17.2 Measurements of flow constants for cement paste and concrete 172
- 17.3 Degradation of concrete 179
- 17.4 Durability of steel in concrete 187
- 17.5 Recommendations for durable concrete construction 192
- 17.6 References 194

Further reading 195

Part Four Bituminous Materials D.G. Bonner 197
Introduction 199

18 Structure 203
18.1 Constituents of bituminous materials 203
18.2 Bitumen 203
18.3 Types of bitumen 205
18.4 Aggregates 208
18.5 References 210

19 Viscosity and deformation 212
19.1 Viscosity and rheology of binders 212
19.2 Measurement of viscosity 213
19.3 Influence of temperature on viscosity 215
19.4 Resistance of bitumens to deformation 218
19.5 Determination of permanent deformation 219
19.6 Factors affecting permanent deformation of bituminous mixes 220
19.7 References 222

20 Strength and failure 223
20.1 The road structure 223
20.2 Modes of failure in a bituminous structure 223
20.3 Fatigue characteristics 226
20.4 References 230

21 Durability 231
21.1 Introduction 231
21.2 Ageing of bitumen 231
21.3 Permeability 233
21.4 Adhesion 234
21.5 References 239

22 Practice and processing 240
22.1 Bituminous mixtures 240
22.2 Recipe and designed mixes 244
22.3 Methods of production 248
22.4 References 249

Part Five Brickwork and Blockwork R.C. de Vekey 251
Introduction 253
Terminology 254

23 Materials 257
23.1 Materials used for manufacture of units and mortars 257
23.2 Other constituents and additives 261
23.3 Mortar 263

23.4 Fired clay bricks and blocks 266
23.5 Calcium silicate units 274
23.6 Concrete units 274
23.7 References 278

24 Masonry construction and forms **280**
24.1 Introduction 280
24.2 Mortar 280
24.3 Walls and other masonry forms 281
24.4 Bond 283
24.5 Specials 284
24.6 Joint style 285
24.7 Workmanship and accuracy 285
24.8 Appearance 286
24.9 References 288

25 Structural behaviour and movement of masonry **289**
25.1 Introduction 289
25.2 Compressive loading 290
25.3 Shear load in the bed plane 296
25.4 Flexure (bending) 298
25.5 Tension 299
25.6 Elastic modulus 300
25.7 Movement and creep of masonry materials 302
25.8 References 305

26 Durability and non-structural properties of masonry **306**
26.1 Introduction 306
26.2 Durability 306
26.3 Chemical attack 307
26.4 Erosion 309
26.5 Thermal conductivity 311
26.6 Rain resistance 312
26.7 Sound transmission 314
26.8 Fire resistance 314
26.9 References 314

Further reading **315**

Part Six Fibre Composites L. Hollaway, D. Hannant **317**
Introduction **319**

Section One Polymers and polymer composites L. Hollaway **321**

27 Polymer and fibre properties and manufacture **322**
27.1 Polymeric materials 322

27.2	Fibres	323
27.3	Processing of thermoplastic polymers	325
27.4	Mechanical properties	326
28	**Polymer composites**	**332**
28.1	Characterization and definition of composite materials	332
28.2	Elastic properties of continuous unidirectional laminae	333
28.3	Elastic properties of in-plane random long-fibre laminae	334
28.4	Macro-analysis of stress distribution in a fibre/matrix composite	334
28.5	Elastic properties of short-fibre composite materials	336
28.6	Laminate theory	337
28.7	Isotropic lamina	337
28.8	Orthotropic lamina	338
28.9	The strength characteristics and failure criteria of composite laminae	339
28.10	References	344
29	**Manufacturing techniques for polymer composite materials**	**345**
29.1	Manufacture of fibre-reinforced thermosetting composites	345
29.2	Manufacture of fibre-reinforced thermoplastic composites	350
29.3	References	351
30	**Durability and design**	**351**
30.1	Temperature	351
30.2	Fire	351
30.3	Moisture	352
30.4	Solution and solvent action	353
30.5	Weather	353
30.6	Design with composites	354
30.7	References	354
31	**The end use of polymers and polymer composites**	**355**
31.1	References	358
Section Two	**Fibre-reinforced cements and concretes** D. Hannant	**359**
32	**Properties of fibres and of matrices**	**361**
32.1	Structure of fibre–matrix interface	362
33	**Structure and post-cracking composite theory**	**365**
33.1	Theoretical stress–strain curves in uniaxial tension	365
33.2	Uniaxial tension – fracture mechanics approach	373
33.3	Principles of fibre reinforcement in flexure	375
33.4	References	378
34	**Composites: Fibres in a cement matrix**	**379**
34.1	Asbestos cement	379
34.2	Glass-reinforced cement (GRC)	380

34.3 Polymer-fibre-reinforced cement 381
34.4 Natural fibres in cement 385
34.5 References 387

35 Fibre-reinforced concrete **388**
35.1 Steel-fibre concrete 388
35.2 Polymer-fibre-reinforced concrete 388
35.3 Glass-reinforced concrete 391

36 Durability **392**
36.1 Durability of asbestos cement 392
36.2 Durability of glass-fibre-reinforced cement 392
36.3 Durability of polymer-fibre-reinforced cement and concrete 393
36.4 Durability of natural-fibre-reinforced concrete 394
36.5 Durability of steel-fibre concrete 394
36.6 References 395

37 Manufacture and uses **396**
37.1 Asbestos cement 396
37.2 Glass-reinforced cement 398
37.3 Polymer-fibre-reinforced cement and concrete 399
37.4 Natural-fibre-reinforced cement 400
37.5 Steel-fibre concrete 400
37.6 References 402

Further reading **403**

Part Seven Timber J.M. Dinwoodie **405**
Introduction **407**

38 Structure of timber **409**
38.1 Structure at the macroscopic level 409
38.2 Structure at the microscopic level 410
38.3 Molecular structure and ultrastructure 417
38.4 Variability in structure 425
38.5 Appearance of timber in relation to its structure 427
38.6 Mass–volume relationships 429
38.7 Moisture in timber 431
38.8 References 435

39 Strength and failure in timber **437**
39.1 Introduction 437
39.2 Sample size 437
39.3 Strength values 439
39.4 Variability in strength values 439
39.5 Interrelationships among the strength properties 439

39.6	Factors affecting strength	440
39.7	Strength, failure and fracture morphology	449
39.8	Working (grade) stresses for timber	457
39.9	References	460
40	**Durability of timber**	**461**
40.1	The physical, chemical and biological agencies	461
40.2	Natural durability	462
40.3	Performance of timber in fire	464
40.4	Flow in timber	466
40.5	Thermal conductivity	471
40.6	References	471
41	**Deformation in timber**	**472**
41.1	Introduction	472
41.2	Dimensional change due to moisture	472
41.3	Thermal movement	475
41.4	Deformation under stress	476
41.5	References	493
42	**Processing of timber**	**494**
42.1	Introduction	494
42.2	Mechanical processing	494
42.3	Chemical processing	502
42.4	Finishes	506
42.5	References	508
	Further reading	509
	Index	510

Contributors

Professor J.M. Illston
10 Merrifield Road
Ford
Salisbury
Wiltshire
SP4 6DF
(Editor)

Dr P.L.J. Domone
Dept of Civil and Environmental Engineering
University College London
Gower Street
London WC1E 6BT
(Concrete)

Dr D.J. Hannant
Dept of Civil Engineering
University of Surrey
Guildford
Surrey GU2 5XH
(Composites – fibre-reinforced cements and concretes)

Professor W.D. Biggs
Beaufort House
Spring Lane
Aston Tirrold
Didcot
Oxon OX11 9EJ
(Fundamentals and metals)

Dr D.G. Bonner
Head of Division
Division of Civil Engineering
University of Hertfordshire
PO Box 109
College Lane
Hatfield
Herts AL10 9AB
(Bituminous materials)

Dr J.M. Dinwoodie
Timber Division
Building Research Establishment
Garston
Watford
Herts WD2 7JR
(Timber)

Professor L. Hollaway
Dept of Civil Engineering
University of Surrey
Guildford
Surrey GU2 5XH
(Composites – polymer composites)

Dr R.C. de Vekey
Building Research Establishment
Garston
Watford
Herts WD2 7JR
(Masonry)

J.M. Illston

Professor John Illston spent the early part of his career as a practising civil engineer before entering higher education. He was involved in teaching and researching into concrete technology and structural engineering as Lecturer and Reader at King's College, London and then Head of Department of Civil Engineering at Hatfield Polytechnic. His interest in his discipline took second place when he became Director of the Polytechnic, but has returned now that he is retired as Professor Emeritus.

W.D. Biggs

After some 20 years in industry, Professor Bill Biggs – a materials scientist – became a University Lecturer in Engineering at Cambridge where he was also Fellow, Tutor and Director of Studies at Christ's College. He was appointed as Professor of Building Technology and Head of the Department of Construction Management at the University of Reading in 1973 and, in 1981, was seconded, part time, to the Science and Engineering Research Council as coordinator for the Specially Promoted Programme of research in construction management. Now retired, he works as a specialist consultant for Buro Happold, Consulting Engineers, Bath.

D. Bonner

Dr David Bonner graduated in civil engineering from Leeds University where he later gained a Ph.D. in Traffic Engineering. Following a period working in the Highways Department of Lincolnshire County Council, he joined Hatfield Polytechnic (now the University of Hertfordshire) where he became Reader in Construction Materials and is presently Head of Division of Civil Engineering. He is a member of the Institution of Civil Engineers.

J.M. Dinwoodie

Dr John Dinwoodie graduated in Forestry from Aberdeen University, and was subsequently awarded his M. Tech. in Non-Metallic Materials from Brunel University, and both his Ph.D. and D.Sc. in Wood Science subjects from Aberdeen University. He is a Senior Principal Scientific Officer at the Building Research Establishment where he is in charge of the Wood Properties Section with special interest in the rheological behaviour of wood and wood products. He was elected a Fellow of the International Academy of Wood Science and is also a Fellow of the Royal Microscopical Society.

P.L.J. Domone

Dr Peter Domone graduated from University College, London in civil engineering, and was subsequently awarded a Ph.D. for his research into tensile strength and tensile creep of concrete. During a period of seven years as a research engineer in the research laboratories of Taylor Woodrow Construction, he developed a particular interest in durability of concrete construction. He joined the staff of the Department of Civil and Environmental Engineering, University College, London, in 1979, and is currently a senior lecturer with interests in cement grouts for offshore construction, non-destructive testing of cement and concrete, and high strength concrete.

D.J. Hannant

Dr David Hannant is a Reader in Construction Materials at the University of Surrey and has been researching and teaching in the field of fibre-reinforced cement and concrete since 1968. He has authored a book, patents and many publications and has been closely involved in the commercial development of fibre-reinforced cement roofing sheets to replace asbestos cement.

L.C. Hollaway

Professor Len Hollaway is Professor of Composite Structures at the University of Surrey and has been engaged in the research and teaching of composites for 25 years. He is the author and editor of a number of books and has written many research papers on the structural and material aspects of fibre/matrix composites.

R.C. de Vekey

Dr Bob de Vekey studied chemistry at Hatfield Polytechnic and graduated with the Royal Society of Chemistry. He subsequently gained a DIC in materials science and a Ph.D. from Imperial College, London on the results of his work at the Building Research Establishment (BRE) on materials. At BRE he has worked on many aspects of building materials research and development and since 1977 has led a section concerned mainly with structural behaviour, testing and safety of brick and block masonry buildings. He has written many papers and advisory publications on building materials and masonry and has been involved in UK and international standards and codes. He is a member of the Institute of Ceramics, the Masonry Society (USA) and is a founder member of the British Masonry Society.

Acknowledgements

First and foremost I want to acknowledge the forbearance and support of my wife who, for the second time, has borne with grace and tolerance my many hours spent immersed in manuscripts. I also want to thank my colleagues, the authors, who accepted my comments with good humour, and accommodated my views with patience and ingenuity; and I greatly appreciate the help extended to me by Nick Clarke in making our co-operation as editors an enjoyable and rewarding experience.

J.M. Illston

I wish to express my appreciation to Dr E.J. Gibson, Head of the former Princes Risborough Laboratory, Building Research Establishment, for permission not only to reproduce many plates and figures from the Laboratory's collection, but also to avail myself of the very willing assistance of the typing, copying, drawing and photographic services of the Laboratory.

Thanks are also due to several publishers for permission to reproduce figures here, including TAPPI.

To the many colleagues who so willingly helped me in some form or other in the production of this part of the text I would like to record my very grateful thanks. In particular I would like to record my appreciation to Dr W.B. Banks, Dr A.J. Bolton, Dr J.D. Brazier, Miss G.M. Lavers, Mr C.B. Pierce and Professor R.D. Preston FRS, for reviewing different chapters of the original manuscript and offering most useful comments; to Mrs A. Miles, Miss J.A. Higgins and Mr G. Moore for much checking of data, reading of drafts and proofs; to Mrs R. Alexander for many long hours of typing the original draft; and lastly to my family for their tolerance and patience over many long months.

J.M. Dinwoodie

Preface

This book is a revised edition of *Concrete, Timber and Metals* which was first published in 1979. Since then there have been advances in the materials of construction and in the information about them. The scope and content of the book have been changed accordingly; there are many additions and much of the original text has been rewritten. Three new materials – bituminous materials, masonry and fibre composites – have been added, and two new authors have updated the content on two out of three of the original materials.

Objectives

The underlying objectives of the book remain unchanged, and, as before, the book is addressed primarily to students taking courses in civil engineering, where we identify a continuing need for the unified treatment of the kind that we have attempted here. We have particularly had in mind the needs of students in the first two years of degree courses, and believe that the book could provide a useful course text covering most if not all of the required information. We also believe that our approach will continue to provide a valuable source of interest and stimulation to both undergraduates and graduates in engineering generally, materials science, building and architecture.

In the past the information on the behaviour of materials has come from three distinct sources. First, mechanical testing of sample specimens has provided values of such properties as strength or elastic modulus with the specific purpose of providing data for structural, or other, analysis. Second, and not to be underestimated, is the combined experiences of the practitioners engaged in the processing, handling and placing of materials. Third, and later, have come the more sophisticated studies of the physical and chemical structures of the materials themselves, in the realm of materials science.

The three sources – empiricism, craft, and science – have, in civil engineering, often remained poorly connected, to the detriment of both the understanding of the materials and of their treatment in practice. It is our purpose to present a more concerted view in which understanding is developed from a knowledge of the structure of the materials, and a logical framework is provided for the craft and empiricism of practice. Thus we hope to lay a sound foundation for the materials technology of the practitioner.

We believe that there is value in comparing the nature and behaviour of one material with another, and, in the first edition of the book, this was done by dividing the content into parts by topic with individual chapters for each material within each part. This is no longer possible with the coverage of six materials, and each part of the book contains all of the text for a single material. Nevertheless, we remain convinced that comparisons of the various structures and of the different behaviours provide an excellent basis for understanding, and we have, as far as possible, followed the same sequence of treatment with the similar chapter headings for each material. The topics are generally as follows:

Structure
Deformation

Strength and failure
Durability
Manufacture and processing

Levels of information

The structure of materials can be described differently depending on the dimensional scale. Three levels have been identified, each of which yields its own kind of information. These levels are given the titles, from the smallest to the largest, molecular, materials structural and engineering. The features of each are described below.

The molecular level

This considers the material at the smallest scale, in terms of atoms or molecules or aggregations of molecules. It is very much the realm of materials science and a general introduction for all materials is given in Part One of the book. The sizes of the particles are in the range of 10^{-7} to 10^{-3} mm. Examples occurring within the materials considered in the book include cellulose molecules in timber, calcium silicate hydrates in hardened cement paste and the variety of polymers, such as polyvinyl chloride, included in fibre composites.

As shown in Part One consideration of the established atomic models of physics leads to useful descriptions of the forms of physical structure, both regular and disordered, and of the ways in which materials are held together. This allows theoretical treatments which in turn open the way to a broader understanding of material behaviour.

Chemical composition is of fundamental importance in determining the physical structure. This may develop with time as chemical reactions continue; for example, the hydration of cement is a very slow process and the structure and properties show correspondingly significant changes with time. Chemical composition is of especial significance for durability which is often determined, as in the cases of timber and metals, by the rate at which external substances such as oxygen or acids react with the chemicals of which the material is made.

Chemical and physical factors come together again in determining whether or not the material is porous, and what degree of porosity is present. In materials such as bricks, timber and concrete, important properties such as strength and rigidity are inversely related to their porosities. Similarly, there is a direct connection between permeability and porosity.

Experimental techniques for the determination of the structure of materials are, at such a small scale, necessarily sophisticated, and include the use of instruments such as electron microscopes and X-ray diffractometers. Some phenomena such as dislocations in metals are directly observable, but more often mathematical and geometrical models are employed to deduce both the structure of the material and the way in which it is likely to behave.

Some engineering analyses, like fracture mechanics, come straight from molecular happenings, but they are the exception. Much more often the information from the molecular level serves to provide mental pictures which aid the engineers' understanding so that they can deduce likely behaviour under anticipated conditions. In the hands of specialists knowledge of the chemical and physical structure may well offer a route to the development of better materials.

Materials structural level

This level is a step up in size from the molecular level, and the material is considered as a composite of different phases, which interact to realize the behaviour of the total material. This may be a matter of separately identifiable entities within the material structure as in cells in timber or grains in metals; alternatively, it may result from the deliberate mixing of disparate parts, in a random manner in concrete or asphalt or some fibre composites, or in a regular way in masonry. Often the material consists of particles such as aggregates distributed in a matrix such as hydrated cement or bitumen. The dimensions of the particles differ enormously from the wall thickness of a wood cell at 5×10^{-3} mm to the length of a brick at 225 mm. Size itself is not an issue; what matters is that the individual phases can be recognized independently.

The significance of the materials structural level lies in the possibility of developing a more general treatment of the materials than is provided from knowledge derived from examination of the total material. The behaviours of the individual phases can be combined in the form of multiphase models which allow the prediction of behaviour outside the range of normal experimental observation. In formulating the models consideration must be given to three aspects.

1. Geometry. The model must recognize that the particulate or disperse phase is scattered or arranged within the matrix or continuous phase. It must take account of the shape and size distribution of the particles and of their overall concentration.
2. State and properties. The chemical and physical states of the phases influence the structure of the total material, and its behaviour is affected by the properties of the phases. For example its rigidity is determined by the elastic moduli of the phases, and the time-dependent deformations depend on the coefficients of viscosity.
3. Interfacial effects. The information under (1) and (2) may not be sufficient because the existence of interfaces between the phases may introduce additional modes of behaviour that cannot be related to the individual properties of the phases. This is especially true of strength, the breakdown of the material often being controlled by the bond strength at an interface.

To operate at the materials structural level requires a considerable knowledge of the three aspects described above. This must be derived from testing the phases themselves, and additionally from interface tests. While the use of the multiphase models is often confined to research in the interest of improving understanding, it is sometimes taken through into practice, albeit mostly in simplified form. Examples include the estimation of the elastic modulus of concrete, and the strength of fibre composites.

The engineering level

At the engineering level the total material is considered; it is normally taken as continuous and homogeneous and average properties are assumed throughout the whole volume of the material body. The materials at this level are those traditionally recognized by construction practitioners, and it is the behaviour of these materials that is the endpoint of this book.

The minimum scale to enable the material to be rightly considered is indicated by the size of the representative cell, which may be taken as the minimum volume of the material that represents the entire material system, including its regions of disorder. The linear dimensions of the representative cells vary considerably from say 10^{-3} mm for metals to 100 mm for concrete and 1000 mm for masonry. Properties measured over volumes greater than the unit cell can be taken to apply to the material at large. If the properties are the same in all directions then the material is isotropic and the representative cell is a cube, while if the properties can only be described with reference to orientation, the material is anisotropic, and the representative cell may be regarded as a parallelepiped.

Most of the technical information on materials used in practice comes from tests on specimens of the total material, prepared and operated on to represent the condition of the material in the engineering structure. The kinds of tests are various, and can be identified under the headings used throughout this book. They include strength and failure, deformation, and durability. The data from the tests give empirical information on the properties which can often be expressed in graphical or mathematical form. In addition the graphs or equations usually give an indication of how the property values are affected by significant variables; such as, the carbon content of steel, the moisture content of timber, the fibre content and orientation in composites or the temperature of asphalt. The quality of information is satisfactory only within the ranges of the variables used in the tests mounted to produce that information. Extrapolation is risky outside those ranges, and the graphs and equations may neither express the physical and chemical processes within the materials, nor provide a high order of accuracy of prediction.

Comparability and variability

Throughout this book we have tried to excite comparison of one material with another. Attention has been given to the structure of each material, with Part One giving a common structural base for all the materials. Although a similar scientific foundation applies to all, the variety of physical and chemical compositions gives rise to great differences in behaviour. The differences are carried through to the engineering level of information and have to be considered by practitioners engaged in the design of structures who must set up formal criteria in determining which materials to use.

Selection of materials

The engineer must consider the fitness of the chosen material for the purpose of the structure being designed. Fitness-for-purpose is the essential criterion in selecting the material, and it is a matter of ensuring that the material will perform adequately both during construction and in service after the structure is completed. The satisfaction of this criterion is likely to include all the main properties covered in this book; the material must be strong enough to make sure that it does not fail under the loads imposed on the structure, the members made of the material must not deform excessively and the material must not degrade significantly during the intended life of the structure. Other aspects of behaviour may also be included in the criterion of fitness-for-purpose; for example, watertightness could be essential, or the speed of construction might be crucial. In addition, aesthetic appearance and the effects on the environment should not be forgotten.

In many circumstances more than one material satisfies the criterion of fitness-for-purpose; for instance, members carrying tension can be made of steel or timber, facing panels can be fabricated from fibre composite, metal, timber or masonry. The matter may be resolved through the engineer making a choice based on his or her judgement on the relative adequacy with which the different materials satisfy the criterion of fitness-for-purpose. This exercise of judgement is not so surprising as it might seem at first sight. Although information is often substantial and understanding well developed, many, and probably most, engineering decisions are made on the basis of incomplete evidence, and the need for expert judgement becomes an everyday matter.

The other criterion that can and usually does resolve the question of which suitable material to use is that of cost. Clearly the estimated cost of the structure must not exceed the money available, and it is often the case that the cheapest design solution is chosen. This is apparently a simple criterion in which a numerical comparison can be made between competing designs. In practice things are not quite so easy as there can, for instance, be difficulties in interpreting the balance between capital and running costs, or in assessing the effects of delays in construction caused by, say, uncertain delivery times of the chosen material.

An alternative criterion is the energy cost of producing and placing materials. Energy costs must include not only the cost of manufacturing the material but also additional costs such as those of transportation and fabrication; this is not a simple matter and comparative material costs cannot be produced as routine. Nevertheless, the need to reduce energy costs is recognized and certain conclusions are accepted. High-strength versions of all the materials covered in this book are sought with the intention of reducing the volume of material for a given structure, normally with a commensurate saving in energy; and lower grade materials are introduced to replace higher grade as, for example, in the partial replacement of cement by the waste material, pulverized fuel ash (fly ash).

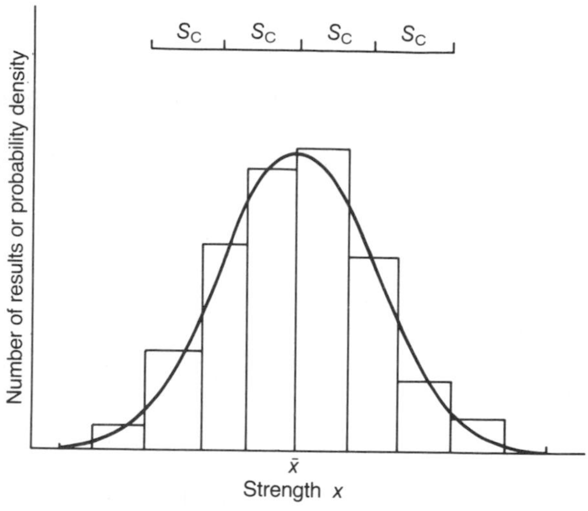

FIGURE 0.1 Histogram and normal distribution of strength.

Variability

As discussed in the last section the practitioner has to consider the criterion of fitness-for-purpose in deciding which material to use. A specific issue within that comparison is the variability of the properties of the material itself. This clearly depends on the uniformity of the material in the structure, which in turn depends on how well it can be made. At one end of the scale, the manufacture of steel is a well developed and closely controlled process so that a particular steel can be readily reproduced and the variability of properties such as strength is small; at the other end unprocessed timber, which in its natural form is full of defects such as knots, inevitably exhibits a wider variation in property values.

Most properties vary according to the normal or Gaussian distribution shown in Figure 0.1. If a number of replicates of supposedly identical samples are tested, say for strength, then a histogram of results can be plotted as shown. This can be represented by the normal bell-shaped mean curve given by the equation

$$y = \frac{1}{S_c\sqrt{(2\pi)}} \exp\left[-\frac{(x - \bar{x})^2}{2S_c^2}\right] \qquad (0.1)$$

where y is the probability density, and x is the variate, in this case the strength. The strength is then expressed in terms of two numbers, namely,

1. the mean strength, $\bar{x}$, where for n samples, $\bar{x} = \Sigma x/n$;
2. the range of strength, given by the standard deviation, S_c, for the strength, given by

$$S_c^2 = \sum \frac{(x - \bar{x})^2}{n - 1}. \qquad (0.2)$$

The standard deviation has the same units as the variate, and expresses the variability of that variate. To allow comparison of different materials or different kinds of the same material the non-dimensional coefficient of variation is used, given by

$$c_V = S_c/\bar{x}. \qquad (0.3)$$

As ungraded timber is more variable than steel we expect, for comparable properties, that it will have a larger coefficient of variation. The variability can also be reduced by processing so that the coefficient of variation for chipboard or fibreboard is appreciably lower than that

TABLE 0.1 Comparison of strengths of construction materials and their coefficients of variation. c = compression, t = tension

Material	*Mean strength N/mm²*	*Coefficient of variation %*	*Comment*
Steel	460 t	2	Structural mild steel
Concrete	40 c	15	Normal weight concrete cube strength at 28 days
Timber	30 t	35	Ungraded softwood
	120 t	18	Knot free, straight grained softwood
	11 t	10	Structural grade chipboard
Fibre cement composites	18 t	10	Continuous polypropylene fibre with 6% volume fraction in stress direction
Masonry	20 c	10	Small walls, brick on bed

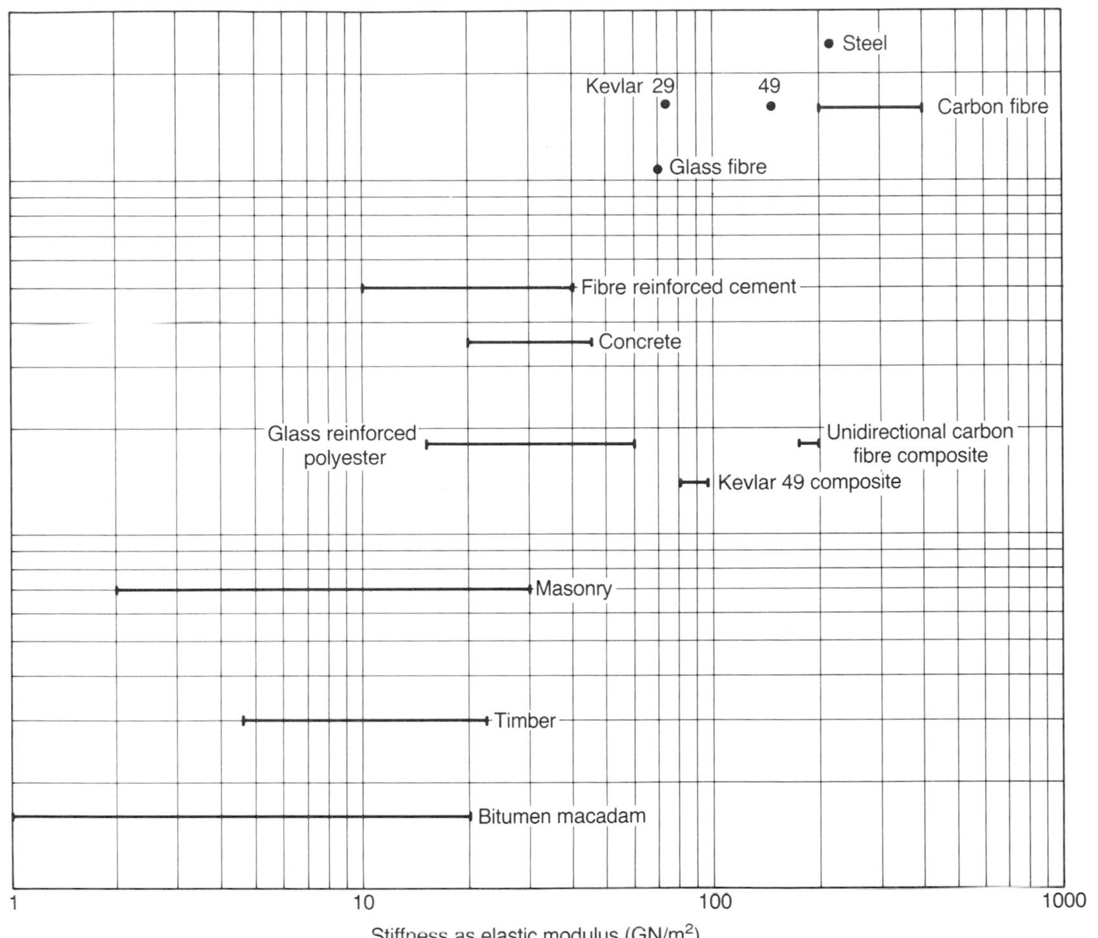

FIGURE 0.2 Ranges of stiffnesses of construction materials.

for ungraded timber. Comparative values for typical mean strengths and their coefficients of variation of materials in this book are given in Table 0.1. It is assumed that the results come from testing a number of samples from the same batch or mix of the typical material.

A further comparison of materials in this book is given in Figure 0.2 which shows the relative stiffnesses, expressed as the elastic modulus E. In this case the range of values is given for the stiffnesses of the variety of types of each material, such as the different species of timber or the different mixes of concrete.

Scope

Although the same framework has been adopted for all six materials in this book, their treatment varies greatly. This is inevitable given the differences between them. This is not only in their structure and properties, but also in their stage of development. It cannot be expected that other materials are as well understood as metals which have a long history of scientific investigation. Similarly, bituminous materials have a more limited literature than concretes, probably because bitumens are extracted, whereas cements are manufactured. The process of production is also significant, and materials controlled under factory conditions such as metals and fibre composites are more sophisticated than those produced in the field such as concrete, asphalt or masonry. In some cases there is overlap between materials. Thus cement is a component of masonry and some fibre composites as well as of concrete; and aggregates occur in both bituminous materials and in concrete.

It is impossible in a single book to cover the field of materials in a fully comprehensive manner; in spite of the expansion to six, not all the materials of construction are included, nor has the attempt been made to introduce design criteria or to provide a compendium of materials data. Neither is this book a manual of good practice. Nevertheless we hope that we have provided a firm foundation on which can be built the further application and practice of materials technology.

Part One

Fundamentals

W.D. Biggs

Introduction

As engineers our job is to design, but any design remains just that and no more until we start to use materials to convert it into a working artefact. There are, basically, three things we need to know about materials.

1. How do they behave in service?
2. Why do they behave in the way that they do?
3. Is there anything we can do to alter their behaviour?

The present chapter is primarily concerned with (2). In it we consider the fundamental elements of which all matter is composed and the forces which hold it together.

The concept of 'atomistics' is not new. The ancient Greeks – and especially Democritus (*c.* 460 BC) – had the idea of a single elementary particle but their science did not extend to observation and experiment. For that we had to wait nearly 22 centuries until Dalton, Avogadro and Cannizzaro formulated atomic theory as we know it today. And very many mysteries remain unresolved, a fact which is as pleasing as it is provoking. So in treating the subject in this way we are reaching a long way back into the development of thought about the universe and the way in which it is put together.

One other important concept is more recent. Engineering is much concerned with change – the change from the unloaded to the loaded state, the consequences of changing temperature, environment, etc. The first scientific studies of change can be attributed to Sadi Carnot (1824), later extended by such giants as Clausius, Joule and others to produce such ideas as the conservation of energy, momentum, etc. Since the early studies were carried out on heat engines it became known as the science of thermodynamics, but if we take a broader view it is really the art and science of managing, controlling and using the transfer of energy – whether the energy of the atom, the energy of the tides or the energy of, say, a lifting rig.

In many engineering courses thermodynamics is treated as a separate topic but, because its applications set rules which no engineer can ignore, a brief discussion is included here. What are these rules? In summary (and rather jocularly) they are:

1. You cannot win, i.e. you cannot get more out of a system than you put in.
2. You cannot break even – in any change something will be lost or, to be more precise, it will be useless for the purpose you have in mind.

All this may be unfamiliar ground so you may skip past it on first reading. But come back to it because it is important. We shall not, in the present part, deal specifically with item (3) above; later parts will deal with this in more specific terms. But what every engineer should remember is that engineering is all about compromise and trade-off. Some properties can be varied – strength is one such – but some, such as density, cannot be varied. If I were designing aircraft I could, in principle, choose between maximum strength and minimum weight. And minimum weight would win because it would ensure a higher payload (let us not forget that engineering is also about money).* But, of course, compromise must be sought and engineering is about finding optimal solutions, not necessarily a 'best' solution. So good luck with your reading. If you really understand the principles much of the rest will be clearer to you. But, in a few short chapters we can do little more than describe the highlights of materials science. A list of suggestions for further reading is given at the end of this part. Unfortunately many books are written by experts and for experts – see the note which prefaces the reading list.

So I must conclude by stating my own simple philosophy – engineering is much too important to be left to engineers.

* An engineer has been defined as a person who can do for £100 what any damn fool could do for £1000.

Chapter one

States of matter

1.1 Fluids
1.2 Solids
1.3 Intermediate behaviour

We conventionally think of matter as solid, liquid or gas but these definitions are not precise and do not fully describe many intermediate types of behaviour.

Our intuitive understanding of these states is, however, based essentially upon one simple concept – the response of a material to an applied force – and from childhood on we recognize two principal classes of behaviour; those materials which flow when a force is applied – fluids (which include both gases and liquids); and those which resist a force – solids. We consider these two main classes first.

1.1 Fluids

Consider first the observable characteristics of a gas.

1. Gases have low density, expand to fill the container, are easily compressed and have low viscosity.
2. Gases diffuse readily into each other and exert a uniform pressure on the walls of the container.

The first set of observations suggests that the gas particles are not in direct contact with each other, the second that they are in constant motion in random directions and at high speeds.

Liquids exhibit most of the above properties; most diffuse into each other readily and their viscosity – although some orders of magnitude higher than that of gases – is still low so that they flow irreversibly under vanishingly small forces. But there are two significant differences. The first is that they are incompressible (hydraulic braking systems depend on this). The second is that they evaporate to form a vapour when heated and return to the liquid state when cooled.

All this suggests that the particles of fluids are in contact but are free to move relative to each other. We shall consider the nature of the interaction between the particles in Chapter 3 but, meanwhile, we can think of a liquid as being similar to people at a well-run cocktail party in which the guests are kept circulating from one group to another by the hostess.

Because the particles are free to move, the application of even a small force causes irreversible flow. In an ideal (Newtonian) liquid the rate of flow $= \mathrm{d}\gamma/\mathrm{d}t$ is proportional to the applied stress τ

$$\frac{\mathrm{d}\gamma}{\mathrm{d}t} = \dot{\gamma} = \beta\tau \tag{1.1}$$

where β = fluidity (Figure 1.1). This is generally written $\tau = \eta\dot{\gamma}$ where η = the coefficient of dynamic viscosity. At higher temperatures the particles possess more energy of their own and the stress required to move them is reduced, i.e. viscosity is highly dependent on temperature (e.g. motor oil, treacle, asphalt).

1.1.1 Diffusion

We noted above that both gases and liquids diffuse into each other. Here, for simplicity,

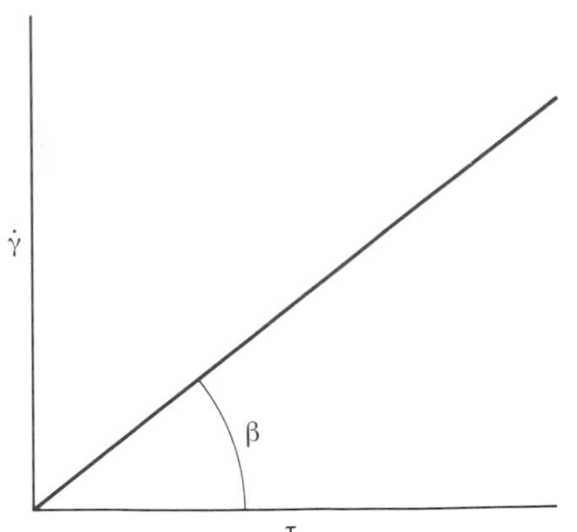

FIGURE 1.1 The schematic relationship between stress and strain rates in an ideal Newtonian fluid.

we consider the diffusion of one gas into another but the same arguments apply broadly to liquids and even to solids under the appropriate conditions.

Diffusion is caused by countless haphazard wanderings of individual atoms or molecules – these continually bump into each other and the atom can rebound in any direction. The path of any individual atom is unpredictable but, if enough make such a movement, the result is a steady and systematic flow.

The mathematical argument is fairly simple, though it is not necessary to pursue it here. Imagine a box containing a partition – on one side there are C_1 particles of gas/unit volume and on the other C_2 where $C_1 > C_2$. As noted above these are moving randomly and exerting a pressure on the partition and, logically, $P_1 > P_2$. Now remove the partition. Both sets will move across the plane into the space formerly occupied by the other, but because of the higher concentration more will move in the direction $C_1 \rightarrow C_2$ and, eventually, a totally random mixture is formed.

Provided we make certain simplifying assumptions it is easy to show that the total flux of particles through the plane J is

$$J = -D\frac{dc}{dx}$$

which is Fick's first law of diffusion. The constant D is known as the diffusion coefficient and is proportional to the average distance travelled by a particle before colliding with another one and the frequency with which this happens. Thus the rate of diffusion is proportional to the concentration gradient dc/dx and is directed down the gradient – hence the minus sign. Both of these follow directly from the statistical nature of the process (see also page 15).

It does not take much imagination to see that temperature will play an important role. At higher temperatures the particles are more active and jump more frequently so that the rate of diffusion increases as the temperature rises and vice versa. This has many important technological consequences, for example, in modifying the properties of metals and alloys by heat treatment.

1.1.2 Vapour–liquid transition

The characteristics of the vapour–liquid transition derive from the work of Van der Waals who pointed out that the perfect gas law relating pressure P, volume V and temperature T, via a constant R, $PV = RT$ neglected two important factors:

1. the volume of the particles themselves;
2. the forces of attraction between the particles.

The first is fairly obvious and we correct by deducting from the volume a term representing the volume of the particles. Thus:

$$P(V - b) = RT.$$

The second is less obvious – the forces of attraction between the particles will have the effect of drawing them closer together, just as if additional pressure were applied. So we must add a correction to P. The magnitude of the force depends on the number of particles within a spherical volume surrounding any given molecule. This is proportional to density or $1/V$. The internal pressure also depends upon the number of molecules in a given volume that are subject to attractive forces, again proportional to $1/V$. Thus this term is written as a/v^2 where a is a constant.

Thus the revised equation (Van der Waals equation) is

$$(P + a/v^2)(V - b) = RT. \quad (1.2)$$

The consequences of this are noteworthy. If we plot P against V for different values of T we obtain a set of isotherms as shown in Figure 1.2. Note that, at low temperatures, each curve has a maximum and minimum; at higher temperatures they become smooth.

The minimum and maximum on each curve are connected by the dotted line. The point C where the minimum and maximum coincide at a point of inflection is the **critical point** and

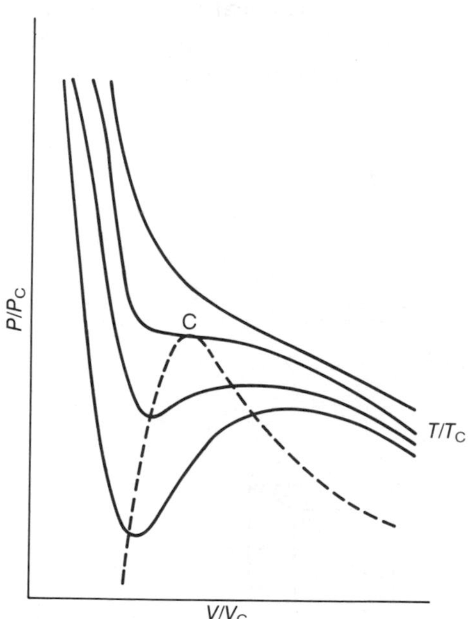

FIGURE 1.2 Isotherms from Van der Waals equation. The values for P, V and T are expressed in terms of their values at the critical point C. In form they are dimensionless and independent of their actual values.

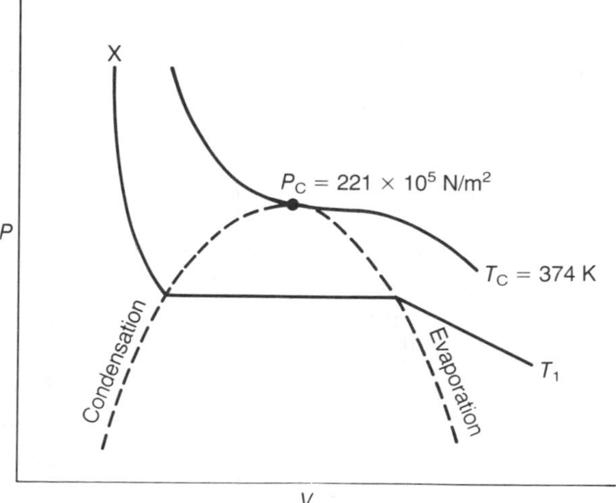

FIGURE 1.3 *P-V-T* curves for water vapour.

denotes the conditions where liquid and vapour can coexist in equilibrium.

The theorem is not totally correct – real materials behave as shown in Figure 1.3 where we note that starting with a liquid at X at some constant temperature T_1 the volume increases as the pressure is reduced. Eventually the liquid becomes saturated with vapour and the volume increases with no change of pressure as a saturated vapour (i.e. vapour saturated with liquid) forms. With further decrease in pressure a true vapour is formed and the liquid is said to have evaporated. The reverse happens if we start with a gas and increase the pressure while keeping temperature constant.

The particles within a liquid (at constant temperature and pressure) may or may not have sufficient thermal energy to escape. Those which escape constitute the vapour and the pressure they exert is the **vapour pressure.** In a closed container an equilibrium is set up between those particles escaping and those returning – this is the **saturation vapour pressure.** When the saturation vapour pressure is equal to or greater than the external pressure the liquid boils. Thus the boiling point is conventionally defined as the temperature to which the liquid must be raised in order for this to occur at atmospheric pressure. Clearly as the atmospheric pressure goes down so does the boiling point – which is why mountaineers never get hot soup.

1.2 Solids

Intuitively the first thing that we notice about a solid is that it resists the application of a force. But so does a liquid, provided that the force is applied equally in all directions – liquids are said to be incompressible. The essential difference is that, unlike gases and liquids, a solid does not appear to flow under load. We shall see later that this is not strictly true; under appropriate conditions all materials will flow but the definition is good enough for our purpose and accords with normal experience.

The reason is simple, the mechanism quite complex. The atoms of which the solid is composed are physically bonded together so that when we apply a force we must displace all the atoms of which the solid is composed, unlike a liquid in which the individual particles can move past each other.

1.2.1 The elastic constants

Before discussing the mechanics and consequences of bonding we should digress a little to define some of the properties which are used to characterize solids.

When a solid is extended or compressed by an external force the dimensions change. Conventionally we express the force P in terms of the area over which it acts, this is known as stress $\sigma = P/A$.

The same convention is used for defining pressure – but whilst pressure is the same as stress, stress is not the same as pressure, since stress may be either tensile or compressive. The units of stress are N/m^2.

Under simple uniaxial tension or compression the material either extends or shortens. Conventionally we express this as strain $\varepsilon = dL/L$, i.e. change in length per unit length. Strain is therefore a ratio and has no dimensions.

For many solids the relationship between stress and strain is linear or, at least, sufficiently linear to provide a first approximation (Figure 1.4(a)). This is known as Hooke's law:

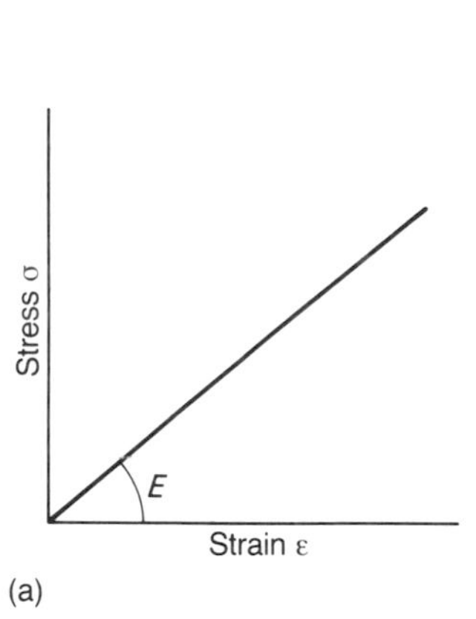

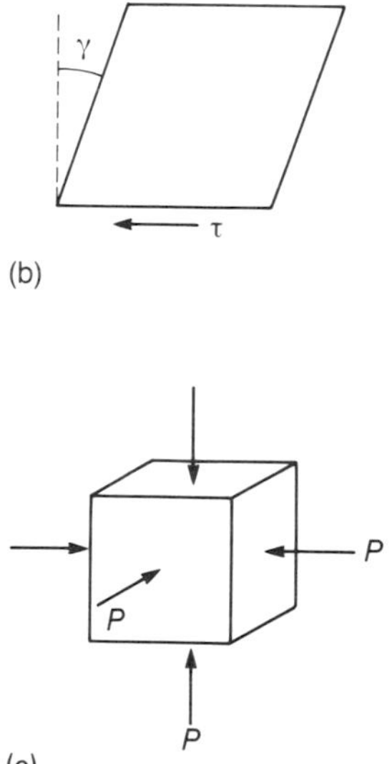

FIGURE 1.4 Elastic constants.

TABLE 1.1 Typical densities and elastic moduli of various materials (arranged in order of decreasing specific stiffness)

	Density ρ (kg/m³) (×10³)	*Young's modulus E (MN/m²) (×10⁶)*	*Specific stiffness E/ρ (m²/sec²) (×10⁶)*
Diamond	3.5	0.8	230
Beryllium	1.8	0.30	170
Alumina Al_2O_3	4.0	0.53	130
Magnesia MgO	3.6	0.28	80
Tungsten carbide WC	15.8	0.72	46
Iron	7.9	0.21	29
Silica and glass	2.5	0.069	28
Titanium	4.5	0.12	26
Spruce (parallel to grain)	0.5	0.013	26
Magnesium	1.74	0.041	24
Aluminium	2.7	0.072	20
Concrete	1.4–2.4	0.01–0.005	6–20
Copper	8.96	0.124	14
Epoxy resin	1.12	0.0045	4
Nylon	1.14	0.003	3

$$\sigma = E\varepsilon \tag{1.3}$$

where E is a material constant known as **Young's modulus** of elasticity and has units of stress, namely N/m^2. Table 1.1 gives some typical values.

Similar relationships apply for other forms of stress. Thus in shear (Figure 1.4(b)) the shear stress τ produces a shear strain γ which is conventionally measured as an angle (and is therefore also dimensionless).

$$\tau = G\gamma \tag{1.4}$$

where G is known as the **shear modulus.**

Under hydrostatic pressure (Figure 1.4(c)) the volume changes. As before we express this non-dimensionally as $\mathrm{d}v/V$ and

$$p = -K\frac{\mathrm{d}v}{V} \tag{1.5}$$

where K is the **bulk modulus.** The minus sign arises as a consequence of the fact that as pressure increases volume decreases.

Young's modulus is a measure of the stress required to produce a given deformation, and engineers often refer to it as the stiffness of the material, for that is what it is. It will be apparent that whereas a liquid can display a bulk modulus it does not possess a shear modulus since it cannot resist shear. Solids, on the other hand, display a bulk modulus and a shear modulus. It is the resistance to shear via the shear modulus that distinguishes between solids and liquids.

1.2.2 Elastic resilience – stored energy

We noted that a linearly elastic (Hookean) material deforms reversibly, i.e. it returns to its original length when the load is removed. The product of stress and strain has the dimensions of energy – in this case **strain energy** which is simply the area under the stress–strain curve

$$U = \tfrac{1}{2}\varepsilon\sigma = \tfrac{1}{2}\sigma^2/E = \tfrac{1}{2}\varepsilon^2 E$$

per unit volume of material. The capacity to store energy on loading and release it on un-

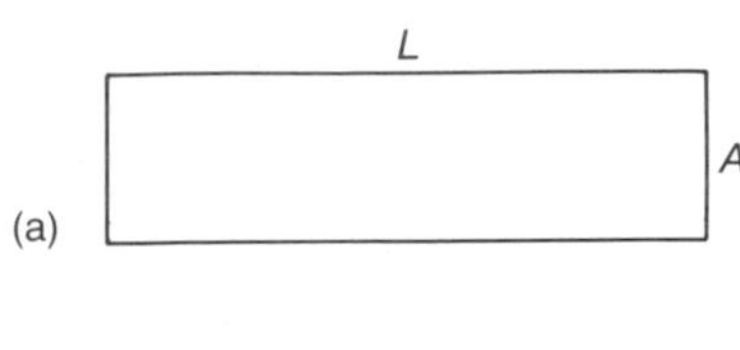

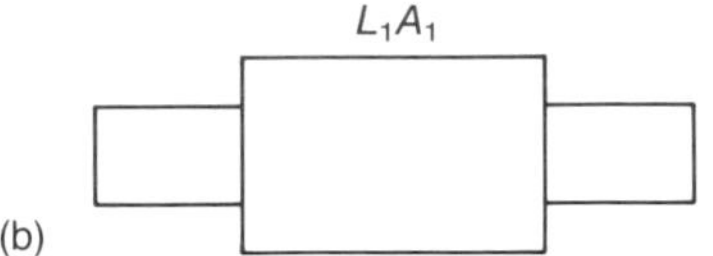

FIGURE 1.5

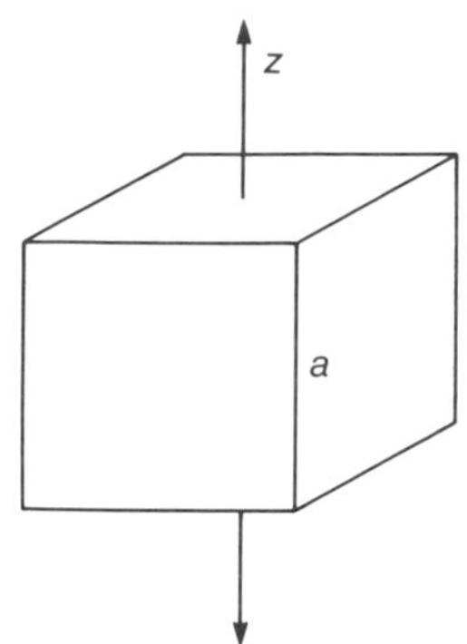

FIGURE 1.6

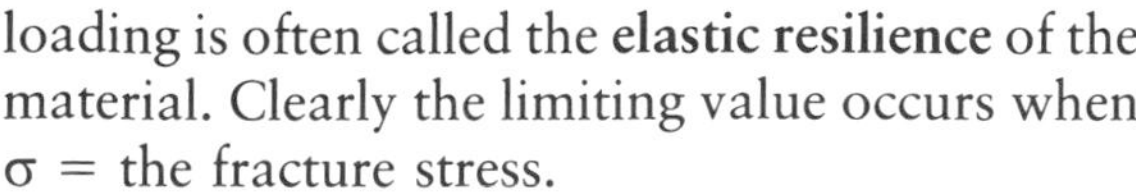

loading is often called the **elastic resilience** of the material. Clearly the limiting value occurs when σ = the fracture stress.

One other feature is worth noting here – whereas stress and strain are independent of cross-sectional shape, elastic resilience is not.

Consider a uniform rod of length L and area A (Figure 1.5(a)). The material has a failure stress σ. At fracture this can store energy amounting to $\frac{1}{2}\sigma^2 E$. Now increase the area to A_1 over a length L_1 (Figure 1.5(b)). The energy absorbed by the unchanged part is

$$\sigma^2 A(L - L_1)/2E$$

and, by the changed part,

$$(\sigma A/A_1)^2 A_1 L_1/2E$$

so that the total energy absorption is

$$\frac{\sigma^2 AL}{2E}\left[1 - \frac{L_1}{L}\left(1 - \frac{A}{A_1}\right)\right]$$

and, since $L_1 < L$ and $A_1 > A$, the resilience is decreased by increasing the area.

1.2.3 Poisson's ratio

Clearly the application of a force displaces the atoms from their normal positions. Thus, in an elastic solid, the application of a longitudinal tension force causes a transverse contraction. The ratio – **Poisson's ratio** – is defined in tension as

$$\nu = \frac{\text{Relative lateral contraction}}{\text{Relative longitudinal extension}}.$$

A cube of side a stressed in the z direction (Figure 1.6) will extend by

$$\delta_z = a\varepsilon_z$$

and

$$\delta_x = \delta_y = -a\nu\varepsilon_z.$$

The final volume is

$$V = (a + \delta_x)(a + \delta_y)(a + \delta_z).$$

Expanding and neglecting higher terms in δ

$$V \approx a^3 + a^2\delta_x + a^2\delta_y + a^2\delta_z,$$

whence the change of volume

$$\mathrm{d}V \approx a^2(\delta_x + \delta_y + \delta_z)$$

TABLE 1.2 Poisson's ratio

Material	ν
Glass	0.23
Concrete	0.2
Steel	0.33
Nylon	0.4
PTFE	0.4
Soft rubber	0.49

and substituting strain for the length change

$$dV \approx a^3\varepsilon_z(1 - 2\nu).$$

In order for volume to remain constant during deformation, i.e. $dV = 0$, we find that $\nu = 0.5$. This represents complete fluidity. Some values are given in Table 1.2. We see that soft rubber comes very close to fluid behaviour but that in all the other materials listed there is a volume change on deformation.

1.3 Intermediate behaviour

We have already emphasized the lack of any dividing line between solids and liquids, the reason being that the response of materials to shear can vary over a wide range. Solids may be either crystalline or amorphous. In a crystalline solid (and metals are an important group) the atoms are arranged in a regular, three-dimensional array or lattice. Amorphous solids do not possess this regularity of structure and we can further subdivide them into glassy and molecular solids.

True glasses are obtained by cooling liquids which, because of their elaborate random molecular configuration, lack the necessary activation energy (see page 14) at the melting point to rearrange themselves in an ordered crystalline array.

The material then retains, even when rigid, a typically glassy structure involving short range order only and resembling, except for its immobility, the structure of the liquid form. Silica gives rise to the commonest form of glass; if cooled sufficiently slowly from the melt it can be obtained in the crystalline form which is more stable thermodynamically than the vitreous state. However, at ordinary cooling rates crystallization does not take place, and the amorphous nature of the solid gives rise to its most important physical property: its transparency. Most non-metallic single crystals are transparent, but in the polycrystalline state light is scattered from internal reflections at flaws and internal boundaries; the material then becomes translucent in thin sections and completely opaque in the mass, as with naturally occurring rocks. Totally amorphous polymers may also be transparent, but most owe their opacity to the presence of crystalline regions (spherulites) within their structure that act as light scatterers.

Molecular solids are best exemplified by soft polymers such as polyethylene which consist of long highly convoluted molecules whose bulk strength depends upon the entanglement of the molecular chains rather than upon three-dimensional bonding.

There are, however, more complex structures involving both solid and liquid phases. One of the most familiar of these structures is the gel, known to most of us from childhood in the form of jellies and lozenges.

Gels are formed when a suspension of very fine particles (usually of colloidal dimensions) in a liquid bonds in a loose structure trapping liquid in its interstices. Depending on the number of links formed, gels can vary from very nearly fluid structures to almost rigid solids. If the links are few or weak, the individual particles have considerable freedom of movement around their points of contact, and the gel deforms easily. A high degree of linkage gives a structure that is hard and rigid in spite of all its internal pores. The most important engineering gel is undoubtedly cement, which develops a highly rigid structure. When water is added to the cement powder, the individual particles take up water of hydration, swell and link up with each other to give rise to a high-strength but permeable gel of complex calcium silicates. A feature of many gels is their very high specific surface area; if the gel is permeable as well as porous, the surface is available for adsorbing large amounts of water vapour, and such a gel is an effective drying agent. Adsorption is a reversible process (see page 37); when the gel is saturated, it may be heated to drive off the water and its drying powers regained. Silica gel is an example of this.

If a gel sets by the formation of rather weak links, the linkages may be broken by vigorous stirring so that the gel liquefies again. When the stirring ceases, the bonds will gradually link up and the gel will thicken and return to its original set. Behaviour of this sort, in which an increase in the applied stress causes the material to act in a more fluid manner, is known as **thixotropy**. Not all gels behave in this manner, or, if they do, it is only at a certain stage of their setting

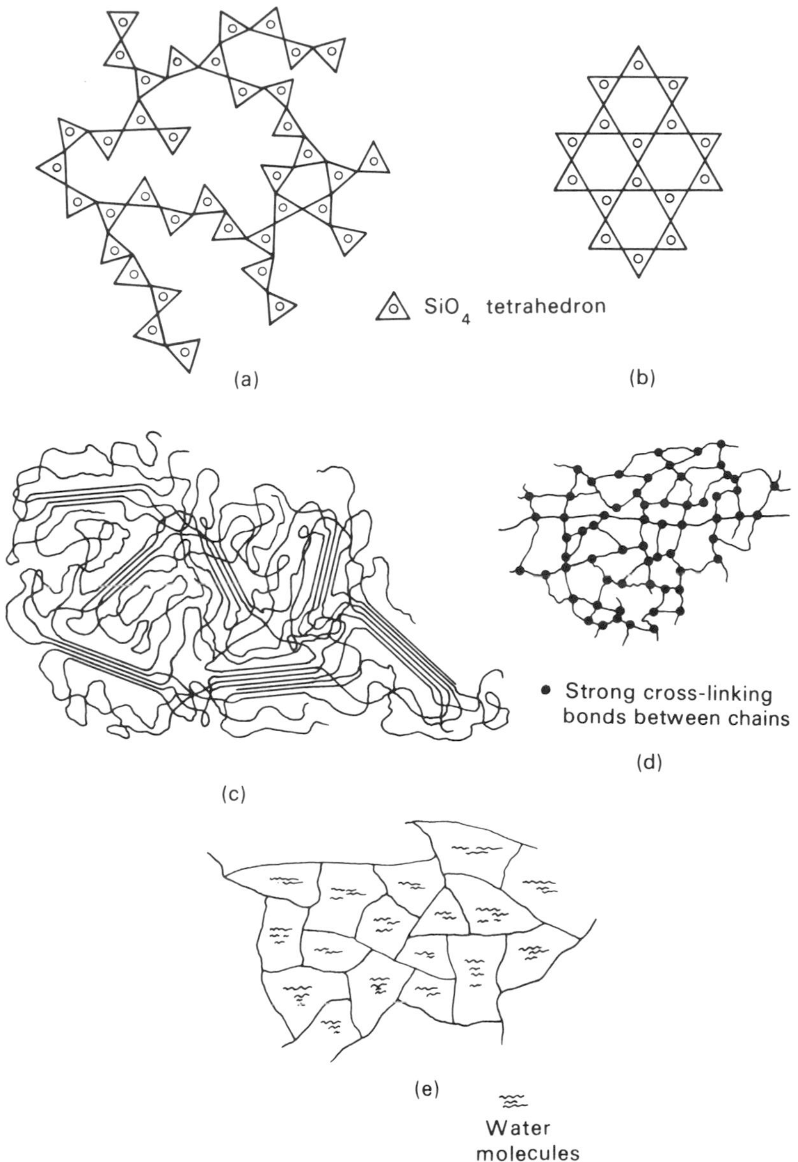

FIGURE 1.7 Schematic structures of some covalent materials: (a) vitreous silica (glass); (b) crystalline silica; (c) thermoplastic polymer showing crystalline regions (spherulites); (d) thermosetting polymer; (e) gel – by comparison with (d), the links between the chains are weak and easily broken.

procedure: hardened concrete will not, alas, heal itself spontaneously after it has cracked, although it exhibits a marked degree of thixotropy at an early state of setting.

The most familiar application of thixotropy is non-drip paints, which liquefy when stirred and spread easily when being brushed on, but which set as a gel as soon as brushing is completed so that dripping or streaks on vertical surfaces are avoided. Clays can also exhibit thixotropy. This is turned to advantage in the mixing of drilling muds for oil exploration: the thixotropic mud serves to line the shaft with an impermeable layer, whilst in the centre it is kept fluid by the movement of the drill and acts as a medium for removing the rock drillings. On the other hand a thixotropic clay underlying major civil engineering works could be highly hazardous.

The reverse effect to thixotropy occurs when an increase in the applied stress causes a viscous material to behave more in the manner of a solid, and is known as **dilatancy**. It is a less familiar but rather more spectacular phenomenon. Cornflour–water mixtures demonstrate the effect over a rather narrow range of composition, when the viscous liquid will fracture if stirred vigorously; it is of short duration, however, since fracture relieves the stress, and the fractured surfaces immediately liquefy and run together again.

Silicone putty (marketed as 'Potty Putty') is also a dilatant; it flows very slowly if left to itself, but fractures if pulled suddenly, and will bounce like a rubber ball if thrown against a hard surface. So far, no engineering applications of dilatancy have been developed. Some structures are illustrated diagrammatically in Figure 1.7.

Chapter two

Energy

2.1 Mixing
2.2 Entropy
2.3 Free energy

Although the engineer conventionally expresses his findings in terms of force, deflection, stress, strain and so on, these are simply that – convention. Fundamentally what he is really dealing with is energy. Any change, no matter how simple, involves an exchange of energy. The mere act of lifting a beam involves a change in the potential energy of the beam, a change in the strain energy held in the lifting cables, an input of mechanical energy from the lifting device which is itself transforming electrical or other energy into kinetic energy. The harnessing and control of energy is at the heart of all engineering.

Thermodynamics teaches us about energy – the fact that all materials possess an *internal* energy associated with the very structure of the atoms of which it is composed, that many processes, such as combustion, can only occur if a given amount of energy – the *activation* energy – is fed in to start the reaction. On the other hand, some changes in behaviour, though thermodynamically correct, proceed so slowly that we may assume the system to be stable. In the present section we examine some of the thermodynamic principles which are of importance to the materials scientist if he wishes to understand the behaviour patterns. Figure 2.1 gives a simple (but rather poor) analogy to some of these ideas. A ball sits in a depression – its potential energy is P_1. It will roll to a lower energy state P_2, if an activation energy is applied. Thereafter it possesses free energy as it rolls down to P_2. But it is losing potential energy all the time and eventually (say, at sea level) it will achieve a stable equilibrium. Note, however, two things. At P_1, P_2, etc. it is 'stable' – actually **metastable** because there are other, more stable states available to it, given the necessary activation energy. What is activation energy – whence does it come? In materials science mostly (but not exclusively) from temperature; as things are heated up the atomic particles react more rapidly and can break out of their metastable state into one where they can now lose energy. What we are trying to identify is the difference between spontaneous changes in state and those changes that need to be driven by the application of some form of energy, usually, but not exclusively, thermal energy – heat.

2.1 Mixing

If whisky and water are placed in the same container they mix spontaneously. And there is no way that we can separate them except by distillation – that is to say by heating them up and collecting the vapours and separating these into alcohol and water. We must, in fact, apply energy to separate them. But, since energy can neither be created nor destroyed, the fact that we must use energy (and quite a lot of it) to restore the status quo must surely pose the question 'Where does the energy come from initially?' The answer is by no means simple but, as we shall see, every particle (whether water or whisky) possesses kinetic energies of motion

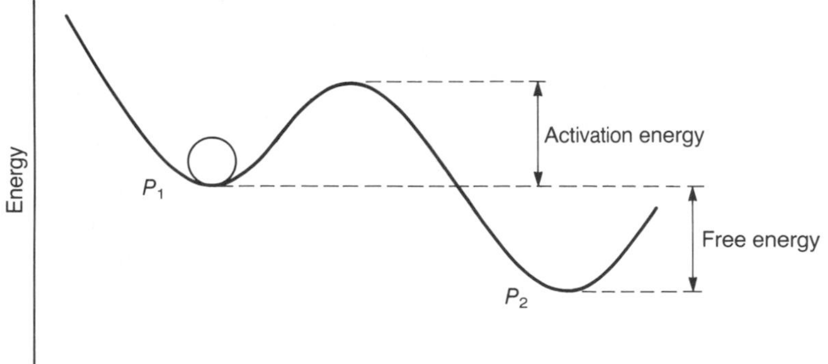

FIGURE 2.1 Schematic illustration of activation energy and free energy.

and of interaction. When a system such as a liquid is left to itself its internal energy remains constant, but when it interacts with another system it will either lose or gain energy. The transfer may involve work or heat or both and the first law of thermodynamics – the conservation of energy and heat – requires that

$$dE = dQ - dW \tag{2.1}$$

where E = internal energy, Q = heat and W = work.

What this tells us is that if we raise a cupful of water from 20°C to 30°C it does not matter how we do it. We can heat it, stir it up with paddles or even put in a whole army of gnomes each equipped with a hot water bottle but the internal energy at 30°C will always be above that at 20°C by exactly the same amount. The first law says nothing about the sequences of changes which are necessary to bring about a change in internal energy.

2.2 Entropy

Classical thermodynamics, as normally taught to engineers, regards entropy as a capacity property of a system which increases in proportion to the heat absorbed at a given temperature. Hence the well known relationship

$$dS \geqslant \frac{dQ}{T}$$

which is a perfectly good definition but does not give a true picture of the meaning of entropy and how it is defined. To a materials scientist entropy has a true physical meaning – it is a measure of the state of disorder in the system. Whisky and water combine; this simply says that, statistically, there are many ways that the atoms can get mixed up and only one possible way in which the whisky can stay on top of (or, depending how you pour it, at the bottom of) the water. Boltzmann showed that the entropy of a system could be represented by

$$S = k \ln W \tag{2.2}$$

where W is the number of ways in which the particles could be distributed and k is a constant (Boltzmann's constant $k = 1.38 \times 10^{-23}$ J/K). The fact that it is logarithmic is important; if the molecules of water can adopt W_1 configurations and those of whisky W_2 the number of possible configurations open to the mixture is not $W_1 + W_2$ but $W_1 \times W_2$. It follows from this that the entropy of any closed system will tend to a maximum since this represents the most probable configuration. You should be grateful for this. As you read these words you are keeping alive by breathing a randomly distributed mixture of oxygen and nitrogen. Now it is statistically possible that at some instant all the oxygen atoms will collect in one corner of the room while you try to exist on pure nitrogen, but only statistically possible. There are so many other possible distributions involving a random arrangement of the two gases that I suspect you will continue to breathe the normal random mixture.

2.3 Free energy

It must be clear that the fundamental tendency for entropy to increase – that is for systems to become more randomized – must be stopped somewhere and somehow. For, if not, the entire universe would break down into chaos. But, as we shall see, the reason for the existence of liquids and solids is that atoms and molecules are not totally indifferent to each other and, under certain conditions and with certain limitations, will associate with each other in a non-random way.

From the first law of thermodynamics the change in internal energy is given by

$$dE = dQ - dW.$$

From the second law the entropy change in a reversible process is

$$TdS = dQ$$

whence

$$dE = TdS - dW \qquad (2.3)$$

In discussing a system subject to reversible changes, such as elastic deformation, it is convenient to use the concept of free energy – that is to say the condition at which the energy is zero at equilibrium. For irreversible changes, it is always negative and is a measure of the driving force leading to equilibrium.

Since a spontaneous change must lead to a more probable state (or else it would not happen) it follows that, at equilibrium, energy is minimized while entropy is maximized.

The Helmholtz free energy is defined as

$$H = E - TS \qquad (2.4)$$

and the Gibbs free energy as

$$G = E + pV - TS \qquad (2.5)$$

and, at equilibrium, both must be a minimum. We shall later (page 25) apply these ideas to the elastic deformation of materials.

Chapter three

Structure of the atom

3.1 Ionic bonding
3.2 Covalent bonding
3.3 Metallic bonding
3.4 Van der Waals bonds

It will be clear that the differences between solids and liquids indicated above are a consequence of the bonding forces between the atoms of which they are composed. In order to discuss these forces we must understand a little about the structure of the atom. For our present purpose a simplified model will be sufficient.

We visualize the simplest atom – that of hydrogen – as consisting of a positively charged nucleus (the proton) with a single, negatively charged particle (the electron) in orbit around it (Figure 3.1(a)). The mass of the proton is about 2000 times that of the electron and the assembly, in its normal state, is electrically neutral. Helium has two protons and two electrons; these two atoms represent rather special cases. The next element, lithium, has 3^+, 3^- but these are arranged now in another shell (Figure 3.1(c)). And so the periodic table of the elements is built up. For reasons which need not concern us here, a structure of particular stability arises when the outermost shell contains eight electrons. The order of filling the various shells is complex and has its origins in the sophisticated concepts of quantum physics. Suffice it to say that these **octets**, as they are known, are found in neon, argon, krypton, xenon, etc. – the **inert gases**, so called because they are just that.

Suppose now we take the atom of sodium. Its structure is shown as 2-8-1 electrons (Figure 3.2). Clearly it can realize the 'octet urge' by losing an electron.

It is then left with a surplus positive charge and is known as an **ion** – in this case a positive ion. Chlorine on the other hand has shells of 2-8-7 electrons and the 'octet urge' can be satisfied if it accepts an electron to become a negative ion. With a little imagination you can probably anticipate what Section 3.1 is all about.

The outermost electrons determine the **valency** – that is to say the number of electrons forming bonds. In the above case, sodium is said to have a valency of 1 and the chemical formula for sodium chloride is NaCl, since chlorine, being able to accept one electron, also has a valency of 1. Oxygen, however, has six valence electrons and needs to borrow two. Since sodium can only donate one we obtain Na_2O. Magnesium has two valence electrons and so the chemical formula for magnesium chloride is $MgCl_2$ and for magnesium oxide MgO. The logic is, or should be, obvious, though it is not always quite so simple since some atoms, such as iron, can exhibit more than one valency.

3.1 Ionic bonding

If an atom (A) with one electron in the outermost shell meets an atom (B) with seven electrons in the outermost shell, then both can attain the octet structure if atom A donates its

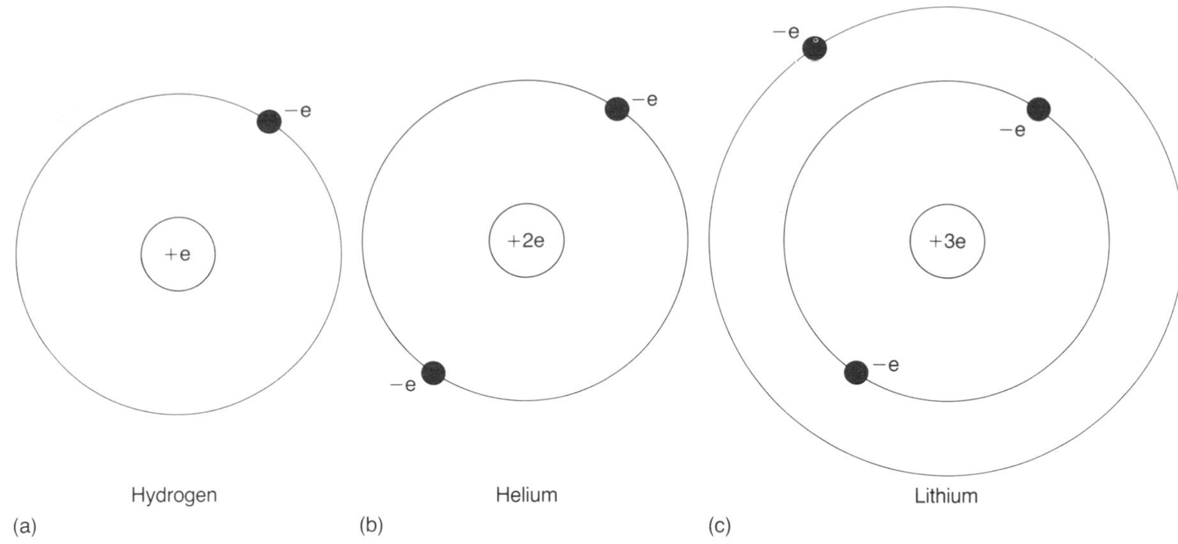

FIGURE 3.1 Schematic illustration of the atomic structures of the first three elements of the periodic table.

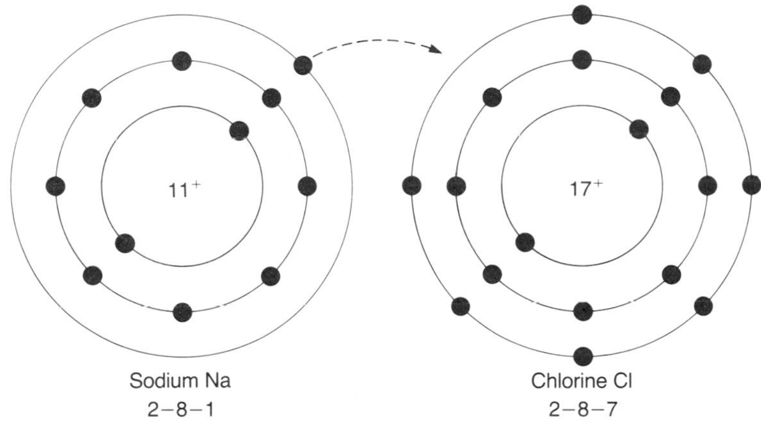

FIGURE 3.2 Schematic representation of ionic bonding.

valence electron to atom B. However, in so doing, the electrical neutrality of the atoms is disturbed: A, with an extra electron, becomes a negatively charged ion and B becomes a positively charged ion.

The two ions are then attracted to each other by the electrostatic force between them and an ionic compound results, the strength of the bond being proportional to $e_A e_B/r$ where e_A, e_B are the charges on the ions and r is the interatomic distance.

The bond is strong, as shown by the high melting point of ionic compounds, and its strength increases, as might be expected, where two or more electrons are donated. Thus the melting point of sodium chloride, NaCl, is 801°C; that of magnesium oxide, MgO, where two electrons are involved, is 2640°C; and that

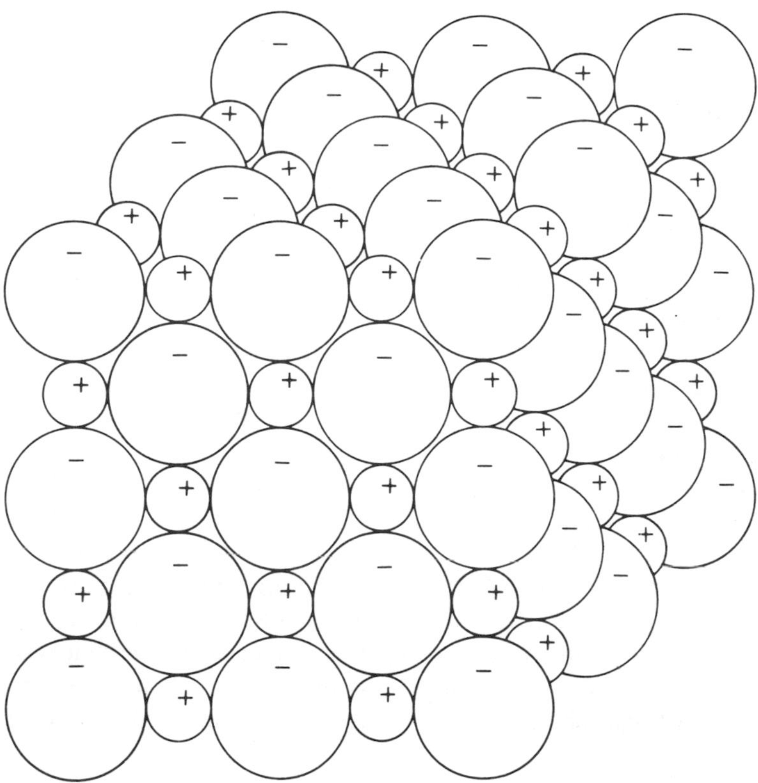

FIGURE 3.3 Non-directional nature of the ionic bond: A^- ions surrounded by B^+ ions, B^+ ions surrounded by A^- ions. This particular arrangement, where each species of ion taken by itself lies on the sites of a face-centred cubic structure, is known as the sodium chloride (NaCl) or rock salt structure.

of zirconium carbide, ZrC, where four electrons are involved, 3500°C. Since the total numbers of electrons and protons in the lattice are the same as those of the individual atoms, the lattice is electrically neutral. The ionic bond is also non-directional: that is to say, when a crystal is built up of large numbers of ions, the electrostatic charges are arranged symmetrically around each ion, with the result that A ions tend to surround themselves with ions of B and vice versa (see Figure 3.3). The pattern adopted then depends on the relative sizes of A and B ions, i.e. how many B ions can be comfortably accommodated around A ions whilst preserving the correct ratio of A ions to B ions in the lattice.

3.2 Covalent bonding

An obvious limitation of the ionic bond is that it can only occur between different atoms, and therefore it cannot be responsible for the bonding of any of the solid elements. Where both atoms are of the electron acceptor type, octet structures can be built up by the sharing of two or more valence electrons between the atoms.

Thus, to take a simple instance, two chlorine atoms can bond together and achieve the octet structure by each contributing one electron to share with the other atom. The interaction may be written:

$$:\underset{\cdot\cdot}{\dot{\mathrm{Cl}}}\cdot + :\underset{\cdot\cdot}{\dot{\mathrm{Cl}}}\cdot \rightarrow :\underset{\cdot\cdot}{\dot{\mathrm{Cl}}}:\underset{\cdot\cdot}{\dot{\mathrm{Cl}}}:$$

Where two electrons are required to make up the octet, the interaction may either be:

$$:\underset{\cdot}{\dot{\mathrm{O}}}: + :\underset{\cdot}{\dot{\mathrm{O}}}: \rightarrow :\underset{\cdot}{\dot{\mathrm{O}}}\vdots\underset{\cdot}{\dot{\mathrm{O}}}:$$

as in the oxygen molecule, or

$$+ :\underset{\cdot}{\dot{\mathrm{S}}}: + :\underset{\cdot}{\dot{\mathrm{S}}}: + :\underset{\cdot}{\dot{\mathrm{S}}}: + \ldots \rightarrow \ldots \underset{\cdot\cdot}{\ddot{\mathrm{S}}}:\underset{\cdot\cdot}{\ddot{\mathrm{S}}}:\underset{\cdot\cdot}{\ddot{\mathrm{S}}}:\underset{\cdot\cdot}{\ddot{\mathrm{S}}}:\ldots$$

as in one form of sulphur, where there is an obvious tendency for the atoms to form up in long chains. Structurally, the elements showing covalent bonding obey what is known as the $8 - N$ Rule. This states that the number of nearest neighbours to each atom is given by $8 - N$ where N is the number of electrons in the outermost shell. Thus chlorine ($N = 7$) has no nearest neighbour and so the atoms pair off as diatomic molecules; with sulphur, selenium and tellurium ($N = 6$) long chains occur; with arsenic, antimony and bismuth ($N = 5$) sheets of atoms occur, and with carbon ($N = 4$) we get a three-dimensional network. Atoms with values of N less than 4 cannot show covalent bonding with their own species, since they would require five nearest neighbours, but have only three electrons available for making up the shared bonds.

The structures are shown schematically in Figure 3.4, and it will be seen that only carbon gives a three-dimensional pattern in which all the bonds are covalent. This reveals the major structural difference between ionic and covalent bonding: the covalent bond, unlike the ionic bond, is saturated by the individual atoms participating in it.

Thus the chlorine molecule is structurally self-sufficient and there is no extension of the covalent bonding between molecules. Similarly, the chains of sulphur and the sheets of bismuth are really large molecules but there is little bonding between the chains or sheets. The result is that the covalent elements (which effectively means the non-metallic elements) have poor

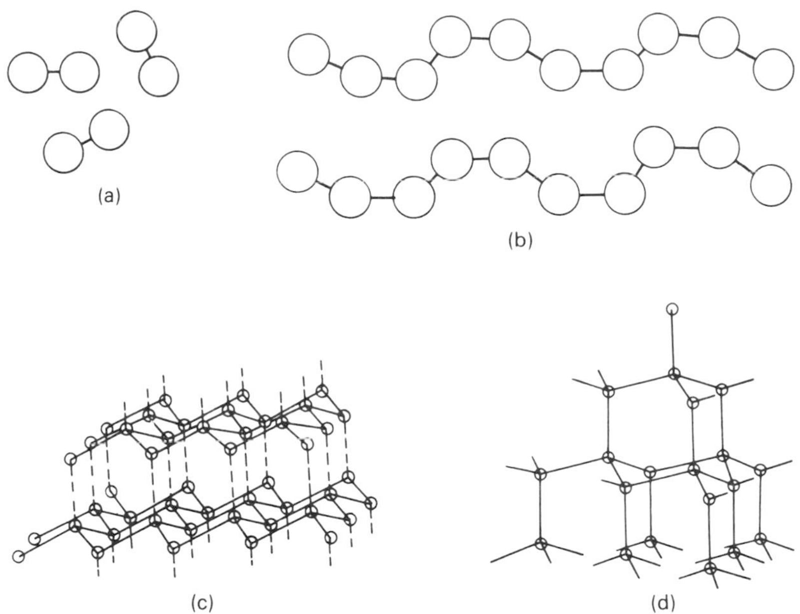

FIGURE 3.4 Schematic structures of elements conforming to the $8 - N$ rule. (a) Chlorine ($N = 7$): individual molecules; (b) tellurium ($N = 6$): spiral chains; (c) antimony ($N = 5$): corrugated sheets; (d) diamond ($N = 4$): three-dimensional crystal.

physical strength, not because the covalent bond itself is weak, but because, with the exception of diamond, they do not form a three-dimensional lattice. In fact, the hardness and high melting point of diamond (3500°C) show that the covalent bond is extremely strong. Covalent bonding is not limited to elements; many compounds are covalent, some simple examples being HCl, H_2O, CH_4 and NH_3. A large number of compounds show partly ionic and partly covalent bonding, e.g. sulphates such as Na_2SO_4 in which the sulphate ion is covalently bonded whilst the bond to the sodium is ionic.

The vast field of industrial polymers is also predominantly concerned with covalent compounds. Individual bonds may exhibit hybrid qualities akin to both ionic and covalent bonding; although in the pure form the two bond types represent different modes of linkage, there is in fact no sharp line of demarcation between them. When elements of high valency combine to form ionic compounds (e.g. the nitrides and carbides of the transition elements), the donor ion may lose three, or even four, electrons to the acceptor ion. The result is a strong polarizing pull exerted by the donor ion on the electrons of the acceptor ion, so that the electrons are sucked back towards the donor and spend more time between the two ions than circling each individually. The bond thus acquires some of the characteristics of the covalent linkage. Compounds of this sort are usually extremely hard and have very high melting points, since they combine in some degree the strength of the covalent bond and the non-directionality of the ionic bond.

3.3 Metallic bonding

The basis of the modern theory of metals was laid as long ago as the year 1900 when Drude and Lorenz put forward the free-electron theory of metals. This suggested that in a metallic crystal the valence electrons are detached from their atoms and can move freely between the positive metallic ions, as shown in Figure 3.5. The positive ions are arranged in a space lattice, and the electrostatic attraction between the positive ions and the negative free electrons

FIGURE 3.5 Schematic 'free-electron' structure for a monovalent metal. In the absence of an electric field the electrons are in ceaseless random motion, but the overall distribution remains uniform over any period of time.

provides the cohesive strength of the metal. The linkage may thus be regarded as a very special case of covalent bonding, in which the urge to attain the octet grouping is satisfied by a generalized donation of the valence electrons to form a 'cloud' which permeates the crystal lattice, rather than by electron sharing between specific atoms (true covalent bonding) or by donation to another atom (ionic bonding).

Since the electrostatic attraction between ions and electrons is non-directional, i.e. the bonding is not localized between individual pairs or groups of atoms, metallic crystals can grow easily in three dimensions, and the ions can approach all neighbours equally to give maximum density of structure.

Crystallographically, these structures are known as 'close-packed' (see page 54); they are geometrically simple by comparison with the structures of ionic compounds and naturally occurring minerals, and it is this simplicity that accounts in a large part for the ductility of the metallic elements.

This theory explains the high thermal and electrical conductivity of metals. Since the valence electrons are not bound to any particular atom, they can move through the lattice under the application of an electric potential, causing a current flow, and can also, by a series of collisions with neighbouring electrons, transmit thermal energy rapidly through the lattice (page 44). Optical properties are also explained by the theory. If a ray of light falls on a metal, the electrons (being free) can absorb the energy of the light beam, thus preventing it from passing through the crystal and rendering the metal opaque. The electrons which have absorbed the energy are excited to high energy levels and subsequently fall back to their original values with the emission of the light energy; in other words the light is reflected back from the surface of the metal, and we can account for the high reflectivity of metals.

The ability of metals to form alloys (of extreme importance to engineers) is also explained by the free-electron theory. We shall discuss this in Chapter 8.

Since the electrons are not bound, when two metals are alloyed there is no question of electron exchange or sharing between atoms in ionic or covalent bonding, and hence the ordinary valency laws of combination do not apply.

The principal limitation then becomes one of atomic size, and providing there is no great size difference (see page 58), two metals can often form a continuous series of alloys or solid solutions from 100% A to 100% B.

The Drude theory has been extensively modified since it was first proposed – only about 1% of the valence electrons are in fact sufficiently free to absorb thermal energy – but the modifications are primarily concerned with conductivity and need not be further considered here.

3.4 Van der Waals bonds

The three strong primary varieties of linkage between atoms all occur because of the need for atoms to achieve a stable electron configuration. However, even when a stable configuration exists already, as in the case of the inert gases, some sort of bonding force must be present since these elements all liquefy and ultimately solidify, albeit at very low temperatures.

Bonds of this nature are universal to all atoms and molecules, but are normally so weak that their effect is negligible when any primary bonds are present. They are knows as Van der Waals bonds, and are one reason why real gases deviate from the ideal gas laws. They arise as follows.

Although in Figure 3.1 we represented the orbiting electrons in discrete shells, the true picture is that of a cloud, the density of the cloud at any point being related to the probability of finding an electron there. Such a picture implies that the electron charge is 'spread' around the atom, and over a period of time the charge may be thought of as symmetrically distributed within its particular cloud.

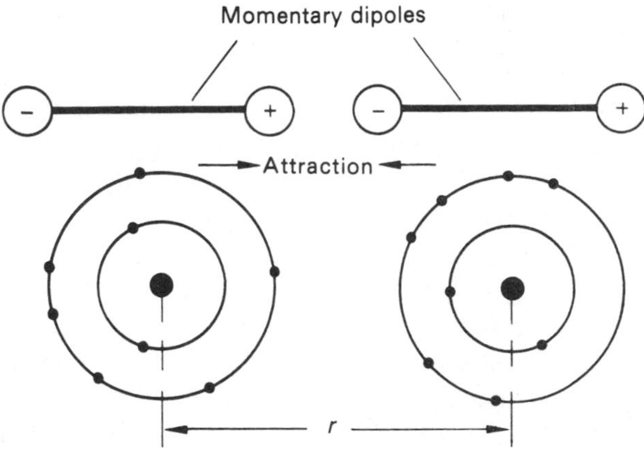

FIGURE 3.6 Weak Van der Waals linkage between atoms arising from fluctuating electronic fields.

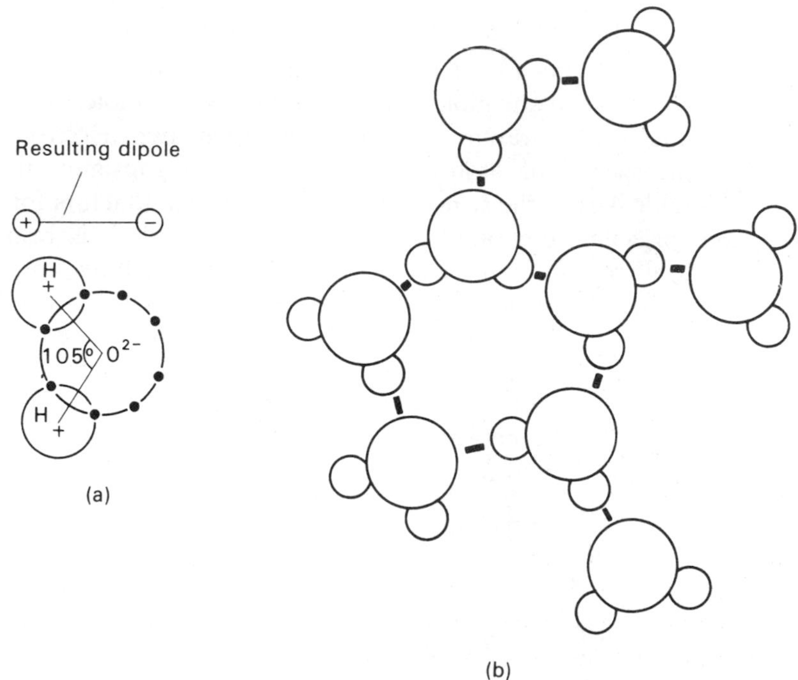

FIGURE 3.7 The hydrogen bond: (a) individual water molecule showing dipole resulting from bond angle; (b) structure of water.

However, the electronic charge is moving, and this means that on a scale of nanoseconds the electrostatic field around the atom is continuously fluctuating, resulting in the formation of a dynamic dipole. When another atom is brought into proximity, the dipoles of the two atoms may interact co-operatively with one another (Figure 3.6) and the result is a weak electrostatic bond. This bond is non-directional.

The attractive force between two atoms is given by the expression

$$F = \frac{\alpha_1 \alpha_2}{r^6}$$

where α_1 and α_2 are the polarizabilities of the two atoms, i.e. the ease with which their electronic fields can be distorted by a unit electric field to form a dipole, and r is the distance between them. Polarizability increases with atomic number, since the outermost electrons (which are responsible for the effect) are further removed from the nucleus and therefore more easily pulled towards neighbouring atoms. This is shown by a comparison of the freezing points of the inert gases He (1 K) and Xe (133 K), or the halogens fluorine (51 K) and iodine (387 K).

As well as this fluctuating dipole, many molecules have permanent dipoles as a result of bonding between different species of atoms. These can play a considerable part in the structure of polymers and organic compounds, where side chains and radical groups of ions can lead to points of predominantly positive or negative charges that will exert an electrostatic attraction to other oppositely charged groups.

The strongest and most important example of dipole interaction occurs in compounds between hydrogen and nitrogen, oxygen or fluorine. It occurs because of the small and simple structure of the hydrogen atom and has in fact become known as the hydrogen bond. When, for example, hydrogen links covalently with oxygen to form water, the electron contributed by the hydrogen atom spends the greater part of its time between the two atoms, and the bond acquires a definite dipole with hydrogen becoming virtually a positively charged ion.

Since the hydrogen nucleus is not screened by any other electron shells, it can attract to itself other negative ends of dipoles, and the result is the hydrogen bond. It is considerably stronger (roughly $\times 10$) than other Van der Waals linkages, but is much weaker (by 10 to 20 times) than any of the primary bonds. Figure 3.7 shows the resultant structure of water, where the hydrogen bond forms a secondary link between the water molecules, and acts as a bridge between two electronegative oxygen ions. This relatively insignificant bond is, then, one of the most vital factors for the benefit and survival of mankind; it is responsible for the abnormally high melting and boiling points of water and for its high specific heat (which affords an essential global temperature control): in its absence water might well be gaseous at ambient temperatures like ammonia or hydrogen sulphide.

Chapter four

Elasticity and plasticity

4.1 Linear elasticity
4.2 Consequences of the theory
4.3 Long-range elasticity
4.4 Viscoelasticity
4.5 Plasticity

We noted earlier that the product of stress and strain has the dimensions of energy. Since thermodynamics teaches us about energy it is convenient to start with the thermodynamics of a deformation process. From the first law (eqn (2.1))

$$dE = dQ - dW$$

and rewrite the second law as

$$dQ = TdS$$

whence

$$dE = TdS - dW.$$

The work done by a force f in extending a bar by dL is $dW = fdL$ so that

$$dE = TdS - fdL.$$

The Helmholtz free energy (eqn (2.4)) is

$$H = E - TS$$

so that a change in free energy

$$dH = dE - TdS - SdT.$$

But if the conditions are such that temperature remains constant, that change is $dH = dE - TdS = fdL$ so that

$$f = \left(\frac{\partial H}{\partial L}\right)_T = \left(\frac{\partial E}{\partial L}\right)_T - T\left(\frac{\partial S}{\partial L}\right)_T. \quad (4.1)$$

This is the **thermodynamic equation of state** for deformation and shows that the force is distributed between a change in internal energy and a change in entropy. We now examine these changes.

4.1 Linear elasticity

The first term of eqn (4.1) implies that at least part of the response to an applied force involves a change in internal energy. In crystalline solids, where the atoms are arranged in orderly ranks in space, the capacity for independent movement is limited and the bulk of the internal energy is to be found in the interaction energies between the atoms.

To keep things simple, let us consider the energies acting between a pair of atoms. Whatever the cause of the energies, they tend to vary as the inverse of the distance between the atoms, raised to some power. So if the distance between the atoms is r, and A, B, m and n are constants that vary with the material and its structure,

the attractive energy $A = r^{-n}$
the repulsive energy $B = r^{-m}$
and the resultant energy $U = Br^{-m} - Ar^{-n}$. (4.2)

These three curves are sketched on Figure 4.1(a). Figure 4.1(b) presents the same information, but in terms of the force F. There are three things to note.

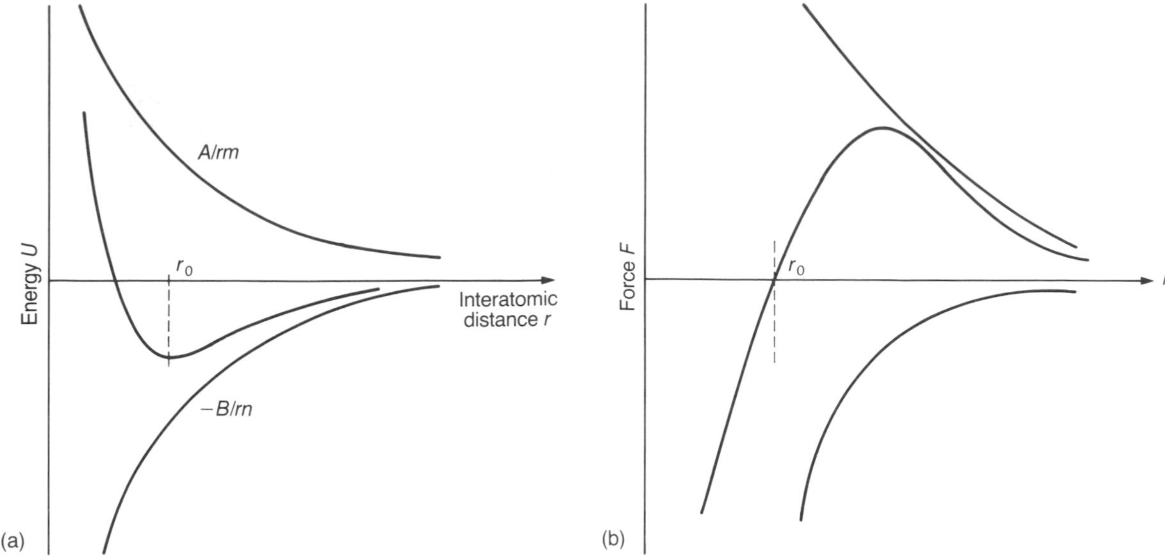

FIGURE 4.1 (a) Condon–Morse curves of energy versus interatomic spacing r; (b) the force acting on an ion as a function of r. r_0 is the mean interatomic spacing.

1. The bond energy U is a continuous function of r. Thus we can express the energy as a series

$$U(r) = U(r_0) + \left(\frac{dU}{dr}\right)_{r_0} + \frac{1}{2}\left(\frac{d^2U}{dr^2}\right)_{r_0} + \ldots$$

where $U(r_0)$ is the energy at $r = r_0$ and the differential is taken at $r = r_0$.
2. The minimum in the curve at r_0 allows us to eliminate the second term since $(dU/dr) = 0$ at a minimum.
3. The displacement is small, so ignore terms higher than r_0^2. Then we find that

$$U(r) = U(r_0) + \frac{1}{2}\left(\frac{d^2U}{dr^2}\right)_{r_0^2}$$

whence

$$F = \frac{dU}{dr} = \left(\frac{d^2U}{dr^2}\right)_{r_0} \mathrm{r} \qquad (4.3)$$

i.e. force is proportional to displacement via a constant (d^2U/dr^2).

In other words, the constant of proportionality is the slope of the $F{:}r$ graph at the equilibrium position where $x = 0$ and $F = 0$, assuming x to be small compared to r_0.

4.2 Consequences of the theory

Having established some mathematical facts about the graphs of force and energy against distance, let us use them to predict some consequences and tie them up with the real world. To a materials scicntist there are a great many consequences but only eight of the most noteworthy are given below.

1. When a material is extended or compressed, the force is proportional to the extension (from eqn (1.3)). This in fact is Hooke's law. The slope of the $F{:}r$ curve at $r = r_0$ is the elastic constant (or stiffness).

2. Since the $F:r$ curve is symmetrical about the equilibrium position, the stiffness of a material will be the same in tension and compression. This is, in fact, the case.
3. At large strains, greater than about 10%, the $F:r$ curve can no longer be considered straight and so Hooke's law should break down. It does.
4. There should be a limit to the tensile strength, since the attractive force between the atoms has a maximum value. This is so.
5. There should be no possibility of failure in compression since the repulsive force between the atoms increases *ad infinitum*. This is so. Under a compressive stress, failure is always in tension or shear.
6. If the atoms vibrate about their equilibrium positions, then their mean separation will increase the more they vibrate. This follows from the trough of the $U:r$ curve being asymmetrical. In fact in materials at any temperature above absolute zero (−273°C), the atoms do vibrate in proportion to the temperature. It follows then that as a material is heated it should expand in all directions. This is so.
7. If the heating process is continued the atoms should reach a degree of vibration that causes them to separate, i.e. the bond is broken. This is what happens when a solid melts.
8. Any degree of vibration by the atoms should reduce the extra amount of energy required to break the bond. In other words the tensile strength should decrease as the temperature increases. This does happen.

4.3 Long-range elasticity

We now consider the second term in eqn (4.1). The structures of specific polymers will be described in Chapter 27. Meanwhile we consider, briefly, the basic type of structure. In its simplest form this consists of a chain, often many units long, of atoms (generally, though not necessarily, of carbon) each of which is covalently bonded to another atom. The structure of polyethylene is shown diagrammatically in Figure 4.2(a).

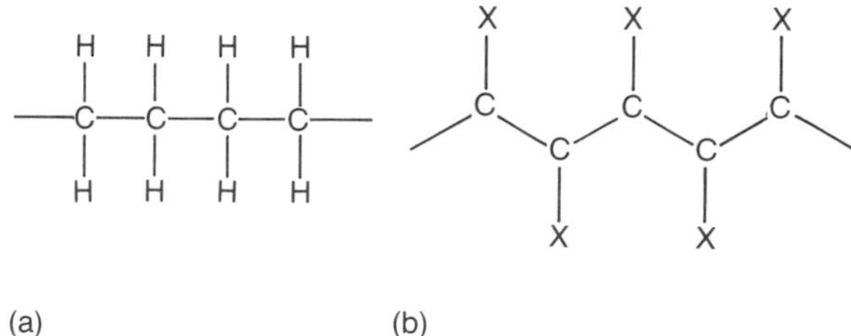

FIGURE 4.2 Polyethylene. (a) Diagrammatic. In (b) X represents two hydrogen atoms, one above and one below the plane of the carbon chain.

But, of course, things are not quite so simple. The carbon bond is not unidirectional but can operate over a volume (Figure 4.2(b)) so that the chain tends to get twisted. Secondly the long chain is a complete molecular entity and, in the simplest case, is not bonded to another chain. We therefore have a structure which looks rather like a tangle of wet spaghetti. But, in addition, at temperatures above a certain level, which is a characteristic property of the polymer, the chains are in constant motion as a result of thermal fluctuations. It is intuitively obvious that the application of a force will cause changes in the internal configuration. A given atom in the molecular chain will not change its neighbours within the chain but it will change its neighbours in adjacent chains several times during the loading–unloading cycle.

Expressed in thermodynamic terms we may state that the unloaded configuration is, or is close to being, the most probable one – in other words this is the equilibrium configuration of maximum entropy. Under load the configuration changes to one that is the most probable for the loaded condition and the entropy changes. It can be shown that the number of possible configurations available to a chain, whether convoluted or not (a straight chain is only one of many possible configurations), is a function of

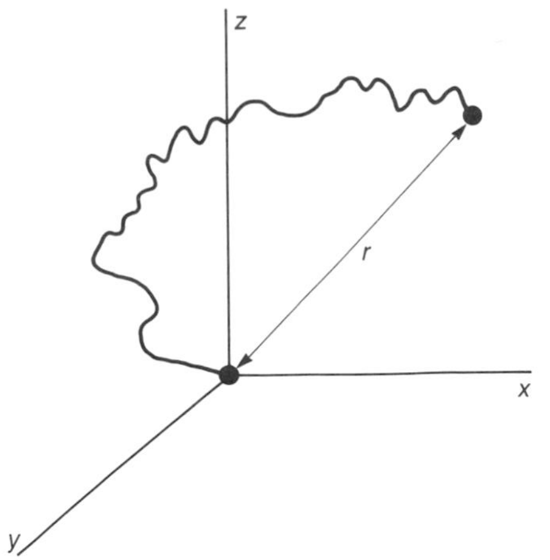

FIGURE 4.3 Schematic representation of a randomly convoluted molecular chain.

its end-to-end length. The number of possible configurations N_c decreases as r increases. This is known as the **configurational entropy** S_c and is given by Boltzmann's equation (eqn (2.2)) here rewritten as:

$$S_c = K \ln N_c \tag{4.4}$$

i.e. the entropy decreases as r increases.

We shall not pursue here the statistical arguments describing the probability of a particular configuration being obtained. This is done fully in standard texts (Treloar, 1949) and here we state only the principles.

1. If the ends of the molecule are moved from their most probable positions the change in entropy causes a force to act along a line joining the ends of the molecule (Figure 4.3).
2. The entropy force increases and is proportional to the absolute temperature. The magnitude of the force is a function of the end-to-end length as represented by a straight line joining the ends. In this it behaves as though it were an elastic spring.

The spring analogy should not, however, be taken too literally. Being statistical in origin the tension in a chain whose endpoints are fixed will be subject to continual fluctuations like the pressure exerted by a gas on the walls of the container.

Similarly, if the molecule is subjected to a constant tension its length will fluctuate. But we see that rubber elasticity is long range and is quite a different thing from the short-range forces which determine Hookean elasticity.

4.4 Viscoelasticity

We have already indicated that it is not possible to draw a sharp dividing line between the mechanical behaviour of liquids and solids. We

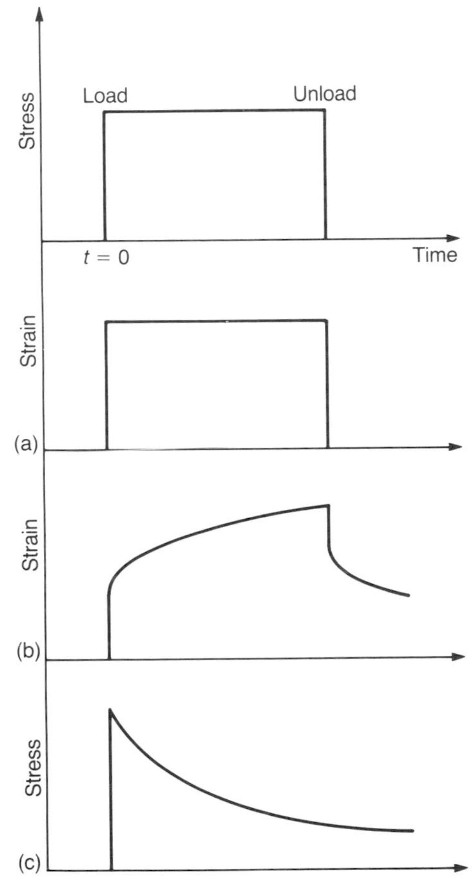

FIGURE 4.4 The behaviour of (a) Hookean; (b) viscoelastic (creep); and (c) viscoelastic (stress relaxation) solids.

shall return to this later in the book but meanwhile we examine one group of materials known as viscoelastics whose behaviour is part liquid and part solid and which is best represented by a combination of the ideal Hookean solid and the ideal Newtonian liquid. This involves a large group of materials (many natural materials); tendon, plant fibres and wood all behave in this way. Of engineering materials, rubbers are the archetype and so are many soft polymers. Here we use simple models to illustrate viscoelasticity.

If an instantaneous stress is applied to a Hookean material the corresponding strain is produced. So long as the load is maintained the strain remains constant (Figure 4.4(a)) and is fully recovered when the load is removed. The behaviour of a viscoelastic material is illustrated in Figure 4.4(b). The strain builds up over a period of time and, when the load is removed, the strain takes time to relax. This behaviour is known as **creep**. A similar phenomenon occurs if the material is subjected to a fixed strain. In a Hookean material stress remains constant for as long as the strain is maintained; in a viscoelastic solid the stress diminishes over a period of time as shown in Figure 4.4(c). This is **stress relaxation.**

The structural reasons for this behaviour need not delay us here as they will be discussed in later chapters dealing with specific materials – cements, polymers and timber especially. Meanwhile we consider a mechanical model (the so-called Maxwell model as shown in Figure 4.5(a)) which is sufficient to define the terms used in the study of viscoelastic materials. It consists of an elastic spring s of modulus M and a piston moving in a fluid F of viscosity η.

Both elements carry equal stress so that

$$\sigma = \sigma_s = \sigma_F$$

and

$$\dot{\varepsilon} = \dot{\varepsilon}_s + \dot{\varepsilon}_F$$

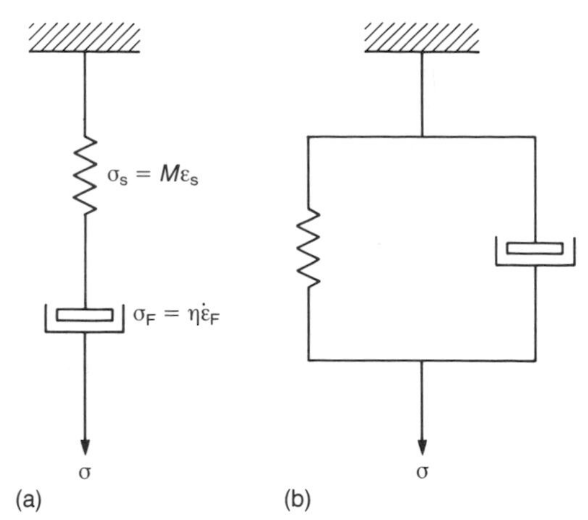

FIGURE 4.5 Viscoelastic models: (a) Maxwell model; (b) Voigt model.

whence

$$\varepsilon = \frac{\sigma}{M} + \int_0^t \frac{\sigma}{\eta} \mathrm{d}t.$$

For a step loading $\sigma = \sigma_0$, for initial stress

$$\varepsilon = \sigma_0\left(\frac{1}{M} + \frac{t}{\eta}\right)$$

or, putting $\eta/M = \tau$,

$$\varepsilon = \frac{\sigma_0}{M}(1 + t/\tau)$$

under constant strain $\varepsilon = \varepsilon_0$, we obtain, by differentiating,

$$\frac{\mathrm{d}\sigma}{\mathrm{d}t} = -\frac{M\sigma}{\eta}$$

having a solution

$$\sigma = \sigma_0 \exp\left(-\frac{ME}{\eta}\right) = \sigma_0 \exp(-t/\tau) \quad (4.5)$$

i.e. under constant strain the stress decays exponentially (Figure 4.4(c)). The ratio t/τ is known as the **relaxation time** (it is in fact that time for the stress to decay to 1/e of its initial value) and is a characteristic of the model.

The relaxation time is an important property

for two reasons. First because it helps us to distinguish between solids and liquids. A perfect solid will support the stress indefinitely, i.e. $\tau = \infty$, but for a liquid, relaxation is virtually instantaneous (for water τ = about 10^{-11} s). In between there is a grey area where stress relaxation may occur in a finite time.

Two cases at least are of importance to engineers. If the strain remains constant (as in a tension bolt clamping two girders together) relaxation may occur without dimensional change. When the material is under constant stress it will respond by a steadily increasing strain and, under prolonged loading, many normally rigid materials such as cement and concrete are prone to creep.

The second reason is the relationship between the relaxation time and the rate of loading t. If the load is applied so fast that the relaxation cannot occur ($t < \tau$) the material will behave elastically but, under slow loading ($t > \tau$), it will flow. This is well shown by 'potty putty' which bounces under impact loading but collapses into a puddle under its own weight when left alone. Many polymeric materials show a similar sensitivity to loading speed.

The Maxwell model is, however, of no use for modelling creep since, under constant load, the spring will be constant under tension and all that will be observed is the flow in the dashpot. It is left as an exercise for the reader to show that the parallel model (Kelvin or Voigt model, as shown in Figure 4.5), where both elements have equal strains but different stresses, leads to the expression

$$\varepsilon = \frac{\sigma_c}{M}[1 - \exp(-t/\tau)] \qquad (4.6)$$

Both models are, of course, simplifications. A real viscoelastic material such as a polymer is composed statistically. Some molecular chains are long, some are short, some behave elastically, some do not.

Thus, to model a real material, we would need to combine large numbers of these simple elements, each having its own relaxation time, to yield a **relaxation spectrum** in which different elements relax at different times. The effect is easily seen by crumpling a piece of cellophane and then watching it try to unfold. This can take many minutes.

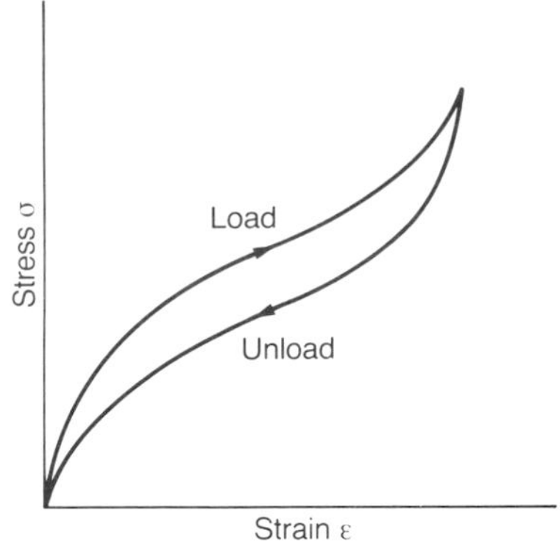

FIGURE 4.6 Loading/unloading curves for a viscoelastic solid.

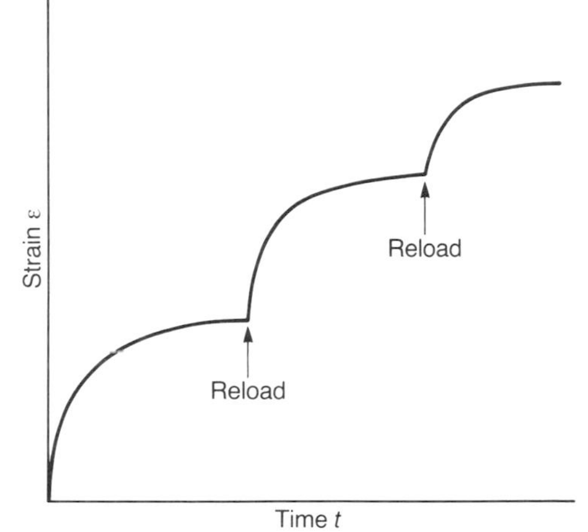

FIGURE 4.7 Boltzmann's superposition principle.

But there are a number of important consequences of viscoelasticity. The first is that the stress–strain relationship is non-linear. We noted that in a Hookean solid the strain energy stored on loading is completely recovered when we unload. Figure 4.6 shows that the energy recovered on unloading is less than that stored on loading. Where has the stored energy gone? It has gone into heat, which explains why, after a few miles in which they are repeatedly loaded and unloaded, car tyres get hot.

The second consequence is known as Boltzmann's superposition theory. This states that each increment of load makes an independent and additive contribution to the total deformation. Thus, under the loading programme shown in Figure 4.7, the creep response is additive and the total creep is the sum of all the units of incremental creep. This has certain consequences when we apply it to the creep behaviour of concrete and soils.

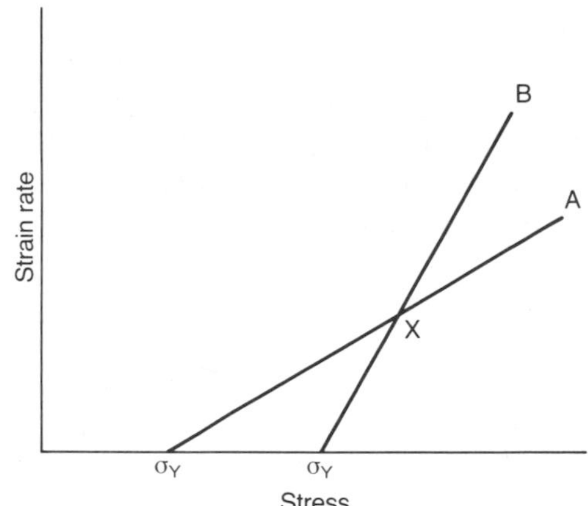

FIGURE 4.8 Flow curves (schematic) for fresh concrete.

4.5 Plasticity

Many materials display **plasticity**; that is to say, when they are deformed the change in shape is permanent and the original dimensions can only be restored by applying a force in the opposite direction. This is a particularly valuable attribute of metals and we shall discuss the reasons in Chapter 9. Meanwhile we consider the more general case as exhibited, for instance, by clays.

We have noted already that the ideal (Newtonian) fluid flows according to

$$\tau = \eta\dot{\gamma}$$

where η is the viscosity. When the fluid contains dispersed particles these perturb the pattern of flow and, for dispersed spheres, the viscosity is now given by Einstein's equation,

$$\eta = \eta_0\left(1 + \frac{5}{2}V\right)$$

where η_0 is the viscosity of the pure fluid and V the volume fraction of particles.

Actual viscosities of suspensions are usually much higher than this because the particles are non-spherical. Thus, for randomly oriented dumb-bells,

$$\eta = \eta_0\left(1 + \frac{3}{2}p^2V\right)$$

where p is the ratio of dumb-bell length to diameter.

The above equations break down still further when the volume fraction of the particles increases to the point where the perturbed regions in the liquid begin to overlap and we find terms in V^2 appearing. We are now in the region of pastes, clays, sand, gravel, etc. where the volume fraction of grains is high, typically $V = 0.65$ for a sand bed and $V = 0.95$ for a mixed sand/gravel bed where the sand can fill the spaces between the grains of gravel.

Clearly the mechanical properties are sensitive to the volume fraction of grains – dry clay becomes plastic when water is added to it. At 30% water each clay particle is separated by a film of water and it can be modelled. With more water the grains float apart to form a slurry.

Pastes and modelling clays, however, are plastic solids rather than viscous fluids. They deform, more or less elastically, up to a certain **yield stress** and can preserve their shape against gravity. This is vital to the moulding of bricks and clay pottery. Above this stress, however, they behave like liquids and deform rapidly. This behaviour is described, approximately, by the Bingham equation

$$\dot{\gamma} = \frac{\sigma - \sigma_Y}{\eta}$$

where σ_Y is the yield stress as shown in Figure 4.8. Tattersall and Banfill (1983) have shown that fresh concrete can be considered as a so-called 'Bingham solid' and instance the difference between two concrete mixes having the flow curves shown in Figure 4.8. At low rates of flow B is less workable than A; the reverse is true at high rates of flow. At X both would be classed as having the same workability.

Chapter five

Surfaces

5.1 Surface energy
5.2 Water of crystallization
5.3 Wetting
5.4 Adhesives
5.5 Adsorption

All materials are bounded by interfaces of varying nature. For the engineer the most important are the liquid–vapour, solid–vapour, solid–liquid and solid–solid interfaces, the last mentioned existing as the boundary either between two differing solid phases in a material (e.g. cement gel and aggregate in concrete) or between two similar crystals which differ only in orientation (e.g. the grain boundaries in a pure metal). Surfaces owe their interest and importance to two simple features: they are areas of abnormality in relation to the structure that they bound (in which sense they may be regarded as a form of imperfection), and they are the only part of the material accessible to chemical change; that is to say all chemical change and, for that matter, most temperature changes take place through the media of surfaces. The importance of surfaces in determining the bulk behaviour of materials naturally depends on the ratio of surface area to the total mass, and this in turn will depend partly on the size and partly on the shape of the individual particles making up the bulk material.

Surface influence probably reaches its zenith with clays, which are composed of platelets that may be as small as 0.1 μm across by 0.01 μm thick.

Platelets have a high surface area/volume ratio by comparison with spheres of equal volume: 1 g of montmorillonite clay (rather smaller than a lump of cube sugar) may contain a total surface area of over 800 square metres! Porous structures such as cement and wood also contain enormous internal surface areas which exercise a considerable effect on their engineering properties.

5.1 Surface energy

All surfaces have one thing in common: the atoms or ions in the surface will be subjected to asymmetric or unsaturated bonding forces (this is particularly the case with solid–vapour and liquid–vapour interfaces), and since bonding is taken to lower their energy (Figure 4.1) they will be in a state of higher energy than interior ions. This excess energy is known as the **surface energy** of the material. In solids the presence of a surface energy is not immediately apparent, since the atoms in the surface are firmly held in position; with liquids, however, the mobile structure permits the individual atoms to respond, and the result is the well-known surface tension effect. Because surfaces are high-energy regions they will always act to minimize their area (and thus lower their energy) when possible; if a soap film is stretched across a frame with a movable wire as in Figure 5.1, the force required to hold the wire in place is

$$F = 2\gamma l$$

where l is the length of the wire, γ is the surface tension of the soap film/air interface and the factor 2 is introduced because the film has two surfaces. It is important to note that surface

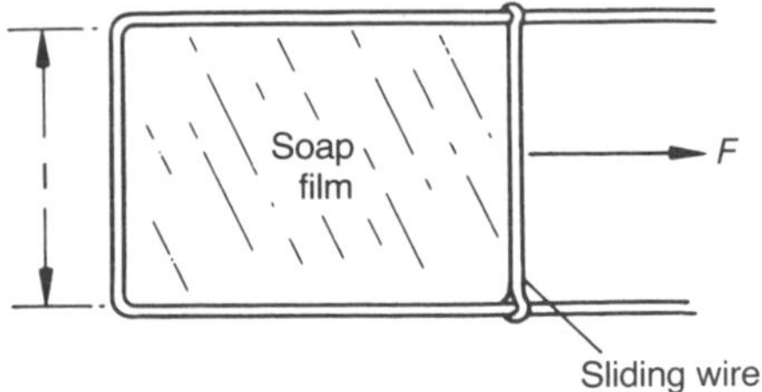

FIGURE 5.1 Equilibrium between soap film and applied force F.

tension differs from an elastic force acting between the surface atoms in that it remains constant whether the film is forced to expand or allowed to contract. This is because the work done in expanding the film is used to bring additional atoms to the surface rather than to increase the interatomic spacing in the surface. Only when the film has become so thin that the two surfaces interact with each other will the force show partial elastic behaviour, by which time the film is on the point of rupture.

5.2 Water of crystallization

It is well known that many ionic crystals contain water molecules locked up in their structure as water of crystallization; such crystals are known in general as hydrates, and their formation can be very important in the development of bulk strength. Both cement and plaster of Paris owe their commercial importance to their ability to take up water and form a rigid mass of interlocking crystals, although in the case of cement the crystals are so small that it becomes an almost philosophical problem to decide whether to classify the structure as a crystalline hydrate or a hydrated gel.

Water and ammonia are the only two molecules that can be taken up as a structural part of crystals, and both for the same reasons: they are small molecules which are strongly polar in nature. The small size permits them to penetrate into the interstices of crystal structures where close packing of ions is not possible. This is particularly the case where the negative counterion is large, such as SO_4 (sulphate), SiO_4 (silicate) or B_4O_7 (borate). It must be emphasized that this process is not to be thought of as a capillary action, analogous to the take-up of large amounts of water by clays; the water molecules are bonded into definite sites within the crystal structure, and the crystal will only form a stable hydrate if ions of the appropriate signs are available and correctly placed to form bonds with the positively and negatively charged regions of the water molecule. We have already mentioned (page 23) the abnormal properties of water as arising from the ability of the molecules to link up by means of hydrogen bonds; the formation of crystalline hydrates is an extension of the same behaviour.

Normally the water molecules cluster round the positive ions in the crystal-forming hydrated ions; this has the effect of making the small ion behave as if it were a good deal larger. As a result, the size difference between the positive and negative ion is effectively reduced, thus making for simpler and more closely packed crystal structures. Water bonded in this manner is very firmly held in many instances so that hydration becomes virtually irreversible. Cement, for example, retains its water of crystallization up to about 300°C.

5.3 Wetting

There are other ways besides reduction in area in which a system of interfaces may reduce its total surface energy; one of the most important technological aspects concerns the behaviour of liquids on solids.

If a droplet of liquid is placed on a solid, the immediate behaviour of the liquid depends on the relative magnitudes of three surface energies: liquid–solid γ_{ls}, liquid–vapour γ_{lv}, and solid–vapour γ_{sv}. At the periphery of the droplet the three energies operate as depicted in Figure 5.2 and the final contour of the droplet will result

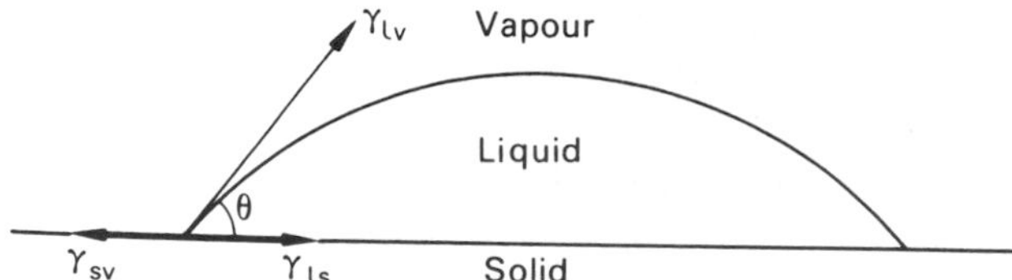

FIGURE 5.2 Surface forces acting at the periphery of a droplet.

when they are in equilibrium resolved parallel to the solid surface, i.e. when

$$\gamma_{sv} = \gamma_{ls} + \gamma_{lv} \cos\theta. \tag{5.1}$$

If

$$\gamma_{sv} \geq \gamma_{ls} + \gamma_{lv}$$

then $\theta = 0°$, and complete wetting of the solid surface occurs; the energy of such a system is obviously lowered when the solid–vapour interface is replaced by a solid–liquid and a liquid–vapour interface. When

$$\gamma_{ls} + \gamma_{lv} > \gamma_{sv} > \gamma_{ls}$$

then $\theta < 90°$ and partial wetting occurs; the resulting force tending to spread the droplet (from eqn (5.1)) is given by

$$\gamma_{sv} - \gamma_{lv} \cos\theta. \tag{5.2}$$

When $\gamma_{sv} < \gamma_{ls}$ (this is comparatively rare, provided that the surfaces are clean) then $\theta < 90°$, and $\gamma_{lv} \cos\theta$ becomes negative, in which case there is little or no tendency to wetting. The rise of water in a capillary tube is a consequence of the ability of water to wet glass. If, in Figure 5.3, θ is the angle of contact between water and glass, the water is drawn up the tube by a circumferential force equal to $2\pi r\gamma_{lv} \cos\theta$. At equilibrium this is balanced by the weight of water in the column; hence

$$2\pi r\gamma_{lv} \cos\theta = \pi r^2 h\rho.$$

For water the density $\rho = 1$, and therefore (neglecting the mass of water contained in the curve of the meniscus)

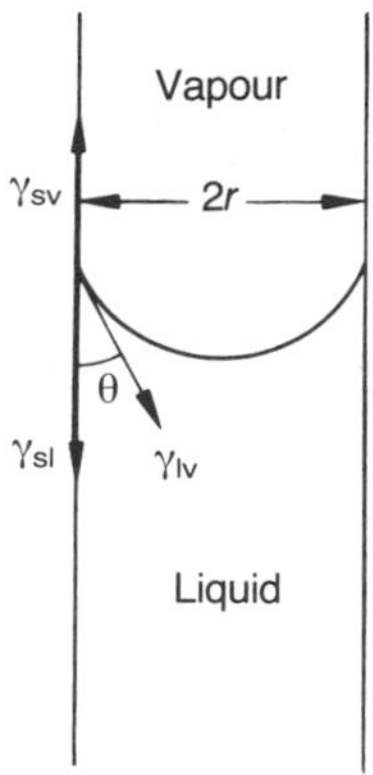

FIGURE 5.3 Capillary rise of liquid up a tube.

$$h = \frac{2\gamma_{lv} \cos\theta}{r}. \tag{5.3}$$

Note that if r is small, h can be very large. If all the pores in brick or concrete were continuous $h \approx 10$ m is theoretically possible. Rising damp indeed! Fortunately the pores are not continuous and evaporation keeps the level lower than this.

5.4 Adhesives

The ability of adhesives to spread and thoroughly wet surfaces is highly important, for example where molten solder or brazing alloy has to penetrate into a thin joint. Furthermore, the adhesion of a liquid to a solid surface is relevant to the performance of adhesives. The work to break away the adhesive (which may be considered as a viscous liquid) from the solid is the work required to create a liquid–vapour and a solid–vapour interface from an equivalent area of liquid–solid interface, i.e. it is the work to totally 'de-wet' the solid surface. Hence the work to cause breakage at the interface is given by

$$W = \gamma_{lv} + \gamma_{sv} - \gamma_{ls}.$$

But

$$\gamma_{sv} - \gamma_{ls} = \gamma_{lv} \cos\theta \tag{5.4}$$

and therefore

$$W = \gamma_{lv}(1 + \cos\theta). \qquad (5.5)$$

Thus the liquid–solid adhesion increases with the ability of the adhesive to wet the solid, reaching a maximum given by

$$W = 2\gamma_{lv}$$

when $\theta = 0°$ and wetting is complete. Under these conditions fracture will then occur within the adhesive, since the energy necessary to form two liquid–vapour interfaces is less than that to form a liquid–vapour and solid–vapour interface.

Surface tension is also the cause of the adhesion between two flat surfaces separated by a thin film of fluid. Where the surface of a liquid is curved (as for example in Figure 5.4) there will be a pressure difference p across it; if the curvature is spherical of radius r, then

$$p = \frac{2\gamma}{r}.$$

In the case of two circular discs, however, the surface of the film has two radii of curvature, as shown in Figure 5.3; r_1 is approximately equal to the radii of the discs and presents a convex surface to the atmosphere whilst $r_2 \approx d/2$ where d is the width of the film between the plates, and presents a concave surface to the atmosphere. The pressure difference between the liquid film and its surroundings is now given by

$$p = \gamma\left(\frac{1}{r_1} - \frac{1}{r_2}\right).$$

If r_2 is small compared with r_1, we can say

$$p \approx -\frac{\gamma}{r_2} + \frac{2\gamma}{d}$$

the negative sign indicating that the pressure is lower within the liquid than outside it.

Since the pressure acts over the whole surface of the discs, the force to overcome it and separate the plates is given by

$$F = \frac{2\pi r_1^2 \gamma}{d}. \qquad (5.6)$$

The magnitude of F thus depends on the factor r_1^2/d, and it is therefore important that joint surfaces should be as flat and closely spaced as possible. Any reader who has tried to pull apart two wet beer glasses will confirm how tenaciously they cling to each other; by contrast, however, they can easily be slid apart since liquid films have little resistance to shear. If we take $d = 0.01$ mm and γ for water as 7×10^{-4} N then $F = 0.4$ N; for two panes of window glass size 30 cm × 20 cm, $F \simeq 8400$ N. The magnitude of these values of F for a liquid

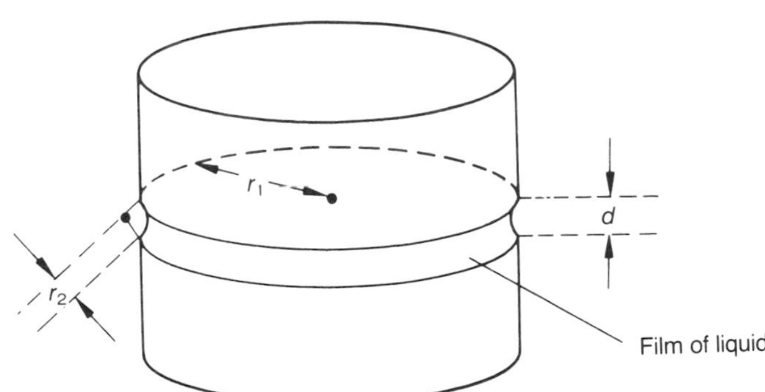

FIGURE 5.4 Adhesive effect of a thin film of liquid between two flat plates. If the liquid wets the surfaces of the discs, then $r_2 \simeq d/2$.

film gives some idea of the potential of adhesives which gain additional strength and rigidity by setting to highly viscous materials on polymerization or solvent evaporation.

5.5 Adsorption

The ability of liquids to wet solids depends very much on the cleanliness of the solid, as anyone with any experience of soldering will appreciate. The presence of any dirt, such as oxide or grease films, will totally alter the balance of surface tensions discussed above and usually results in complete prevention of wetting.

Clean surfaces, in fact, are so rare as to be virtually non-existent, since the broken bonds will readily attract to themselves any foreign atoms or molecules that have a slight affinity for the surface material. This effect is known as **adsorption**, and by satisfying or partially satisfying the unsaturated surface bonds it serves to lower surface energy. Adsorption is a dynamic process; that is to say molecules are constantly alighting on and taking off from the surface.

Different molecules adsorb with varying degrees of intensity, depending on the nature of the bond that is able to form at the interface, and the strength of the bond may be expressed in terms of ϕ_a, the energy of adsorption. As in the case of interatomic bonds, a negative value of ϕ_a is taken to indicate a positive adsorption; that is to say the molecules are attracted to the interface, and the surface tension is lowered thereby. A positive value of ϕ_a indicates a repulsive interaction and the molecules avoid the surface. Typical plots of ϕ_a against the spacing of the adsorbed layer away from the surface are given in Figure 5.5; they closely resemble Condon–Morse curves (Figure 4.1) and their shape is due to the same circumstance of equilibrium between attractive and repulsive forces, although the attraction is far weaker than that of the principal interatomic bonds.

If the adsorbing molecule is non-polar and does not react chemically with the surface, absorption (if it occurs) will be by Van der Waals bonds, and the minimum value of ϕ_a is small (curve 2 in Figure 5.5). If on the other hand the molecule is strongly polar (as is the case with water or ammonia), the electrostatic forces between the surface and the charged portion of the molecule give rise to stronger bonding; if a chemical reaction occurs as part of the bonding mechanism (e.g. when fatty acid in a

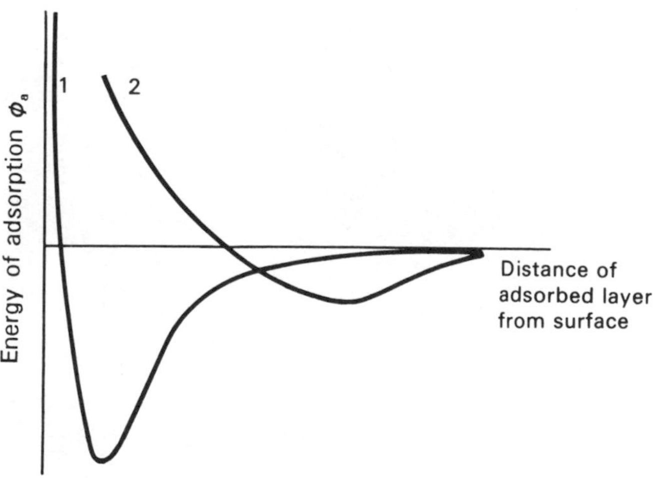

FIGURE 5.5 Energies of adsorption for different adsorption mechanisms: curve 1, chemisorption; curve 2, physical adsorption.

lubricant forms an adsorbed layer of metallic soap on a metal surface), the bonding is still stronger (curve 1) and the effect is referred to as **chemisorption.**

The behaviour of water is of particular importance in this context. Because of its ability to form hydrogen bonds with neighbouring molecules, water adsorbs rapidly and strongly on most solid surfaces. Despite the tenacity with which such a layer is held (clay does not lose all its adsorbed water until heated to 300°C), the interaction cannot be thought of as chemisorption; rather it is in a sense a halfway stage to solution or alternatively to the taking up of crystalline water of hydration. Bonding is strong enough to maintain a surface layer perhaps several molecules thick, but the affinity is not sufficient for the molecules to penetrate into the interstices of the structure.

The physical nature of such a film is difficult to visualize; it cannot be thought of as a fluid in the accepted sense of the term even when more than one molecule thick (as in the case of the clays and cements). Yet the molecules are mobile in this situation. They will not desorb readily, but they can diffuse along the surface under the impetus of pressure gradients.

Such movements, occurring over the vast internal surface area of cement gels, are primarily responsible for the slow creep of concrete under stress. The ability of water molecules to penetrate solid–solid interfaces in clays and build up thick adsorbed layers results in the swelling of clays and has caused (and may well continue to cause) considerable structural damage to buildings erected on clays that are liable to behave in this manner. The readiness with which water will adsorb on surfaces is turned to account in the use of porous silica gel and molecular sieves as drying agents.

Chapter six

Fracture

6.1 Theoretical strength
6.2 Microcrack theory
6.3 The Griffith criterion
6.4 Fracture mechanics

We should first try to define what we mean by the term 'fracture'. It is often used synonymously with the term 'failure' but the two are not, necessarily, describing the same process. Failure (in the sense that a component is rendered unfit for further service) can occur without fracture – as, for instance, by excessive deformation (e.g. in creep) or by reduction of load supporting area (e.g. by wear or corrosion). Fracture, quite specifically, requires that new surfaces shall be created within the body and, since the creation of new surfaces requires that energy shall be supplied, the process of fracture is one which involves the supply of energy.

In the following we shall concern ourselves with one mode of energy supply, namely the supply of strain energy from a source external to the system which is going to fracture. Furthermore, we shall only consider uniaxial stressing though the theory can quite easily be extended to cover the case of multiaxial stressing.

6.1 Theoretical strength

We can estimate the theoretical strength of a crystalline solid in a number of ways. The simplest is to assume a totally homogeneous body which is, at all points, uniformly stressed to its breaking point. All the interatomic bonds must break simultaneously as the body changes from the solid to the vapour phase. Since the heat of vaporization is quite easy to measure experimentally we can, by this means, set an upper limit to the strength. If we assume that the solid obeys the rules of Hookean elasticity right up to final separation, this gives a value of about $E/5$.

If, however, we take a more reasonable view of the force–displacement curve and assume it to be sinusoidal at the interatomic level (which, in fact, it very nearly is) we get about $E/20$ as the theoretical strength. Other estimates, based upon various assumptions about the shape of the force–displacement curve, give values between these, so it seems not unreasonable to take a value of about $E/10$ as a good working estimate.

Real solids show very much lower values than this when they are tested in bulk form. Glasses and ceramics break, with little or no measurable deformation, at stresses of about $E/1000$. Ductile materials like metals and many polymers start to deform at about the same value and break at, perhaps, $E/100$. Very strong metals may reach $E/50$ and a few, carefully prepared, materials have approached the theoretical estimate.

6.2 Microcrack theory

The problem of the discrepancy was tackled by A.A. Griffith in about 1923. Griffith worked on glass which, for the moment, can be taken as the

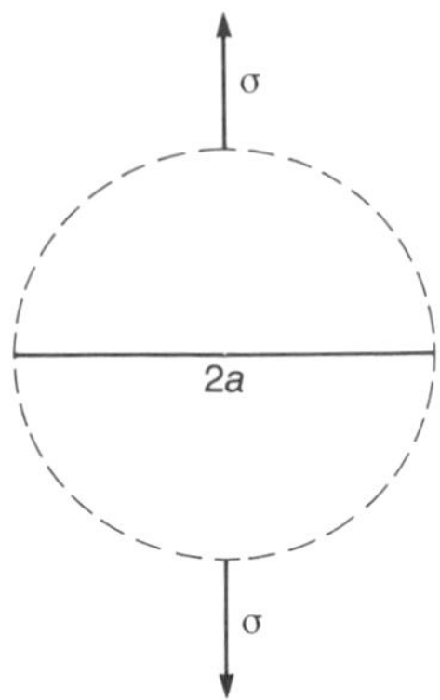

FIGURE 6.1 Schematic of crack in uniformly loaded plate.

archetypal 'brittle' material as one which shows no 'useful' deformation prior to fracture.*

Griffith suggested that the discrepancy might be explained if it were assumed that, in a 'brittle' material, there existed small cracks which effectively weaken the material.

In a series of papers Griffith presented two quite distinct ways of looking at the problem. Here we consider only one of these – the 'thermodynamic' way – once again involving a balance of energies.

Consider a plate of unit thickness containing a crack of length $2a$ under applied stress and assume that there is no stress in a circular region around the crack (Figure 6.1). The strain energy for this volume may be written

$$U = \frac{\sigma^2}{2E}(\pi a^2)$$

and if the crack extends at each end by da the strain energy released is

$$dU = a^2 + 2a da$$

if we neglect higher terms in da.

This is opposed by the surface energy S per unit area and, since we are creating four new surfaces, we obtain

$$\frac{d}{da}\left(\frac{\pi a^2 \sigma^2}{E}\right) = \frac{d}{da}(4Sa)$$

whence

$$\sigma = \sqrt{\frac{2ES}{\pi a}} \simeq \sqrt{\frac{ES}{a}}. \qquad (6.1)$$

6.3 The Griffith criterion

In order that any physical change may take place it is essential that two conditions be satisfied:

1. a 'thermodynamic' condition that the change must take place in such a way as to minimize the total energy of the system (thus a car on a hill will, generally, roll down);
2. a 'mechanical' condition which ensures that there is some mechanism which permits (1). The car must have wheels.

We now examine the Griffith criterion to see if it provides for these. If we consider the two

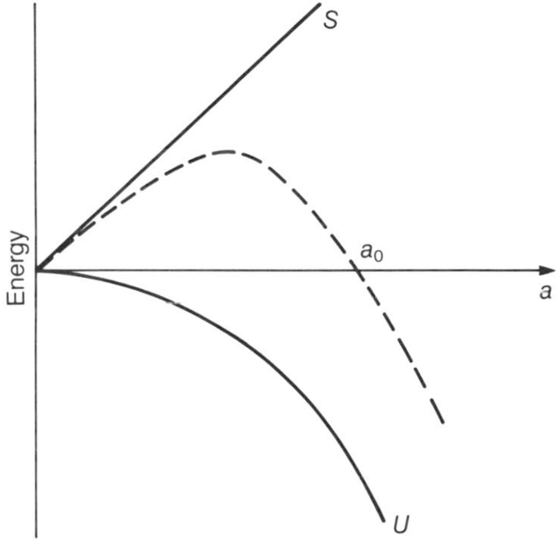

FIGURE 6.2 Energy balance in Griffith's theory of fracture. a_0 is the critical crack length.

* The term 'useful' here means just what it says. No engineering component works at an absolute value of stress, it works at a stress which gives deformations which can be accommodated. These may be accommodated in the whole of the structure (motor car doors do have to close when four students get in) or they may be purely local (as at a small stress raiser). Usable strength is more important than absolute strength.

terms – strain energy and surface energy – as a function of crack length we obtain something like Figure 6.2.

The dashed curve shows that an instability condition is achieved at some critical length a_0 when the rate of release of strain energy equals the rate at which work is expended in creating a new surface. For cracks shorter than a_0 energy must be supplied; beyond a_0 the energy available exceeds that which is needed.

A crack which has reached the critical length and thus satisfies the Griffith equation must continue to satisfy it as it grows since an increase in a_0 can only decrease the stress which is necessary to propagate the crack. In fact the crack will not only grow but its rate of growth will be accelerated as the elastic energy required by crack growth substantially exceeds that required.

In this way, a fast unstable fracture is achieved under a falling, or even zero, applied stress. In extreme cases the energy is so much in excess of that required that the crack can produce additional surfaces by forking and splitting to produce a 'shatter' type of crack. Providing there is enough strain energy to 'pay' for additional surface there is no limit to the amount of surface that can be produced. Thus the 'thermodynamic' requirement is easily seen to be achieved.

The 'mechanical' requirement is not quite so easy. In effect, it requires that a relatively low level of strain energy in the plate shall be concentrated at the crack tip, to a level which equals the theoretical strength of the bond. Or, to put it another way, that the surface energy term be explicable in terms of purely local strains. Consider the most probable shape of the crack tip. In an ideal elastic solid it cannot be very different from that shown in Figure 6.3 where bond (*a*) has just broken and (*b*) has been strained almost to breaking point. The elastic strain at (*b*) must be accommodated in the next group of bonds (*c*, *d*, *e*, . . .) each of which is displaced from its equilibrium spacing.

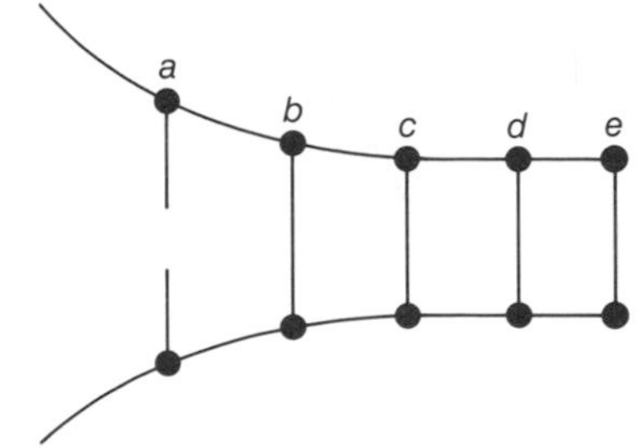

FIGURE 6.3 Schematic of the situation at the tip of a crack.

When (*b*) finally breaks, each successive pair of bonds now adopts the configuration possessed by its predecessor in the series and the sum of all these strain increments equals the fracture strain of (*b*). This then is the interpretation of surface energy, namely that the fracture of a given pair of bonds can only arise as result of localized strain in the adjacent lattice and the theoretical strength must be reached here.

Thus we may conclude that for fully brittle solids the theory satisfies the above conditions and that it represents both a necessary and sufficient criterion. But it is worth noting here that the surface energy, as outlined here, is only a minimum requirement.

It should, of course, be obvious that failure in this way cannot occur in compression since the applied forces would tend to close that crack rather than open it. The mechanism is much more complicated and many materials such as glass, stone, brick and concrete are strong in compression even though they are weak in tension.

For materials which can undergo plastic flow the Griffith condition above is not sufficient. This arises because the stress at the tip of the crack may not be sufficiently large to satisfy eqn (6.1). Indeed Orowan (1948–49) has shown that this can only occur when the tip radius of the crack is of the order of the atomic spacing as intimated above. We shall say a little more about this later.

There is, however, one important lesson to be

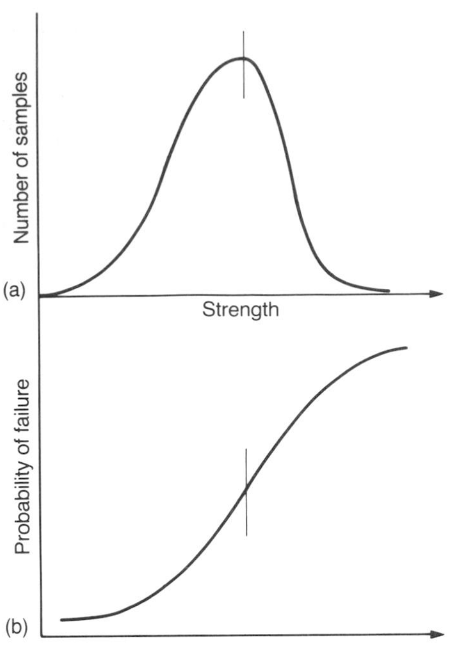

FIGURE 6.4 Strength of brittle solids: (a) distribution of measured strengths; (b) cumulative probability of failure under load.

learned here. Materials which behave in this way do not have a single valued tensile strength. Both the size and the distribution of the defects are wholly random so that the stress at fracture is determined by the size and location of the largest defect in the sample. And since no two samples are exactly alike, if we test 50 samples our measured strengths will show a Gaussian distribution as shown in Figure 6.4. The concept of a mean strength is sometimes useful but we must remember what it actually means. If we replot the data as a cumulative probability curve, as shown in Figure 6.4, the mean stress simply means a stress at which 50% of the samples may be expected to fail which is not a very good design parameter! There are ways of dealing with the problem but the only really safe thing to do is to never subject these materials to tension. The classical arched and domed styles of architecture developed from this restriction – one which troubles many engineers today.

TABLE 6.1 Toughness G_c and fracture toughness K_c

Material	G_c *kJ/m²*	K_c *MN/m³ᐟ²*
Pure ductile metals	100–1000	100–350
High strength steels	15–120	50–150
Mild steel	100	150
GFRP	10–100	20–50
Polyethylene	6–8	1
Reinforced concrete	0.2–4.0	10–15
Common timbers*	0.5–2.0	0.5–1.0
Mass concrete	0.03	0.2
Glass	0.01	0.8

* Crack parallel to grain.

6.4 Fracture mechanics

It was generally thought at one time that the microcrack theory applied only to elastic materials containing flaws – glass, concrete, fired clay products, ceramics, etc. Doubts started to arise when welded steel ships, oil rigs, pressure vessels and even aircraft displayed the same type of behaviour – a crack propagating at high speed with little or no prior deformation in materials normally thought of as ductile, i.e. capable of plastic deformation.

For this plastic work would be considerably greater than the surface energy. So we must replace S in eqn (6.1) by another term G_c which we shall not try to define too closely but merely state that it represents the total of all the energies absorbed in making the crack. It is a property of the material and is the toughness of the material. Since we continue to define it in terms of unit area of crack it has dimensions J/m^2. Table 6.1 gives some typical values and it will at once be apparent why copper, say, is tough and glass is not.

Rewriting the Griffith equation for a crack of length a then gives*

* A rigorous mathematical solution of the conditions around the crack tip shows that the Griffith condition is too high by a factor of 2, so we lose it from the numerator.

$$\sigma = \left(\frac{EG_c}{\pi a}\right)^{1/2}$$

or, as it is now more generally written,

$$\sigma\sqrt{\pi a} = \sqrt{EG_c}. \tag{6.2}$$

The left-hand side includes all the 'engineering' factors and says that when a material containing a crack of length a is subjected to a stress σ fast fracture will occur. The right-hand side contains the constants which depend upon the material. The important thing to note is that the critical combination of crack length and stress at which fast fracture occurs is a material constant.

The term $\sigma\sqrt{\pi a}$ crops up so often that it is often abbreviated to a single symbol K having units $N/m^{3/2}$ and is called the **stress intensity factor**. Fast fracture then occurs when K reaches a critical value K_c known as the **fracture toughness**.

Reference

Orowan, E. (1948–49) Fracture and strength of Solids. *Reports on Progress in Physics* **12**, 185.

Chapter seven

Electrical and thermal conductivity

Although electrical conductivity is not a constraint in structural design, thermal conductivity is important and perhaps nowhere more so than in the shell of the building. Nonetheless, we shall briefly consider electrical conductivity since it provides a basis for the more complex ideas of thermal conductivity.

Some typical values of electrical and thermal conductivities are given in Table 7.1. It can be seen that:

1. metals are good conductors of heat and electricity;
2. non-metals are poor conductors;
3. there is an approximate relationship between electrical and thermal conduction in metals. This is not true of non-metals.

The structure of the metallic bond was described on page 22 as an 'electron cloud' and as long as no electrostatic field is applied, the free electrons in a metal behave in much the same way as the particles in a gas – they move around randomly and collide elastically with each other and with the stationary ions in the lattice. But when an electrostatic field is applied, the electrons drift preferentially and, being negatively charged, they 'drift' towards the positive pole, though the random motion still remains. In drifting, they collide more frequently with the stationary ions. This provides a resistance to drift and this resistance is proportional to the drift.

The force F tending to accelerate each electron is

$$F = Ee$$

where e is the electronic charge and E is the electrostatic field.

The bodily movement of the electrons, (i.e. the current density) J, for unit area of cross-section can be expressed as

$$J = neV_a$$

where n is the number of free electrons, and V_a is the **drift velocity**. Since metals contain a large number of free electrons the flux is high. Thus, as Ohm's law states, current is directly proportional to potential difference and inversely proportional to resistance $I = V/R$. Since non-metals are either ionically or covalently bound, there are, effectively, no free electrons so that their low conductivity is at once apparent.

Thermal conductivity in metals follows much the same general argument though here it is not the bodily movement of electrons but rather the transference of heat energy by collision. The analysis is, however, much more complicated but it is intuitively obvious that the higher the temperature, the greater the excitation of the

TABLE 7.1 Electrical and thermal conductivities. Gases are at STP; other substances are at 273 K

	Electrical resistivity ρe $M\Omega\ m$	*Thermal conductivity* $K(t)$ W/mK	*Wiedemann–Franz ratio*
Air	–	24.1×10^{-3}	–
Oxygen	–	24.4×10^{-3}	–
Nitrogen	–	24.4×10^{-3}	–
Brick	2×10^{6}	0.6	10^{13}
Concrete	2×10^{6}	1.5	10^{13}
Glass	10	1.0	10^{10}
Polythene	10^{11}	0.25	10^{8}
Al alloy	48×10^{-9}	150	26.4
Copper	16×10^{-9}	390	22.9
Lead	182×10^{-9}	35	23.3
Silver	15×10^{-9}	418	23.0
Steel	112×10^{-9}	50	20.5

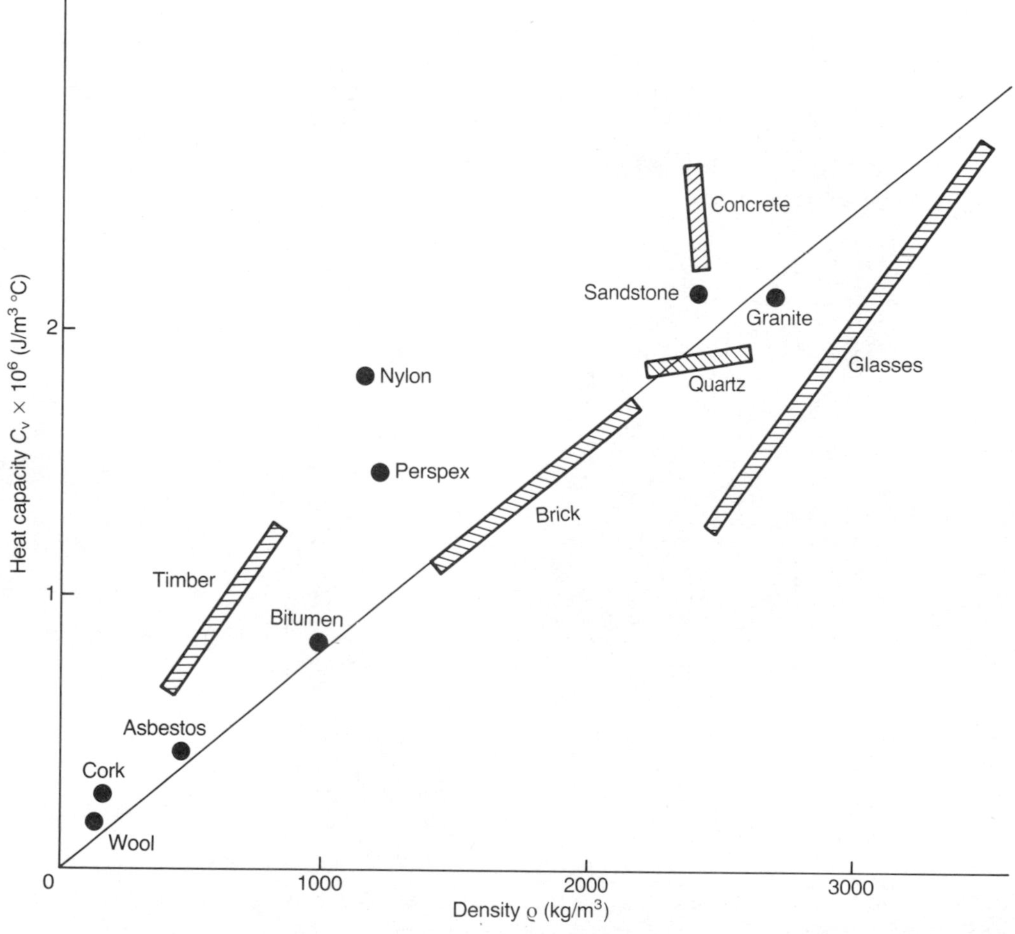

FIGURE 7.1 Thermal capacities of various substances.

electrons and the larger the number of collisions. Since, in metals, both thermal and electrical conductivities have their origins in the same structural features the proportionality noted in Table 7.1 is not surprising. It is known as the Wiedemann–Franz ratio and has a theoretical, constant value of 24.5×10^{-1} J/sec/K^2 at a given temperature.

The thermal conductivity of non-metals is more complex still since it involves totally random movement of the lattice and, in fact, approximates quite closely to the situation in a perfect gas. What is important to note, however, is that the thermal conductivity is controlled largely by the product of the density and the specific heat at constant volume C_v. This is called the **heat capacity** and Figure 7.1 shows that light materials with an open structure are better insulators than heavy, compact materials.

The effect of moisture on thermal conductivity is at once obvious. If the pores are filled, the water acts as a bridge and since the conductivity of water is many times greater than that of air, the resulting conductivity is greater. At the same time, water is denser and has a higher specific heat so that the heat capacity also increases.

Further reading

General

Ashby, M.F. and Jones, D.R.H. (1980) *Engineering Materials*, Vols 1 and 2, Pergamon, Oxford. Certainly a book to be dipped into. Perhaps a little detailed for easy reading but with a set of excellent case studies which illustrate the engineer's approach.

Gordon, J.E. (1978) *Structures – or Why Things Don't Fall Down*, Harmondsworth, Middlesex. An excellent and very readable account. Read it on the bus or in the bath. It will tell you more than many hours of library study.

Petrowski, H. (1982) *To Engineer is Human*, Macmillan, London. Petrowski considers what it is like to be an engineer in the twentieth century and lays some emphasis on the things that have gone wrong. Not a book for those lacking in self-confidence but good (and easy) reading.

Van Vlack, L.H. (1989) *Elements of Materials Science and Engineering*, 6th edn, Addison Wesley, New York. Fairly elementary but expands upon matters dealt with in this part.

The symposium *Design Life of Buildings* (Institution of Civil Engineers, 1985, Thomas Telford, London) is scarcely a textbook but the papers cover many aspects of the engineer's profession. Well worth a glance at those papers that may interest you.

Specialist

Cottrell, A.H. (1964) *The Mechanical Properties of Matter*, John Wiley, New York. First class, scientific and of much wider coverage than the title suggests. Essential reading for any student wishing to follow up the concepts herein and highly desirable reading for all students of all branches of engineering.

Freudenthal, A.M. (1950) *The Inelastic Behaviour of Engineering Materials and Structures*, John Wiley, New York. Old now but still very readable in the way it deals with materials in relation to their structures. Not easy to read, but good.

Treloar, L.R.G. (1949) *The Physics of Rubber Elasticity*, Clarendon Press, Oxford. Old now and pretty hard going, but the classic work on the subject. Perhaps overtaken by Aklonis, J.J. and MacKnight, W.J.L. (1983) *Introduction to Polymer Viscoelasticity*, 2nd edn, John Wiley, New York.

Angrist, S.W. and Hepler, L. (1973) *Order and Chaos*, Harmondsworth, Middlesex. A helpful (and non-mathematical) introduction to thermodynamics. Recommended as bedtime reading.

Houwink, R. and De Decker, H.K. (eds) (1973) *Elasticity, Plasticity and Structure of Matter*, 3rd edn, Cambridge University Press, Cambridge. You need to be pretty strong-minded for this. It's not widely read but, oddly, it's the one that the present author always turns to for information which is not listed elsewhere. Where else could you find out about the rheology of baker's dough or of liquid paints, gelatins and glues or soaps? They may not be 'engineering' as defined by your average university lecturer but they are all materials and it never does to assume that the findings of one discipline are inapplicable to another.

Tattersall, G.H. and Banfill, P.F.G. (1983) *The Rheology of Fresh Concrete*, Pitman, London. Very highly specialized – for budding experts only.

Part Two

Metals and Alloys

W.D. Biggs

Introduction

I cannot do better than quote from the seminal work *A History of Metals* by Professor Leslie Aitchison:

> It is generally held today that the contemporary way of living in all the more advanced societies is almost entirely based upon the use of metals; it would certainly be difficult to conceive of modern life without them. Some . . . have even gone so far as to assert that the development of civilisation . . . is the direct consequence of usefully employing metallic materials. The complete acceptance of such an opinion might involve us in an examination of what is meant by the term civilisation, a matter that is quite outside our subject. It seems better therefore to avoid any such debatable topic and to agree on the simpler statement that the possession of metals has decisively contributed towards raising man's standard of living . . .

But it is clear that metals, and especially useful metals, have been known longer than was at one time supposed and they came into employment very gradually indeed. Stone tools were adequate for most early cultures and where metals were available – usually by chance findings – their uses were not known. The spread was very slow – probably a thousand years in any given area – and even slower to spread to other cultures. To talk of a 'Stone Age', a 'Bronze Age' or an 'Iron Age' leads only to confusion and misconception unless the region is also clearly identified. But, by the eighth century BC, the Greek writer Hesiod had distinguished between the 'Ages' and this is repeated in the Book of Daniel (*c.* 166 BC). Metals, then, have a long and venerable history, though not always a praiseworthy one. In the fifth century BC Herodotus wrote that 'iron had been sent us for our woe', a plaint re-echoed by Pliny in the first century AD 'for it brings death more speedily to our fellow man'.

My own philosophy of metals comes close to that of Rudyard Kipling:

> Gold is for the mistress – silver for the maid
> Copper for the craftsman – cunning at his trade,
> 'Good!' said the Baron, sitting in his hall,
> 'But Iron – Cold Iron – is master of them all.'

That is the trouble with having been reared in Sheffield. But it has not hurt my sense of engineering or my love of general metallurgy.

Most metals occur in nature as oxides, sulphides, carbonates, etc. **Extraction metallurgy** is the process of converting these ores into metals. The basic chemistry is mostly fairly simple. The problem is that of doing it on a large enough scale to make the end product economically viable. But when the finished product goes into service and is exposed to its working environment the process is reversed and the metal reverts to the oxidized state, i.e. it rusts or corrodes. Thus there are two tasks, namely to get the raw materials into the metallic state and then to keep them that way. The origins of extraction metallurgy go back to prehistory and many discoveries must have been made accidentally when a piece of rock was subjected to the reducing atmosphere of the camp fire and a piece of metal resulted. Copper, lead and tin were among the earliest to be produced in this way and, at an early stage, bronze – an alloy of copper and tin – appeared on the scene and was much prized, not only for its hardness but also from the fact that it could be melted and cast into complex shapes. Brass (copper and zinc) was made at around the same time.

Iron was a relative latecomer. It was not possible to reach the high temperatures (*c.* 1533°C) needed to melt iron and early iron was produced by mixing a pasty mass with a slag composed of oxides and silicates and hammering this mass, while still hot and pasty, to make something like **wrought iron**. The first breakthrough was the introduction of a forced air blast to raise the temperature and liquid iron was then possible. The product, however, contained about 4% carbon picked up from the furnace fuel, and this lowered the melting point and so made it easy for the metal to be cast into moulds. However this **cast iron** was brittle and so could not be used for the same purpose as forged sponge iron.

The problem of reducing the carbon content was solved in the eighteenth century by Cort who produced wrought iron by controlled oxidation and these two materials, wrought iron and cast iron, remained the staple constructional materials until the latter part of the nineteenth century. The delicate control needed to produce mild steel with about 0.25% carbon was only achieved when Bessemer developed his converter process which involved blowing cold air through molten metal to oxidize the impurities (including carbon) and then to add controlled amounts of carbon and other elements to the relatively pure liquid iron. The first commercial converter went into operation in 1859 and, once some problems of scale had been solved, converters increased in size. Since the conversion process, from start to finish, took only about an hour or so, the age of mass production had begun.

The converter process was followed by the open-hearth process which was capable of even greater output. Here oxidation of the carbon was achieved by the controlled addition of iron oxide in a large shallow furnace heated by a preheated air blast. Both processes – though greatly refined – form the basis of modern practice.

The availability of electricity led to the commercial production of aluminium in 1886 and nowadays many other metals, such as magnesium, calcium and sodium, are produced using electric power. It is also used for the refinement of crude, smelted copper, for instance. These developments have, in turn, led to production methods for the 'modern' metals such as titanium, zirconium and niobium.

Metals need to be shaped if they are to fulfil the engineer's needs. This is the area of **mechanical metallurgy** (see Chapter 10), involving the understanding of such processes as hot working, cold working and joining. Many of these processes remained small-scale until the development of steam power in the Industrial Revolution increased the power of man's arm and ever larger pieces of metal could be hammered or forged to shape. The rolling mill, developed in the eighteenth century, revolutionized the shapes that could be obtained and the speed with which they could be produced; and many new methods, such as drawing and extrusion, developed from these early forming processes.

Physical metallurgy (Chapter 8) deals with the structure of metals and alloys with the aim of designing and producing those internal structures which give the desired properties, and provides the substance of much of what follows.

Chapter eight

Physical metallurgy

8.1 Grain structure
8.2 Atomic structure of metals
8.3 Solutions and compounds

8.1 Grain structure

Probably the greatest single breakthrough in our understanding of the properties of metals was made by Sorby who, in the latter part of the nineteenth century, perfected a technique by which the structure of metals could be examined under an optical microscope. Despite many advances since that time, **metallography**, as it is known, remains the most widely used tool of the metallurgist. Figure 8.1 shows the structure of a pure metal which is seen to consist of an assembly of minute, interlocked grains and we now examine how, and why, this type of structure develops.

We noted earlier in Chapter 1 that, in a liquid, the atoms are in a state of constant motion and change positions frequently. As a liquid cools the motion of the atoms becomes more sluggish and, sooner or later, the atoms arrange themselves into a pattern which forms the nucleus of the solid material. The kinetics of nucleation are quite complex – it is sufficient simply to note that nucleation of the solid almost always begins from an impurity particle in the melt. Let us not worry too much about the conditions for nucleation of a solid crystal but rather concern ourselves with the mechanism. Suppose we assume that a solid nucleus has formed within a liquid melt and that it has the geometrical configuration of an elementary cube of atoms. The corners of the cube lose heat faster than the edges so that atoms from the melt attach themselves to the corners first, then to the edges and last of all to the faces of the elementary cube. Thus a branching pattern or **dendrite** is built up from each nucleation site (Figure 8.2) and dendrites will grow from each until they are stopped by interference from other dendrites. Eventually the liquid is used up by infilling between the arms of the dendrites and the characteristic polycrystalline structure results (Figure 8.1). There are two important facts to note here:

1. the orientation of the atoms differs from grain to grain, *but*
2. within each grain the atoms are arranged in a regular lattice so that at each grain boundary there is a line of mismatch in the atomic arrangement.

In practice few metals are really pure (and it would be prohibitively expensive to make them so) and certain impurities tend to segregate in the grain boundaries. Some consequences of this will be examined later.

8.2 Atomic structure of metals

It will be recalled from Chapter 3 that the generalized nature of the metallic linkage results in the development of crystalline structures in

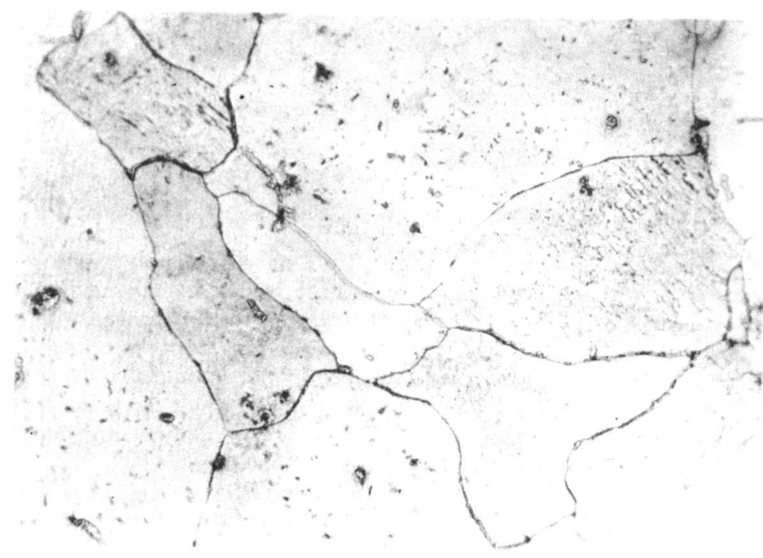

FIGURE 8.1 The microstructure of Armco iron.

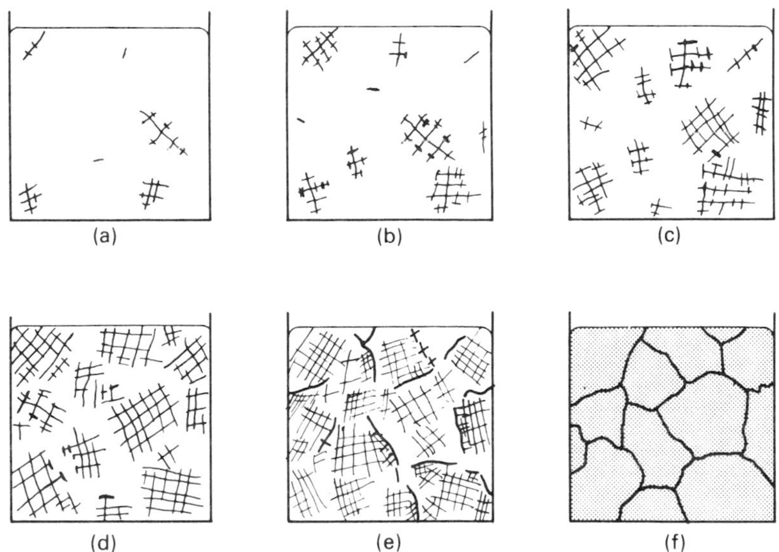

FIGURE 8.2 Solidification of a metal by dendritic growth (schematic).

which each ion is bound to all its immediate neighbours. Metal ions, therefore, tend to pack as closely as possible and this limits the common crystal structures of pure metals (in which all of the ions are of equal size) to three. Compare this with the enormous range of structures met with in ionic and covalent solids. We consider the ions as incompressible – like billiard balls – and find how these may be packed together to achieve maximum density. If we begin with one sphere the maximum number of other spheres which can be packed around it in one plane is

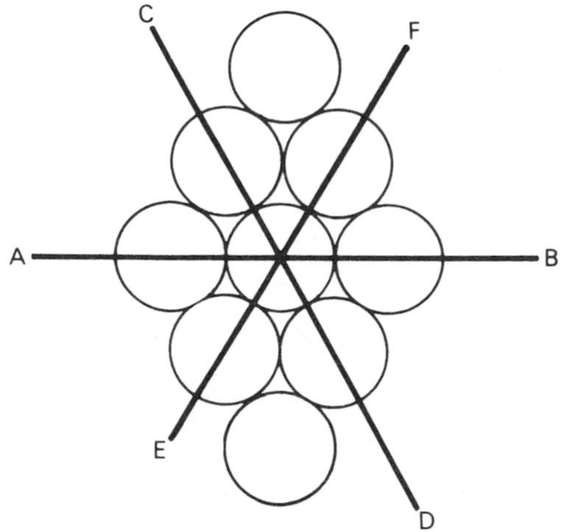

FIGURE 8.3 Close-packed directions in a close-packed plane of spheres.

six (Figure 8.3). By continuing the plane, a close-packed plane can be built up. There are now two possible arrangements for the next plane provided that each sphere is in contact with three spheres below. The second layer is placed in the dimples at BBBB..., etc. But two choices occur when a third plane is to be formed. The spheres may either be placed in positions vertically above the original spheres ABABAB... or they may be placed in the unoccupied dimples CCCC, which are above neither the first nor the second layer, to give ABCABC... (Figure 8.4). At first sight these differences in stacking may appear to be trifling but they have important consequences. We define these structures in terms of a unit cell and visualize the metal as composed of an array of such cells. The ABABAB... arrangement gives us the hexagonal close-packed (hcp) structure illustrated in Figure 8.5. The ABCABC... arrangement we define as face-centred cubic (fcc) and although at first sight this does not appear to be close packed, a view on the diagonal plane XYZ (Figure 8.6) shows that it is. These two structures represent the closest possible packing of spheres of equal size. In each case the

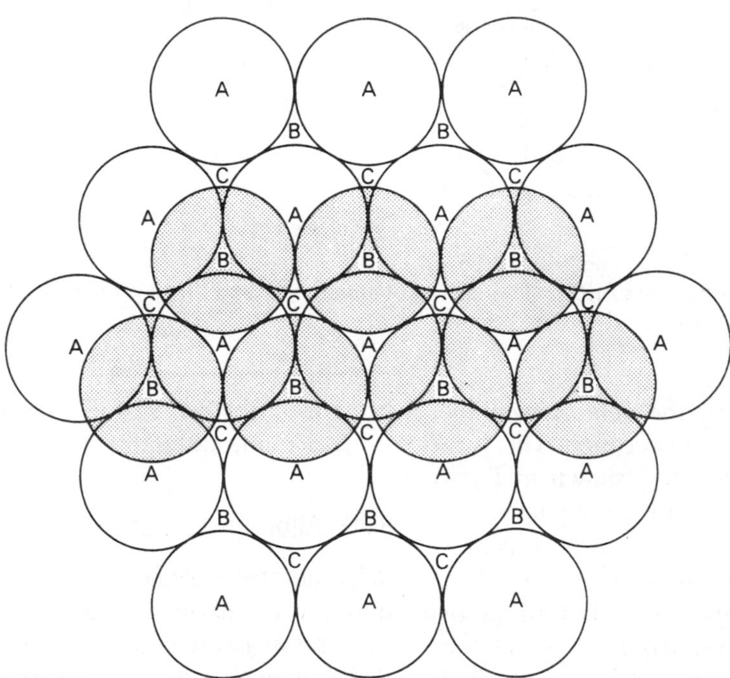

FIGURE 8.4 The B spheres (shaded) rest on the A spheres. A third close-packed layer may then rest on the B spheres either directly above the A spheres or in C positions.

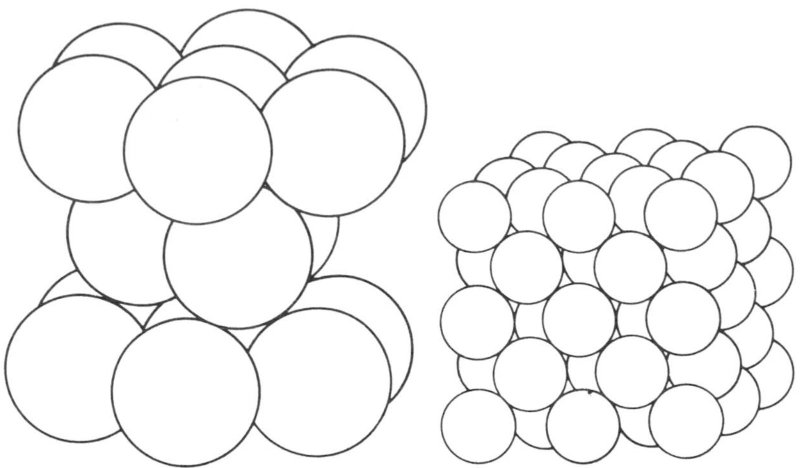

FIGURE 8.5 (a) The close-packed hexagonal structure. (b) The face-centred cubic structure. (From W. Hume-Rothery and G.E. Raynor (1956) *The Structure of Metals and Alloys*, by permission of the Institute of Metals.)

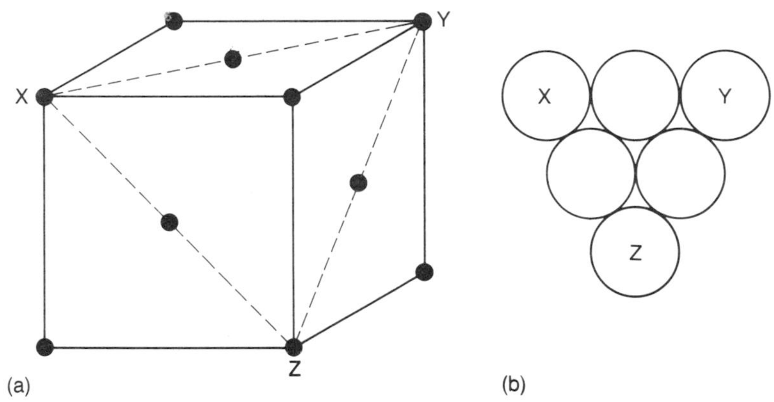

FIGURE 8.6 Face-centred cubic structure: (a) location of atomic sites and (b) view on XYZ plane showing close packing.

spheres occupy 74% of the volume available.

There is, inevitably, one exception. This is the body-centred cubic cell (bcc) shown in Figure 8.7. Here the spheres are not close packed.

Metals crystallizing in the above forms are:

fcc aluminium, copper, nickel, iron (above 910°C), lead, silver, gold.
hcp magnesium, zinc, cadmium, cobalt, titanium.
bcc iron (below 910°C), chromium, molybdenum, niobium, vanadium.

8.2.1 Allotropy (or polymorphism)

Why do these differences occur? Why is aluminium fcc and magnesium hcp? The answer is that the structure is that which gives the crystal the least energy, though this structure need not, necessarily, be close packed. The energy dif-

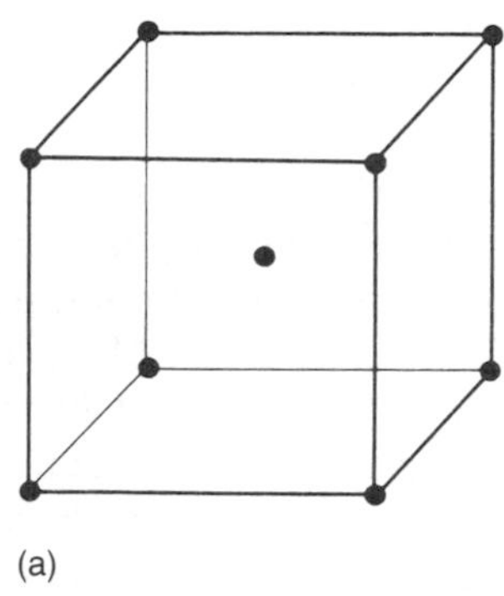

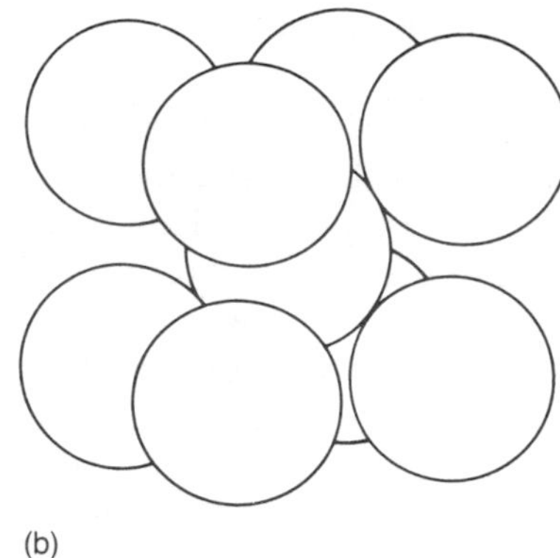

FIGURE 8.7 The body-centred cubic structure: (a) expanded unit cell and (b) sphere model of unit cell. (From W. Hume-Rothery and G.E. Raynor (1956) *The Structure of Metals and Alloys*, by permission of the Institute of Metals.)

ference between different structures is often very small and the crystal structure which has the lowest energy at one temperature may not have the lowest energy at another. These various forms are called allotropes. Thus tin changes its structure at about 18°C and becomes a highly brittle, powdery material. This caused the buttons to fall off the coats of Napoleon's army in Russia and leakage of the soldered cans of food on Scott's Antarctic expedition. Fortunately for modern users of tin, the nucleation process for this change is slow and tin can be cooled well below 18°C. Perhaps of more importance industrially, the change from fcc to bcc in iron at 910°C forms the foundation of the metallurgy of steel.

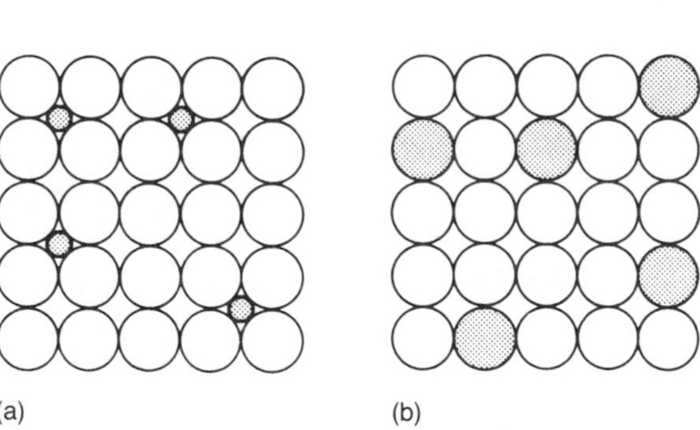

FIGURE 8.8 Solid solutions: (a) interstitial and (b) substitutional.

FIGURE 8.9 Relatively coarse pearlite in a plain carbon steel (×200). (From A.R. Bailey (1967) *The Structure and Strength of Metals*, by permission of Metallurgical Services Laboratories Ltd.)

8.3 Solutions and compounds

Very few metals are used in the pure state – they are nearly always **alloyed** with other elements to obtain better mechanical properties. The alloying elements dissolve in the basis metal to form **solid solutions**. These are in many ways akin to liquid solutions. Some elements dissolve readily, some with more difficulty; iron can only dissolve 0.007% carbon at room temperature, but copper can dissolve 30% zinc to make brass, and in the copper–nickel system (including Monel metal, cupronickel, etc.) there is complete solubility.

There are two principal classes of solid solution. In one, small atoms (such as carbon and nitrogen) fit into the spaces between the larger atoms. This is an **interstitial solid solution** (Figure 8.8(a)). The solubility of the small atoms is generally limited, but the effects on properties can be dramatic. In the other class, the dissolved atoms are similar in size to those of the host metal and they simply replace some of the lost atoms to produce a **substitutional solid solution** (Figure 8.8(b)). The classic example is copper–nickel where the sizes of the ions have been calculated to be approximately 12.7 and 12.5 nm respectively. Substitutional solid solutions may be random (they mostly are) or ordered depending upon what sort of neighbours the ions find most comfortable in energy terms.

But some atoms are too big to fit comfortably into the lattice and others are too small, though not small enough to achieve interstitial solubility. In either case, the energy of the lattice is increased and the surplus is rejected, usually as an **intermediate compound**, such as iron carbide (Fe_3C) in steel, or $CuAl_2$ in the 2000 series of aluminium alloys (see Chapter 12). Generally such compounds are hard and brittle and exert a 'reinforcing' effect upon the soft matrix. Figure 8.9 shows Fe_3C in carbon steel and it will be noted that the 'reinforcement' is occurring at the microscopic level of resolution. Some intermediate compounds are used in their own right such as tungsten carbide for cutting tools and tantalum carbide in 'superalloys' which can operate at temperatures of 1200°C as, for example, in gas turbines.

The metallurgist refers to these compounds as 'phases'; a phase is simply a material, or region of material, which has the same properties. Water is a phase, so is whisky. Whisky and water form a uniform solution – another single phase. Add ice and you have a two-phase mixture, because the properties of ice differ from those of water. Much of the science of physical metallurgy is concerned with phases and with the interaction between them, but a full discussion is beyond the scope of this chapter and the reader is referred to the standard texts such as Cottrell (1967).

Chapter nine

Mechanical properties of metals

9.1 Stress–strain behaviour
9.2 Tensile strength
9.3 Ductility
9.4 Plasticity
9.5 Dislocation energy
9.6 Strengthening of metals
9.7 Plastic design

Metallurgists tend to divide properties into two groups – **structure insensitive** and **structure sensitive.** Structure insensitive properties are wholly invariant – they are associated with the properties of the atoms themselves and the primary forces between them. They do not depend on the arrangement of the atoms. The principal properties here are elastic modulus, density and, to a lesser extent, some chemical, electrical and thermal characteristics. As the name implies the structure sensitive properties are wholly dependent upon the past history; whether hot rolled or cold rolled, whether heated and cooled and if so, how. For all of these processes disturb the atomic arrangement and these disturbances are reflected in changes in properties. From the designer's point of view the most important structure sensitive properties are the **yield strength** and the **fracture strength.**

9.1 Stress–strain behaviour

In the basic tension test metals and alloys deform as shown in Figure 9.1. Up to A the behaviour is essentially elastic (see Chapter 1) but at A it changes. This is variously called the yield point (YP), the yield stress (YS), the limit of proportionality (LP) or the elastic limit (EL). We shall use the first – yield point – not because it is the most descriptive but because it (or yield stress) is most widely used in specifications. Below the yield point the material returns to its original dimensions on unloading. Beyond the yield point it is permanently deformed. Try squeezing a beer can, first lightly, and it takes no notice, then squeeze it hard and it stays deformed.

In more scientific terms once the yield is passed and the material is unloaded it travels back down the line BC and there is a permanent deformation OC; this permanent deformation is known as plasticity. But here is the interesting fact. Once you reload it to B it goes on as before. In other words, if we took a new beer can it would start to deform at stress A. If we take another, load it to B and then unload it, it will not start to deform again until stress B is reached. What an interesting phenomenon! Overload a metal and it gets stronger. We call this **strain hardening** or **work hardening.** It was the principal method used by early blacksmiths to produce harder, stronger bronze and iron by cold hammering and, as we shall see, it is of immense importance (and comfort) to the structural engineer since it forms the basis of what is known as 'plastic design' of structural steelwork.

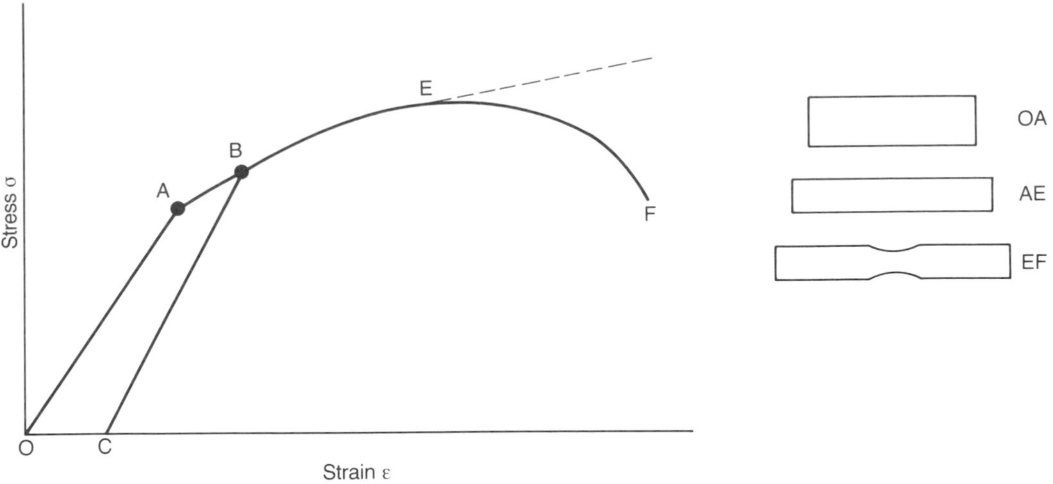

FIGURE 9.1 Tensile stress–strain curve (schematic). From O to A the bar remains substantially constant in shape; from A to E it lengthens but reduces uniformly; at E it forms a 'neck' at which fracture eventually occurs.

9.2 Tensile strength

At point E in Figure 9.1 the stress falls away. This occurs because, as the material starts to deform locally, a waist or neck is produced at which fracture will eventually occur. Because of the reduction in diameter less force is needed to sustain a given stress, hence the drop. But, conventionally, stress is defined as load/original area so that the net result is that the breaking stress (F) appears to be lower than the maximum. However, in the early days of testing, the change in behaviour at E was readily observed and was described as the **ultimate tensile strength**, a term which is still in use. Its value is of little concern in design.

If the reduction in area is measured and the true stress (i.e. load/actual area) is calculated, the dashed curve is obtained – which looks intelligible. This value is rarely determined except for research purposes.

9.3 Ductility

The reduction in area of the specimen and the total elongation at fracture are both conventionally used as measures of ductility, and as yield strength and tensile strength increase, ductility decreases. The same will apply to cold worked materials – as the yield strength is raised ever closer to the tensile strength the reserve of ductility diminishes and, in the limit, the material will snap under heavy cold working. This is familiar to anyone who has broken a piece of wire by continually bending and rebending it.

Failure by fatigue occurs after a member or component has been subjected to reversing or fluctuating stress even when the maximum applied stress is below that normally required to cause fracture and, indeed, even below the yield strength of the material.

Fatigue always starts from a stress raiser such as a notch (see Chapter 6) though there may be a less obvious focal point. Thus in standing machinery subjected to many reversals fatigue starting from one machining groove a little deeper than the rest is not unknown or uncommon. The appearance of a fatigue fracture is quite characteristic – it shows a series of ripples spreading from the focal point. These

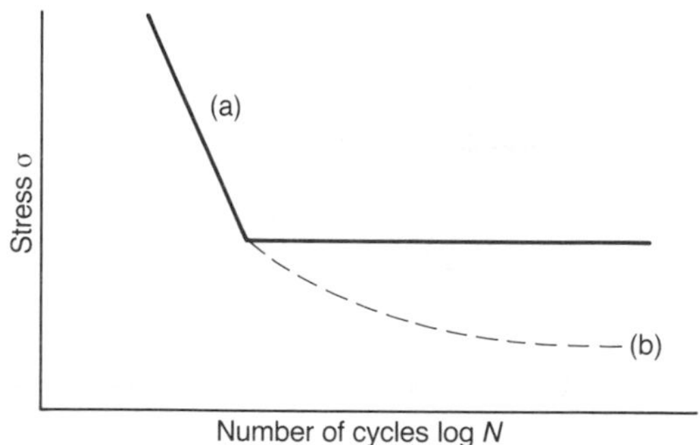

FIGURE 9.2 Fatigue (schematic).

correspond to progress in crack growth and, when the crack is large enough, fast fracture follows.

In laboratory tests a plot of the stress range versus cycles to failure generally appears as shown in Figure 9.2(a). This would seem to imply a limiting stress below which fatigue failure will not occur. This is, however, an assumption which should be treated with great caution, for even under the most moderately corrosive conditions (e.g. a 'normal' urban atmosphere) the curve of Figure 9.2(b) is more typical.

With much reservation it may be stated that, in most buildings, the designer has little to fear from fatigue in the structure itself though such cases as the collapse of the oil rig Alexander Keilland in 1980, due to fatigue failure in one of the legs, cannot be ignored. Welded joints, if not carefully made, are particularly at risk because of the adventitious introduction of stress raisers in the form of unwelded areas. Certainly individual components such as bolts may be at risk under live load conditions. Fatigue is an important consideration in bridge design.

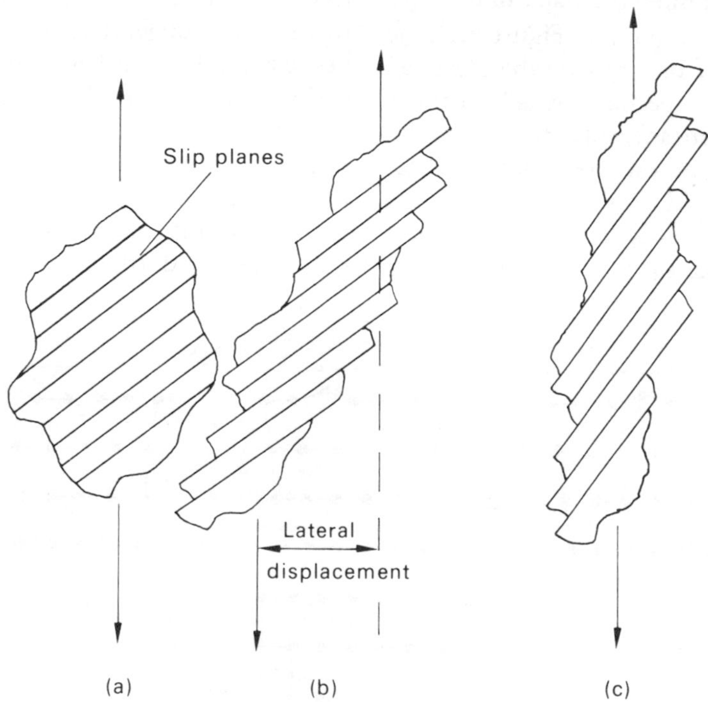

FIGURE 9.3 (a) Crystal under stress. (b) Free unconstrained yielding results in considerable lateral displacement. (c) Rotation of slip planes during deformation permits elongation with very little overall lateral movement.

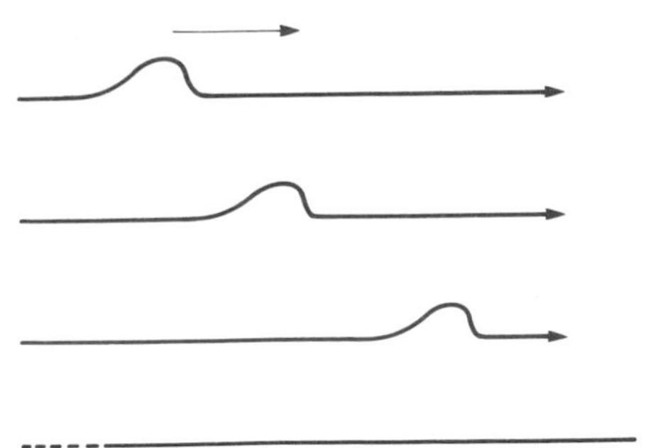

FIGURE 9.4 How to move a heavy carpet.

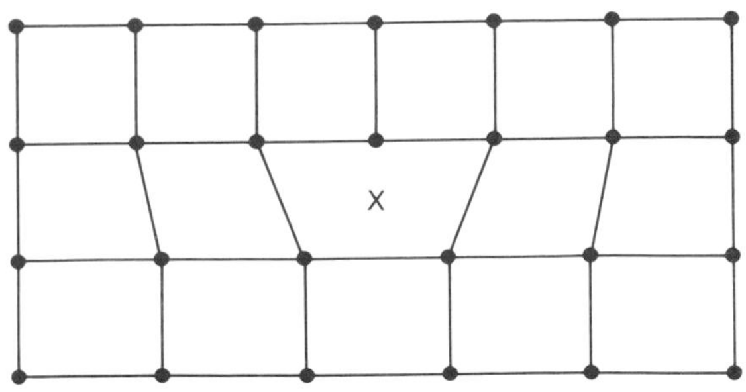

FIGURE 9.5 Schematic diagram of dislocation.

9.4 Plasticity

This is one of the most important properties of metals and one that we should all be grateful for. If you run your car into a tree, the wing will be seriously deformed. But you do not necessarily need a new wing since the old one can be successfully hammered back into shape.

Clearly, at the yield point (see Figure 9.1), the behaviour changes from recoverable (elastic) deformation to one of permanent deformation. Early observations on specially prepared samples suggested that, at the yield point, whole rows of atoms had slid bodily past each other rather like a pack of cards (Figure 9.3). This is known as **slip**. Further theoretical consideration suggested that the energy required to break a whole chain of atomic bonds was far greater than the forces applied at yield and an alternative mechanism was sought. Suppose you want to move a heavy carpet lying on a rough floor. The way not to do it is to try to move it bodily – the frictional forces over the whole area are considerable. The right way is to create a small ripple in the carpet and then to work it across to the other edge. The force required is small because the friction between carpet and floor is easily overcome locally (Figure 9.4).

This is almost precisely the mechanism we now believe to exist in metals where we visualize a mismatch in the atomic stacking as shown in Figure 9.5. It is called a **dislocation** and, because only one bond (that at x) is unsatisfied, the

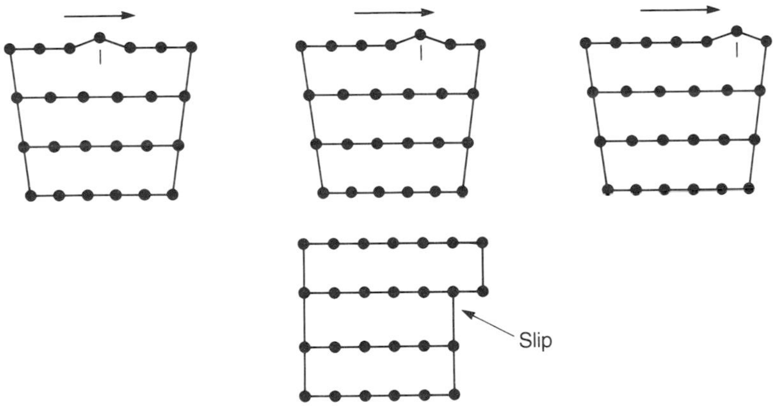

FIGURE 9.6 Movement of a dislocation to produce one unit of slip.

application of a small shearing force causes the dislocation to move to produce one unit of slip (Figure 9.6). You will see that the dislocation represents a boundary; on one side the material has slipped, on the other it has not and for this reason it is known as a **line defect** and is conventionally represented by the symbol ⊥.

Except in specially prepared laboratory samples, dislocations, in large numbers, are always present. They result from the chaotic conditions during solidification when atoms are attaching themselves to, and detaching themselves from, the advancing solid–liquid interface. However, dislocations can also be generated when the metal is stressed. The exact mechanism is complex but suffice it to say that under an applied stress the pre-existing dislocations can move and more dislocations can be created.

It is, however, important to note that dislocations can only move on certain atomic planes within the lattice. These are known as **slip planes**. The hcp metals have a fairly restricted number of slip planes; the bcc and fcc metals have many.

9.5 Dislocation energy

The atoms at the core of the dislocation are displaced from their proper positions. We can express this in terms of a strain. It is approximately 0.5 so that the stress is of the order of $G/2$ where G is the shear modulus and the strain energy per unit volume is about $G/8$. In order to minimize the energy the dislocation line tries to be as short as possible – it behaves as if it were an elastic band under a tension T. If we now assume that the radius of the core is about the size of the atom b, the volume of the core, per unit length, is πb^2 whence

$$T = \frac{\pi G b^2}{8} \approx \frac{G b^2}{2}.$$

T is actually very small but, relative to the size of the dislocation, it is large and it plays an important role in determining the way in which obstacles of one sort or another can obstruct dislocations.

9.6 Strengthening of metals

The critical property in design is the yield stress so that, in using the term 'strengthening' we are concerned with the various ways in which we can make slip more difficult since if the material requires a higher stress to produce yield then the safe working stress is correspondingly increased. We now consider some of the ways in which this is done.

9.6.1 Grain boundaries

It was noted above that, within a single grain, the atomic arrangement is regular but changes at a grain boundary. A dislocation which has reached a grain boundary cannot move until the shear stress, resolved on to the new slip plane and in the new slip direction, reaches the value needed to continue movement; and other dislocations will pile up behind it in a traffic jam. The stress on the leading dislocation is a simple function of the number of dislocations in the pile-up. In a coarse grained structure many dislocations can pile up and the critical stress is reached early, whereas in a fine grained structure the length of the pile-up is smaller and more stress must be applied from external forces, i.e. the yield point is raised. Control of grain size is generally achieved by 'inoculating' the liquid metal with a metal which forms a solid oxide. The particles of oxide then act as nucleation sites for crystal growth.

9.6.2 Strain hardening

Metals, especially those in the fcc and bcc systems, have many different planes on which slip (i.e. dislocation movement) occurs. But none of these are markedly different from the others and, under increasing stress, all dislocations try to move at once. If the slip planes intersect each

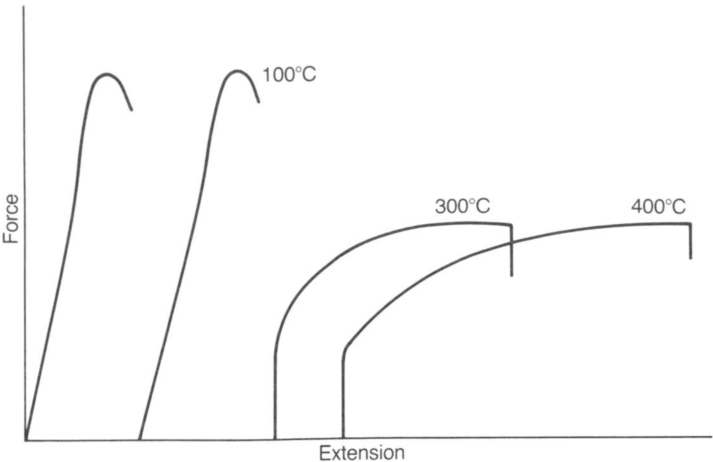

FIGURE 9.7 Load–extension curves for heavily cold worked copper reheated to various temperatures. (After K.J. Pascoe (1978) *An Introduction to the Properties of Engineering Materials*, Van Nostrand Reinhold.)

other (as indeed they do) the dislocations on one slip plane act as a barrier to dislocations trying to move across them. The traffic pile-up is now considerable; it is equivalent to trying to go through a crossroads which is already full of stalled traffic. Very much more stress needs to be applied to get things moving again and strain hardening is one of the most effective ways of raising the yield strength of a metal, though if carried too far, it results in fracture as we have seen.

Since each dislocation is a region of higher strain in the lattice, the situation is not thermodynamically stable and comparatively little energy is required to cause a redistribution and cancellation of the dislocation arrays. The energy is most conveniently supplied in the form of heat which gives the atoms enough energy to move spontaneously and to form small areas which are relatively free of dislocations. This is called **recovery** but, since the dislocation density is only slightly reduced, the yield strength and ductility remain almost unchanged. The major change involves **recrystallization**. New grains nucleate and grow, the material is restored to its original dislocation density and the yield point returns to its original value. This process (see Figure 9.7) involves heating to temperatures of around 0.6 T_m (where T_m is the melting point in K) and is known as **annealing**. In addition to overcoming the effects of work hardening, this is an important way of controlling grain size. We shall later see (page 68) the importance of annealing in the preparation of metals and alloys for commercial use.

9.6.3 Dispersion hardening

By far the most powerful way of impeding dislocation movement, and hence of increasing the yield strength, is to disperse hard and often brittle particles throughout the structure so that the dislocations in the softer matrix are arrested and then must find a way round. But there are limitations and perhaps the following analogy will help to explain what these are.

Bitumen is a soft substance which, if left alone, will flow under its own weight and will most certainly flow under load. And yet it is used for roads. This is only possible because it is

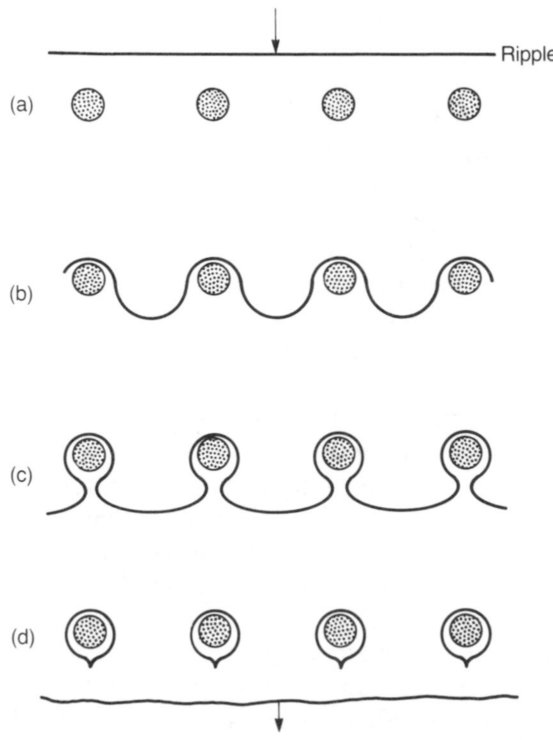

FIGURE 9.8 Schematic diagram of the progress of a ripple which (a) approaches obstacles, (b) is deflected, (c) curls around them and (d) passes through leaving a disturbed area.

mixed with a hard aggregate. Let us suppose that the aggregate is supplied as a fine 'flour'; this will offer little or no resistance to flow since it will be carried along by the bitumen matrix, rather as fine sand is carried along by water. At the other extreme, assume that the same amount of aggregate is supplied in the form of a few large boulders. The bitumen will simply flow in between them. Between these two extremes there lies a region where the particles are small enough and sufficiently close together to restrict flow.

And so it is in metals. By various means, the metallurgist is able to produce dispersions of hard particles of such a size and of such a spacing that the movement of dislocations is impeded with a consequent increase in yield strength. This facility is used in heat-treated steels and in certain aluminium alloys. The process is shown schematically in Figure 9.8. If you imagine a stream with a small ripple which must pass through a series of obstacles you will have the idea.

Our understanding of this process has led to one of the greatest advances in metallurgy over the last 30 years. It was once believed that the jet engine was not possible because no metal

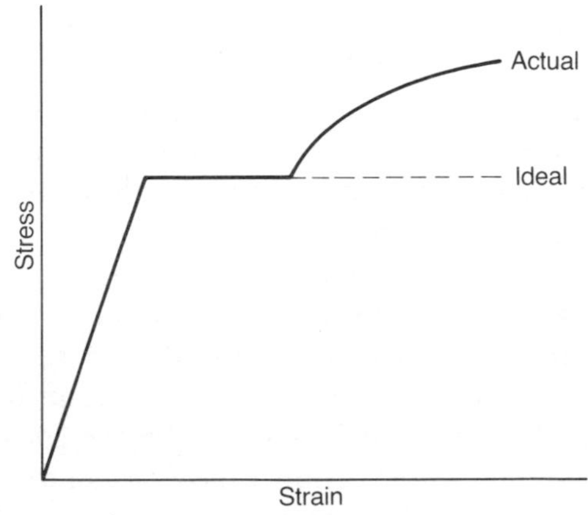

FIGURE 9.9 Stress–strain curve of ideal elastic–plastic solid.

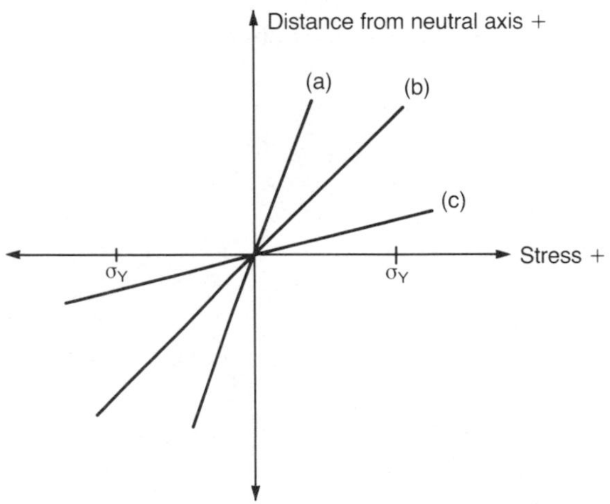

FIGURE 9.10 Stress distribution on the cross-section of a rectangular beam.

could retain a suitably high yield strength at the temperatures involved. The fact that it has been done as a result of an understanding of the mechanisms of dispersion hardening provides a salutary lesson to all engineers who should distinguish very carefully between what is certainly impossible and what is only probably impossible. You cannot change the fundamental laws of mathematics or of thermodynamics, but it is surprising what you can do if you really understand what is going on inside a material.

9.7 Plastic design

Here we consider an aspect of design concerned, primarily, with steel since that is the structural engineer's most used material, but the concept is applicable quite generally.

At the yield stress structural steel shows a discontinuity in the stress–strain curve. Figure 9.9 shows the curve schematically and we idealize the situation as shown. It may seem to be over-idealized: but it is not when we consider the amount of deflection which we can tolerate in a structure. We describe the curve as elastic–ideally plastic. Consider a beam in bending – the surface fibres carry the greatest stress and there is no stress at the neutral axis. So the surface fibres yield first when the yield stress σ_Y is reached. In Figure 9.10 curve (a) represents the fully elastic state while curve (b) represents the state at which the surface fibres yield. However, this is not the limiting case since the inner fibres are still behaving elastically. On further loading more and more of these yield until, at curve (c), yield has spread across the whole cross-section. This is known as **plastic collapse** and it can be shown that the **fully plastic moment** at this stage is 1.5 times the limiting elastic moment. And note that, once an element of the material has yielded, strain hardening takes over and that element is now stronger than it was before so that the load is now passed to the next, unyielded, element.

Here, then, is a powerful design tool. At its best elastic design is always fraught with guesswork – it is impossible to take proper account of irregularities such as notches, misfits, self stresses, etc. But if we assume – as indeed we can – that the material takes care of these things and by yielding and strain hardening produces greater strength where it is needed, all will be well. Professor Jacques Heyman sums it up well when he says that we may be clever engineers but we sleep the sounder in our beds for knowing that the material is cleverer than we are. But never be over-confident of this – treat your material with respect and it will not let you down. Treat it with disdain and it will – suddenly and often catastrophically.

Chapter ten

Mechanical metallurgy

10.1 Castings
10.2 Hot working
10.3 Cold working
10.4 Joining

We now look at the various ways in which metals and alloys may be prepared for industrial use. The subject is complex and the treatment here is, necessarily, brief. Further information may be found in, for example, Thomas (1970). Nonetheless, it is of some importance to the designer. Figure 10.1 outlines the processing route for most of the commoner metals and alloys used in structural engineering.

10.1 Castings

Most metals are produced by melting and casting in moulds. The mould may be shaped and dimensioned to the final size or it may simply be a prism which is intended for further processing.

The general process of solidification of a molten metal has already been described. When intended for further processing the metal will solidify in a rather coarse grain structure and will contain a number of casting defects such as porosity, shrinkage and cavities. These are not disastrous because further processing will rectify them. Shaped castings need more care – they are normally degassed and the grain size needs to be carefully controlled if the desired mechanical properties are to be achieved.

10.2 Hot working

The working of metals and alloys depends upon plasticity. They can be heavily deformed, especially in compression, without breaking. For steel structural members the most usual method is by hot rolling between shaped rolls at temperatures around 1000°C or more. After rolling, the members are left to cool naturally and, during this process, a heavy film of iron oxide (mill scale) develops. Thus steel sections delivered 'as rolled' need to be shot blasted or sand blasted before receiving any protective coating (see page 74).

Many familiar articles, e.g. engine crankshafts, are **forged** into shape. This involves placing a hot blank into one half of a shaped mould and then impressing the other half of the mould on to the blank. This is generally done under impact using such methods as drop forging, die stamping, etc. Many metals can be extruded and this has the advantage that very long lengths with complex sections can be produced. Aluminium glazing bars are a familiar example.

10.3 Cold working

Because of their ductility many metals and alloys can be cold worked, that is to say, shaped at temperatures below the recrystallization temperature. This creates an immense number of dislocations and, as a consequence, the metal becomes harder and its yield point is raised.

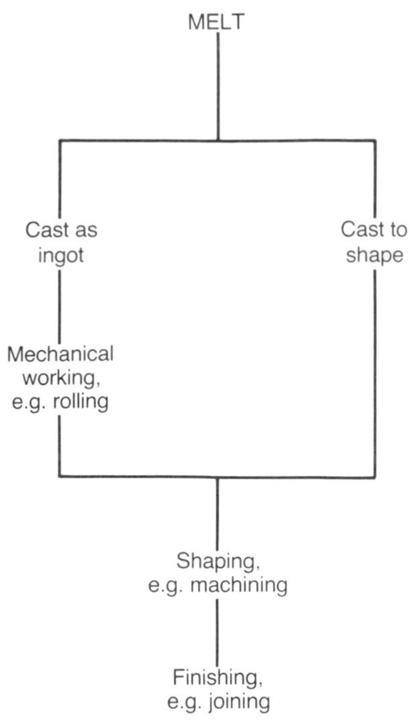

FIGURE 10.1 Processing of the commoner engineering materials.

Indeed, for pure metals and some alloys it is the only way of increasing the yield strength.

There are many different processes. Cold rolling is extensively used to produce sheet material, while high strength wire, as used for cables, is cold drawn by pulling through a tapered die. Metal sheets are shaped into cups, bowls or motor car parts by deep drawing or stretch forming (Figure 10.2).

Clearly there comes a limit beyond which the ductility is exhausted and the metal will fracture. If further cold work is required the metal must be annealed by heating it to a temperature where recrystallization occurs when the original ductility is restored and further working is possible. Some metals can be cold extruded.

10.4 Joining

Although adhesive bonding may be used for joining metals, the commonest methods are welding, brazing, soldering or inserting metal pins such as rivets and bolts.

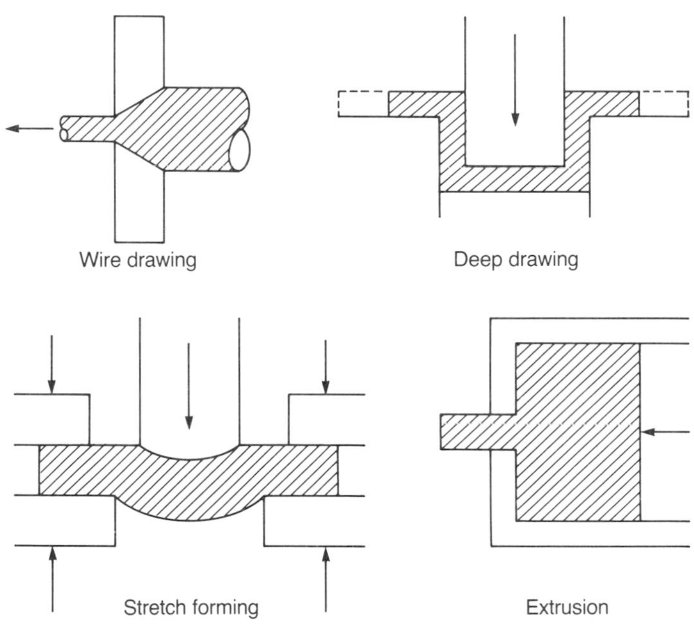

FIGURE 10.2 Some methods of metal forming.

10.4.1 Welding

It is beyond the scope of the present work to list the various welding processes that are available (but see, for instance, Houldcroft (1977)). All welding involves essentially the same sequence of operations at the joint; the material is raised, locally, to the melting point, additional metal may or may not be added and the joint is then allowed to cool naturally. Whatever the material or process all welds should comply with the two following ideal requirements.

1. There should be complete continuity between the parts to be joined and every part of the joint should be indistinguishable from the parent metal. In practice this is rarely achieved though welds giving satisfactory performance can be made.
2. The joining material should have metallurgical properties which are no worse than those of the parent metal. This is largely the concern of the supplier of welding consumables though poor welding practice can significantly affect the final product.

During welding a temperature gradient is created in the parent material. This gradient ranges from the melting point at the fusion zone to ambient temperature at some point distant. The quality of the joint is affected by:

1. the structure and properties of the weld metal;
2. the structure and properties of that part of the parent material which has undergone a significant thermal cycle (the heat affected zone).

Both are significantly affected by the rate of cooling after welding – the slower the rate of cooling the closer the structure is to equilibrium. Cooling occurs, principally, by conduction in the parent material and since the thermal conductivity of a metal is a fixed property the controlling factor is the thermal mass, i.e. the thickness and size of the material to be welded. The greater the thermal mass the faster the cooling rate.

10.4.2 Brazing and soldering

Both processes involve jointing by means of a thin film of a material which has a lower melting point than that of the parent material and which, when melted, flows into the joint, often by capillary action, to form a thin film. A good brazed or soldered joint should have a strength which is not too different from that of the parent material but, as shown later, quite high forces are needed to break a film of liquid provided the film is thin enough. This is not quite the whole explanation but is a very significant part of it. The rest is associated with the behaviour of materials under complex stress conditions, biaxial and triaxial, and is beyond the scope of this chapter. See, for instance, Cottrell (1964).

10.4.3 Pinning

For some materials (such as cast iron and wrought iron) bolting or riveting are the only possible ways of making joints. Both rely on friction – the tightened bolt forces the two members together and the friction between nut and bolt at the threads holds it in place. In riveting, the hot rivet is hammered into prepared holes. As it cools it contracts and develops a tensile stress which effectively locks the members together. High strength friction grip (HSFG) bolts used in structural steelwork combine both aspects – the bolt is prestressed to a given level and this tensile prestress acts in the same way as does the tensile stress in a rivet.

Chapter eleven

Oxidation and corrosion

11.1 Dry oxidation
11.2 Wet corrosion
11.3 Control of corrosion
11.4 Protection against corrosion

Corrosion can be divided into two areas – dry oxidation and wet corrosion.

11.1 Dry oxidation

The earth's atmosphere is an oxidizing one and, of the metals, only gold and silver are found in the native (i.e. unoxidized) state. The reaction is often written

$$M + O \rightarrow MO$$

where M is the metal and O is oxygen. But, in fact, there are two steps. The metal forms an ion, releasing electrons

$$M \rightarrow M^{++} + 2e^-$$

and the electrons are absorbed by oxygen to form an ion

$$O + 2e^- \rightarrow O^{--}.$$

At the surface the oxygen ions attach themselves to the surface to form a thin layer of oxide. Thereafter the metal ions $M^{++} + 2e$ must diffuse outwards to meet O^{--} at the outer surface or the oxygen ions diffuse inwards. The rate of oxidation is determined by whichever reaction can proceed the faster and, to a great extent, this is controlled by the thickness and structure of the oxide skin.

In some metals the oxide occupies less volume than the metal from which it was formed and if brittle (and oxides usually are) it will crack and split, exposing fresh metal. In others the oxide occupies more volume and it will tend to wrinkle and spring away, again exposing fresh metal.

In some cases, however, the oxide volume matches the metal volume and thin, adherent films form which act as barriers to further oxidation. This is true of aluminium, chromium and nickel, the last two metals being essential components of so-called 'stainless steel' for that very reason.

11.2 Wet corrosion

In the presence of moisture the situation changes drastically and the loss of metal by corrosion becomes appreciable. It has been estimated that in the UK the annual corrosion bill for either replacement or prevention is around £5000 million.

As in dry oxidation the basic mechanism involves ionization but, if the ions are soluble in the corroding medium (usually, but not necessarily, water), the metal steadily corrodes. Consider a simple cell in which two electrodes, both of the same metal, are connected via a battery and placed in a suitable electrolyte (Figure

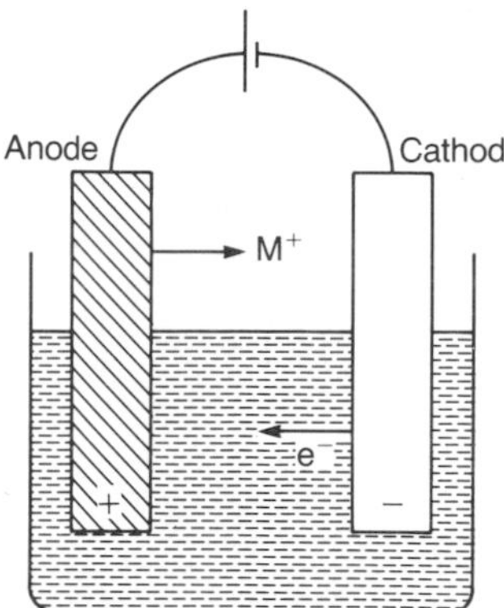

FIGURE 11.1 A simple cell.

11.1). The battery pumps out electrons which increase the negativity of the cathode while, at the same time, electrons are leaving the anode in order to maintain the flow of current:* the electrolyte completes the circuit and the metal ions go into solution and flow across to try to neutralize the surplus negative charge on the cathode. Thus the anode corrodes and the metal ions collect on the cathode. This is, in fact, a simple electroplating cell and is used to produce metals of a high degree of purity. 'Electrolytic' copper used for its high electrical conductivity is one example.

However, in some cases, the metal ions react with the electrolyte. Iron is one example and if we were to set up a cell similar to that in Figure 11.1 we would obtain the following reactions

$$Fe \rightarrow Fe^{++} + 2e^-$$

$$H_2O \rightarrow H^+ + (OH)^-$$

$$2H^+ + 2e^- \rightarrow H_2$$

at the anode and, at the cathode,

$$Fe^{++} + 2(OH)^- \rightarrow Fe(OH)_2.$$

* This is an area of fine confusion. The current is determined by the flow of electrons which, because they are negatively charged, means a flow towards the positive pole. But, by convention, the current is assumed to flow from positive to negative. Here we are considering the phenomenon in terms of the physics, not in terms of electrical engineering.

Iron hydroxide $Fe(OH)_2$ either deposits away from the cathode or, if it deposits on the cathode, it does so as a loose deposit giving no protection. It is, in fact, that orange, slimy oxide you often see on, say, sheet piling in stagnant water. But, since

$$Fe(OH)_2 \rightarrow FeO + H_2O$$

evaporation of water to the air leaves the more conventionally recognized rust – iron oxide, FeO.

But, you should say, in order to achieve this you needed a battery to drive the reactions along and the reinforcing bars in structural concrete are not connected to a battery and yet they still rust. Why?

In these circumstances, the whole subtlety of the process often makes it difficult to establish what is happening, and many large books have been written about it. This is not surprising, as nearly every case of corrosion involves some departures from the ideal but here we can only consider a few of the more general phenomena.

11.2.1 Electrochemical series

The process of ionization itself produces a change in electric potential and this can be

TABLE 11.1 Standard electrode potentials

Electrode	*Voltage*
Na^+	+2.71 base, anodic, corrodes
Al^{+++}	+1.66
Zn^{++}	+0.76
Fe^{++}	+0.46
Ni^{++}	+0.25
Sn^{++}	+0.14
H^+	0.00 reference
Cu^{++}	−0.34
Ag^+	−0.80
Pt^{++}	−1.20
Au^{+++}	−1.50 noble, cathodic

Note: Conventions differ as to which are negative and which are positive in the series. This does not matter too much since it is the relative position that is important. The convention adopted here is that commonly used in the USA; it is more directly associated with the text.

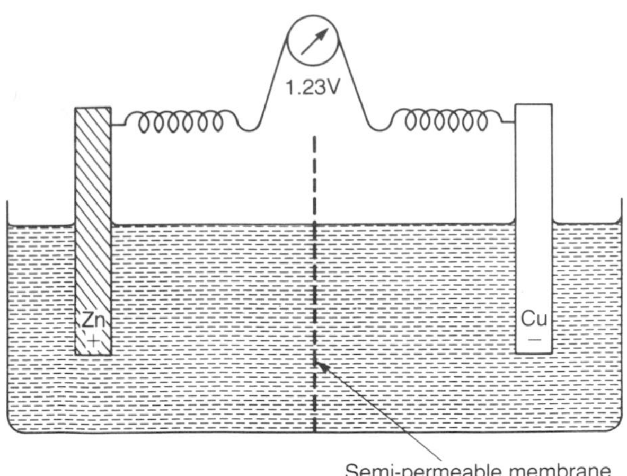

FIGURE 11.2 A Daniell cell.

measured relative to some convenient reference value. The reference value usually selected is that of the ionization of hydrogen

$$H \rightarrow H^+ + e^-$$

and the emf produced by a given metal relative to this reaction gives the **electromotive series**. An abbreviated version is given in Table 11.1. Metals which are more positive than the reference value are anodic and will corrode, metals which are relatively cathodic will not. And one of the first batteries for generating electricity was the Daniell cell (Figure 11.2) containing a zinc anode (which corroded) and a copper cathode (which did not).

With zinc at +0.76 V and copper at −0.47 V the cell produced an output of 1.23 V which was steady and wholly reproducible and, in the past, a freshly set up Daniell cell formed the standard against which all other measuring instruments were calibrated. However, we are talking here about a series developed under laboratory conditions. In the real world the nature of the electrolyte – sea water, boiler water, etc. – may change the order of merit. Table 11.2 gives an example. When pairs of metals are immersed in sea water, one will become the cathode and unreactive, the other becomes the anode and

TABLE 11.2 Galvanic series in sea water

Magnesium	Anodic, corrodes
Zinc	
Aluminium	
Mild steel	
Cast iron	
Lead	
Tin	
60–40 Brass	
70–30 Brass	
Copper	
Nickel	
Silver	
Stainless steel (18Cr 8Ni)	
Monel metal (70Ni 30Cu)	Cathodic, noble

reacts (i.e. corrodes). The table shows that brass and stainless steel fittings would form a cell in which the brass would corrode. Other situations which are more commonly found in construction are listed in Blyth (1990). These also include metal–non-metal cells such as steel–concrete, etc.

11.2.2 Cells

The above is an extreme example of a composition cell, i.e. a galvanic cell which arises as a result of the energy difference between two metals. But there are ways in which a composition cell can be used to advantage.

The most familiar is the use of zinc to galvanize steel. Table 11.2 shows that zinc is more anodic than iron and on exposure to the atmosphere the zinc corrodes first, thereby protecting the steel. The same system is used for buried pipelines where zinc slabs are connected to the steel pipe and are periodically replaced when they corrode. The converse occurs with chromium plating. Chromium is more cathodic than iron so that if a small pit appears in the chromium the steel underneath rusts away quite rapidly. The phenomenon will be familiar to the owners of elderly cars.

There are, however, some variations whose origins are, at first sight, less obvious. In the so-

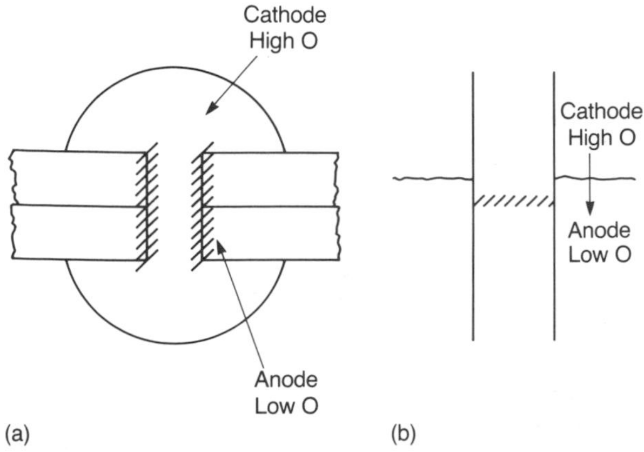

FIGURE 11.3 Concentration cells: (a) at riveted connection; (b) waterline corrosion.

called **concentration cell** preferential corrosion is a consequence of a difference in the constitution of the electrolyte itself.

The reaction

$$2H_2O + O_2 + 4e^- \rightarrow 4(OH)^-$$

removes electrons and these must be supplied from adjacent areas which are deficient in oxygen. These act as the anode and hence corrode. Thus, in a riveted or bolted connection corrosion will occur in the inaccessible (i.e. oxygen-poor) areas as indicated in Figure 11.3. A classic case is the 'waterline' corrosion of steel piling in stagnant water. Here the surface layers of the water are richer in oxygen and become the cathode; and the lower, oxygen-deficient layers are anodic and corrosion occurs locally. Much the same mechanism applies to pitting corrosion where the oxygen-poor region at the bottom of the pit is anodic and the pit therefore tends to deepen, often leading to premature failure by fatigue or brittle fracture.

11.3 Control of corrosion

Of all the problems facing the design engineer the management and control of corrosion is one of the most intractable. But it cannot be too firmly stressed that the problems start on, and must be tackled on, the drawing-board. There are three requirements, all easy in theory but difficult in practice.

1. Understand the environment in which the metal must work, whether polluted or not, whether facing or away from pervading sources of corrosion, whether wet and/or humid or dry, whether these conditions are stable or variable. Thus, given adequate cover and 'normal' working conditions steel reinforcement in concrete should not corrode. But it does – often because of sloppy workmanship and poor inspection leading to inadequate and over-porous cover. And, of course, if it is a motorway bridge, a combination of the excessive use of de-icing salts with inadequate drainage will speed up corrosion.
2. Consider the 'design life'. How long before the first major maintenance? Are you designing a throw-away structure like a modern motor car or are you designing a bridge for a century of service? And, if the component is not expected to outlive the structure as a whole, how easy is it to inspect and replace?
3. Select the most appropriate method of control. You will, of course, be excused for imagining that the 'most appropriate' method is that one which involves the longest life. You will, of course, be wrong. In the commercial world the most appropriate means of control is that one which produces the longest life at the least annual cost. So, on the whole, you would be best to master such matters as payback, rate of return, and discounted cash flow before deciding upon an appropriate technology.

11.4 Protection against corrosion

11.4.1 Design

At ambient temperatures corrosion occurs only if moisture is present. Thus, surfaces should be

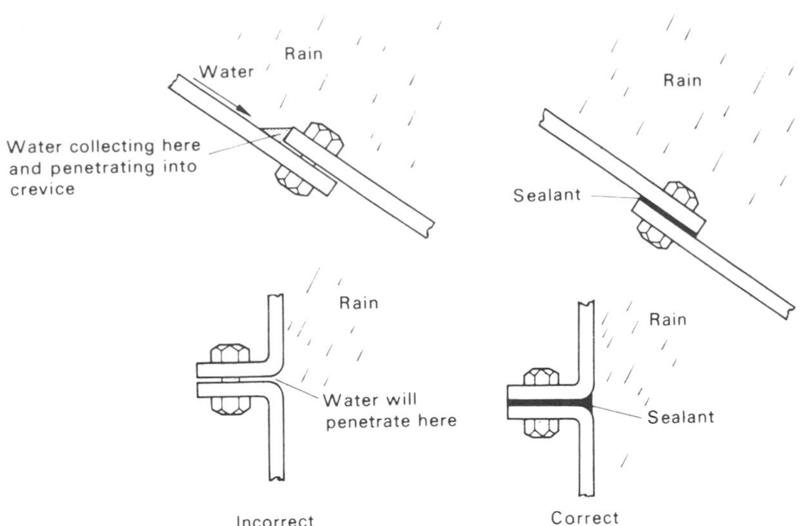

FIGURE 11.4 Design of joints to minimize corrosion risks. Note that small relative movements at joints can quickly abrade away any protective coatings of primer or paint.

exposed as little as possible to moisture and arranged so as to dry out quickly after wetting. In practice all surfaces are at risk, vertical surfaces suffer 'run off', flat surfaces retain moisture on their upper side and can attract dew and condensation on the lower. Water retention by V, H and other channel sections is obvious and drain holes should be provided if mechanically acceptable. Overlaps and joints should be arranged to avoid the formation of water channels (Figure 11.4). Porous materials which can retain moisture should not be in contact with metals.

Steel which has been allowed to rust on site poses a threat, for the methods available to clean the steel are usually less than adequate and some rust will inevitably remain at the bottom of the pits formed during rusting. These will contain sufficient active material for rusting to continue below any paint film. The only real remedy is not to let rusting start by protecting the steel by priming coats as an integral part of the manufacturing process and, if these are damaged during erecting, to repair the damage as soon as possible.

Remember also that structures need maintenance and the design should ensure that this can be carried out effectively.

11.4.2 Isolation from the environment

This is done by applying one or more protective coatings to a suitably prepared surface. Some metallic coatings simply form a protective barrier, e.g. nickel or chromium on steel. Other coatings (e.g. zinc, cadmium and aluminium) are anodic with respect to steel and provide sacrificial protection.

Organic coatings such as paints, pitch, tar, etc. form a protective barrier and are most commonly used, often in conjunction with a metallic primer. There are now so many different types of paint available that it would be impossible to summarize the virtues and limitations here. For steelwork the publications of the British Constructional Steelwork Association provide excellent guidance for the practising engineer.

It must be emphasized that all paint coatings even of the highest quality and meticulous application are only as good as the quality of the preceding surface preparation. Application, whether by brushing or spraying, should always be carried out on dry surfaces and in conditions of low humidity.

11.4.3 Cathodic protection

In addition to the use of sacrificial anodes, cathodic protection can be achieved by the use of an external power source to make the metal cathodic to its surroundings. Inert anodes are used, commonly carbon, titanium, lead or platinum. The process is not without its problems. Thus, in many cases, the cost of replacement anodes is greater than the cost of the impressed power supply.

In buried structures, secondary reactions with other nearby buried structures may enhance, rather than control, corrosion and there is the possibility of hydrogen evolution at the cathode. This can diffuse into the metal and embrittle it. Nonetheless, this method of cathodic protection has been quite widely used in marine environments, especially on offshore oil rigs. Similarly, considerable attention has also been paid to the application of cathodic protection to concrete reinforcement.

Chapter twelve

Metals, their differences and uses

12.1 The extraction of iron
12.2 Cast irons
12.3 Steel
12.4 Aluminium and alloys
12.5 Copper and alloys
12.6 Design for minimum weight

Metals are divided into ferrous (based on iron) and non-ferrous (based on metals other than iron). The principal ferrous alloys in use today are those of iron and carbon – cast iron and steel. The cast irons contain more than 1.7% C, steels contain up to about 1.5% with structural steels containing only about 0.25% C. The main non-ferrous alloys of interest in civil and structural engineering are those based on aluminium and copper.

12.1 The extraction of iron

Like all metals, iron is extracted from naturally occurring ores. These are actually quite complex chemical compounds but, for simplicity, we shall assume that their starting material is iron oxide. As noted in the introduction high temperatures (*c.* 1600°C) are needed to allow the reaction

$$FeO + C \rightarrow Fe + CO,$$

the carbon monoxide being evolved into the air. This produces **pig iron** which contains a large amount of carbon and being industrially useless requires further processing. The pig is remelted, often with scrap iron or steel and, by controlled oxidation using an air blast, the carbon is reduced to 2–4%. This is **cast iron** which, as its name implies, is cast directly into sand or metal moulds.

12.2 Cast irons

These are used in a variety of applications, the major consumption being in pipes and fittings for services, but in civil engineering an important use is for tunnel segments and mine shaft tubing. The engineer should, however, be aware that cast iron was one of the predominant structural materials in the nineteenth century and will be found as beams, columns and arches in many rehabilitation and refurbishment projects. As we shall see it should be treated with respect. There are four principal types:

White cast iron

The carbon is here combined as hard, brittle iron carbide Fe_3C. This makes it structurally undesirable and its main use is for applications where high resistance to wear and abrasion is required.

Grey cast iron

Most of the carbon is present in the form of free graphite flakes. This makes it softer and easier to machine. It has good rigidity and compressive strength.

Nodular or ductile irons

The flakes in grey cast iron act as internal notches and the metal is brittle in tension. Graphite may be induced to form spherulites by the addition of certain alloying elements. These irons have good strength, toughness and ductility.

Malleable irons

These are produced from white irons by annealing which results, again, in nodules of graphite. Depending on the process used, and the composition, they may be described as whiteheart or blackheart (this derives from the appearance of the fracture surface). Both have good strength and resistance to impact.

All cast irons are extremely difficult to weld and, all too often, the welds are unreliable and of poor strength. Unless specialist advice is available the engineer should use brazing rather than welding. Riveting is possible, but again needs care for fear of rupturing the iron. Bolting is the safest method of joining.

12.3 Steel

Steel making involves some very complex thermochemistry but the basic reaction is simply that of reducing the carbon content still further (for structural steels down to about 0.2%) by a process of controlled oxidation:

$$Fe_3C + O \rightleftharpoons Fe + CO,$$

the CO being lost to the atmosphere. To keep the reaction moving to the right a considerable amount of oxygen must be used; if not removed this would form hard, brittle iron oxide FeO and we would revert to square one. Thus when the desired carbon content is reached the residual oxygen is 'fixed' as an oxide which, after a period of resting, rises to the surface and is removed as slag. The metals commonly used to achieve this are manganese and silicon and steels treated in this way are known as **killed** steels. Manganese is added for another reason. One of the most persistent impurities, and one which is difficult to eliminate economically, is sulphur. This forms iron sulphide FeS which, if present (even in small quantities), leads to a defect known as **hot shortness** in which the steel cracks disastrously if it is stressed when hot. Even contraction stresses on cooling can lead to irredeemable cracking. The manganese addition counteracts this, and so even the simplest steels contain silicon and manganese.

There is one more important feature to note here. Steels, and especially structural steels, can fail in a wholly brittle manner at quite ordinary temperatures. Figure 12.1 shows the curve of energy absorption for a typical structural steel and it will be seen that, over quite a modest drop of temperature, the ductility (i.e. the fracture toughness) diminishes. The test normally used is the Izod or Charpy test in which a

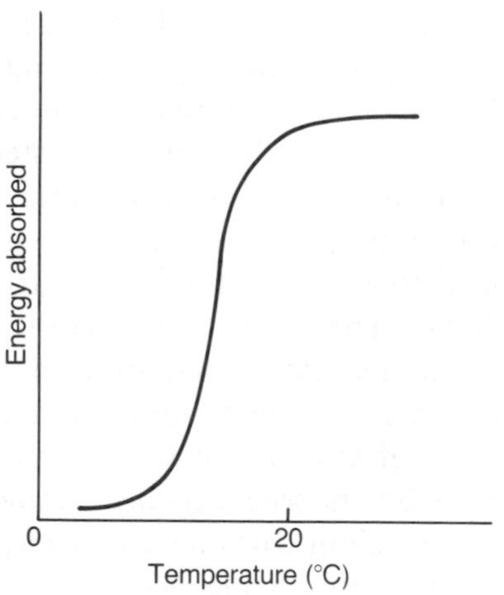

FIGURE 12.1 Energy absorption of structural steel (schematic).

TABLE 12.1 Structural steels (BS 4360: 1990)

Chemical composition

Grade	*C* %	*Si* %	*Mn max* %	*P max* %	*S max* %	*Nb max* %	*V max* %	*Normal supply condition*
40	0.16	0.10/0.50	1.50	0.04	0.03	–	–	Normalized
43	0.16	0.10/0.50	1.50	0.04	0.03			Normalized
50	0.18	0.10/0.50	1.50	0.04	0.03	0.10	0.10	Normalized
55	0.22	0.10/0.50	1.60	0.04	0.03	0.10	0.20	Normalized

Note: The above data are summaries of some of the main features only. For full details the British Standard should be consulted.

notched bar is struck by a hammer of known momentum. Even though this phenomenon appears to have been first noted by I.K. Brunel in 1847 we are still very hazy about the reasons. What we do know, however, is that a high ratio of manganese to carbon provides a useful insurance so that in Table 12.1 we give extracts from the relevant British Standards for structural steels for normal and for low temperature use.

The terminology used to describe steels is traditional and far from exact. With up to about 0.25% carbon they are 'mild steel' or 'low carbon steel' (structural steels come into this category). Between about 0.3% and 0.6% C they are 'medium carbon steels' or often 'carbon steels'. Above about 0.6% they are 'high carbon steels'. If elements (other than the normal Mn and Si) are added they become 'alloy steels' and, if certain elements (notably Cr and Ni) are added in quantity, 'stainless steels'.

We need to consider further the traditional terminology. The early microscopic studies were, essentially, developed from mineralogy where, because of the wide variation in chemical composition of minerals, it was not possible to define each by its true chemical name. Thus, the impure calcium carbonate becomes calcite, impure magnesium oxide becomes magnesite, and so on. Sometimes the geographical source of the mineral was used, e.g. dolomite, and sometimes the name of the mineralogist who identified it (gibbsite). Early metallographers followed the same scheme. Those grains of iron showing white in Figure 12.2 contain little or no carbon (hence ferrite); the carbon is found, as lamellae, in the darker areas. At about 0.8% C the microstructure consists wholly of these lamellae and, when prepared for microscopical examination, such steels reflect the light like mother-of-pearl. Hence pearlite. We shall need to come back to some of these terms later in connection with stainless steels.

12.3.1 Structural steel

Table 12.2 gives some details from standard specifications. It will be noted that there are four grades: 40, 43, 50 and 55. These numbers are related to the minimum tensile strength (400, 430, 500 and 550 N/mm^2 respectively). There are a few points to note.

1. The specified minimum yield strength in grades 43 and 50 can be obtained by various combinations of carbon and manganese.
2. Sulphur and phosphorous are both deleterious. Maximum permissible values are always specified.
3. Structural steels are normally delivered annealed (i.e. slowly cooled in a furnace) or normalized (cooled in air). The term 'as rolled' implies no further treatment.

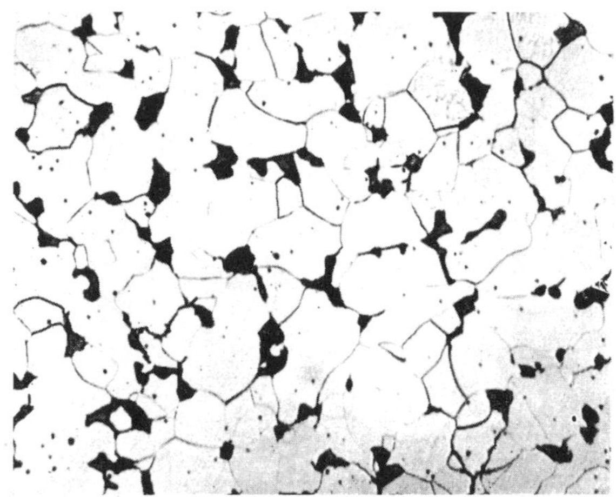

FIGURE 12.2 Typical microstructure of a low-carbon (structural) steel.

TABLE 12.2 Mechanical properties of steel

Grade	*Tensile strength N/mm²*	*Minimum yield strength for thickness shown N/mm²*		*Minimum elongation %*	*Minimum Charpy V-notch, impact*	
		<16 mm	*>100 mm*		*Temp °C*	*Energy J*
40	340/500	260	205	25	−50	27
43	430/580	275	225	22	−50	27
50	490/640	355	305	20	−50	27
55	550/700	450	400	19	−50	27

4. Note that, in Table 12.2, the specified yield strength decreases with size of section. This is the **size effect**, and arises from the fact that thick sections cool more slowly than thin ones and the Fe_3C is more evenly distributed.

All structural steels are readily weldable though some care is needed in the higher grades 50 and 55 (see below).

12.3.2 Heat treated steels

With a carbon content greater than about 0.3% the properties of steel can be varied by heat treatment, that is to say, by fast cooling (generally by quenching in oil or water) from a higher temperature followed by reheating to temperatures not exceeding about 650°C (tempering). The fast cooling produces a hard, brittle micro-

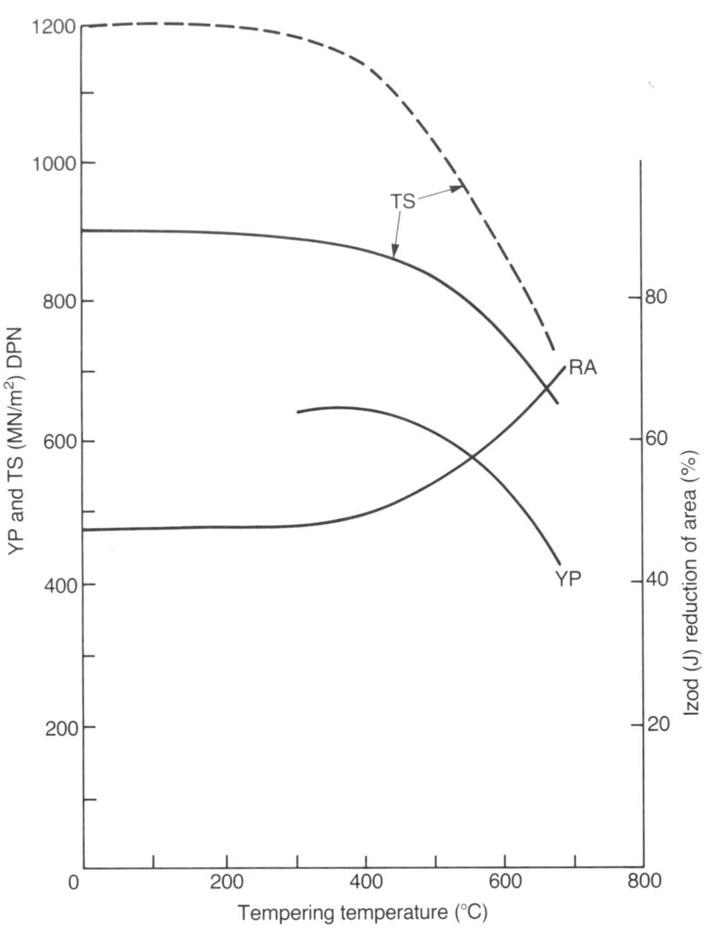

FIGURE 12.3 Variation in properties of 1% Ni steel with varying tempering temperatures. TS: tensile strength; RA: reduction in area; YP: yield point. (From O.H. Wyatt and D. Dew-Hughes (1974) *Metals, Ceramics and Polymers*, by permission of Cambridge University Press.)

structure (martensite) which is of little use except for a few applications such as cutting tools or cutlery. The structure is, however, metastable and the reheating causes the carbon to be redistributed evenly throughout the matrix which is thereby softened and becomes more ductile. By varying the tempering temperature (Figure 12.3) great control over the properties can be achieved.

Such steels do not, however, find great application in structural engineering. High strength friction grip (HSFG) bolts are supplied in the hardened and tempered condition and it follows that these should not be reheated (e.g. by welding or flame cutting) or the effects of the heat treatment may well be cancelled.

It is, however, important to note that the higher strength structural steels (Grades 50 and 55) can also harden in the same way. Welding, and especially flame cutting, of these grades should be undertaken with some caution and due respect for the specification and any recommendations by the manufacturer of the welding consumables.

12.3.3 Stainless steel

The term 'stainless steel' covers a whole range of ferrous alloys all of which contain at least 12% of chromium which produces a stable passive oxide film. Other alloying elements, notably nickel and molybdenum, may also be present. (See also BS 1449: 1967.) There are three basic types, grouped according to metallurgical structure.

1. Martensitic. The 410 series are low carbon steels containing 13% chromium. They are hard and since they retain a cutting edge they are particularly used for cutlery.
2. Ferritic. These (the 430 series) also contain 13% chromium but with very low carbon.
3. Austenitic. The 300 series are low carbon with a basic composition of 18% Cr and 8% Ni though other additions may be made.

All these steels will corrode in solutions low in oxygen. The austenitic steels are the most resistant to pitting corrosion, though they may suffer from stress corrosion cracking in chloride solutions at slightly elevated temperatures. Type 316 (18Cr 10Ni 3Mo) is recommended for all external applications. Ferritic steels should be limited to internal uses.

For all practical purposes, martensitic and ferritic stainless steels should be regarded as unweldable since both undergo significant changes in structure and properties as a result of the thermal cycle. Ordinarily, austenitic stainless steels can be welded (BS 2926: 1984) but can suffer from a form of intergranular attack (weld decay) and grades recommended for welding (i.e. stabilized by the use of titanium) should be specified.

12.4 Aluminium and alloys

Aluminium and its alloys are used both structurally and decoratively. Typical applications include cladding, roofing, window frames, window and door furniture, etc. The high cost, however, is still a limiting factor and aluminium can only compete with, say, steel where the inherent properties of the material – lightness, strength, durability and appearance – must be exploited. The most economical structures are those having a high ratio of self-weight/live load – roofs, footbridges, long span structures – and where the lightness of the material offers advantages in transport, handling and erection. Its comparatively high durability makes it attractive in polluted and coastal areas where its high initial cost may be offset by reduced maintenance. Aluminium alloys may be cast or wrought while structural sections are produced almost exclusively by extrusion.

TABLE 12.3 International designations of wrought aluminium alloys (BS 1470: 1987)

Composition

The first of four digits in the designation indicates the alloy group as follows:

Aluminium 99% or greater	1×××
Principal alloy – copper	2×××
Principal alloy – manganese	3×××
Principal alloy – silicon	4×××
Principal alloy – magnesium	5×××
etc.	

The second digit indicates alloy modifications. If this is zero it indicates the original alloy. The last two digits serve only to identify the different alloys in this group – thus 2014 refers to Al, 4% Cu, + Si, Mg, while 2024 refers to Al, 4% Cu + Mg 1%.

Temper

There are many subdivisions here. The reader is referred to the BS for details. However, the main groups are:

F	As fabricated. There are no special requirements for mechanical properties.
O	Annealed. The lowest strength for wrought products, to improve ductility in cast products.
H	Strain hardened. The H is always followed by two digits to indicate the level of strain hardening.
T	Thermally treated. To produce stable temper other than F, O or H. The T is followed by one or more digits indicating the specific treatment.

Because the modulus is significantly lower than that of steel (70 kN/m^2 compared with 210 kN/m^2) the deflection under a given load is correspondingly greater and, for deflection limited designs, deeper beams must be used. At the same time, of course, the density of aluminium is significantly lower than that of steel (2.7 against 7.9 kg/m^3) so that specific moduli E/ρ are not so very different (aluminium 20, steel 29).

The term 'aluminium' is normally used to include aluminium alloys and the alloys of particular interest are those whose properties can be changed by heat treatment. Earlier we noted that plastic flow, by dislocation movement, can be impeded by suitable barriers. The classic example here is the original alloy Al–4% Cu, i.e. Duralumin or Dural, first developed in 1906 upon which the whole of the aircraft industry depended, and, in more sophisticated form, still depends.

When heated to around 550°C the copper enters into solid solution in the aluminium and remains in solution when the alloy is rapidly cooled. But, even at room temperature, a hard intermediate compound $CuAl_2$ forms and, because the particles are small (actually submicroscopic) and evenly dispersed throughout the matrix, they offer maximum resistance to dislocation movement and the yield stress is consequently considerably higher than that of pure aluminium (Figure 12.4). This process, often known as ageing, can be speeded up by reheating to temperatures of about 150°C. But, if reheated to too high a temperature (*c.* 250°C) the minute particles of $CuAl_2$ coalesce and clump together. They are then more widely separated and the slip dislocation can pass easily between them and the yield strength is correspondingly reduced. This is known as overageing. Modern alloys are more sophisticated but the same principles apply.

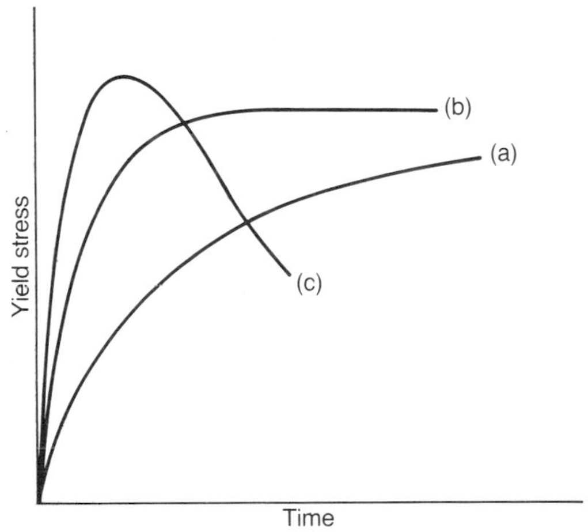

FIGURE 12.4 Ageing of Al–Cu alloy (schematic): (a) untreated; (b) correctly aged; (c) over-aged.

Unlike mild steel, aluminium alloys do not show a definitive yield point and, for design purposes, the working stress is usually defined as that stress at which a small, but acceptable, amount of plastic deformation has occurred. This is known as the proof stress, generally defined as the stress corresponding to a plastic deformation of 0.2%.

The thermal expansion of aluminium and its alloys is nearly twice that of steel but the lower modulus means that the thermal stress developed by a given rise in temperature is less in aluminium than in steel.

The durability of aluminium alloys is, generally, greater than that of steel but their corrosion resistance depends upon their composition and heat treatment, the fully heat treated alloys being generally the most susceptible to corrosion and needing, therefore, some protection.

It will be clear that welding of heat treated aluminium alloys is not without its problems since the thermal cycle will, inevitably, produce an over-aged structure in the parent metal. And, although techniques for welding are now well established, bolting, and to a lesser extent riveting, are preferred, especially for joints made on site.

Steel bolts may be used but should be protected by a zinc coating. Cold riveting, using rivets up to 22 mm diameter, is often used and there are many varieties – some solid, some hollow – but limitations of size and the lower shear strength of aluminium require that, compared with steel, more rivets are used.

Most normal structural forms are available and special sections can be produced by extrusion more readily than in steel, though at some cost, and these are really only justified when large quantities are needed. On the other hand, the use of special sections perhaps allows the designer more freedom and scope.

12.5 Copper and alloys

The principal use of copper is in applications where its high thermal and electrical conductivity are important – domestic water services, heating, sanitation, etc. But its high resistance to corrosion combined with the pleasing colour of its oxide film has seen much demand for roofs, cladding and flashing. Decorative schemes make considerable use of the wide range and variety of colours available in copper alloys. Two alloys are widely used:

12.5.1 Brasses

These are alloys of copper and zinc with other additions to produce enhanced strength or corrosion resistance. Two main classes are used: alpha brasses, nominally 70Cu 30Zn, and alpha-beta, nominally 60Cu 40Zn. Neither are heat treatable, both are difficult to weld and are better soldered or brazed.

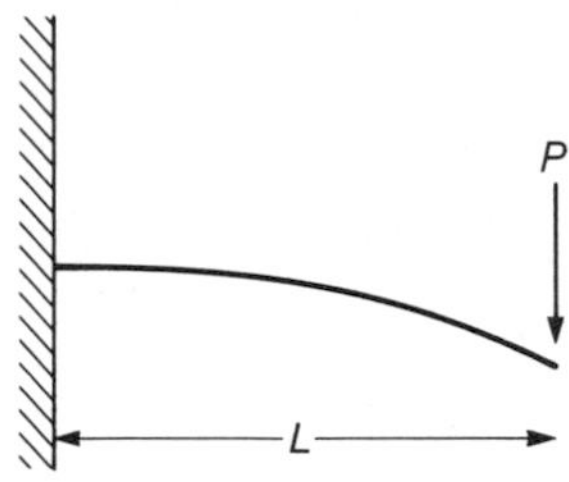

FIGURE 12.5 A simple cantilever.

12.5.2 Bronzes

Basically alloys of copper and tin but with a whole range of possible additions to produce alloys with specific protection – thus phosphor-bronze, aluminium-bronze, silicon-bronze, etc. **Gunmetal** is bronze containing zinc. All have high corrosion resistance, and many are weldable by inert gas processes.

12.6 Design for minimum weight

An important aspect to consider here is that of designing for minimum weight. Although at first sight this may appear to be no more than an intellectual exercise it is often a good exercise to see what is the least amount of material needed to carry the design loads. It also produces some interesting comparisons between materials. Consider the simple cantilever shown in Figure 12.5. Its deflection is given by

$$\delta = \frac{PL^3}{3EI} \qquad (12.1)$$

where I is the second moment of area having units of (length)^4. Rewrite as

$$\delta = \frac{PL^3}{3Ex^4}$$

where x is a unit of length. The weight is

$$W = \rho AL = \rho Lx^2$$

whence

$$x^4 = \frac{W^2}{\rho^2 L^2}.$$

TABLE 12.4 Materials in decreasing order of efficiency in bending. Units as in Table 1.1 in Part One

Timber	4.55
Aluminium	10.0
GFRP*	11.25
Titanium	12.86
Steel	17.17
Concrete	21.82
Copper	25.60

* Mean values for glass-fibre-reinforced plastics.

Substituting and rearranging

$$W = \left(\frac{PL^5}{3\delta}\right)^{1/2} \frac{\rho}{E^{1/2}}$$

so that, for a given set of design conditions (P, L, δ) W is minimized by minimizing $\rho/E^{1/2}$. Let us take the data in Table 1.1 in Part One and compare various materials on the basis of what is often called the 'efficiency' of the material.

We see that, in terms of material efficiency, timber is outstanding, closely followed by glass-reinforced plastic and aluminium. All three have competed for use in applications where weight is costly – aircraft, sailing dinghies, racing cars, etc. – and, indeed, in small-scale building – squash rackets, golf clubs, tables and chairs, and so on. So why are bicycles not made of timber? They once were but metals (and polymers) can be easily shaped into tubes and since the second moment of area, I, of a tube is about 18 times greater than that of a solid bar of the same stiffness this dominates in eqn (12.1).

We take these thoughts one stage further. With energy conservation a matter of prime importance we should consider the energy cost of the materials that we use. Not simply the energy per tonne but rather the energy cost of buying one unit of engineering property.

Accurate data for energy consumption are hard to come by and usually untrustworthy since they rarely include the energy used to win the material and the cost of transport. But, for what they are worth (and they are all from the same source so they are at least self-consistent), the cost in kJ of buying one unit of elasticity is: sawn timber – 53; mass concrete – 124; brick – 167; steel – 1598; aluminium – 9180. This stresses a point made earlier. Do not regard any property as an absolute. For each gain in some property there is a cost to be paid in another. The engineer's task is that of achieving the best trade-off.

Further reading

Though not, perhaps, essential, the student should, at least, glance at standard specifications. Those of relevance to the present part are:

BS 1449: 1982: *Stainless and heat resisting steels*
BS 1470: 1987: *Aluminium and alloys*
BS 4360: 1990: *Weldable structural steels*
BS 5950: 1985: *The structural use of steelwork*

Brunel, I.K. in evidence to the Royal Commission appointed to inquire into the application of iron to railway structures. Report, HMSO, 1849.

Cottrell, A.H. (1964) *The Mechanical Properties of Matter*, John Wiley, London. Particularly good for the treatment of multiaxial stressing and for plastic design.

Cottrell, A.H. (1967) *An Introduction to Metallurgy*, Edward Arnold, London. Thorough but probably more detailed than required. Worth dipping into.

Pascoe, K.J. (1978) *An Introduction to the Properties of Engineering Materials*, Van Nostrand Reinhold, New York. Very much a beginner's text.

Gordon, J.E. (1978) *Structures*, Penguin, Harmondsworth, Middlesex. Very readable, very informative. Lays stress on what engineers do and why they do it. Keep it by your bedside.

Blyth, A. (ed.) (1990) *Specification*, Architectural Press and Building Publications, London. Very straightforward and oversimplified but extremely useful as reference.

Aitchison, L. (1960) *A History of Metals*, Macdonald and Evans, London.

Houldcroft, P.T. (1977) *Welding Process Technology*, Cambridge University Press, Cambridge.

Chilton, J.P. (1963) *Principles of Metallic Corrosion*, Royal Institute of Chemistry, London.

Evans, U.R. (1960) *The Corrosion and Oxidation of Metals*, Edward Arnold, London. Size and cost also make this a reference book, but it is the classic textbook on the subject.

Thomas, G.G. (1970) *Production Technology*, Oxford University Press, Oxford.

British Constructional Steelwork Association (1986) *Guides for Protection against Corrosion in Steelwork*.

Part Three

Concrete

P.L. Domone

Introduction

Concrete is a ubiquitous material and its versatility, comparative cheapness and energy efficiency have ensured that it is of great and increasing importance for all types of construction throughout the world. Even in structures where other materials such as steel or timber form the principal structural elements, concrete will normally still have an important role, for example in the foundations.

The hardened properties are obviously of paramount importance, and, as we shall see, depend on a very complex structure. However, unlike other major structural materials which are delivered in a ready-to-use state, civil engineers are responsible for the manufacture of concrete from its constituent materials – cement, aggregates, water and admixtures – and its transport, placing and compaction. We shall not be discussing production practice in any detail, but a knowledge of the behaviour when fresh or still plastic is necessary since this has a crucial bearing on the hardened properties. A further complication is that, even when hardened, the concrete structure and properties are not static, but continue to change with time. For example, about 50–60% of the ultimate strength is developed in 7 days, 80–85% in 28 days, and small but measurable increases in strength have been found in 30-year-old concrete.

Despite its current popularity, concrete is not just a modern material; various forms of it have been used for several millenia. Mortars and concretes made from lime, sand and gravels dating from about 5000 BC have been found in Eastern Europe, and similar mixtures were used by the ancient Egyptians and Greeks some three to four thousand years later. However, it was the Romans who first made concrete with a hydraulic cement, i.e. one which reacts chemically with the mix water, and is therefore capable of hardening under water and is subsequently insoluble. The cement was a mixture of lime and volcanic ash from a source near Pozzuoli. This ash contained silica and alumina in an active form which combined chemically with the lime; the term **pozzolana** is still used to describe such materials. Concretes produced by combining this cement with aggregates were used in many of the great Roman structures, for example in the foundations and columns of aqueducts, and, in combination with pumice, a lightweight aggregate, in the arches of the Colosseum and in the dome of the Pantheon in Rome.

Lime concretes were used in some structures in the Middle Ages and after, but it was not until the early stages of the Industrial Revolution in the second half of the eighteenth century that a revival of interest in the material led to any significant developments. In 1756, John Smeaton required a mortar for use in the foundations and masonry of the Eddystone Lighthouse, and, after many experiments, he found that a mixture of burnt Aberthau blue lias, a clay-bearing limestone from South Wales, and an Italian pozzolana produced a suitable hydraulic cement.

In the 1790s, James Parker developed and patented 'Roman cement' (a confusing name since it bore little resemblance to the cement of Roman times). This was made from nodules of a calcareous clay from North Kent, which were broken up, burnt in a kiln or furnace, and then ground to a powder to produce the cement. Alternative sources of suitable clay were soon identified, and production of significant quantities continued until the 1860s. The cement was used in many of the pioneering civil engineering structures of the period, such as Brunel's Thames Tunnel and the foundation of Stephenson's Britannia Bridge over the Menai Straits.

Roman cement, and some others of a similar type developed at about the same time, relied on using a raw material which was a natural mixture of clay and calcareous minerals. Methods of producing an 'artificial' cement from separate clay- and lime-bearing materials were therefore sought, resulting in the patenting by Joseph Aspdin in 1824 of Portland cement. A mixture of clay and calcined (or burnt) limestone was further calcined until carbon dioxide was expelled, and the product was then ground into the fine cement powder. This had hydraulic cementitious properties when mixed with water, and was called Portland cement because Aspdin considered the hardened product to have a resemblance to Portland stone. In 1828, Brunel found the hardened mortar to be three times stronger than that made from Roman cement, and he used it for repairs in the Thames Tunnel. However, Portland cement was relatively expensive, and it did not become widespread in use until larger scale production processes were developed. In particular, the replacement of single-shaft kilns by continuous-process rotary kilns in the 1890s was critical. Increasingly larger capacity kilns have met the enormous worldwide demand of the twentieth century. A measure of the importance of Portland cement is that it was the subject of one of the first British Standards (BS 12) in 1904, subsequently revised several times. Although the constituent materials have remained essentially the same, refinements in the production processes, in particular higher burning temperatures and finer grinding, and a greater knowledge of cement chemistry and physics have led to steadily increasing quality and uniformity of the cement.

Chapter thirteen

Constituent materials of concrete

13.1 Portland cements
13.2 Admixtures
13.3 Cement replacement materials
13.4 Aggregates
13.5 References

Throughout this section of the book the term concrete will refer to composite mixtures formed from Portland cement, water and aggregate. The aggregates form the bulk of the volume, typically 70–80%. Other materials, such as admixtures or partial cement replacement materials, may also be added to the basic constituents. Setting and hardening of the concrete occurs by a chemical reaction between the cement and the water called **hydration.** In this chapter we shall describe the composition and nature of the constituent materials, the processes of hydration and the hydration products. In subsequent chapters we shall go on to consider the properties of the composite concrete.

13.1 Portland cements

13.1.1 Manufacture

We have already seen in the introduction that cement is made from a mixture of clay and calcareous raw materials. The essential ingredients are lime and silica, and these occur abundantly in suitable forms as chalk (or limestone) and clay (or shale) respectively. Occasionally they even occur in a single raw material such as marl. Clays in particular contain additional but lesser amounts of other minerals, chiefly oxides of aluminium, iron, magnesium, sodium and potassium; the first two have a significant effect on the manufacture and composition of the resulting cement.

The manufacturing process is basically simple, although high temperatures are involved. Initially the chalk and clay are reduced to particle sizes of 75 μm or less, and then intimately mixed in a slurry (in the so-called wet process) or blended and transported in an air stream (in the dry process). The blend is then fed into the upper end of a long (up to 200 m), gently sloping rotating kiln of up to 6 m diameter. The kiln is heated to about 1500°C at its lower end by burning a jet of oil or powdered coal. As the material moves down the kiln it undergoes successive changes as it becomes progressively hotter. First, water is evaporated (in the dry process less energy is required for this, and hence the process is more economical). At about 600°C the calcium carbonate of the chalk decomposes to give quicklime (CaO) and gaseous carbon dioxide, which is given off. Finally, fusion reactions start at about 1200°C and calcium silicates, calcium aluminates and smaller amounts of other compounds are formed. The oxides of iron, aluminium and magnesium from the clay assist this process by acting as a flux and enabling the calcium silicates to be formed at considerably lower temperatures than would otherwise be possible. The material emerges from the kiln as a clinker with particle sizes of the order of a few millimetres. This is cooled and a few per cent of gypsum (calcium sulphate dihydrate, $CaSO_4.2H_2O$) is added before the mixture is then ground to a fine powder. Grinding is continued until most particles are in the size range of 2–80 μm, equivalent to a total specific surface area of the order of 300 m^2/kg. The ground clinker and gypsum are often the sole constituents of the final Portland cement, although some countries, such as those in Western Europe, allow the addition of up to 5% of an inert filler such as limestone dust.

13.1.2 Composition

Cement chemists use a shorthand notation for the principal oxides in the cement:

$$CaO \text{ (lime)} = C, \quad SiO_2 \text{ (silica)} = S,$$

$$Al_2O_3 \text{ (alumina)} = A, \quad Fe_2O_3 \text{ (iron oxide)} = F$$

Four main compounds, sometimes called **phases**, are formed in the fusion process:

Tricalcium silicate	$3CaO.SiO_2$	in short C_3S
Dicalcium silicate	$2CaO.SiO_2$	in short C_2S
Tricalcium aluminate	$3CaO.Al_2O_3$	in short C_3A
Tetracalcium aluminoferrite	$4CaO.Al_2O_3.Fe_2O_3$	in short C_4AF

Strictly, C_4AF is not a true compound, but represents the average composition of a solid solution.

Each grain of cement consists of an intimate mixture of these compounds, but it is not possible to determine the amounts of each by direct chemical analysis; instead an oxide analysis is carried out, and the compound composition then calculated from the oxide proportions using equations developed by Bogue (1929), which, in the shorthand form, are:

$$\%C_3S = 4.07C - 7.60S - 6.72A - 1.43F - 2.85\bar{S} \quad (13.1)$$

$$\%C_2S = 2.87S - 0.754C_3S \quad (13.2)$$

$$\%C_3A = 2.65A - 1.69F \quad (13.3)$$

$$\%C_4AF = 3.04F \quad (13.4)$$

$\bar{S} = SO_3$, and the value of C should be the total from the oxide analysis less the free lime, i.e. that not compounded. Also, the above equations apply to the more common case of $A/F > 0.64$; with lower alumina, alternative equations should be used. See, for example, Soroka (1979).

The approximate range of oxide composition that can be expected for Portland cements is given in the first column of figures in Table 13.1. It can be seen that CaO and SiO_2 are the principal oxides, with the ratio of CaO and SiO_2 normally being about three to one by weight. The principal compounds are C_3S and C_2S, and these together normally amount to about three-quarters of the cement. The composition of any one cement will depend on the quality and proportions of the raw materials, and will therefore vary from one cement works to another, and even with time from a single works. Cements A, B, C and D in Table 13.1 are typical individual cements, and it is apparent that relatively small variations in the oxide composition result in very large differences in the compound composition. As we will see, such variations have considerable effects on the hydration process and hardened cement properties, and therefore careful control of the raw materials and manufacturing processes is vital if cement of uniform quality is to be produced. Cement A can be considered to have a 'typical' or 'average' composition for Portland cement; cements B, C and D are common and useful variations of this, i.e. higher early strength, low heat and sulphate

TABLE 13.1 Compositions of Portland cements

	Range	*Cement A*	*Cement B*	*Cement C*	*Cement D*
Oxides (% by weight)					
CaO	60–67	66	67	64	64
SiO_2	17–25	21	21	22	23
Al_2O_3	3–8	7	5	7	4
Fe_2O_3	0.5–6.0	3	3	4	5
$Na_2O + K_2O$	0.2–1.3				
MgO	0.1–4.0				
Free CaO	0–2	1	1	1	1
SO_3	1–3	2	2	2	2
Potential compound composition (% by weight)					
C_3S		48	65	31	42
C_2S		24	11	40	34
C_3A		13	8	12	2
C_4AF		9	9	12	15

resisting properties respectively, which we shall discuss in Section 13.1.4.

The cement compounds exist in a complex and impure semi-crystalline form. (The impure forms of C_3S and C_2S in cement are commonly called alite and belite respectively.) The Bogue equations assume pure compounds, and therefore are only an approximate, but useful, estimate of the compound composition. For this reason the calculated values are sometimes known as the potential compound composition. Results from X-ray micro-analysis have shown that, in particular, the Bogue equations underestimate the proportion of alite by an average of about 8%, and Taylor (1989) has suggested modifications to the equations to account for this.

13.1.3 Hydration

For an initial period after mixing, the fluidity or consistency of the cement/water paste remains relatively constant. In fact, a small but gradual loss of fluidity occurs, but this can be recovered on remixing. At a time called the initial set, normally between two and four hours after mixing at normal temperatures, the mix starts to stiffen at a much faster rate. However, it still has little or no strength, and hardening, or strength gain, does not start until after the final set, which occurs some hours later. The rate of strength gain is rapid for the next one or two days, and continues, but at a steadily decreasing rate, for at least a few months.

The cement paste also gets warm, particularly during the setting and early hardening period. In other words, the hydration reactions are exothermic, and measurement of the rate of heat output at constant temperature gives curves of the form shown in Figure 13.1. On mixing, there is a high but very short peak (A) in the heat output rate, lasting only a few minutes. This quickly declines to a low constant value for the dormant period, when the cement is relatively inactive; this may last for up to two or three hours. The rate then starts to increase rapidly, at a time corresponding roughly to the initial set, and reaches a broad peak (B), some time after the time of final set. It then gradually declines, with sometimes a further sharp peak (C) after one or two days.

The hydration reactions causing this behaviour involve all four main compounds simultaneously, and the hydration products also interact with each other. The processes are extremely complex, and even now are not fully

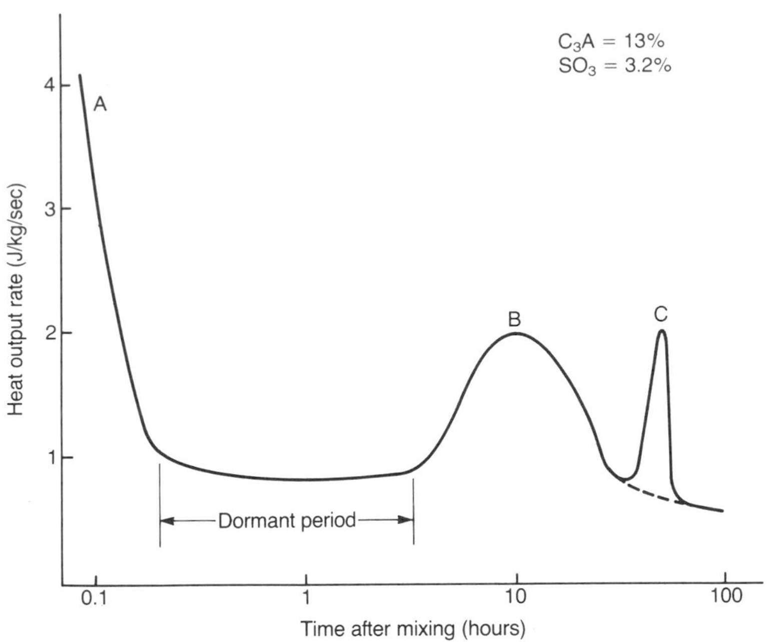

FIGURE 13.1 Typical rate of heat output from Portland cement during hydration at constant temperature (Forester, 1970).

understood, but the following simplified description, considering each of the compounds in turn, is nevertheless valuable.

The main contribution to the first peak (A) is thought to be rehydration of calcium sulphate hemihydrate, which arises from the decomposition of the gypsum in the grinding process (Bensted, 1986). Gypsum is reformed:

$$C\bar{S}.0.5H + 3H \rightarrow C\bar{S}H_2 \qquad (13.5)$$

($H = H_2O$ in shorthand form)

Additional contributions to this peak come from the hydration of the free lime, the heat of wetting, heat of solution and the initial reactions of the aluminate phases. The aluminates are particularly important. In a pure form, C_3A reacts very rapidly forming mainly a crystalline hydrate with six molecules of water:

$$C_3A + 6H \rightarrow C_3AH_6. \qquad (13.6)$$

This reaction is fast enough to result in a flash set of the cement or concrete in a few minutes. It therefore must be moderated, or retarded, which is why the gypsum is added to the cement before grinding. This reacts with the C_3A to form calcium sulphoaluminate, often called **ettringite**:

$$C_3A + 3C\bar{S}H_2 + 26H \rightarrow C_3A.3C\bar{S}.H_{32}. \qquad (13.7)$$

Although the ettringite is insoluble and crystallizes out, the reaction is relatively slow, and does not cause flash setting. Usually about 3–4% gypsum by weight of the cement is added, and this is used up some time after the first 24 hours or so after mixing; the exact time depends on the relative amounts of C_3A and gypsum. The straightforward reaction of the C_3A then takes over, and secondary transformation of the ettringite into a monosulphate form ($C_3A.C\bar{S}.H_{16}$) occurs. This results in the sharp peak (C) which can sometimes be observed towards the tail of the heat output curve (Figure 13.1), but this only occurs in cements with a substantial C_3A content, i.e. more than about 12%.

The C_4AF phase reacts over similar timescales, and the reaction also involves an intermediate compound with the gypsum. The products have a variable composition, but the high and low sulphate forms approximate to $C_3(A.F).3C\bar{S}.H_{32}$ and $C_3(A.F).C\bar{S}.H_{16}$ respectively, i.e. similar to the C_3A products. The reactions or products contribute little of significance to the overall cement behaviour.

The two calcium silicates form the bulk of hydrated material once these initial reactions are completed, and are responsible for most of the significant behaviour, strength and other properties of the hardened cement. The C_3S (or, more accurately, the alite) is the faster to react, producing a tricalcium disilicate hydrate and calcium hydroxide

$$2C_3S + 6H \rightarrow C_3S_2H_3 + 3CH. \quad (13.8)$$

Most of the main peak (B) in the heat evolution curve (Figure 13.1) results from this reaction, and it is the calcium silicate hydrate (often simply referred to as C-S-H) that is responsible for the strength of the hardened cement paste (hcp).

The C_2S (or, strictly, the belite) reacts more slowly, but produces identical products:

$$2C_2S + 4H \rightarrow C_3S_2H_3 + CH. \quad (13.9)$$

This reaction contributes little heat in the timescales of Figure 13.1.

The cumulative amounts of individual products formed over timescales a few days longer than those of Figure 13.1 are shown in Figure 13.2. The dominance of the C-S-H after a day or so is readily apparent, and this is accompanied by an increase in calcium hydroxide. There is some evidence that in the absence of the sulphate from the gypsum the formation of the C-S-H from the alite and belite would be considerably slower than the observed rate (Mehta *et al.*, 1979).

The timescales and the contributions of the reactions of the individual compounds to the

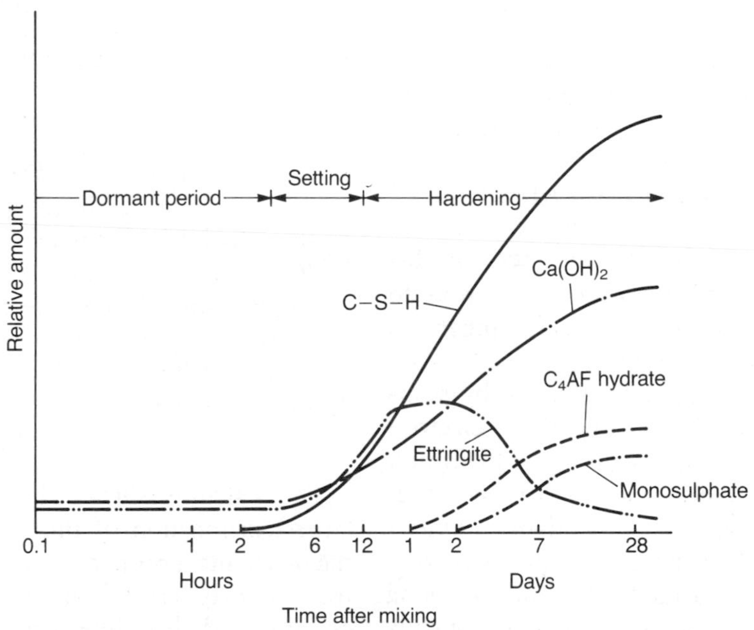

FIGURE 13.2 Typical hydration product development in Portland cement paste (Soroka, 1979).

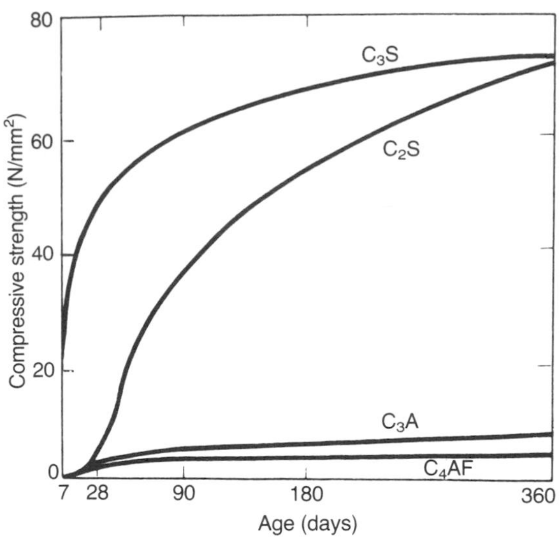

FIGURE 13.3 Development of strength of pure compounds from Portland cement (Bogue, 1955).

development of the cement strength are shown in Figure 13.3. This further emphasizes the long-term nature of the strength-giving reactions of the calcium silicates, particularly of the belite. In fact the reactions can never be regarded as complete, and the extent of their completeness is called the **degree of hydration.**

In common with most chemical processes, increasing temperature accelerates all of the above reactions. With decreasing temperature, hydration will continue even below 0°C, but stops completely at about −10°C. We will discuss the effect of temperature in relation to cement and concrete strength development in Chapter 14.

Numerous studies have been made by scanning, transmission and analytical electron microscopy of the mechanisms of the hydration and the resulting microstructure. It is clear that the process takes place at the solid–liquid interface, and the products have a complex structure with an enormous surface area. The following simplified summary is illustrated schematically in Figure 13.4.

1. After mixing, the fresh cement particles are dispersed throughout the mix water either as single grains or small flocs. The spacing depends on the amount of mix water, i.e. the water/cement ratio.
2. During the so-called dormant period, ettringite is being formed at the cement surface, in the form of sharp needles or rods.
3. At the end of the dormant period, i.e. at about the time of initial set, the ettringite from adjacent cement particles has begun to interfere, and C-S-H hydrate with a spicular (cigar-shaped) crumpled-foil form has started to appear. The solid layers of the foil are typically two or three molecules thick.
4. During subsequent hydration a dense continuous gel of C-S-H hydrate is formed between the particles, resulting in the increasing strength. Also, large hexagonal crystals of calcium hydroxide are deposited. Some larger pores remain unfilled between the grains, and fresh unhydrated cement is left in the centre of the grains.

13.1.4 Structure of hardened cement paste

It follows from the description of hydration in the last section that hardened cement paste (hcp) consists of:

1. a residue of unhydrated cement, at the centre of the original grains;
2. the hydrates, chiefly calcium silicates (C-S-H) but also some calcium aluminates, sulphoaluminates and ferrites;
3. crystals of calcium hydroxide (sometimes called **calcite**);
4. the unfilled residues of the spaces between the cement grains, called **capillary pores.**

The calcium silicate hydrates occupy the largest proportion of the volume, and govern the mechanical properties. Their structure varies from poorly crystalline fibres to a reticular or crumpled sheet-like network. The most important feature of this is its colloidal scale

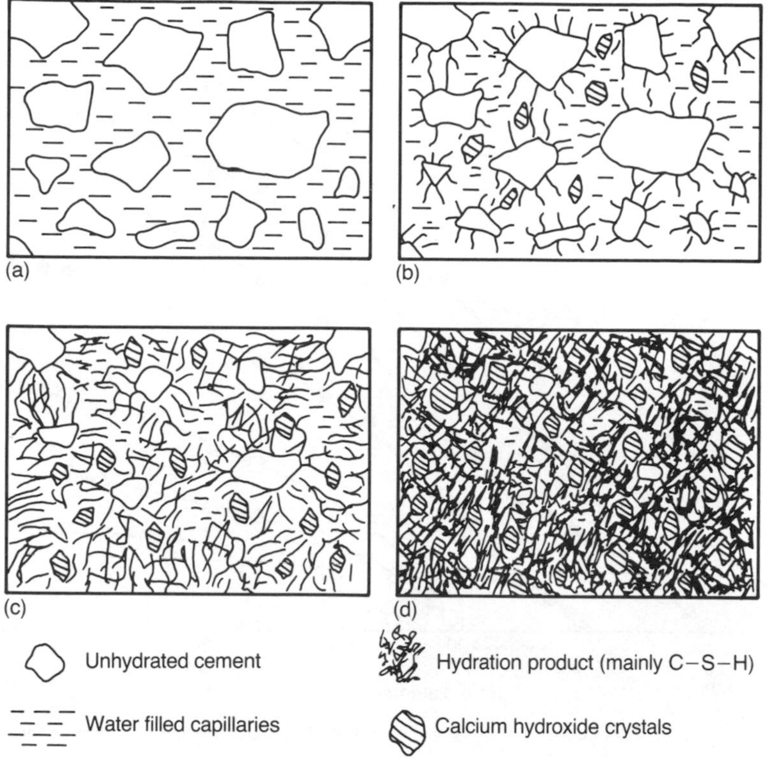

FIGURE 13.4 Schematic of the development of microstructure in hydrating cement paste: (a) fresh cement and water; (b) initial set – interlocking of weak C-S-H product, some $Ca(OH)_2$ crystals; (c) two to three days old – strength from denser C-S-H between unhydrated cement and capillary voids; (d) mature paste – denser C-S-H around $Ca(OH)_2$ crystals, residue of unhydrated cement and capillary voids.

and extremely high surface area, estimated to be between 100 and 700 m^2/gm, i.e. about a thousand times greater than the cement particles from which it has been formed. The spaces between the particles (known as **gel pores**) are typically 0.5 to 5 nm wide, and occupy about 27% of the C-S-H volume. It is important that these gel pores are not confused with the capillary pores, which are on average about two orders of magnitude larger. In practice, however, there is a continuous distribution of pore sizes, as shown in Figure 13.5 for pastes with different initial water/cement ratios.

13.1.5 Strength of hardened cement paste

The strength of hcp derives from van der Waals type forces between the hydrate layers. Although these forces are of relatively low magnitude, the integrated effect over the enormous surface areas is considerable.

We have described the structure of the hcp in qualitative terms, but a quantitative estimate of the relative amounts of the major components, i.e. unhydrated cement, hydrated gel and capillary pores, is required to more fully understand the influence of such factors as initial water/cement ratio and age on the hcp properties, particularly strength. Much of the early work in this area was done by Powers in the 1950s, and his model is still useful. It is not possible in the

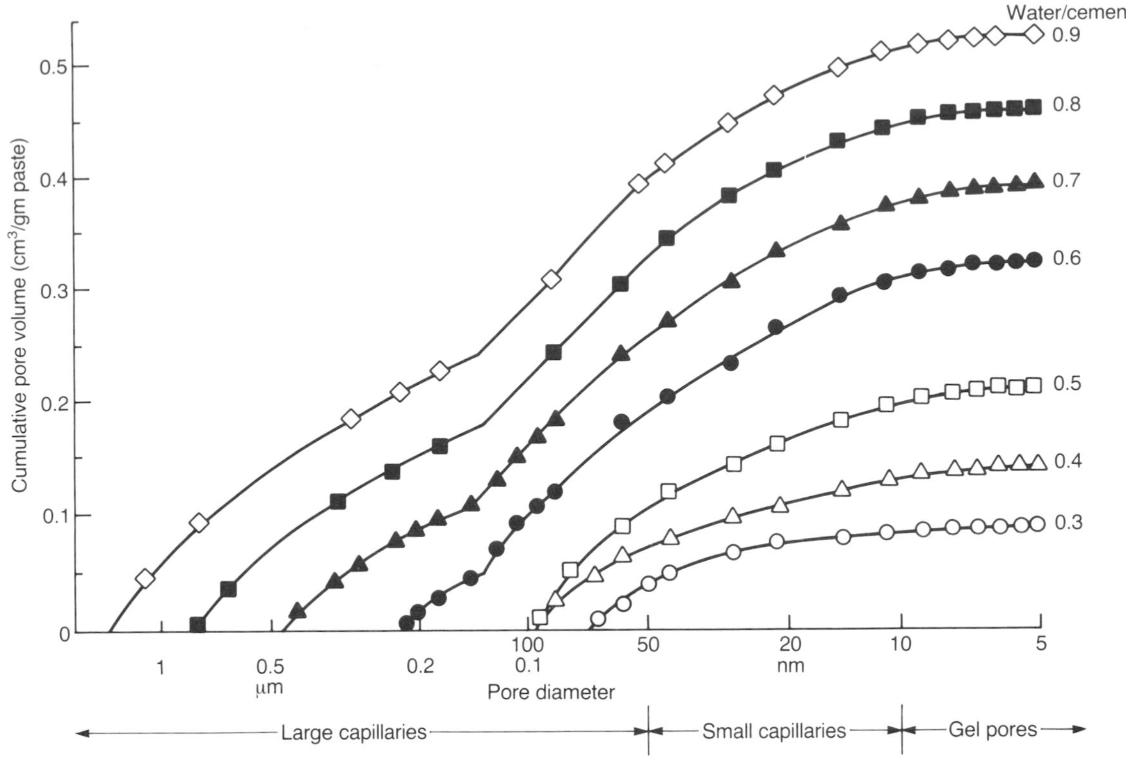

FIGURE 13.5 Pore size distribution in 28-day-old hydrated cement paste (Mehta, 1986).

space available here to describe this and its subsequent modifications in full, but the important features are as follows.

1. The hydration takes place at constant volume, i.e. the combined volume of the unhydrated cement, cement gel and capillary space in the hcp is the same as that of the freshly mixed unhydrated cement and water. The total volume can therefore be calculated from the water/cement ratio and the relative densities of the unhydrated cement (3.17) and water (1.0).
2. The gel is the same regardless of the stage of hydration at which it is formed, the type of cement and the water/cement ratio. The following are constants:
   (a) The unhydrated cement chemically combines with about 23% of its own weight of water.
   (b) The relative density of the gel solids = 2.43.
   (c) The relative density of the gel including pores = 1.76.
3. From the relative densities, it can be seen that the gel (including pores) occupies a space about 1.8 times that of the unhydrated cement. If the total space available is too small, then hydration will stop when the products grow to fill this space, i.e. complete hydration can never occur. If the total space available is large, then it will never be filled up even with 100% hydration, and there will always be some remaining capillary pores, the volume of which will increase with increasing initial volume, i.e. higher

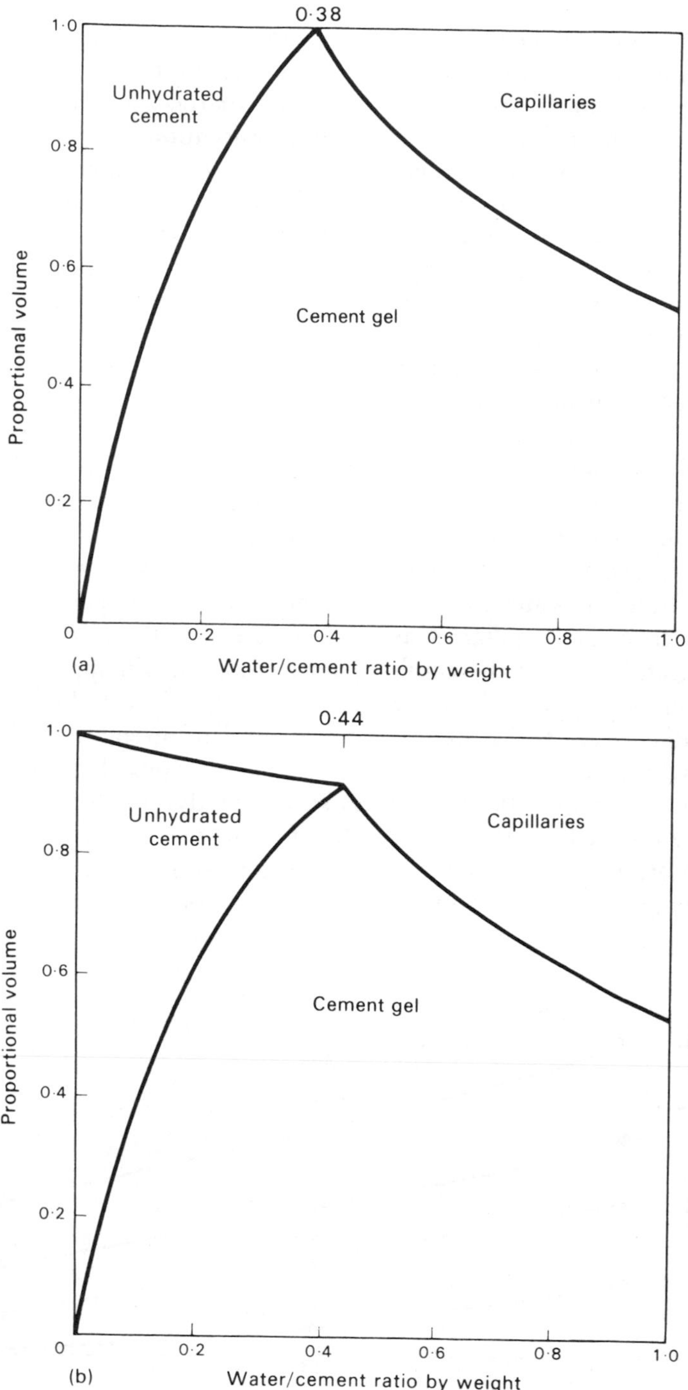

FIGURE 13.6 Composition of hydrated cement paste at the final stage of hydration after prolonged storage (a) in water, (b) sealed (Hansen, 1970).

water/cement ratio. There is obviously a unique water/cement ratio at which the products of 100% hydration exactly fit into the total available space; this can be calculated to be 0.38. It is also possible to calculate the relative volumetric proportions that result from complete hydration at any water/cement ratio, and the result is shown in Figure 13.6(a). (It is a useful exercise for the reader to verify a few points on this diagram for him/herself from the above data.)

4. In deriving Figure 13.6(a) it has been assumed that sufficient water is available for the hydration. A check using the relative densities shows that the volume of the solid products of hydration is about 93% of the initial volume of unhydrated cement and water with which it chemically combines during hydration. Therefore water must be drawn into the gel from the capillaries as hydration proceeds, and some of the capillaries will empty unless an external source of water is available, e.g. if the hcp is immersed in water. Figure 13.6(a) therefore applies to this condition. If, on the other hand, the paste is sealed, i.e. there is no gain or loss of water, then the capillaries will progressively empty, and if the initial water/cement ratio is too low then there is insufficient water and hydration will cease before it might be affected by lack of space for the gel. This process is known as **self-desiccation.** The break-even value for the water/cement ratio in this case is calculated to be 0.44, and Figure 13.6(b) shows the relative volume proportions for various water/cement ratios when the hcp is sealed. (Again, it is a useful exercise for the reader to verify some points on this graph for him/herself.)

It is important to emphasize that Figures 13.6(a) and (b) apply to the final hydrated state, but, as pointed out in Section 13.1.3, the hydration reactions rarely, if ever, reach 100% completion. In reality, therefore, any paste will contain less cement gel and more unhydrated cement and capillaries than values taken from Figure 13.6, but will approach these values with increasing age. The unhydrated cement is not detrimental to strength, and can be beneficial in that it is exposed if the paste or concrete is subsequently cracked or fractured, and can therefore form new hydrates to seal the crack and restore some structural integrity provided, of course, some water is present. No other

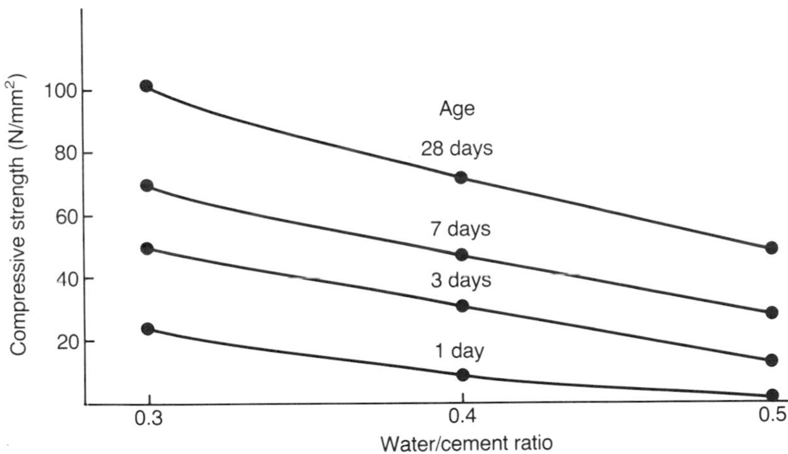

FIGURE 13.7 Compressive strength development of Portland cement paste stored in water (Domone and Thurairatnam, 1986).

common structural materials have this self-healing property.

Figure 13.7 shows the effect of water/cement ratio and age on paste strength. Decreasing water/cement ratio and increasing age result in increasing compressive strength (σ) and, as explained above, these two factors also result in decreasing capillary volume, often expressed as porosity (*P*); the relationship between the two was shown by Powers (1958) to be of the form

$$\sigma = k(1 - P)^3 \qquad (13.10)$$

Powers' experiments were on 'normally' cured pastes, i.e. in water at ambient temperatures and pressures, with variations in porosity obtained by varying the water/cement ratio. This resulted in porosities ranging from about 25 to 50%. Porosities down to about 2% were obtained by Roy and Gouda (1975) by curing pastes with water/cement ratios down to 0.093 at higher temperatures (up to 250°C) and pressures (up to 350 N/mm^2). Figure 13.8 shows that at these very low porosities they achieved compressive strengths of more than 600 N/mm^2, with Powers' results being consistent with their relationship of the form

$$\sigma = A \log(P/P_{crit}) \qquad (13.11)$$

where A is a constant and P_{crit} is a critical porosity giving zero strength, shown by Figure 13.8 to be about 55%.

The size of the pores rather than their total volume has also been shown to be an important factor. Birchall *et al.* (1981) reduced the volume of the larger pores (greater than about 15 μm diameter) by incorporating a polymer in pastes of water/cement ratios of about 0.2 and curing initially under pressure. The resulting 'macro-defect free' (MDF) cement had compressive strengths of 200 N/mm^2 and above, with flexural strengths of 70 N/mm^2, a much higher fraction of compressive strength than in 'normal' pastes or concrete.

Obviously the extremes of porosities or strengths cannot be achieved in concretes produced on a large scale by conventional civil engineering practice, but they do indicate important relationships; we shall discuss concrete strength in detail in Chapter 16.

13.1.6 Water in hcp and drying shrinkage

The large surface areas in the gel give the hcp a considerable affinity for water, and make its overall dimensions water-sensitive, i.e. loss of water results in shrinkage, which is largely recoverable on regain of water. This behaviour can be explained by considering the ways in

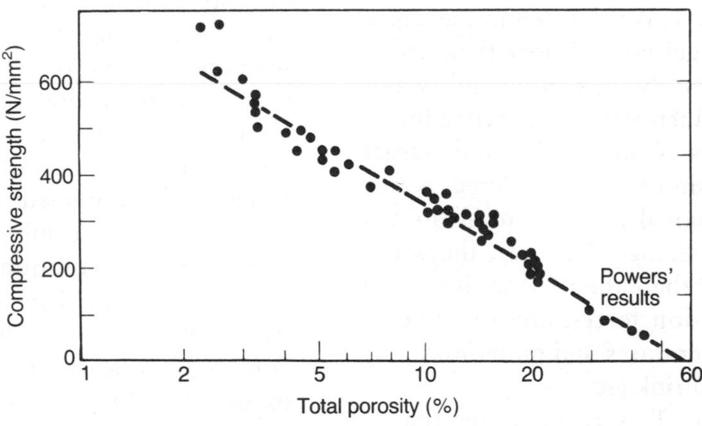

FIGURE 13.8 The dependence of strength of hardened cement paste on porosity (Roy and Gouda, 1975).

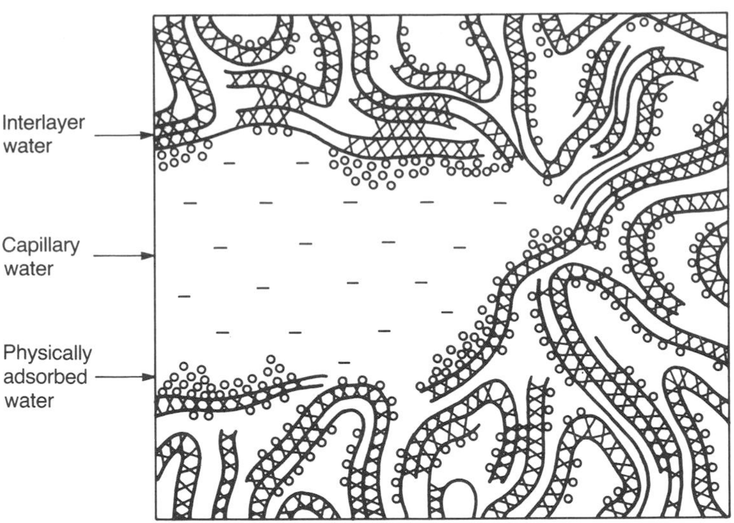

FIGURE 13.9 Schematic of types of water within calcium silicate hydrate (Feldman and Sereda, 1970).

which the water is contained in the paste, and it is useful to classify it into types depending on the degree of difficulty of its removal. The sites of the water are illustrated in the diagram of the gel structure shown in Figure 13.9.

1. Water vapour. The larger voids may only be partially filled with water, and the remaining space will contain water vapour at a pressure in equilibrium with the relative humidity and temperature of the surrounding environment.
2. Capillary water. This is located in the capillary and larger gel pores (wider than about 5 nm) and can be thought of as bulk water free from the influence of the attractive forces of solid surfaces. Water in the voids larger than about 50 nm can be considered as free water as its removal does not result in any overall volume change; however, the water in pores smaller than about 50 nm is subject to capillary tension forces, and its removal at normal temperatures and humidities may result in some shrinkage.
3. Adsorbed water. This is the water that is close to the solid surfaces, and under the influence of surface attractive forces. Up to five molecular layers of water can be held, giving a maximum total thickness of about 1.3 nm. A large proportion of this water can be lost on drying to 30% relative humidity, and this loss is the main contributing factor to drying shrinkage.
4. Interlayer water. This is the water in gel pores narrower than about 2.6 nm; it follows from (3) that such water will be under the influence of two surfaces, and will therefore be more strongly held. It can be removed only by strong drying, for example, at elevated temperatures and/or relative humidities less than 10%, but its loss results in considerable shrinkage, the van der Waals forces being able to pull the solid surfaces closer together.
5. Chemically combined water. This is the water that has combined with the fresh cement in the hydration reactions discussed in Section 13.1.3. This is not lost on drying, but is only evolved when the paste is decomposed by heating to high temperatures in excess of 1000°C.

The above divisions should not be thought of as having distinct boundaries; and there is a considerable overlap between the removal of water of different states, resulting in a continuous loss of water and shrinkage as the relative humidity is reduced. We will describe the factors influencing shrinkage, its magnitude and suggested mechanisms when discussing concrete deformation in Chapter 15.

13.1.7 Other types of Portland cement

The relative timescales of the dormant period, setting and gain of strength govern the operations that must be adopted in concrete practice, for example in transporting and placing the concrete, or in formwork removal. The figures already given for these properties are typical of average quality Portland cement, but it is often useful for the engineer to be able to modify the cement to produce a concrete to more closely suit the particular application. One way of achieving this is to alter the compound composition by varying the type and quantities of raw materials used in the cement manufacture. For example, if a cement with a higher C_3S and lower C_2S content is produced, as in cement B in Table 13.1, this will have a higher rate of strength gain than cement A (but it should be noted that this does not mean rapid **setting**). Rapid hardening properties can also be achieved by finer grinding of the cement, giving an increased surface area exposed to the mix water, and a combination of the two modifications is often used in practice. A consequence of the rapid hardening is a higher rate of heat output in the early stages of hydration.

Another example is cement C from Table 13.1. This has a lower C_3S and higher C_2S content which results in a lower rate of heat of hydration output in the first few days after placing, and may therefore be of value in large pours to reduce the risk of thermal cracking from substantial temperature differentials. For obvious reasons, such a cement is often known as **low heat cement**, but it has the disadvantage of a low rate of gain of strength.

Cement D in Table 13.1 has a very low C_3A content, and is an example of a **sulphate resisting** cement. If sulphates from external sources, such as groundwater, come into contact with the hcp, degradation can occur. Depending on the form of the sulphate, reactions can take place with both the free calcium hydroxide and the hydrated calcium aluminates. However, the most critical reaction is typified by that between the sulphate ions and the hydrated monosulphate aluminate:

$$C_3A.C\bar{S}.H_{18} + 2CH + 2\bar{S} + 12H \rightarrow C_3A.3C\bar{S}.H_{32} \quad (13.12)$$

Thus ettringite is reformed, but crucially the reaction is expansive and can therefore lead to disruption, cracking and loss of strength in the relatively brittle, low tensile strength hcp; a low C_3A content cement therefore increases the long-term sulphate resistance.

One further variation is worth mentioning, that of **white cement**. The grey colour of most Portland cements is largely due to ferrite in the C_4AF phase, which derives from the ferrite in the clay or shale used in the cement manufacture. The use of non-ferrite-containing material, such as china clay, results in a near zero C_4AF content cement, which is almost pure white, and therefore attractive to architects for exposed finishes.

As we shall see, it is also possible to modify the concrete properties by using either admixtures or cement replacement materials, described in the next two sections respectively.

13.2 Admixtures

Admixtures are chemicals that are added to the concrete immediately before or during mixing and significantly change its fresh, early age or hardened state to advantage. Only small quantities are required, typically 1 to 2% by weight of the cement. Their popularity and use have increased considerably in recent years; it is estimated that in 1989 about 40% of all concrete produced in the UK contained an admixture, and in some places, notably North America, Australia and Japan, the proportion is even higher.

An extremely large number of commercial products are available, which are usually classified or grouped according to mode of action rather than chemical type. We shall consider four main classes, namely plasticizers, accelerators, retarders and air entraining agents, and briefly mention others.

13.2.1 Plasticizers

Plasticizers, also called **workability aids**, increase the fluidity or workability of a cement paste or concrete. They are also known as **water-reducers** since they can produce a concrete with the same workability at a lower water/cement ratio, hence increasing the strength or durability with the same cement content. Alternatively, a similar strength can be produced with a lower cement content.

There are two broad groups, both polymers:

1. normal plasticizers, which are usually based on lignosulphonates or hydroxycarboxylic acids, and
2. super- or high-range plasticizers, which are either modified lignosulphonates or based on sulphonated melamine or naphthalene formaldehydes.

To give an example of their effectiveness, Rixom *et al.* (1988) have reported that for a concrete with a cement content of 325 kg/m^3 and a water/cement ratio of 0.55, the slump (see Chapter 14) was increased from 75 mm to 135 mm by a 'standard' dose of plasticizer. The slump could then be returned to 75 mm by reducing the water/cement ratio to 0.5, thereby increasing the strength.

As their name implies, superplasticizers can be used to produce even greater increases in workability, resulting in the so-called 'flowing' concrete which is very easy to handle and compact. The superplasticizer properties are such that the concrete does not segregate, as it would if the high workability was produced by increasing either the amount of water or normal plasticizer. The water reduction effects of superplasticizers are such that they can also be used to produce high-strength, low water/cement ratio (less than 0.4) mixes with an adequate workability without an excessively high cement content. The effects of these admixtures will be considered further after discussing workability in Chapter 14.

The plasticizing action of both normal and superplasticizers is due to the absorption of the molecules of the admixture on to the surface of the cement grains and early hydration products, each admixture molecule being orientated with an ionic group outwards. This gives the surface a uniform electrical potential, normally negative and of the order of a few millivolts. The cement particles then mutually repel each other, thereby breaking up any flocs, as illustrated in Figure 13.10. The particles also become surrounded by a layer of water molecules associated with

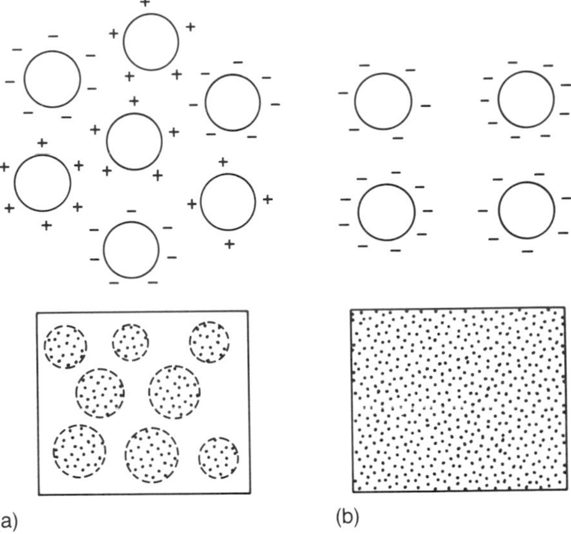

FIGURE 13.10 Schematic of dispersing action of plasticizing admixtures: (a) flocculated particles; (b) dispersed particles after admixture addition (Mindess and Young, 1981).

the admixture, and the overall effect is one of greater lubrication and hence increased fluidity of the paste or concrete.

A significant secondary effect results from the adsorbed molecules of the admixture acting as a partial barrier to the mix water. This may lengthen the dormant period and decrease the early hydration rate of the C_3S. Plasticizers may therefore also act as retarders to the setting and early strength gain. Mechanical properties and durability at later ages appear largely unaffected and are similar to those expected for a plain concrete of the same water/cement ratio, with two relatively minor exceptions.

1. There is some evidence of a slight increase in 28-day strength, attributed to the dispersion of the particles causing an increased surface area of cement being exposed to the mix water (Hewlett, 1988).
2. Some plasticizers entrain about 1–2% air because they lower the surface tension of the mix water. This will reduce the density and strength of the concrete, but may have a beneficial effect on other properties, as we shall see when discussing air entraining agents in Section 13.2.4.

The mechanism of action of both normal and superplasticizers is essentially similar, but, as mentioned above, superplasticizers can be used to greater effect without increasing any tendency of the mix to segregate. This is probably due to the larger, colloidal size of the long chain particles of the admixture which obstructs the bleed water channels in the concrete. They do, however, suffer from the disadvantage that their plasticizing action only lasts for a limited time after addition to the concrete, typically 30 to 60 minutes.

13.2.2 Accelerators

An accelerator is used to increase the rate of hardening of the cement paste, thus enhancing the early strength, perhaps thereby allowing early removal of formwork, or reducing the curing time for concrete placed in cold weather.

Calcium chloride ($CaCl_2$) has historically been very popular as it is readily available and

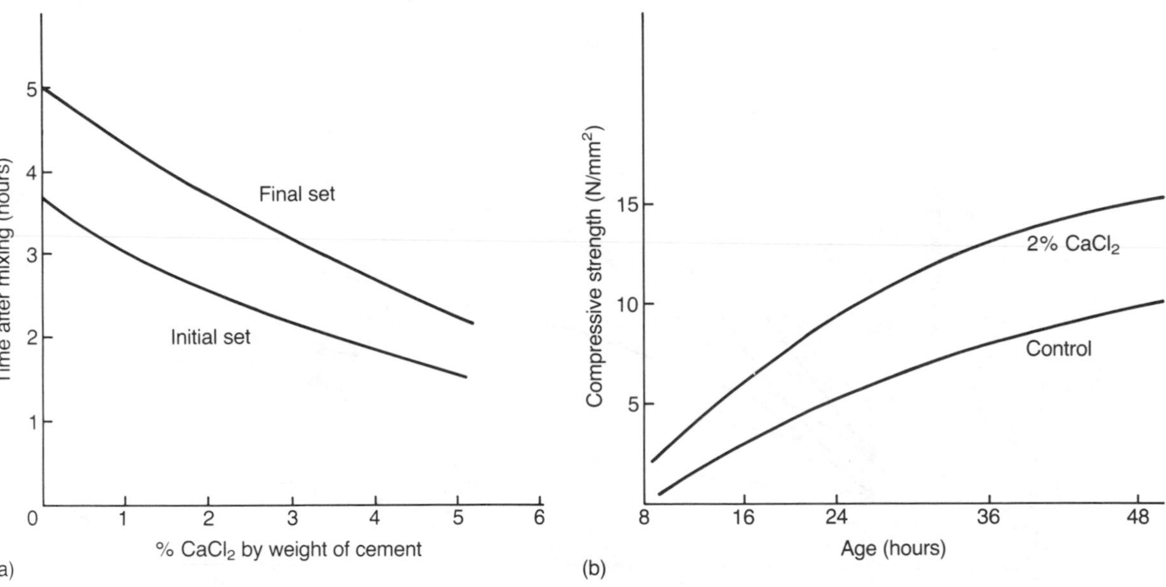

FIGURE 13.11 Typical effects of calcium chloride admixture on (a) setting times, and (b) early strength of concrete (Dransfield and Egan, 1988).

very effective. Figure 13.11(a) shows that it accelerates both the initial and final set, and Figure 13.11(b) shows that a 2% addition by weight of cement can result in very significant early strength increases. This effect diminishes with time, and the long-term strength is similar to that of non-accelerated concrete.

The exact mechanism of the acceleration is not clear, but it would seem that the $CaCl_2$ becomes involved in the hydration reactions involving C_3A, gypsum and C_4AF, and acts as a catalyst in the C_3S and C_2S reactions (Ramachandran *et al.*, 1981). It is, however, clear that the C-S-H produced is modified by the presence of the $CaCl_2$. At a given degree of hydration, the gel formed in a paste containing $CaCl_2$ has a higher surface area than that in a plain paste, which leads to increased creep and shrinkage. There is also evidence that the long-term resistance to sulphates or freeze–thaw conditions is reduced.

Of great significance is the increased vulnerability of embedded steel to corrosion due to the presence of the chloride ions. This has led to the use of $CaCl_2$ being prohibited in reinforced and prestressed concrete, and to the development of alternative chloride-free accelerators, such as calcium formate. This appears to have a similar range of effects on concrete properties. We shall discuss the corrosion of steel in concrete in some detail when considering durability in Chapter 17.

13.2.3 Retarders

Retarders delay the setting time of a mix, and examples of use include:

1. counteracting the accelerating effect of hot weather, particularly if the concrete has to be transported over a long distance;
2. controlling the set in large pours, where concreting may take several hours, to achieve concurrent setting of all the concrete, hence

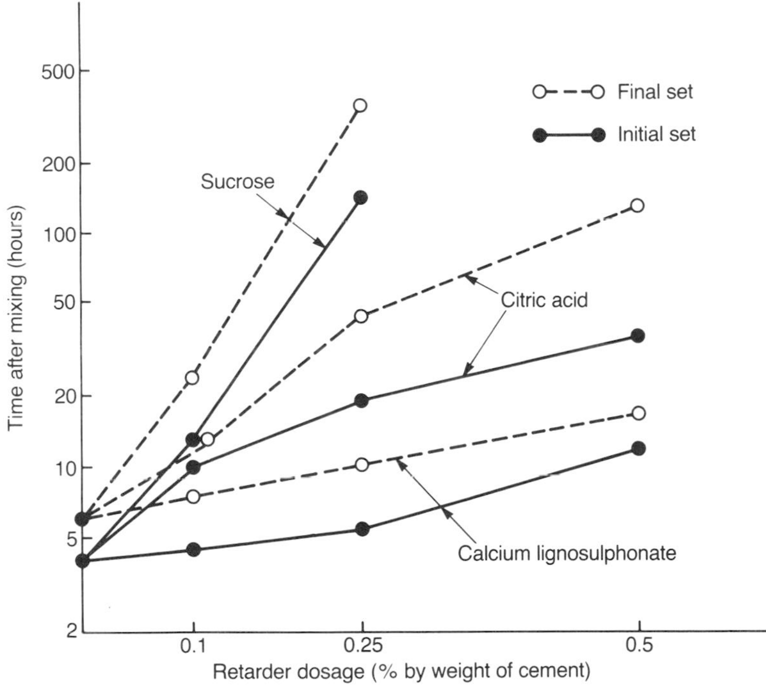

FIGURE 13.12 Influence of retarders on the setting times of cement paste (Ramachandran *et al.*, 1981).

avoiding cold joints and discontinuities, and achieving uniform strength development.

The retardations resulting from varying doses of three different retarding chemicals are shown in Figure 13.12. Sucrose and citric acid are very effective retarders, but it is difficult to control their effects, and lignosulphonates, often with a significant sugar content, are preferred. The retarding action of normal plasticizers such as some lignosulphonates and carboxylic acids has already been mentioned; most commercial retarders are based on these compounds, and therefore have some plasticizing action as well.

Temperature, mix proportions, fineness and composition of the cement and time of addition of the admixture all affect the degree of retardation, and it is therefore difficult to generalize.

13.2.4 Air entraining agents

Air entraining admixtures are organic materials which, when added to the mix water, entrain a controlled quantity of air in the form of microscopic bubbles in the cement paste component of the concrete. The bubble diameters are generally less than about 0.1 mm, and they are sufficiently stable to be unchanged during the placing, compaction, setting and hardening of the concrete. Entrained air should not be confused with entrapped air which is normally present as the result of incomplete compaction of the concrete, and usually occurs in the form of larger irregular cavities.

The major reason for entraining air is to provide freeze–thaw resistance to the concrete. Moist concrete contains free water in entrapped and capillary voids, which expands on freezing, setting up disruptive internal bursting stresses. Successive freeze–thaw cycles, say, over a winter, may lead to a progressive deterioration. Entrained air voids, uniformly dispersed throughout the hcp, provide a reservoir for the water to expand into when it freezes, thus reducing the disruptive stresses. Entrained air volumes of only about 4–7% by volume of the concrete are required to provide effective protection (Figure 13.13). Apart from air volume, an important parameter is the spacing factor, defined as the average maximum distance from any point in the paste to the edge of the bubble. This should not exceed 0.2 mm.

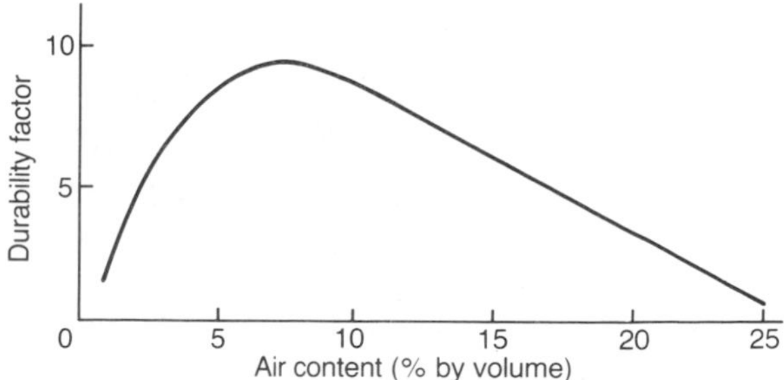

FIGURE 13.13 Effect of air entrainment on the durability factor of concrete, a measure of the freeze–thaw resistance. A high factor indicates a high durability (Mindess and Young, 1981).

Air entrainment has two important secondary effects.

1. There is a general increase in the workability of the mix, the bubbles seeming to act like small ball-bearings. The bubbles' size means that they can compensate for the lack of fine material in a coarse sand, which would otherwise produce a concrete with poor cohesion. Aggregate gradings will be discussed in Section 13.4.
2. The increase in porosity results in a drop in strength, by a factor of about 6% for each 1% of air. This must therefore be taken into account in mix design, but the improvement in workability means the loss can at least be partly offset by reducing the water content and hence the water/cement ratio.

As we have seen, plasticizers often entrain some air due to their surfactant properties. However, a variety of other organic substances are more effective and are therefore normally used, notably vinsol resins extracted from wood pulp. They are, in effect, foaming agents, which

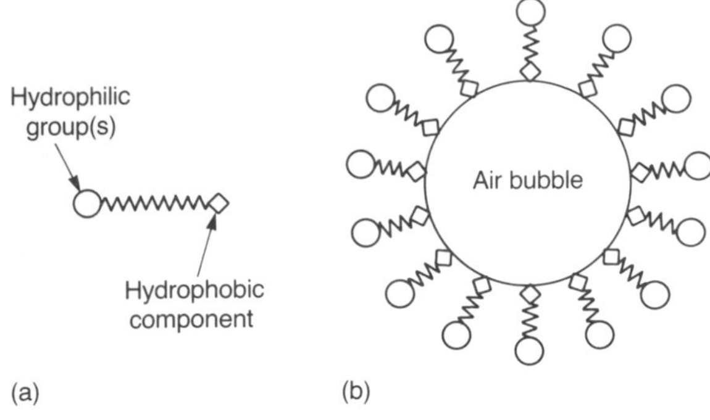

FIGURE 13.14 Schematic of air entrainment by surface active molecules: (a) surface active molecule; (b) stabilized air bubble (Mindess and Young, 1981).

reduce the surface tension of the mix water, and the bubbles are produced during the concrete mixing. The long chain molecules have a **hydrophilic** or water-loving group on one end, and a **hydrophobic** or water-hating group on the other. The molecules therefore align themselves radially on the surface of the bubble, with their hydrophilic groups in the water and their hydrophobic groups in the air, thus providing the bubble stability. This effect is shown schematically in Figure 13.14.

Air entraining agents have little influence on the hydration reactions, at least at normal dosages, and therefore have no effect on the resulting concrete properties other than those resulting from the physical presence of the voids, as described above.

13.2.5 Other admixtures

As we have seen, some admixtures have useful secondary effects in addition to their main function, and some combined action products are marketed, notably:

1. water reducing and air entraining agents;
2. water reducing and retarding agents; and
3. water reducing and accelerating agents.

Other admixtures include waterproofers, bonding agents and pigments for producing coloured concrete; there are a number of texts which contain information on these, and give a more detailed treatment of the admixtures we have described, notably Rixom and Mailvaganam (1986) and Hewlett (1988).

13.3 Cement replacement materials

As the name implies, cement replacement materials can be used as a substitute for some of the Portland cement in a concrete; partial cement replacement materials is therefore a more accurate name. The terms 'mineral admixtures' or 'additives' are sometimes used, but the materials should not be confused with the admixtures described in the preceding section. As we shall see, the materials can give useful modifications to the concrete properties for certain applications, and, as they are often waste products from other industries, they can also lead to greater economy.

13.3.1 Pozzolanic behaviour

Naturally occurring pozzolanic materials were used in early concretes as mentioned in the introduction to this part of the book. A pozzolanic material is one which contains active silica (SiO_2) and is not cementitious in itself but will, in a finely divided form and in the presence of moisture, chemically react with calcium hydroxide at ordinary temperatures to form cementitious compounds. The key to the pozzolanic behaviour is the structure of the silica; this must be in a glassy or amorphous form with a disordered structure, which is formed, for example, in the rapid cooling of a volcanic magma. A uniform crystalline structure, such as is found in silica sand, is not chemically active.

When a pozzolanic material is used in conjunction with a Portland cement, the calcium hydroxide that takes part in the pozzolanic reaction is that produced from the cement hydration (see Section 13.1.3); further quantities of calcium silicate hydrate are produced:

$$S + CH + H \rightarrow C\text{-}S\text{-}H. \quad (13.13)$$

The products of this secondary reaction cannot be distinguished from those of the primary cement hydration, and therefore make their own contribution to the strength and other properties of the hardened cement paste.

13.3.2 Types of material

The main cement replacement materials in use worldwide are:

1. pulverized fuel ash (pfa), called fly ash in several countries: the ash from pulverized coal used to fire power stations, but only selected ashes have a suitable composition and particle size range for use in concrete;
2. ground granulated blast furnace slag (ggbs): slag from the 'scum' formed in iron smelting in a blast furnace, ground to a similar fineness to Portland cement;
3. condensed silica fume (csf), often called microsilica; very fine particles of silica condensed from the waste gases given off in the production of silicon metal;
4. natural pozzolans; some volcanic ashes and diatomaceous earth;
5. calcined clay and shale; clay and shale minerals heat treated to produce pozzolanic silica;
6. rice husk ash; ash from the controlled burning of rice husks after the rice grains have been separated.

The first three of these are the most commonly used, and although the following comments are mainly confined to these, the basic principles discussed apply to the others. All three are commercially available as individual materials, and in several countries blends of ggbs and pfa with Portland cement are also marketed. These blended cements avoid having to store, weigh and mix the extra material, but the user has no control over the blend proportions.

TABLE 13.2 Typical oxide compositions of cement replacement materials

Oxide	*pfa*		*ggbs*	*csf*	*Portland cement*
	Low lime	*High lime*			
	(% by weight)				
SiO_2	48	40	36	97	20
Al_2O_3	27	18	9	2	5
Fe_2O_3	9	8	1	0.1	4
MgO	2	4	11	0.1	1
CaO	3	20	40	–	64
Na_2O	1	–	–	–	0.2
K_2O	4	–	–	–	0.5

13.3.3 Chemical and physical composition

Typical chemical compositions are given in Table 13.2. All of the materials contain substantially greater quantities of silica than does Portland cement, but more importantly, most of this is in the active amorphous form in each case. Csf is almost entirely active silica.

Two of the materials, high lime pfa and ggbs, also contain large quantities of CaO. This also takes part in the hydration reaction, and therefore neither material is a true pozzolan, and both are to a certain extent self-cementing. The reactions are very slow in the neat material, but they are much quicker in the presence of the cement hydration, which seems to act as a form of catalyst. Because of the contributions of their own CaO, both materials can be used at high cement substitution rates (up to 90%), whereas the practical limit for low lime pfa is about 40% and for csf is about 25%.

Physical properties are shown in Table 13.3. Pfa and csf have significantly lower specific gravities than Portland cement, and therefore substitution of the cement on a weight-for-weight basis will result in a greater volume of paste. The particle sizes of pfa and ggbs are approximately similar to cement ; pfa in particular

TABLE 13.3 Typical physical properties of cement replacement materials

	pfa	*ggbs*	*csf*	*Portland cement*
Specific gravity	2.1	2.9	2.2	3.15
Particle size range (microns)	10–150	3–100	0.01–0.5	0.5–100
Specific surface area (m^2/kg)	350	400	15 000	350

consists of near spherical particles, but particles of both materials have smooth surfaces, which results in some increase of fluidity of cement paste or work-ability of concrete when partially replacing the cement (see Section 14.1). Csf also has near spherical particles, but in a size range some three orders of magnitude lower, giving a much higher surface area. This results in a substantial loss of workability when csf is used in concrete if no other alterations are made to the mix. Either increased water (and hence loss of strength) or a plasticizer is therefore required to maintain workability. The latter is the preferred option, and with a sufficient dosage of super plasticizer to disperse the fine particles, a combination of excellent workability with good cohesion and low bleed can be obtained.

13.3.4 The rate of pozzolanic reaction

The C-S-H production from the pozzolanic reaction is secondary to that from the Portland cement, and results in a delay in the exothermic heat output, as shown for a low lime pfa in Figure 13.15. The behaviour of mixes with high lime pfa and ggbs is intermediate between that of cement and cement plus pfa for similar replacement levels, but it is difficult to produce typical figures as the behaviour varies considerably with pfa, slag and cement from different sources. The heat reduction is beneficial in reducing thermal cracking in large concrete pours, and therefore these materials can be used as an alternative to low heat Portland cements. We shall discuss this further in Chapter 14.

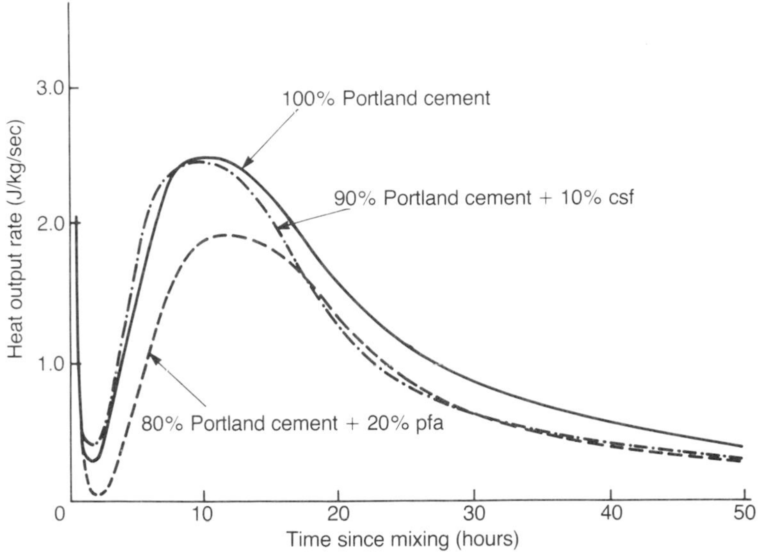

FIGURE 13.15 Typical heat output during hydration of opc paste with cement replacement materials (Meland, 1983).

With csf the delay is not as great due to its high surface area and active silica content. In addition the C_3S hydration seems to be accelerated, probably due to the small csf particles acting as nucleation sites for the deposition of C-S-H. The net effect is one of increase and acceleration of the heat output, at least at fairly low replacement levels, as shown in Figure 13.15.

13.3.5 Hardened structure and strength

Compared to pastes of the same water/solids ratio, the secondary nature of the pozzolanic reaction results in lower early age strengths as shown in Figure 13.16 for a typical low lime pfa mix. As with heat output, high lime pfa and ggbs mixes will be intermediate in behaviour, but again it is difficult to produce typical data.

For the reasons described above, mixes with fairly low csf replacement levels have an enhanced strength throughout, and with all three cement replacement materials the strengths at later ages tend to be somewhat higher than those of plain Portland cement pastes. The slower pozzolanic reaction therefore seems to be more effective in reducing the overall hcp porosity. In addition, the transition zone between the aggregate and the hcp in concrete, a weakness in plain Portland cement concretes, is strengthened by the pozzolanic reaction, particularly with csf. This enhances the overall concrete strength, and is particularly valuable when producing high-strength concrete. This is discussed further in Section 13.4 and Chapter 16.

13.3.6 Other properties

Pastes, mortars and concretes containing cement replacement materials have, in general, similar properties to plain Portland cement mixtures of the same strength. Therefore when we discuss properties, such as modulus, creep and shrinkage, in later sections, the relationships to strength apply equally well to pfa, ggbs or csf mixes and plain Portland cement mixes. The materials have an important influence on some aspects of durability, as we shall see in Chapter 17.

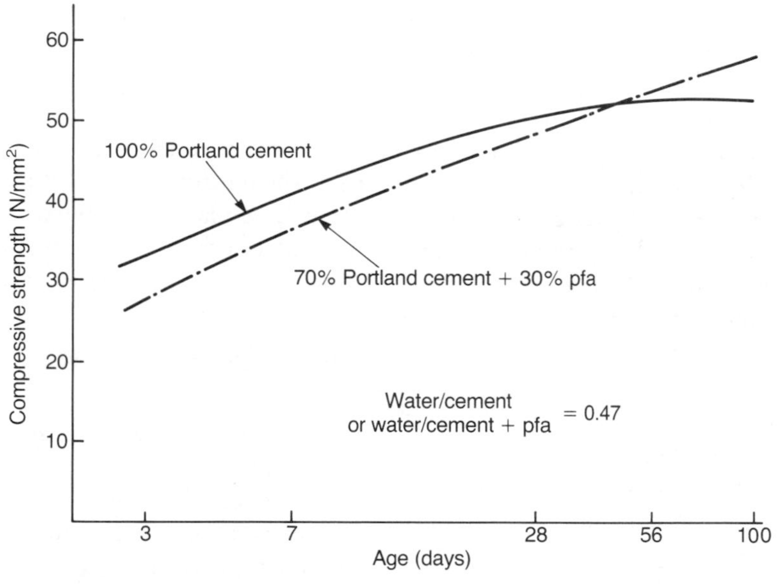

FIGURE 13.16 Strength development of concrete with and without low lime pfa (Bamforth, 1980).

13.4 Aggregates

As we have seen, hardened cement paste (hcp) has strength and other properties that could make it suitable for use as a construction material in its own right, but it suffers from two main drawbacks – dimensional instability, in particular high creep and shrinkage, and cost. Both of these disadvantages are overcome, or at least modified, by adding aggregates to the cement paste, thus producing concrete. The objective is to use as much aggregate as possible, binding the particles together with the hcp. This means that the largest possible aggregate size should be used, with a continuous grading of particle sizes from the fine sand up to the coarse stones; this minimizes the void content of the aggregate mixture and therefore the amount of hcp required. Normally the aggregates occupy about 70–80% of the total concrete volume.

With one or two notable exceptions, the aggregates can be thought of as being inert fillers; for example, they do not hydrate, and they do not swell or shrink. They are distributed throughout the hcp, and it is sometimes useful to regard concrete as a two-phase material of either coarse aggregate dispersed in a mortar matrix, or coarse and fine aggregate dispersed in an hcp matrix. Models based on this two-phase material are of value in describing deformation behaviour, as discussed in Chapter 15, but, when cracking and strength are being considered, a three-phase model of aggregate, hcp and the transition or interfacial zone between the two (about 50 μm wide) is required, since the transition zone is often the weakest phase, and cracking initiates within it. This will be discussed when considering concrete strength in Chapter 16. In this section we shall first describe the various types of most commonly used aggregates and how they are classified, and then consider some of their most important properties when used in concrete.

13.4.1 Types of aggregate

Aggregates can be obtained either from natural sources, such as gravel deposits and crushed rocks, or specifically manufactured for use in concrete. It is convenient to group them in terms of their density or specific gravity.

Normal density aggregates

Many different natural materials have been used for making concrete, including gravels, igneous rocks such as basalt and granite and the stronger sedimentary rocks such as limestone and sandstone. The mineral constituents are not generally of great importance, provided the rock has sufficient integrity and strength. (The exception is certain forms of active silica, the importance of which will be discussed when describing alkali–silica reaction in Chapter 16.) All these rocks have specific gravities within a limited range, approx. 2.55–2.75, and therefore all produce concretes with similar densities, normally in the range 2250–2450 kg/m^3 depending on the mix proportions.

Gravels from suitable deposits in river valleys or shallow coastal waters have particles which for the most part are of a suitable size for direct use in concrete, and therefore only require washing and grading before use. Bulk rock sources, e.g. granite, require crushing to produce suitable size material. The particles are therefore sharp and angular, distinctly different from the naturally rounded particles in a gravel; we will see later that particle shape has a significant effect on fresh and hardened concrete properties.

Lightweight aggregates

Lightweight aggregates are used to produce lower density concretes, which are advantageous in reducing the self-weight of structures and also have better thermal insulation than normal weight concrete. The reduced specific gravity is obtained from air voids within the aggregate particles. Pumice, a naturally occurring volcanic rock of low density, has been used since Roman times, but it is only available at a few locations, and artificial lightweight aggregates are now widely available. They are of three main types:

1. sintered pulverized fuel ash, formed by heating the pelletized ash from pulverized coal used in power stations until partial fusion and hence binding occurs;
2. expanded clay or shale, formed by heating suitable sources of clay or shale until gas is given off and trapped in the semi-molten mass;
3. foamed slag, formed by directing jets of water, steam and compressed air on to the molten slag from blast furnaces.

In each case, both fine and coarse aggregates can be produced, and many different products are available, particularly in Europe and North America. Because they all achieve lower specific gravity by increased porosity, they all result in an overall lowering in the concrete strength, the penalty to be paid for the lower density. The quality and properties of different aggregates vary considerably, and therefore produce different strength/density relationships, illustrated in Figure 13.17.

Lightweight aggregates are not as rigid as normal weight aggregates, and therefore produce concrete with higher elastic modulus, creep and shrinkage. As with strength, the properties depend on the lightweight aggregate type and source, and also whether lightweight fines or natural sands are used.

Heavyweight aggregates

Where concrete of high density is required, for example in radiation shielding, heavyweight aggregates can be used. Densities of 3500 to 4500 kg/m^3 are obtained by using barytes (a barium sulphate ore), and about 7000 kg/m^3 by using steel shot.

13.4.2 Classification

Within each of the types described above, aggregates are classified principally by size and type. Any sample of aggregate will contain a

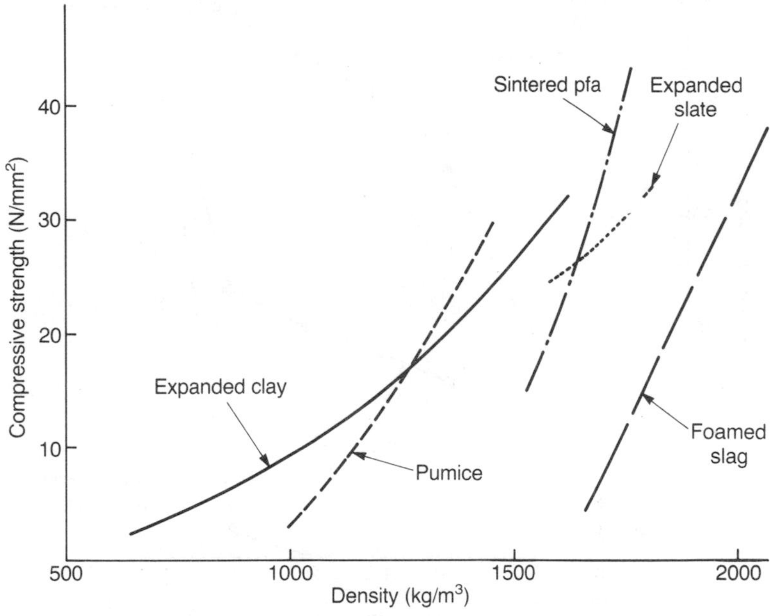

FIGURE 13.17 Typical strength versus density relationships for concretes containing selected lightweight aggregates (from aggregate supplier's information).

continuous spectrum of sizes from the smallest to the largest, and these are divided into fractions for both classification and for combining in the optimum proportions for a particular mix. The main division is that between fine and coarse aggregate at a particle size of 5 mm. For further subdivisions, standard sieves are used, ranging from 75 μm to 37.5 mm in a logarithmic progression, each sieve having twice the aperture size of the previous one.

Normal-density aggregates in particular may contain a range of particle shapes, from well rounded to angular, but it is usually considered sufficient to classify the aggregate as uncrushed, i.e. coming from a natural gravel deposit, or crushed, i.e. coming from a bulk source.

13.4.3 Properties

Apart from specific gravity, which, as mentioned above, chiefly influences the density of the concrete, the main aggregate properties influencing fresh or hardened concrete properties are shape and grading, porosity and absorption, elasticity, strength and surface characteristics affecting the bond to the hardened cement paste.

Sieve analysis using the range of sieves given above will result in a grading curve for either individual aggregate fractions or their combination, usually plotted as the total amount of material passing a particular sieve versus sieve size, the latter normally on a log scale. Typical gradings for a fine aggregate (or sand) and a crushed granite coarse aggregate with a 10 mm maximum size are shown in Figure 13.18, together with a combined grading for 45% of the fine and 55% of the coarse aggregate. Also given are the voids contents for each material and the combination. The importance of using a combined continuous grading to obtain a low voids content is apparent, the combination shown giving the minimum voids content. We shall mention some further grading require-

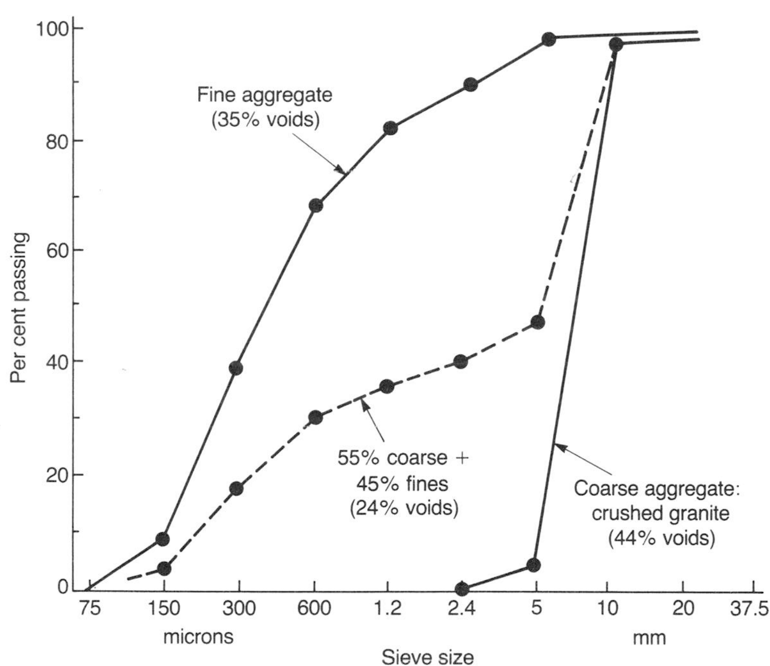

FIGURE 13.18 Typical grading curves for fine, coarse (10 mm) and combined aggregate.

ments when discussing bleeding of newly placed concrete in Chapter 14.

Grading curves take no account of particle shape, but this does influence the voids content of the aggregate sample – more rounded particles will pack more efficiently and will therefore have a lower voids content. According to Dewar (1983) it is sufficient to use only three numbers to characterize an aggregate for mix design purposes – specific gravity, mean particle size and voids content in the loosely compacted state.

We have mentioned the high porosity of lightweight aggregates, but normal weight aggregates also contain some pores (typically 1–2% by volume) which can absorb and hold water. Before concrete mixing, the aggregate can therefore be in one of four moisture conditions:

1. completely (oven) dry, i.e. all pores empty;
2. air dry, i.e. pores partially filled;
3. saturated surface dry, i.e. all pores full but no excess water;
4. wet, i.e. excess water.

In the fresh concrete, aggregate in the first two conditions will absorb some of the mix water, and in the fourth condition will add to it. The third state is perhaps most desirable, but is difficult to achieve except in the laboratory. Of prime importance to the subsequent concrete properties is the amount of water available for cement hydration, i.e. the amount that is non-absorbed or 'free'; therefore, to ensure that the required free water/cement ratio is obtained, it is necessary to allow for the aggregate moisture condition when calculating the amount of mix water. If the aggregate is drier than saturated surface dry, extra water must be added; if it is wetter, then less mix water is required.

Since the aggregate occupies most of the concrete volume, its elastic properties have a major influence on the elastic properties of the concrete, as we shall discuss in Chapter 15. The reduction in strength of the concrete resulting from the use of the porous, lower strength lightweight aggregate has been discussed above. Normal weight aggregates are generally considerably stronger than the hcp, and therefore do not have a major influence on the strength of most concretes. However, in high-strength concrete (with strengths in excess of, say, 70–80 N/mm^2) aggregate strength and the effect of the transition zone between the aggregate and the hcp become increasingly important.

13.5 References

Bamforth, P.B. (1980) *Proc. Instn Civ. Engnrs*, Part 2 **69**, Sept., 777–800.

Bensted, J. (1986) *Proceedings of Conduction Calorimetry Meeting*, King's College, London, 11 Dec.

Birchall, J.D., Howard, A.J. and Kendall, K. (1981) *Nature*, Vol. 289, Jan., pp. 388–90.

Bogue, R.H. (1929) *Ind. Engng Chem. Analyt.*, Edn 1, No. 4, 192–7.

Bogue, R.H. (1955) *Chemistry of Portland Cement*, Van Nostrand Reinhold, New York.

Dewar, J.D. (1983) *Proceedings of the ERMCO Congress*, London, Paper W8B(2), pp. 1–8.

Domone, P.L. and Thurairatnam, H. (1986) *Magazine of Concrete Research*, **38**, No. 136, Sept., 129–38.

Dransfield, J.M. and Egan, P. (1988) In *Cement Admixtures: Use and Applications* (ed. P.C. Hewlett), Longman, Essex (2nd edn), pp. 102–29.

Feldman, R.F. and Sereda, P.J. (1970) *Eng. J. (Canada)*, **53**, No. 8/9.

Forester, J. (1970) *Cement Technology*, May/June, 95–9.

Hansen, T.C. (1970) *Proc. Amer. Conc. Inst.*, **67**, 404.

Hewlett, P.C. (ed.) (1988) *Cement Admixtures: Use and Applications*, Longman, Essex (2nd edn).

Mehta, P.K. (1986) *Concrete: Structure, Properties and Materials*, Prentice-Hall, New Jersey.

Mehta, P.K., Pirtz, D. and Polivka, M. (1979) *Cement and Concrete Research*, **9**, No. 4, 439–50.

Meland, I. (1983) *Proceedings of CANMET/ACI First International Conference on the Use of Fly Ash, Silica Fume, Slag and Other Mineral By-Products in Concrete*, American Concrete Institute Publication, SP-79, V2, pp. 665–76.

Mindess, S. and Young, J.F. (1981) *Concrete*, Prentice-Hall, New Jersey.

Powers, T.C. (1958) *J. Amer. Ceramic Soc.*, **41**, No. 1, 1–6.

Ramachandran, V.S., Feldman, R.F. and Beaudoin, J.J. (1981) *Concrete Science*, Heyden and Sons, London.

Rixom, M.R. and Mailvaganam, N.P. (1986) *Chemical*

Admixtures for Concrete, E. & F.N. Spon, London (2nd edn).

Rixom, M.R., Howarth, I.M. and Waddicor, M.J. (1988) In *Cement Admixtures: Use and Applications* (ed. P.C. Hewlett), Longman, Essex (2nd edn), pp. 15–27.

Roy, D.M. and Gouda, G.R. (1975) *Cement and Concrete Research*, 5, No. 2, March, 153–62.

Soroka, I. (1979) *Portland Cement Paste and Concrete*, Macmillan, London.

Taylor, H.F.W. (1989) *Advances in Cement Research*, 2, No. 6, April, 73–7.

Chapter fourteen

Fresh and early age properties of concrete

14.1 Fresh properties
14.2 Behaviour after placing
14.3 Strength gain and temperature effects
14.4 References

Civil engineers are responsible for the production, transport, placing, compacting and curing of fresh concrete. Without adequate attention to all of these the potential hardened properties of the mix, such as strength and durability, will not be achieved in the finished structural element. It is important to recognize that it is not sufficient simply to ensure that the concrete is placed correctly; the behaviour and treatment of the concrete during the period before setting, typically some six to ten hours after casting, and during the first few days of hardening have a significant effect on the long-term performance.

It is beyond the scope of this book to discuss the operations and equipment used to batch, mix, handle, compact and finish the concrete. The aim of these practices is to produce a homogeneous structure with minimum air voids as efficiently as possible; it is also necessary to ensure that the concrete is then stable and achieves its full, mature properties. We therefore need to consider the properties when freshly mixed, between placing and setting, and during the early stages of hydration.

14.1 Fresh properties

14.1.1 General behaviour

The main properties of interest in the freshly mixed concrete during handling, placing and compacting are the following.

1. Fluidity. It must be capable of being handled and of flowing into the formwork and around any reinforcement, with the assistance of whatever equipment is available. For example, concrete for a lightly reinforced shallow floor slab need not be as fluid as that for a narrow, heavily reinforced column.
2. Compactability. All, or nearly all, of the air entrapped during mixing and handling should be capable of being removed by the compacting system being used, such as poker vibrators.
3. Stability or cohesiveness. The concrete should remain as a homogeneous uniform mass. For example, the mortar should not be so fluid that it segregates from the coarse aggregate.

The first two of these properties, fluidity and compactability, are generally combined into the property called **workability**. In general, higher workability concretes are easier to place and handle, but if this high workability is obtained, for example, by an increased water content, then a lower strength and durability will result. It is therefore normal practice to use the lowest workability consistent with efficient handling and placing in the particular application, thereby increasing the need for a proper understanding of the fresh structure and properties.

As mentioned in Chapter 13, most of the concrete (about 70–80% of the volume) consists of fine and coarse aggregate. The remainder is cement paste, which in turn consists of 30–50% by volume of cement, the rest being water. Cement paste, mortar and concrete are all therefore concentrated suspensions of particles of varying sizes. Surface attractive forces are significant in relation to gravitational forces for the cement particles, but less so for the aggregate particles, and the main resistance to flow comes from interference and friction between them. There is considerable evidence that the behaviour of fresh paste, mortar and concrete all approximate reasonably closely to the Bingham model described in Chapter 6 and illustrated in Figure 14.1. Flow only starts when the applied shear stress reaches a yield value (τ_y) sufficient to overcome the interparticle interference effects, and at higher stresses the shear rate varies approximately linearly with shear stress, the slope defining the plastic viscosity (μ).

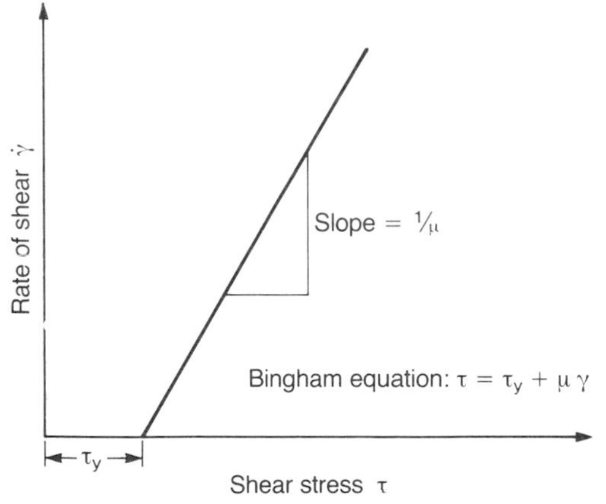

FIGURE 14.1 The Bingham model of fluid behaviour.

14.1.2 Workability measurements

Two point tests

To quantify the workability of a concrete, it is necessary to determine the two Bingham constants τ_y and μ. In practice, absolute measurement of τ_y and μ for concrete is difficult, as conventional instruments such as concentric cylinder viscometers are far too small to accommodate the aggregate particles. A test system based on measuring the torque required to turn an impeller in a bowl of concrete has therefore been devised (Tattersall and Banfill, 1983). Two versions are available, employing different impellers, illustrated in Figure 14.2. A helical impeller is used for high workability mixes, and an H-shaped impeller rotating on its own axis and circulating in a planetary motion in the concrete is preferred for low workability mixes. Torque is measured for a number of impeller speeds, and from the resulting plot of torque versus speed a yield torque (denoted g) and slope (denoted h) corresponding to the Bingham yield stress and plastic viscosity can be obtained (Figure 14.3). Because at least two data points are required to define the torque/speed relationship, the test is known as the two point workability test.

The values of g and h depend both on the concrete properties and the apparatus geometry, but provided the latter is kept constant then different concretes can be compared. Lower values of g and h indicate a more fluid mix, and, in particular, reducing g lowers the resistance to flow at low shear stresses, e.g. under self-weight when being poured, and reducing h tends to decrease the cohesion of the mix. Some of the more important effects of variation of mix proportions and constituents on g and h, shown schematically in Figure 14.4, are as follows.

1. Increasing the water content whilst keeping the proportions of the other constituents constant decreases both g and h.
2. Adding a plasticizer or superplasticizer

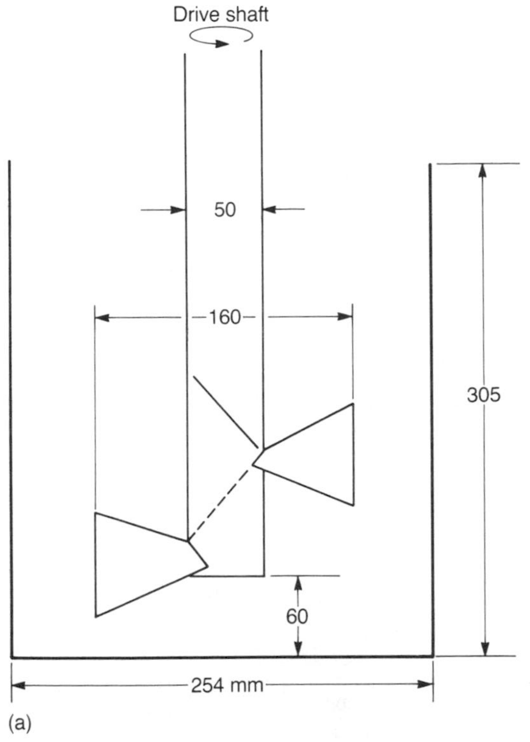

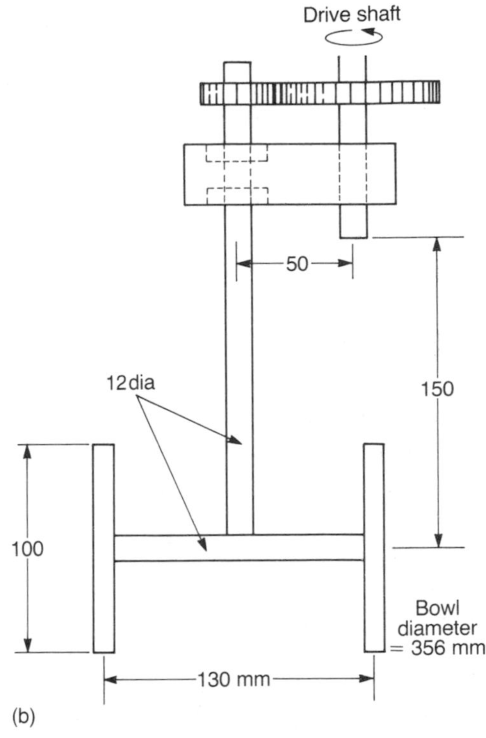

FIGURE 14.2 Two point workability test systems for concrete (Tattersall and Banfill, 1983): (a) helical impeller for high workability mixes; (b) H-shaped impeller with planetary drive for low workability mixes.

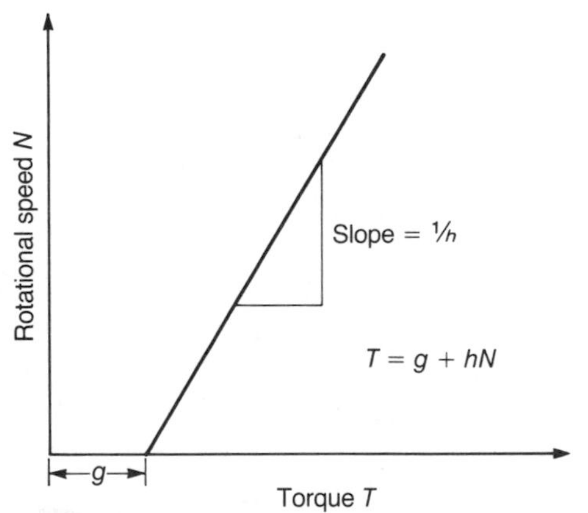

FIGURE 14.3 Interpretation of results from two point workability tests on concrete.

decreases g but leaves h relatively constant, i.e. they preferentially reduce yield stress. The effect is more marked with superplasticizers, which means that the yield stress can be considerably reduced, giving greatly increased flow properties under self-weight, whilst maintaining the plastic viscosity and hence the cohesion of the mix.

3. Increasing the fine/coarse aggregate ratio will normally increase g and decrease h, but for some mixes opposite effects can occur.
4. Replacing some of the cement with pfa or ggbs will generally decrease g, but h may either increase or decrease, depending on the initial mix proportions.

Single point tests

Prior to the understanding of concrete as Bingham material, a number of simple but arbitrary tests for workability had been devised, some of which are still in common use. The simplest, and crudest, is the slump test (Figure 14.5(a)). The concrete is placed in the frustum

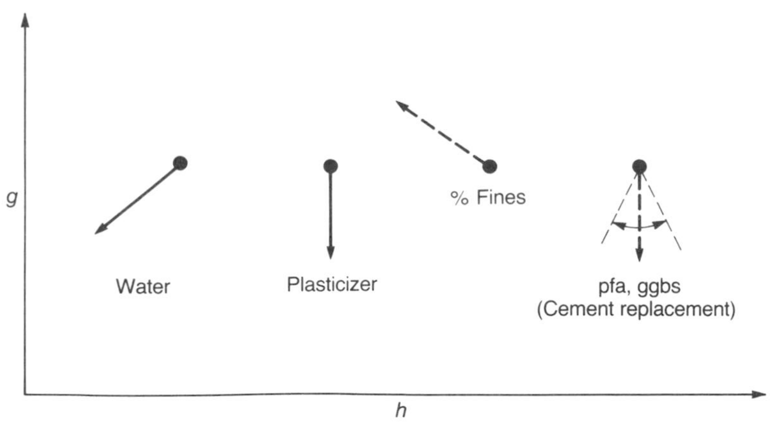

FIGURE 14.4 Typical effects of increases in quantities of individual mix components of concrete on *g* and *h*.

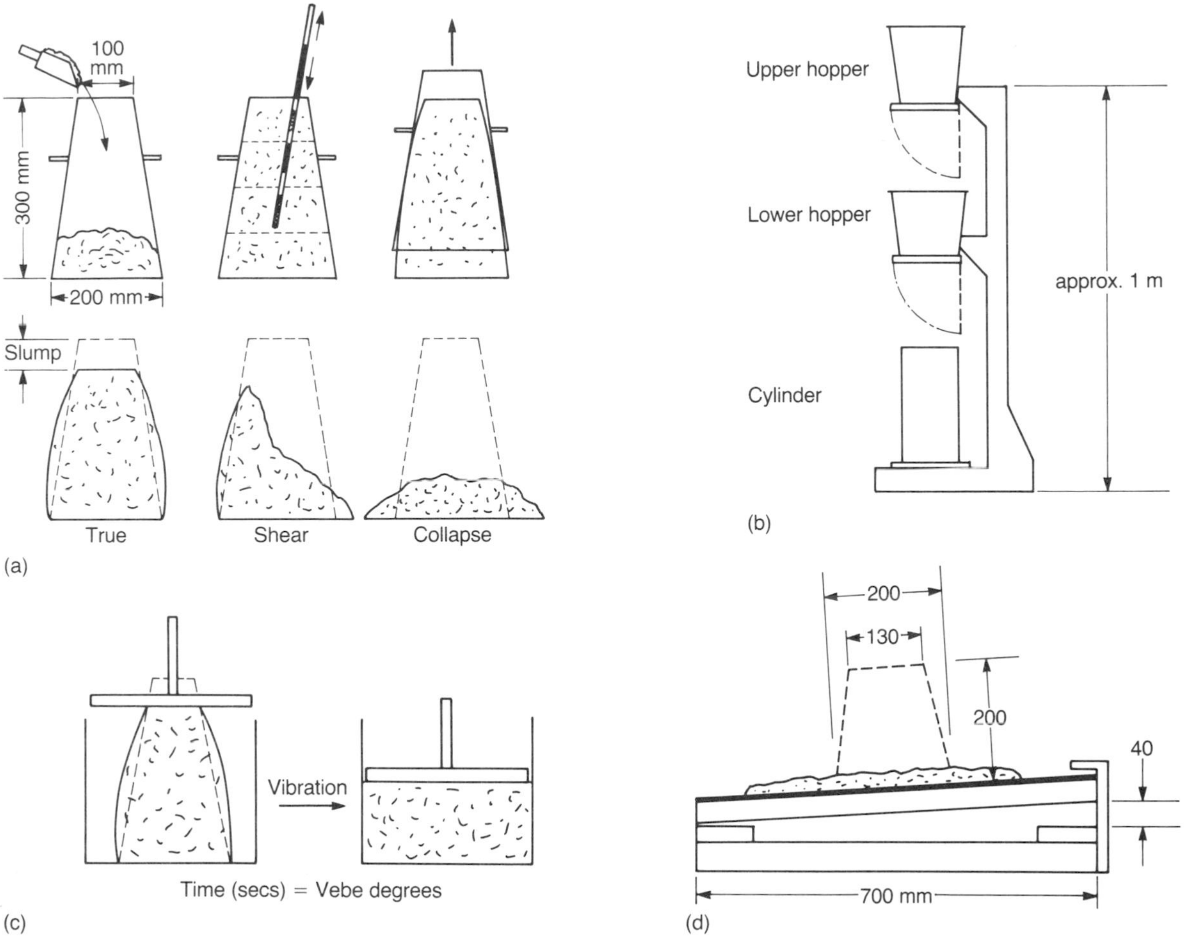

FIGURE 14.5 Single point workability tests for concrete: (a) slump; (b) compacting factor; (c) Vebe; (d) flow table.

of a steel cone and hand tamped in three layers. The cone is lifted off, and the slump is defined as the downward movement of the concrete. For the test to be valid, the concrete should retain the overall shape of the cone and not collapse; this gives an upper limit to the workability that can be tested. Slumps from zero to about 175 mm can be measured. Also, mixes with a tendency to segregate can produce a shear collapse; if this occurs, the test should be repeated. As a general guide, mixes with slumps ranging from about 10 mm upwards can be handled with conventional site equipment, with higher slumps (100 mm and above) being required to ensure full compaction of the concrete in areas with limited access or congested reinforcement. However, some zero slump mixes have sufficient workability for some applications.

The compacting factor test (Figure 14.5(b)) is able to distinguish between zero slump mixes. Concrete is placed in an upper hopper, dropped into a lower hopper to bring it to a standard state, and then allowed to fall into a cylinder. The resulting degree of compaction of the concrete is then measured by comparing its weight with the weight of concrete in the cylinder when fully compacted. The compacting factor is defined as the former divided by the latter; values in the range 0.7 to 1 are obtained. The closer the value approaches 1, the higher the workability.

In the Vebe test (Figure 14.5(c)), the response of the concrete to vibration is determined. The Vebe time is defined as the time taken to completely remould a sample of concrete from a slump test carried out in a cylindrical container. Standard vibration is applied, and remoulding times from 1 to about 25 secs are obtained, with higher values indicating decreased workability. It is often difficult to define the end point of complete remoulding with a sufficient degree of accuracy.

To differentiate between mixes whose workability is too high for the slump test, a flow table test has been devised (Figure 14.5(d)). A hand tamped sample of the concrete is formed by a smaller version of a slump cone in the centre of a wooden board covered by a steel plate. This is hinged along one side to a base board. The opposite side is then raised 40 mm and allowed to drop under its own weight 15 times, and the resulting diameter of the concrete measured; a spread of 400 mm indicates medium workability, and 500 mm high workability.

All of the above tests are single point tests, i.e. they give only a single test value. As we have seen, two points are required to define the workability, and therefore none of the tests can truly represent the workability of the concrete. Furthermore they measure the response of the concrete to specific, but arbitrary and different, test conditions. The slump, Vebe and flow table tests provide a measure of the consistency or mobility of the concrete; the slump test after a standard amount of work has been done on the concrete, the Vebe test during a standard energy input, and the flow table with some combination of the two. The compacting factor test comes closest to assessing the compactability of the concrete, but the amount of work done on the concrete in falling into the cylinder is much less than the energy input from practical compaction equipment such as a poker vibrator.

There is some degree of correlation between the results of these tests, as shown in Figure 14.6, but since none of the tests measure a fundamental property of the concrete the correlation is quite broad. In some specific instances, comparison of results can even be misleading; for example, consider the results of Table 14.1. Ranking in order of increasing 'workability' gives

by slump	B-C-A
by compacting factor	A-B-C
by Vebe	B-A-C.

The result therefore depends on the choice of test, which is far from satisfactory.

Despite these limitations, single point tests,

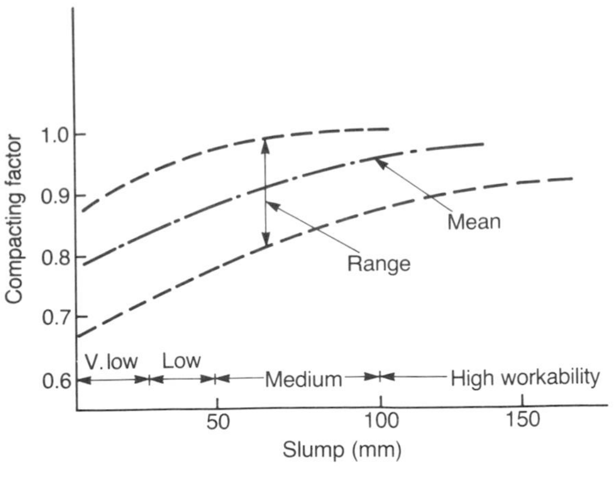

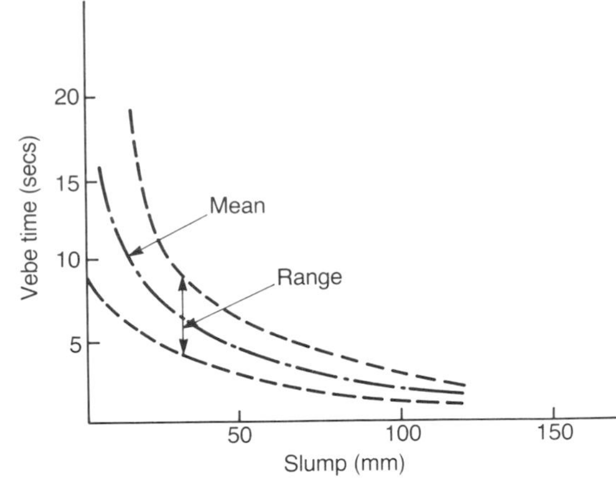

FIGURE 14.6 Correlations between compacting factor, Vebe time and slump.

TABLE 14.1 Single point workability test results (Ritchie, 1962)

Mix	*w/c*	*Cement content (kg/m³)*	*Slump (mm)*	*cf**	*Vebe (secs)*
A	0.45	520	80	0.85	3.5
B	0.55	385	50	0.92	6.5
C	0.69	270	55	0.95	2.5

* Compacting factor.

particularly the slump test, remain popular. As this is carried out at low shear rates, it seems to have a better correlation with g than with h, slump increasing with decreasing values of g. Reference to changes in g in Figure 14.4 will show the way in which slump will vary with changes in mix composition, etc. The main reason for the continuing popularity of the slump test may be its simplicity. For quality control of concrete production, if only one variable is considered of significance, e.g. water content, it can be a useful way of assessing variations.

14.2 Behaviour after placing

Between the time of placing and the final set, a period that can last several hours, concrete is in a plastic, semi-fluid state. The constituent materials are still relatively free to move and, as they are of differing relative density, they can do so due to gravity. The denser aggregate and cement particles tend to settle and the mix water has a tendency to migrate upwards. This can give rise to three interrelated phenomena – bleeding, plastic settlement and plastic shrinkage.

14.2.1 Bleeding

The process of the upward migration or upward displacement of water is known as bleeding. Its most obvious manifestation is the appearance of a layer of water on the top surface of concrete shortly after it has been placed; this can amount to 2% or more of the total depth of the concrete. In time this water either evaporates or is re-absorbed into the concrete with continuing hydration, thus resulting in a net reduction of the original concrete volume. This in itself may not be of concern in many cases, but there are two other effects of bleeding that can give greater problems, illustrated in Figure 14.7(a). Firstly, the cement paste at or just below the top surface of the concrete becomes water rich and therefore hydrates to a weak structure, a phenomenon known as surface laitance. This is

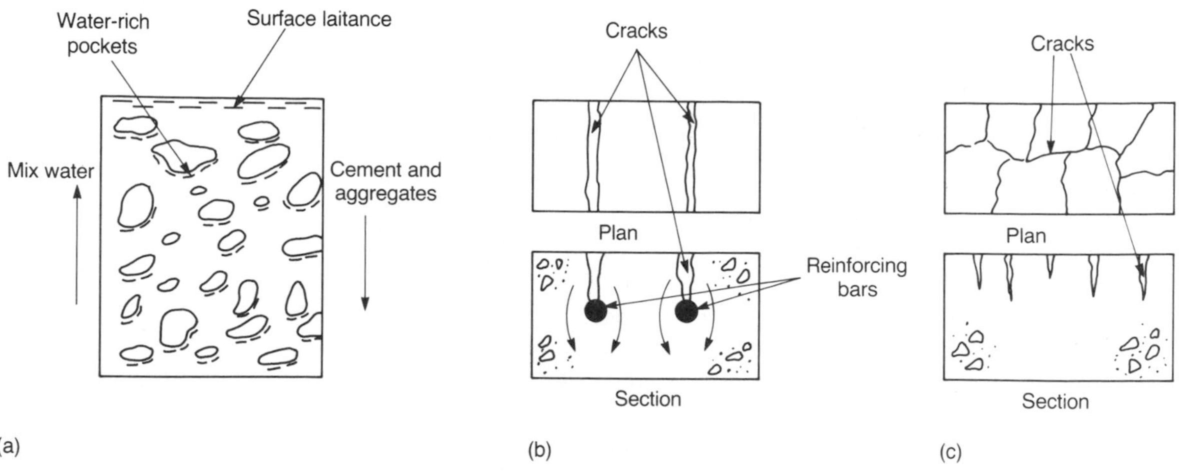

FIGURE 14.7 Effects of movement in freshly placed concrete: (a) bleeding; (b) plastic settlement cracking; (c) plastic shrinkage cracking.

a problem in, for example, floor slabs which are required to have a hard wearing surface. Secondly, the upward migrating water can be trapped under aggregate particles, causing a local weakening of the transition zone between the paste and the aggregate (which may already be a relatively weak part of the concrete) and hence an overall loss of concrete strength.

14.2.2 Plastic settlement

The overall settlement of the concrete will result in greater movement in the fresh concrete near the top surface of a deep pour. If there is any local restraint to this movement from, say, horizontal reinforcing bars, then plastic settlement cracking can occur, in which vertical cracks form along the line of the bars, penetrating from the surface to the bars (Figure 14.7(b)).

14.2.3 Plastic shrinkage

Bleed water arriving at an unprotected concrete surface will be subject to evaporation; if the rate of evaporation is greater than the rate of arrival of water at the surface, then there will be a net reduction in water content of the surface concrete, and plastic shrinkage, i.e. drying shrinkage whilst the concrete is still plastic, will occur. The restraint of the mass of concrete will cause tensile strains to be set up in the near surface region, and as the concrete has near zero tensile strength, plastic shrinkage cracking may result. The cracking pattern, illustrated in Figure 14.7(c), is a fairly regular 'crazing', and is therefore distinctly different from that resulting from plastic settlement.

Any tendency to plastic shrinkage cracking will be encouraged by greater evaporation rates of the surface water which occurs, for example, with higher concrete or ambient temperatures, or if the concrete is exposed to wind.

14.2.4 Methods of reducing bleed and its effects

A major cause of excessive bleed is the use of a poorly graded aggregate, with a lack of fine material below a particle size of 300 µm being most critical. This can be remedied by increasing the sand content, but if this is not feasible for other reasons, or if a particularly coarse sand has to be used, then air entrainment can be an effective substitute for the fine particles.

Higher bleeds may also occur with higher

workability mixes, and if very high workabilities are required, it is preferable to use super plasticizers rather than high water contents, as discussed in Section 13.2.1. Condensed silica fume, with its very high surface area, is also an effective bleed control agent.

Bleed, however, cannot be entirely eliminated, and so measures must be taken in practice to reduce its effects. Plastic settlement and plastic shrinkage cracks that occur soon after placing the concrete can be eliminated by revibrating the surface region, particularly in large flat slabs. All concretes, however, must have adequate curing; that is, they must be protected from moisture loss from as soon after placing as possible, and for the first few days of hardening. Curing methods include:

1. spraying or ponding the surface of the concrete with water;
2. protecting exposed surfaces from wind and sun by windbreaks and sunshades;
3. covering surfaces with wet hessian and/or polythene sheets;
4. applying a curing membrane, usually a spray-applied resin seal, to the exposed surface; this prevents moisture loss, and weathers away in a few weeks.

14.3 Strength gain and temperature effects

14.3.1 Effect of curing temperature

We mentioned in Section 13.1.3 that the hydration reactions between cement and water are temperature-dependent and their rate increases with curing temperature. Typical effects of curing temperature on concrete strength development are shown in Figure 14.8, in which the following features can be seen.

1. At early ages the rate of strength gain increases with curing temperature, as would be expected.

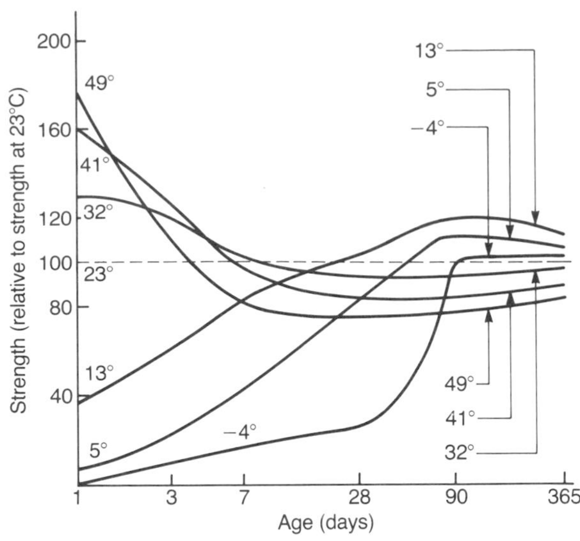

FIGURE 14.8 Effect of curing temperature on concrete strength (Portland cement, w/c = 0.4) (Klieger, 1958).

2. At later ages, however, higher strengths are obtained from the concrete cured at lower temperatures. Explanations of this behaviour have been conflicting, but it would seem that, as similar behaviour is obtained with cement paste, the C-S-H gel more rapidly produced at the higher temperatures is less uniform and hence weaker than that produced at the lower temperatures. There also appears to be an optimum temperature for maximum long-term strength, in this case 13°C; this optimum has been found to vary for different types of cement.
3. The hydration reactions proceed at temperatures below the freezing point of water, 0°C. In fact they only cease completely at about −10°C. However, the concrete must only be exposed to such temperatures after a significant amount of the mix water has been incorporated in the hydration reactions, since the expansion of free water on freezing will disrupt the immature, weak concrete. A degree of hydration equivalent to a strength

of 3.5 N/mm^2 is considered sufficient to give protection against this effect.

14.3.2 Maturity

Since the degree of cement hydration depends on both time and temperature, it might be expected that maturity, defined as the product of time and curing temperature, would show some correlation with strength. For the reasons given above, −10°C is taken as the datum point for temperature, and hence

$$\text{maturity} = \Sigma\, t \cdot (T + 10)$$

where t and T are the time (normally in hours) and curing temperature (in °C) respectively. Figure 14.9 shows maturity plotted against strength for three different but constant curing temperatures, −1, 21 and 43°C. It can be seen that concrete at all three temperatures has similar strength/maturity values at low maturities, but subsequently the maturities for the lowest temperature give higher strength values. In addition, initial curing for even a few hours at temperatures higher or lower than that for subsequent curing alters the strength/maturity relationship.

The maturity concept is useful when estimating the strength of concrete in a structure from the strength of laboratory samples cured at a different temperature. However, the limitations of the temperature range, as illustrated in Figure 14.9, must be borne in mind.

14.3.3 Heat of hydration effects

As well as being temperature-dependent, cement hydration is exothermic, and in Section 13.1.3 we discussed in some detail the rate of heat output at constant temperature (i.e. isothermal) conditions in relation to the various hydration reactions. The opposite extreme to the isothermal condition is adiabatic (i.e. perfect insulation or no heat loss), and in this condition the exothermic reactions result in heating of a cement paste, mortar or concrete. This leads to progressively faster hydration, heat output rate and temperature rise, the result being substantial temperature rises in relatively short timescales (Figure 14.10). The temperature rise

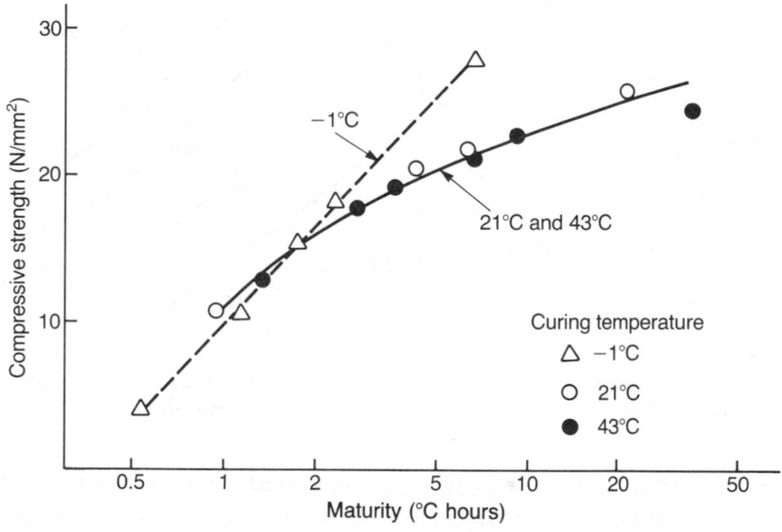

FIGURE 14.9 Strength versus maturity relationship for a concrete cured at three different temperatures (Carino *et al.*, 1983).

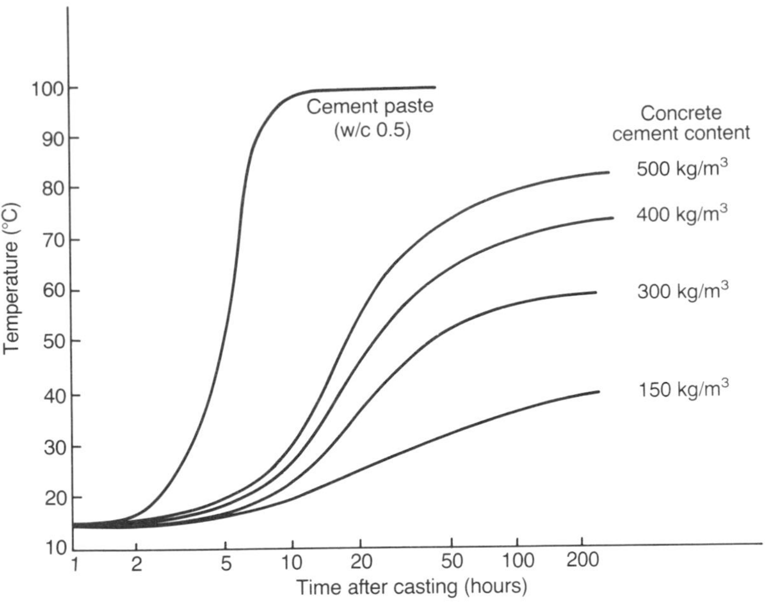

FIGURE 14.10 Typical temperature rise during curing under adiabatic conditions for a neat cement paste and concrete with varying cement content (Bamforth, 1988).

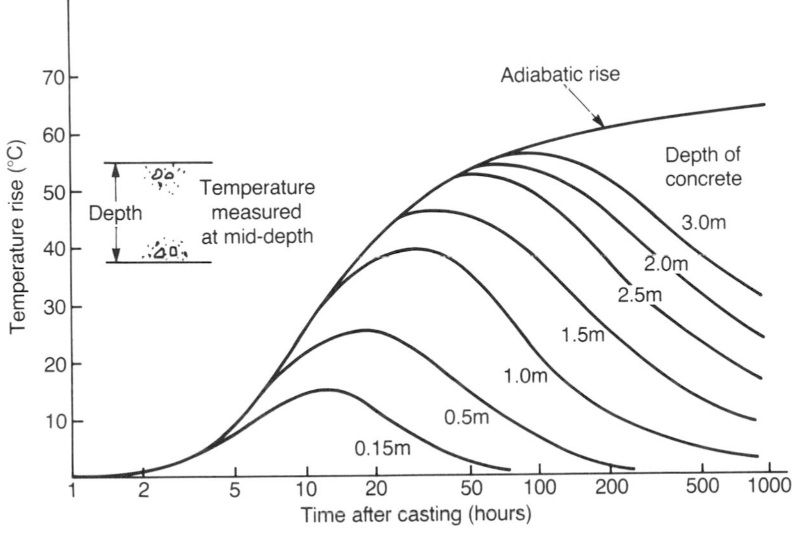

FIGURE 14.11 The effect of depth of a concrete pour on temperature rise at mid-depth during hydration (placing temperature = 20°C, Portland cement content = 400 kg/m³) (Browne and Blundell, 1973).

in concrete is less than that in cement paste as the aggregate acts as a heat sink and there is less cement to react. An average rise of 13°C per 100 kg of cement per m^3 of concrete has been suggested for typical structural concretes.

When placed in a structure, the concrete will lose heat to its surrounding environment either directly or through formwork, and it will

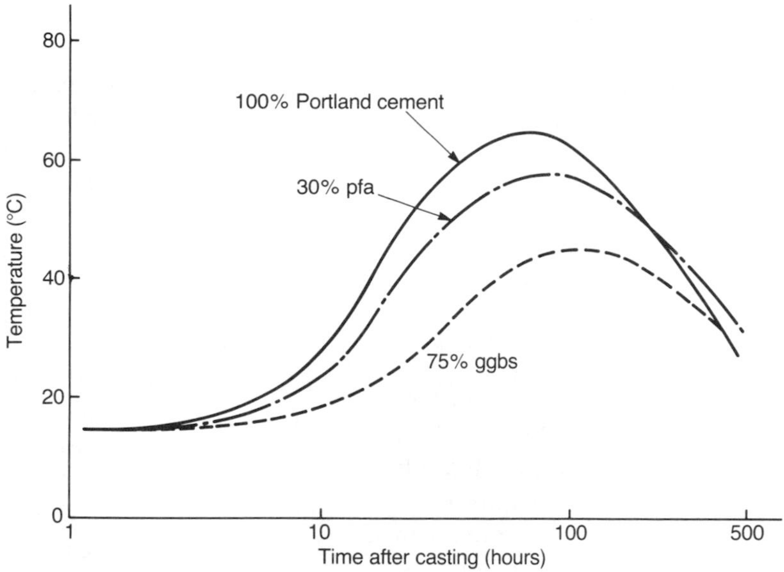

FIGURE 14.12 Temperature variation at mid-height of a 2.5 m deep pour during hydration of concrete made with 100% Portland cement, 70% Portland cement + 30% pfa and 25% Portland cement + 75% ggbs (Bamforth, 1980).

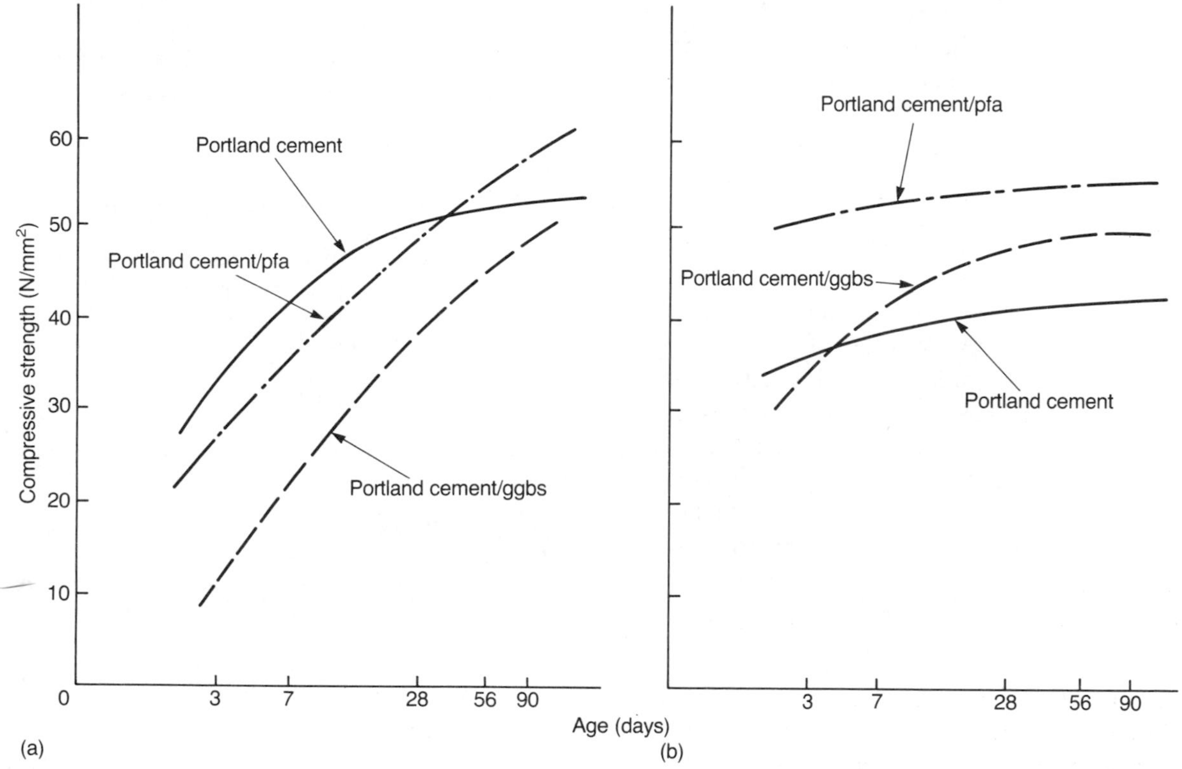

Compressive strength (N/mm²)
60
50
40
30
20
10
0
Portland cement
Portland cement/pfa
Portland cement/ggbs
3
7
28
56
90
(a)
Portland cement/pfa
Portland cement/ggbs
Portland cement
3
7
28
56
90
Age (days)
(b)

FIGURE 14.13 Strength development of concrete made with 100% Portland cement, 70% Portland cement + 30% pfa and 25% Portland cement + 75% ggbs when subjected to: (a) standard curing at 20°C; and (b) the curing cycle shown in Figure 14.12 (Bamforth, 1980).

therefore not be under either truly adiabatic or isothermal conditions, but in some intermediate state. This results in some rise in temperature within the pour followed by cooling to ambient. Typical temperature/time profiles for the centre of pours of varying depths are shown in Figure 14.11; it can be seen that the central regions of a pour with an overall thickness in excess of about 1.5 to 2 m will behave adiabatically for the first few days after casting.

Such behaviour has two important effects.

1. The cool down from the peak temperature conditions will result in thermal contraction of the concrete, which if restrained will result in tensile stresses which may be sufficiently large to crack the concrete. Restraint can result from the structure surrounding the concrete, e.g. the soil underneath a foundation, or from the outer regions of the concrete pour itself, which will have been subject to greater heat losses, and therefore will not have reached the same peak temperatures, or from reinforcement within the concrete. The amount of restraint will obviously vary in different structural situations.

   As an example, a typical coefficient of thermal expansion for concrete is 10×10^{-6} per °C, and therefore a thermal shrinkage strain of 300×10^{-6} would result from a cool down of 30°C. Taking a typical elastic modulus for the concrete of 30 kN/mm^2, and assuming complete restraint with no relaxation of the stresses due to creep, the resulting tensile stress would be 9 N/mm^2, well in excess of the tensile strength of the concrete, which would therefore have cracked.

   It is therefore necessary in pours of any substantial size to limit the temperature differentials. Insulation by way of increased formwork thickness or thermal blankets will have some beneficial effect, but, more commonly, or in addition, low heat mixes are used. Low heat Portland cement was mentioned in Chapter 13, but, more conveniently, partial cement replacement by pulverized fuel ash (pfa) or ground granulated blast furnace slag (ggbs) is an effective solution, as shown in Figure 14.12. These materials were also described in Chapter 13.
2. Much of the concrete will have hydrated for at least a few days after casting at temperatures higher than ambient, and the long-term strength may therefore be reduced, due to the effects described above. Typical effects of this on strength development are shown in Figure 14.13. By comparing Figure 14.13(a) and (b) it can be seen that pfa and ggbs mixes do not suffer the same strength losses as the 100% Portland cement mixes. The importance of determining the concrete properties after being subjected to such 'temperature matched curing' has received increasing attention in recent years.

14.4 References

Bamforth, P.B. (1980) *Proc. Instn Civ. Engnrs*, Part 2, **69**, Sept., 777–800.

Bamforth, P.B. (1988) *Proceedings of Asia Pacific Conference on Roads, Highways and Bridges*, Hong Kong, Sept.

Browne, R.D. and Blundell, R. (1973) *Proceedings of Symposium on Large Pours for RC Structures*, University of Birmingham, Sept., pp. 42–65.

Carino, N.J., Lew, H.S. and Volz, C.K. (1983) *J. Amer. Concrete Inst.*, **80**, No. 2, March–April, 93–101.

Klieger, P. (1958) *Proc. Amer. Concrete Inst.*, **54**, No. 12, 1063–81.

Ritchie, A.G.B. (1962) *Magazine of Concrete Research*, **14**, No. 40, March, 37–42.

Tattersall, G.H. and Banfill, P.F.G. (1983) *The Rheology of Fresh Concrete*, Pitman Books, London.

Chapter fifteen

Deformation of concrete

15.1 Drying shrinkage
15.2 Carbonation shrinkage
15.3 Thermal expansion
15.4 Stress–strain behaviour
15.5 Creep
15.6 References

Deformation of concrete results both from environmental effects, such as moisture movement and heat, and from applied stress, both short- and long-term. A general view of the nature of the behaviour is given in Figure 15.1, which shows the strain arising from a uniaxial compressive stress applied to the concrete in a drying environment. The stress is applied at a time t_1, and held constant until removal at time t_2. Before applying the stress, there is a net contraction in volume of the concrete, or shrinkage, associated with the drying. The dotted extension in this curve beyond time t_1 would be the subsequent behaviour without load, and the effects of the load are therefore the differences between this curve and the solid curves. Immediately on loading there is an instantaneous strain response, which for low levels of stress is approximately proportional to the stress, and hence an elastic modulus can be defined. With time, the compressive strain continues to increase at a decreasing rate. This increase, after allowing for shrinkage, represents the creep strain. Although reducing in rate with time, the creep does not tend to a limiting value.

On unloading, there is an immediate strain recovery, which is often less than the instantaneous strain on loading. This is followed by a time-dependent creep recovery, which is less than the preceding creep, i.e. there is a permanent deformation, but, unlike creep, this reaches completion in due course.

In this chapter we shall discuss the mechanisms and the factors influencing the magnitude of the components of this behaviour, i.e. shrinkage, elastic response and creep, and also consider thermally induced stresses. There are two causes of shrinkage, drying and carbonation, and both will be discussed. We shall also outline methods of predicting drying shrinkage, elastic modulus and creep. We shall for the most part be concerned with the behaviour of hardened cement paste and concrete when mature, but some mention of age effects will be made.

15.1 Drying shrinkage

15.1.1 Drying shrinkage of hardened cement paste

In Section 13.1.6 the broad divisions of water in hardened cement paste were described; loss of this water results in a net contraction, or drying shrinkage of the paste. Even though shrinkage is a volumetric effect, it is normally measured in the laboratory or on structural elements by determination of length change, and it is therefore expressed as a linear strain.

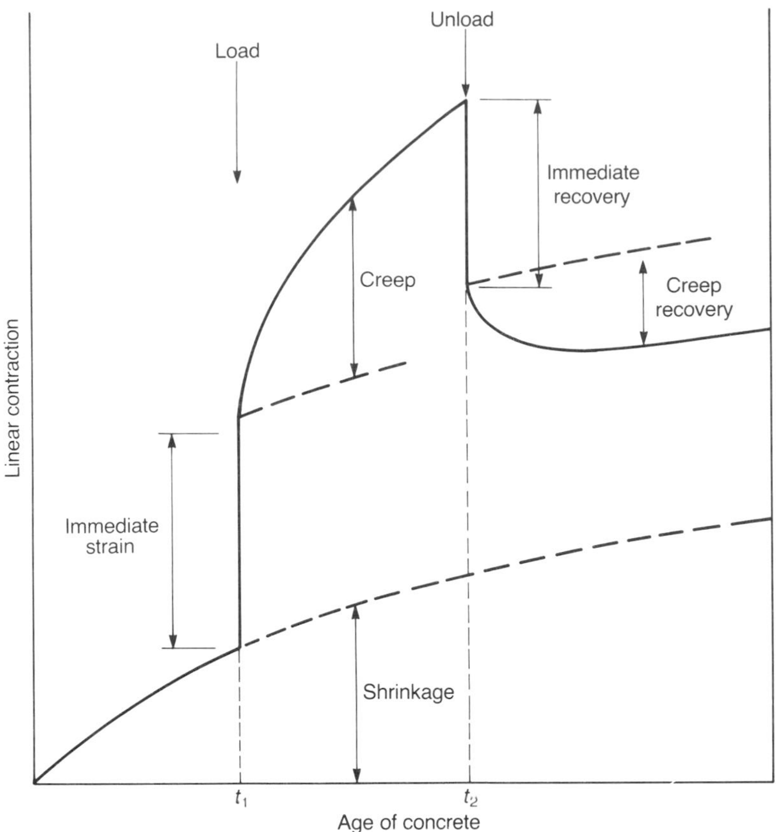

FIGURE 15.1 The response of concrete to a compressive stress applied in a drying environment.

A considerable complication in interpreting and comparing drying shrinkage measurements is that specimen size will affect the result. Water can only be lost from the surface and therefore the inner core of a specimen will act as a restraint against overall movement; the amount of restraint and hence the measured shrinkage will therefore vary with specimen size. In addition, the rate of moisture loss, and hence the rate of shrinkage, will depend on the rate of transfer of water from the core to the surface. The behaviour of hcp discussed in this section is therefore based on experimental data from specimens with a relatively small cross-section.

A schematic illustration of typical shrinkage behaviour is shown in Figure 15.2. Maximum shrinkage occurs on the first drying, and a considerable part of this is irreversible, i.e. is not recovered on subsequent rewetting. Further drying and wetting cycles result in more or less completely reversible shrinkage; hence the important distinction between reversible and irreversible shrinkage.

Also shown in Figure 15.2 is a continuous, but relatively small, swelling of the hcp on continuous immersion in water. The water content first increases to make up for the self-desiccation during hydration (see Section 13.1.6), and to keep the paste saturated. Secondly, additional water is drawn into the C-S-H structure to cause the net increase in volume. This is a characteristic of many gels, but in hcp the expansion is

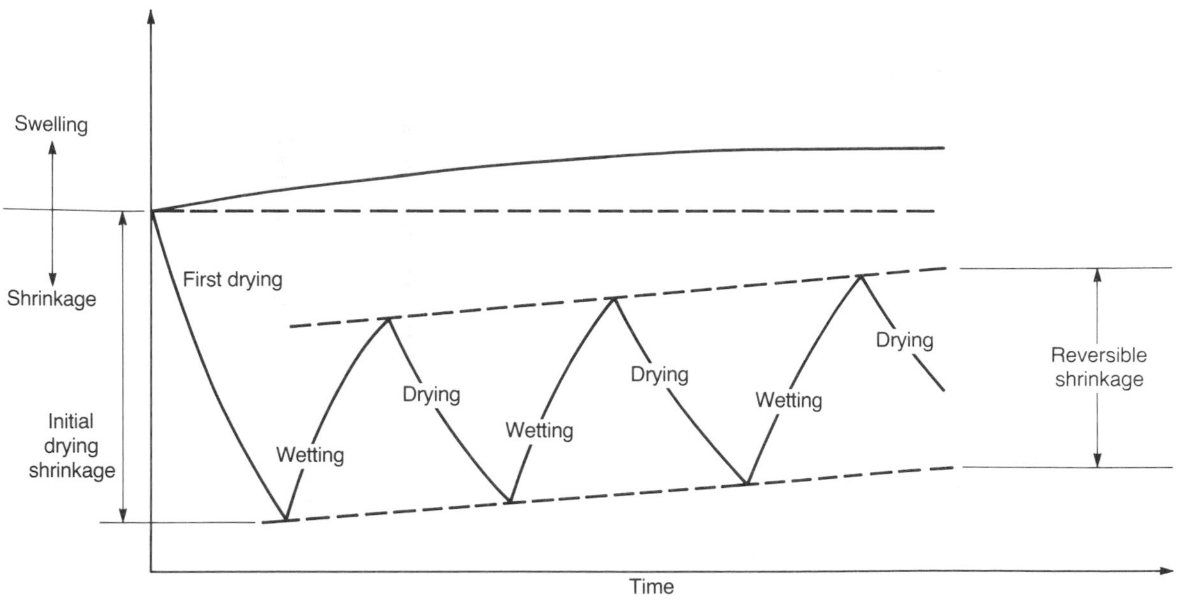

FIGURE 15.2 Schematic of volume changes in cement paste or concrete due to alternate cycles of drying and wetting.

resisted by the skeletal structure so that the swelling is small compared to the drying shrinkage strains.

In principle, the stronger the hcp structure, the less it will respond to the forces of swelling or shrinkage. This is confirmed by the results shown in Figure 15.3, in which the increasing total porosity of the paste is, in effect, decreasing strength. It is interesting that the reversible shrinkage appears independent of porosity, and the overall trend of increased shrinkage on first drying is entirely due to the irreversible shrinkage.

The variations in porosity shown in Figure 15.3 were obtained by testing pastes of different water/cement ratios. As we have seen, reduction in porosity also results from greater degrees of hydration of pastes with the same water/cement ratio, but the effect of the degree of hydration on shrinkage is not so simple. The obvious effect should be that of reduced shrinkage with age of paste if properly cured; however, the unhy-

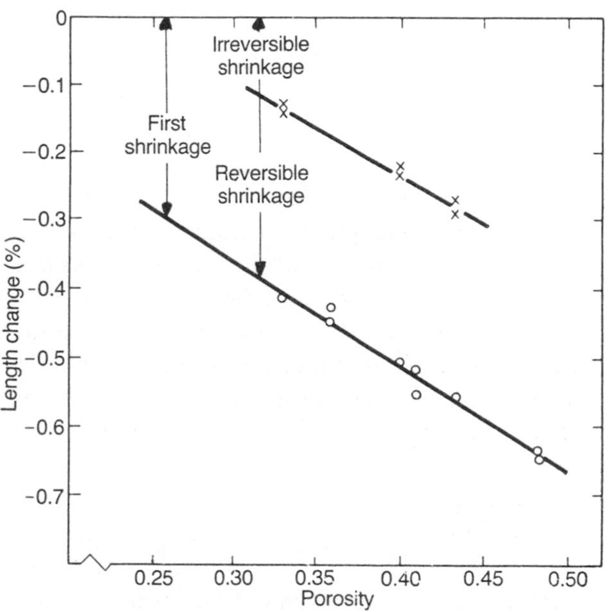

FIGURE 15.3 Reversible and irreversible shrinkage of hcp after drying at 47% relative humidity (Helmuth and Turk, 1967).

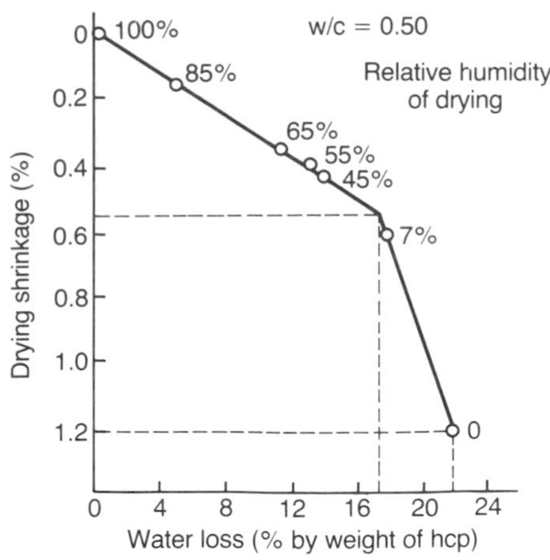

FIGURE 15.4 The effect of water loss on drying shrinkage of hardened cement paste (Verbeck and Helmuth, 1968).

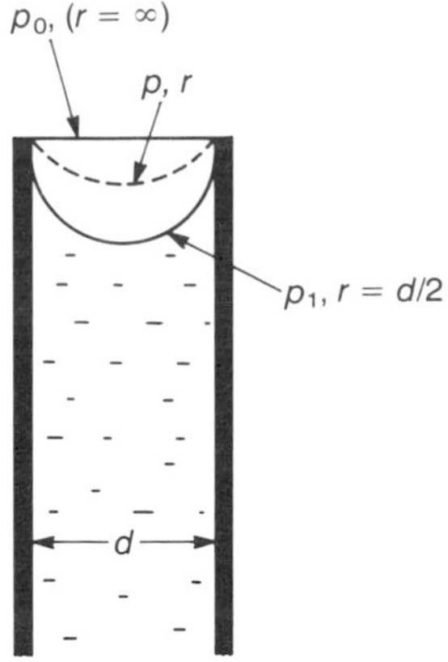

FIGURE 15.5 Relationship between the radius of curvature and vapour pressure for water in a capillary (Soroka, 1979).

drated cement grains provide some restraint to the shrinkage, and as their volume decreases with hydration, an increase in shrinkage would result. Another argument is that a more mature paste contains more water of the type whose loss causes greater shrinkage, e.g. less capillary water, and so loss of the same amount of water from such a paste would cause more shrinkage. It is thus difficult to predict the net effect of age on the shrinkage of any particular paste.

Since shrinkage results from water loss, the relationship between the two is of interest. Typical data are given in Figure 15.4, which shows that there is a distinct change of slope with moisture losses at relative humidities of less than about 10%. This implies that there is more than one mechanism of shrinkage; as other tests have shown two or even three changes of slope, it is likely that in fact several mechanisms are involved.

15.1.2 Mechanisms of shrinkage and swelling

Four principal mechanisms have been proposed for shrinkage and swelling in cement pastes. The following is a summary of the main features of each.

Capillary tension

Free water surfaces in the capillary and larger gel pores (see Section 13.1.5) will be in surface tension, and when water starts to evaporate due to a lowering of the ambient vapour pressure, the free surface becomes more concave and the surface tension increases (Figure 15.5). The relationship between the radius of curvature, r, of the meniscus and the corresponding vapour pressure, p, is given by Kelvin's equation

$$\ln(p/p_0) = 2T/R\theta\rho r \qquad (15.1)$$

where p_0 is the vapour pressure over a plane surface, T is the surface tension of the liquid, R is the gas constant, θ is the absolute temperature and ρ the density of the liquid.

The tension within the water near the meniscus can be shown to be $2T/r$, and this tensile stress must be balanced by compressive stresses in the surrounding solid. Hence the evaporation which causes an increase in the tensile stress will subject the hcp solid to increased compressive stress which will result in a decrease in volume, i.e. shrinkage. The diameter of the meniscus cannot be smaller than the diameter of the capillary, and the pore therefore empties at the corresponding vapour pressure, p_1. Hence on exposing a cement paste to a steadily decreasing vapour pressure, the pores gradually empty according to their size, the widest first. Higher water/cement ratio pastes with higher porosities will therefore shrink more, thus explaining the general form of Figure 15.3. As a pore empties, the imposed stresses on the surrounding solid reduce to zero, and so full recovery of shrinkage would be expected on complete drying. Since this does not occur, it is generally accepted that other mechanisms become operative at low humidities, and that this mechanism only applies at relative humidities above about 50%.

Surface tension or surface energy

The surface of both solid and liquid materials will be in a state of tension due to the net attractive forces of the molecules within the material. Work therefore has to be done against this force to increase the surface area, and the surface energy is defined as the work required to increase the surface by unit area.

Surface tension forces induce compressive stresses in the material of value $2T/r$ (see above) and in the hcp solids, whose average particle size is very small, these stresses are significant. Adsorption of water molecules on to the surface of the particles reduces the surface energy, hence reducing the balancing internal compressive stresses, leading to an overall volume increase, i.e. swelling. This process is also reversible.

There are differing opinions as to the importance of this effect and its contribution to the overall shrinkage. It is likely that, as the greatest change in surface energy occurs when water molecules are adsorbed or desorbed on to dry or nearly dry surfaces, then any contributions will be more significant at low vapour pressures.

Disjoining pressure

Figure 15.6 shows a typical gel pore, narrowing from a wider section containing free water in contact with vapour to a much narrower space between the solid in which all the water is under the influence of surface forces. The two layers are prevented from moving apart by an interparticle van der Waals type bond force. The adsorbed water forms a layer about five molecules or 1.3 nm thick on the solid surface at saturation, which is under pressure from the surface attractive forces. In regions narrower than twice this thickness, i.e. about 2.6 nm, the interlayer water will be in an area of hindered adsorption. This results in the development of a swelling or disjoining pressure, which is balanced by a tension in the interparticle bond.

On drying, the thickness of the adsorbed water layer reduces, as does the area of hindered ad-

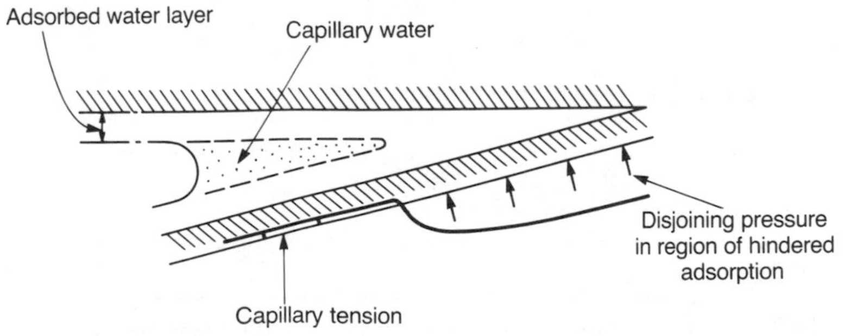

FIGURE 15.6 Water forces in a gel pore in hardened cement paste (Bazant, 1972).

sorption, hence reducing the disjoining pressure. This results in an overall shrinkage.

Movement of interlayer water

The mechanisms described above concern the free and adsorbed water. The third type of evaporable water, the interlayer water, may also have a role. Its intimate contact with the solid surfaces and the tortuosity of its path to the open air suggest that a steep hygrometric energy gradient is needed to move it, but also that such movement is likely to result in significantly higher shrinkage than the movement of an equal amount of free or adsorbed water. It is likely that this mechanism is associated with the steeper slope of the graph in Figure 15.4 at the lower relative humidities.

The above discussions apply to the reversible shrinkage only, but the reversibility depends on the assumption that there is no change in structure during the humidity cycle. This is highly unlikely, at least during the first cycle, because

1. the first cycle opens up interconnections between previously unconnected capillaries, thereby reducing the area for action of subsequent capillary tension effects;
2. some new interparticle bonds will form between surfaces that move closer together as a result of movement of adsorbed or interlayer water, resulting in a more consolidated structure at a decreased total system energy.

Opinion is divided on the relative importance of the above mechanisms and their relative contribution to the total shrinkage. These differences of opinion are clear from Table 15.1, which shows the mechanisms proposed by four main authors, and the suggested humidity levels over which they act. Readers are referred to the reference list for further study.

15.1.3 Drying shrinkage of concrete

Effect of aggregate

The drying shrinkage of concrete is less than that of neat cement paste because of the restraining influence of the aggregate, which, apart from a few exceptions, is dimensionally stable under changing moisture states. The amount of restraint provided depends on two main factors, the volume concentration of the aggregate and its modulus of elasticity.

The effect of aggregate volume is shown in Figure 15.7. Unhydrated cement grains also act as a restraint and are therefore included in the total aggregate volume figure. It is apparent that normal concretes have a shrinkage of some 10 to 30% of that of neat paste. The effect of aggregate stiffness is shown in Figure 15.8. Normal density aggregates are stiffer and therefore give more restraint than lightweight aggregates, and therefore lightweight aggregate

TABLE 15.1 Summary of suggested shrinkage mechanisms (Soroka, 1979)

<table>
<tr><th rowspan="2">Source</th><th colspan="11">Relative humidity (%)</th></tr>
<tr><th>0</th><th>10</th><th>20</th><th>30</th><th>40</th><th>50</th><th>60</th><th>70</th><th>80</th><th>90</th><th>100</th></tr>
<tr><td rowspan="2">Powers (1965)</td><td colspan="11">← Disjoining pressure →</td></tr>
<tr><td colspan="5"></td><td colspan="6">← Capillary tension →</td></tr>
<tr><td>Ishai (1965)</td><td colspan="5">← Surface energy →</td><td colspan="6">← Capillary tension →</td></tr>
<tr><td>Feldman and Sereda (1970)</td><td colspan="4">← Interlayer water →</td><td colspan="7">← Capillary tension and surface energy →</td></tr>
<tr><td>Wittman (1968)</td><td colspan="5">← Surface energy →</td><td colspan="6">← Disjoining pressure →</td></tr>
</table>

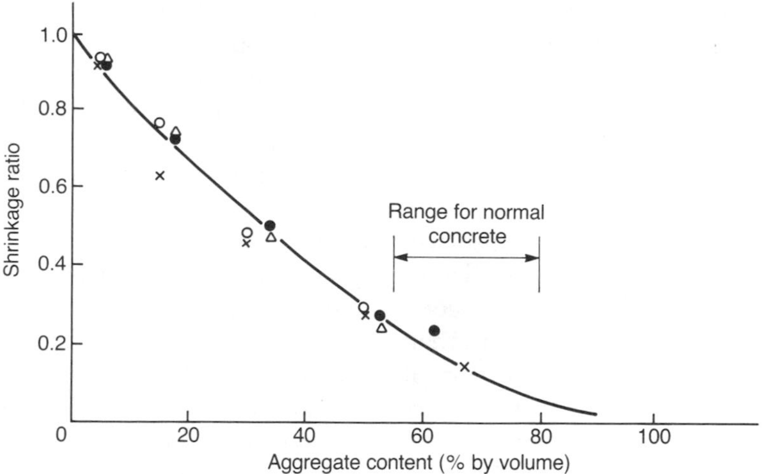

FIGURE 15.7 Influence of aggregate content in concrete on the ratio of the shrinkage of concrete to that of neat cement paste (Pickett, 1956).

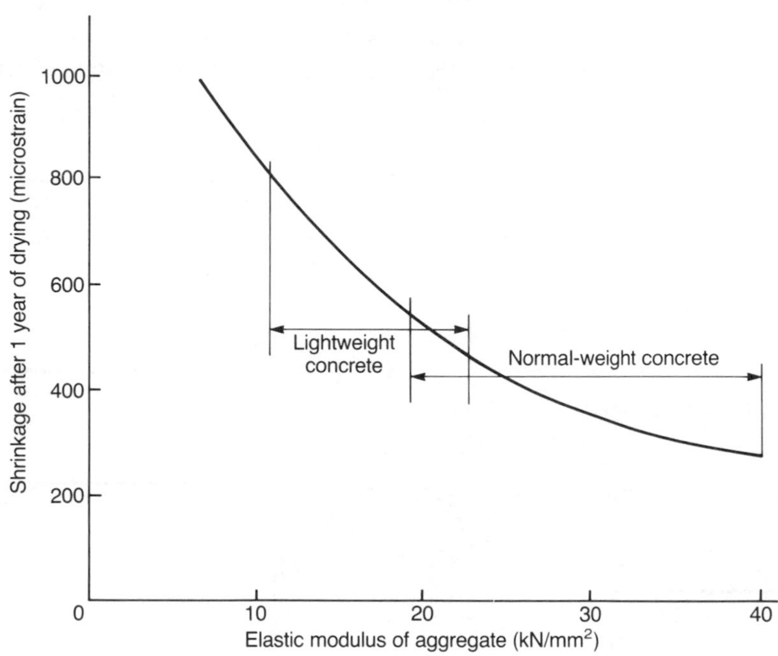

FIGURE 15.8 The effect of aggregate stiffness on concrete shrinkage (Mindess and Young, 1981).

concretes will tend to have a higher shrinkage than normal density concretes of similar volumetric mix proportions.

The combined effects of aggregate content and stiffness are contained in the empirical equation

$$\varepsilon_c/\varepsilon_p = (1 - g)^n \qquad (15.2)$$

where ε_c and ε_p are the shrinkage strains of the concrete and paste respectively, g is the aggregate volume content, and n is a constant which depends on the aggregate stiffness, and has been found to vary between 1.2 and 1.7.

Effect of specimen geometry

The size and shape of a concrete specimen will influence the rate of moisture loss and the degree of overall restraint provided by the central core, which will have a higher moisture content than the surface region. The rate and amount of shrinkage and the tendency for the surface zones to crack are therefore affected.

In particular, longer moisture diffusion paths lead to lower shrinkage rates. For example, a member with a large surface area to volume ratio, e.g. a T beam, will dry and therefore shrink more rapidly than, say, a beam with a square cross-section of the same area. In all cases, however, the shrinkage process is protracted. In a study lasting 20 years, Troxell *et al.* (1958) found that in tests on 300 mm × 150 mm diameter cylinders made from a wide range of concrete mixes and stored at relative humidities of 50 and 70%, an average of only 25% of the 20-year shrinkage occurred in the first two weeks, 60% in three months, and 80% in one year.

The effects of shrinkage are shown diagrammatically in Figure 15.9, which represents a section of a long cylindrical member drying radially. If successive cylindrical elements were free to slide over each other longitudinally, then the moisture gradient would result in the free shrinkage of Figure 15.9(b). The material is, of course, continuous and the restraint of the long cylinder results in a uniform observed strain across the section and an elastic strain distribution as in Figure 15.9(c). With no creep, this would result in a similarly shaped stress distribution, with the balance between the outer

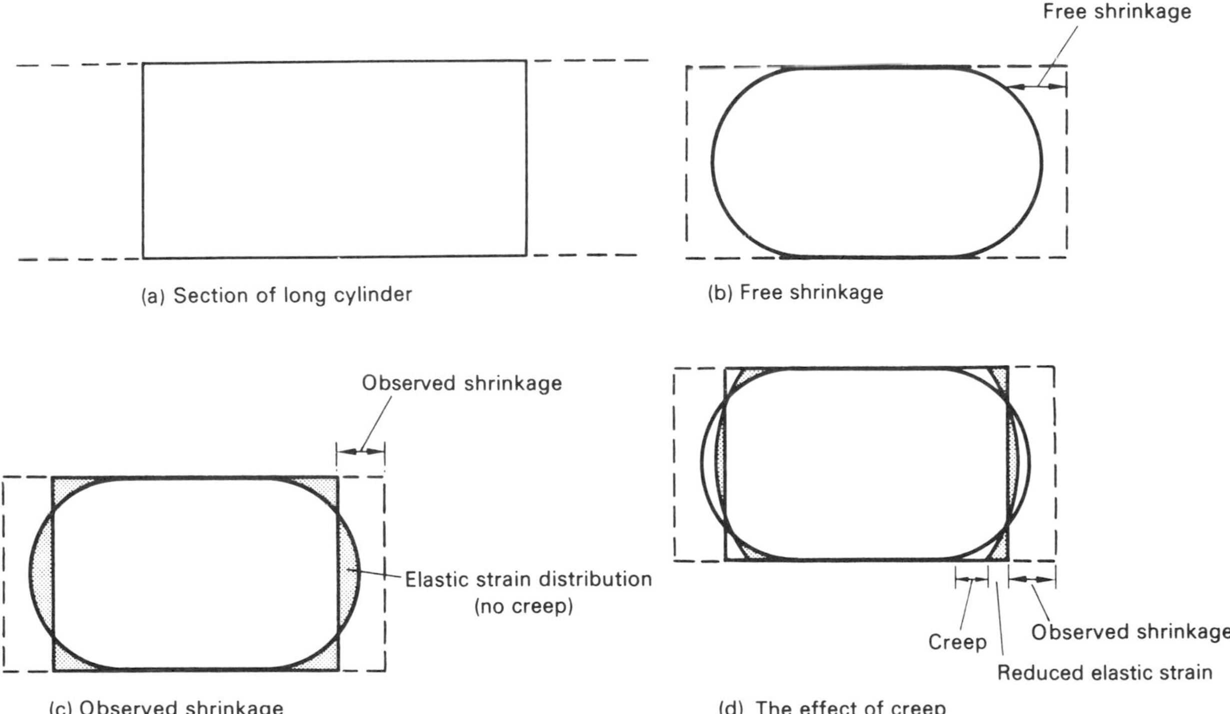

FIGURE 15.9 Internal strain distribution in a long cylinder drying radially.

zone tensile stresses and the core compressive stresses being such to ensure equilibrium. The tensile stresses may therefore result in surface cracking. Fortunately, creep effects in concrete over the long timescales involved are significant, and the strains and stresses are thereby reduced, as shown in Figure 15.9(d). The implication of this sequence is that the measured so-called shrinkage is, in reality, a combination of free shrinkage, elastic and creep strains.

Effect of cement type

A study in the USA using 199 different Portland cements, mostly classified as ordinary Portland cement, found that the shrinkage of concrete specimens made with otherwise identical mixes varied between 150 and 400 microstrain after eight weeks' drying (Blaine, 1968). A statistical analysis showed that changes in C_3A and sulphate content were responsible for the greatest variations in shrinkage, but some other variables such as alkali content and fineness also had a significant effect. The main conclusion that should be drawn is that the composition of the cement is important, but it is difficult to predict its effects.

15.1.4 Prediction of shrinkage

It is often necessary during structural design to make an estimate of the long-term drying shrinkage or swelling of a structural element; a number of methods are available for this, all based on empirical data. We have seen that shrinkage and swelling depend on the concrete composition, the member geometry and the surrounding environment, and any prediction method should take all these factors into account. A good example of a relatively straightforward method is included in The British Standard Code of Practice for Structural Concrete (BS 8110: 1985). From a single graph (Figure 15.10) a value of either the ultimate or six-month shrinkage or swelling is obtained for any given ambient humidity and member geometry. The latter is expressed as an effective section thickness, defined as twice the cross-sectional area divided by the exposed perimeter. The value of shrinkage or swelling applies to a concrete made with a high quality, dense, non-shrinking aggregate, and with an initial water content of about 190 kg/m^3. For different water contents, the shrinkage is assumed to be directly proportional to the water content, provided this is within the range 150 to 230 kg/m^3 (which covers most structural concrete). For other aggregates, which may themselves be liable to shrinkage or have a lower stiffness (e.g. lightweight aggregates) the value from Figure 15.10 should be modified accordingly, for example using relationships such as that shown in Figure 15.8.

15.2 Carbonation shrinkage

Carbonation shrinkage differs from drying shrinkage in that its cause is chemical, and it does not result from loss of water from the hcp or concrete. Carbon dioxide, when combined with water as carbonic acid, attacks most of the components of the hcp, and even the very dilute carbonic acid resulting from the low concentrations of carbon dioxide in the atmosphere can have significant effects. The most important reaction is that with the calcium hydroxide:

$$H_2CO_3 + Ca(OH)_2 = CaCO_3 + 2H_2O \quad (15.3)$$

Thus water is released and there is an increase in weight of the paste. There is an accompanying shrinkage, and the paste also increases in strength and decreases in permeability. The most likely mechanism to explain this behaviour is that the calcium hydroxide is dissolved from more highly stressed regions, resulting in the shrinkage, and the calcium carbonate crystallizes out in the pores, thus reducing the permeability and increasing the strength.

The rate and amount of carbonation depend

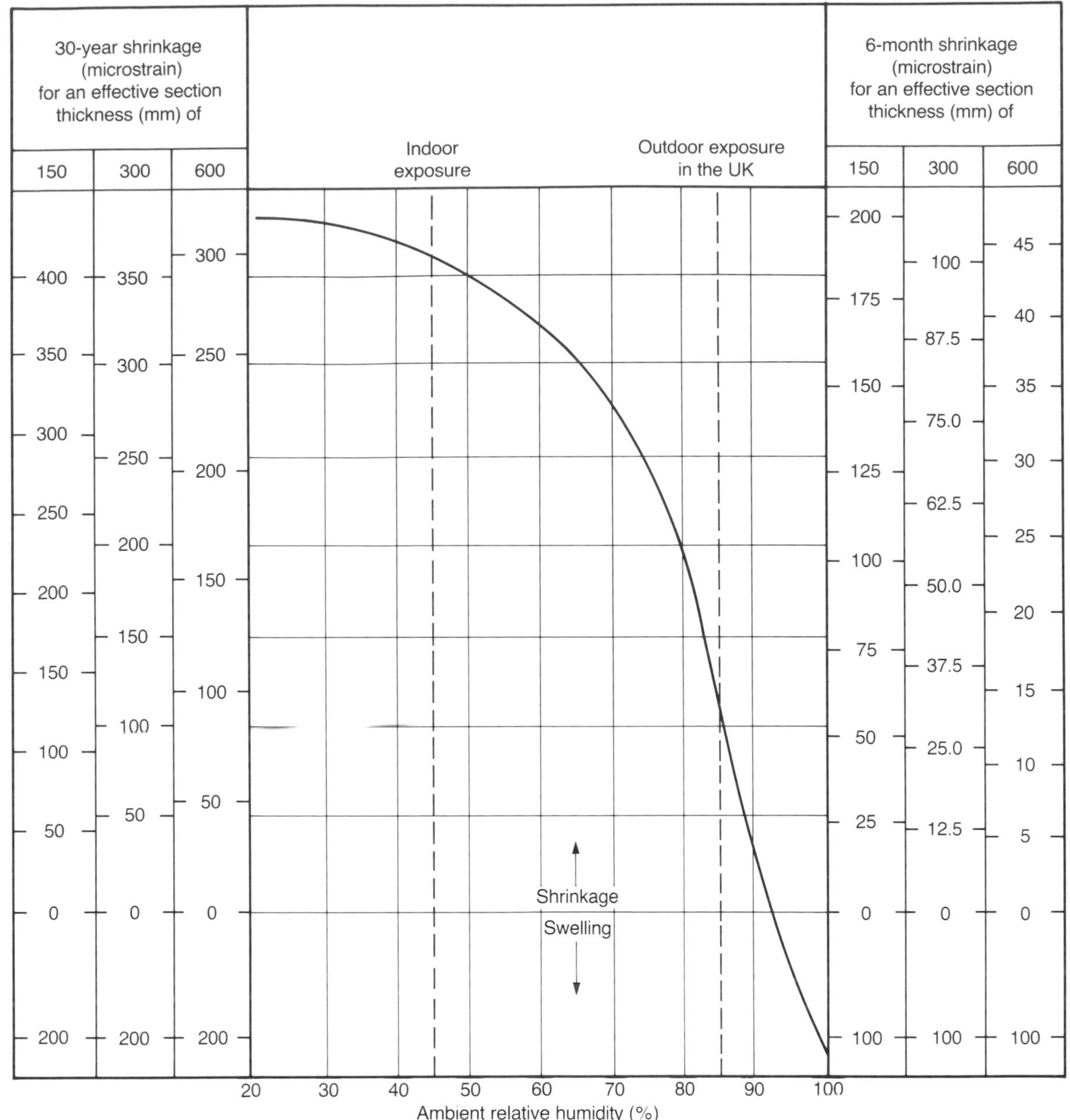

FIGURE 15.10 Prediction of shrinkage and swelling of high quality dense-aggregate concrete (from BS 8110: Part 2: 1985).

in part on the relative humidity of the concrete. If it is saturated, then the carbonic acid will not penetrate the concrete, and no carbonation will occur; if it is very dry, then no carbonic acid is available. Maximum carbonation shrinkage occurs at humidities of 25–50% and it can be of the same order of magnitude as drying shrinkage. The porosity of the concrete is also an important controlling factor. With average-strength concrete, provided it is well compacted and cured, the carbonation front will only penetrate a few centimetres in many years, and with high-strength concrete even less. However, much greater penetration can occur with poor quality concrete or in regions of poor compaction, and this can lead to substantial problems if the concrete is reinforced, as we shall see in Chapter 17.

15.3 Thermal expansion

In common with most other materials, cement pastes and concretes expand on heating. Knowledge of the coefficient of thermal expansion is needed in two main situations; firstly to calculate stresses due to thermal gradients arising from heat of hydration effects or continuously varying diurnal temperatures, and secondly to calculate overall dimensional changes in structures such as bridge decks due to ambient temperature variations.

The measurement of thermal expansions on laboratory specimens is relatively straightforward, provided sufficient time is allowed for thermal equilibrium to be reached (at most a few hours). However, the in-situ behaviour is complicated by the observation that, unlike most other materials, the thermal movement is time-dependent, and, as with shrinkage, it is difficult to estimate movement in structural elements from those on laboratory specimens.

15.3.1 Thermal expansion of cement paste

The coefficient of thermal expansion of hcp varies between about 10 and 20 $\times 10^{-6}$ per °C, depending mainly on the moisture content. Figure 15.11 shows typical behaviour, with the coefficient reaching a maximum at about 70% rh. The value at 100% rh, i.e. about 10×10^{-6} per °C, probably represents the 'true' inherent value for the paste itself. The time-dependence of the behaviour is demonstrated by the initial expansion on an increase in temperature showing some reduction over a few hours with the temperature held constant.

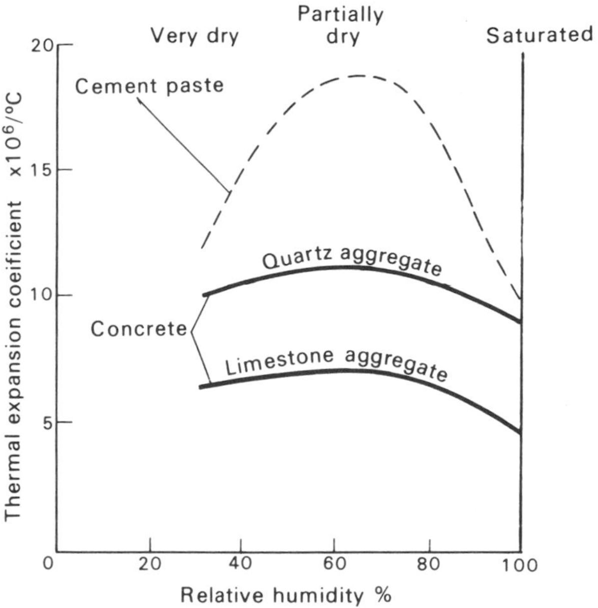

FIGURE 15.11 The effect of dryness on the thermal expansion of hardened cement paste and concrete (Meyers, 1950).

Explanations for this behaviour have all involved the role of water, and relate to the disturbance of the equilibrium between the water vapour, the free water, the freely adsorbed water, the water in areas of hindered adsorption and the forces between the layers of gel solids. Any disturbances will have a greater effect at intermediate humidities, when there is a substantial amount of water present with space in which to move. On an increase in temperature, the surface tension of the capillary water will decrease, and hence its internal tension and the corresponding compression in the solid phases will decrease, causing extra swelling, as observed. However, changes in internal energy with increased or decreased temperature will stimulate internal flow of water, causing the time-dependent volume change in the opposite sense to the initial thermal movement mentioned above.

15.3.2 Thermal expansion of concrete

The thermal expansion coefficients of the most common rock types used for concrete aggregates vary between about 6 and 10×10^{-6} per °C, i.e. lower than either the 'true' or 'apparent' values for cement paste. The thermal expansion coefficient for the concrete is therefore lower than that for cement paste, as shown in Figure 15.11. Furthermore, since the aggregate occupies 70 to 80% of the total concrete volume, there is a considerable reduction of the effects of humidity that are observed in the paste alone, to the extent that a constant coefficient of thermal expansion over all humidities is a reasonable approximation. The value depends on the concrete mix proportions, chiefly the cement paste content, and the aggregate type; for normal mixes the latter tends to dominate. Figure 15.12 shows the thermal expansion coefficient for the concrete plotted against that for the aggregate.

Values such as those given in Figure 15.12 apply over a temperature range of about 0 to 60°C. At higher temperatures, the differential stresses set up by the different thermal expansion coefficients of the paste and aggregate can lead to internal microcracking and hence non-linear behaviour. We shall discuss this further when considering fire damage in Chapter 17.

15.4 Stress–strain behaviour

15.4.1 Elasticity of the hardened cement paste

Hardened cement paste has a near linear compressive stress–strain relationship for most of

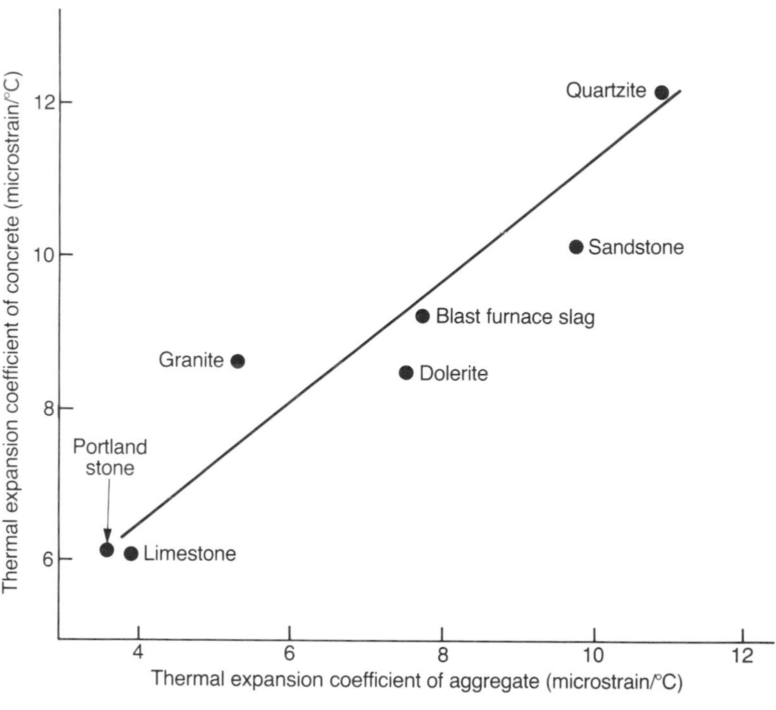

FIGURE 15.12 Thermal expansion of concrete made from different aggregates (aggregate : cement = 6 : 1) (Bonner and Harper, 1951).

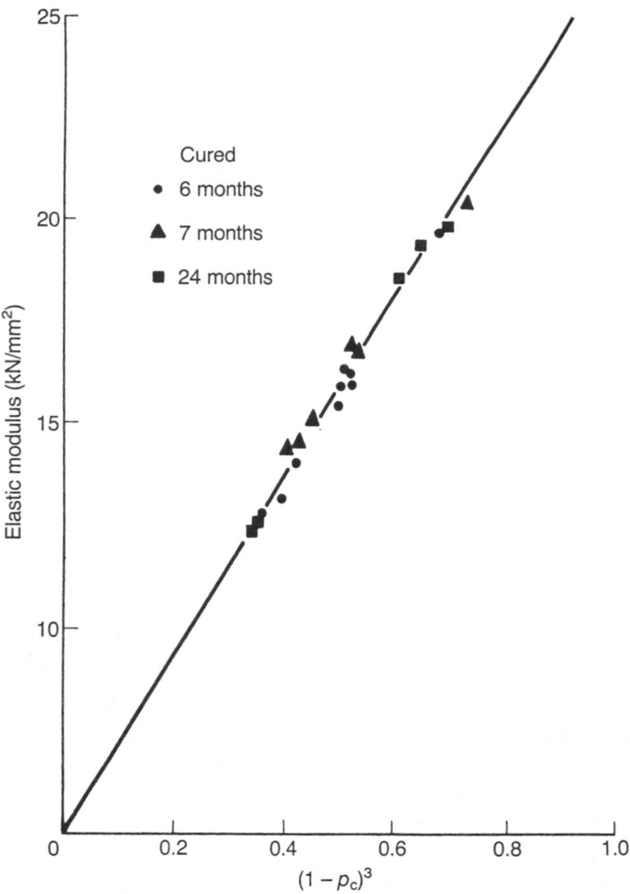

FIGURE 15.13 The effect of capillary porosity on the elastic modulus of hardened cement paste (Helmuth and Turk, 1966).

its range and therefore a modulus of elasticity can readily be determined from stress–strain data. Water-saturated pastes generally have a slightly higher modulus than dried pastes, indicating that some of the load is carried by the water in the pores. Nevertheless, the skeletal lattice of the paste carries most of the load, and the elastic response is governed by the lattice properties. As might therefore be expected, the elastic modulus (E_p) is highly dependent on the capillary porosity (p_c), as shown in Figure 15.13, and the relationship can be expressed as

$$E_p = E_g(1 - p_c)^3 \qquad (15.4)$$

where E_g is the modulus when $p_c = 0$, i.e. it represents the modulus of elasticity of the gel itself.

This is a parallel expression to eqn (13.10) for the strength of the paste, and therefore it is to be expected that the same factors will influence both strength and modulus. This is indeed the case; for example, Figure 15.14 shows that decreasing water/cement ratio and increasing age both increase the elastic modulus, a directly comparable effect to that on strength shown in Figure 13.8.

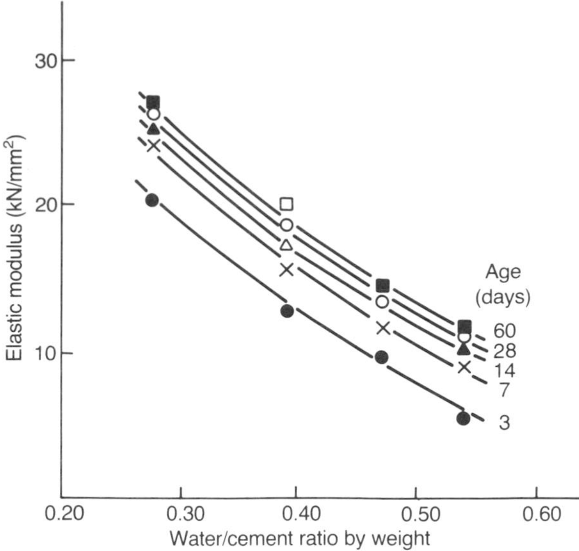

FIGURE 15.14 Effect of water/cement ratio and age on the elastic modulus of hardened cement paste (Hirsch, 1962).

15.4.2 Models for concrete behaviour

Concrete is, of course, a composite multiphase material, and its elastic behaviour will depend on the elastic properties of the individual phases – unhydrated cement, cement gel, water, coarse and fine aggregate – and their relative proportions and geometrical arrangements. The real material is too complex for rigorous analysis, but if it is considered as a two-phase material consisting of hcp and aggregate, then analysis becomes possible, and instructive.

The model for the concrete behaviour requires the following.

1. The property values for the phases; in this simple analysis, three are sufficient:
   (a) the elastic modulus of the aggregate, E_a;
   (b) the elastic modulus of the hcp, E_p; and
   (c) the volume concentration of the aggregate, g.
2. A suitable geometrical arrangement of the phases; three possibilities are shown in Figure 15.15. All the models consist of unit cubes. Models A and B have the phases arranged as adjacent layers, the difference being that in A the two phases are in parallel, and therefore undergo the same strain, whereas in B the phases are in series and are therefore subjected to the same stress. Model C has the aggregate set within the paste such that its height and base area are both equal to $\sqrt{g}$, thus complying with the volume requirements. This intuitively is more satisfactory in that it bears a greater resemblance to concrete.

Analysis of the models is not intended to give any detail of the actual distribution of stresses and strains within the concrete, but to predict average or overall behaviour. Three further assumptions are necessary for the analysis which follows:

1. the applied stress remains uniaxial and compressive throughout the model;

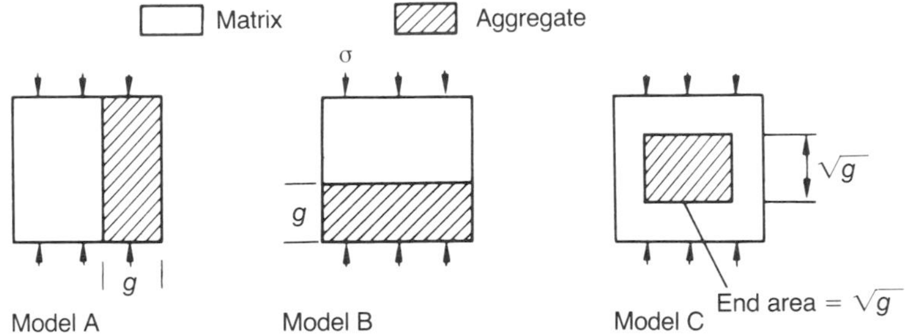

FIGURE 15.15 Simple two-phase models for concrete (Hansen (1960) and Counto (1964)).

2. the effects of lateral continuity between the layers can be ignored;
3. any local bond failure or crushing does not contribute to the deformation.

Model A

Strain compatibility
The strain in the concrete, ε_c, is equal to the strain in the aggregate, ε_a, and the paste, ε_p, i.e.

$$\varepsilon_c = \varepsilon_a = \varepsilon_p. \quad (15.5)$$

Equilibrium
The total force is the sum of the forces on each of the phases. Expressed in terms of stresses and areas this gives

$$\sigma_c \cdot 1 = \sigma_a \cdot g + \sigma_p \cdot (1 - g). \quad (15.6)$$

Constitutive relations
Both of the phases and the concrete are elastic, hence

$$\sigma_c = \varepsilon_c \cdot E_c \qquad \sigma_a = \varepsilon_a \cdot E_a$$
$$\sigma_p = \varepsilon_p \cdot E_p. \quad (15.7)$$

Substituting into eqn (15.6) from eqn (15.7) gives

$$\varepsilon_c \cdot E_c = \varepsilon_a \cdot E_a \cdot g + \varepsilon_p \cdot E_p \cdot (1 - g)$$

and hence, from eqn (15.5)

$$E_c = E_a \cdot g + E_p \cdot (1 - g). \quad (15.8)$$

Model B

Equilibrium
The stresses in both phases and the composite are equal, i.e.

$$\sigma_c = \sigma_a = \sigma_p. \quad (15.9)$$

Strains
The total displacement is the sum of the displacements in each of the phases; expressed in terms of strain this gives

$$\varepsilon_c = \varepsilon_a \cdot g + \varepsilon_p \cdot (1 - g). \quad (15.10)$$

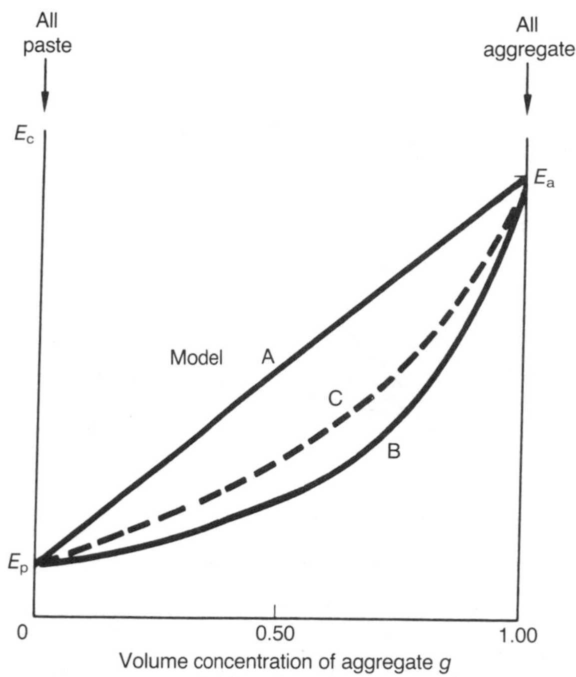

FIGURE 15.16 The effect of volume concentration of aggregate on elastic modulus of concrete calculated from simple two-phase models.

Substituting from eqns (15.7) and (15.9) into (15.10) and rearranging gives

$$\frac{1}{E_c} = \frac{g}{E_a} + \frac{(1 - g)}{E_p}. \quad (15.11)$$

Model C

This is a combination of two layers of hcp alone in series with a third layer of hcp and aggregate in parallel, as in model A. Repetition of the above two analyses with substitution of the appropriate geometry and combination gives:

$$\frac{1}{E_c} = \frac{(1 - \sqrt{g})}{E_p} + \frac{\sqrt{g}}{E_a \cdot \sqrt{g} + E_p \cdot (1 - \sqrt{g})} \quad (15.12)$$

Figure 15.16 shows the predicted results from the three models for varying aggregate concentrations and typical relative values of E_p

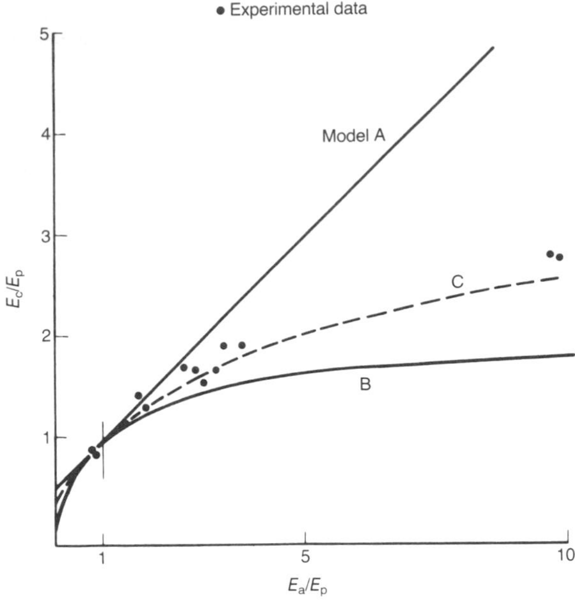

FIGURE 15.17 Prediction of elastic modulus of concrete (E_c) from the modulus of the cement paste (E_p) and the aggregate (E_a) for 50% volume concentration of aggregate.

and E_a. Models A and B give upper and lower bounds respectively to the concrete modulus, with model C giving intermediate values. The effect of aggregate stiffness is shown in non-dimensional form in Figure 15.17, on which some typical experimental results are also plotted. It is clear that with soft aggregates in which $E_a/E_p < 1$, e.g. lightweight aggregates, all three models give a reasonable fit, but for normal aggregates which are stiffer than the paste, i.e. $E_a/E_p > 1$, model C is preferable.

15.4.3 Observed stress–strain behaviour of concrete

The stress–strain behaviour of both the hcp and aggregate is substantially linear over most of the range up to maximum. However, the composite concrete, although showing intermediate stiffness as predicted from the above analysis, is markedly non-linear over most of its length (Figure 15.18(a)). Furthermore, successive unloading/loading cycles to stress levels below

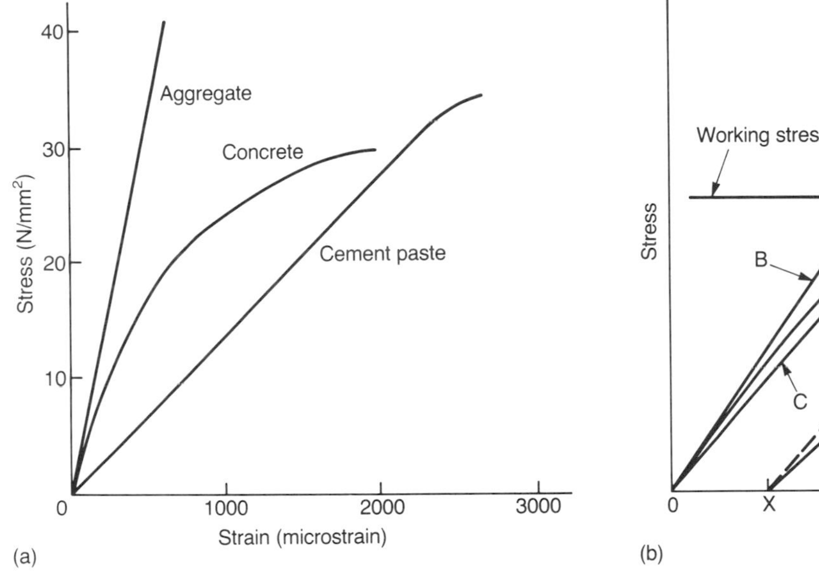

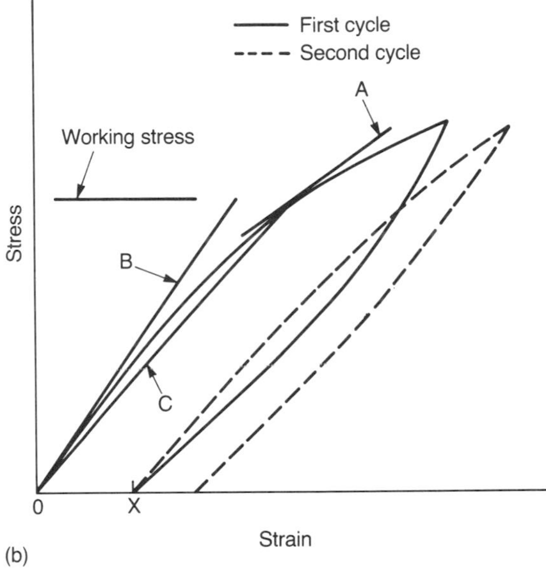

FIGURE 15.18 Stress–strain relationships for cement paste, aggregates and concrete: (a) typical behaviour of hcp, aggregate and concrete (Neville, 1971); (b) typical short-term behaviour of concrete.

ultimate show substantial, but diminishing, hysteresis loops, and residual strains at zero load (Figure 15.18(b)).

The explanation for this behaviour lies in the contribution of microcracking to the overall concrete strains, i.e. assumption (3) in the above analysis is invalid. As we have seen in Chapter 13, the transition zone between the aggregate and the hcp or mortar is a region of relative weakness, and in fact some microcracks will be present in this zone even before loading. The number and width of these will depend on such factors as bleeding characteristics and the amount of drying or thermal shrinkage. As the stress level increases, these cracks will increase in length, width and number, causing progressively increasing non-linear behaviour. This eventually leads to complete breakdown and failure, and therefore we will postpone more detailed discussion of cracking until the next chapter.

Subsequent cycles of loading will not tend to produce or propagate as many cracks as the initial loading, provided the stress levels of the first or previous cycles are not exceeded. This explains the diminishing size of the hysteresis loops shown in Figure 15.18(b).

15.4.4 Elastic modulus of concrete

The non-linear stress–strain curve for concrete means that a number of different elastic modulus values can be defined. These include the slope of the tangent to the curve at any point (giving the **tangent modulus**) or the slope of the line between the origin and a point on the curve (giving the **secant modulus**).

Two types of test are used to determine the modulus, **static** and **dynamic**. A static test involves loading to a typical working stress, say 40% of ultimate, and measuring the corresponding strain. Cylindrical or prism specimens are usually used, loaded longitudinally, and with a length at least twice the lateral dimension. Strain measurements are usually taken over the central section of the specimen to avoid end effects. To minimize hysteresis effects, the specimens are normally subjected to a few cycles of load before the strain readings are taken over a load cycle lasting about five minutes. It is usual to calculate the static secant modulus (E_s) from these readings. (Line C in Figure 15.18b.)

The dynamic test is completely different in nature. A specimen, typically a 500 mm long by 100 mm square cross-section prism, is balanced at its mid-point and excited by a variable frequency electromagnetic exciter in contact with it at one end, as shown in Figure 15.19. A piezoeletric pick-up at the other end detects the induced vibrations, and the signal from this is amplified and displayed. The exciting frequency is varied until the fundamental resonant frequency (n) is obtained, indicated by maximum amplitude of the pick-up signal at the same

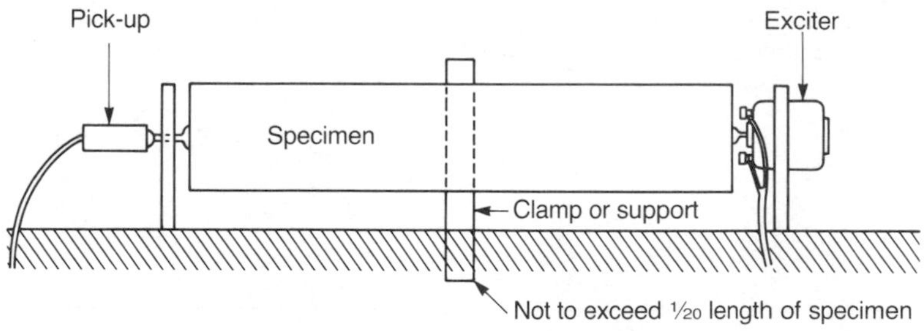

FIGURE 15.19 Test arrangement for the measurement of dynamic elastic modulus by longitudinal vibration (from BS 1881: Part 209: 1990).

frequency as the input signal. The dynamic elastic modulus (E_d) is then calculated from the formula:

$$E_d = 4 \cdot n^2 \cdot l^2 \cdot \rho \qquad (15.13)$$

where ρ is the density of the concrete and l the specimen length.

The dynamic modulus test gives reproducible results, and also benefits from being non-destructive. The forces applied to the concrete are extremely small, and so the problems of non-linearity in the static test do not arise. It is reasonable to assume that the value obtained approximates to the tangent modulus at the origin of the stress–strain curve. (Line B in Figure 15.18b.)

As might therefore be expected, the dynamic modulus is higher than the static secant modulus of the same concrete. Also, both will increase with age and decreasing water/cement ratio of the concrete, for the reasons outlined when discussing the paste modulus. The effects of these two factors combine into an increase of modulus with compressive strength, for example, in the relationships shown in Figure 15.20 between static and dynamic modulus and strength (British Standards Institution, 1985). Also shown is the expected range for values of the former, which is high mainly because of the likely variation of aggregate modulus. The advantage of the relationship shown in Figure 15.20 is that an estimate of modulus can be made for, say, initial design purposes, without any knowledge of the aggregate type or mix proportions. The disadvantage is the likely deviation of the modulus from this average figure

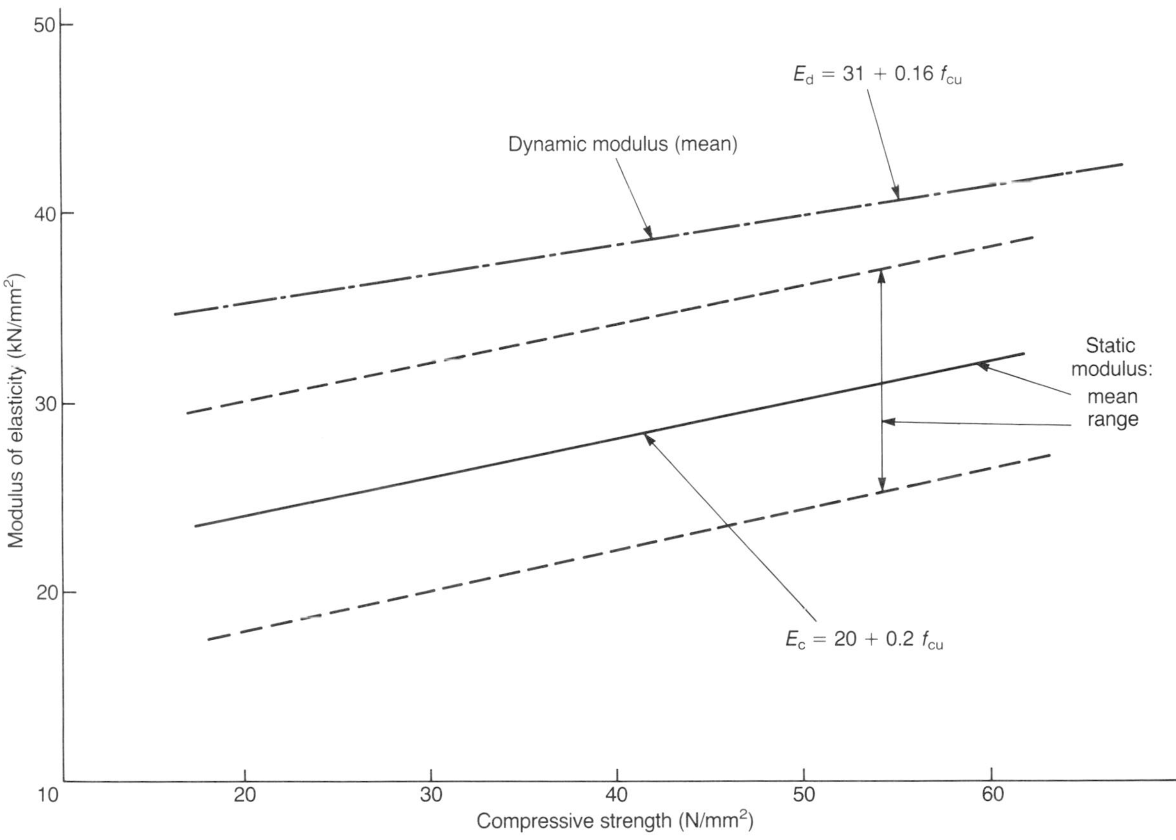

FIGURE 15.20 The relationship between compressive strength and static and dynamic elastic moduli of normal weight concrete (from BS 8110: Part 2: 1985).

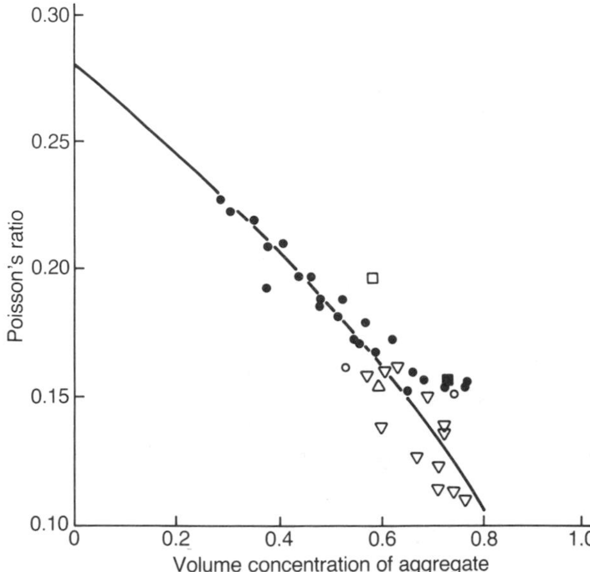

FIGURE 15.21 The effect of aggregate concentration on Poisson's ratio of concrete (gravel aggregates) (Anson and Newman, 1966).

in practice. Hence, if a more precise value of modulus is required, then either the analytical approach using the aggregate modulus and mix proportions, as outlined above, can be used, or specimens of concrete made with the particular aggregate should be tested.

15.4.5 Poisson's ratio

The Poisson's ratio of water-saturated cement paste varies between 0.25 and 0.3; on drying it reduces to about 0.2. It seems to be largely independent of water/cement ratio, age and strength. The addition of aggregate again modifies the behaviour, and for concrete lower values are obtained with increasing aggregate content, as shown in Figure 15.21.

15.5 Creep

The general nature of the creep behaviour of concrete was illustrated in Figure 15.1. The

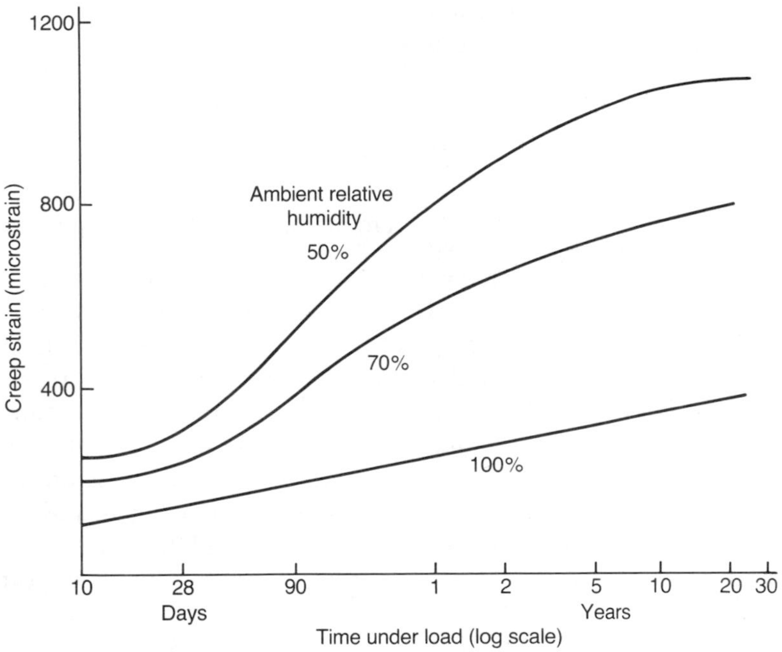

FIGURE 15.22 Creep of concrete moist-cured for 28 days, then loaded and stored at different relative humidities (Troxell *et al.*, 1958).

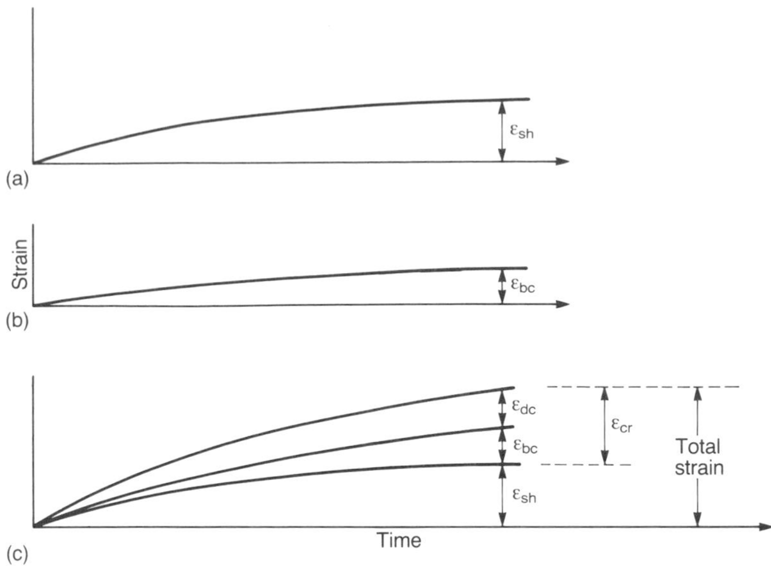

FIGURE 15.23 Definitions of shrinkage, creep and combined behaviour for hardened cement paste and concrete: (a) free shrinkage (no load); (b) basic creep (no drying); (c) loading and drying.

magnitude of the creep strains is as great or greater than the elastic strains on loading, and they therefore often have a highly significant influence on structural behaviour. Also, the creep does not appear to tend to a limit, as shown in Figure 15.22 for tests of 30 years duration. This figure also shows that the creep is substantially increased when the concrete is simultaneously drying, i.e. creep and shrinkage are interdependent. This leads to the definitions of creep strains shown in Figure 15.23. Free shrinkage (ε_{sh}) is defined as the shrinkage of the unloaded concrete in the drying condition, and basic creep (ε_{bc}) as the creep of a similar specimen under load but not drying, i.e. sealed so that there is no moisture movement to or from the surrounding environment. The total strain (ε_{tot}) is that measured on the concrete whilst simultaneously shrinking and creeping, and therefore, as stated above, it is found that

$$\varepsilon_{tot} > \varepsilon_{sh} + \varepsilon_{bc}. \qquad (15.14)$$

The difference, i.e. $\varepsilon_{tot} - (\varepsilon_{sh} + \varepsilon_{bc})$, is called the drying creep (ε_{dc}). It follows that the total creep strain (ε_{cr}) is given by

$$\varepsilon_{cr} = \varepsilon_{dc} + \varepsilon_{bc}. \qquad (15.15)$$

15.5.1 Factors influencing creep

Apart from the increase in creep with simultaneous shrinkage just described, the following factors have a significant effect on creep.

1. A reduced moisture content before loading, which reduces creep. In fact, completely dried concrete has very small, perhaps zero, creep.
2. The level of applied stress; for any given concrete and loading conditions, the creep is found to increase approximately linearly with the applied stress up to stress/strength ratios of about 0.4 to 0.6 (different studies have indicated different limits). It is therefore often useful to define the specific creep as the creep strain per unit stress in this region. At higher stress levels increased creep is observed.

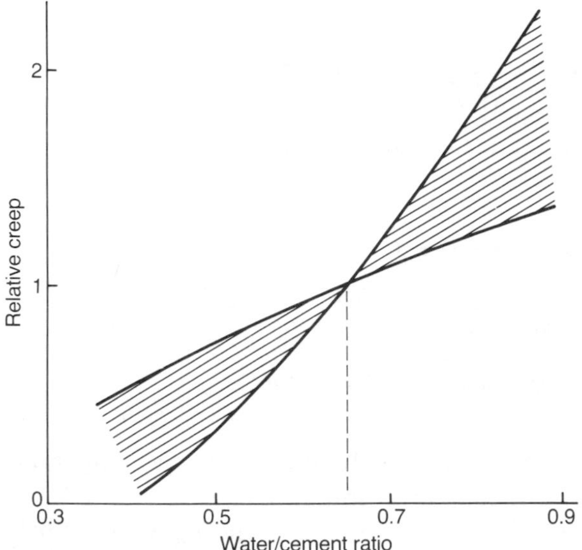

FIGURE 15.24 Range of results for effect of water/cement ratio on creep of concrete relative to creep at a water/cement ratio of 0.65 (Wagner (1958) quoted by Neville and Brooks (1987)).

3. Increasing concrete strength, which decreases the creep. This is illustrated in Figures 15.24 and 15.25, which show the effects of water/cement ratio and age at loading on relative creep values.
4. Increasing temperature, which increases the creep significantly (Figure 15.26).
5. The aggregate volume concentration, illustrated in Figure 15.27, which shows that the aggregate is inert as regards creep, and hence the creep of concrete is less than that of cement paste. This is therefore directly comparable to the shrinkage behaviour shown in Figure 15.7. Neville (1964) suggested a relationship between the creep of the concrete (C_c) and that of neat cement paste (C_p) of the form

$$C_c/C_p = (1 - g)^n \qquad (15.16)$$

where g = volume fraction of unhydrated cement and aggregate and n = constant.

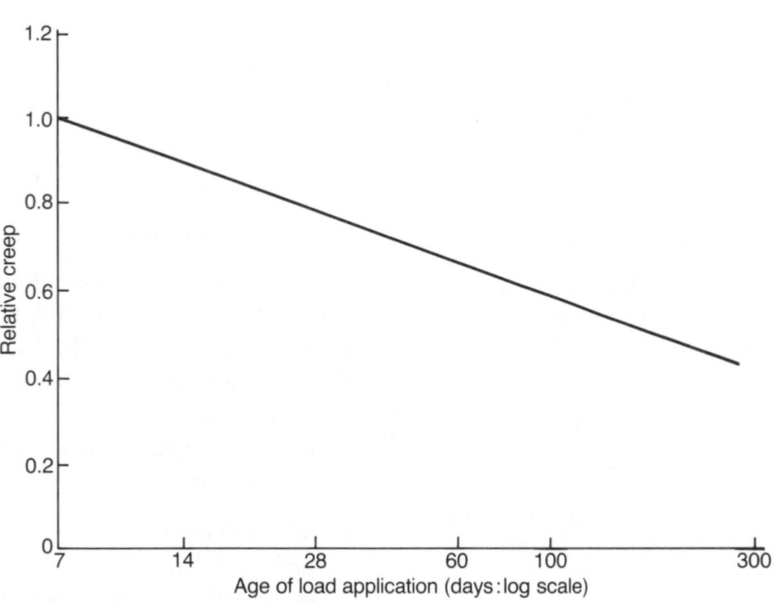

FIGURE 15.25 The effect of age at load application on creep of concrete stored at 75% relative humidity (creep relative to that for concrete loaded at seven days) (L'Hermite, 1959).

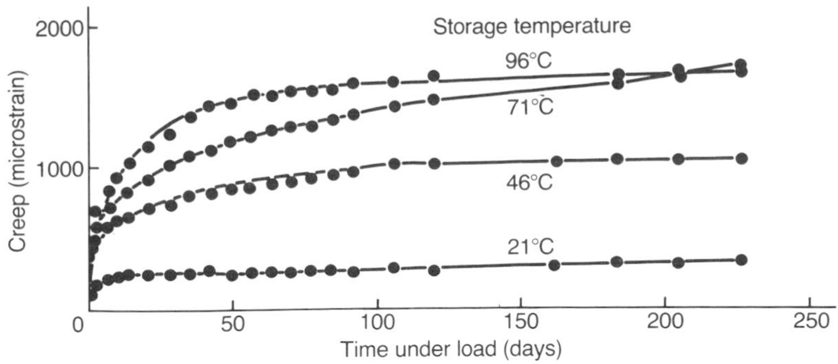

FIGURE 15.26 The effect of temperature on concrete creep (Nasser and Neville, 1965).

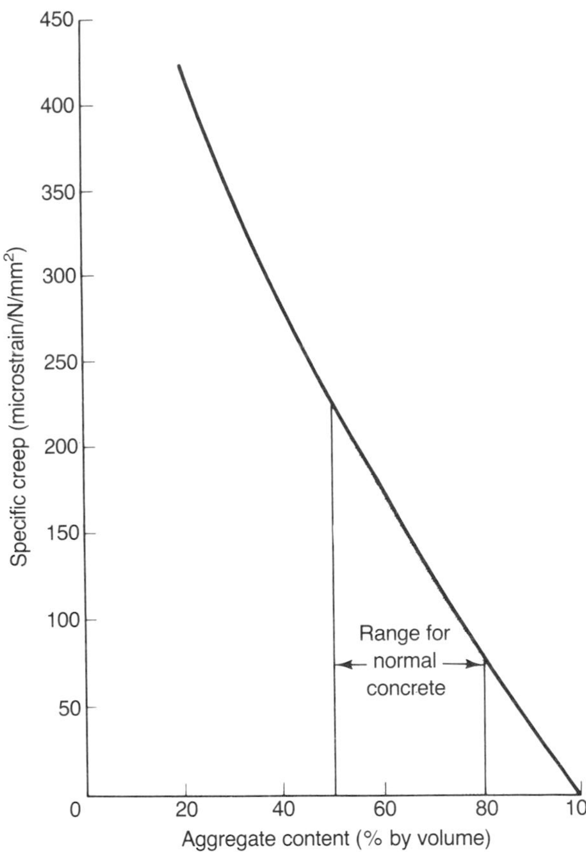

FIGURE 15.27 The effect of aggregate content of concrete on creep (Concrete Society, 1973).

Not surprisingly, this is directly comparable to eqn (15.2) for shrinkage.

6. The elastic modulus of the aggregate, shown in Figure 15.28, which is also comparable to the shrinkage behaviour (Figure 15.8).

15.5.2 Mechanisms of creep

Since the creep process is occurring within the cement paste, and the moisture content and movement have a significant effect on its magnitude, it is not surprising that the mechanisms proposed for creep have similarities with those proposed for shrinkage and discussed in Section 15.1.2. As with shrinkage, it is likely that a combination of the mechanisms now outlined is responsible.

Moisture diffusion

The applied stress causes changes in the internal stresses and strain energy within the hcp, resulting in an upset to the thermodynamic equilibrium; moisture then moves down the induced free energy gradient, implying a movement from smaller to larger pores, which can occur at several levels:

1. in capillary water as a rapid and reversible pressure drop;
2. in adsorbed water moving more gradually from zones of hindered adsorption – this movement should be reversible;

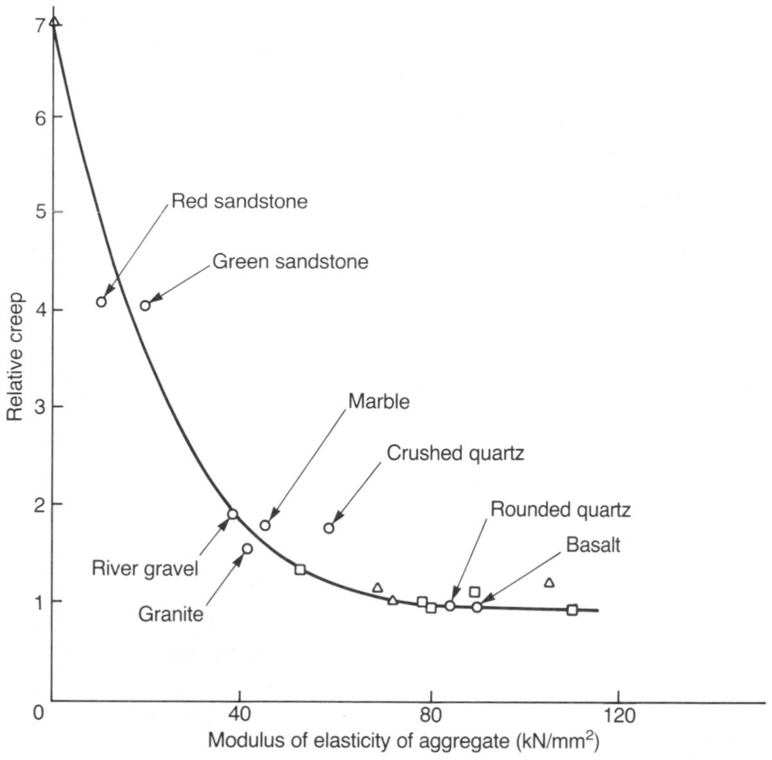

FIGURE 15.28 The effect of the modulus of elasticity of aggregate on relative creep of concrete (equals 1 for an aggregate with a modulus of 69 kN/mm^2, coarse aggregate content = 45–55% by volume) (Concrete Society, 1973).

3. in interlayer water in diffusing very slowly out of the gel pores. Some extra bonding may then develop between the solid layers, and so this process may not be completely recoverable.

In sealed concrete, there are always sufficient voids to allow the moisture movement, hence basic creep can occur with this mechanism. With simultaneous drying, all of the processes are much enhanced, hence explaining drying creep.

Structural adjustment

Stress concentrations arise throughout the hcp structure because of its heterogeneous nature, and consolidation to a more stable state without loss of strength occurs at these points by either:

1. viscous flow, with adjacent particles sliding past each other; or
2. local bond breakage, closely followed by reconnection nearby after some movement.

Concurrent moisture movement is assumed to disturb the molecular pattern, hence encouraging a greater structural adjustment. The mechanisms are essentially irreversible.

Microcracking

We have seen that hcp and concrete contain defects and cracks before loading, and propagation of these and the formation of new cracks will contribute to the creep strains, particularly at higher levels of stress. This is the most likely explanation of the non-linearity of creep strain with stress at high stress levels. In a drying concrete, the stress gradient arising from the moisture gradient is likely to enhance the cracking.

Delayed elastic strain

The 'active' creeping component of the hcp or concrete, i.e. mainly the water in its various forms in the capillary or gel pores, will be acting in parallel with inert material that will undergo elastic response only. In hcp this will be solid gel particles, the unhydrated cement particles, and the calcium hydroxide crystals, augmented in concrete with the aggregate particles. The stress in the creeping material will decline as the load is transferred to the inert material, which then deforms elastically as its stress gradually increases. The process acts in reverse on removal of the load, so that the material finally returns to its unstressed state; thus the delayed elastic strain would be fully recoverable in this model.

15.5.3 Prediction of creep

As with shrinkage, it is often necessary to estimate the likely magnitude of the creep of a structural element at the design stage. There are several methods available for this; all are based on empirical data, and take into account the main factors that influence creep, i.e. age, strength and modulus of elasticity of the concrete at loading, ambient humidity, member size and applied stress. A good example of such a method is included in The British Standard Code of Practice for Structural Concrete (BS 8110: 1985).

The ultimate (30-year) creep strain (ε_{cc}) is calculated from the expression:

$$\varepsilon_{cc} = \frac{\text{Applied stress}}{E_{c,t}} \times \phi \qquad (15.17)$$

where $E_{c,t}$ = elastic modulus of the concrete at the age of loading, t, and ϕ = 30-year creep coefficient.

For normal weight concrete $E_{c,t}$ can be calculated from the expression:

$$E_{c,t} = E_{c,28}(0.4 + 0.6f_{cu,t}/f_{cu,28}) \qquad (15.18)$$

where $f_{cu,28}$ = compressive cube strength at 28

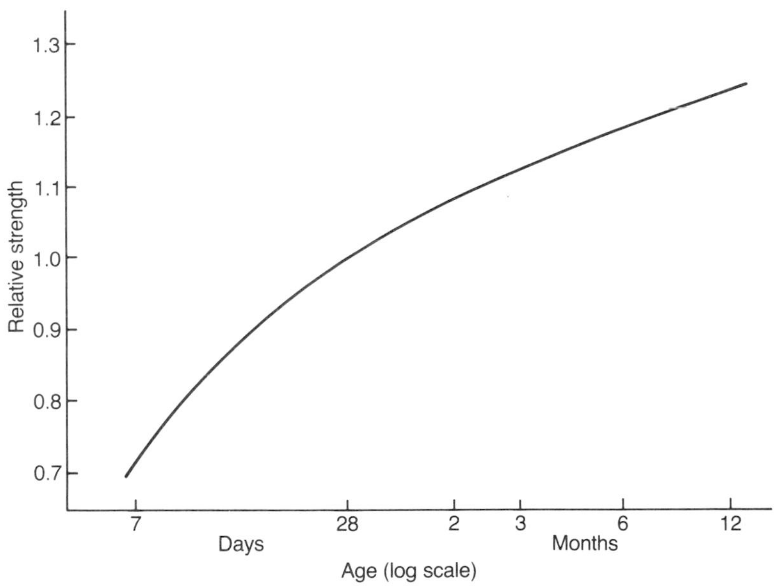

FIGURE 15.29 The development of compressive strength of concrete relative to strength at 28 days (from BS 8110: Part 2: 1985).

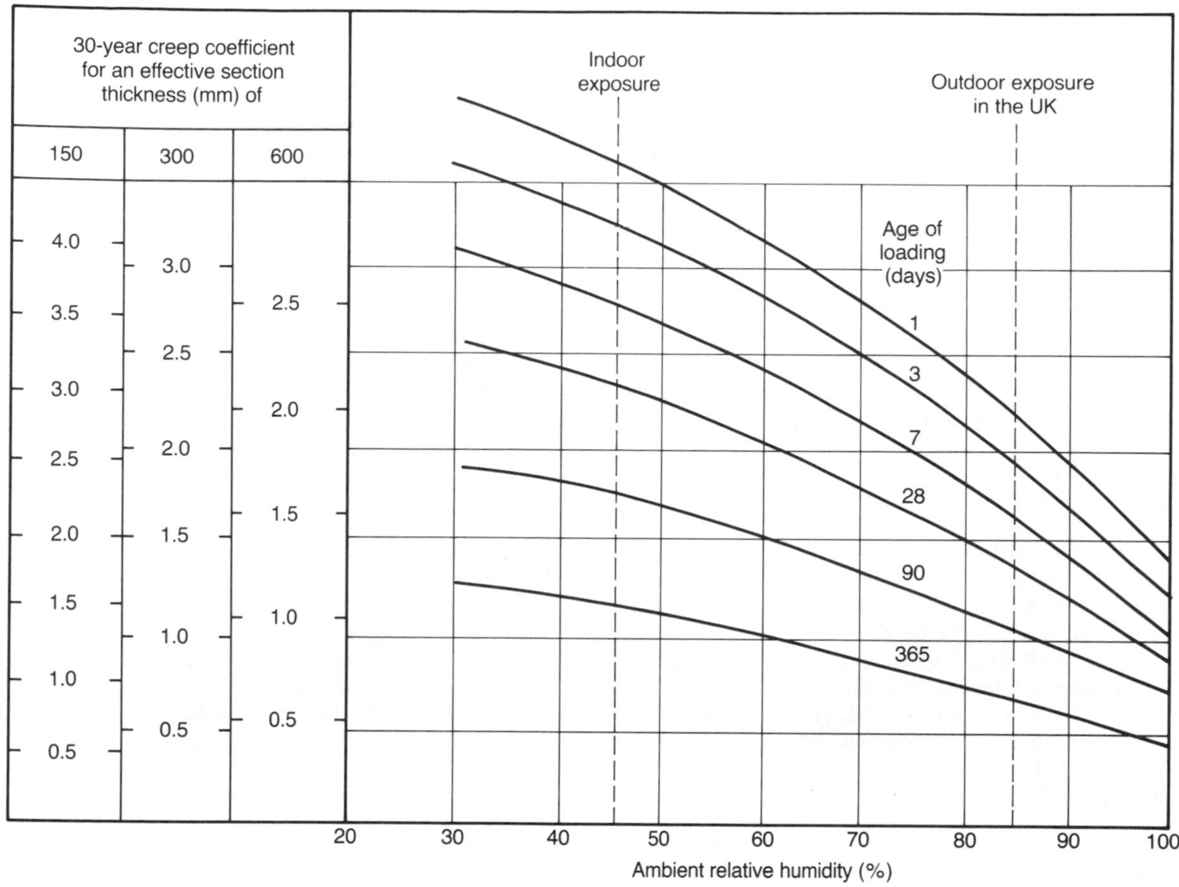

FIGURE 15.30 Prediction of creep coefficient for normal weight concrete (from BS 8110: Part 2: 1985).

days, $f_{cu,t}$ = compressive cube strength at the age of loading, t, which can be found from the 28-day cube strength by the relationship shown in Figure 15.29, and $E_{c,28}$ = elastic modulus of the concrete at 28 days, which can be obtained from the cube strength by the relationship shown in Figure 15.20, i.e.

$$E_{c,28} = 20 + 0.2 f_{cu,28} \qquad (15.19)$$

If the concrete contains lightweight aggregate, then the value obtained for $E_{c,t}$ should be multiplied by $(\rho/2400)^2$, where ρ is the density of the concrete.

The 30-year creep coefficient, ϕ, is obtained from Figure 15.30 for the particular effective section thickness (defined as twice the cross-sectional area divided by the exposed perimeter) and ambient relative humidity. If drying is prevented by immersion in water or by sealing, the effective section thickness should be taken as 600 mm. If estimates of creep at earlier times are required, then it is assumed that 40%, 60% and 80% of the 30-year creep occur in the first month, six months and 30 months under load respectively.

15.6 References

Anson, M. and Newman, K. (1966) *Magazine of Concrete Research*, 18, 125.

Bazant, Z.P. (1972) *Cement and Concrete Research*, **2**, 1–16.

Blaine, R.L. (1968) *International Colloquium on the Shrinkage of Neat Cements and Concretes*, RILEM/Cembureau, Madrid, Paper I-M.

Bonner, D.C.R. and Harper, F.C. (1951) *National Building Studies*, Technical Paper No. 7, HMSO, London.

British Standards Institution (1990) BS 1881: *Methods of testing concrete. Part 209: Recommendations for the measurement of dynamic modulus of elasticity.*

British Standards Institution (1985) BS 8110: *Structural use of concrete. Part 2: Code of practice for special circumstances.*

Concrete Society (1973) *The Creep of Structural Concrete*, Technical Report No. 101, London.

Counto, U.J. (1964) *Magazine of Concrete Research*, **16**, No. 48, Sept., pp. 129–38.

Feldman, R.F. and Sereda, P.J. (1970) *Engng J.*, **53**, 53–9.

Hansen, T.C. (1960) *Proceedings of Swedish Cement and Concrete Research Institute*, **31**.

Helmuth, R.A. and Turk, D.M. (1966) *Symposium on Structure of Portland Cement Paste*, Highway Research Board, Special Report 90, National Academy of Sciences, Washington.

Helmuth, R.A. and Turk, D.M. (1967) *Journal of the Portland Cement Association*, Research and Development Laboratories, **9**.

Hirsch, T.J. (1962) *Proc. Amer. Conc. Inst.*, **59**, March, 427.

Ishai, O. (1965) *Proceedings of the Conference on Structure of Concrete and Its Behaviour Under Load*, Cement and Concrete Association, London, Sept., pp. 345–64.

L'Hermite, R. (1959) *RILEM Bulletin*, No. 1, 21–5, Paris, March.

Meyers, S.L. (1950) *Proceedings of the Highway Research Board*, **30**, 193.

Mindess, S. and Young, J.F. (1981) *Concrete*, Prentice-Hall, New Jersey.

Nasser, K.W. and Neville, A.M. (1965) *Proc. Amer. Conc. Inst.*, **62**, pp. 1527–79.

Neville, A.M. (1964) *Magazine of Concrete Research*, **16**, No. 46, March, 21–30.

Neville, A.M. (1971) *Amer. Conc. Inst. Monograph*, Hardened Concrete: Physical and Mechanical Properties, Detroit, **6**, p. 100.

Neville, A.M. and Brooks, J.J. (1987) *Concrete Technology*, Longman Scientific and Technical, Harlow.

Pickett, G. (1956) *J. Amer. Conc. Inst.*, **52**, 581–90.

Powers, T.C. (1965) *Proceedings of the Conference on Structure of Concrete and Its Behaviour Under Load*, Cement and Concrete Association, London, Sept., pp. 319–44.

Soroka, I. (1979) *Portland Cement Paste and Concrete*, Macmillan, London.

Troxell, G.E., Raphael, J.M. and Davis, R.E. (1958) *Proc. Amer. Soc. Test and Mater.*, **58**, 1101–20.

Verbeck, G.J. and Helmuth, R.A. (1968) *Proceedings of the Symposium on the Chemistry of Cement*, Tokyo, **3**, pp. 1–37.

Wagner, O. (1958) *Deutscher Auschuss fur Stahlbeton*, No. 131, 74.

Wittman, F.H. (1968) *Mater. Struct.*, **1**, No. 6, 547–52.

Chapter sixteen

Strength and failure of concrete

16.1 Strength tests
16.2 Factors influencing strength
16.3 Cracking and fracture in concrete
16.4 Strength under multiaxial loading
16.5 References

Strength is probably the most important single property of concrete, since the first consideration in structural design is that the structural elements must be capable of carrying the imposed loads. The maximum value of stress in a loading test is usually taken as the strength, even though under compressive loading the test piece is still whole (with substantial internal cracking) at this stress, and complete breakdown subsequently occurs at higher strains and lower stresses. Strength is also important because it is related to several other important properties which are more difficult to measure directly, and a simple strength test can give an indication of these properties. For example, we have already seen the relation of strength to elastic modulus; we shall discuss durability in the next chapter, but in many cases a low permeability, low porosity concrete is the most durable, and, as discussed when we considered the strength of cement paste in Chapter 13, this also means it has high strength.

In structural situations concrete will be subject to one of a variety of types of loading, resulting in different modes of failure. Knowledge of the relevant strength is therefore important; for example, in columns or reinforced concrete beams, the compressive strength is required; for cracking of a concrete slab the tensile strength is important. Other situations may require torsional strength, fatigue or impact strength or strength under multiaxial loading. As we shall see, most strength testing involves the use of a few, relatively simple tests, generally not related to a particular structural situation. Procedures enabling data from the tests described in this chapter to be used in design have been obtained from empirical test programmes at an engineering scale on large specimens. The reader is referred to texts on structural design for a description of these design procedures.

In discussing aggregates in Chapter 13, we introduced a three-phase model for concrete – the phases being the hardened cement paste, the aggregate and the transition zone between the two. It is useful to have this model in mind when considering strength since the transition zone (about 50 μm wide) is generally the weakest phase, and cracking and failure initiate within this. In fact in many cases, such as after drying shrinkage, there will be cracks present before loading. As loading increases, either in tension or compression, cracks in the transition zone propagate into the hcp, resulting in paths through

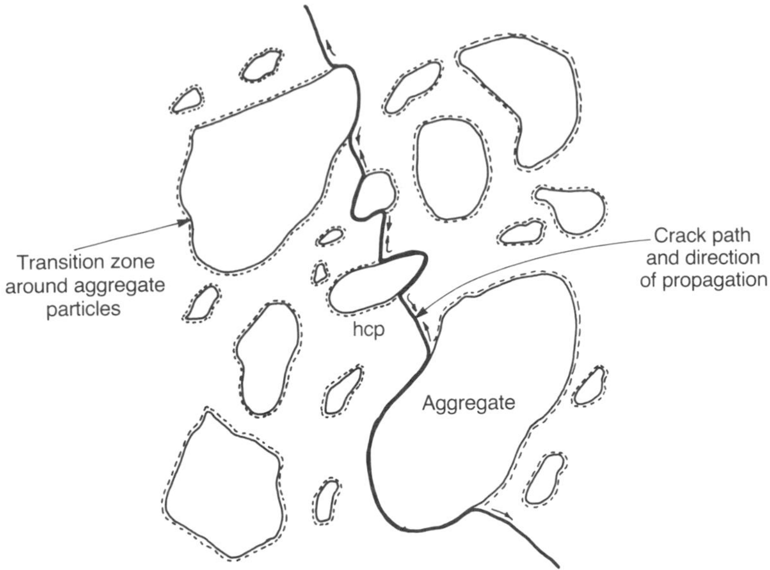

FIGURE 16.1 Typical crack path through normal-strength concrete.

the concrete such as that shown in Figure 16.1.

In this chapter we shall describe the most common test methods used to assess concrete strength, discuss the factors influencing the results obtained from them, and then return to a more detailed consideration of the cracking and fracture processes taking place within the concrete. Finally, we shall briefly discuss strength under multiaxial loading situations.

16.1 Strength tests

16.1.1 Compressive strength

The simplest compressive strength test uses a concrete cube, and this is the standard test in the UK (BS 1881: 1983). The cube must be sufficiently large to ensure that an individual aggregate particle does not unduly influence the result; 100 mm is recommended for maximum aggregate sizes of 20 mm or less, 150 mm for maximum sizes up to 40 mm. The cubes are usually cast in lubricated steel moulds, accurately machined to ensure that opposite faces are smooth and parallel. The concrete is fully compacted by external vibration or hand tamping, and the top surface trowelled smooth. After demoulding when set, the cube is normally cured under water at constant temperature until testing.

The cube-testing machine has two heavy platens through which the load is applied to the concrete. The bottom one is fixed and the upper one has a ball seating which allows rotation to match the top face of the cube at the start of loading. This then locks in this position during the test. The load is applied to a pair of faces which were cast against the mould, i.e. with the trowelled face to one side. This ensures that there are no local stress concentrations which would result in a falsely low average failure stress. A very fast rate of loading gives overhigh strengths, and a rate to reach ultimate in a few minutes is recommended. It is vital that the cube is properly made and stored; only then will the test give a true indication of the properties of the concrete, unaffected by such factors as poor compaction, drying shrinkage cracking, etc.

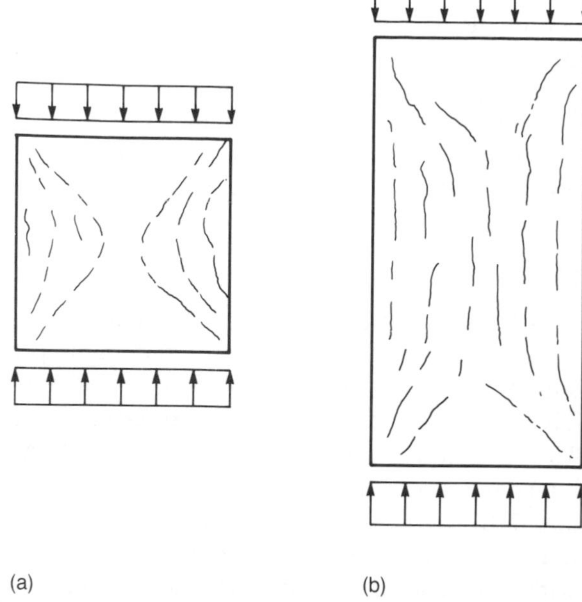

FIGURE 16.2 Cracking patterns during testing of concrete specimens in compression: (a) cube; (b) cylinder (height/diameter = 2).

The cracking pattern within the cube (Figure 16.2(a)) produces a double pyramid shape after failure. From this it is immediately apparent that the stress within the cube is far from uniaxial. The compressive load induces lateral tensile strains in both the steel platens and the concrete due to the Poisson effect. The mismatch between the elastic modulus of the steel and the concrete and the friction between the two result in lateral restraint forces in the concrete near the platen. This concrete is therefore in a triaxial stress state, with consequent higher failure stress than the true, unrestrained strength. This is the major objection to the cube test. The test is, however, relatively simple, and capable of comparing different concretes. (We shall consider triaxial stress states in more detail in Section 16.5).

An alternative test, which at least partly overcomes the restraint problem, uses cylinders; this is popular in North America and in many other parts of the world. Cylinders with a height/diameter ratio of 2, normally 300 mm high by 150 mm diameter, are tested vertically; the effects of end restraint are much reduced over the central section of the cylinder, which fails with near uniaxial cracking (Figure 16.2(b)), indicating that the failure stress is much closer to the uniaxial unconfined compressive strength. As a rule of thumb, it is generally assumed that the cylinder strength is about 80% of the cube strength, but this ratio has been found to depend on several factors, particularly the strength level. For example, L'Hermite (1955) has suggested a ratio of cylinder to cube strength (f_{cu} in N/mm^2) of

$$0.76 + 0.2 \log_{10}(f_{cu}/19.6). \qquad (16.1)$$

The general relationship of height/diameter ratio (h/d) to the strength of cylinders is shown in Figure 16.3. This is useful in, for example, interpreting the results from testing cores cut from a structure, where h/d often cannot be controlled. It is preferable to avoid an h/d ratio of less than 1, where sharp increases in strength are obtained, and high values, although giving closer estimates of the uniaxial strength, result

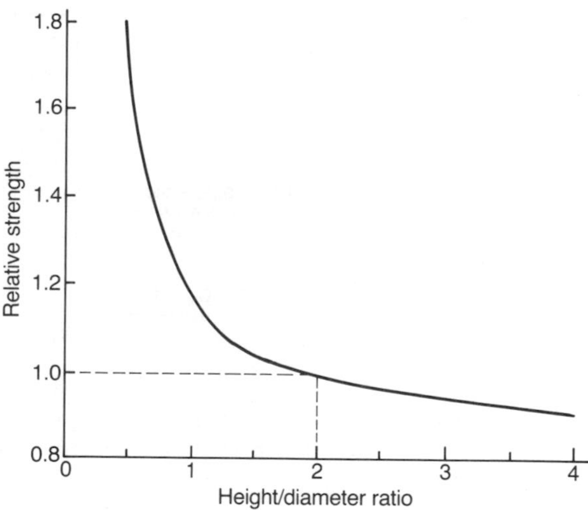

FIGURE 16.3 General relationship between height/diameter ratio and compressive strength of a concrete cylinder (Gonnerman, 1925).

in excessively long specimens which can fail due to slenderness ratio effects.

Testing cylinders has one major disadvantage; the top surface is finished by a trowel and is not plane and smooth enough for testing, and it therefore requires further preparation. It can be ground, but this is very time consuming, and the normal procedure is to cap it with a thin (2–3 mm) layer of a fluid cement paste of high early strength, applied a day or two in advance of the test. Apart from the inconvenience of having to carry this out, the failure load is sensitive to the capping, and therefore it is a source of potential error.

16.1.2 Tensile testing

Direct testing of concrete in uniaxial tension, as shown in Figure 16.4(a), is more difficult than for, say, steel or timber. Relatively large cross-sections are required to be representative of the concrete, and, because the concrete is brittle, it is difficult to grip and align. Eccentric loading and failure at or in the grips is then difficult to avoid. A number of gripping systems have been developed, but these are somewhat complex, and their use is confined to research laboratories. For more regular purposes, one of two indirect tests is preferred.

Flexural test

A rectangular prism, usually of square cross-section ($b \times d$) of side 100 or 150 mm, is simply supported over a span (L) of 400 or 600 mm. The load is applied at the third points (Figure 16.4(b)), and since the tensile strength of the concrete is much less than the compressive strength, failure occurs when a flexural tensile crack at the bottom of the beam, normally within the constant bending moment zone, propagates upwards through the beam. If the total failure load is P, and the maximum tensile stress

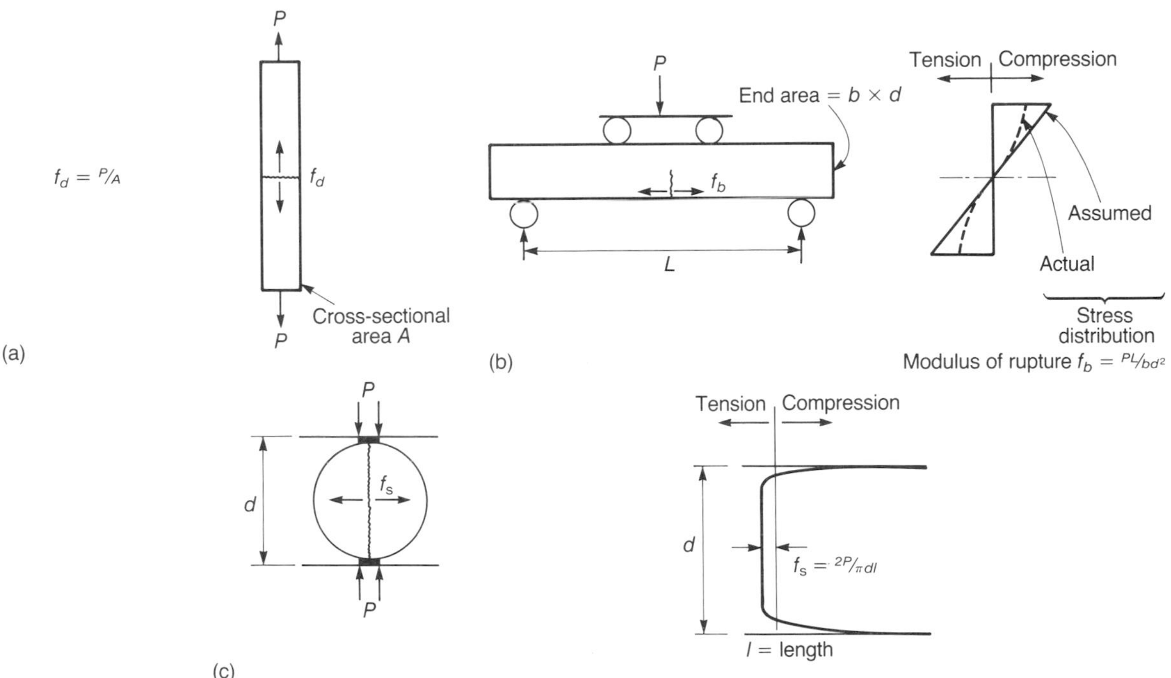

FIGURE 16.4 Tensile tests for concrete: (a) direct tension test; (b) flexural test; (c) splitting test.

in the concrete is f_b, then analysis based on simple beam-bending theory and linear elastic stress distribution up to failure gives

$$f_b = \frac{P \cdot L}{b \cdot d^2}. \qquad (16.2)$$

f_b is known (somewhat confusingly) as the **modulus of rupture**.

Since concrete is a non-linear material, the assumption of linear stress distribution is not valid, and the stress calculated from eqn (16.1) is higher than that actually developed in the concrete, as shown in Figure 16.4(b). The strain gradient in the specimen may also inhibit the crack growth. For both of these reasons the modulus of rupture is greater than the direct tensile strength.

Splitting test

A concrete cylinder, normally the same size as that used for compressive testing, i.e. 300 mm long (l) by 150 mm diameter (d), is placed on its side in a compression testing machine and loaded across its vertical diameter (Figure 16.4(c)). Hardboard or plywood strips are inserted between the cylinder and the platens to ensure even loading over the full length.

The theoretical distribution of horizontal stress on the plane of the vertical diameter, shown in Figure 16.4(c), is a near uniform tension (f_s), with local high compression stresses at the top and bottom. Failure occurs by a split or crack along this plane, the specimen falling into two neat halves. The cylinder splitting strength is defined as the magnitude of near uniform tensile stress on the vertical plane, which is given by

$$f_s = \frac{2 \cdot P}{\pi \cdot l \cdot d} \qquad (16.3)$$

The state of stress in the cylinder is biaxial rather than uniaxial, and this, together with the local zones of compressive stress at the extremes, results in the value of f_s being higher than the uniaxial tensile strength. However, the test is very easy to perform with standard equipment used for compressive strength testing, and gives consistent results; it is therefore very useful.

16.1.3 Relationship between strength measurements

The relationship between cube and cylinder strengths has already been discussed above.

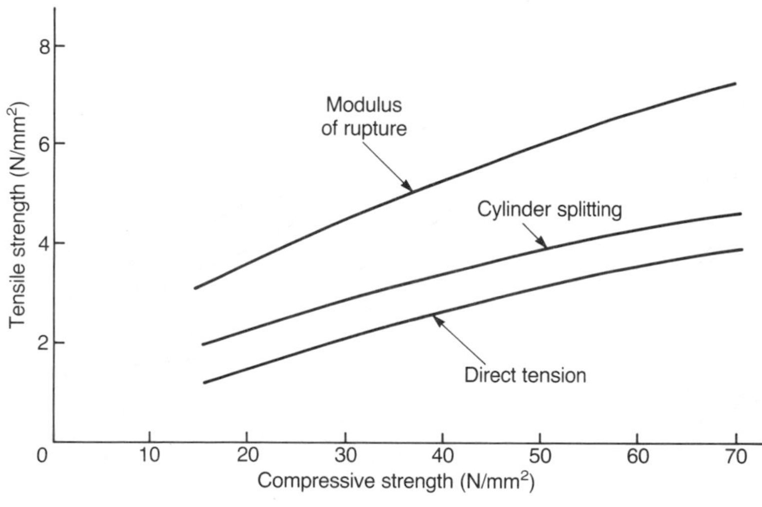

FIGURE 16.5 Typical relationships between tensile and compressive strengths of concrete (Carasquillo *et al.* (1981) and Price (1951)).

Typical relationships between direct and indirect tensile strengths and compressive strengths are shown in Figure 16.5, from which it can be seen that the ratio of each of the tensile strengths to the compressive strength depends on the strength level. The modulus of rupture gives the highest strength, varying between 10 and 20% of the cube strength (the higher value applies to lower strengths). The cylinder splitting strength is between 6.5 and 11% of the cube strength, and the direct tensile strength is the lowest of all, varying between about 6 and 8% of the cube strength.

16.2 Factors influencing strength

16.2.1 Water/cement ratio

In Chapter 13 we saw that the strength of cement paste is governed by its porosity, which in turn depends on the water/cement ratio and degree of hydration. Concrete strength depends on the strength of the paste, to a lesser extent on the aggregate properties, and, most importantly, the strength of the transition zone between the paste and the aggregate, as already discussed in Chapter 13. The strength of this zone is also dependent on the water/cement ratio, and therefore this is one of the main factors determining the concrete strength. This was first recognized

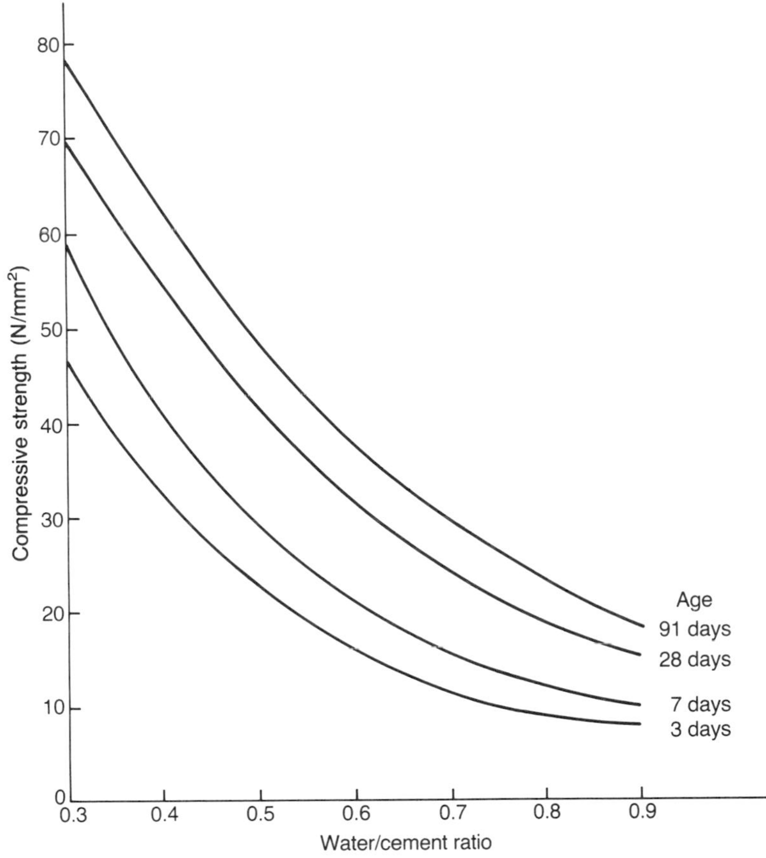

FIGURE 16.6 Typical effect of age and water/cement ratio on concrete strength (Portland cement, uncrushed aggregate) (Building Research Establishment, 1988).

by Abrams who, in 1918, demonstrated an inverse relationship with concrete strength (f_c) of the form:

$$f_c = \frac{k_1}{k_2} \text{ w/c} \qquad (16.4)$$

where w/c = water/cement ratio, and k_1 and k_2 are empirical constants which depend on age, curing regime, type of cement, amount of air entrainment, test method and, to a limited extent, aggregate type and size. This relationship has become known as Abrams' law, although it is not strictly a law, being based on empirical observations.

Most mix design methods use Abrams' law, or curves based on it, to estimate the water/cement ratio required for a given strength. Sets of curves are often used, such as those shown in Figure 16.6, derived from a widely used UK mix design method. The curves shown apply for concrete made with a typical Portland cement and 20 mm uncrushed gravel. In effect, the curves represent different combinations of k_1 and k_2, although these are not normally calculated.

It is important to recognize the limits of applicability to Abrams' law. Abrams himself showed the relationship was valid for water/cement ratios of up to 2 or more. However, at these high water/cement ratios the paste itself is extremely fluid, and it is very difficult to achieve a homogeneous, cohesive concrete without significant segregation. In practice, water/cement ratios in excess of 1 are rarely used.

At the other end of the scale, concretes with water/cement ratios less than about 0.3 are too dry to handle and compact efficiently, and even at values between 0.3 and about 0.4 the high cement content required for adequate workability may have undesirable side effects such as excessive temperature rise due to heat of hydration. It is, however, apparent from data such as those shown in Figure 13.7 that the paste itself is readily capable of achieving strengths of over 100 N/mm^2 at water/cement ratios of 0.3 or less, and in recent years it has been possible to produce concretes of such strengths by one or more of the following methods.

1. Using a plasticizer or superplasticizer to achieve adequate workability without excessive paste (and hence cement) content.
2. Incorporating a partial cement replacement material, which, whilst giving only a limited increase in the strength of the paste itself, seems to have a proportionally greater benefit to the strength of the transition zone, primarily a result of the long-term pozzolanic reaction. Microsilica at dosage levels of 5–10% cement replacement seems particularly beneficial.
3. Selection of the aggregate to have high inherent strength and good bond characteristics, already briefly mentioned in Chapter 13, and further discussed below.

With this approach, concretes with water/cement or cementitious material ratios of 0.26 or less and compressive strengths in excess of 130 N/mm^2 have been successfully produced and placed with conventional mixing, transporting and compaction methods, but with considerable attention given to high standards of site practice and supervision and quality control (A.C.I., 1984).

16.2.2 Effect of age

The degree of hydration increases with age, leading to the effect of age on strength apparent from Figure 16.6. It is important to remember that, as discussed in Chapter 13, the hydration reactions are never complete, and, in the presence of moisture, concrete will continue to gain strength for many years, although, of course, the rate of increase after such times will be very small.

16.2.3 Temperature

As we discussed in Chapter 14, a higher temperature maintained throughout the life of a

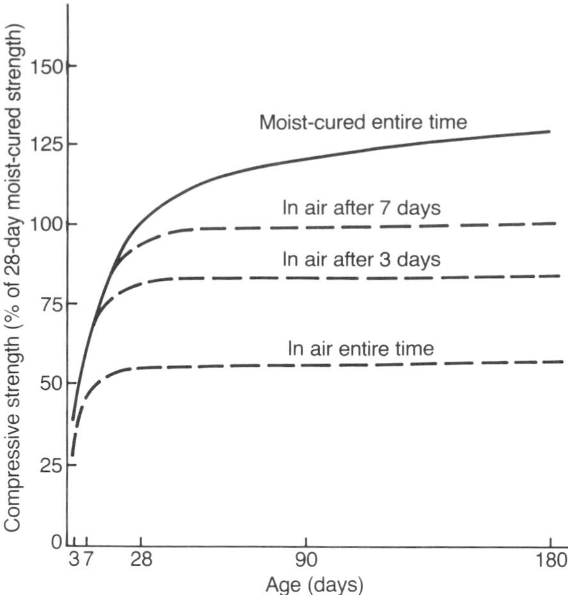

FIGURE 16.7 The influence of curing conditions on concrete strength (Portland Cement Association, 1968).

concrete will result in higher short-term strengths but lower long-term strengths. Also, an early age heating/cooling cycle from heat of hydration effects can lead to lower long-term strength, but the effect can be reduced or even eliminated by the incorporation of pulverized fuel ash or ground granulated blast furnace slag. We shall discuss the effect of transient high temperatures when considering the durability of concrete in fire in Chapter 17.

16.2.4 Humidity

The necessity of a humid environment for adequate curing has already been discussed; for this reason concrete stored in water will achieve a higher strength than if cured in air for some or all of its life, as shown in Figure 16.7. Also, specimens cured in water will show a significant increase in strength (5% or more) if allowed to dry out for a few hours before testing.

16.2.5 Aggregate properties, size and volume concentration

We have already seen that for normal aggregate it is the strength of the paste/aggregate bond or transition zone that has a dominant effect on concrete strength; the aggregate strength itself is generally significant only in very high strength concrete or with the relatively weaker lightweight aggregates. The transition zone properties are primarily dependent on the overall concrete properties (e.g. mix proportions, control of bleeding) rather than the aggregate properties, but Struble *et al.* (1980) have concluded that with some carbonate and siliceous aggregates there is evidence that the structure and chemistry of the transition zone are influenced by both the aggregate mineralogy and surface. Also, increased surface roughness can improve the bond, probably due to mechanical interlocking. For this reason, and also the increased mechanical interlocking of the aggregate particles themselves, concretes made with crushed rocks are typically some 15% stronger than those made with uncrushed gravels, provided all other mix proportions are the same.

The use of a larger maximum aggregate size reduces the concrete strength, again provided all other mix proportions are the same. The reduction is greater at lower water/cement ratios and larger aggregate sizes (Figure 16.8). The larger aggregates have a lower overall surface area with a weaker transition zone, and this has a more critical effect on the concrete strength at the lower water/cement ratios. In fresh concrete, the decreased surface area with the increased aggregate size leads to increased workability for the same mix proportions, and therefore for mix design at constant workability the water content can be reduced and a compensating increase in strength obtained.

Increasing the volumetric proportion of aggregate in the mix will, at constant water/cement ratio, produce a relatively small increase in concrete strength (Figure 16.9). This has been at-

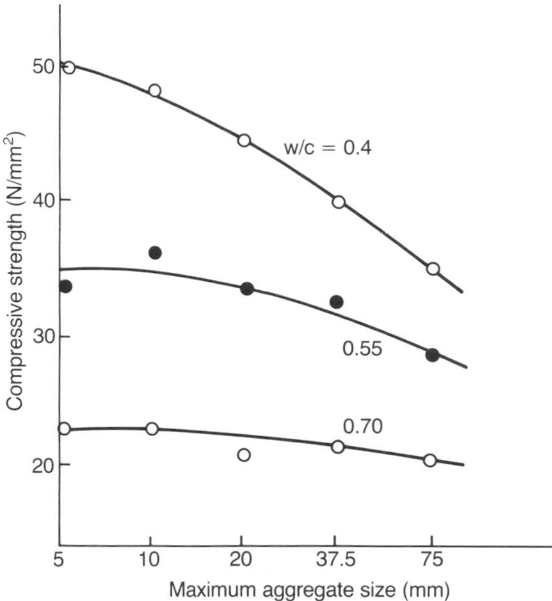

FIGURE 16.8 The effect of aggregate size and water/cement ratio on concrete strength (Cordon and Gillespie, 1963).

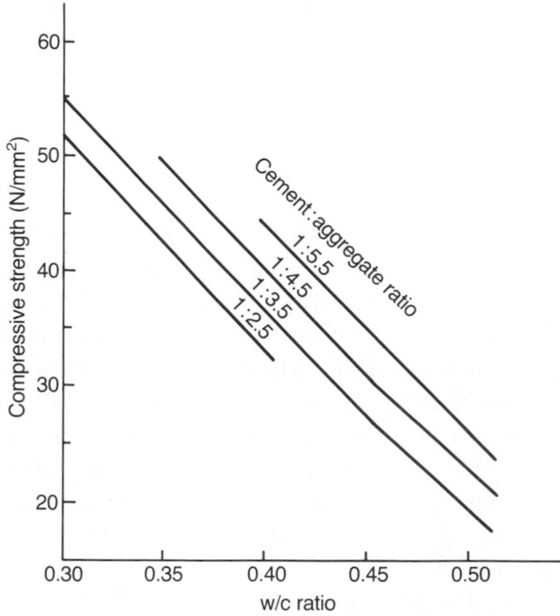

FIGURE 16.9 The effect of aggregate concentration and water/cement ratio on concrete strength (Erntroy and Shacklock, 1954).

tributed, at least in part, to the increase in aggregate concentration producing a greater number of secondary cracks prior to failure, which require greater energy, i.e. higher stress, to reach fracture. This effect is only valid if the paste content remains high enough to at least fill the voids in the coarse/fine aggregate system, thereby allowing complete consolidation of the concrete. This therefore imposes a maximum limit to the aggregate content for practical concretes.

16.3 Cracking and fracture in concrete

16.3.1 Development of microcracking

As we discussed in Chapter 15, the non-linear stress–strain behaviour of concrete in compression is largely due to the increasing contribution of microcracking to the strain with increasing load. Four stages of cracking behaviour have been identified, illustrated in Figure 16.10(a). Below 30% of ultimate load, the transition zone cracks remain stable, and the stress–strain curve remains approximately linear (Stage 1). As the stress increases beyond 30% of ultimate, the cracks begin to increase in length, width and number, causing non-linearity, but are still stable and confined to the transition zone (Stage 2). At loads above 50% ultimate (Stage 3), the cracks start to spread into the matrix and become unstable at loads approaching 75% ultimate, resulting in further deviation from linearity. Above 75% ultimate (Stage 4), spontaneous and unstable crack growth becomes increasingly frequent, leading to very high strains. Also at this stage the excessive cracking results in transverse strains increasing at a faster rate than the longitudinal strains, resulting in an overall increase in volume (Figure 16.10(b)).

Complete breakdown, however, does not occur until strains significantly higher than those at maximum load are reached. Figure 16.11 shows stress–strain curves from strain

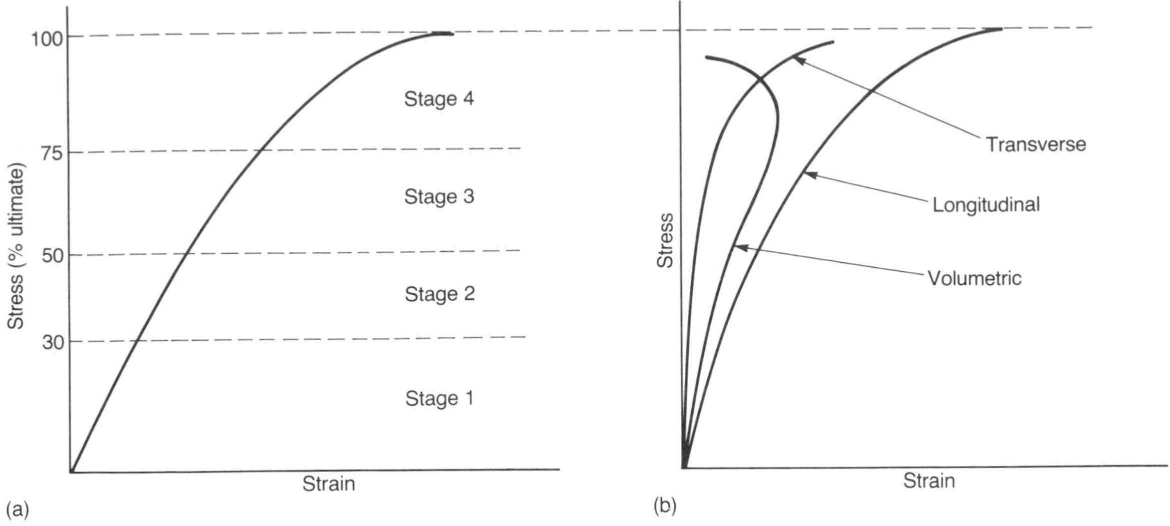

FIGURE 16.10 Stress–strain behaviour of concrete under compressive loading: (a) from Glucklich (1965); (b) from Newman (1966).

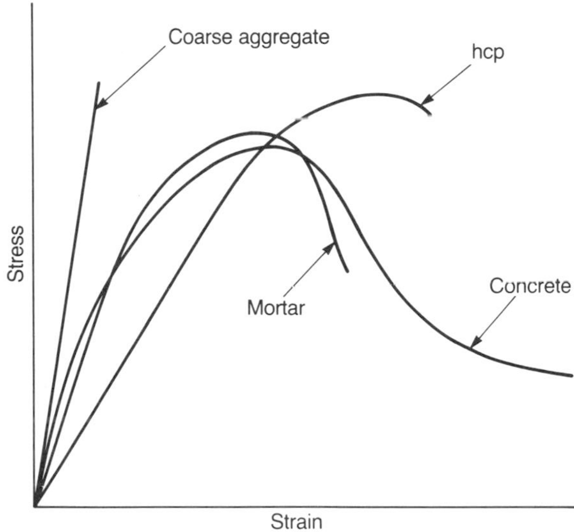

FIGURE 16.11 Typical stress–strain characteristics of aggregate, hardened cement paste, mortar and concrete under compressive loading (Swamy and Kameswara Rao, 1973).

controlled tests on paste, mortar and concrete. The hcp has a small descending branch after maximum stress; with the mortar it is more distinct, but with the concrete it is very lengthy. During the descending region, excess cracking and slip at the paste–aggregate interface are occurring before the cracking through the hcp is sufficiently well developed to cause complete failure.

16.3.2 Creep rupture

We discussed in Section 15.5.2 the contribution of microcracking to creep. This increases with stress level to the extent that if a stress sufficiently close to the short-term ultimate is maintained then failure will eventually occur, a process known as **creep rupture**. There is often an acceleration in creep rate shortly before rupture. The behaviour can be shown by stress–strain relationships plotted at successive times after loading, giving an ultimate strain envelope, shown for compressive and tensile loading in Figures 16.12(a) and (b) respectively. The limiting stress below which creep rupture will not occur is about 70% of the short-term maximum for both compression and tension.

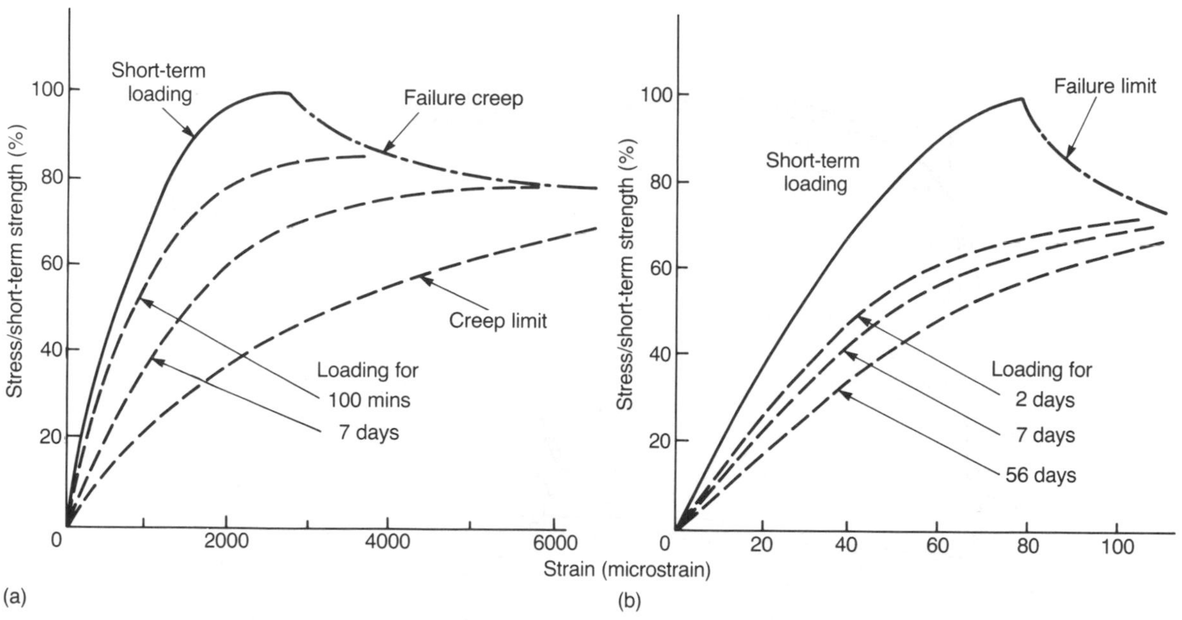

FIGURE 16.12 The effect of sustained compressive and tensile loading on the stress–strain relationship for concrete: (a) compressive loading; (b) tensile loading (Rusch (1960) and Domone (1974)).

16.3.3 The fracture mechanics approach

Griffith's theory for the fracture of materials and its consequent development into fracture mechanics was described in general terms in Chapter 6. Not surprisingly, there have been a number of studies attempting to apply linear fracture mechanics to concrete, with variable results; the American Concrete Institute (1980) have suggested three main reasons for the difficulties encountered.

1. Failure in compression, and to a lesser extent in tension, is controlled by the interaction of many cracks, rather than by the propagation of a single crack.
2. Cracks in cement paste or concrete do not propagate in straight lines, but follow tortuous paths around cement grains, aggregate particles etc., which both distort and blunt the cracks.
3. Concrete is a composite made up of cement paste, the transition zone and the aggregate, and each has its own fracture toughness (K_C), in themselves difficult to measure. There is also disagreement on the size of concrete specimen necessary to determine an overall fracture toughness.

Despite these difficulties, K_C values for cement paste have been estimated as lying in the range 0.1 to 0.5 $MN/m^{3/2}$, and for concrete between about 0.45 and 1.40 $MN/m^{3/2}$ (Mindess and Young, 1981). K_C for the transition zone seems to be smaller, about 0.1 $MN/m^{3/2}$, confirming the critical nature of this zone. Comparison of these values with those in Table 6.1 shows the brittle nature of concrete.

16.4 Strength under multiaxial loading

So far in this chapter our discussions on compressive strength have been concerned with the effects of uniaxial loading, i.e. where σ_1 (or σ_x)

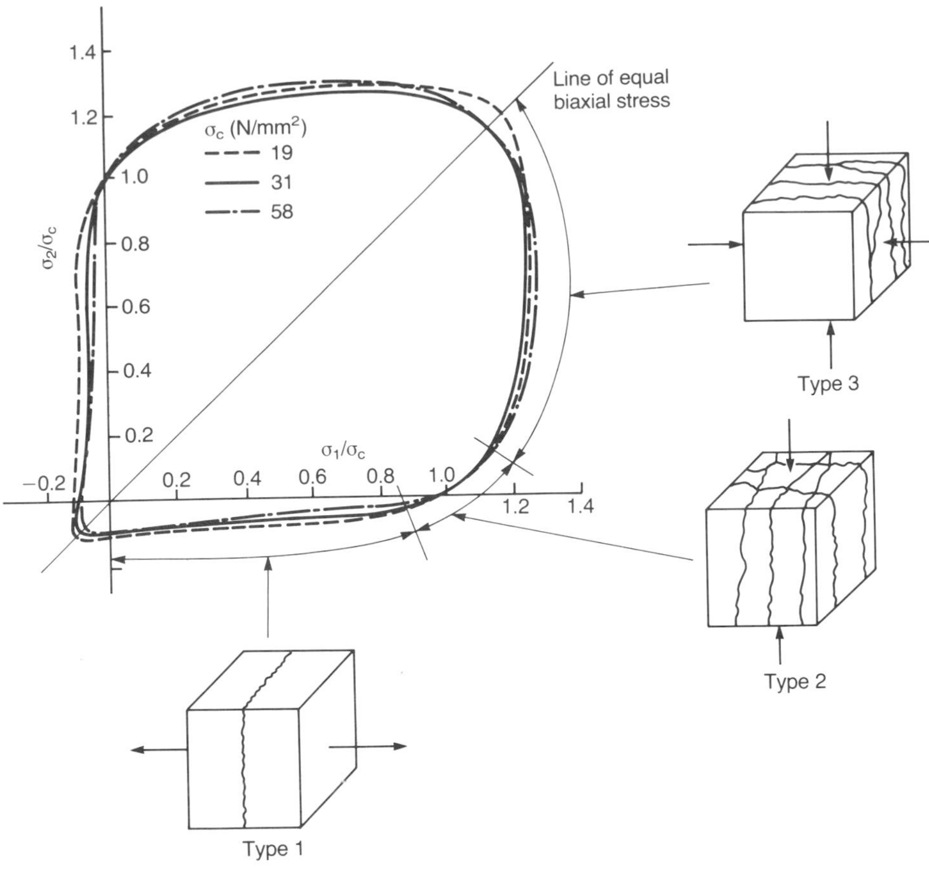

FIGURE 16.13 Failure envelopes and typical fracture patterns for concrete under biaxial stresses σ_1 and σ_2, relative to uniaxial stress σ_c (Kupfer *et al.* (1969) and Vile (1965)).

is finite, and the orthogonal stresses σ_2 (or σ_y) and σ_3 (or σ_z) are both zero. In many, perhaps most, structural situations concrete will be subject to a multiaxial stress state (i.e. σ_2 and/or σ_3 as well as σ_1 are finite). This can result in considerable modifications to the failure stresses, primarily by influencing the cracking pattern.

A typical failure envelope under biaxial stress (i.e. $\sigma_3 = 0$) is shown in Figure 16.13, in which the applied stresses, σ_1 and σ_2, are plotted non-dimensionally as proportions of the uniaxial compressive strength, σ_c. Firstly, it can be seen that concretes of different strengths behave very similarly when plotted on this basis. Not surprisingly, the lowest strengths in each case are obtained in the tension–tension quadrant. The effect of combined tension and compression is to reduce considerably the compressive stress needed for failure even if the tensile stress is significantly less than the uniaxial tensile strength. The cracking pattern over most of this region (Type 1 in Figure 16.13) is a single tensile crack, indicating that the failure criterion is one of maximum tensile strain, with the tensile stress enhancing the lateral tensile strain from the compressive stress. In the region of near uniaxial compressive stress, i.e. close to the compressive stress axes, the cracking pattern

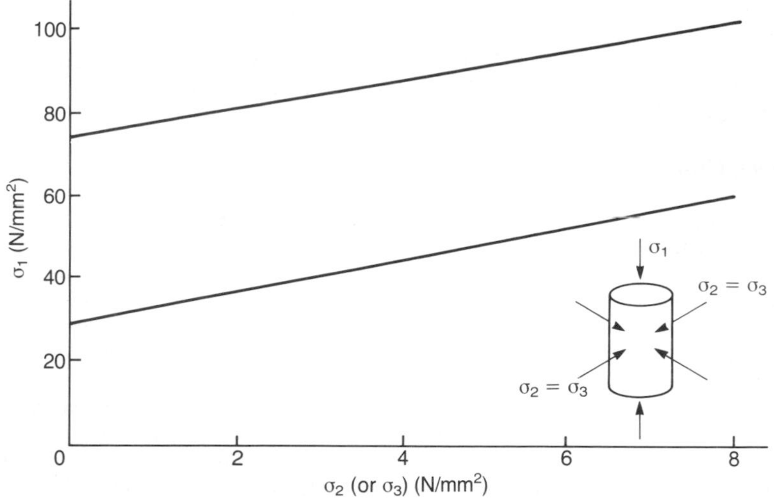

FIGURE 16.14 The effect of lateral confining stress (σ_2, σ_3) on the axial compressive strength (σ_1) of concretes of two different strengths (FIP/CEB, 1990).

(Type 2) is essentially the same as that in the central region of the cylinder shown in Figure 16.2, i.e. the cracks form all around the specimen approximately parallel to the compressive load. In the compression–compression quadrant, the cracking pattern (Type 3) becomes more regular, with the cracks forming in the plane of the applied loads, splitting the specimen into slabs. Under equal biaxial compressive stresses, the failure stress is somewhat larger than the uniaxial strength. Both Type 2 and Type 3 crack patterns also indicate a limiting tensile strain failure criterion, in the direction perpendicular to the compressive stress(es).

With triaxial stresses, if all three stresses are compressive then the lateral stresses (σ_2 and σ_3) act in opposition to the lateral tensile strain produced by σ_1. This in effect confines the specimen, and results in increased values of σ_1 being required for failure, as illustrated in Figure 16.14 for the case of uniform confining stress (i.e. $\sigma_2 = \sigma_3$); the axial strength ($\sigma_{1\text{ult}}$) can be related to the lateral stress by the expression

$$\sigma_{1\text{ult}} = \sigma_c + K \cdot \sigma_2 \text{ (or } \sigma_3) \qquad (16.5)$$

where K has been found to vary between about 2 and 4.5.

We have already seen in Section 16.1.1 that when a compressive stress is applied to a specimen by the steel platen of a test machine, the lateral (Poisson effect) strains induce restraint forces in the concrete near the platen due to the mismatch in elastic modulus between the concrete and the steel. This is therefore a particular case of triaxial stress, and the cause of the higher strength of cubes compared to longer specimens such as cylinders.

16.5 References

American Concrete Institute Committee 224 (1980) *Concrete International*, **2**, No. 10, 35–70.

American Concrete Institute Committee 363 (1984) *J. Amer. Conc. Inst.*, **81**, July–Aug., 364–411.

British Standards Institution (1983) BS 1881: *Part 116: Method for determination of compressive strength of concrete cubes.*

Building Research Establishment (1988) *Design of normal concrete mixes*, Report BR106, Dept. of Environment/Dept. of Transport, London.

Carasquillo, R.L., Nilson, A.H. and Slate, F.O. (1981) *J. Amer. Conc. Inst.*, **78**, No. 3, May–June, 171–8.

Cordon, W.A. and Gillespie, H.A. (1963) *J. Amer. Conc. Inst.*, **60**, No. 8, 1029–50.

Domone, P.L. (1974) *Magazine of Concrete Research*, **26**, No. 88, Sept., 144–52.

Erntroy, H.C. and Shacklock, B.W. (1954) *Proceedings of the Symposium on Mix Design and Quality Control of Concrete*, Cement and Concrete Association, London, pp. 55–73.

FIP/CEB (1990) State-of-the-art report on high strength concrete, Thomas Telford, London.

Glucklich, J. (1965) *Proceedings of the International Conference on Structure of Concrete and Its Behaviour Under Load*, Cement and Concrete Association, London, Sept., pp. 176–89.

Gonnerman, H.F. (1925) *Proc. Amer. Soc. Test and Mater.*, **25**, Pt II, 237–50.

Kupfer, H., Hilsdorf, H.K. and Rusch, H. (1969) *Proc. Amer. Conc. Inst.*, **66**, 660.

L'Hermite, R. (1955) *Institut Technique du Batiment et des Travaux Publics*, Paris.

Mindess, S. and Young, J.F. (1981) *Concrete*, Prentice-Hall, New Jersey.

Newman, K. (1966) Concrete systems, in *Composite Materials* (ed. L. Hollaway), Elsevier, London.

Portland Cement Association (1968) *Design and Control of Concrete Mixes*, 11th edn, Stokie, Illinois, USA.

Price, W.H. (1951) *J. Amer. Conc. Inst.*, **47**, 429.

Rusch, H. (1960) *J. Amer. Conc. Inst.*, **57**, No. 1, July, 1–29.

Struble, L., Skalny, J. and Mindess, S. (1980) *Cement and Concrete Research*, **10**, No. 2, March, 277–86.

Swamy, R.N. and Kameswara Rao, C.B.S. (1973) *Cement and Concrete Research*, **3**, No. 4, July, 413–28.

Vile, G.W.D. (1965) *Proceedings of the International Conference on Structure of Concrete and Its Behaviour Under Load*, Cement and Concrete Association, London, Sept., pp. 275–88.

Chapter seventeen

Durability of concrete

17.1 Transport mechanisms through concrete
17.2 Measurements of flow constants for cement paste and concrete
17.3 Degradation of concrete
17.4 Durability of steel in concrete
17.5 Recommendations for durable concrete construction
17.6 References

Durability can be defined as the ability of a material to remain serviceable for at least the required lifetime of the structure of which it forms a part. However, many structures do not have a well-defined lifetime, and in such cases the durability should be such that the structure remains serviceable more or less indefinitely, given reasonable maintenance. Initially, concrete was regarded as having an inherently high durability, but more recent experiences have shown that this is not necessarily the case. Degradation can result from either the environment to which the concrete is exposed, for example frost damage, or from internal causes within the concrete, as in alkali–aggregate reaction. It is also necessary to distinguish between degradation of the concrete itself and loss of protection and subsequent corrosion of the reinforcing or prestressing steel contained within it.

The rate of most of the degradation processes is controlled by the rate at which moisture, air or other aggressive agents can penetrate the concrete. This is a unifying theme when considering durability, and for this reason we shall first consider the various transport mechanisms through concrete – steady-state flow, diffusion and absorption – their measurement and the factors which influence their rate. We shall then discuss the main degradation processes, firstly of concrete – chemical attack by sulphates, sea water, acids and alkali–silica reaction, and physical attack by frost and fire – and then the corrosion of embedded steel. We shall thereby show how potential problems in all of these areas can be eliminated, or at least minimized, by due consideration to durability criteria in the design and specification of new structures. By way of illustration, some typical recommendations are included at the end of the chapter. Ignorance of, or lack of attention to, such criteria in the past has led to a thriving and expanding repair industry in recent years; it is to be hoped that today's practitioners will be able to learn from these lessons and reduce the need for such activities in the future. It is beyond the scope of this book to discuss inspection and repair methods; publications on this subject are now extensive, and some useful reviews are listed in the Further Reading section.

17.1 Transport mechanisms through concrete

As we have seen, hardened cement paste and concrete contain pores of varying types and sizes, and therefore the transport of materials through concrete can be considered as a particular case of the more general phenomenon of

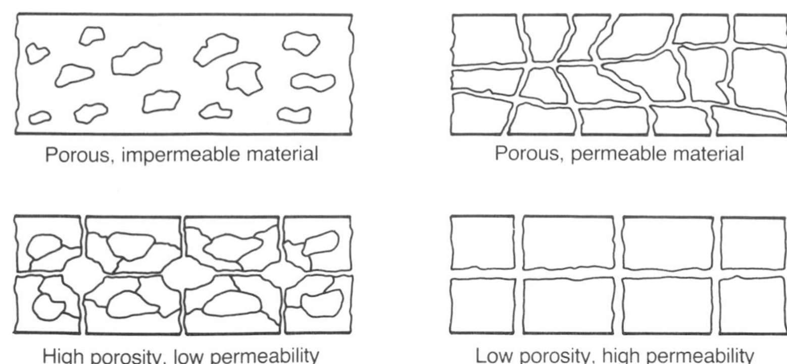

FIGURE 17.1 Illustration of the difference between permeability and porosity (Concrete Society, 1988).

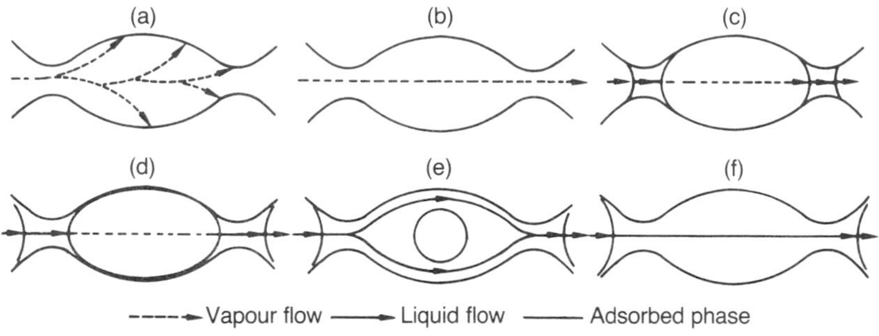

FIGURE 17.2 Mode of moisture transport through a typical pore (Rose, 1965).

flow through a porous medium. The rate of flow will not depend simply on the porosity, but on the degree of continuity of the pores. The term **permeability** is often loosely used to describe this general property (although we shall see that it also has a more specific meaning); Figure 17.1 illustrates the difference between permeability and porosity.

The flow processes depend on the degree of saturation of the cement paste or concrete, as illustrated in Figure 17.2, which represents the various stages of flow through an idealized single pore with a neck at each end. At very low humidities, the moisture is in the vapour state and is adsorbed on to the dry surfaces of the paste (Stage (a)). As the humidity increases, the adsorption becomes complete, and flow then takes place as direct vapour movement through the pore due to a pressure or concentration gradient, in the manner of inert gas (Stage (b)). The next stage (c) occurs when the humidity is sufficient for water to condense in the restricted part of the pore; this shortens the path for vapour transfer, thus increasing the rate of movement. The condensed water zones extend with rising humidity (Stage (d)) and the flow is augmented by transfer in the adsorbed layers.

Straightforward liquid flow under a pressure gradient eventually occurs, initially in the incompletely saturated state (Stage (e)), and finally in the completely saturated state (Stage (f)). In addition, movement of ions or dissolved gases will occur through saturated pores under a concentration gradient.

Three processes can therefore be distinguished, each of which has an associated 'flow constant', as follows.

1. Flow or movement of a fluid under a pressure differential. The flow passages through concrete and the flow rates are sufficiently small for the flow of either a liquid or gas to be laminar, and hence it can be described by Darcy's law:

$$u_x = -K\frac{\partial h}{\partial x} \qquad (17.1)$$

where, for flow in the x-direction, u_x = mean flow velocity, $\partial h/\partial x$ = rate of increase in pressure head in the x-direction, and K is a constant called the **coefficient of permeability**, the dimensions of which are [length]/[time], e.g. m/sec.

The value of K depends on both the pore structure within the concrete and the properties of the permeating fluid. The latter can, in theory, be eliminated by using the intrinsic permeability (k), given by

$$k = \frac{K\mu}{\rho_w} \qquad (17.2)$$

where μ = coefficient of viscosity of the fluid and ρ_w = unit weight of the fluid. k has dimensions of $[\text{length}]^2$, and should be a property of the porous medium alone and therefore applicable to all permeating fluids. However, for liquids it depends on the viscosity being independent of the pore structure, and for hcp with its very narrow flow channels in which a significant amount of the water will be subject to surface forces this may not be the case. Furthermore, comparison of k values from gas and liquid permeability tests has shown the former to be between 5 and 60 times higher than the latter, a difference attributed to the flow pattern of a gas in a narrow channel differing from that of a liquid (Bamforth, 1987). It is therefore preferable to consider permeability in terms of K rather than k, and accept the limitation that the values given apply to one permeating fluid only, normally water.

2. Movement of ions, atoms or molecules under a concentration gradient, a process of diffusion, which is governed by Fick's law:

$$P = -D\frac{\partial C}{\partial x} \qquad (17.3)$$

where, for the x-direction, P = transfer rate of the substance per unit area normal to the x-direction, $\partial C/\partial x$ = concentration gradient and D is a constant called the diffusivity, which has the dimensions of $[\text{length}]^2/[\text{time}]$, e.g. m^2/sec.

Defining the diffusivity in this way treats the porous solid as a continuum, but the complex and confining pore structure within concrete means that D is an effective, rather than a true, diffusion coefficient. We are also interested in more than one type of diffusion process, for example moisture movement during drying shrinkage, or de-icing salt diffusion through saturated concrete road decks. Furthermore, in the case of moisture diffusion (in, say, drying shrinkage) the moisture content within the pores will be changing throughout the diffusion process. There is, however, sufficient justification to consider D as a constant for any one particular diffusion process, but it should be remembered that, as with the permeability coefficient K, it is dependent on both the pore structure of the concrete and the properties of the diffusing substance.

3. Adsorption and absorption of a liquid into empty or partially empty pores by capillary attraction. It has been shown analytically and experimentally that the depth of penetration (x) is proportional to the square root of the time (t), i.e.

$$x = S \cdot t^{1/2} \qquad (17.4)$$

where S is a constant called the sorptivity, which has the dimensions of [length]/$[\text{time}]^{1/2}$, e.g. mm/scc$^{1/2}$.

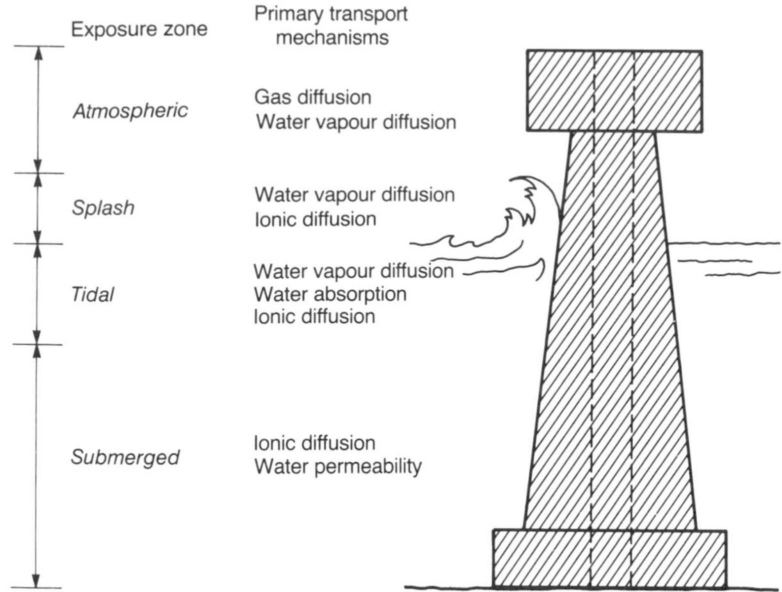

FIGURE 17.3 Primary transport mechanisms in the various exposure zones of a concrete offshore structure (Concrete Society, 1988).

The applicability of these mechanisms in practice is illustrated by the case of an offshore concrete structure, which is exposed to a range of different environments. Figure 17.3 shows the predominant mechanisms in the respective exposure zones.

17.2 Measurements of flow constants for cement paste and concrete

17.2.1 Permeability

Permeability is commonly measured by subjecting the fluid on one side of a concrete specimen to a pressure head, and measuring the steady-state flow rate that eventually occurs through the specimen, as illustrated in Figure 17.4. The specimen is normally a circular disc, the sides of which are sealed to ensure uniaxial flow. If the fluid is incompressible, i.e. it is a liquid such as water, the pressure head gradient through the specimen is linear, and Darcy's equation reduces to

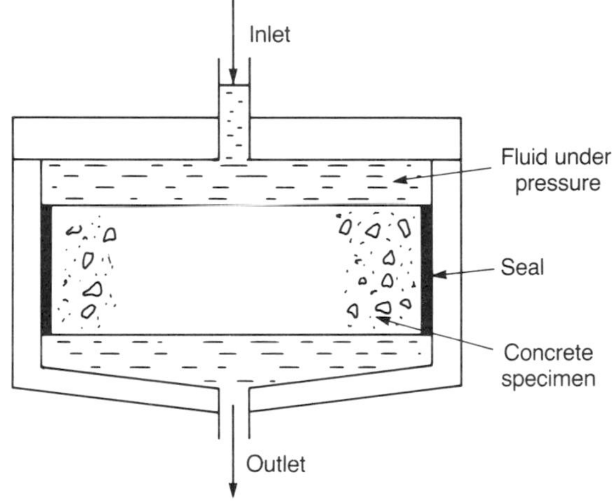

FIGURE 17.4 Typical test system for measurement of concrete permeability under steady-state flow.

$$\frac{\Delta Q}{\Delta A} = \frac{-K \cdot \Delta P}{l} \tag{17.5}$$

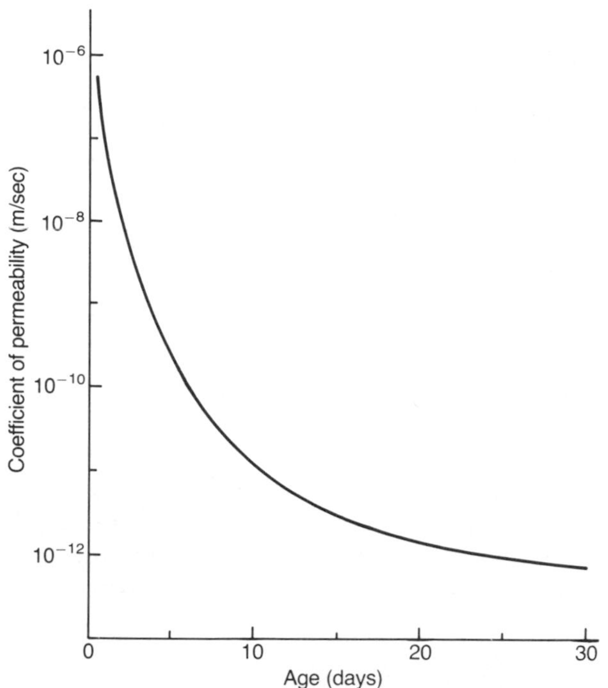

FIGURE 17.5 The effect of hydration on the permeability of cement paste (water/cement = 0.7) (Powers *et al.*, 1954).

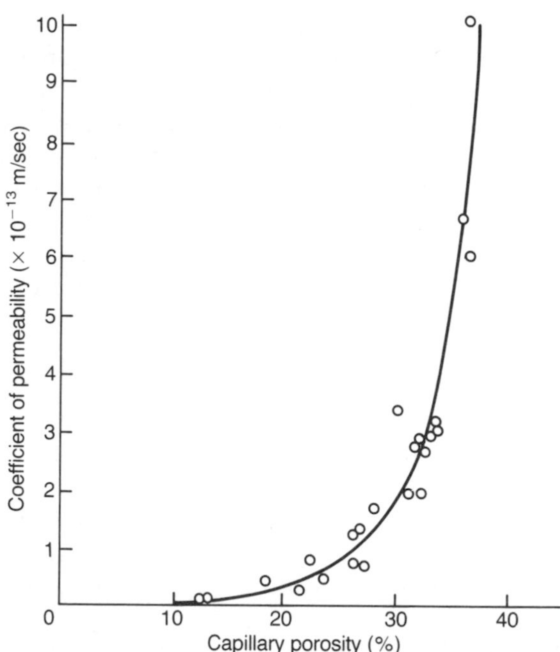

FIGURE 17.6 The relationship between permeability and capillary porosity of hardened cement paste (Powers, 1958).

where ΔQ = volumetric flow rate, ΔA = total cross-sectional area of flow perpendicular to the x-direction, ΔP = pressure head and l = flow path length.

Much of the fundamental work on the permeability of cement paste to water was carried out by Powers in the 1950s. As the cement hydrates, the hydration products infill the skeletal structures, blocking the flow channels and hence reducing the permeability. As might be expected from our earlier description of cement hydration in Section 13.1.3, the reduction of permeability is high at early ages, when hydration is proceeding rapidly. In fact it reduces by several orders of magnitude in the first 2–3 weeks after casting (Figure 17.5).

Although permeability and porosity are not necessarily related, as demonstrated in Figure 17.1, there is a general non-linear correlation between the two for cement paste, as shown

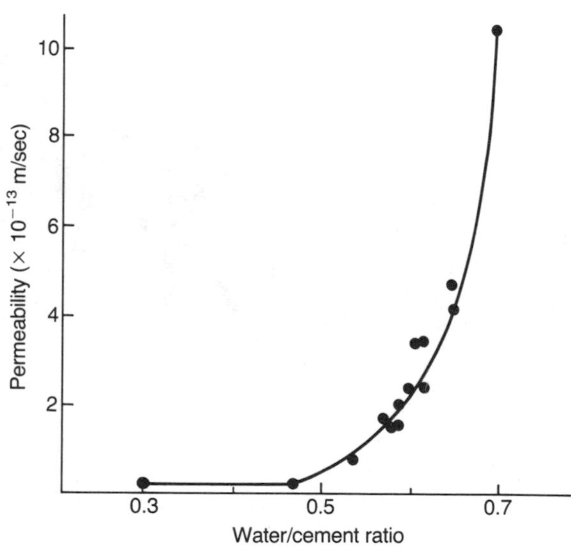

FIGURE 17.7 The relationship between the permeability and water/cement ratio of mature cement paste (93% hydrated) (Powers *et al.*, 1954).

in Figure 17.6. The greatest reduction in permeability occurs for porosities reducing from about 40 to 25%, where increased hydration product reduces both the pore sizes and the flow channels between them. Further hydration product, although still reducing porosity significantly, results in much lower changes in the permeability. This explains the general form of Figure 17.5, and also accounts for the effect of water/cement ratio on permeability shown in Figure 17.7 for a constant degree of hydration. At water/cement ratios above about 0.55 the capillary pores form an increasingly continuous system, with consequent large increases in permeability.

It is apparent from the above arguments and from Section 13.1.5 that high strength and low permeability both result from low porosity, and in particular a reduction in the volume of the larger capillary pores. In general, higher strength implies lower permeability, although the relationship is not linear, and may be different for

TABLE 17.1 Comparison between permeabilities of rocks and cement paste (Powers, 1958)

Type of rock	*Permeability (m/sec)*	*Water/cement ratio of cement paste of same permeability*
Dense trap	2.47×10^{-14}	0.38
Quartz diorite	8.24×10^{-14}	0.42
Marble	2.39×10^{-13}	0.48
Marble	5.77×10^{-12}	0.66
Granite	5.35×10^{-11}	0.70
Sandstone	1.23×10^{-10}	0.71
Granite	1.56×10^{-10}	0.71

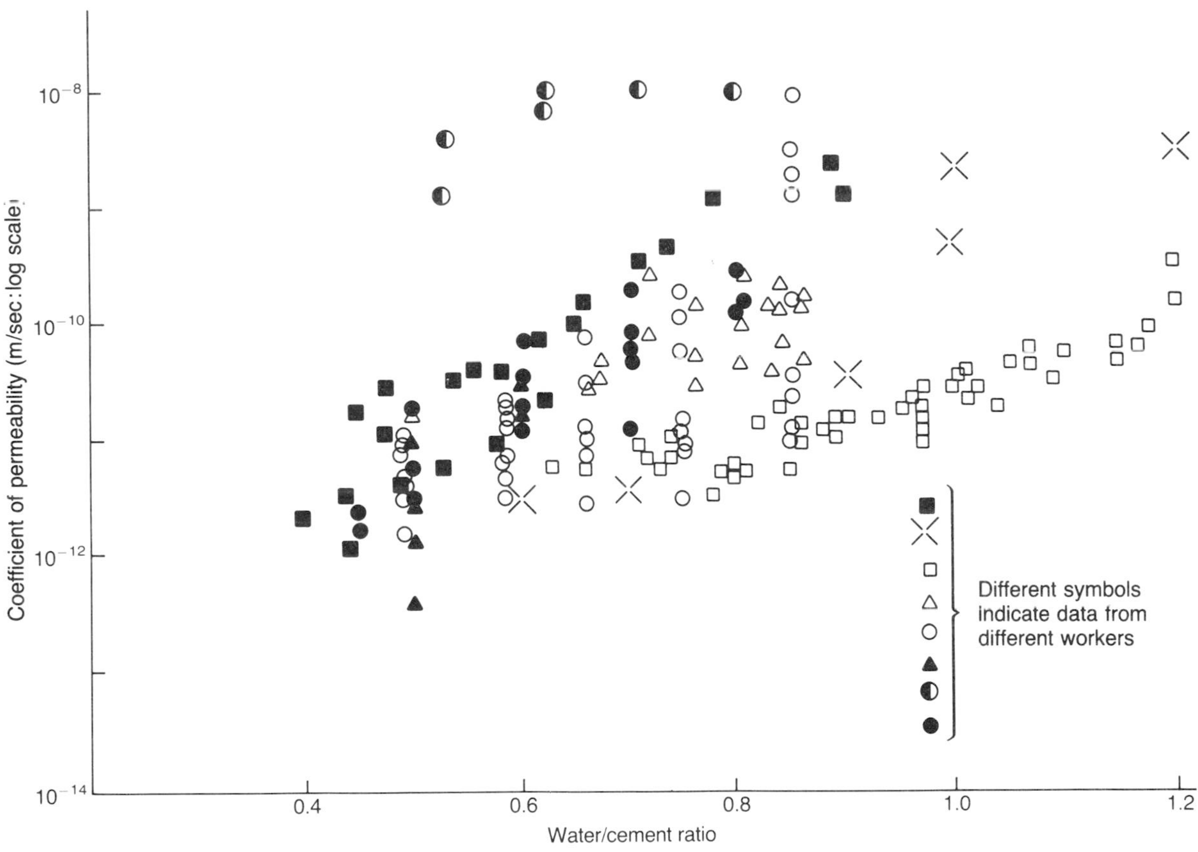

FIGURE 17.8 Comparison between test results of permeability of concrete to water (Lawrence, 1985).

different curing histories and cement types.

The permeability of the concrete will also be influenced by the permeability of the aggregate. Many of the rock types used for natural aggregates have permeabilities of the same order as that of cement paste (Table 17.1), despite having relatively low porosities. Lightweight aggregates, which are highly porous, can have much higher permeabilities. However, in practice the permeability of the composite concrete is often found to be substantially higher than that of either the aggregate or the paste, as can be seen by comparing the data for concrete shown in Figure 17.8 with those for aggregate and cement paste in Table 17.1 and Figure 17.7 respectively. This is primarily due to the presence of defects or cracks, particularly in the weaker transition zone at the cement/aggregate interface. Larger aggregates, with larger transition zones, exaggerate the effect.

As with cement paste, similar factors control both the permeability and strength of the concrete, and it is therefore possible to produce low permeability by attention to the same factors required to produce high strength. These include using a low water/cement ratio (Figure 17.8) and an adequate cement content, and ensuring proper compaction and adequate curing; in addition, the properties of the transition zone may be improved by the use of cement replacement materials (see Section 13.3.5), although longer curing periods are necessary to ensure continuance of the pozzolanic reaction. The avoidance of microcracking from thermal or drying shrinkage strains and premature or excessive loading is also important.

17.2.2 Diffusivity

The principle of diffusivity testing is relatively simple. A high concentration of the diffusant is placed on one side of a suitable specimen (normally a disc) of hcp, mortar or concrete, and the diffusion rate calculated from the increase of concentration on the other side. In the case of gas diffusion, the high concentration side may be an atmosphere of the pure gas; in the case of salts, a high concentration aqueous solution would be used. The test is therefore similar to the permeability test without the complication of high pressure. It is generally found that, after an initial period for the diffusant to penetrate through the specimen, the concentration on the 'downstream' side increases linearly with time. The diffusivity will change if the moisture content of the concrete changes during the test, and so the specimens must be carefully conditioned before testing.

Diffusivity measurements on cement paste have generally been carried out on relatively mature specimens. As might be expected, higher water/cement ratios lead to higher diffusivities; for example, Page *et al.* (1981) have found values for chloride ion diffusivity through saturated cement paste at 25°C of 2.6, 4.4 and 12.4×10^{-12} m^2/sec for water/cement ratios of 0.4, 0.5, and 0.6 respectively. In addition, the diffusivity of the 0.5 water/cement ratio paste was reduced to 1.47×10^{-12} m^2/sec for a mix containing 30% pfa and 0.41×10^{-12} m^2/sec for a mix with 70% ggbs.

Cement replacement materials have also been found to reduce the diffusivity of concrete, as shown by the data in Table 17.2. Although the reductions are substantial, it should be noted that diffusivity tests are carried out on saturated concrete, and therefore they will not show any

TABLE 17.2 Diffusivities of concrete made with combinations of Portland cement and cement replacement materials (Bamforth and Pocock, 1990) (Concrete compressive strength approx. 35 N/mm^2 throughout)

Cement	*Chloride ion diffusivity (m^2/sec)*
Portland cement	1.75×10^{-12}
70% Portland cement + 30% pfa	0.41×10^{-12}
50% Portland cement + 50% ggbs	0.15×10^{-12}
92% Portland cement + 8% csf	0.32×10^{-12}

influence of poor curing, which will be more critical with mixes containing cement replacement materials, as already mentioned.

17.2.3 Sorptivity

Sorptivity can be calculated from measurements of penetration depth, and tests are carried out on samples in which penetration is restricted to one direction only, such as cylinders with the curved surface sealed with a suitable bitumen or resin coating. The penetration depth at a particular time can be measured by splitting a sample open, but this requires a considerable number of samples to obtain a significant number of results. Alternatively, it can be estimated from weight gain, providing the concrete's porosity is known; this can be conveniently found by drying the specimen after the test. Such tests can only be carried out in the laboratory, either on specimens cast for this purpose, or on cores cut from structural concrete.

Sorptivity results obtained by Bamforth and Pocock (1990) are shown in Figure 17.9. They measured the variation of sorptivity with depth by slicing cores cut from concrete slabs 28 days old which had been moist cured for 4 days and then air cured for 24 days. They found that the sorptivity decreased with depth, attributed to the air drying causing imperfect curing of the surface zone. However, although similar strength mixes containing cement replacement materials had similar sorptivities in the 15 mm

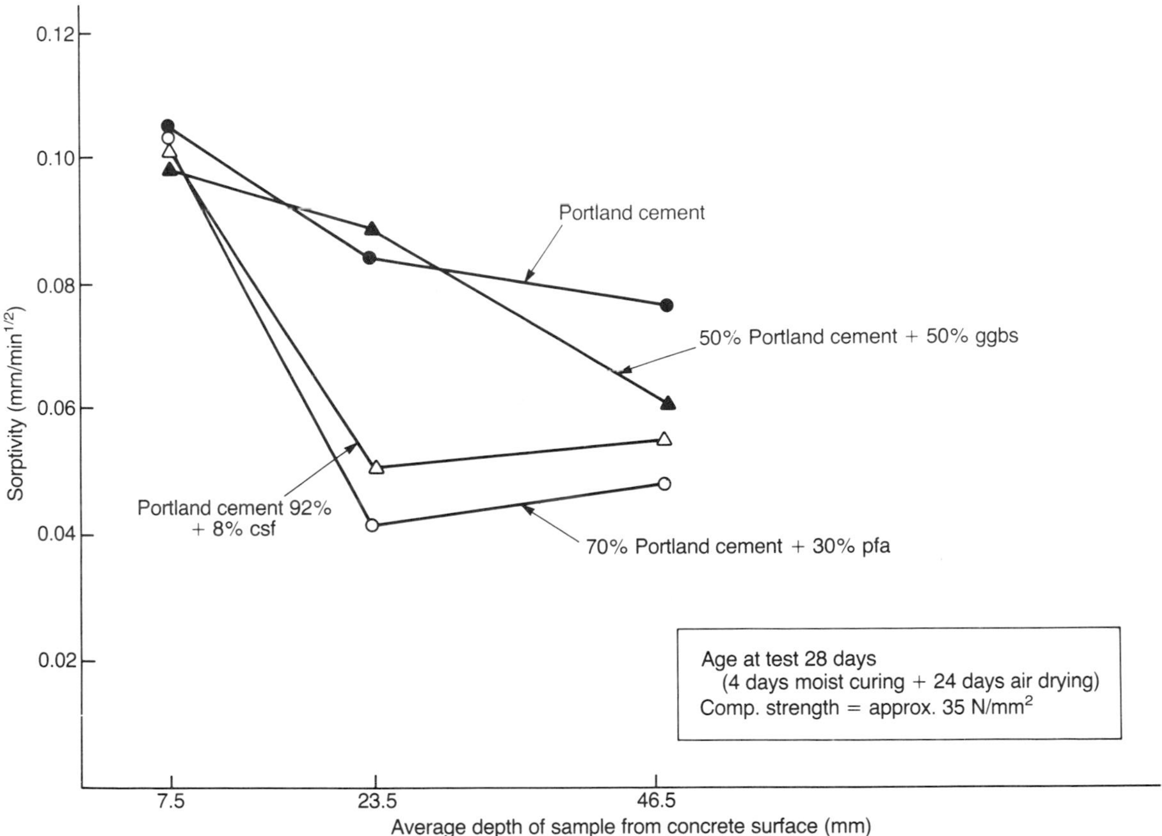

FIGURE 17.9 Variation of sorptivity with distance from cast surface of concrete made with Portland cement and cement replacement materials (Bamforth and Pocock, 1990).

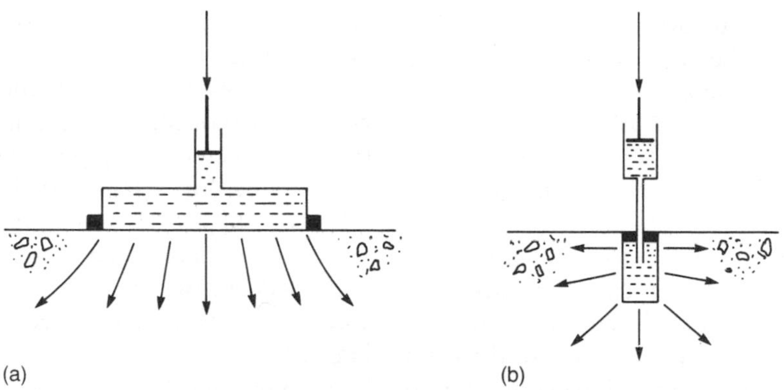

FIGURE 17.10 Techniques for surface permeability and absorption measurements on in-situ concrete.

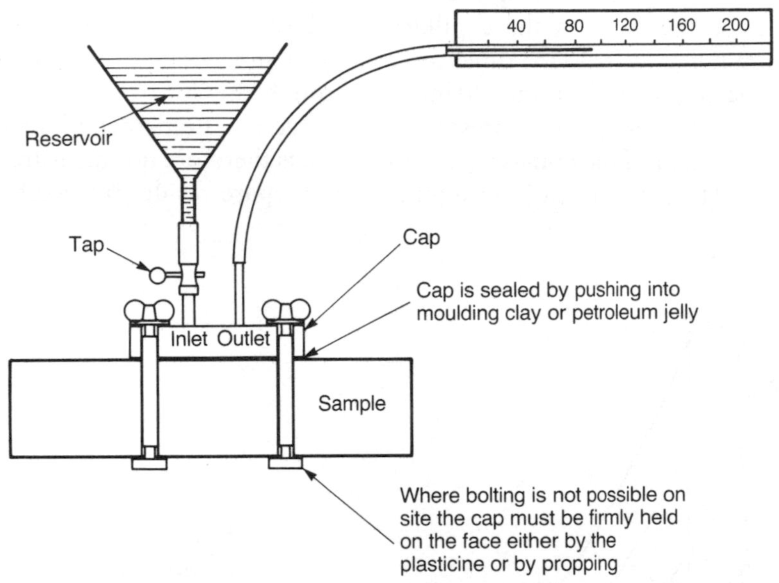

FIGURE 17.11 Initial Surface Absorption Test system (Concrete Society, 1988).

thick surface zone, they generally had lower values than the plain Portland cement concrete at greater depth, indicating the advantages to be gained from these materials with sufficient curing.

A number of tests have been developed to measure the absorption and permeability characteristics of in-situ concrete whilst still in the structure, i.e. avoiding the need to cut cores. These all measure the penetration rate of a fluid (normally air or water) into the concrete, either through the concrete surface with the fluid contained in a chamber fixed to the concrete (Figure 17.10(a)) or outwards from a hole drilled into the concrete, with the fluid delivered via a small tube or needle inserted in the hole (Figure 17.10(b)). Depending on the fluid pressure, which varies from test to test, estimates are made of either the absorption or permeability characteristics of the surface zone, or some combination of the two.

A commonly used test of this type is the Initial Surface Absorption Test (ISAT for short), shown in Figure 17.11. A cap is clamped to the concrete surface and a reservoir of water is set up with a constant head of 200 mm. The reservoir is connected through the cap to a capillary tube set level with the water surface. At the start of the test, water is allowed to run through the cap (thus coming into contact with the concrete surface) and to fill the capillary tube. The rate of absorption is then found by closing off the reservoir and observing the rate of movement of the meniscus in the capillary tube. Readings are taken at standard times after the start of the test (typically 10 mins, 20 mins, 30 mins, 1 hour and 2 hours), and expressed as flow rate per surface area of the concrete, e.g. in units of ml/m²/sec. The rate drops off with time, and in general increases with the sorptivity of the concrete.

Typical results showing the effect of water/cement ratio of the concrete and the duration of the initial water curing period on the 10 minute ISAT value for tests carried out on concrete 28 days old are shown in Figure 17.12. Not surprisingly, decreasing water/cement ratio and increased curing time both decrease the ISAT values; the results clearly reinforce the importance of curing.

In common with the other tests of this type, the ISAT has two main disadvantages. Firstly, the results depend on the moisture state of the concrete at the start of the test, which is particularly difficult to control if the test is carried out in situ. Secondly, the flowpath of the fluid through the concrete is not unidirectional but diverges; a fundamental property of the concrete is therefore not measured, and it is difficult to compare results from different test systems.

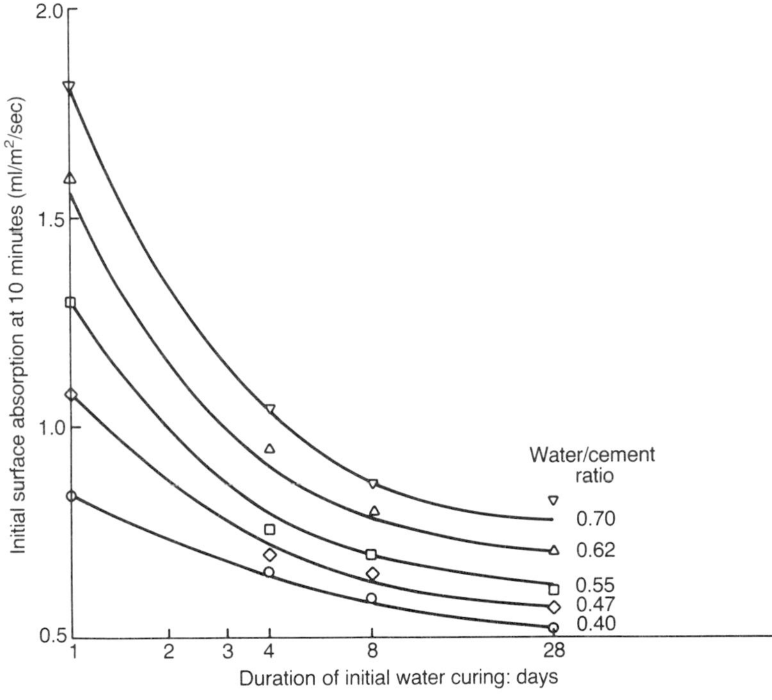

FIGURE 17.12 Effect of water/cement ratio and initial curing on surface absorption measured by the ISAT test (Dhir *et al.*, 1987).

However, the tests all measure some property of the surface layers of the concrete and, as we shall see, this is all important in ensuring good durability.

17.3 Degradation of concrete

The degradation agencies that affect concrete can be divided into two broad groups:

1. those whose action is initially chemical, before subsequently leading to loss of physical integrity, including sulphates, sea water, acids and alkali–silica reactions;
2. those which directly lead to physical effects, such as frost and fire.

Each of these is now discussed.

17.3.1 Attack by sulphates and sea water

We have seen in Section 13.1.1 that a controlled amount of calcium sulphate, in the form of gypsum, is added to Portland cement during its manufacture to control the setting process. Extra sulphates can arise from contaminated aggregates, a particular problem in some Middle Eastern countries, or from sulphate bearing ground-water, particularly from clay soils, coming into contact with the concrete, for example in the foundations of structures. We briefly described the nature of the resulting durability problem when discussing sulphate resisting Portland cement in Section 13.1.7. The sulphates and the hydrated aluminate phases in the hardened cement paste react to form ettringite, according to eqn (13.12), now repeated:

$$C_3A \cdot C\bar{S} \cdot H_{18} + 2CH + 2\bar{S} + 12H \rightarrow C_3A \cdot 3C\bar{S} \cdot H_{32} \quad (13.12)$$

This is an expansive reaction, causing disruption.

With sulphates other than calcium sulphate, reactions can also occur with the calcium hydroxide in the hcp, forming gypsum, which may cause a loss of stiffness and strength of the paste, thereby contributing to the degradation. For example, the reaction with sodium sulphate is:

$$Na_2SO_4 + Ca(OH)_2 + 2H_2O \rightarrow CaSO_4 \cdot 2H_2O + 2NaOH \quad (17.6)$$

With magnesium sulphate, a similar reaction takes place, but the magnesium hydroxide formed is relatively insoluble and poorly alkaline; this reduces the stability of the calcium silicate hydrate which is also attacked:

$$MgSO_4 + Ca(OH)_2 + 2H_2O \rightarrow CaSO_4 \cdot 2H_2O + Mg(OH)_2 \quad (17.7)$$

$$3MgSO_4 + 3CaO \cdot 2SiO_2 \cdot 3H_2O + 8H_2O \rightarrow 3(CaSO_4 \cdot 2H_2O) + 3Mg(OH)_2 + 2SiO_2 \cdot H_2O \quad (17.8)$$

Thus the severity of attack depends on the type of sulphate; magnesium sulphate is more damaging than sodium sulphate, which, in turn, is more damaging than calcium sulphate. In each case the rate of attack increases with the amount of sulphate present, for example its concentration in the groundwater, but the rate of increase in intensity reduces above about 1% concentration. Also, the rate of attack will be faster if the sulphates are replenished, for example if the concrete is exposed to flowing groundwater.

Concrete which has been attacked has a whitish appearance; damage usually starts at edges and corners, followed by progressive cracking and spalling, eventually leading to complete breakdown. Although this stage can be reached in a few months in laboratory tests, it normally takes several years in the field.

For any given concentration and type of sulphate, the rate and amount of the deterioration increase with:

1. the C_3A content of the cement, hence the low C_3A content of sulphate resisting Portland cement;
2. lower cement content and higher water/cement ratio of the concrete; higher quality

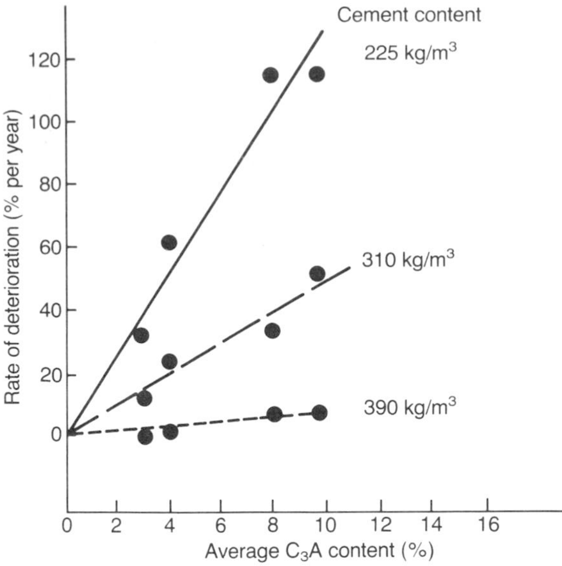

FIGURE 17.13 The effect of C_3A content of cement and cement content of concrete on deterioration in a soil containing 10% Na_2SO_4 (Verbeck, 1968).

concrete is less vulnerable due to its lower permeability. This is a more significant factor than the C_3A content, as shown in Figure 17.13.

The rate and amount of deterioration are decreased by the incorporation of cement replacement materials, which can decrease the permeability, reduce the amount of free lime in the hcp, and effectively 'dilute' the C_3A.

Sea water contains sulphates, along with other salts, and its action on concrete has some similarities to that of pure sulphate solutions, with the addition of some interactive effects. The total soluble salt content is typically about 3.5% by weight, the principal ionic contributors being 2.0% Cl^-, 1.1% Na^+, 0.27% SO_4^{--}, 0.12% Mg^{++} and 0.05% Ca^{++}. The sulphates react as described above, but the severity of the attack is not as great as for sulphates acting alone and there is little accompanying expansion. This is due to the presence of chlorides; gypsum and ettringite are more soluble in a chloride solution than in pure water, and therefore tend to be leached out of the concrete by the sea water. The magnesium ions participate in the reactions as in equations (17.7) and (17.8), and a feature of sea water damaged concrete is the presence of white deposits of $Mg(OH)_2$, often called **brucite**. In experiments on concrete permanently saturated with sea water, a form of calcium carbonate called **aragonite** has also been found, arising from the reaction of dissolved carbon dioxide with calcium hydroxide. The brucite and aragonite can have a pore-blocking effect, effectively reducing the permeability of the concrete near the surface (Buenfeld and Newman, 1984).

As illustrated in Figure 17.3, the transport of salts into concrete in a marine structure, or their leaching from it, may be a permeability, diffusion or absorption controlled process. In the areas subject to wetting and drying cycles, salts will crystallize as the water evaporates, which may lead to disruption from the pressure exerted by the crystals. These areas therefore tend to be more vulnerable. This can be compounded by damage from freeze–thaw cycles or wave action, depending on the environment.

The key to elimination or at least reduction of all of these problems is, not suprisingly, the use of a low permeability concrete, perhaps combined with some limits on the C_3A content of the cement, or the use of cement replacement materials. However, for the reasons given above, the degadration processes in many climates do not cause rapid deterioration, which explains why concrete of even relatively modest quality has a long and distinguished history of use in marine structures, both coastal and offshore.

The salts in sea water can contribute to two other, potentially much more critical, degradation processes, namely alkali–aggregate reaction and corrosion of embedded steel. Both are discussed later.

17.3.2 Acid attack

We have seen that the hardened cement paste binder in concrete is alkaline, and therefore no Portland cement concrete can be considered acid resistant. However, it is possible to produce a concrete which is adequately durable for many common circumstances by giving attention to low permeability and good curing. In these circumstances, attack is only considered significant if the pH of the aggressive medium is less than about 6.

Examples of acids that commonly come into contact with concrete are dilute solutions of CO_2 and SO_2 in rain water in industrial regions, and CO_2 bearing groundwater from moorlands. The acids attack the calcium hydroxide within the cement paste, converting it, in the case of CO_2, into calcium carbonate and bicarbonate. The latter is relatively soluble, and leaches out of the concrete, destabilizing it. The process is thus diffusion controlled, and progresses at a rate approximately proportional to the square root of time. The rate of attack also increases with reducing pH.

As mentioned above, the quality of the concrete is the most important factor in achieving acid resistance, but concretes containing cement replacement materials also seem to have greater resistance, probably because of the lower calcium hydroxide content as a result of the pozzolanic reaction. In cases where some extra acid resistance is required, such as in floors of chemical factories, the surface can be treated with diluted water glass (sodium silicate), which reacts with the calcium hydroxide forming calcium silicates, blocking the pores. In more aggressive conditions, the only option is to separate the acid and the concrete by, for example, applying a coating of epoxy resins or other suitable paint systems to the concrete.

17.3.3 Alkali–aggregate reaction

We described the general nature and composition of natural aggregates in Chapter 13. Among many other constituents, they may contain silica, silicates and carbonates, which in certain mineral forms can react with the alkalis (sodium, potassium and calcium hydroxide) in hydrated Portland cement paste. The product is a gel which absorbs water and swells to a sufficient extent to cause cracking and disruption of the concrete. The most common and important reaction involves active silica, and is known as alkali–silica reaction (ASR for short).

For the reaction to occur, both active silica and alkalis must be present. In its reactive form, silica occurs as the minerals opal, chalcedony, crystobalite and tridymite and as volcanic glasses. These can be found in some flints, limestones, cherts and tuffs. The sources of such aggregates include parts of the USA, Canada, South Africa, Scandinavia, Iceland, Australia, New Zealand and the midlands and south west of England. Only a small proportion of reactive material in the aggregate (as low as 0.5%) may be necessary to cause disruption to the concrete.

In unhydrated opc, the Na_2O and K_2O are present in small but significant quantities (see Table 13.1), either as soluble sulphates (Na_2SO_4 and K_2SO_4) or a mixed salt $(Na,K)_2SO_4$. There is also a small amount of free CaO, which is subsequently supplemented by $Ca(OH)_2$ from the hydration reactions of C_3S and C_2S. During hydration, these sulphates take part in a reaction with the aluminate phases in a similar way to gypsum (see Section 13.1.3), the product again being ettringite with sodium, potassium and hydroxyl ions going into solution:

$$(Na,K)_2SO_4 + \underset{(C_3A)}{3CaO \cdot SiO_2} + Ca(OH)_2 \rightarrow \underset{\text{(calcium sulphoaluminate, ettringite)}}{3CaO \cdot SiO_2 \cdot 3CaSO_4 \cdot 32H_2O} + \underset{\text{(in solution)}}{Na^+, K^+, OH^-} \quad (17.9)$$

The resulting pH of the pore water is 13–14, higher than that of saturated calcium hydroxide solution alone.

Alkalis may also be contributed by external sources, such as aggregate impurities, sea water or road de-icing salts.

The reaction between the active silica and the alkalis, which forms the alkali–silicate gel,

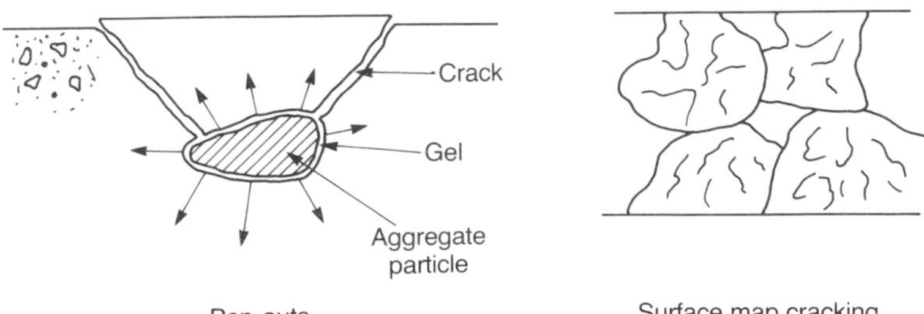

FIGURE 17.14 Typical cracking patterns resulting from alkali–silica reaction.

occurs first at the aggregate/cement paste interface. The nature of the gel is complex and not fully understood. However, it is clear that it is a mixture of sodium, potassium and calcium silicates. It is soft, but on contact imbibes a large quantity of water by osmosis and swells considerably. The hydraulic pressure that is developed leads to overall expansion of the concrete and can be sufficient to cause cracking of the aggregate particles, the hcp and the transition zone between the two.

Continued availability of water causes enlargement and extension of the cracks which eventually reach the outer surface of the concrete, forming either pop-outs if the affected aggregate is close to the surface, or more extensive crazing, or map cracking, on the concrete surface, as illustrated in Figure 17.14.

The whole process is often very slow, and the cracking can take years to develop in structural concrete; over the last 10 to 15 years many cases have been identified from which it is apparent that the problem is more widespread than previously thought. This has generated much research, and even though laboratory tests have somtimes not satisfactorily explained all field observations, the most important factors influencing the amount and rate of reaction can be summarized as follows.

1. The amount of alkalis available. (This is normally expressed as the total weight of sodium oxide equivalent = Na_2O + $0.658K_2O$.) The reaction rate and amount increase with increasing alkali level, but test data such as those shown in Figure 17.15 indicate that there is a threshold level below which no disruption will occur, even with reactive aggregates. This is typically about 3.5–4 kg/m^3 of concrete, which corresponds to a lower limit of about 0.6% by weight of cement. Cements with a sodium oxide equivalent of less than this are called low-alkali cements.
2. The amount of reactive silica. Typical effects from tests on mortars are shown in Figure 17.16. Four types of behaviour can be identified.
   (a) Region A: the reactive silica content is low and gel growth after the concrete has hardened is insufficient to cause cracking.
   (b) Region B: the reaction continues after the concrete has hardened, at an intensity sufficient to cause cracking. There is an excess of alkalis, and the reaction continues until all the active silica has been used up.
   (c) Region C: there is an excess of silica over alkalis, and the reaction continues until all the alkalis have been used up or their concentration falls below the threshold level.
   (d) Region D: the reactive silica content is very high and the reaction is so rapid that by the time the concrete has hardened the rate of gel growth is too slow to induce cracking.

At the common boundary of regions B and C

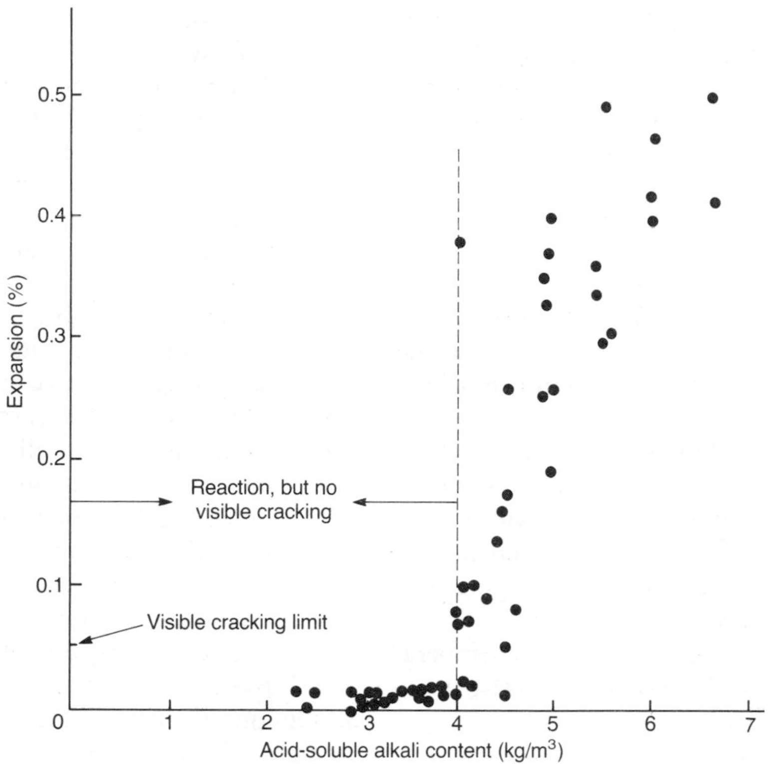

FIGURE 17.15 Effect of acid-soluble alkali content of concrete on expansion and cracking after 200 days from alkali–silica reaction (tests at critical silica/alkali ratio) (Hobbs, 1986).

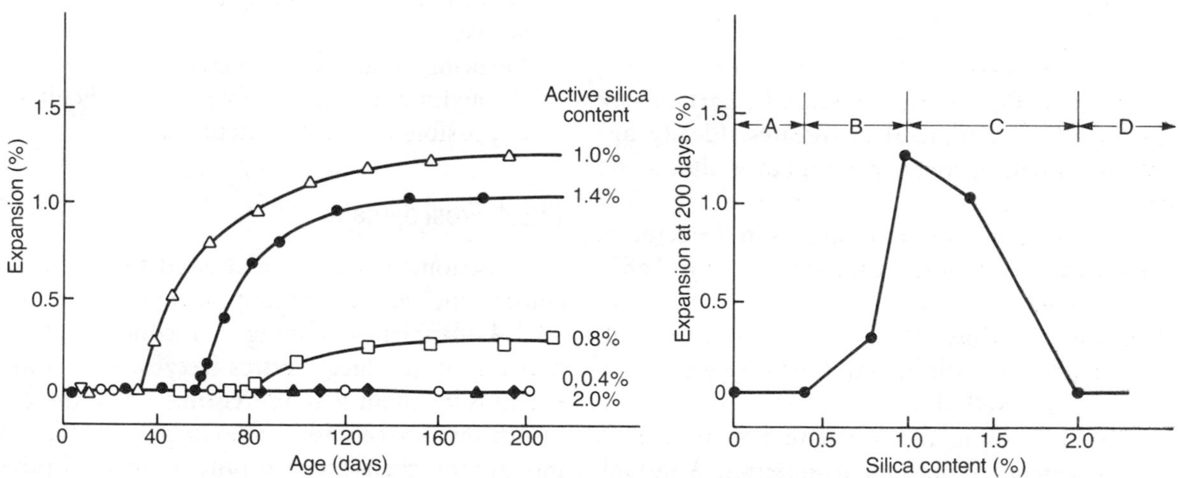

FIGURE 17.16 Effect of age and active silica content on expansion of mortars due to alkali–silica reaction (opaline silica, w/c = 0.53, A/c = 3.75, Na_2O = 4.4 kg/m^3) (Hobbs, 1988).

the expansion reaches a maximum; this is the point at which the amount of reactive silica is just sufficient to react with all the alkalis present, and is sometimes referred to as the point of pessimum behaviour.

3. The aggregate particle size, which affects the amount of reactive silica exposed to the alkali; fine particles therefore produce more rapid and greater expansion.
4. The gel composition. There is evidence that $Ca(OH)_2$ in the gel is necessary, but the overall effect of gel composition is not fully understood.
5. The availability of moisture. The gel swelling will cease if the relative humidity within the concrete falls below 75%. This will depend on the environment and the concrete permeability. Alternative wetting and drying may be the most harmful.
6. The ambient temperature. Higher temperatures accelerate the reaction, at least up to 40°C.

Once started, ASR is almost impossible to eliminate, and therefore extensive rebuilding or strengthening of a structure may be required. It follows that it is important to reduce or eliminate the risk of ASR occurring by careful materials selection and concrete mix design. Preventive measures include the following.

1. Avoiding the use of reactive aggregates. This is more difficult than it sounds, particularly with mixed mineral aggregates. Ideally aggregates of proven performance should be used.
2. Limiting the amount of alkalis in the cement. Recommendations (Concrete Society, 1987) include:
   (a) using a low-alkali cement, i.e. with alkali content of less than 0.6% by weight, as discussed above;
   (b) combining the Portland cement with a cement replacement material. Although pfa and ggbs can contain high total alkali levels, the extent to which this contributes to the total alkalinity of the pore water appears to be small when they are combined with a high alkalinity Portland cement, and therefore the effective total alkalinity is reduced. Also, ggbs contains a form of silica which reacts slowly with the alkalis to give a non-expansive product, and for mixes with at least 50% Portland cement replacement by ggbs, higher total alkalis can be tolerated. With csf, which is very finely divided active silica, the opposite effect occurs; the reaction is accelerated so that it is essentially completed whilst the concrete is in its fluid, fresh state, rendering the expansion harmless. However, the exact mechanisms and quantitative nature of the role of cement replacement materials are complex and unclear, and are the subject of continuing research.
3. Limiting the total alkali content of the concrete. Alkalis from all sources (cement, de icing salts, etc.) should total less than 3.0 kg/m^3 of concrete. Partial substitution of the Portland cement with pfa or ggbs can be used to achieve this figure; at least 25% substitution should be used, and their own alkali content can be ignored, as discussed above.
4. Ensuring that the concrete remains dry throughout its life – obviously difficult or impossible in many structures.

17.3.4 Frost damage

Frost action, which we discussed briefly when considering air entraining agents in Section 13.2.4, can cause damage to concrete when moisture in the larger pores freezes. Free water expands by about 9% on freezing, and if there is insufficient space within the concrete to accommodate this then internal, potentially disruptive pressures will result. Successive cycles of freezing and thawing can cause progressive and cumulative damage, which takes the form of cracking and spalling, initially of the concrete surface.

It is the water in the larger capillary pores and entrapped air voids that has the critical effect; the water in the much smaller gel pores (see Chapter 13) is adsorbed on to the C-S-H surfaces, and does not freeze until the temperature falls to about −78°C. However, after the capillary water has frozen it has a lower thermodynamic energy than the still-liquid gel water, which therefore tends to migrate to supplement the capillary water, thus increasing the disruption. The disruptive pressure is also enhanced by osmotic pressure. The water in the pores is not pure, but is a solution of calcium hydroxide and other alkalis, and perhaps chlorides; pure water separates out on freezing, leading to salt concentration gradients and osmotic pressures which increase the diffusion of water to the freezing front.

The magnitude of the disruptive pressure depends on the capillary porosity, the degree of saturation of the concrete and the pressure relief provided by a nearby free surface or escape boundary. The extent of this pressure relief will depend on:

1. the permeability of the material;
2. the rate at which ice is formed; and
3. the distance from the point of ice formation to the escape boundary. In saturated cement paste, the disruptive pressures will only be relieved if the point of ice formation is within about 0.1 mm of an escape boundary. A convenient way of achieving this is by use of an air entraining agent (see Section 13.2.4), which entrains air in the form of small discrete bubbles at an average spacing of about 0.2 mm.

As we saw in Chapter 13, the capillary porosity of a cement paste or concrete, and hence its susceptibility to frost attack, can be reduced by lowering the water/cement ratio and ensuring that by proper curing the hydration is as com-

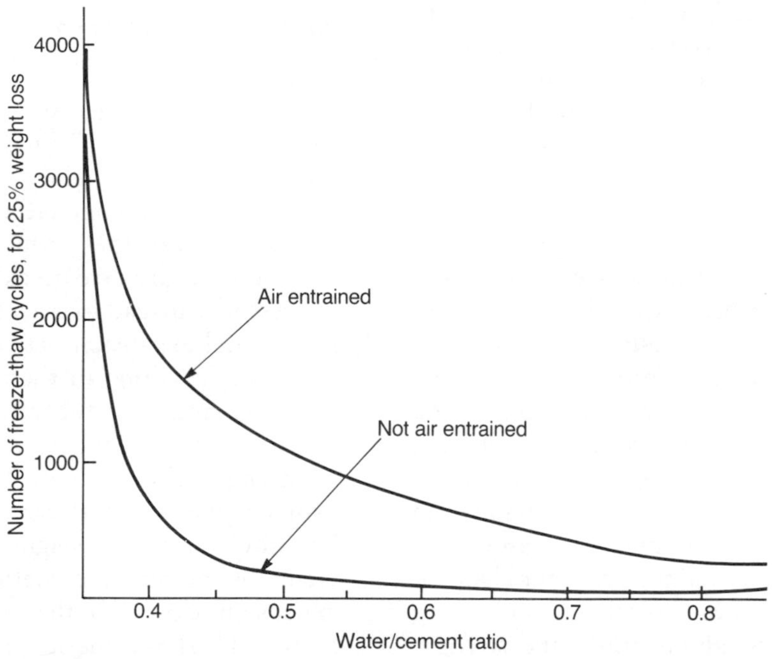

FIGURE 17.17 The effect of air entrainment and water/cement ratio on the frost resistance of concrete moist-cured for 28 days (US Bureau of Reclamation, 1955).

plete as possible. Bleeding, which results in local high porosity zones, should also be minimized. The combined effects of air entrainment and water/cement ratio are illustrated in Figure 17.17.

Certain aggregates are themselves susceptible to frost action, and their use must be avoided if a durable concrete is to be achieved. The first sign of damage caused by aggregate disruption is normally pop-outs on the concrete surface. Vulnerable aggregates include some limestones and porous sandstones; these generally have high water absorption, but other rocks with high absorption are not vulnerable. Similar arguments of pore size and distribution for cement paste apply to the aggregates; for example, it has been found that pores of about 4 to 5 microns are critical, since these are large enough to permit water to enter but not large enough to allow dissipation of disruptive pressure. Aggregate size is also a factor, with smaller particles causing less disruption, presumably because the average distance to an escape boundary on the aggregate surface is less. The only satisfactory way of assessing an aggregate is through its performance when incorporated in concrete, using field experience or laboratory testing.

17.3.5 Fire resistance

Concrete is incombustible and does not emit any toxic fumes when exposed to high temperatures. It is thus a favoured material, both in its own right and as protection for steelwork, when structural safety is being considered. However, although it can retain some strength for a reasonable time at high temperatures, it will eventually degrade, the rate of degradation depending on the maximum temperature, the concrete constituents and the size of the element.

Figure 17.18 shows typical behaviour. For temperatures up to about 500°C the strength reduction is relatively gradual, but thereafter the decline is more rapid giving almost total loss

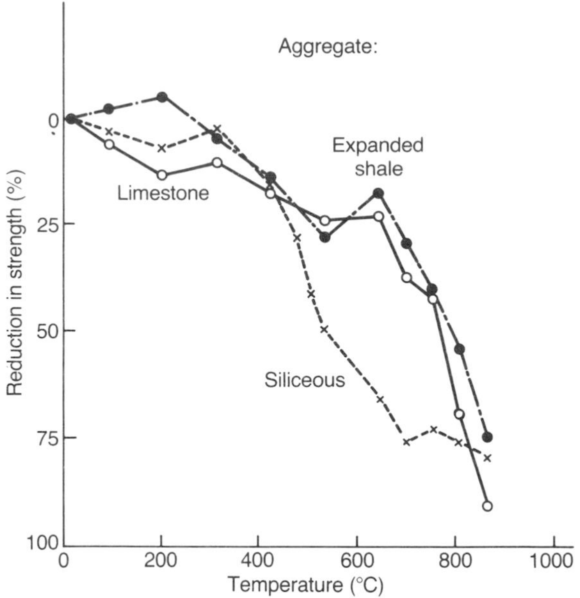

FIGURE 17.18 The effect of temperature and aggregate type on the compressive strength of concrete heated and tested hot (average initial strength = 28 N/mm^2) (Abrams, 1971).

approaching 1000°C. There are three main contributions to the degradation as follows.

1. Evaporation of water within the concrete, which starts at 100°C, and continues with progressively more tightly held water being driven off. If the concrete is initially saturated and also of low permeability, then the steam cannot disperse quickly, and build-up of pressure can lead to cracking and spalling.
2. Differential expansion between the hcp and aggregate, resulting in thermal stresses and cracking, initiated in the transition zone. This is mainly responsible for the more rapid loss of strength above about 500°C, and also explains the superior performance of the limestone and lightweight aggregate concrete; the former has a coefficient of thermal expansion closer to that of the hcp (see Section 15.3) and the latter is less stiff and hence the thermal stresses are lower. Lightweight aggregates have the additional advan-

tage of decreasing the thermal conductivity of the concrete, thus delaying the temperature rise in the interior of a structural member.

3. Breakdown of the hydrates in the hcp, which is not complete until the temperature approaches 1000°C, but results in a total loss of strength at this point.

17.4 Durability of steel in concrete

Nearly all structural concrete contains steel, either in the form of reinforcement to compensate primarily for the low tensile and shear strength of the concrete, or as stressed pre-tensioned tendons which induce stresses in the concrete to oppose those due to the subsequent loading. Sound concrete provides an excellent protective medium for the steel, but this protection can be broken down in some circumstances, leaving the steel vulnerable to corrosion. It is of great significance that the corrosion products, namely rust in various forms, occupy a considerably greater volume than the original steel. Rusting in the concrete can therefore cause cracking and spalling of the concrete covering the steel, followed by more rapid corrosion of the exposed steel and eventual loss of structural integrity. Such corrosion has caused extensive and increasing degradation of some concrete structures throughout the world in the last 30 years or so.

In this section we shall first describe the general nature of the corrosion process of steel in concrete, before going on to consider the factors that control its onset and subsequent rate.

17.4.1 General principles of the corrosion of the steel in concrete

The electrochemical nature of the corrosion of steel was described in Chapter 11, but it is worth summarizing the main reactions here:

at the anode

$$2Fe \rightarrow 2Fe^{++} + 4e^- \quad (17.10)$$

electron conductance

$$4e\ (\text{anode}) \rightarrow 4e\ (\text{cathode}) \quad (17.11)$$

at the cathode

$$4e + O_2 + 2H_2O \rightarrow 4OH^- \quad (17.12)$$

at some distance from the surface

$$2Fe^{2+} + 4OH^- \rightarrow \underset{\text{ferrous hydroxide, black rust}}{2Fe(OH)_2} \quad (17.13)$$

followed by

$$4Fe(OH)_2 + O_2 \rightarrow \underset{\text{ferric hydroxide, red rust}}{2Fe_2O_3 \cdot H_2O} + H_2O \quad (17.14)$$

For iron or steel rusting in oxygenated water or moist air, the water on or near the metal surface acts as the electrolyte of the corrosion cell, and the anode and cathode are close together, e.g. across a single crystal or grain; the oxide is formed and deposited away from the surface, as illustrated in Figure 17.19, allowing the corrosion to be continuous. In concrete, the electrolyte is the pore water in contact with the steel, and, as we have seen, this is normally highly alkaline (pH = 12–13) due to the $Ca(OH)_2$ from the cement hydration and the small amounts of Na_2O and K_2O in the cement. In such a solution, the primary anodic product is not Fe^{++} as in reaction (17.10) but is Fe_3O_4, which is deposited at the metal surface as a tightly adherent thin film, and stifles any further corrosion. The steel is said to be passive, and

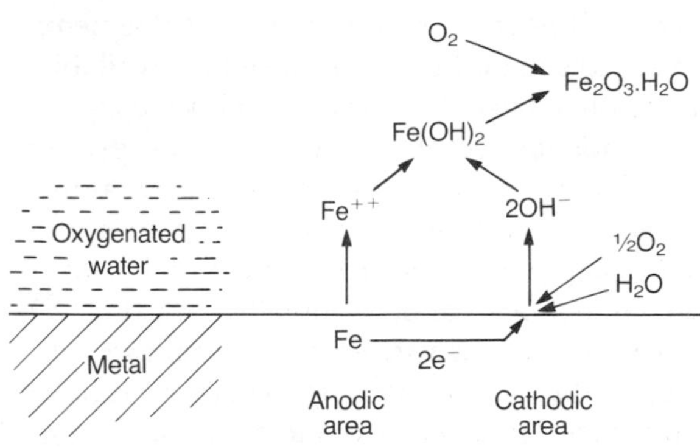

FIGURE 17.19 Spacial arrangement of corrosion reactions of iron in moist air or oxygenated water.

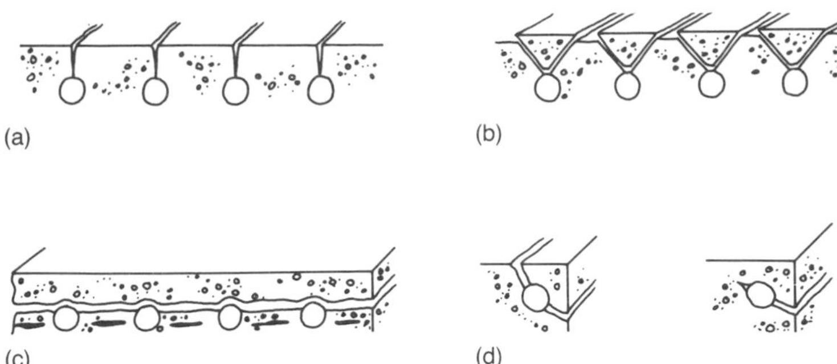

FIGURE 17.20 Different forms of damage from steel corrosion: (a) cracking; (b) spalling; (c) lamination; (d) corner effects (Browne, 1985).

thus sound concrete provides an excellent protective medium. However the passivity can be destroyed by either

1. a loss of alkalinity by carbonation of the concrete, in which the calcium hydroxide is neutralized by carbon dioxide from the air, producing calcium carbonate; or
2. chloride ions, e.g. from road de-icing salts or sea water.

Either of these can therefore create conditions for the corrosion reactions (17.10) to (17.13) or (17.14) to occur. The corrosion can be localized, for example in load induced cracks in the concrete, leading to pitting, or the corrosion cells can be quite large, for example if anodic areas have been created by penetration of chlorides into a locally poorly compacted area of concrete. However, it is important to remember that oxygen and water must still be available at the cathode to ensure reaction (17.12) continues.

As mentioned above, the corrosion products (ferric and ferrous hydroxide) have a much larger volume than the original steel, by about 2 to 3 times, and hence lead to bursting pressures in the concrete and, eventually, cracking. This damage can take various forms, as illustrated in Figure 17.20. The steel is then completely unprotected, and the corrosion can be very fast and destructive.

Since the carbon dioxide or chlorides will normally have to penetrate the concrete cover before the corrosion can be initiated, the total time to concrete cracking will consist of two parts, illustrated in Figure 17.21:

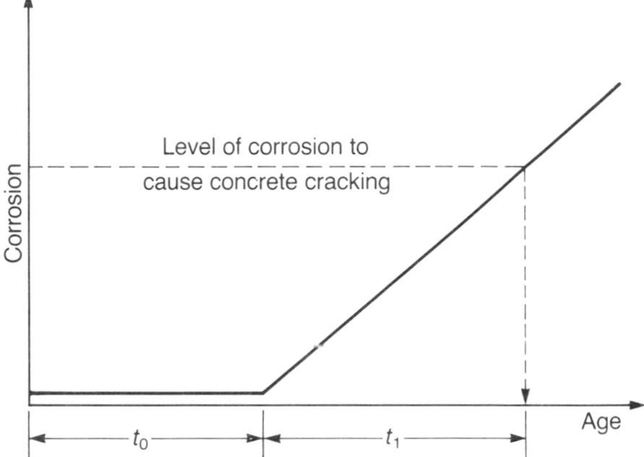

FIGURE 17.21 The two stages of corrosion damage: t_0 = time to initiation of corrosion, t_1 = time for sufficient corrosion to crack the concrete cover (Browne, 1983).

1. the time (t_0) for the depassivating agents (the carbon dioxide or chlorides) to reach the steel and initiate the corrosion;
2. the time (t_1) for the corrosion to then reach critical levels, i.e. sufficient to crack the concrete, which depends on the subsequent corrosion rate.

The processes for carbonation-induced corrosion and chloride-induced corrosion are considered separately.

17.4.2 Carbonation-induced corrosion

We discussed carbonation and its associated shrinkage in Chapter 15. Atmospheric carbon dioxide, when dissolved in the pore water in concrete, reacts rapidly with the calcium hydroxide produced during the cement hydration, forming calcium carbonate, and reducing the pH from 12 or more to about 8. There are also some reactions between the carbon dioxide and the other hydrates, but these are not significant in this context.

The carbonation reaction occurs first at the surface of the concrete and then progresses inwards, further supplies of carbon dioxide diffusing through the carbonated layer. The reaction is therefore a diffusion controlled process, as confirmed by Richardson (1988) whose extensive analysis showed that the carbonation depth (x) and time (t) are related by the simple expression

$$x = k \cdot t^{1/2} \qquad (17.15)$$

where k is a constant closely related to the diffusion characteristics of the concrete. The value of k depends on several factors, chiefly:

1. The degree of saturation of the concrete. It is necessary for the carbon dioxide to be dissolved in the pore water, and so concrete which has been dried by storing at low relative humidities will not carbonate. At the other extreme, the diffusion will be slow in concrete completely saturated with water, and so the fastest advance of the carbonation front occurs in partially saturated concrete at relative humidities of between 50 and 70%. Thus concrete surfaces which are sheltered will carbonate faster than those exposed to direct rainfall.
2. The pore structure of the concrete. It has

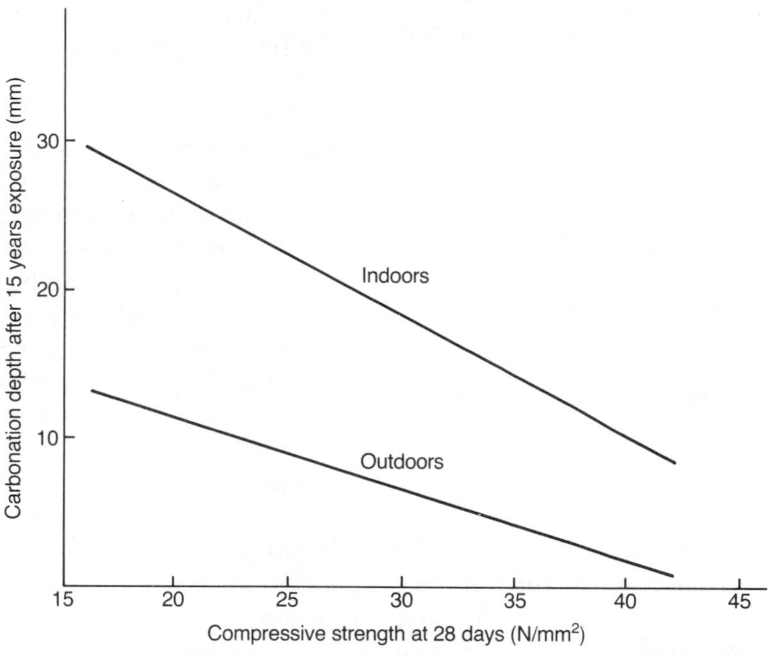

FIGURE 17.22 The relationship between carbonation depth and concrete strength (Nagataki *et al.*, 1986).

been suggested by Parrott (1987) that relating carbonation depth to concrete strength, as in Figure 17.22, is a useful way of combining the effects of water/cement ratio, cement content and incorporation of cement replacement materials.

Although cement replacement materials can result in lower overall porosity with full curing, incomplete curing can lead to higher porosity; the pozzolanic reaction can also reduce the calcium hydroxide content before carbonation, and so some care should be exercised when using these materials.

3. The carbon dioxide content of the environment.

Observed rates of carbonation, such as those shown in Figure 17.22, are such that with high-quality, well-cured concrete the carbonated region, even after many years' exposure to normal atmospheric conditions, is restricted to within 20–30 mm of the concrete surface. It is difficult to estimate or predict the rate of corrosion once the steel has been depassivated, and therefore design recommendations are aimed at ensuring that the depth and quality of concrete cover are sufficient to achieve a sufficiently long initiation period, t_0.

17.4.3 Chloride-induced corrosion

There are four common sources of the chlorides:

1. calcium chloride, a cheap and effective accelerator (see Section 13.2.2);
2. contamination in aggregates;
3. sea water, for coastal or marine structures; and
4. road de-icing salts, a particular problem on bridge decks.

In the first two cases the chlorides will be included in the concrete on mixing; if they are present in significant quantities the steel may never be passivated, and the initiation period, t_0, will be zero. Calcium chloride, or any chloride-containing admixture, is no longer permitted in concrete containing steel, but small amounts of chlorides from aggregates can be tolerated, because they participate in a reaction with the aluminate phases of the cement, and therefore no longer exist as chloride ions. Typical 'threshold' limits (expressed as chloride ion by weight of cement) are 0.2% for concrete made with sulphate resisting Portland cement; and 0.4% for concrete made with Portland or low heat Portland cement. More chlorides can be tolerated with the latter group as these cements contain higher proportions of aluminates.

Chlorides from sea water or de-icing salts have to penetrate the concrete cover in sufficient quantities to depassivate the steel before the corrosion is initiated: t_0 is finite in these circumstances. The transport mechanisms may be governed by the permeability in the case of, say, concrete permanently submerged in sea water; diffusivity, where salts are deposited on to saturated concrete; or sorptivity, where salts are deposited on to partially saturated concrete. The work of Bamforth and Pocock (1990), already discussed in Section 17.2.3, has indicated the importance of the absorption process in the early stages of contamination of concrete subject to salt spray, with the diffusion process being more important at later stages.

These processes result in chloride profiles such as those shown in Figure 17.23(a). Their form and magnitude depend on time of exposure, the exposure conditions and the concrete properties, with the properties of the cover zone being critical in ensuring that t_0 is as long as possible. Lower sorptivities and diffusivities, and hence increased values of t_0, are associated with lower water/cement ratios, higher cement contents and efficient curing. There is also evidence that the use of cement replacement materials, particularly pulverized fuel ash, can reduce the chloride penetration significantly, as shown in Figure 17.23(b).

Although recommendations for concrete cover and quality are aimed at extending the period t_0

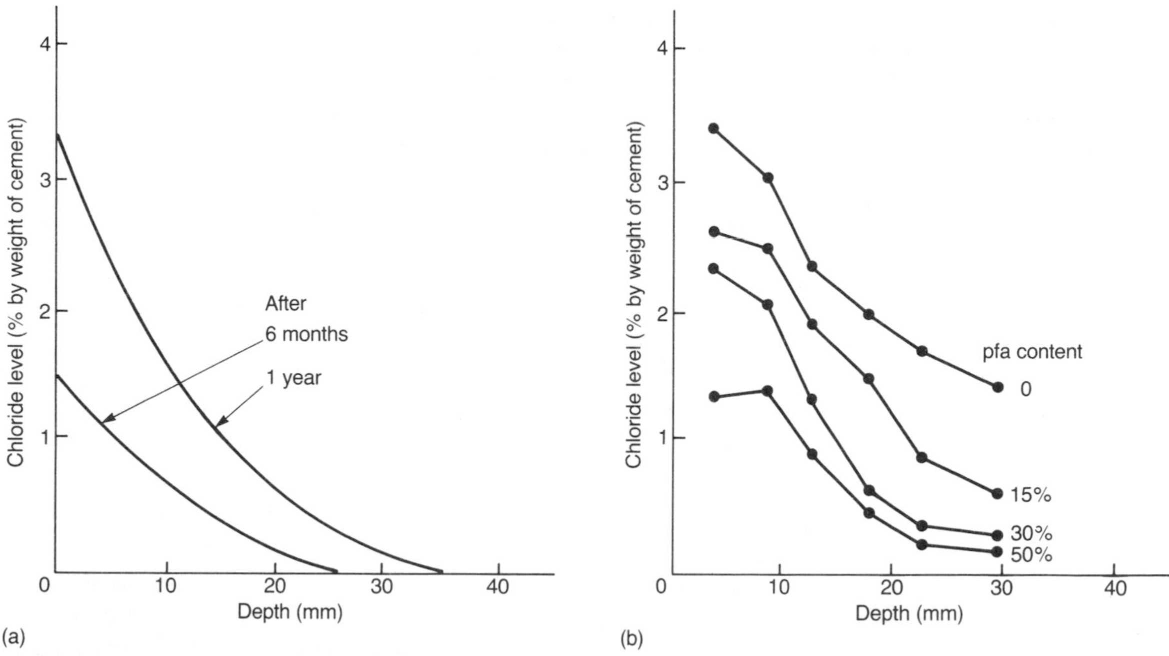

FIGURE 17.23 Chloride concentration profiles in concrete after marine exposure in tidal/splash zone: (a) the effect of exposure period (Portland cement concrete, moist-cured for 3 days, exposed from 28 days) (Bamforth and Pocock, 1990); (b) the effect of pfa (moist-cured for 1 day, exposed from 28 days for 2 years) (Thomas *et al.*, 1990).

as far as possible, there are circumstances in which it is impossible to prevent corrosion being initiated. Much research has therefore been carried out to determine the factors which control the rate of corrosion. These have been found to include the following.

1. The spacing and relative size of the anode and cathode in the corrosion cell. Relatively porous areas of a concrete member, such as a poorly compacted underside of a beam, will allow rapid penetration of chlorides, depassivating a small area of steel to form the anode. The reinforcement throughout the structure is normally electrically continuous, and so the remainder forms a large area cathode, resulting in a concentration of corrosion current, and hence a high corrosion rate, at the anode.
2. The availability of oxygen and moisture, particularly to sustain the cathodic reaction. If the supply of either is reduced, then the corrosion rate is reduced. Hence little corrosion occurs in completely dry concrete, and only very low rates in completely and permanently saturated concrete through which diffusion of oxygen is difficult.
3. The electrical resistivity of the electrolyte of the corrosion cell, i.e. the concrete. High resistivities reduce the corrosion current and hence the rate of corrosion, but increasing moisture content, chloride content and porosity all reduce the resistivity.

If the circumstances are such that protection against corrosion cannot be guaranteed by selection of the materials and proportions of the concrete, depth of cover and attention to

TABLE 17.3 British Standard recommendations for concrete exposed to sulphates (BS 8110: 1985)

Class	*Sulphate concentration in*		*Type of cement*	*Min cement content kg/m³*	*Max water/cement ratio*
	Soil %	*Groundwater gm/litre*			
1	<0.2	<0.3	Portland cement	No limit	No limit
2	0.2–0.5	0.3–1.2	Portland cement	330	0.50
			Portland cement + 25–40% pfa	310	0.55
			Portland cement + 70–90% ggbs		
			Sulphate resisting Portland cement (srpc)	280	0.55
3	0.5–1.0	1.2–1.5	Portland cement + 25–40% pfa	380	0.45
			Portland cement + 70–90% ggbs		
			srpc	330	0.50
4	1.0–2.0	2.5–5.0	srpc	370	0.45
5	>2.0	>5.0	srpc + protective coating	370	0.45

sound construction practice, then any of the following extra protective measures may be taken:

1. the addition of a corrosion inhibiting admixture such as calcium nitrite to the fresh concrete;
2. the use of corrosion-resistant stainless steel reinforcement bars, or epoxy-coated conventional bars;
3. applying a protective coating to the concrete, to reduce chloride and/or oxygen ingress;
4. cathodic protection of the reinforcement, i.e. applying a voltage from an external source sufficient to ensure that all of the steel remains permanently cathodic (see Section 11.4.3).

17.5 Recommendations for durable concrete construction

Most national codes of practice give due attention to durability criteria. Their requirements follow from the understanding of the degradation processes and the factors which influence their rate that have been discussed in this chapter, and typical examples are included in The British Standard Code of Practice for Structural Concrete (BS 8110).

Recommendations for the constituents and proportions of concretes to be exposed to sulphates are shown in Table 17.3. The environment is divided into five classes, depending on the concentration of the sulphates; no distinction between the types of sulphate is made. The need for an increasing quality of concrete and a less vulnerable cement, i.e. either sulphate resisting Portland cement or Portland cement

TABLE 17.4 Exposure conditions for concrete (BS 8110: 1985)

Environment	*Exposure conditions for concrete surfaces*
Mild	Protected against weather or aggressive conditions.
Moderate	Sheltered from severe rain or freezing. Subject to condensation. Continuously under water. In contact with non-aggressive soils.
Severe	Exposed to severe rain, alternate wetting and drying or occasional freezing.
Very severe	Exposed to sea water spray, de-icing salts, corrosive fumes or severe freezing whilst wet.
Extreme	Exposed to abrasive action, flowing water with pH less than 4.5, machinery or vehicles.

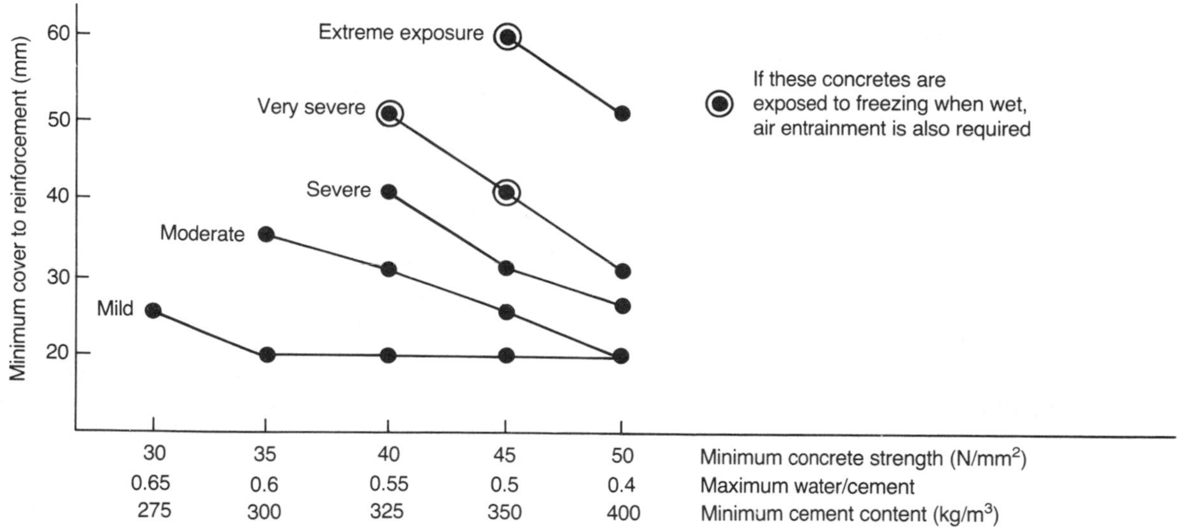

FIGURE 17.24 Requirements for concrete quality and cover to steel for the exposure conditions in Table 17.3 (BS 8110: 1985).

with pfa or ggbs, with increasing sulphate concentration is apparent. In the most extreme conditions (Class 5), a protective coating on the concrete is also required.

Other exposure conditions are combined into an overall classification of the environment from mild to extreme, as in Table 17.4. The requirements for both the concrete and the minimum cover to embedded steel are shown in Figure 17.24. Different combinations of cover, concrete quality and air entrainment are acceptable for any exposure condition. If pfa or ggbs is used, the value for minimum cement content is taken to be that of the cement plus replacement material, and the strength level must also be achieved.

TABLE 17.5 Recommended minimum periods of curing and protection (BS 8110: 1985)

Type of cement	*Ambient conditions* after casting*	*Minimum period of curing and protection* — *Average concrete surface temperature* *5 to 10°C*	*above 10°C*
Portland cement, srpc	average	4 days	3 days
	poor	6 days	4 days
All except Portland cement and srpc, and all with ggbs or pfa	average	6 days	4 days
	poor	10 days	7 days
All	good	no special requirements	

* Ambient conditions: good = damp and protected
poor = dry and unprotected
average = intermediate between good and poor.

The importance of adequate curing is shown by the requirements of Table 17.5. In anything less than the ideal conditions of a fully protected, damp environment, additional measures must be taken for several days, with longer periods being required if cement replacement materials are used.

Recommendations for more particular durability problems, such as the avoidance of alkali–silica reaction, have already been discussed.

17.6 References

Abrams, M.S. (1971) *Temperature and Concrete*, Amer. Conc. Inst. Special Publication No. 25, pp. 33–58.

Bamforth, P.B. (1987) *Magazine of Concrete Research*, **39**, No. 138, March, 3–11.

Bamforth, P.B. and Pocock, D.C. (1990) *Proceedings of Third International Symposium on Corrosion of Reinforcement in Concrete Construction*, Elsevier Applied Science, pp. 119–31.

British Standards Institution (1985) BS 8110: *The structural use of concrete. Part 1: Code of practice for design and construction.*

Browne, R.D. (1983) *Proceedings of the Symposium on Durable Concrete*, Institute of Concrete Technology, London.

Browne, R.D. (1985) *Proceedings of Seminar on Improvements in Concrete Durability*, Institute of Civil Engineers, London, pp. 97–130.

Buenfeld, N. and Newman, J.B. (1984) *Magazine of Concrete Research*, **36**, No. 127, June, 67–80.

Concrete Society (1987) *Alkali–silica reaction: minimising the risk of damage to concrete*, Technical Report No. 30, London.

Concrete Society (1988) *Permeability testing of site concrete*, Technical Report No. 31, London.

Dhir, R.K., Hewlett, P.C. and Chan, Y.N. (1987) *Magazine of Concrete Research*, **39**, No. 141, Dec., 183–95.

Hobbs, D.W. (1986) *Magazine of Concrete Research*, **38**, No. 137, Dec., 191–205.

Hobbs, D.W. (1988) *Alkali–Silica Reaction in Concrete*, Thomas Telford, London.

Lawrence, C.D. (1985) Concrete Society Materials Research Seminar on Serviceability of Concrete, Slough, July, published in Concrete Society (1988) above.

Nagataki, S., Ohga, H. and Kim, E.K. (1986) *Proceedings of the 2nd International Conference on Fly Ash, Silica Fume, Slag and Natural Pozzolans in Concrete*, Amer. Conc. Inst. Special Publication SP-91, pp. 521–40.

Page, C.L., Short, N.R. and El Tarras, A. (1981) *Cement and Concrete Research*, **11**, No. 3, 395–406.

Parrott, L.J. (1987) *A Review of Carbonation in Reinforced Concrete*, Cement and Concrete Association, Slough.

Powers, T.C. (1958) *J. Amer. Ceramic Soc.*, **41**, 1–6.

Powers, T.C., Copeland, L.E., Hayes, J.C. and Mann, H.M. (1954) *J. Amer. Conc. Inst.*, **5**, 285–98.

Richardson, M.G. (1988) *Carbonation of Reinforced Concrete: Its Causes and Management*, CITIS Ltd, Dublin.

Rose, D.A. (1965) *RILEM Bulletin*, No. 29.

Thomas, M.D.A., Matthews, J.D. and Haynes, C.A. (1990) *Proceedings of Third International Symposium on Corrosion of Reinforcement in Concrete Construction*, Elsevier Applied Science, pp. 198–212.

US Bureau of Reclamation (1955) Concrete Laboratory Report No. C-810, Denver, Colorado.

Verbeck, G.J. (1968) in *Performance of Concrete* (ed. E.G. Swenson), University of Toronto Press.

Further reading

General texts

Lea, F.M. (1970) *The Chemistry of Cement and Concrete*, 3rd edn, Edward Arnold, London.

Mehta, P.K. (1986) *Concrete: Structure, Properties and Materials*, Prentice-Hall, New Jersey.

Murdock, L.J., Brook, K.M. and Dewar, J.D. (1991) *Concrete Materials and Practice*, 6th edn, Edward Arnold, London.

Neville, A.M. (1981) *Properties of Concrete*, 3rd edn, Longman Scientific and Technical, Harlow.

Neville, A.M. and Brooks, J.J. (1987) *Concrete Technology*, Longman Scientific and Technical, Harlow.

Ramachandran, V.S., Feldman, R.F. and Beaudoin, J.J. (1981) *Concrete Science*, Heyden & Son Ltd, London.

Specialist texts

Hewlett, P.C. (ed.) (1988) *Cement Admixtures: Use and Applications*, 2nd edn, Longman, Harlow.

Hobbs, D.W. (1988) *Alkali–Silica Reaction in Concrete*, Thomas Telford, London.

Mays, G.C. (1992) *Durability of Concrete Structures: Investigation, Repair, Protection*, E. & F.N. Spon, London.

Neville, A.M., Dilger, W.H. and Brooks, J.J. (1981) *Creep of Plain and Structural Concrete*, Construction Press, London.

Pullar-Strecker, P. (1987) *Corrosion Damaged Concrete: Assessment and Repair*, Butterworths, London.

Richardson, M.G. (1988) *Carbonation of Reinforced Concrete: Its Causes and Management*, CITIS Ltd, Dublin.

Rixom, M.R. and Mailvaganam, N.P. (1986) *Chemical Admixtures for Concrete*, 2nd edn, E. & F.N. Spon, London.

Swamy, R.N. (1986) 'Cement replacement materials', Vol. 3 of *Concrete Technology and Design*, Surrey University Press.

Tattersall, G.H. (1991) *Workability and Quality Control of Concrete*, E. & F.N. Spon, London.

Tattersall, G.H. and Banfill, P.F.G. (1983) *The Rheology of Fresh Concrete*, Pitman Books, London.

Taylor, H.F.W. (1990) *Cement Chemistry*, Academic Press, London.

Part Four

Bituminous Materials

D.G. Bonner

Introduction

The term 'bituminous materials' is generally taken to include all materials consisting of aggregate bound with either bitumen or tar. Materials of this kind are used almost exclusively in road construction. However, bitumen and tar on their own have other uses in construction. For example bitumen is used in roofing materials and as a protective/waterproof coating. This part will concentrate on the use of bituminous materials in road construction.

The use of tar in road building materials began to grow significantly in the UK just after the turn of the century following the advent of the pneumatic tyre and the motor vehicle. Up to that time, roads were constructed following the principles developed by Macadam using water-bound, graded aggregate. Under the action of pneumatic tyres and the higher speeds of motor vehicles, a great deal of dust was generated on macadam roads which led to the use of tar as a dressing to bind the surface. Tar was eminently suitable for this purpose since it could be made sufficiently fluid, by the use of heat, to be sprayed, but stiffened on cooling. Furthermore, it protected the road from the detrimental effects of water. The benefits of using tar were quickly realized and a range of 'coated stone' materials, or 'tarmacadams', were developed.

References to natural sources of bitumen date back to biblical times. However, the first use of natural rock asphalt for paving roads was in the middle of the nineteenth century. The first refinery bitumens to be used in this country came from the Mexican oilfields around 1913. But it was the opening of the Shell Haven refinery in 1920 which gave rise to the rapid development of bitumen for road construction. Bitumen was found to be less temperature-susceptible than tar. Thus it is less soft than an equivalent grade of tar at high temperatures, making it more resistant to deformation, and less stiff than tar at low temperatures, making it less brittle and more resistant to cracking. As the performance required of bituminous materials increased, due to the increase in quantity and weight of traffic, bitumen became more widely used than tar. Although tar-bound materials predominated during the Second World War due to difficulties in importing crude oil, the introduction of North Sea gas in the late 1960s dramatically reduced the production of crude coal tar. Now the use of tar in road construction is limited to tar/bitumen blends for surface dressing and dense tar surfacing used in areas such as car parks where the greater resistance of tar to diesel and oil spillage is an advantage. Therefore the following chapters will deal only with bitumen.

A very wide range of bituminous mixtures have evolved to suit the wide variety of circumstances in which they are used. They vary according to their bitumen content and grade as well as their aggregate grading and size. However, they can all be classified into two groups, namely asphalts and macadams. (Here it should be noted that the term 'asphalt' is used with its European meaning, i.e. a particular type of mixture of bitumen and aggregate. In North America, 'asphalt' means bitumen.) Figure IV.1 illustrates the fundamentally different characteristics of asphalts and macadams. Asphalts rely on their dense, stiff mortar for strength and

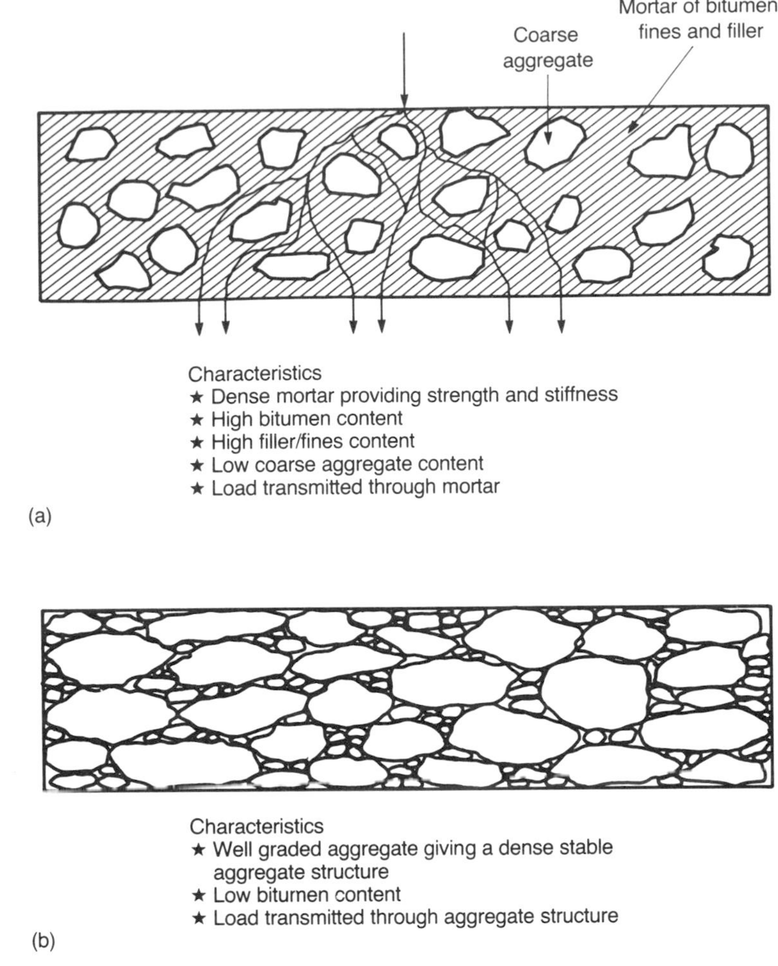

FIGURE IV.1 The essential features of asphalts and macadams: (a) asphalt; (b) macadam.

stiffness, whereas macadams rely on the stability of the aggregate through its grading. Thus the role of bitumen is quite different in each case, and the properties of asphalts are more strongly dependent on the nature of the bitumen than the properties of macadams. However, although Figure IV.1 portrays two very different types of material, there is in fact almost a continuous spectrum of materials between these two extremes. Thus there are asphalts which have a larger coarse aggregate content than suggested in Figure IV.1 so that the overall aggregate grading is more continuous and the materials resemble macadams in that respect. Similarly there are macadam mixes which are dense and contain more bitumen, and tend towards the model for asphalts. This will be discussed in more detail in Chapter 22.

Bituminous materials are used in so-called ‘flexible’ construction. The alternative is ‘rigid’ construction where the road consists essentially of a concrete slab. In flexible construction there are a number of layers to the road structure each having a specific function. Figure IV.2 illustrates

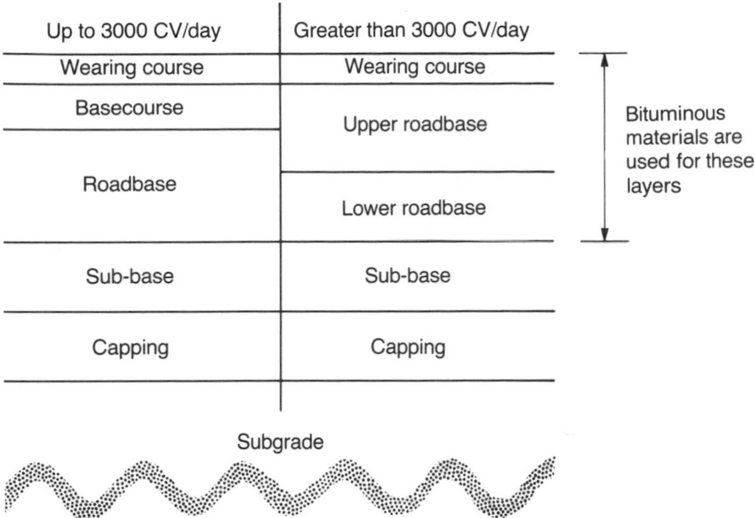

FIGURE IV.2 The structure of a flexible road according to the daily flow of commercial vehicles.

those layers and where bituminous materials may be used. The nature of the materials will vary according to their position and function in the structure. Thus both the wearing course and basecourse may be asphalts but the properties required of the wearing course at the surface are different from those required just below the surface in the basecourse. Therefore a wearing course asphalt differs from a basecourse asphalt. Also particular types of material are selected according to their suitability. Thus when traffic loads are very high, an asphalt roadbase may not provide sufficient resistance to deformation, but would give the necessary resistance to fatigue cracking. Therefore asphalt is used at the bottom of the roadbase where tensile stresses inducing cracks are greatest, and macadam is used for the upper part to provide improved resistance to deformation. This will be discussed more fully in Chapter 20.

Chapter eighteen

Structure

18.1 Constituents of bituminous materials
18.2 Bitumen
18.3 Types of bitumen
18.4 Aggregates
18.5 References

18.1 Constituents of bituminous materials

Bituminous materials consist of a graded aggregate bound together with bitumen. Thus they are two-phase materials and their properties depend upon the properties of the individual phases as well as the mix properties. The two phases are quite different in nature. Whilst the aggregate is stiff and hard, the bitumen is flexible and soft and is particularly susceptible to temperature change. Therefore the proportion of bitumen in the mix has a great influence on the mix properties and is crucial in determining the performance of the material.

Bitumen may be supplied in a number of forms either to facilitate the mixing and laying process or to provide a particular performance. Aggregates may come from a wide range of rock types or from artificial sources such as slag. The grading of the aggregate is important and ranges from continuous grading for mix types known as macadams through to gap grading for mixes known as asphalts. The very fine component of the aggregate (passing 75 microns) is called filler. Although the graded aggregate will normally contain some material of this size it is usually necessary to provide additional filler in the form of limestone dust, pulverized fuel ash or ordinary Portland cement.

18.2 Bitumen

18.2.1 Sources

There are two sources of bitumen: natural deposits and refinery bitumen.

Natural asphalts

Bitumen occurs naturally, formed from petroleum by geological forces, and always in intimate association with mineral aggregate. Types of deposit range from almost pure bitumen to bitumen-impregnated rocks and bituminous sands with only a few per cent bitumen.

Rock asphalt consists of porous limestone or sandstone impregnated with bitumen with a typical bitumen content of 10%. Notable deposits are in the Val de Travers region of Switzerland and the 'tar sands' of North America.

Lake asphalt consists of a bitumen 'lake' with finely divided mineral matter dispersed throughout the bitumen. The most important deposit of this type, and the only one used as a source of road bitumen in the UK, is the Trinidad Lake. The lake consists of an area of some 35 ha and extends to a depth of 100 m. Asphalt is dug from the lake, partially refined by heating to 160°C in open stills to drive off water, then filtered, barrelled and shipped. The material consists of 55% bitumen, 35% mineral matter and 10% organic matter. It is too hard in this form to use directly on roads and is usually blended with refinery bitumen.

Refinery bitumen

This is the major source of bitumen in the UK. In essence, bitumen is the residual material left after the fractional distillation of crude oil. Crudes vary in their bitumen content. The lighter paraffinic crudes, such as those from the Middle East and North Sea, have a low bitumen content which must be obtained by further processes after distillation. Heavier crudes, known as asphaltic crudes, such as those from the United States, contain more bitumen which is more easily extracted.

18.2.2 Manufacture

The process of refining crude oil yields a range of products as shown in Figure 18.1. These products are released at different temperatures with the volatility decreasing and viscosity increasing as the temperature rises. Bitumen is the residual material but its nature will depend on the distillation process and, in particular, on the extent to which the heavier oils have been removed. If the residual material contains significant amounts of heavy oils, it will be softer than if the heavy oils had been more thoroughly extracted. Modern refinery plant is capable of very precise control which enables bitumen to be produced consistently at a required viscosity.

18.2.3 Chemistry and molecular structure

Bitumen is a complex colloidal system of hydrocarbons and their derivatives which is soluble in trichloroethylene. The usual approach to determination of the constituents of a bitumen is through use of solvents. It may be subdivided into the following main fractions:

1. carbenes – fraction insoluble in carbon tetrachloride;
2. asphaltenes – fraction insoluble in light aliphatic hydrocarbon solvent, e.g. heptane;
3. maltenes – fraction soluble in heptane.

The last two fractions predominate and the maltenes may be further subdivided into resins (that part adsorbed on an active powder such as Fuller's earth) and oils. The asphaltenes have the higher molecular weight but their exact nature is dependent on the type of solvent and the volume ratio of solvent to bitumen. If small amounts of solvent are used, resins, which form part of the maltene fraction, may be adsorbed on to the asphaltene surfaces, yielding a higher percentage of asphaltene. Although they may vary according to method of extraction, the appearance of asphaltenes is always of a dark brown to black solid which is brittle at room temperature. They have a complex chemical

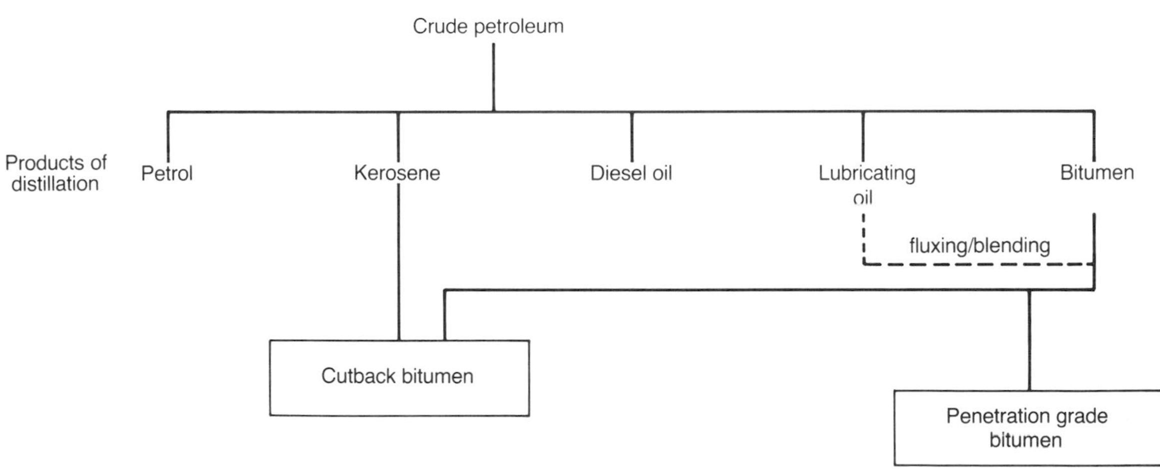

FIGURE 18.1 Preparation of refinery bitumens.

composition but consist chiefly of condensed aromatic hydrocarbons and include complexes with nitrogen, oxygen, sulphur and metals such as nickel and vanadium. The structure of asphaltenes is not known with certainty. One suggestion is of two-dimensional condensed aromatic rings, short aliphatic chains and naphthenic rings combined in a three-dimensional network (Dickie and Yen, 1967). Another suggestion is that there are two different molecular types, one being a simple condensed aromatic unit and the other consisting of collections of these simple units (Speight and Moschopedis, 1979). It is likely that all of these may exist in bitumens from different sources since the nature of the molecules present in a crude oil will vary according to the organic material from which the crude was formed, and to the type of surrounding geology.

Maltenes contain smaller molecular weight versions of asphaltenes called resins and a range of hydrocarbon groups known as 'oils' including olefins, naphthenes and paraffins. The aromatic oils are oily and dark brown in appearance and include naphtheno-aromatic type rings. The saturated oils are made up mainly of long straight saturated chains and appear as highly viscous whitish oil.

Bitumen is normally described as a colloidal system where the asphaltenes are solid particles in the form of a cluster of molecules or micelles in a continuum of maltenes (Girdler, 1965). Depending on the degree of dispersion of the micelles in the continuous phase, the bitumen may be either a sol, where there is complete dispersal, or a gel, where the micelles are flocculated into flakes. Bitumens with more saturated oils of low molecular weight have a predominantly gel character. Those with more aromatic oils, which are more like asphaltenes, have a predominantly sol character.

In terms of their influence on the properties of bitumen, asphaltenes constitute the body of the material, the resins provide the adhesive and ductile properties, and the oils determine the viscosity and rheology.

Although bitumens are largely complex mixtures of hydrocarbons, there are other elements present. The high molecular weight fraction contains significant amounts of sulphur, the amount of which influences the stiffness of the material. Oxygen is also present, and some complexes with oxygen determine the acidity of the bitumen. This is important in determining the ability of the bitumen to adhere either to aggregate particles or to road surfaces.

18.3 Types of bitumen

18.3.1 Penetration grades

Refinery bitumens are produced with a range of viscosities and are known as penetration grade

TABLE 18.1 Specification for penetration grade bitumens (*The Shell Bitumen Handbook*, 1990)

Property		*Test method*	*Grade of bitumen*		
			40 pen HD	*50 pen*	*100 pen*
Penetration at 25°C dmm*		BS 2000: Part 49	40 ± 10	50 ± 10	100 ± 20
Softening point, °C	min	BS 2000: Part 58	58	47	41
	max		68	58	51
Loss on heating for 5 h at 163°C		BS 2000: Part 45			
(a) loss by mass, %	max		0.2	0.2	0.5
(b) drop in penetration, %	max		20	20	20
Solubility in trichloroethylene, % by mass	min	BS 2000: Part 47	99.5	99.5	99.5
Permittivity at 25°C and 1592 Hz	min	BS 2000: Part 357	2.630	2.630	2.630

* 1 dmm = 0.1 mm

bitumens. The term derives from the test which is used to characterize them according to hardness. The range of penetration grades for road bitumens is from 15 to 450, although the most commonly used are in the range 50 to 200. The range is produced partly through careful control of the distillation process and partly by fluxing 'residual' bitumen with oils to the required degree of hardness. The specification for penetration grade bitumens is contained in BS 3690 Part 1(4). Table 18.1 indicates a range of tests with which penetration grade bitumens for road purposes must comply. These bitumens are specified by their penetration value (BS 2000: Part 49: 1983) and softening point (BS 2000: Part 58: 1983) which indicate hardness and viscosity respectively. However, they are designated only by their penetration, e.g. 50 pen bitumen has a penetration of 50 ± 10. In addition there are limits for loss on heating (BS 2000: Part 45: 1983) which ensures that there are no volatile components present whose loss during preparation and laying would cause hardening of the bitumen, and solubility (BS 2000: Part 47: 1983), which ensures that there are only negligible amounts of impurity. The permittivity test (BS 2000: Part 357: 1983) measures the dielectric constant for the material which has been shown to be related to the weathering characteristics.

18.3.2 Oxidized bitumens

Refinery bitumen may be further processed by air blowing. This consists of introducing air under pressure into a soft bitumen under controlled temperature conditions. The oxygen in the air reacts with certain compounds in the bitumen resulting in the formation of compounds of higher molecular weight. Thus the asphaltene content increases at the expense of the maltene content, resulting in harder bitumens which are also less ductile and less temperature-susceptible. Although these bitumens are mostly used for industrial applications such as roofing and pipe coatings, there is a road bitumen produced by this process known as heavy duty bitumen. It is regarded as a penetration grade bitumen and is included in Table 18.1 (40 pen HD).

18.3.3 Cutbacks

Penetration grade bitumen is thermoplastic and thus its viscosity varies with temperature. At ambient temperature it can be more or less solid and to enable it to be used for road construction it must be temporarily changed into a fluid state. This may simply be achieved by raising the temperature. However, for surface dressing and some types of bituminous mixture it is necessary

TABLE 18.2 Specification for cutback bitumens (BS 3690: Part 1: 1989)

Property		*Test method*	*Grade of cutback*		
			50 sec	*100 sec*	*200 sec*
Viscosity (STV) at 40°C, 10 mm cup, secs		BS 2000: Part 72	50 ± 10	100 ± 20	200 ± 40
Distillation		BS 2000: Part 27			
(a) distillate to 225°C, % by volume	max		1	1	1
360°C, % by volume			10 ± 3	9 ± 3	7 ± 3
(b) penetration at 25°C of residue from distillation to 360°C, dmm*		BS 2000: Part 49	100 to 350	100 to 350	100 to 350
Solubility in trichloroethylene, % by mass	min	BS 2000: Part 47	99.5	99.5	99.5

* 1 dmm = 0.1 mm

to have a fluid binder that can be applied and mixed at relatively low temperatures, but have an adequate hardness after laying. Cutback bitumens are penetration grade bitumens which have their viscosity temporarily reduced by dilution in a volatile oil. After application the volatile oil evaporates and the bitumen reverts to its former viscosity.

The curing time and viscosity of cutbacks can be varied according to the volatility of the diluting oil and the amount of diluent used. In the UK cutbacks are manufactured using 100 or 200 pen bitumen with kerosene. Three grades are produced to comply with a viscosity specification based on the standard tar viscometer (STV). Table 18.2 from BS 3690 shows that cutbacks also must comply with solubility, distillation and recovered penetration requirements. The last two are to ensure that the diluent will evaporate at the required rate and that the residual bitumen will have an appropriate hardness for the performance requirements.

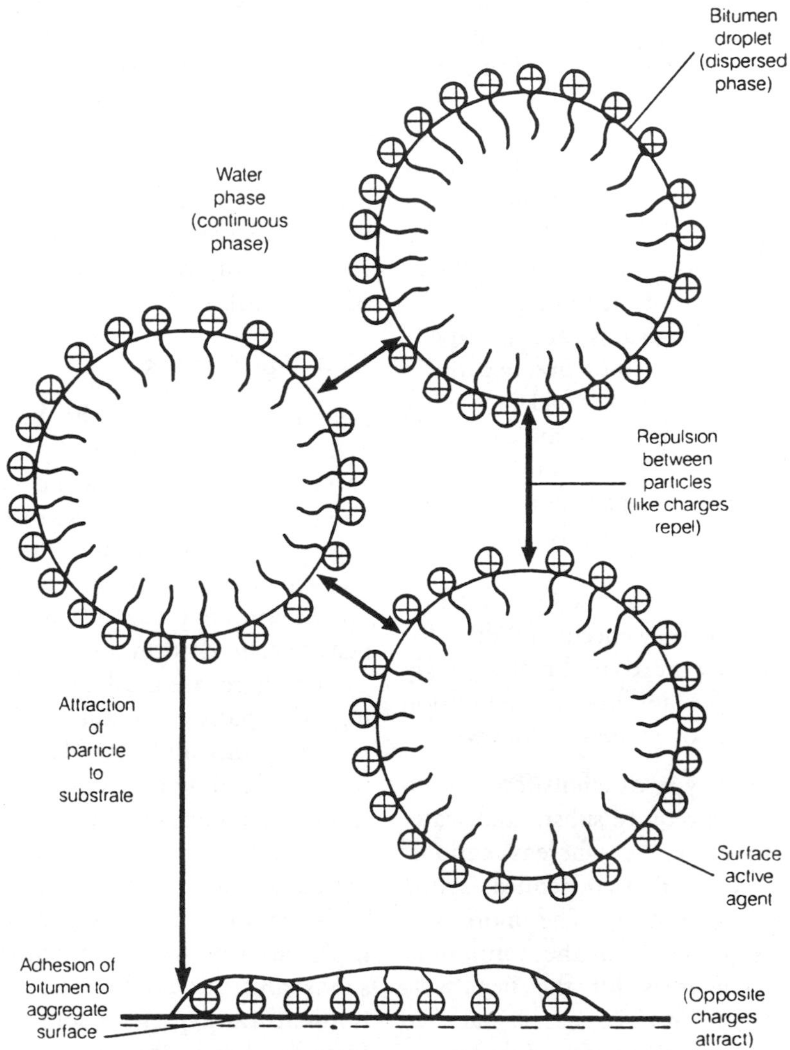

FIGURE 18.2 Schematic diagram of charges on bitumen droplets (*The Shell Bitumen Handbook*, 1990).

18.3.4 Emulsions

An emulsion is a two-phase system consisting of two immiscible liquids, one being dispersed as fine globules within the other. A bitumen emulsion consists of discrete globules of bitumen dispersed within a continuous phase of water, and is a means of enabling penetration grade bitumens to be mixed and laid.

Dispersal of the bitumen globules must be maintained electrochemically using an emulsifier which consists of a long hydrocarbon chain terminating with either a cationic or an anionic functional group. The hydrocarbon chain has an affinity for bitumen, whereas the ionic part has an affinity for water. Thus the emulsifier molecules are attracted to the bitumen globules with the hydrocarbon chain binding strongly to the bitumen leaving the ionic part on the surface of the globule as shown in Figure 18.2. Each droplet then carries a like surface charge depending on the charge of the ionic part of the emulsifier. Cationic emulsions are positively charged and anionic emulsions are negatively charged. The globules therefore repel each other making the emulsion stable. Cationic emulsions are preferred because they also aid adhesion, the positively charged bitumen globules being strongly attracted to the negatively charged aggregate surface.

Emulsions must satisfy two conflicting requirements in that they need stability for storage but also may need to break quickly when put into use. The stability of an emulsion depends on a number of factors as follows.

1. The quantity and type of emulsifer present. Anionic emulsions require substantial water loss before they break, whereas cationic emulsions break by physicochemical action before much evaporation. The more free emulsifier ions there are in the continuous phase, the easier it is for the negatively charged aggregate surface to be satisfied without attracting the bitumen globules.
2. Rate of water loss by evaporation. This in turn depends on ambient temperature, humidity and wind speed as well as rate and method of application.
3. The quantity of bitumen. Increasing the bitumen content will increase the breaking rate.
4. Size of bitumen globules. The smaller their size, the slower will be the breaking rate.
5. Mechanical forces. The greater the mixing friction or, in the case of surface dressing, the rolling and traffic action, the quicker the emulsion will break.

The viscosity of emulsions is important because a large proportion of emulsions are applied by spray. The viscosity increases with bitumen content and is very sensitive for values greater than about 60%. The chemistry of the aqueous phase is also important with viscosity being increased by decreasing the acid content or increasing the emulsifier content. The viscosity for road emulsions is specified in BS 434 Part 1.

18.4 Aggregates

Aggregates make up the bulk of bituminous materials; the percentage by weight ranges from about 92% for a wearing course asphalt to about 96% for an open-textured macadam. The aggregate has important effects on the strength and stiffness of bituminous mixtures. In more open-textured types of mix, the strength and resistance to deformation are largely determined by the aggregate grading with the bitumen acting principally as an adhesive. Here the grading is continuous and provides a dense packing of particles leading to a stable aggregate structure. In denser mixes, aggregate grading is again important, but the properties are largely determined by the matrix of fines and bitumen.

The majority of aggregates used in bituminous mixes are obtained from natural sources, either sands and gravels or crushed rock. The only non-natural aggregate source is slag, and blast furnace slag is the most commonly used. As with concrete, aggregates in bituminous mixes are regarded as inert fillers. However, whereas in concrete both the aggregate and the hcp are relatively stiff, in a bituminous mix, the bitumen is very soft compared to the aggregate. Therefore the role of the aggregate in determining mix stiffness and strength is more important in bituminous mixtures.

Three size ranges are recognized in aggregates for bituminous mixes. These are coarse, fine and filler. Coarse material is that retained on a 2.36 mm sieve, fine material passes 2.36 mm but is retained on the 75 micron sieve, and the filler is the material passing 75 microns.

18.4.1 Properties

The importance of grading has already been mentioned. In addition, aggregates suitable for use in bituminous mixes must have sufficient strength to resist the action of rolling during construction. For surfacing materials, they must also be resistant to abrasion and polishing in order to provide a skid-resistant surface. Here the shape and surface texture of aggregate particles are important.

Figure 18.3 gives typical grading curves for a dense macadam and an asphalt wearing course. The curve for the macadam clearly shows the continuous nature of the grading, whereas that for the asphalt shows a gap grading with a lack of material in the range 600 microns to 10 mm. This is typical of an asphalt where the 'mortar' of fines and filler bound with bitumen characterizes the material, the coarse aggregate providing the bulk.

The strength of aggregate is assessed in two ways. For resistance to crushing, the aggregate crushing value test is used. This test (BS 812: Part 110: 1990) determines the extent to which an aggregate crushes when subjected to a steadily increasing load up to 40 tonnes. The test sample consists of single-sized particles, 10–14 mm, and the amount of fines produced in the test is expressed as a percentage of the original sample. A variation of this test for weaker aggregates is the 10% fines test. Here the maximum crushing

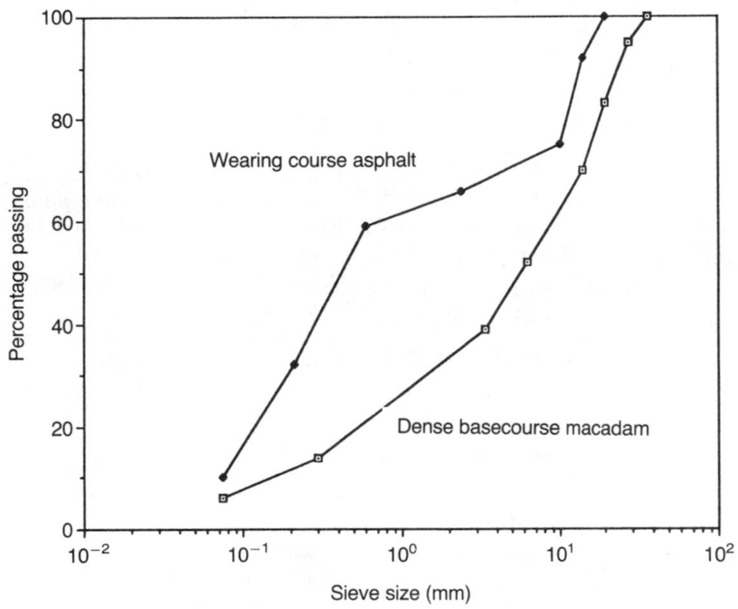

FIGURE 18.3 Aggregate grading curves.

FIGURE 18.4 Measurement of macrotexture using the sand patch test.

load which will produce 10% fines from the original single-sized sample is determined. The importance of this test is to assess the extent of crushing which may occur during compaction.

Resistance to impact loads is also required for road aggregates. The impact value test (BS 812: Part 112: 1990) determines the response of aggregate to blows from a heavy hammer. Once again the outcome of the test is the percentage of fines produced from the original single-sized sample.

The skid resistance of a road surface is provided largely by the aggregate exposed at the surface. There are two components which are referred to as macrotexture and microtexture. The macrotexture is the overall road surface roughness which arises from the extent to which there are spaces between aggregate particles. This is a function of mix proportions. For example, an asphalt provides an extremely low macrotexture because the coarse aggregate content is low and coarse particles are immersed in the fines/filler/bitumen mortar. Consequently, a layer of single-sized aggregate particles is rolled into the surface to provide the required macrotexture. These are precoated with a film of bitumen to improve adhesion to the asphalt surface and are known as coated chippings. Macadams on the other hand have a lower proportion of fines and filler and provide a rough surface.

Macrotexture is measured in terms of texture depth using the sand patch test (BS 598: Part 105: 1990). The test involves spreading a known volume of sand in a circular patch over the road surface until it can be spread no further. The sand fills the spaces between aggregate particles as shown in Figure 18.4. The diameter of the patch is measured and, knowing the volume of sand, the average depth can be calculated.

Microtexture refers to the surface texture of individual particles and varies according to the type of aggregate. Here it is important not only to use an aggregate which has a rough surface texture, but also which will retain that texture under the action of traffic. This is assessed using the polished stone value test (BS 812: Part 114: 1989). Here samples of aggregate are subjected to a simulated wear test, where a pneumatic tyre runs continuously over the aggregate particles under the abrasive action of emery powder. The skidding resistance of the samples is determined after the test using the pendulum skid tester.

18.5 References

British Standard 2000: Part 27: 1982: *Distillation of cutback asphaltic (bituminous) products.*

British Standard 2000: Part 45: 1983: *Loss on heating of bitumen and flux oil.*

British Standard 2000: Part 47: 1983: *Solubility of bituminous binders.*

British Standard 2000: Part 49: 1983: *Penetration of bituminous materials.*

British Standard 2000: Part 58: 1983: *Softening point of bitumen (ring and ball).*

British Standard 2000: Part 72: 1982: *Viscosity of cutback bitumen and road oil.*

British Standard 2000: Part 357: 1983: *Permittivity of bitumen.*

British Standard 434: Part 1: 1984: *Bitumen road emulsions (anionic and cationic). Part 1: Specification for bitumen road emulsions.*

British Standard 812: Part 114: 1989: *Method for determination of polished stone value.*

British Standard 3690: Part 1: 1989: *Bitumens for building and civil engineering. Part 1: Specification for bitumens for road purposes.*

British Standard 598: Part 105: 1990: *Methods of test for the determination of texture depth.*

British Standard 812: Part 110: 1990: *Methods for determination of aggregate crushing value.*

British Standard 812: Part 112: 1990: *Methods for determination of aggregate impact value.*

Dickie, T.P. and Yen, T.F. (1967) Macrostructure of asphaltic fractions by various instrumental methods. *Analytical Chemistry*, **39**.

Girdler, R.B. (1965) Constitution of asphaltenes and related studies. *Proceedings of the Association of Asphalt Paving Technologists*, **34**.

Speight, J.G. and Moschopedis, S.E. (1979) Some observations on the molecular 'nature' of petroleum asphaltenes. *American Chemical Society*, Division of Petroleum Chemistry, **24**.

The Shell Bitumen Handbook (1990) Shell Bitumen UK.

Chapter nineteen

Viscosity and deformation

19.1 Viscosity and rheology of binders
19.2 Measurement of viscosity
19.3 Influence of temperature on viscosity
19.4 Resistance of bitumens to deformation
19.5 Determination of permanent deformation
19.6 Factors affecting permanent deformation of bituminous mixes
19.7 References

19.1 Viscosity and rheology of binders

The viscosity of a liquid is the property that retards flow so that when a force is applied to the liquid, the higher the viscosity, the slower will be the movement of the liquid. The viscosity of bitumen is dependent upon both its chemical make-up and its structure. In sol-type bitumens, the asphaltene micelles are well dispersed within the maltene continuum. The viscosity depends on the relative amounts of the asphaltenes and maltenes, decreasing as the asphaltene content reduces. In gel-type bitumens, where the asphaltene micelles have aggregated, the viscosity is higher and dependent upon the extent of the aggregation. The degree of dispersion of the asphaltenes is controlled by the relative amounts of resins, aromatics and saturated oils. If there are sufficient aromatics they form a stabilizing layer around the asphaltene micelles, promoting the dispersion. However, if they are not present in sufficient quantity the micelles will tend to join together. A schematic representation of the two states is shown in Figure 19.1 (*The Shell Bitumen Handbook*, 1990). In practice most bitumens are somewhere between these two states. The maltene continuum is influenced by the saturated oils which have low molecular weight and consequently a low viscosity. These saturates have little solvent power in relation to the asphaltenes, so that as the saturate fraction increases, there is a greater tendency for the asphaltenes to aggregate to form a gel structure. Thus a high proportion of saturates on the one hand tends to reduce viscosity because of their low molecular weight, but on the other hand encourages aggregation of the asphaltene micelles which increases viscosity. The relative importance of these two opposing effects depends on the stabilizing influence on the asphaltenes of the aromatics.

The asphaltenes exert a strong influence on viscosity in three ways. Firstly, the viscosity increases as the asphaltene content increases. Secondly, the shape of the asphaltene particles governs the extent of the change in viscosity. The asphaltene particles are thought to be formed from stacks of plate-like sheets of aromatic/naphthenic ring structures. These sheets are held together by hydrogen bonds. However, the asphaltenes can also form into extended sheets and combine with aromatics and resins so that particle shape varies. Thirdly, the asphaltenes may tend to aggregate, and the greater the degree of aggregation the higher is the viscosity.

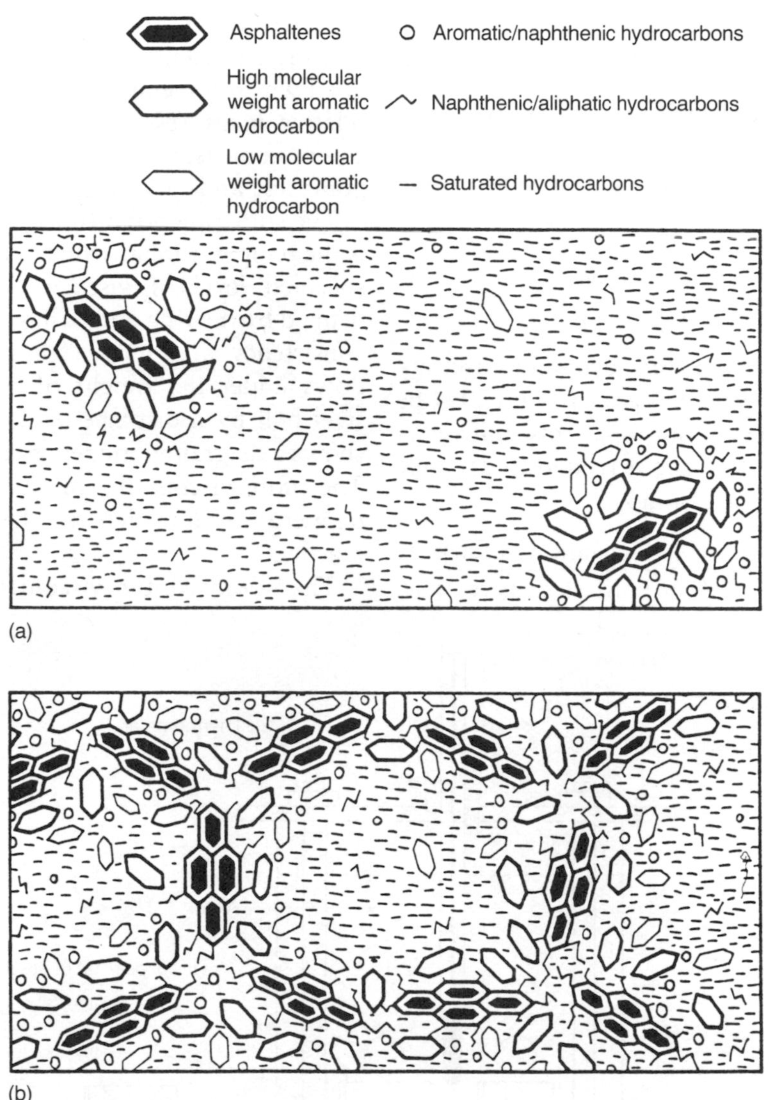

FIGURE 19.1 The structure of bitumen: (a) schematic diagram of a sol-type bitumen; (b) schematic diagram of a gel-type bitumen (*The Shell Bitumen Handbook*, 1990).

19.2 Measurement of viscosity

An absolute measure of viscosity can be determined using the sliding plate viscometer. If a thin film of bitumen is held between two parallel plane surfaces, and one surface is moved parallel to the other, the movement is resisted by the bitumen, according to its viscosity. The force of resistance, F, depends on the area of the surfaces, A, the distance between them, d, and the speed of movement of one plate relative to the other, V, such that

$$F = \eta\frac{AV}{d}$$

The factor η is the coefficient of viscosity, and is given by

$$\eta = \frac{F}{A} \div \frac{V}{d}$$

$$= \frac{\text{Shear stress}}{\text{Rate of strain}}.$$

This is known as the dynamic viscosity and has units of Pa sec. Viscosity may also be measured in units of mm^2/sec. This unit refers to kinematic viscosity and is related to dynamic viscosity by the expression:

$$\text{Kinematic viscosity} = \frac{\text{Dynamic viscosity}}{\text{Mass density}}.$$

However, it is not necessary to know absolute viscosity, and a number of tests have been developed which are empirical and provide arbitrary relative measures of viscosity. The two most common measures of viscosity are the softening point test and the standard tar viscometer.

The softening point (BS 2000: Part 58: 1983) is the temperature at which a bitumen reaches a specified level of viscosity. This viscosity is defined by the ring and ball test apparatus as the consistency at which a thin disc of bitumen flows under the weight of a 10 mm diameter steel ball by a distance of 25 mm. Figure 19.2 shows a diagrammatic representation of the test. The more viscous the bitumen, the higher the temperature at which this level of viscosity is reached.

The standard tar viscometer, as the name

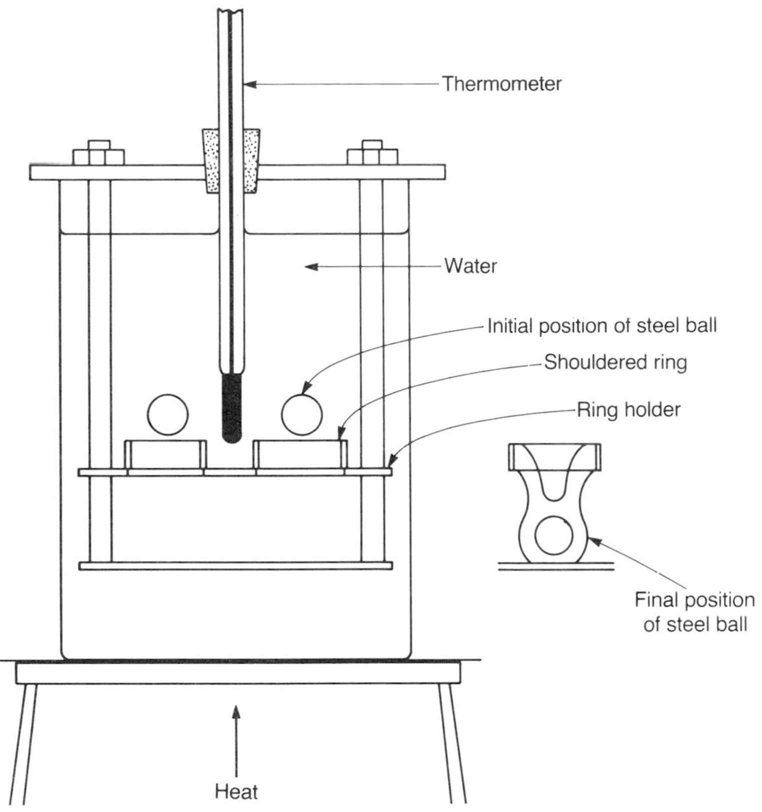

FIGURE 19.2 Apparatus for ring and ball test.

implies, is normally used to assess the viscosity of tars. Tars have a greater range of viscosity than bitumens, extending to lower values, and the test allows for this range by permitting a variation in test temperature. The test involves the measurement of the time taken for 50 ml of the tar to run out of a cup through a standard orifice (BS 2000: Part 72: 1982). Results obtained at different test temperatures selected to ensure that the efflux time lies between 10 and 140 sec are related to a common equiviscous temperature scale. The viscosity defined for this scale is that at which 50 ml flows out in 50 sec. The test is not used for penetration grade bitumens since these are too viscous to reach the defined viscosity except at very high temperatures which cannot confidently be converted to the empirical equiviscous temperature scale. However, the test is used for cutback bitumens. The efflux time depends on kinematic viscosity, and the test results may be converted to absolute viscosity in Pa sec according to:

$$\eta = \text{flow time} \times \text{density} \times \text{constant}.$$

For cutback bitumens, using a cup with a 10 mm orifice, the constant is 0.40.

Another test which is commonly applied to bitumens, and is the basis for their characterization, is the penetration test. The test measures hardness, but this is related to viscosity. The test consists of measuring the depth to which a needle penetrates a sample of bitumen under a load of 100 g over a period of 5 sec at a temperature of 25°C. Thus the test differs from the previous two in that, rather than determining an equiviscous temperature, the viscosity is determined at a particular temperature.

However, because bitumen is viscoelastic, the penetration will depend on the elastic deformation as well as the viscosity. Therefore, since viscosity changes with temperature, different bitumens may have the same hardness at 25°C but different hardnesses at other temperatures. It is the varying elasticity of bitumens which prevents correlation between these empirical tests.

19.3 Influence of temperature on viscosity

Bitumens are thermoplastic materials so that they soften as the temperature rises but become hard again when the temperature falls. The extent of the change in viscosity with temperature varies between different bitumens. It is clearly important, in terms of the performance of a bitumen in service, to know the extent of the change in viscosity with temperature. This is referred to as temperature susceptibility and, for bitumens, is determined from the penetration value, P, and softening point temperature, T. These are related empirically by the expression:

$$\log P = AT + k$$

where A is the temperature susceptibility of the logarithm of penetration and k is a constant. From this relationship, an expression has been developed (Pfeiffer and Van Doormaal, 1936) which relates A to an index, known as the penetration index, PI, such that for road bitumens the value of PI is about zero.

$$A = \frac{\mathrm{d}(\log P)}{\mathrm{d}T} = \frac{20 - \mathrm{PI}}{10 + \mathrm{PI}} \cdot \frac{1}{50}.$$

It has been determined that, for most bitumens, the penetration at their softening point (SP) temperature is about 800. Thus if the penetration at 25°C and the softening point temperature are known, the PI can be evaluated from:

$$\frac{\mathrm{d}(\log P)}{\mathrm{d}T} = \frac{\log 800 - \log P}{\mathrm{SP} - 25}$$

$$= \frac{20 - \mathrm{PI}}{10 + \mathrm{PI}} \cdot \frac{1}{50}.$$

For example, for a 50 pen bitumen with a softening point of 48°C,

$$\frac{\mathrm{d}(\log P)}{\mathrm{d}T} = \frac{\log 800 - \log 50}{48 - 25}$$

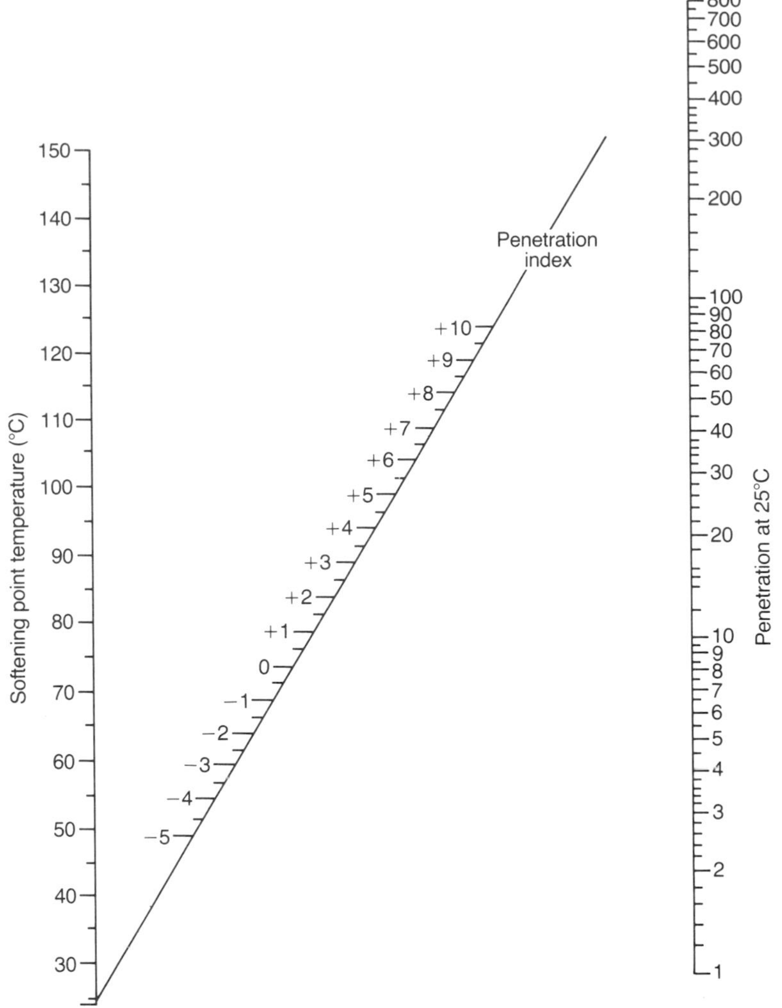

FIGURE 19.3 Nomograph to evaluate penetration index from softening point and penetration (Pfeiffer and Doormaal, 1936).

$$= \frac{1.204}{23} = 0.0523.$$

Therefore:

$$0.0523 = \frac{20 - \text{PI}}{10 + \text{PI}} \cdot \frac{1}{50}$$

giving:

$$\text{PI} = 1.7.$$

Pfeiffer and Van Dormaal produced a nomograph (Figure 19.3) to evaluate the above expression, and it can be seen that for the above example a similar result is obtained.

Bitumens for road use normally have a PI in the range −2 to +2. If the PI is low, bitumens are more Newtonian in their behaviour and become very brittle at low temperatures. High PI bitumens have marked time-dependent elastic

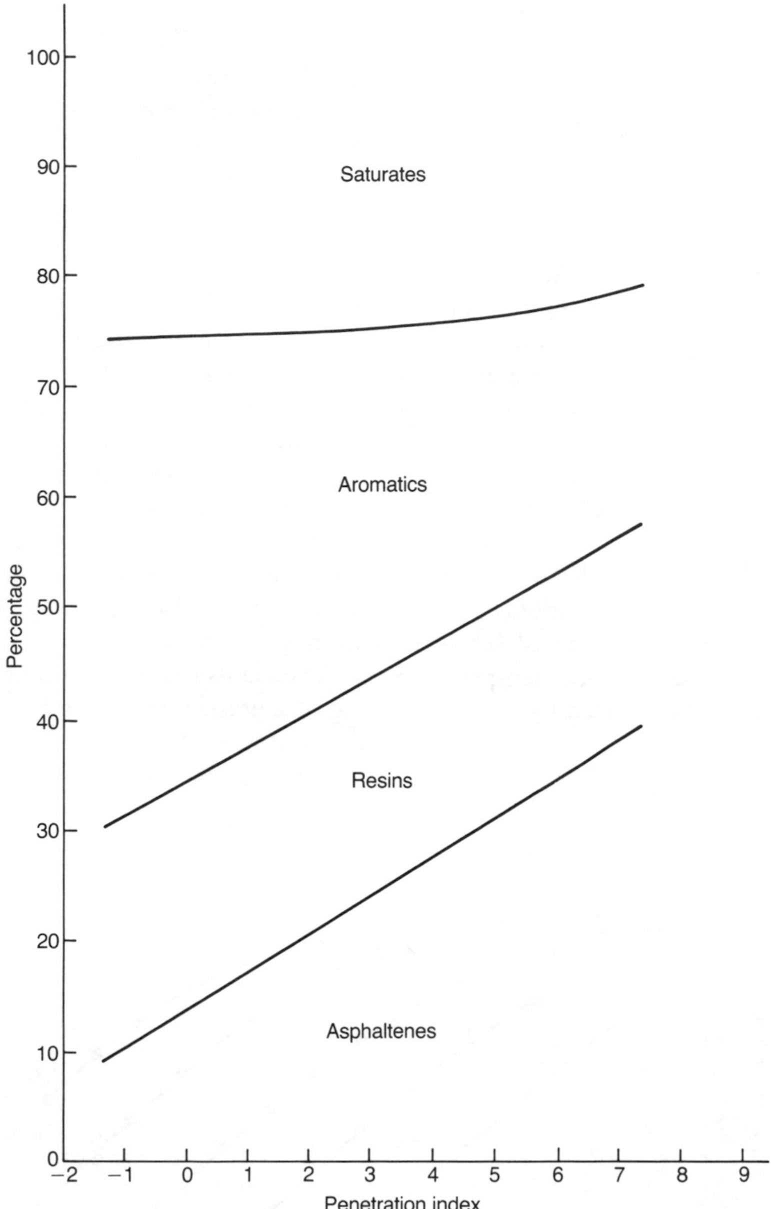

FIGURE 19.4 Relationship between chemical composition and penetration index (Lubbers, 1985).

properties and give improved resistance to permanent deformation.

The influence of chemical composition on temperature susceptibility is illustrated in Figure 19.4. In general the PI increases as the asphaltenes increase at the expense of the aromatics. This change can be achieved by controlled air blowing. Heavy duty bitumen (40 pen) is produced by this technique and has a PI of about 2.5. As a consequence, mixes incorporating this bitumen have a better resistance to deformation.

19.4 Resistance of bitumens to deformation

Since bitumen is a viscoelastic material, the response to an applied load depends on the size of the load, the temperature, and the duration of its application. In other words there is no simple relationship between stress and strain. Therefore it is difficult to predict the elastic modulus of bitumen. However, this modulus is of crucial importance in determining the resistance of a bituminous mixture to permanent deformation. Therefore if the performance of a mix is to be assessed, it is necessary to obtain a value for elastic modulus. Van der Poel (1954) has introduced the concept of stiffness modulus to take account of the viscoelastic nature of bitumen. This modulus is dependent on both temperature and time of loading, and is given by:

$$S_{t,T} = \frac{\sigma}{\varepsilon_{t,T}}$$

where σ is the tensile stress and $\varepsilon_{t,T}$ is the resultant strain after loading time at temperature T. Figures 19.5 and 19.6 illustrate the effect of loading time and temperature for bitumens of different PI. For low PI bitumens (Figure 19.5) the stiffness is constant for very short loading times and virtually independent of temperature. This represents elastic behaviour. For longer loading times the curves have a consistent slope of 45° and have a significant variation with temperature indicating viscous behaviour. The effect of increasing PI can be seen by comparing Figures 19.5 and 19.6. High PI bitumens are much stiffer at high temperatures and longer loading times. Thus under conditions which are more likely to give rise to deformation, namely slow moving or stationary traffic and high temperatures, a high PI bitumen offers greater resistance to deformation by virtue of its higher stiffness.

When considering a bituminous mix, consisting of a graded aggregate bound with bitumen, the stiffness of the mix is dependent on the stiffness of the bitumen and the quantity of

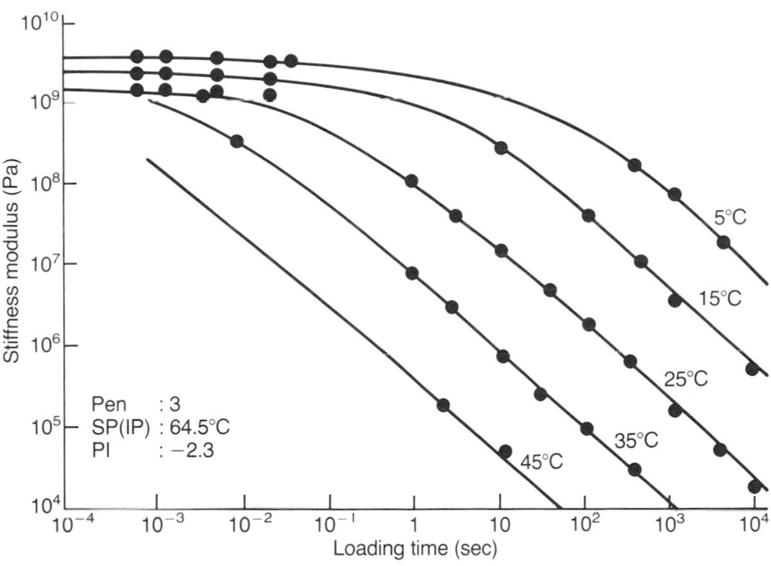

FIGURE 19.5 The effect of temperature and loading time on stiffness of a low PI bitumen (*The Shell Bitumen Handbook*, 1990).

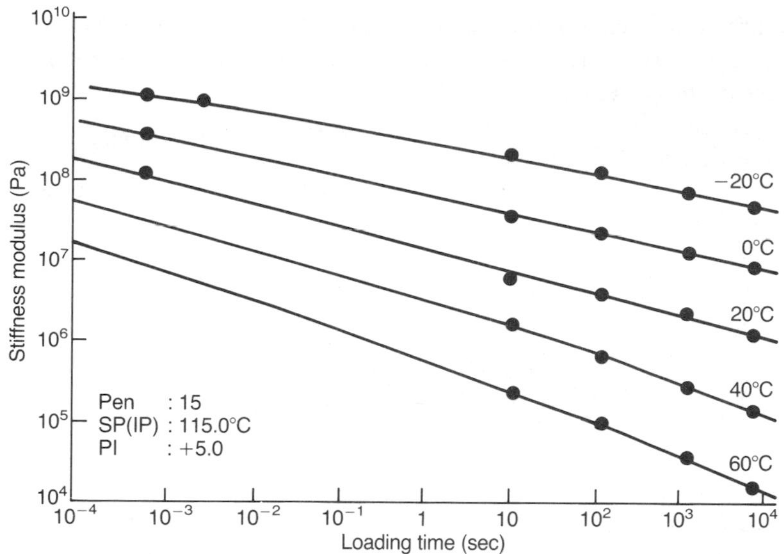

FIGURE 19.6 The effect of temperature and loading time on stiffness of a high PI bitumen (*The Shell Bitumen Handbook*, 1990).

aggregate in the mix (Van der Poel, 1955). The quantity of aggregate depends on its grading, particle shape and texture, and method of compaction.

19.5 Determination of permanent deformation

Rutting of bituminous pavements is the most common type of failure in the UK. It is therefore important to be able to predict the deformation for a bituminous mix and this depends on the low stiffness response, that is the stiffness at long load times. Two tests which have been commonly used to determine fundamental values of stiffness are the creep test and the repeated load triaxial test.

In the creep test, a uniaxial load of 0.1 MPa is applied to a cylindrical specimen for 1 hour at 40°C. During the test, deformation is measured as a function of time. The stiffness, S_{mix}, of the mix may then be determined from:

$$S_{mix} = \frac{\text{Applied stress}}{\text{Axial strain}}.$$

Although simple, and giving good correlation with rutting measurements, the test does not employ a confining stress. In-situ materials will clearly be confined and the effect of the confining stress on the vertical strain may be important.

The repeated load triaxial test overcomes this disadvantage and simulates more closely the actual conditions of stress in a bituminous pavement layer. This test is similar to that used in soil mechanics. A cylindrical specimen with a height/diameter ratio of at least 2.5 : 1 is subjected to a static confining pressure whilst a cyclic vertical stress is applied. The resulting vertical and horizontal strains can be measured and stiffness deduced. However, the good correlation between creep and rutting tests has led to the creep test being more commonly used.

A model has been developed (Hills *et al.*, 1974) linking creep results and rutting as follows:

$$R = \frac{C_m \times H \times \sigma_{av}}{S_{mix}}$$

where R = rut depth, C_m = correlation factor varying between 1 and 2, H = layer thickness, σ_{av} = average stress in the pavement, related to wheel load and stress distribution, and S_{mix} = stiffness of the mix as determined from the creep test.

19.6 Factors affecting permanent deformation of bituminous mixes

19.6.1 Bitumen viscosity

When a stress is applied to a bituminous material, both the aggregate particles and the bitu-

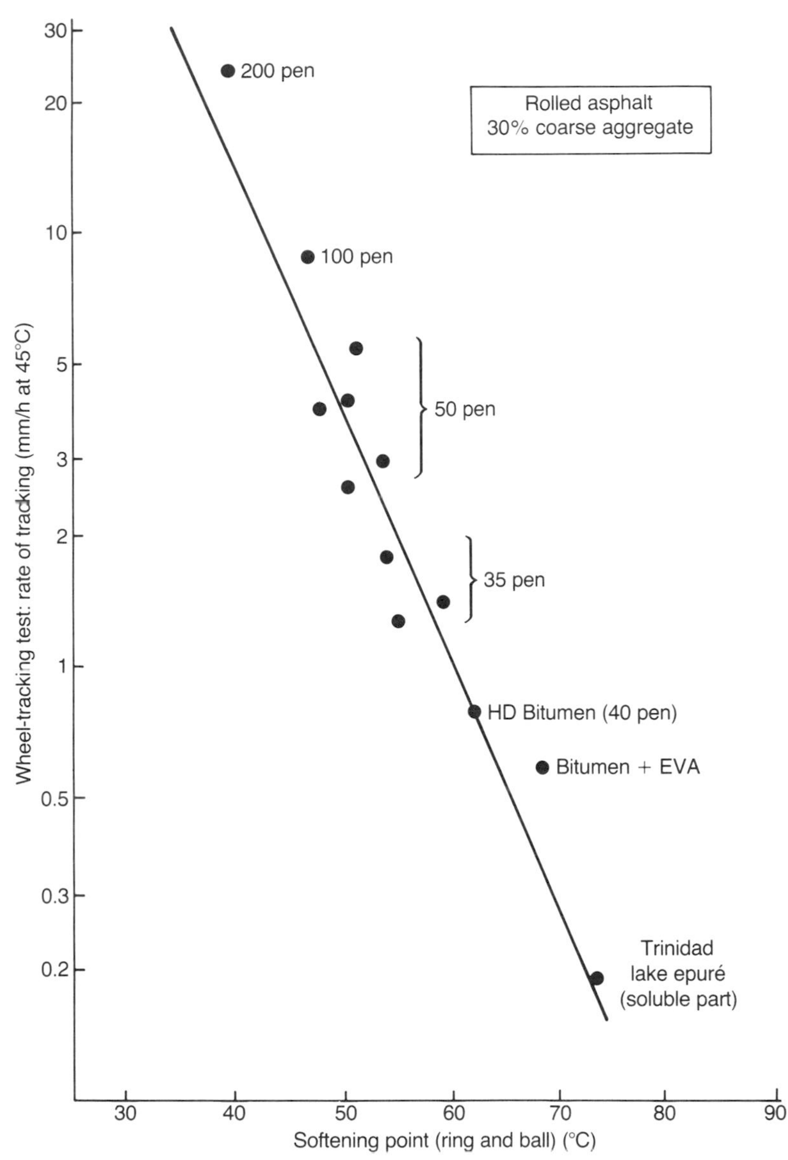

FIGURE 19.7 Effect of softening point of binder on resistance to deformation (Szatkowski, 1980).

men will be subjected to the stress. But the aggregate particles, being hard and stiff, will undergo negligible strain, whereas the bitumen, being soft, will undergo considerable strain. Thus the deformation is associated with movement in the bitumen and the extent of the movement will depend on its viscosity. Figure 19.7 shows how the rate of deformation, as measured by the wheel-tracking test, varies with the softening point of the bitumen. It can be seen that a reduction in softening point of 5°C will approximately double the deformability.

19.6.2 Aggregate

Bituminous mixtures which utilize a continuously graded aggregate – macadams – rely mainly on aggregate particle interlock for their resistance to deformation. Thus the grading and particle shape of the aggregate are major factors governing deformation. The characteristics of the fine aggregate are particularly important in gap-graded materials which rely on a dense bitumen and fines mortar for their strength. These are the asphalt mixes. Sand particles can vary considerably from spherical glassy grains in dune sands, to angular and relatively rough grains from some pits. Mixes made with a range of sands all at the same bitumen content have been shown to give deformations, when tested in the laboratory wheel-tracking test, that varied by a factor of 4 from the best to the worst sand (Knight *et al.*, 1979).

19.6.3 Temperature

Figure 19.8 shows permanent strain against number of test cycles in a repeated load triaxial test. It can be seen that permanent strain increases with temperature. This is due to the reduction in viscosity of bitumen and consequent reduction in bitumen stiffness. The figure also indicates the effect of the aggregate grading. At low temperatures, the permanent strain in the asphalt and macadam are the same. Here the high degree of aggregate particle interlock in the macadam and the high viscosity bitumen in the asphalt provide a similar resistance to deformation. However, at higher temperatures, the asphalt deforms more because its stiff-

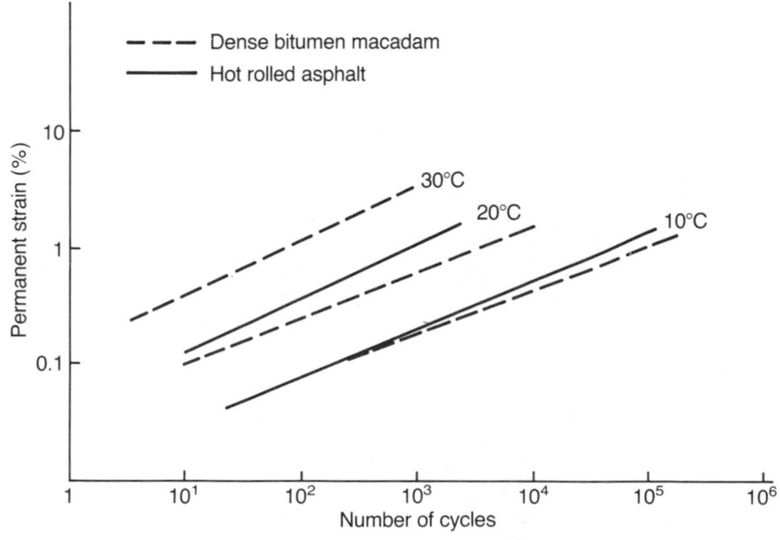

FIGURE 19.8 Comparison of permanent strain for dense macadam and hot rolled asphalt base mixes (Brown, 1978).

ness is reduced by the reduced bitumen viscosity, which is not compensated by the aggregate interlock effect. In the macadam, although the bitumen will also be less stiff, the aggregate grading continues to provide a compensating resistance to deformation.

19.7 References

British Standard 2000: Part 58: 1983: *Softening point of bitumen (ring and ball).*

British Standard 2000: Part 72: 1982: *Viscosity of cutback bitumen and road oil.*

Brown, S.F. (1978) Material characteristics for analytical pavement design. In *Developments in Highway Pavement Engineering – 1*, Applied Science Publishers, London.

Hills, J.F., Brien, D. and Van de Loo, P.J. (1974) *The correlation of rutting and creep tests on asphalt mixes*, Institute of Petroleum, IP-74-001.

Knight, V.A., Dowdeswell, D.A. and Brien, D. (1979) Designing rolled asphalt wearing courses to resist deformation. In *Rolled Asphalt Road Surfacings*, ICE, London.

Lubbers, H.E. (1985) *Bitumen in de weg- en waterbouw.* Nederlands Adviesbureau voor bitumentopassingen.

Pfeiffer, J.Ph. and Van Doormaal, P.M. (1936) The rheological properties of asphaltic bitumens. *Journal of Institute of Petroleum*, **22**.

Szatkowski, W.S. (1980) Rolled asphalt wearing courses with high resistance to deformation. In *Rolled Asphalt Road Surfacings*, ICE, London.

The Shell Bitumen Handbook (1990) Shell Bitumen UK.

Van der Poel, C. (1954) A general system describing the viscoelastic properties of bitumen and its relation to routine test data. *Journal of Applied Chemistry*, **4**.

Van der Poel, C. (1955) Time and temperature effects on the deformation of bitumens and bitumen mineral mixtures. *Journal of the Society of Plastics Engineers*, **11**.

Chapter twenty

Strength and failure

20.1 The road structure
20.2 Modes of failure in a bituminous structure
20.3 Fatigue characteristics
20.4 References

20.1 The road structure

A flexible road structure consists of a number of layers of different materials illustrated in Figure IV.2 of the Introduction. In structural terms, the purpose of the road is to distribute the applied load from the traffic to a level which the underlying subgrade can bear. The stresses induced by the loads are high at the surface but reduce with depth. Thus, the surfacing material must be of high quality, but at greater depths below the surface, economies can be achieved by using materials of lower strength.

20.2 Modes of failure in a bituminous structure

Roads deteriorate in a number of ways, but broadly there are two forms of failure. Firstly, the road surface may deteriorate. This may be through breakdown of the surface material either generally, for example through fretting or stone loss, or locally when a pot hole develops as a result of a local weakness. Alternatively, the surface texture of the wearing course may be reduced, through polish or abrasion, so that the skidding resistance drops below an acceptable level.

Secondly, the road structure deteriorates. It is this structural deterioration which will be discussed here. The key feature of such deterioration is that it is gradual, and develops with the continued application of wheel loads. In the early stages, the rate of deterioration is very small and the structural changes are not perceptible and are difficult to measure. But with continued service, signs of structural change become clearer and the rate of deterioration accelerates. There are two modes of breakdown which are illustrated in Figure 20.1. Firstly, permanent deformation occurs in the wheel tracks. This 'rutting' is associated with deformation of all the pavement layers and is linked to a loss of support from the underlying subgrade. Deformation within the bituminous layers is an accumulation of the small irrecoverable part of the deformation caused by each wheel load. It is a function of the viscoelastic nature of the bitumen together with the mechanical support offered by the grading of the aggregate. The second mode of failure is cracking, which appears along the wheel tracks. The cracking is caused by the tensile strain developed in the bound layers as each wheel load passes. It is therefore a function of both the size of tensile strain, and the repetitive nature of the loading; that is a fatigue failure. It is important to note, as Figure 20.1 shows, that the cracking initiates at the base of the bound layer. This is where the tensile stresses are highest as shown in Figure 20.2. It follows that, by thc time the

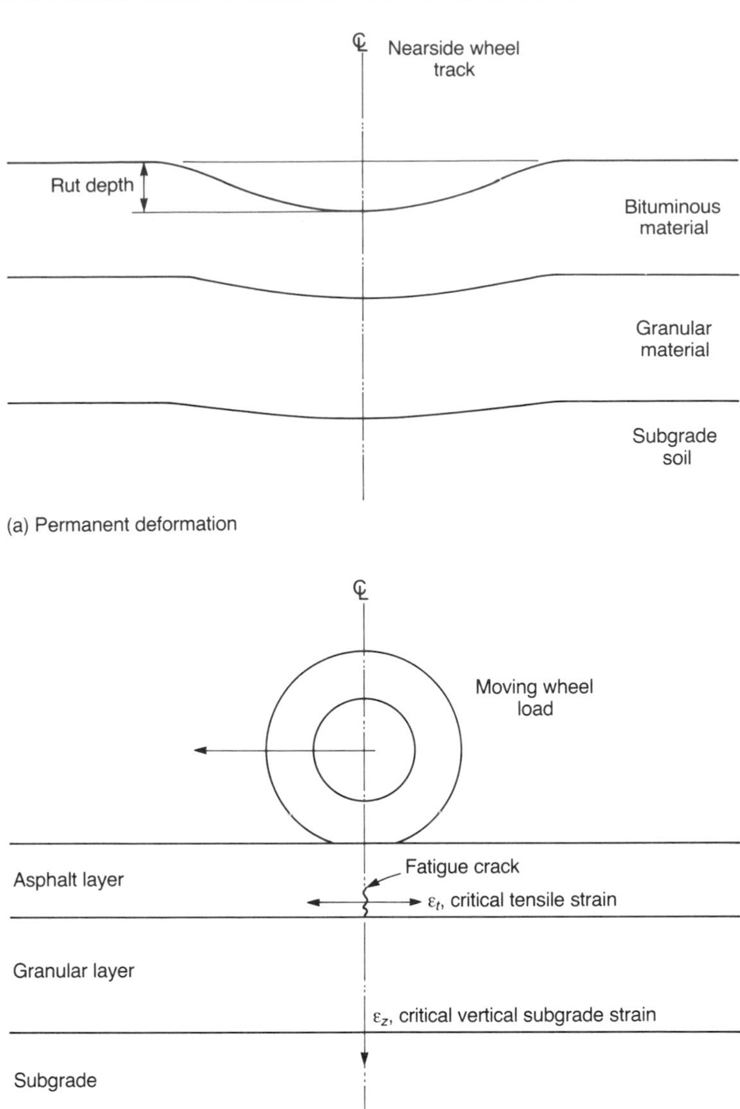

FIGURE 20.1 Modes of failure and critical strains in a flexible pavement (Brown, 1980).

cracking is visible at the surface, the damage has been present for some time.

In both modes of failure, the breakdown is caused by (a) the repetitive nature of the loading, and (b) by the development of excessive strains in the structure. This leads to the notion that, if failure can be defined, the life of a road can be determined provided that the loading can be assessed and the performance of the materials evaluated. Alternatively, the structural

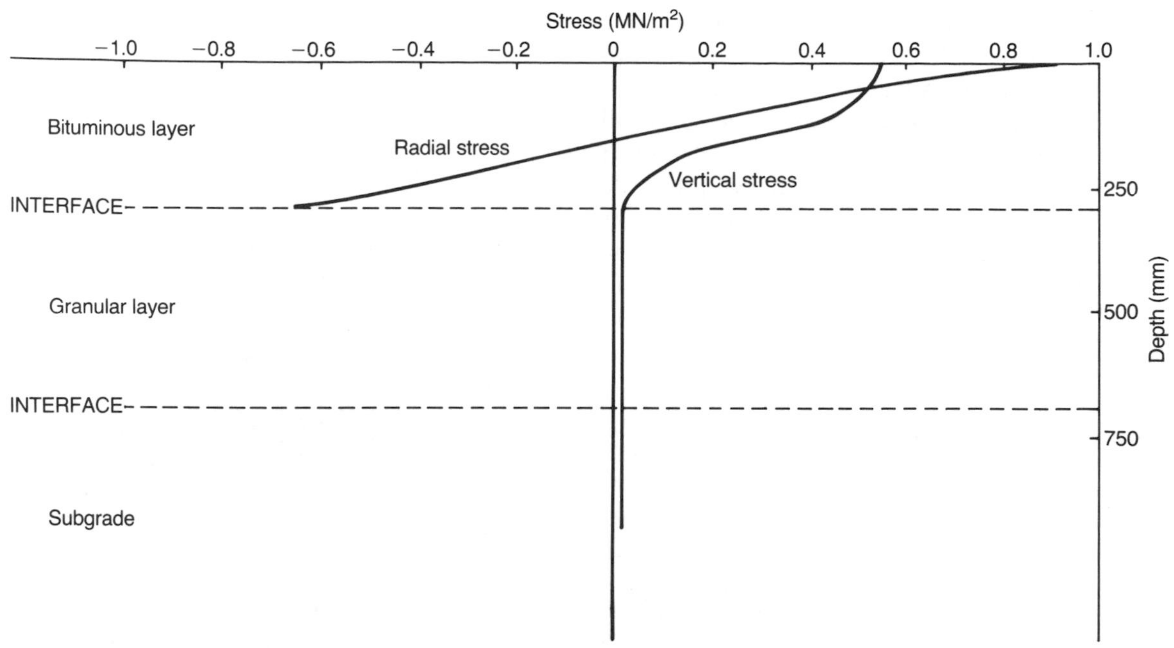

FIGURE 20.2 Variation of vertical and radial stresses below the centreline of a 40 kN wheel load acting over a circular area of radius 160 mm, with a contact pressure of 0.5 MN/m^2 (Peattie, 1978).

design of the road together with the make-up of the materials to give required properties may be determined, in order to provide a given life. In either case, it is necessary to define failure. In most civil engineering structures, structural failure renders the structure unusable and is often associated with collapse. However, whilst roads may become less comfortable to drive on and less safe, they do not, except in very extreme cases, become unusable. Therefore failure for roads must be identified in terms of serviceability and/or repairability; that is, the extent of cracking and deformation must be defined which is just acceptable to drivers and/or which represents a condition which may be economically restored by repair. A definition is provided, in terms of both modes of failure, which identifies two conditions. Table 20.1 shows that

TABLE 20.1 Criteria for determining pavement condition (Department of Transport, 1983, Advice Note HA/25/83. Reproduced with permission of the Controller of HMSO. © Crown copyright.)

Wheel-track cracking	*Wheel-track rutting under a 2 m straight edge*			
	Less than 5 mm	*From 5 mm to <10 mm*	*From 10 mm to <20 mm*	*20 mm or greater*
None	Sound	Sound	Critical	Failed
< half width or single crack	Critical	Critical	Critical	Failed
> half width	Failed	Failed	Failed	Failed

if any cracking is visible at the surface, then the road is regarded as being at critical condition or as having failed. Here the term 'critical' means that failure is imminent but the road still has sufficient structural capability to support strengthening and to provide an extended life from the strengthened road. If there are no signs of cracking, then the condition is defined in terms of the extent of permanent deformation. Thus, if the rut depth reaches 20 mm, the road is regarded as having failed.

20.3 Fatigue characteristics

The development of permanent deformation has already been discussed. Here the fatigue characteristics of bituminous mixes, leading to cracking, will be examined. Fatigue cracking arises from the fact that under repeated applications of tensile stress/strain, a bituminous material will eventually fracture. The higher the level of stress and strain applied, the smaller the number of load applications before cracking occurs. For a particular level of stress and strain, the mix proportions and nature of the bitumen dictate the number of cycles before cracking occurs.

A number of laboratory tests have been developed to assess the fatigue characteristics of bituminous materials. The tests, illustrated in Figure 20.3, are flexure tests and simulate the repeated bending action in the stiff bound layer of a pavement caused by the passage of each wheel load. The number of load cycles which a particular specimen can endure before failure depends on a number of factors discussed below.

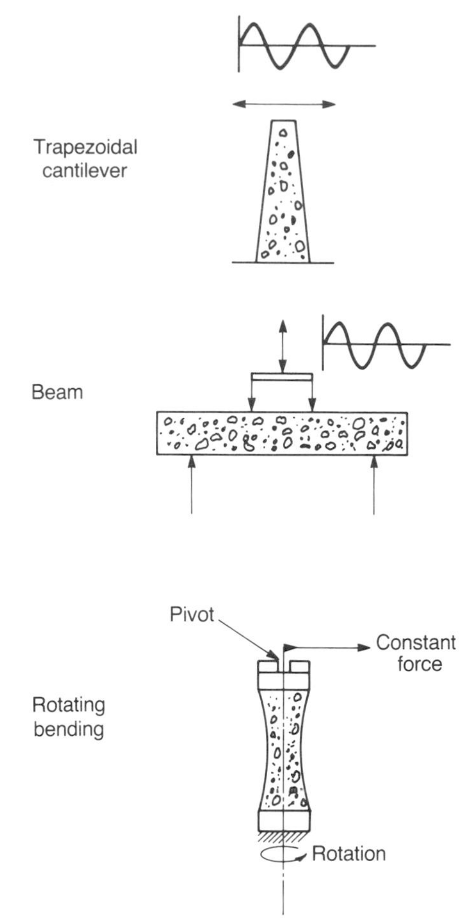

FIGURE 20.3 Methods for fatigue testing of bituminous materials (Brown, 1978).

20.3.1 Stress and strain conditions

Fatigue tests may be conducted in two ways. They may be constant stress tests, where each load application is to the same stress level regardless of the amount of strain developed. Alternatively they may be constant strain tests, where each load application is to the same strain level regardless of the amount of stress required.

These two alternatives produce quite different results. Figure 20.4(a) shows the general pattern of results from constant stress tests. Each line represents a different test temperature, i.e. a different stiffness, and it can be seen that mixes with higher stiffness have longer lives. Figure 20.4(c) shows the general pattern of results from constant strain tests. Again each line represents a different temperature or stiffness and it can be seen that the outcome is reversed, with the mixes of higher stiffness having the shortest lives. This contrast may be explained in terms of

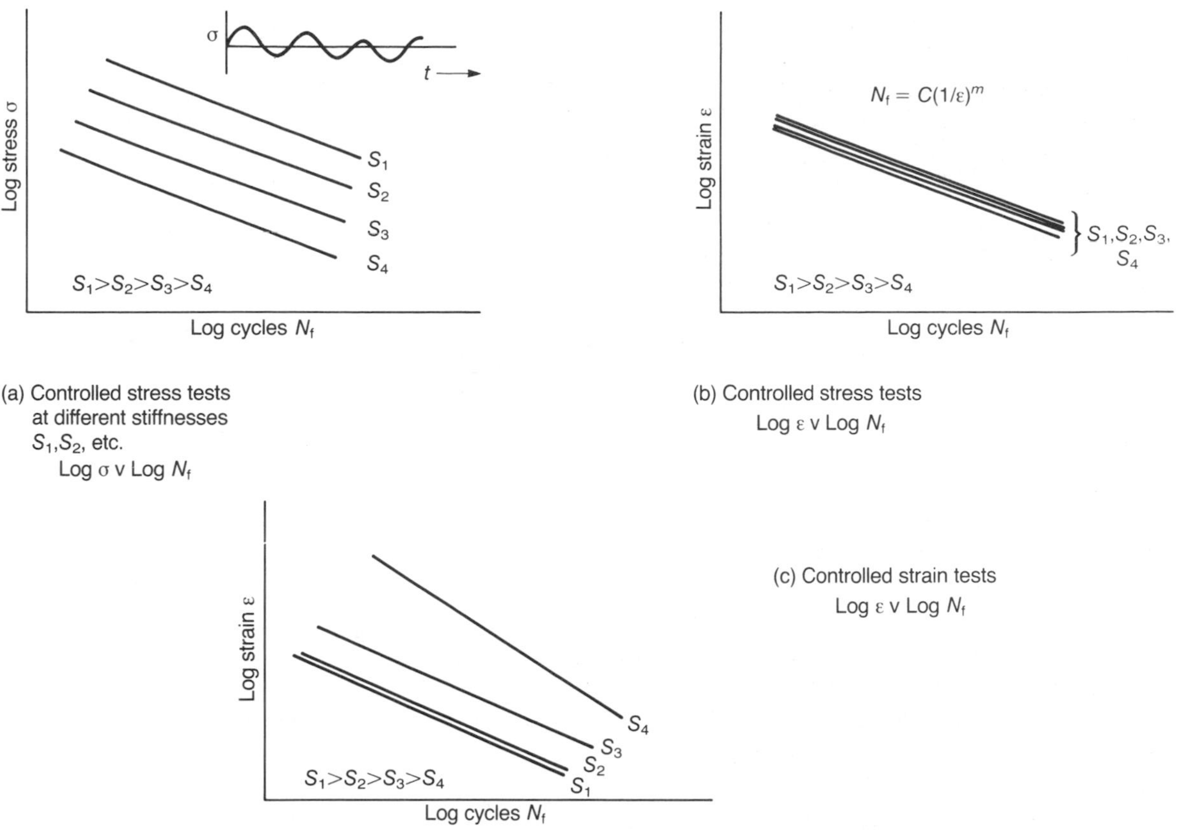

FIGURE 20.4 Fatigue lines representing number of cycles to failure, N_f, under different test conditions (Brown, 1980).

the failure mechanism. Cracks initiate at points of stress concentration and propagate through the material until fracture occurs. If the stress level is kept constant, the stress level at the tip of the crack continues to be high so that propagation is rapid. However, in a constant strain test, the development of a crack causes a steady reduction in the applied stress level because the cracks contribute more and more to the strain as they propagate. Thus the stress at the crack tips reduces and rate of propagation is slow. Thus it is important to establish which test condition is most relevant to actual pavement behaviour. It has been shown (Monismith and Deacon, 1969) that strain control is appropriate to thin layers (for example surfacing layers), whereas stress control is appropriate to thicker structural layers. This is because pavements are subject to a stress controlled loading system, so that the main (and normally thick) structural layers are stress controlled. However, the thin surface layer must move with the lower structural layers and so is effectively subject to strain control. Nevertheless, under low temperature conditions giving high stiffness, crack propagation is relatively quick even under strain controlled loading so that the difference between the two loading conditions is small.

20.3.2 The strain criteria

If the results of a controlled stress test are expressed in terms of an equivalent strain then the log–log plot of strain against number of load

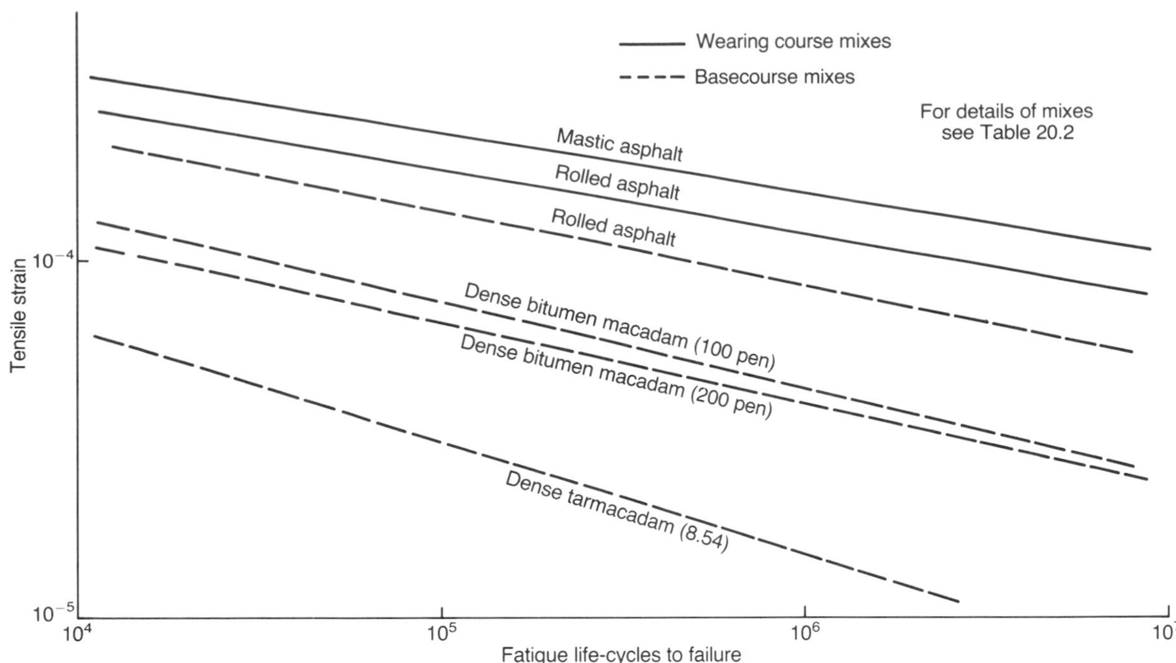

FIGURE 20.5 Fatigue lines under controlled stress conditions for a range of bituminous mixes (Brown, 1980).

TABLE 20.2 Details of mixes represented in Figure 20.5 (Brown, 1980)

Description of mix	*Coarse aggregate (% by mass)*	*Fine aggregate (% by mass)*	*Filler (% by mass)*	*Binder (% by mass)*	*Mean void content (%)*	*Fatigue line constants*	
						C	*m*
Mastic asphalt wearing course	42 crushed rock	23 limestone	20 limestone	15:70/30 TLA[a]/20 pen bit.	0	1.1×10^{-15}	5.5
Rolled asphalt wearing course	30 crushed rock	53.2 sand	8.9 limestone	7.9 45 pen	2.9	1.3×10^{-14}	5.1
Rolled asphalt basecourse	65 crushed rock	29.3 sand	–	5.7 45 pen	4.0	3.2×10^{-8}	3.2
Dense bitumen macadam basecourse	62 crushed rock	28.6 crushed rock	4.7 crushed rock	4.7 100 pen	6.8	2.0×10^{-11}	3.8
Dense bitumen macadam basecourse	62.3 crushed rock	28.7 crushed rock	4.7 crushed rock	4.3 200 pen	6.9	2.5×10^{-12}	4.0
Dense tar macadam basecourse	61.7 crushed rock	28.4 crushed rock	4.7 crushed rock	5.2 B54	7.5	1.0×10^{-7}	2.7

[a] Trinidad Lake asphalt.

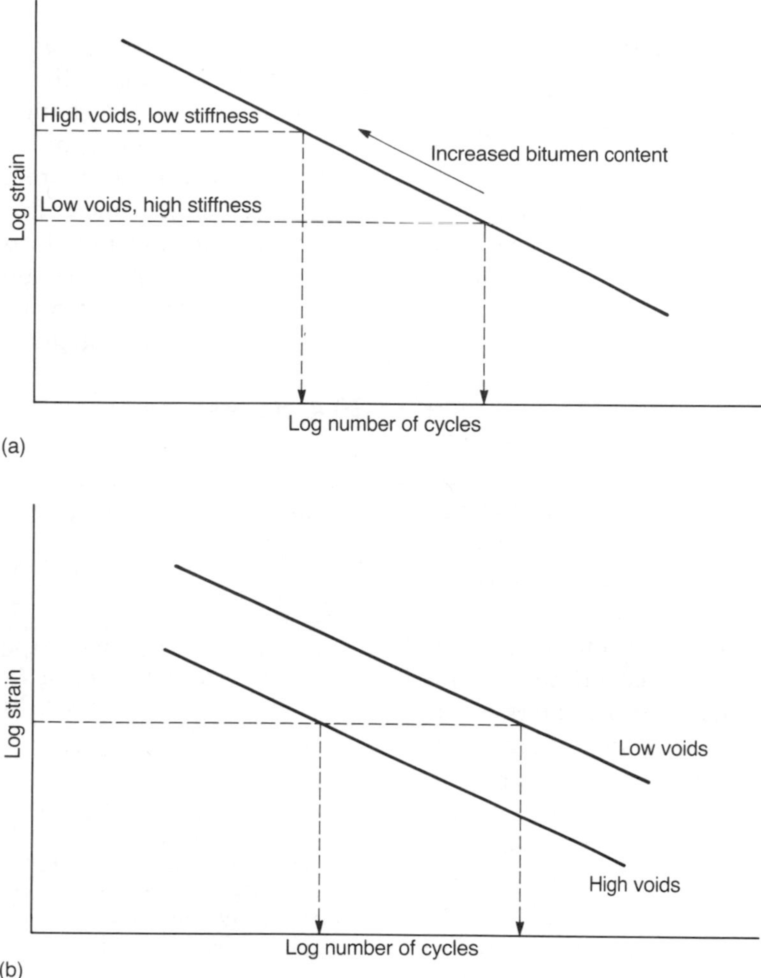

FIGURE 20.6 The influence of voids on fatigue life.

cycles produces a single linear relationship for all test conditions for a particular mix as shown in Figure 20.4(b). In other words the relationship is independent of mix stiffness. This suggests that strain is the principal criterion governing fatigue failure, and it has been demonstrated (Cooper and Pell, 1974) that flexure tests on a wide range of mixes produce unique fatigue lines for each mix. The general relationship defining the fatigue line is:

$$N_f = C\left(\frac{1}{\varepsilon}\right)^m$$

where N_f is the number of load cycles to initiate a fatigue crack, ε is the maximum applied tensile strain, and C and m are constants depending on the composition and properties of the mix.

The fatigue lines for a range of mixes are shown in Figure 20.5 together with details of the mix compositions in Table 20.2.

20.3.3 Effect of mix variables

A large number of variables associated with the mix affect the fatigue line. However, it has been shown (Cooper and Pell, 1974) that two variables are of prime importance. These are:

1. the volume of bitumen in the mix;
2. the viscosity of the bitumen as measured by the softening point.

As the volume of bitumen increases up to 15%, the fatigue life increases, and as the bitumen becomes more viscous, with softening point increasing up to 60°C, the fatigue life also increases.

Other factors are important in so far as they affect the two main variables. The void content of the mix has an effect on the volume of bitumen. The total void content is in turn affected by the particle shape and grading of the aggregate, the compactive effort, and the temperature. In other words there is a link between workability, compactive effort and void content which is controlled by the bitumen content. However, whilst a higher bitumen content improves fatigue life, it also reduces stiffness which leads to increased strain. Figure 20.6 illustrates the double influence of void content. Figure 20.6(a) shows the effect that an increased content has on stiffness. The stiffness is reduced which increases the strain under constant stress conditions causing a shift to the left along the fatigue line. Thus the fatigue life is reduced. Figure 20.6(b) shows the influence that void content has on the fatigue line, so that for the same strain the fatigue life is reduced as void content increases. The change in position of the fatigue line corresponds to a change in material type, as was seen in Figure 20.5, whereas the shift along a fatigue line due to a stiffness change corresponds to a change in degree of compaction. However, in practice, both effects occur if the change in void content is associated with a change in bitumen content.

20.4 References

Brown, S.F. (1978) Material characteristics for analytical pavement design. In *Developments in Highway Pavement Engineering – 1*, Applied Science Publishers, London.

Brown, S.F. (1980) An introduction to the analytical design of bituminous pavements. Department of Civil Engineering, University of Nottingham.

Cooper, K.E. and Pell, P.S. (1974) *The effect of mix variables on the fatigue strength of bituminous materials*, Transport and Road Research Laboratory, Laboratory Report 633.

Department of Transport (1983) Departmental Advice Note HA/25/83.

Monismith, C.L. and Deacon, J.A. (1969) Fatigue of asphalt paving mixtures. *Journal of Transport Engineering Division, ASCE*, **95**.

Peattie, K.R. (1978) Flexible pavement design. In *Developments in Highway Pavement Engineering – 1*, Applied Science Publishers, London.

Chapter twenty-one

Durability

21.1 Introduction
21.2 Ageing of bitumen
21.3 Permeability
21.4 Adhesion
21.5 References

21.1 Introduction

Durability is the ability to survive and continue to give an acceptable performance. In the case of roads, it is necessary that the structure should survive for the specified design life although it is accepted that not all aspects of performance can be sustained for this duration without some restorative maintenance. The design guide for UK roads suggests a design life of 40 years (Department of Transport, 1987), although this can only be achieved in stages as shown in Figure 21.1. The durability of a flexible road structure depends on the durability of the materials from which it is constructed, in particular the bitumen-bound materials. Bituminous materials may deteriorate in a number of ways. The bitumen itself will harden with exposure to oxygen and temperature effects, the aggregate may not be of sufficient quality so that some individual particles may break down, or there may be loss of adhesion between the bitumen and aggregate particles. These forms of deterioration are caused by weathering and the action of traffic. These agents act at the road surface which is particularly vulnerable. However, deterioration can also occur in the body of the material and this is controlled by the permeability of the material.

21.2 Ageing of bitumen

The ageing or hardening of bitumen is an inevitable result of exposure of bitumen to the atmosphere. The rate of hardening will depend on the conditions and the nature of the bitumen. There are two main processes which occur: oxidation and loss of volatiles.

21.2.1 Oxidation

In the oxidation process, oxygen molecules from the air combine with the resins to form asphaltenes. Thus there is an increase in the polar, high molecular weight fraction at the expense of the lower molecular weight resins. The result is an increase in viscosity of the bitumen. Also, the bitumen becomes unstable due to the discontinuity which develops between the saturates and the rest of the components. This instability causes a lack of cohesion within the bitumen which will lead to cracking. The rate of oxidation is highly dependent on temperature, and is rapid at the high temperatures used for mixing and laying bituminous materials.

21.2.2 Loss of volatiles

Loss of volatiles will occur if there is a substantial proportion of low molecular weight components in the bitumen and if the bitumen is subjected to high temperatures. However, for penetration grade bitumens the loss of volatiles is relatively small.

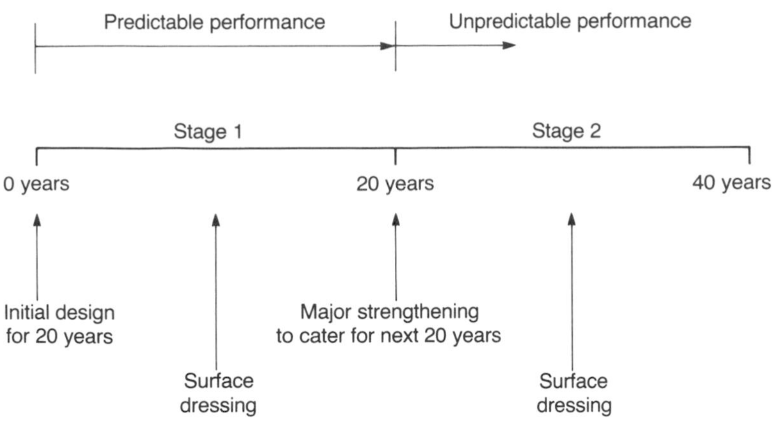

FIGURE 21.1 The life of a flexible road.

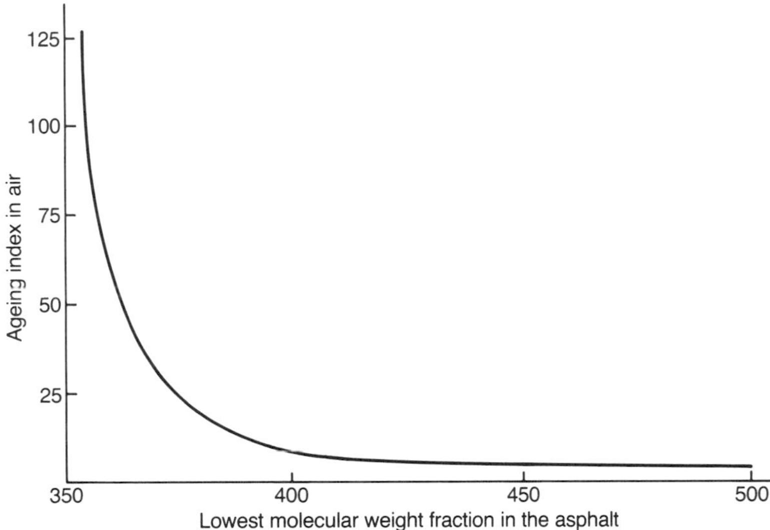

FIGURE 21.2 Influence of initial molecular weight on durability (Griffin *et al.*, 1959).

21.2.3 Ageing index

The hardening of bitumen results in a lowering of penetration, an increase in softening point and an increase in penetration index. Therefore an excessive amount of hardening will cause the material to be brittle at low temperatures and vulnerable to cracking. A convenient means of evaluating the ability of a bitumen to resist hardening is to use the microfilm durability test (Griffin *et al.*, 1955). The test consists of ageing films of bitumen 5 microns thick on glass plates in an oven at 225°F for two hours. The hardening which occurs is determined by measuring the viscosity of the material before and after this exposure with the sliding plate microviscometer. The ratio of the viscosity of the aged asphalt to that of the original asphalt is the ageing index.

Ageing index is strongly influenced by the

initial molecular weight of the asphalt. Figure 21.2 shows that ageing index can be large in asphalts with low molecular weight. A satisfactory durability (ageing index less than 10) can be obtained if components with a molecular weight less than 400 are eliminated.

In practice, the ageing of bitumen is most marked during the mixing process because high temperatures are involved. For example, the penetration value of a 50 pen bitumen will fall to between 30 and 40 depending on the duration of the mixing and the temperature used; subsequent high temperature storage will cause further ageing. Thus the penetration value could be reduced by as much as a half. Ageing of bitumen on the road is generally a much slower process. This is because the temperatures are much lower and the availability of oxygen is restricted by the permeability of the mix. In more open-textured mixes with a large volume of interconnected voids, air can readily permeate the material allowing oxidation to occur. Macadams generally fall into this category. However, in dense mixes such as asphalts, the permeability is low and there will be very little movement of air through the material. In both cases, ageing will be more rapid at the surface than in the bulk of the material because there is a continual availability of oxygen and the surface will reach higher temperatures.

21.3 Permeability

Permeability is an important parameter of a bituminous mixture because it controls the extent to which both air and water can migrate into the material. The significance of exposure to air was described in the previous section. Water may also bring about deterioration by causing the bitumen to strip from the aggregate particles, or causing breakdown of the aggregate particles themselves. Furthermore, permeability controls the extent of frost damage. Thus permeability may be regarded as a measure of durability.

21.3.1 Measurement and voids analysis

The measurement of permeability is, in essence, a simple task, achieved by applying a fluid under pressure to one side of a specimen of a bituminous mixture and measuring the resulting flow of fluid at the opposite side. Both air and water have been used as the permeating fluid. A

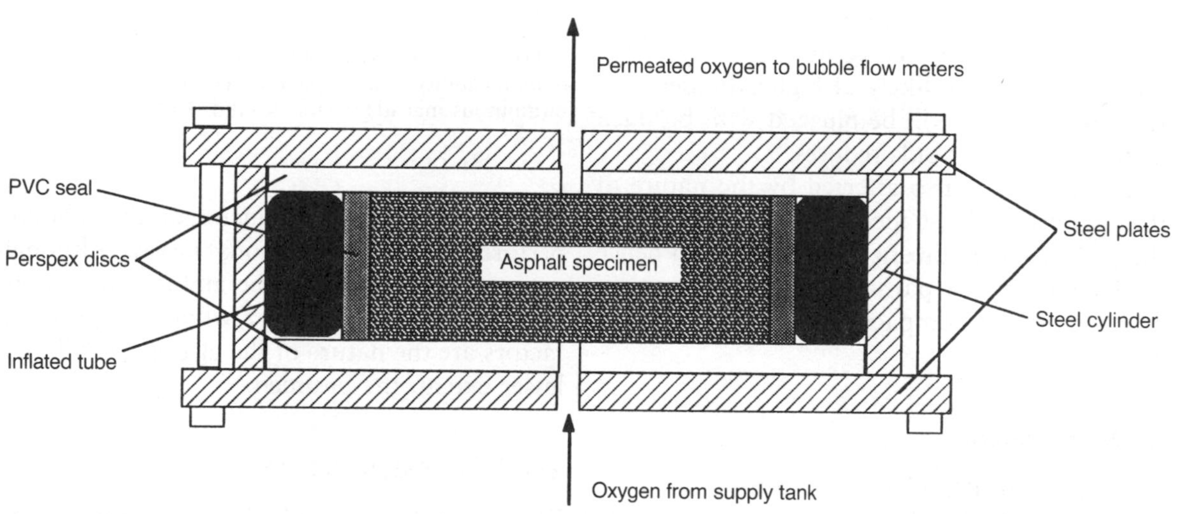

FIGURE 21.3 Schematic diagram of permeability test cell.

permeability cell developed for the measurement of permeability of concrete, shown in Figure 21.3, has been used successfully to measure the permeability of hot rolled asphalt to oxygen (Robinson, 1991). Here a constant fluid pressure is maintained. By contrast a falling head permeameter has been used (Khalid, 1990) with water as the permeating fluid.

21.3.2 Factors affecting permeability

The permeability of a bituminous mixture depends on a large number of factors. Of particular importance is the quantity of voids, the distribution of void size and the continuity of the voids. Figure 21.4 shows how permeability varies with total voids in the mix for an open-textured bituminous macadam. It can be seen that the permeability is more sensitive to void content at high binder contents. This is likely to be due to the size and continuity of pores. At low binder contents, the pores are large and although a reduction in the volume of voids will tend also to reduce the pore size, the size will remain sufficiently large to permit high permeability. At high binder contents, however, the pores are relatively small and a reduction in the volume of voids will cause a significant change in pore size with a much greater effect on permeability. A change in continuity of the voids is also more likely at higher binder contents when pores will be plugged with bitumen as the volume of voids reduces.

The voids are also affected by the nature of the aggregate. The shape, texture and grading of the particles will govern the packing and hence void content at a particular bitumen content. The amount of compactive effort employed is also important.

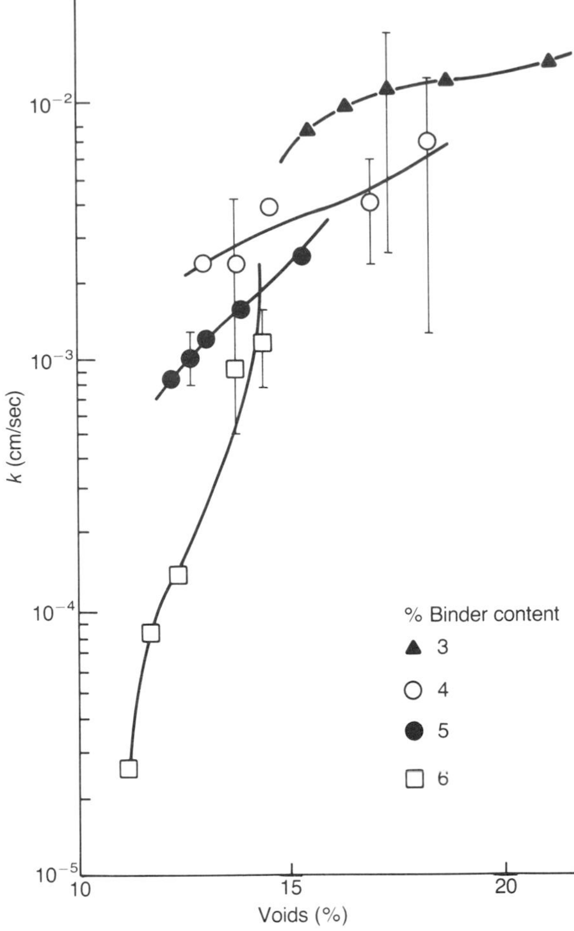

FIGURE 21.4 Relationship between the coefficient of permeability, k, and voids content of an open-textured bituminous macadam mix (Khalid, 1990).

21.4 Adhesion

The quality of the adhesion of a bitumen to an aggregate is dependent on a complex assemblage of variables. Table 21.1 identifies a number of factors which have an influence on the adhesion performance of bituminous mixes. Although some of these relate to the ambient conditions and aspects of the mix as a whole, the principal factors are the nature of the aggregate and, to a lesser extent, the bitumen.

21.4.1 The nature of the aggregate

The mineralogical and physical nature of the aggregate particles has an important bearing on

TABLE 21.1 Material properties and external influences which can act singularly or together to affect the adhesion and stripping resistance of a bituminous mix

Aggregate properties	*Bitumen properties*	*Interactive mix properties*	*External influences*
Mineralogy	Composition and source	Compaction	Annual precipitation*
Surface texture	Durability and weathering	Grading	Relative humidity*
Porosity	Viscosity	Permeability	pH of water*
Surface coatings and dust	Curing time	Binder content	Presence of salts*
Mechanical durability	Oxidation	Cohesion	Temperature*
Surface area	Electrical polarity	Film thickness	Temperature cycling*
Absorption	Use of additives	Filler type	Light, heat and radiation*
Moisture content		Type of mix	Traffic
Abrasion pH		Method of production	Construction practice
Weathering grade		Use of additive	Design
Exposure history			Workmanship
Shape			Drainage
Additives			

* Factors considered uncontrollable.

adhesion, with the adhesive capacity being a function of chemical composition, shape and structure, residual valency, and the surface area presented to the bitumen.

Generalizations about the effect of mineralogy are difficult because the effects of grain size, shape and texture are also important. However, there seem to be a preponderance of reports of failures with the more siliceous aggregates such as granites, rhyolites, quartzites, siliceous gravel and cherts. The fact that good performance with these materials has also been reported, and that failures in supposedly good rock types such as limestones and basic igneous rocks have occurred, emphasizes the complexity of the various material interactions. Therefore caution should be exercised when attempting to make generalizations on the adhesion performance of aggregates of different or even similar mineralogy.

The surface character of each individual aggregate type is important particularly in relation to the presence of a residual valency or surface charges. Aggregates with unbalanced surface charges possess a surface energy which can be attributed to a number of factors including broken coordination bonds in the crystal lattice, the polar nature of minerals, and the presence of absorbed ions. Such surface energy will enhance the adhesive bond if the aggregate surface is coated with a liquid of opposite polarity.

Absorption of bitumen into the aggregate depends on several factors including the total volume of permeable pore space, and the size of the pore openings. The presence of a fine microstructure of pores, voids and microcracks can bring about an enormous increase in the absorptive surface available to the bitumen. This depends on the petrographic characteristics of the aggregate as well as its quality and state of weathering.

It is generally accepted that rougher surfaces exhibit a greater degree of adhesion. A balance is, however, required between the attainment of good wettability of the aggregate (smooth surfaces being more easily wetted), and a rougher surface which holds the binder more securely once wetting is achieved. The presence of a rough surface texture can mask the effects of mineralogy.

21.4.2 The nature of the bitumen

The important characteristics of the bitumen affecting adhesion to aggregate are its viscosity and surface tension, and its polarity.

The viscosity and surface tension will govern the extent to which bitumen is absorbed into the pores at the surface of the aggregate particles. Both these properties are altered with temperature, and mixing of aggregate and bitumen is always done at high temperature – up to 180°C for 50 pen bitumen – in order that the bitumen coats the aggregate surface readily.

Bitumen will also chemically adsorb on to aggregate surfaces. Strongly adsorbed bitumen fractions have been identified at the bitumen–aggregate interface forming a band of the order of 180 Å thick. Ketones, dicarboxylic anhydrides, carboxylic acids, sulphoxides and nitrogen-bearing components have been found in this layer (Ensley, 1975). The strongly adsorbed components have been found to have sites capable of hydrogen bonding to the aggregate, though in the presence of water the available bonds prefer the more active water. A migration of some bitumen components to the interface is inferred and therefore a dependence on binder composition, mixing temperature and viscosity. Figure 21.5 illustrates the process, with molecules of bitumen at the surface aligned in the direction of polarity of the substrate (aggregate), usually a negative surface. The zone of orientation of bitumen molecules extends for a thickness of several thousand molecules.

21.4.3 Mechanisms for loss of adhesion

Breakdown of the bond between bitumen and aggregate, known as stripping, may occur for a number of reasons. However, the principal agencies are the action of traffic, weathering and moisture, and these often act in combination.

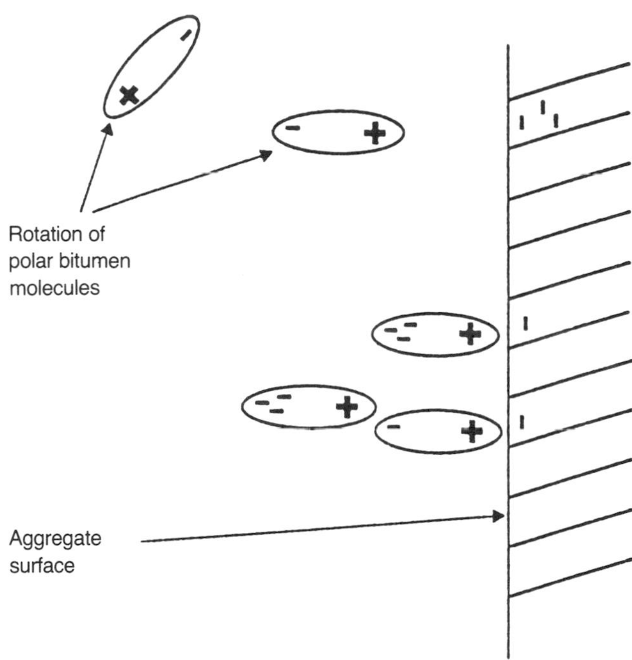

FIGURE 21.5 Adsorption of bitumen molecules to the aggregate surface (Ensley, 1975).

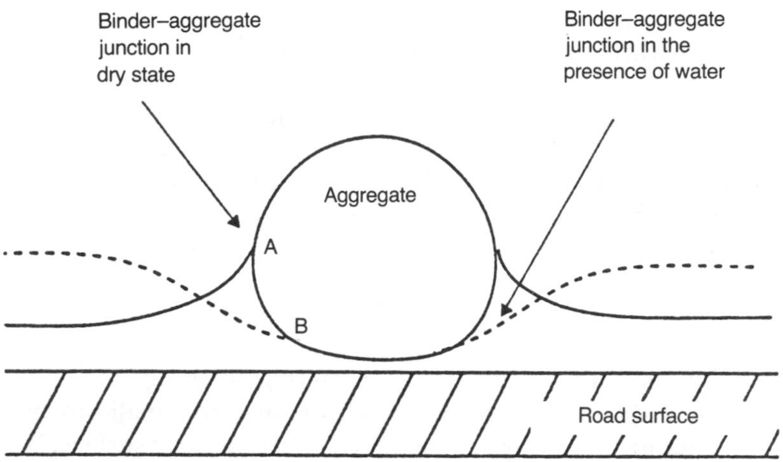

FIGURE 21.6 Retraction of the binder–water interface over the aggregate surface in the presence of water (Majidzadeh and Brovold, 1968).

Weathering may affect the aggregate itself but is a strong influence on the bitumen causing ageing through exposure to ultra-violet light. The consequent loss of ductility of the bitumen will render it more vulnerable to brittle fracture and the coating of aggregate particles may be broken.

The effect of moisture is more significant since it causes loss of adhesion in a number of ways (Hargreaves, 1987). A number of mechanisms have been postulated for adhesion loss and most involve the action of water. These are described below and each may occur depending on the circumstances.

Displacement
This occurs when the bitumen retracts from its initial equilibrium position as a result of contact with moisture. Figure 21.6 illustrates the process in terms of an aggregate particle embedded in a bituminous film (Majidzadeh and Brovold, 1968). Point A represents the equilibrium contact position when the system is dry. The presence of moisture will cause the equilibrium point to shift to B leaving the aggregate particle effectively displaced to the surface of the bitumen. The positions of points A and B will depend on the type and viscosity of bitumen.

Detachment
This occurs when the bitumen and aggregate are separated by a thin film of water or dust though no obvious break in the bitumen film may be apparent. Although the bituminous film coats

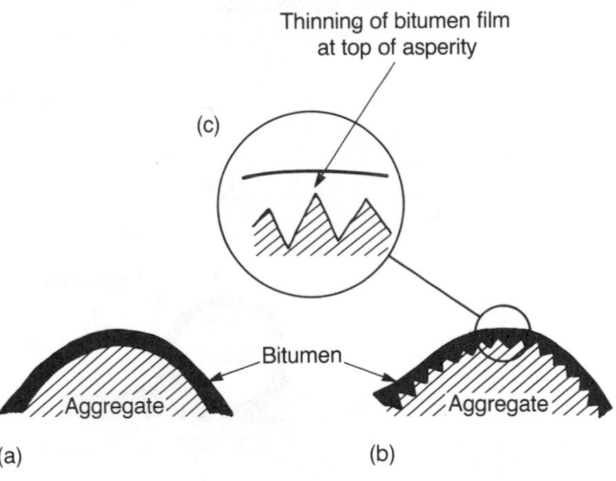

FIGURE 21.7 Thinning of the bitumen film on an aggregate with rough surface texture (b, c). Smooth aggregates (a) retain an unstressed and even film.

the aggregate particle, no adhesive bond exists and the bitumen can be clearly peeled from the surface.

Film rupture
This occurs when the bitumen fully coats the aggregate but where the bitumen film thins, usually at the sharp edges of the aggregate particle (Figure 21.7).

Blistering and pitting
If the temperature of bitumen at the surface of a road rises, its viscosity reduces. This reduced viscosity allows the bitumen to creep up the surface of any water droplets which fall on the surface, and may eventually form a blister (Figure 21.8). With further heating, the blister can expand and cause the bitumen film to rupture leaving a pit.

Spontaneous emulsification
Water and bitumen have the capacity to form an emulsion with water as the continuous phase. The emulsion formed has the same negative charge as the aggregate surface and is thus repelled. The formation of the emulsion depends on the type of bitumen, and is assisted by the presence of finely divided particulate material such as clay materials, and the action of traffic.

Hydraulic scouring
This is due principally to the action of vehicle tyres on a wet road surface. Water can be pressed into small cavities in the bitumen film in front of the tyre and, on passing, the action of the tyre sucks up this water. Thus a compression–tension cycle is invoked which can cause disbonding.

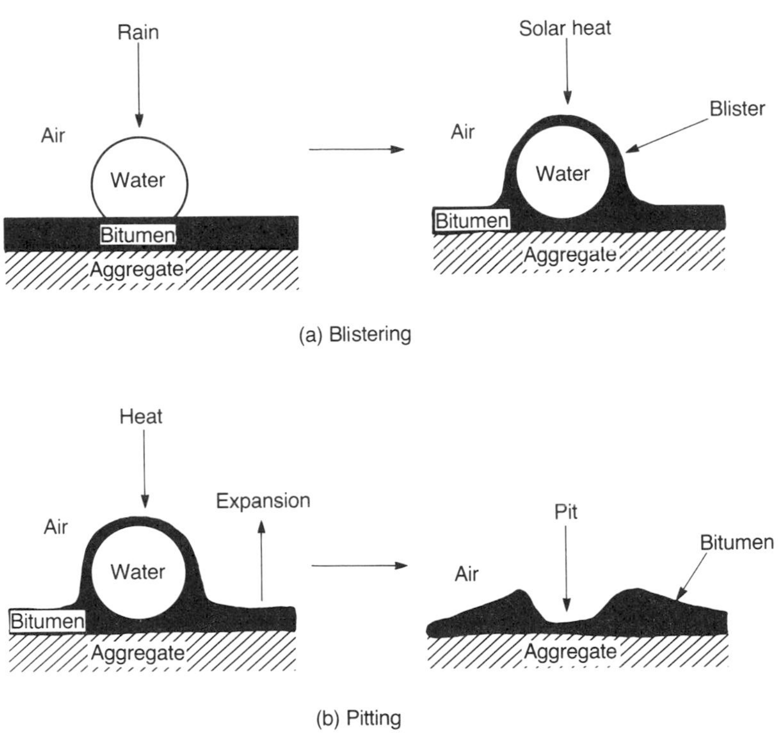

FIGURE 21.8 Formation of blisters and pits in a bituminous coating (Thelan, 1983).

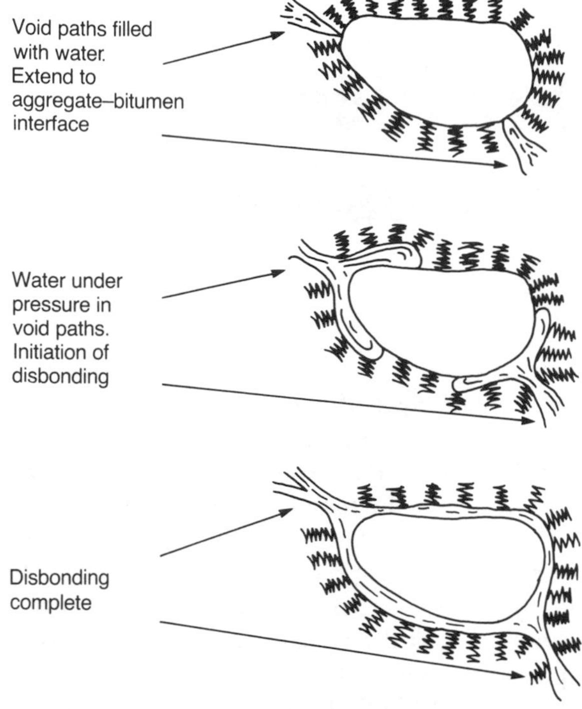

FIGURE 21.9 Pore pressure disbonding mechanism (McGennis *et al.*, 1984).

Pore pressure

This mechanism is most important in open or poorly compacted mixes. Water can become trapped in these mixes as densification takes place by trafficking. Subsequent trafficking acts on this trapped water and high pore pressures can result. This generates channels at the interface between bitumen and aggregate (Figure 21.9) and eventually leads to disbonding (BS 594: 1985).

Chemical disbonding

Diffusion of moisture through the bituminous coatings can lead to the layers of water building up in the interfacial region.

21.5 References

British Standard 594: 1985: *Hot rolled asphalt for roads and other paved areas. Part 1: Specification for constituent materials and asphalt mixtures.*

Department of Transport (1987) Departmental Standard HD 14/87.

Ensley, E.K. (1975) Multilayer absorption with molecular orientation of asphalt on mineral aggregate and other substrates. *Journal of Applied Chemistry and Biotechnology*, **25**.

Griffin, R.L., Miles, T.K. and Penther, C.J. (1955) Microfilm durability test for asphalt. *Proceedings of the Association of Asphalt Paving Technologists*, **24**.

Griffin, R.L., Simpson, W.C. and Miles, T.K. (1959) Influence of composition of paving asphalt on viscosity, viscosity–temperature susceptibility, and durability. *Journal of Chemical and Engineering Data*, **4**.

Hargreaves, A. (1987) An investigation of the premature failure of bituminous macadam wearing courses with particular reference to the effects of moisture and aggregate quality. Ph.D. thesis, Hatfield Polytechnic.

Khalid, H. (1990) Permeability: implications in asphalt mix design. Highways Asphalt 90 Supplement, *Highways*, Faversham House Group.

Majidzadeh, K. and Brovold, F.N. (1968) *State of the art: Effect of water on bitumen–aggregate mixtures.* Highway Research Board, Publication 1456, Special Report 98.

McGennis, R.B., Kennedy, T.W. and Machemehl, R.B. (1984) *Stripping and moisture damage in asphalt mixtures.* Research Report 253.1, Project 3-9-79-253, Centre for Transportation Research, University of Texas, USA.

Robinson, D. (1991) An investigation into wearing course failure on the A414 Breakespeare Way, Hemel Hempstead. Unpublished project report, Hatfield Polytechnic.

Thelan, E. (1983) *Surface energy and adhesion properties in asphalt–aggregate systems.* Highway Research Board Bulletin, 911.

Chapter twenty-two

Practice and processing

22.1 Bituminous mixtures
22.2 Recipe and designed mixes
22.3 Methods of production
22.4 References

22.1 Bituminous mixtures

There are a very large number of bituminous mixtures which vary according to density, bitumen content, bitumen grade, and aggregate size and grading. However, they can all be classified into two groups, namely asphalts and macadams.

22.1.1 Asphalts

Asphalts are dense materials and are characterized by their high bitumen content and high filler/fines content. They derive their strength and stiffness from a dense stiff mortar of bitumen, filler and fines. The coarse aggregate content is relatively low so that the overall particle size distribution is gap-graded. Figure IV.1(a) of the Introduction illustrates these features and it can be seen that the material transmits load through the mortar continuum. This mortar, being rich in bitumen, is expensive and the coarse aggregate serves to increase the volume of the mortar with a cheap material, thereby reducing the overall cost. The binder used for asphalt will normally be 50 or 70 pen and may either be penetration grade bitumen or a blend of bitumen with pitch or lake asphalt. Because of the hardness of the binder and the higher filler/fines content, the workability is low, and high temperatures have to be used to mix, lay and compact the material. Freshly laid wearing course asphalt (known as hot rolled asphalt) presents a smooth surface with coarse aggregate particles submerged with the mortar. In order to provide a skid-resistant surface, coated chippings are rolled into the surface. This too adds to the cost. Asphalts have a very low permeability, and are capable of transmitting high stresses whilst providing some ductility. They are therefore very durable, and normally used where traffic loads are high or durability is important.

There are three groups of asphalt mixtures (BS 594: 1985). Group 1 mixes are for roadbases, base courses and regulating courses and their composition requirements are shown in Table 22.1. Group 2 mixes are designed mixes for wearing courses. These may be either type F (incorporating fine sand) or type C (incorporating crushed rock or slag fines which are more coarsely graded). Tables 22.2(a) and (b) give the composition requirements. The binder content of these mixes is determined from a design process which will be described in the following section. Group 3 mixes are recipe mixes for wearing courses. Again types F and C are specified and Tables 22.3 and 22.4 give the composition requirements. The binder contents for type F mixes should be related to the climatic conditions and volume of traffic. In the majority

TABLE 22.1 Composition of roadbase, basecourse and regulating course hot rolled asphalt mixtures (BS 594: 1985)

Column number	*1*	*2*	*3*
Designation*	50/14†	50/20†	60/20
Nominal thickness of layer (mm)	35 to 65	45 to 80	45 to 80
Percentage by mass of total aggregate passing BS test sieve			
50 mm	–	–	–
37.5 mm	–	–	–
28 mm	–	100	100
20 mm	100	90 to 100	90 to 100
14 mm	90 to 100	65 to 100	30 to 65
10 mm	65 to 100	35 to 75	–
6.3 mm	–	–	–
2.36 mm	35 to 55	35 to 55	30 to 44
600 µm	15 to 55	15 to 55	10 to 44
212 µm	5 to 30	5 to 30	3 to 25
75 µm	2 to 9	2 to 9	2 to 8
Binder content, % by mass of total mixture for:			
Crushed rock or steel slag	6.5	6.5	5.7
Gravel	6.3	6.3	5.5
Blast furnace slag: bulk density (kg/m^3)			
1440	6.6	6.6	5.7
1360	6.7	6.7	5.9
1280	6.8	6.8	6.0
1200	6.9	6.9	6.1
1120	7.1	7.1	6.3

* The mixture designation numbers (e.g. 50/14 in column 1) refer to the nominal coarse aggregate content of the mixture/nominal size of the aggregate in the mixture respectively.
† Suitable for regulating course.

of cases material complying with Schedules 1A, 2A and 3A (see Table 22.3) should be used, but in cold, elevated wet conditions, or for more lightly trafficked roads, materials to Schedules 1B, 2B and 3B should be used.

22.1.2 Macadams

Macadams range from dense mixes to open-textured mixes. They are characterized by a relatively low binder content and a continuously graded aggregate.

Macadams rely on the packing and interlock of the aggregate particles for their strength and stiffness. The binder coats the aggregate and acts as a lubricant when hot and an adhesive and waterproofer when cold. The grade of binder used is softer than for asphalts being 100 or 200 pen. Figure IV.1(b) of the Introduction illustrates these features and it can be seen that the material transmits load through the aggregate structure. Because of their lower binder content, macadams are cheaper than asphalts. In general macadams have a higher void content than asphalts so they are more permeable and less durable. They lack ductility and are generally used on less heavily trafficked roads.

Macadams are classified according to the nominal size of the aggregate, the grading of the aggregate and the intended use of the material (BS 4987: 1988). The main mixes available are:

TABLE 22.2 Composition of design type hot rolled wearing course mixtures (a) type F and (b) type C (BS 594: 1985)
(a)

Column number	*4*	*5*	*6*	*7*
Designation*	30/14	40/14	40/20	55/20
Nominal thickness of layer (mm)	40	50	50	50
Percentage by mass of total aggregate passing BS test sieve				
28 mm	–	–	100	100
20 mm	100	100	95 to 100	90 to 100
14 mm	85 to 100	90 to 100	50 to 85	35 to 80
10 mm	60 to 90	50 to 85	–	–
6.3 mm	–	–	–	–
2.36 mm	60 to 72	50 to 62	50 to 62	35 to 47
600 μm	45 to 72	35 to 62	35 to 62	25 to 47
212 μm	15 to 50	10 to 40	10 to 40	5 to 30
75 μm	8.0 to 12.0	6.0 to 10.0	6.0 to 10.0	4.0 to 8.0
Maximum percentage of aggregate passing 2.36 mm and retained on 600 μm BS test sieves	14	12	12	9
Minimum target binder content, % by mass of total mixture†	6.5	6.3	6.3	5.3

* The mixture designation numbers (e.g. 30/14 in column 4) refer to the nominal coarse aggregate content of the mixture/nominal size of the aggregate in the mixture respectively.
† In areas of the country where prevailing conditions are characteristically colder and wetter than the national average the addition of a further 0.5% of binder may be beneficial to the durability of the wearing courses.

(b)

Column number	*8*	*9*	*10*
Designation*	30/14	40/14	40/20
Nominal thickness of layer (mm)	40	50	50
Percentage by mass of total aggregate passing BS test sieve			
28 mm	–	–	100
20 mm	100	100	95 to 100
14 mm	85 to 100	90 to 100	50 to 85
10 mm	60 to 90	50 to 85	–
6.3 mm	–	–	–
2.36 mm	60 to 72	50 to 62	50 to 62
600 μm	25 to 45	20 to 40	20 to 40
212 μm	15 to 30	10 to 25	10 to 25
75 μm	8.0 to 12.0	6.0 to 10.0	6.0 to 10.0
Minimum target binder content, % by mass of total mixture†	6.5	6.3	6.3

* The mixture designation numbers (e.g. 30/14 in column 8) refer to the nominal coarse aggregate content of the mixture/nominal size of the aggregate in the mixture respectively.
† In areas of the country where prevailing conditions are characteristically colder and wetter than the national average the addition of a further 0.5% of binder may be beneficial to the durability of the wearing courses.

TABLE 22.3 Composition of recipe type F hot rolled asphalt wearing course mixtures (BS 594: 1985)

Column number	*11*	*12*	*13*	*14*
Designation*	30/14	40/14	40/20	55/20
Nominal thickness of layer (mm)	40	50	50	50
Percentage by mass of total aggregate passing BS test sieve				
28 mm	–	–	100	100
20 mm	100	100	95 to 100	90 to 100
14 mm	85 to 100	90 to 100	50 to 85	35 to 80
10 mm	60 to 90	50 to 85	–	–
6.3 mm	–	–	–	–
2.36 mm	60 to 72	50 to 62	50 to 62	35 to 47
600 μm	45 to 72	35 to 62	35 to 62	25 to 47
212 μm	15 to 50	10 to 40	10 to 40	5 to 30
75 μm	8.0 to 12.0	6.0 to 10.0	6.0 to 10.0	4.0 to 8.0
Maximum percentage of aggregate passing 2.36 mm and retained on 600 μm BS test sieves	14	12	12	9
Binder content, % by mass of total mixture for:				
Crushed rock or steel slag				
Schedule 1A	7.8	7.0	7.0	5.8
Schedule 1B	8.3	7.5	7.5	6.3
Gravel				
Schedule 2A	7.5	6.5	6.5	–
Schedule 2B	8.0	7.1	7.1	–
Blast furnace slag: bulk density (kg/m^3)				
Schedule 3A				
1440	7.9	7.2	7.2	–
1360	8.0	7.3	7.3	–
1280	8.1	7.4	7.4	–
1200	8.2	7.5	7.5	–
1120	8.3	7.6	7.6	–
Schedule 3B				
1440	8.4	7.7	7.7	–
1360	8.5	7.8	7.8	–
1280	8.6	7.9	7.9	–
1200	8.7	8.0	8.0	–
1120	8.8	8.1	8.1	–

* The mixture designation numbers (e.g. 30/14 in column 11) refer to the nominal coarse aggregate content of the mixture/nominal size of the aggregate in the mixture respectively.

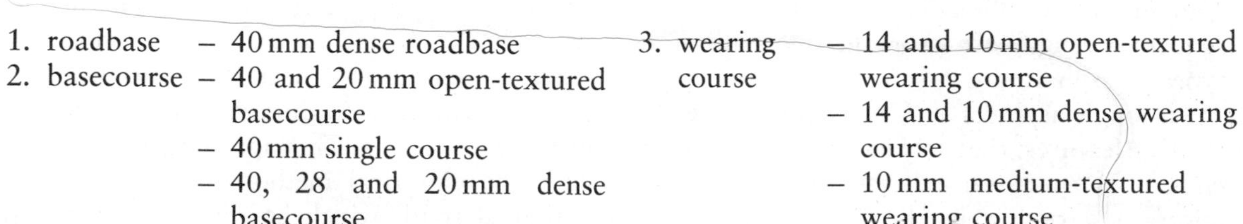

1. roadbase – 40 mm dense roadbase
2. basecourse – 40 and 20 mm open-textured basecourse
   – 40 mm single course
   – 40, 28 and 20 mm dense basecourse
3. wearing course – 14 and 10 mm open-textured wearing course
   – 14 and 10 mm dense wearing course
   – 10 mm medium-textured wearing course

TABLE 22.4 Composition of recipe type C hot rolled asphalt wearing course mixtures (BS 594: 1985)

Column number	*15*	*16*	*17*
Designation*	30/14	40/14	40/20
Nominal thickness of layer (mm)	40	50	50
Percentage by mass of total aggregate passing BS test sieve			
28 mm	–	–	100
20 mm	100	100	95 to 100
14 mm	85 to 100	90 to 100	50 to 85
10 mm	60 to 90	50 to 85	–
6.3 mm	–	–	–
2.36 mm	60 to 72	50 to 62	50 to 62
600 μm	25 to 45	20 to 40	20 to 40
212 μm	15 to 30	10 to 25	10 to 25
75 μm	8.0 to 12.0	6.0 to 10.0	6.0 to 10.0
Binder content, % by mass of total mixture for:			
Crushed rock	7.8	7.0	7.0
Steel slag	6.8	6.2	6.2
Blast furnace slag: bulk density (kg/m^3)			
1440	7.8	7.0	7.0
1360	7.9	7.2	7.2
1280	8.1	7.4	7.4
1200	8.3	7.6	7.6
1120	8.5	7.8	7.8

* The mixture designation numbers (e.g. 30/14 in column 15) refer to the nominal coarse aggregate content of the mixture/nominal size of the aggregate in the mixture respectively.

– 6 mm fine-textured wearing course.

(The last two mixes are referred to as coarse cold asphalt and fine cold asphalt even though they are macadams.)

For the open-textured mixes, the fines content is low (less than 15%), whereas for the medium- and fine-textured materials the fines content is higher (40–60% and more than 75% respectively). The dense materials have a closely specified aggregate grading and a low voids content (about 4%). Their density and consequent strength are more in line with some types of asphalt.

Although asphalts and macadams have distinctive features, they in fact represent opposite ends of a spectrum of materials. This range covers a variation in the proportions of the constituents and the void content and is illustrated in Figure 22.1. It can be seen that in the middle of the range the roadbase asphalts and dense macadams are not so different from one another.

22.2 Recipe and designed mixes

The majority of bituminous mixtures are recipe mixes. In other words, the mixtures are put together according to prescribed proportions laid down in the appropriate British Standard. These mix proportions have been derived through experience in use and, provided the separate ingredients meet their specifications, the mix will provide the required performance in most situations. This approach is consistent with the empirical method for the structural design of roads which has predominated until

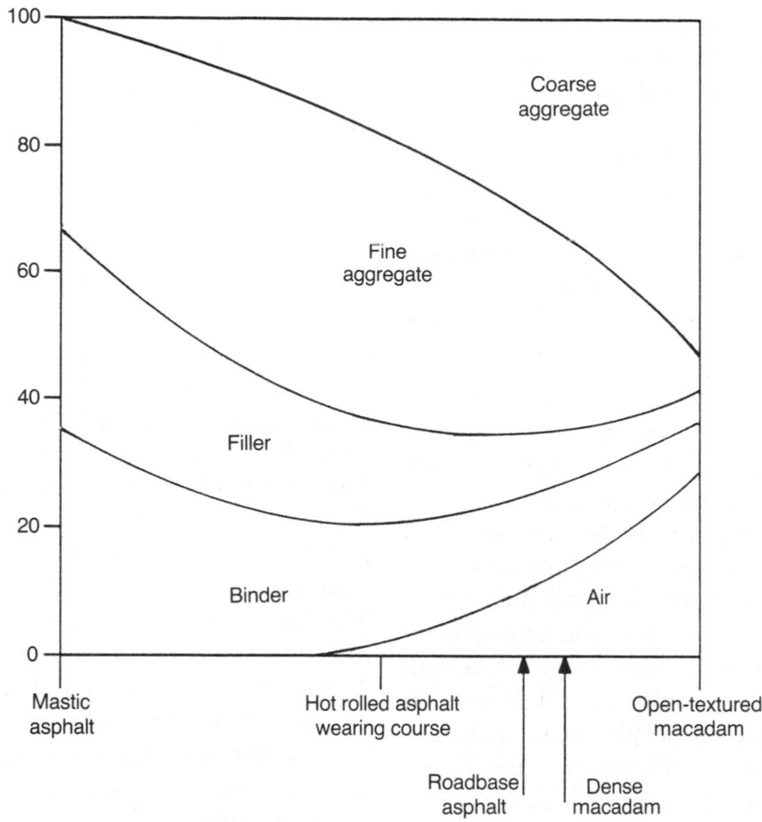

FIGURE 22.1 Constituent proportions of various bituminous materials.

relatively recently. Thus an empirical chart to determine the thickness of roadbase was used which depended on the roadbase material having the same mix proportions as the materials in the roads from which the design chart was originally established.

It is important to note that tests for compliance of recipe mixes can only be compositional tests and tests of the nature of individual ingredients. Typically, these materials are broken down to determine binder content and the aggregate grading. It is axiomatic that there are no tests of the properties of the material produced or of its performance.

Recipe mixes provide a satisfactory performance in many cases and there is some advantage in the simplified approach which recipe mixes offer. However, there are limitations to the use of recipe mixes which match the limitations of empirical structural design of roads. These are as follows.

1. Non-specified materials cannot be used. For example, a locally available sand may not meet the grading requirements of the specification but may produce a satisfactory mix. Recipe mixes preclude any assessment of the properties of a mix containing that sand.
2. Modified binders cannot be used. The use of chemical additives in binders can give useful enhancements to their properties. The

absence of any end-test of recipe mixes prevents the evaluation of these changes.
3. No procedure is available to assess causes of failure.
4. No procedure is available to optimize the mix proportions. This is particularly important as far as the bitumen is concerned because this is the most expensive ingredient and has a strong bearing on the performance of mixes, especially those which are more dense.

These drawbacks have led to the development of a procedure for the design of bituminous mixes, which has occurred in parallel with the development of analytical procedures for the structural design of roads. An analytical approach to road design enables the determination of the thickness of the road through an analysis of its behaviour under the applied load. This clearly requires a knowledge of certain properties of the materials and it follows that materials will have to be produced with particular characteristics. However, the design system, with material properties feeding into the analysis, has not yet been fully developed and what are now called designed mixes are in fact only partially designed.

The procedure for mix design (BS 598: Part 107: 1990) is based upon the Marshall test which was originally developed in the USA for designing mixes for use on airfield runways. The objective of the procedure is to determine an optimum binder content from a consideration of:

1. mix strength (stability);
2. mix density;
3. mix deformability (flow).

Test samples of binder/aggregate mixtures are prepared using the materials to be used in the field. The aggregate grading is kept constant and samples with a range of binder contents are produced. The samples are prepared and compacted in a standard way into moulds 101.6 mm in diameter and 70 mm high. The state of compaction achieved is determined by measuring the bulk density and calculating the compacted aggregate density. At low binder contents the mix will lack workability and the densities will be correspondingly low. At high binder contents, aggregate will effectively be displaced by bitumen, and again the densities will be low. Each of these measures of density will thus produce an optimum binder content as shown in Figures 22.2(a) and (b).

To test the strength and resistance to deformation of the material, the specimens are heated to 60°C and subjected to a compression test using special curved jaws which match the curved sides of the specimens as shown in Figure 22.3. Thus the load is applied radially. The jaws of the machine are driven together at a constant rate of 50 mm per minute until the maximum load is obtained which is termed the 'stability'. The deformation of the sample at this maximum load is also recorded and termed the 'flow'. Typical plots of stability and flow against binder content are shown in Figures 22.2(c) and (d). The stability plot gives a third optimum binder content, and the design binder content is obtained from the average of this and the optima from the two density plots. The flow at this design binder content can then be read off. Minimum values of stability and flow are specified according to the amount of traffic which the road will carry.

In evaluating mixes it is helpful to consider the Marshall quotient, Q_m. This is derived from the stability and flow:

$$Q_m = \frac{\text{Stability}}{\text{Flow}}.$$

Thus Q_m bears some resemblance to a modulus (stress/strain) and may be taken as a measure of mix stiffness. It has been found to correlate well with wheel-tracking tests to assess deformation resistance. Since stability is used to determine the optimum binder content, the design procedure may be regarded as determining stiffness at optimum binder content, and the larger the value of Q_m, the more resistant the mix will be to deformation.

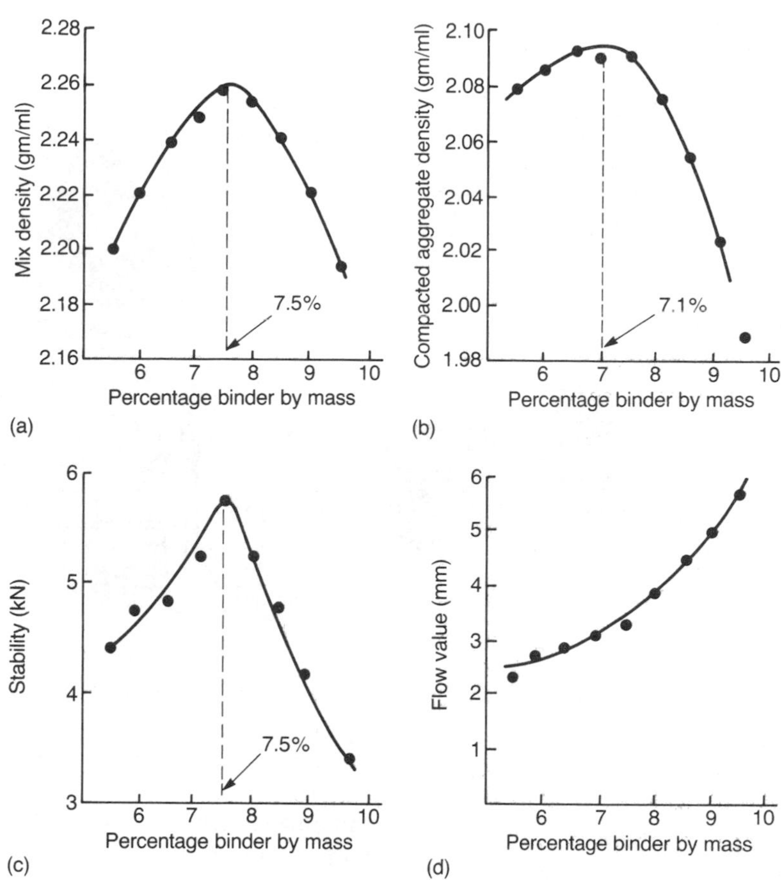

FIGURE 22.2 Analysis of mix design data from the Marshall test.

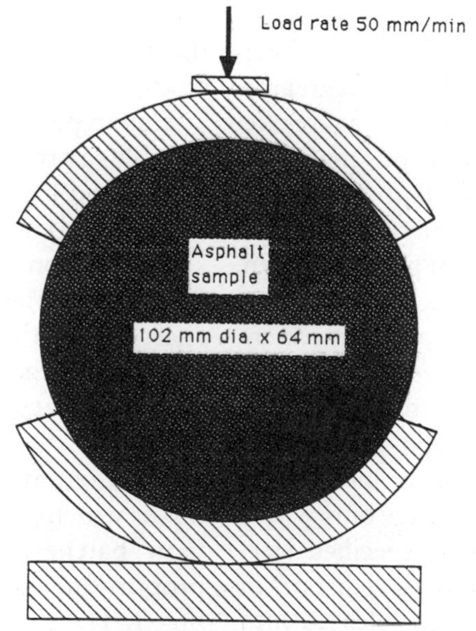

FIGURE 22.3 Testing arrangement for a Marshall asphalt design.

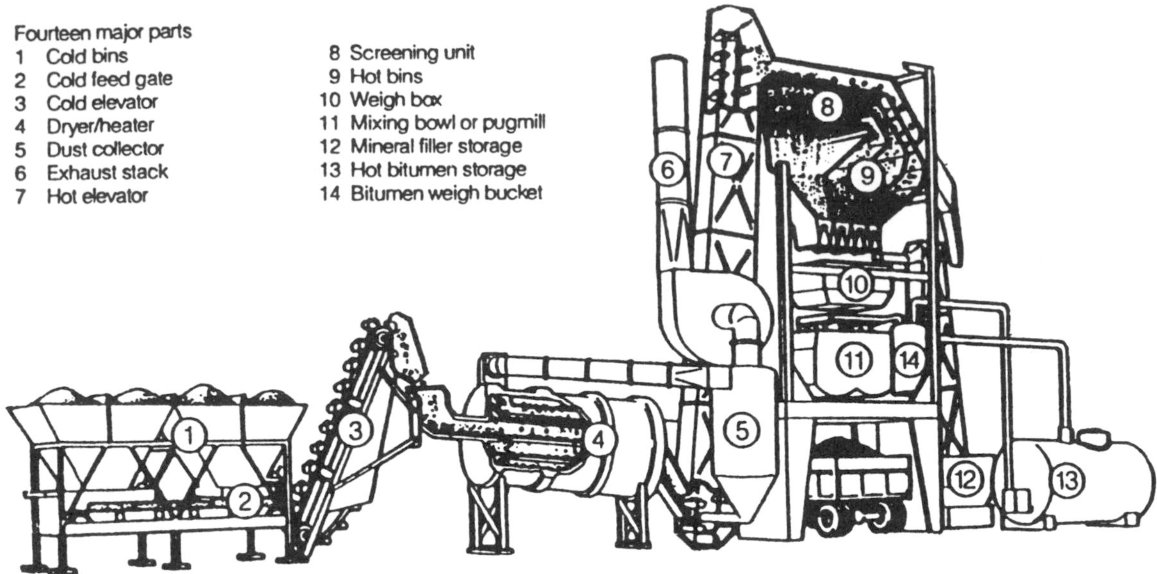

FIGURE 22.4 Schematic diagram of an indirectly heated batch mixing plant (*The Shell Bitumen Handbook*, 1990).

22.3 Methods of production

The process of manufacture of bituminous materials involves three stages. Firstly, the aggregates must be proportioned to give the required grading, secondly the aggregates must be dried and heated and thirdly the correct amount of binder must be added to the aggregate and mixed to thoroughly coat the aggregate particles and produce a homogeneous material.

The most common type of plant in the UK is the indirectly heated batch mixing plant. A schematic diagram of this type of plant is shown in Figure 22.4. The aggregate is blended from cold bins and passed through a rotary drier/heater. Here the moisture is driven off and the aggregate temperature raised to the prescribed mixing temperature for the type of material being produced. The aggregate is then transported by hot elevator to hot storage bins where it is separated into fractions of specified size. Aggregates are released into the weigh box in the desired proportions and then released into the mixer. Bitumen heated to the prescribed temperature is also introduced to the mixer, the quantity being determined using a weigh bucket or volumetrically using a flow meter. The mixing time varies up to 60 seconds but should be as short as possible in order to limit oxidation of the binder. After mixing, the material is discharged directly into a wagon.

This type of plant is very versatile, being capable of producing both asphalt and macadam mixes, and being able to easily adjust to a wide range of mix specifications.

A variation on this type of plant is to dry and heat the aggregate in batches before being charged into the mixer. This eliminates the need for hot aggregate storage but the proportioning of the cold aggregate needs to be very carefully controlled.

An alternative type of mixer is the drum mixer which gives continuous production rather than batches. Here the cold aggregates are proportioned and conveyed directly into a drum mixer. The drum has two zones. The first zone is where drying and heating occur, and in the second zone the bitumen is introduced and the mixing takes place. The advantages of this type of plant are that the amount of dust emission is reduced, the process is simpler and, above all, the rate of production can be very high – up to 500 tonnes per hour. This is advantageous where large quantities of the same type of material are required, but it is difficult to change production to a different mix.

Acknowledgements

Extracts from British Standards are reproduced with the permission of BSI. Complete copies of the standard can be obtained by post from BSI Sales, Linford Wood, Milton Keynes, MK14 6LE.

22.4 References

British Standard 594: 1985: *Hot rolled asphalt for roads and other paved areas. Part 1: Specification for constituent materials and asphalt mixtures.*

British Standard 4987: 1988: *Coated macadam for roads and other paved areas. Part 1: Specification for constituent materials and for mixtures.*

British Standard 598: Part 107: 1990: *Method of test for the determination of the composition of design wearing course asphalt.*

The Shell Bitumen Handbook (1990) Shell Bitumen UK.

Part Five

Brickwork and Blockwork

R.C. de Vekey

Introduction

This part outlines the history of masonry and explains the terminology used. The following chapters cover: starting materials, composition and manufacturing processes for the components of masonry; structural forms, architecture and detailing; structural behaviour and response to actions such as wind and movement; and durability and other important properties in relation to heat, noise, fire and rain and weather.

The title 'Brickwork and blockwork' has been chosen to emphasize that these materials are the most common of this type used in construction at the present time. The term 'masonry' has recently been widened from its traditional meaning of structures built of natural stone to encompass all structures produced by stacking, piling or bonding together discrete chunks of rock, fired clay, concrete, etc. to form the whole, and 'masonry', in this wider sense, is what these chapters are about.

Second to wood, masonry is probably the oldest building material used by man and it certainly dates from the ancient civilizations of the Middle East and was used widely by the Greeks and Romans. Early cultures used mud building bricks and very little of their work has survived, but stone structures such as the Egyptian pyramids, Greek temples and many structures made from fired clay bricks have survived for thousands of years. The Romans used both fired clay bricks and hydraulic (lime/pozzolana) mortar and spread this technology over most of Europe.

The basic principle of masonry is of building stable bonded (interlocked) stacks of handleable pieces. The pieces are usually chosen or manufactured to be of a size and weight that one person can place by hand but, where additional power is available, larger pieces may be used which give potentially more stable and durable structures. This greater stability and durability is conferred by the larger weight and inertia which increases the energy required to remove one piece and makes it more resistant to natural forces such as winds and water as well as human agency. There are four main techniques for achieving stable masonry.

1. Irregularly shaped and sized but generally laminar pieces are chosen and placed by hand in an interlocking mass (e.g. dry stone walls).
2. Medium to large blocks are made very precisely to a few sizes and assembled to a basic grid pattern either without mortar or with very thin joints (e.g. ashlar).
3. Small to medium units are made to normal precision in a few sizes and assembled to a basic grid pattern and the inaccuracies are taken up by use of a packing material such as mortar (e.g. normal brickwork).
4. Irregularly shaped and sized pieces are both packed apart and bonded together with adherent mortar (e.g. random rubble walls).

Only type (4) structures depend wholly on the mortar for their stability; all the other types rely largely on the mechanical interlocking of the pieces. Figure V.1 shows typical examples.

These descriptions are given to emphasize that most traditional masonry owes much of its strength and stability to interlocking action,

FIGURE V.1 The main types of masonry: (a) dry stone walls, (b) ashlar, (c) jointed brick and blockwork and (d) rubble masonry.

weight and inertia while the mortar, when present, is not acting as a glue but as something to fill in the gaps resulting from the imperfect fitting together of the pieces. Most contemporary masonry is type (3) and modern mortars do have an adhesive role but much of the strength still derives from the mass and interlocking of shapes and it is important to remember this in design.

It is also important to remember that, although the wall is the most useful and effective masonry structure, many other structural forms are used such as columns, piers, arches, tunnels, floors and roads. Normal plain masonry must be designed such that the predominant forces put it into compression since it cannot be relied on to resist tensile forces. If, however, tension structures such as cantilevers, earth-retaining walls and beams are required, masonry may be reinforced or post-tensioned in the same way as concrete.

Terminology

Components

Units – pieces of stone, brick, concrete or calcium silicate which may be assembled to make masonry. Usually, but not invariably, they are in the form of rectangular parallelepipeds.

Mortar – a material that is plastic (flows) when fresh but sets hard over a period of hours to

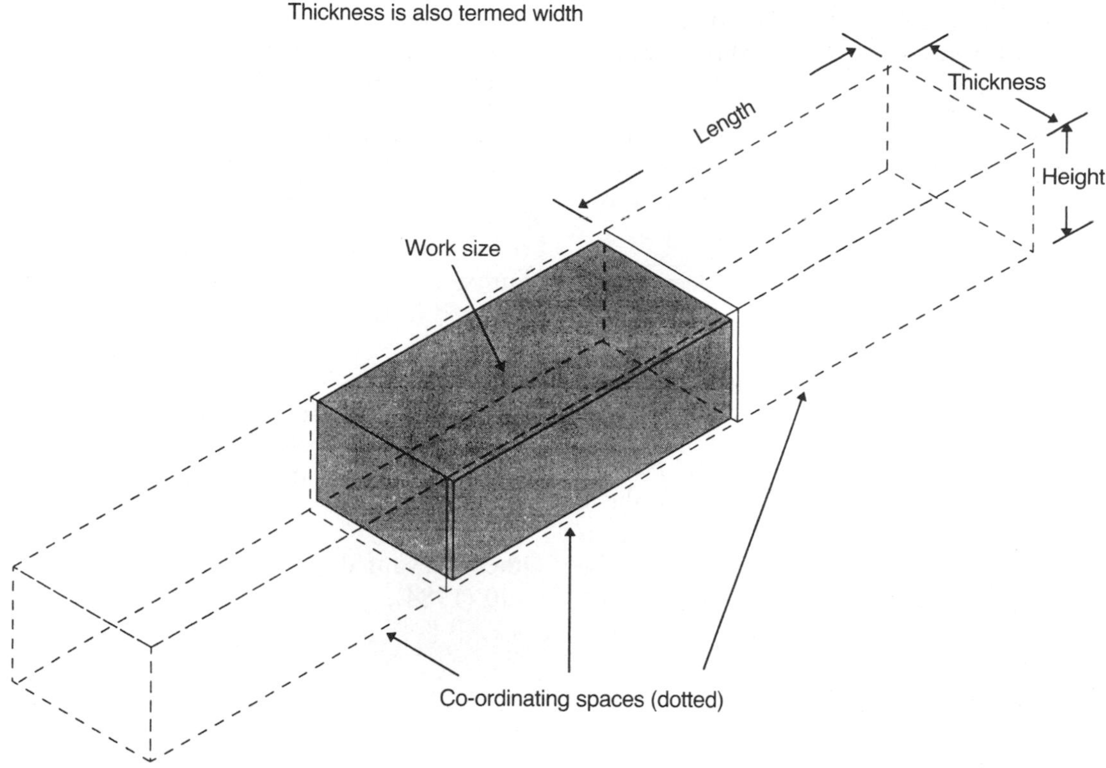

FIGURE V.2 Masonry dimensions.

days. Its purpose is to fill the gaps caused by variations in the size and shape of units such that the masonry is stable and resists the flow of air and water. Mortar is compounded from a binder and a filler (usually sand).

Binder – a finely ground material which when mixed with water reacts chemically and then sets hard and binds aggregates into solid masses.

Size and dimensions (Figure V.2)

Work size – the size of a masonry unit specified for its manufacture, to which its actual size should conform within specified permissible deviations. As a rough guide for the following sections bricks are considered to be units with face dimensions of up to 337.5 mm long × 112.5 mm high and with a maximum depth of 225 mm, while blocks are larger units up to face dimensions of 1500 mm × 500 mm. UK units are smaller than these limits. A standard UK brick is 215 mm long × 65 mm high and with a depth of 102.5 mm. There is no standard block size but the commonest size is 440 mm long × 215 mm high and with a depth of 100 mm with a limiting size of 650 mm for any dimension for standard concrete units.

Coordinating size – the size of a coordinating space allocated to a masonry unit, including allowances for joints and tolerances. This co-ordination grid into which they fit is generally 10 mm larger for each dimension.

Units

Units may be produced in a number of forms.

Solid – having no designed voids (holes, depressions or perforations) other than those inherent in the material.

Frogged – with a depression (or frog) in one or both of the bed faces where the total volume of the frog(s) does not exceed 20% of the gross volume.

Cellular – having one or more deep holes or depressions in from one bed face with an aggregate volume exceeding 20% of the gross volume and which do not penetrate through to the other side.

Perforated – having one or more holes passing from one face to the opposite face. UK products have vertical perforations, i.e. the holes pass from one bed face to the other and will be vertical when laid normally in a stretcher bonded wall. Horizontally perforated clay blocks are, however, not uncommon in continental Europe.

Hollow – having one or more formed holes or cavities which pass through the units.

Specials (special shapes) – a range of standard bricks for curves, non-right-angled corners, plinths, cappings, etc., are available. They are described in BS 4729 (1990).

General

Fair-faced – masonry, within the variability of individual units, precisely flat on the visible face. This is normally only possible on one side of solid walls.

Other relevant definitions are contained in BS 6100 (1984).

Chapter twenty-three

Materials

23.1 Materials used for manufacture of units and mortars
23.2 Other constituents and additives
23.3 Mortar
23.4 Fired clay bricks and blocks
23.5 Calcium silicate units
23.6 Concrete units
23.7 References

23.1 Materials used for manufacture of units and mortars

23.1.1 Sands and fillers

Sand

Sand is used widely as a constituent of masonry in mortar, in concrete units and sandlime units, in grouts and renders. It is a mixture of rock particles of different sizes from about 10 mm diameter down to 75 μm diameter.

Sand is usually extracted from recent naturally occurring alluvial deposits such as river beds and sea beaches or from older deposits from alluvial or glacial action. In some areas it may be derived from dunes or by crushing quarried rocks. The chemical and geological composition will reflect the area from which it is derived. The commonest sands are those based on silica (SiO_2), partly because of its wide distribution in rocks such as sandstones and the flint in limestones, and partly because silica is hard and chemically resistant. Other likely constituents are clay, derived from the decomposition of feldspars, calcium carbonate ($CaCO_3$), in the form of chalk or limestone from shells in some marine sands, and micas in sands from weathered granites. Crushed rocks such as crushed basalts and granites will reflect their origins.

Sands should be mostly free of particles of clay (around 75–30 μm) which cause unsatisfactory shrinkage characteristics and chemical interactions with binders. Most of the constituents of sand are relatively chemically inert to environmental agents but chalk or limestone particles will be dissolved slowly by mild acids and clays may react in time with acids or alkalis. Most sand constituents are also fairly hard and are resistant, in themselves, to mechanical abrasion and erosion by dust in wind and water.

Mortar and rendering sands

Mortar sand must contain no particles with a diameter greater than about half the thinnest joint thickness, i.e. around 5 mm. It should also have a good range of particle sizes from the largest to the smallest (a good grading) since this leads to good packing of the particles to give a dense, strong mass resistant to erosion, permeation and chemical attack. Many naturally occurring alluvial deposits fall naturally into the required grading and may be used as dug or just with a few coarser particles screened off. These are usually termed pit sands. Sands that are outside the normal range must be sieved to remove coarse fractions and washed to remove excess clay particles.

The shape of the particles is also important for mortar sands. Very flaky materials such as slates and micas are not very suitable as it is dif-

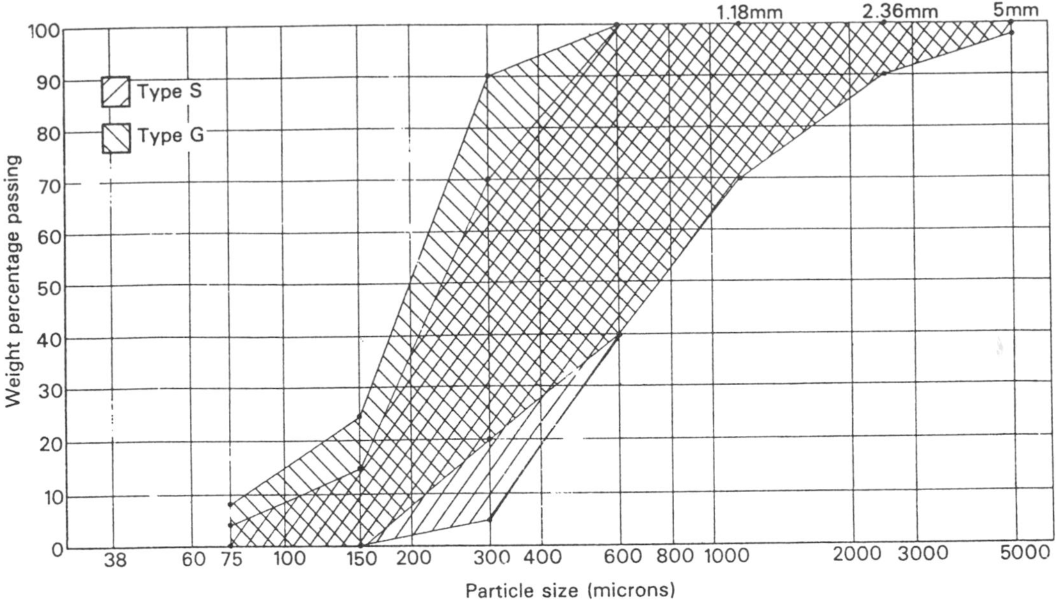

FIGURE 23.1 Grading curves for S and G sands.

TABLE 23.1 Typical chemical composition ranges of pfa (weight %)

Range	SiO_2	Al_2O_3	Fe_3O_4	CaO	MgO	K_2O	Na_2O	TiO_2	SO_3	Cl
Minimum	45	24	7	1.1	1.5	2.8	0.9	0.8	0.3	0.05
Maximum	51	32	11	5.4	4.4	4.5	1.7	1.1	1.3	0.15

ficult to make them workable. Very absorbent materials are also unsatisfactory for dry-mixed mortars since they cause rapid falls in workability by absorbing the mixing water. They may be suitable for mixes based on wet premixed lime-sand 'coarse stuff'. Sand may be sieved into fractions and regraded but this is rarely done for a mortar sand. Figure 23.1 shows the grading curves for the sands allowed under BS 1200 (1976). This gives two allowed grades, S for structural use and G, with slightly wider limits, for general purposes.

Rendering mixes require sands with broadly similar characteristics to mortars but a good grading is even more important to avoid shrinkage cracking and spalling.

Concreting sands

See Section 13.4.

Ground sand

Finely ground silica sand is used particularly in the manufacture of autoclaved aerated cement (AAC) materials.

Pfa

Pulverized fuel ash is the main by-product of modern coal-fired electricity generating stations which burn finely ground coal. Typical composition ranges are given in Table 23.1 and fuller information is available in Central Electricity Generating Board (1972).

Chalk (calcium carbonate; $CaCO_3$)

In a finely ground state chalk is used as a filler and plasticity aid in masonry cement and some grouts.

23.1.2 Clays

Clay is a very widely distributed material which is produced by weathering and decomposition of acid alumino-silicate rocks such as the feldspars, granites and gneisses. Typical broad types are the kaolin group of which kaolinite has a composition $Al_2O_3.2SiO_2.2H_2O$, the montmorillonite group of which montmorillonite itself has the composition $Al_2O_3.4SiO_2.nH_2O$, and the clay micas which typically have a composition $K_2O.MgO.4Al_2O_3.7SiO_2.2H_2O$.

They will frequently contain iron, which can substitute for the aluminium, and other transition metals. The clays used for clay brick manufacture are normally only partly actual clay minerals, which impart the plasticity when wetted, the balance being made up of other minerals. Brick earths, shales, marls, etc. mostly contain finely divided silica, lime and other materials associated with the particular deposit, e.g. carbon in coal measure shales. Most brick clays contain iron compounds which give the red, yellow and blue colours to fired bricks. Table 23.2 gives the compositions of some typical clays in terms of their content of oxides and organic matter (coal, oil, etc.).

The properties of clays are a result of their layer structure which comprises SiO_4 tetrahedra bonded via oxygen to aluminium atoms which are also bonded to hydroxyl groups to balance the charge. The layers form loosely bound flat sheet-like structures which are easily parted and can adsorb and bond lightly to varying amounts of water between the sheets. As more water is absorbed the clay swells and the intersheet bond becomes weaker, i.e. the clay becomes more plastic and allows various shaping techniques to be used.

23.1.3 Aggregates

Natural aggregates, sintered pfa nodules, expanded clay and foamed slag are described in Section 13.4. Other aggregates used particularly for unit manufacture are the following.

1. Furnace clinker, a partially fused ash from the bottom of solid fuelled industrial furnaces.
2. Furnace bottom ash. Most large modern furnaces, especially those used to raise steam in power stations, burn finely ground coal dust as a dust/air mixture. A proportion of the ash sinters together in the gas stream, then falls to the base of the furnace as par-

TABLE 23.2 Chemical compositions of some typical clays (weight %)

Broad type	*SiO_2*	*Al_2O_3*	*Fe_3O_4*	*CaO*	*MgO*	*X_2O*[1]	*CO_2*	*H_2O*	*Organic matter*
London brick	49.5	34.3	7.7	1.4	5.2	–	–	–	1.9
Blue clay	46.5	38.0	1.0	1.2	–	–	–	–	13.3
Loam	66.2	27.0	1.3	0.5	–	–	–	–	5.0
Fletton clay	50.0	16.0	7.0	10.0	1.0	3.0	–	6.0	6.0
Marl	33.0	10.0	3.0	26.0	3.5	–	20.5	4.0	–
Burnham clay	42.9	20.9	5.0	10.8	0.1	0.3	8.1	6.9	5.0
Red brick clay	49.0	24.0	8.0	7.0		1.0	11.0	–	
Gault clay	44.0	15.0	6.0	17.0		–	–	18.0	–
Washed china clay	46.0	40.0	–	1.0		–	–	13.0	–
Stourbridge fireclay	65.0	22.0	2.0	1.0		–	–	10.0	–

[1] X = alkali metal, e.g. sodium or potassium.

ticles too large to stay suspended in the gas stream. This clinker-like material is termed furnace bottom ash.

3. Perlite. Volcanic ash is deposited as a fine glassy dust and can be converted to a lightweight aggregate by hot sintering.
4. Pumice, a light foamed rock formed when volcanic lava cools. It is normally imported from volcanic regions such as Italy.

23.1.4 Binders

The binder is the component which binds together mixtures of sands, aggregates, fillers, plasticizers, pigments, etc. used to make mortars, concrete units, sandlime units and grouts. All those used widely are based on: hydraulic cements which react chemically with water at normal factory/site temperatures; lime–silica mixtures which react only in the presence of high-pressure steam; or lime which sets slowly in air by carbonation. Because they must be finely divided to be able to penetrate the spaces between sand grains and to react in some way to give the change from a formable plastic material to a hard adhesive, they must inherently be more chemically reactive than the other components. Their chemical reactivity is their weakness in that they often react with chemicals in the environment with resultant deterioration.

Ordinary Portland cement (opc)

Currently, the most popular binder for general purposes is opc. Related products are rapid hardening Portland cement and sulphate resisting Portland cement. The chemistry and manufacturing methods of hydraulic cements are covered more fully in Part Three.

Masonry cement

A factory prepared mixture of opc with a fine inert filler/plasticizer (around 20%) and an air entraining agent to give additional plasticity is supplied as masonry cement. It is intended solely for mixing with sand and water to make bedding mortars. The fine powder is normally ground chalk but a wide range of inert and semi-inert materials can be substituted. In the future Portland cements blended with pulverized fuel ash (pfa) may well be used for mortars either as masonry cements or as blended cements.

Hydraulic lime

Impure lime was widely used in the past and is gaining popularity for repairing historic buildings to match the existing mortar. It is basically a quicklime – calcium oxide – produced by heating impure limestone to a high temperature. The impurities, usually siliceous or clay, lead to the formation of a proportion of hydraulically active compounds such as calcium silicates or aluminates. The mortar is made as normal by gauging (mixing in prescribed proportions) with sand and water but there will be some emission of heat while the lime is slaking.

Quicklime (CaO)

The pure oxide was used widely in the past for mortars for stonework. It is prepared in the same way as hydraulic lime mortar but since it does not have any setting action in the short term it may be kept for days or weeks provided it is covered and prevented from drying out. The wet mix with sand is termed 'coarse stuff'. Contemporary lime mortar may be made from hydrated lime ($Ca(OH)_2$) but is otherwise similar. The initial setting action of this mortar depends only on dewatering by contact with the units so it is not suitable for construction of slender structures which require rapid development of flexural strength. Over periods of months or years the lime in this mortar carbonates and hardens to form calcium carbonate as in eqn (23.1), but it is never as hard or durable as properly specified hydraulic cement mortars.

$$Ca(OH)_2 + CO_2 \rightarrow CaCO_3 + H_2O \tag{23.1}$$

Most of the hydraulic cements may be blended

with pure hydrated lime in various proportions to make hybrid binders which give mortars with a lower strength and rigidity but still maintain the plasticity of the 1:3 binder:sand ratio. This leads to mortars which are more tolerant of movement and more economical.

Sandlime

The binder used for sandlime bricks and autoclaved aerated concrete (AAC) blocks is lime (calcium hydroxide, $Ca(OH)_2$) which reacts with silica during autoclaving to produce calcium silicate hydrates. The reaction, in a simplified form, is:

$$Ca(OH)_2 + SiO_2 \rightarrow CaSiO_3, H_2O \tag{23.2}$$

The lime is usually added directly as hydrated calcined limestone or may be derived in part from opc which is also incorporated in small quantities to give a green strength to the unit.

23.2 Other constituents and additives

Organic plasticizers

Many organic compounds improve plasticity, or workability, of mortars, rendering mortars, infilling grouts and concrete used for manufacture of units. All the classic mortar plasticizers operate by causing air to be entrained as small bubbles. These bubbles fill the spaces between the sand grains and induce plasticity. Typical materials are based on Vinsol resin, a by-product of cellulose pulp manufacture, or other naturally available or synthetic detergents. They are surfactants and alter surface tension and other properties. Super plasticizers, used only for concrete and grout mixes, plasticize by a different mechanism which does not cause air entrainment. Section 13.2.1 gives more information.

Latex additives

A number of synthetic copolymer plastics may be produced in the form of a 'latex', a finely divided dispersion of the plastic in water usually stabilized by a surfactant such as a synthetic detergent. Generally the solids content is around 50% of the dispersion. At a temperature known as the film-forming temperature, they dehydrate to form a continuous polymer solid. When combined with hydraulic cement mixes these materials have a number of beneficial effects: they increase adhesion of mortar to all substrates; increase the tensile strength and durability; reduce the stiffness and the permeability. Because of these effects they are widely used in flooring screeds and renders but are also used to formulate high-bond mortars and waterproof mortars. The better polymers are based on copolymerized mixtures of butadiene, styrene and acrylics. Polyvinylidene dichloride (PVDC) has also been marketed for this application but it can lose chlorine which can attack buried metals. Polyvinyl acetate (PVA) is not suitable as it is unstable in moist conditions. Polyvinyl propionate has been found to give less satisfactory flow properties than the acrylic copolymers. These materials should never be used with sands containing more than 2% of clay or silt particles. Dosage is usually in the range of 5–20% of the cement weight. Table 23.3 gives some properties of common types from data in de Vekey (1975) and de Vekey and Majumdar (1977).

Pigments

Through-coloured units and mortars of particular colours may be manufactured either by selecting suitably coloured natural sands and binders or by adding pigments. Units may also be coloured by applying surface layers but this is more common for fired clay than for concrete or calcium silicate units. Pigments are in the form of inert coloured powders of a similar fineness to the binder so thus tend to dilute the mix and reduce strength. Most pigments should be limited to a maximum of 10% by weight of the binder in mortars and carbon black to 3%. Some typical pigments are listed in Table

TABLE 23.3 Latex polymer additives

Chemical name: polymer of or copolymer of	*Reaction product with cement slurry*	*Properties of polymer/cement[1] as proportion of neat cement paste*			
		Elastic modulus		*Flexural strength*	
		Air[2]	*Water[2]*	*Air[2]*	*Water[2]*
Vinyl acetate	Acetate ions	0.62[3]	0.59[3]	1.60[3]	0.66[3]
Vinyl propionate	None	0.62[3]	0.74	1.24[3]	1.22[3]
Butadiene and styrene	None	0.51	0.71	1.00[3]	1.63[3]
Vinylidene dichloride	Chloride ions	0.66[4]	0.84[4]	1.52[4]	1.36[4]
Acrylic acid and styrene	None	0.59	0.69	1.56	1.95
Acrylic acid	None	0.40	0.65	1.29	1.91
Acrylic acid and methacrylic acid	None	0.32	0.73	1.44	1.68

[1] Properties are for an opc cement paste with a w/c ratio of 0.3 and a polymer solids/cement ratio of 0.1 after storage for two years.
[2] Storage conditions are air at 65% relative humidity or water at 20°C.
[3] These figures are the mean of two products.
[4] These figures are the mean of four products.

TABLE 23.4 Pigments suitable for mortars and units

Pigment type (name/description)	*Probable formula (if known)*	*Lightfastness (colour change)*
Synthetic red iron oxide	Fe_2O_3	None
Synthetic yellow iron oxide		None
Synthetic black iron oxide	FeO (or Fe_3O_4)	None
Synthetic brown iron oxide	Fe_2O_3, xH_2O	None
Natural brown iron oxide	Fe_2O_3, xH_2O	None
Chromium oxide green	Cr_2O_3	None
Carbon black (concrete grade)	C	None
Cobalt blue	–	None
Ultramarine blue	–	None
Phthalocyanine green	Copper phthalocyanine	Severe
Dalamar (hansa) yellow	–	Significant

23.4 from information in ASTM task group C09.03.08.05 (1980). Only pigments resistant to alkali attack and wettable under test mix conditions are included.

Retarders

Retarders are used to delay the initial set of hydraulic cement mortars. They are generally polyhydroxycarbon compounds. Typical examples are sugar, lignosulphonates and hydroxycarboxylic acids.

Accelerators

Accelerators have been marketed, usually based on calcium chloride ($CaCl_2$), which is used in small amounts in concrete block manufacture. Alternatives such as calcium formate ($Ca(CHO_2)_2$) may be satisfactory. Accelerators are not effective when building with mortar in frosty weather and are no substitute for proper protection of the work.

More data on these materials are given in Section 13.2.2.

23.3 Mortar

Mortar has to cope with a wide range of, sometimes conflicting, requirements. To obtain optimum performance the composition must be tailored to the application. The broad principles are as follows.

1. Mortars with a high content of hydraulic cements are stronger, denser, more impervious and more durable, bond better to units under normal circumstances and harden rapidly at normal temperatures. They also lead to a high drying shrinkage and rigidity of the masonry. They are likely to cause shrinkage cracks if used with shrinkable low-strength units particularly for long lightly loaded walls such as parapets and spandrels.
2. Mortars with decreased content of hydraulic cements are weaker and more ductile and thus more tolerant of movement. They are matched better to low-strength units but at the cost of a reduction in strength, durability and bond. There is a corresponding reduction in shrinkage and hardening rate.
3. Mortars made with sharp, well-graded sands can have very high compressive strength, low permeability and generally good bond but poor workability, while fine loamy sands give high workability but generally with reduced compressive strength and sometimes reduced bond.
4. Lime addition confers plasticity and, particularly for the wet stored mixes, water retentivity – the ability of the mortar to retain its water in contact with highly absorbent bricks – which facilitates the laying process and makes sure that the cement can hydrate. Lime mortars perform poorly if subjected to freezing while in the green (unhardened) state but, when hardened, are very durable. Lime is white and thus tends to lighten the colour of the mortar. In some circumstances it can be leached out and may cause staining.
5. Air entrainment improves the frost resistance of green mortar and allows lower water/cement ratios to be used but such plasticized mixes may be less durable and water-retentive than equivalent lime mixes. Air entrained mixes also need careful manufacture and control of use since over-mixing gives very high air contents, and retempering (adding more water and reworking the mix) can lead to very poor performance due to the high porosity of the set dry mortar.
6. Pigment addition weakens mortar and the content should never exceed 10% of the weight of the cement in the mortar. Carbon black is a special case and should be limited to 3%.
7. Polymer latex additives can markedly improve some properties, such as bond, flexural strength and resistance to permeation by water and air but they are costly and should only be used where there is a particular requirement.
8. Retarders are widely used in the manufacture of ready-mixed mortars, delivered to site in the same way as ready-mixed concrete. The retarder is dosed as required by the supplier to give a 'pot life' of between 1 and 3 days. Care is needed in the use of retarded mortars, especially in hot weather, because if they dry out too rapidly the curing process never takes place and the mortar never hardens.

23.3.1 Properties of unset mortar

The important properties of unset mortar are the workability, i.e. how easy it is to handle and place on to the masonry; the pot life, i.e. how long it may be used for after mixing; the water retentivity, i.e. how good it is at retaining water against the suction of the units; the setting time; and the hardening rate. Associated parameters are the cement content, water content (often expressed as the water/cement ratio w/c) and the air content. Test methods are given in BS 4551 (1980), RILEM (1978) and ISO (1991).

The workability is measured in terms of the slump, consistence or the flow. The slump test is seldom now used for mortar. Consistence is measured by the dropping ball test. Flow is measured on a standard 254 mm diameter (ASTM) flow table.

Water retentivity is measured by weighing the amount of water extracted from a dropping ball mould full of mortar by weighted layers of filter paper through two layers of cotton gauze. The consistence retentivity is measured by repeating the dropping ball test on the dewatered mortar.

Air content may be measured by weighing a known volume (0.5 l) of mortar and then calculating, using data on the relative densities and proportions of the constituents, from the following formula:

$$A = 100(1 - K\rho) \qquad (23.3)$$

where A is the air content, ρ is the relative density of the mortar and K is derived from:

$$K = \frac{\left[\frac{M_1}{d_1} + \frac{M_2}{d_2} + \ldots + M_w\right]}{M_1 M_2 + \ldots + M_w}$$

where $M_1, M_2, \ldots$, etc. are the relative masses of the constituents of the mortar of relative densities (specific gravities) d_1, d_2, etc., and M_w is the relative mass of water. The sum of all the values of M_1, $M_2 \ldots$ and M_w will be equal to 1. For precise measurements it is necessary to measure the specific gravity of all the constituents separately by use of the density bottle method. If this cannot be done the following default values are suggested: opc 3.12, masonry cement 3.05, silica sand 2.65, white hydrated building lime 2.26, grey hydrated lime 2.45. Alternatively the pressure method can be used. All the methods are detailed in BS 4551 (1980). The water content can be determined independently on fresh mortar by rapid oven drying of a weighed quantity. Recently a simple site test has become available to independently measure cement content of fresh and unhardened mortars (Southern, 1989). A quantity of mortar is weighed and dissolved in a prediluted and measured volume of acid. The cement content can be calculated from the temperature rise measured with an electronic thermometer.

23.3.2 Properties of hardened mortar

The important properties of hardened mortar are the density, permeability, Young's modulus, compressive strength, flexural strength, bond strength to units and drying shrinkage. The durability is determined, indirectly, by the combination of other properties. Most of these properties may be measured by tests given in standards BS 4551 (1980), RILEM (1978) and ISO (1991).

The compressive strength is measured by a cube-crushing test and the flexural strength is measured by the three point bend (or modulus of rupture) test. The modulus of rupture (MOR) is based on the formula:

$$\text{MOR} = \frac{3 \cdot P \cdot L}{2\, b \cdot d^2} \qquad (23.4)$$

where P is the maximum load applied, L is the span of the support rollers, b is the width of the prism and d is the depth of the prism.

The bond strength to typical units is conven-

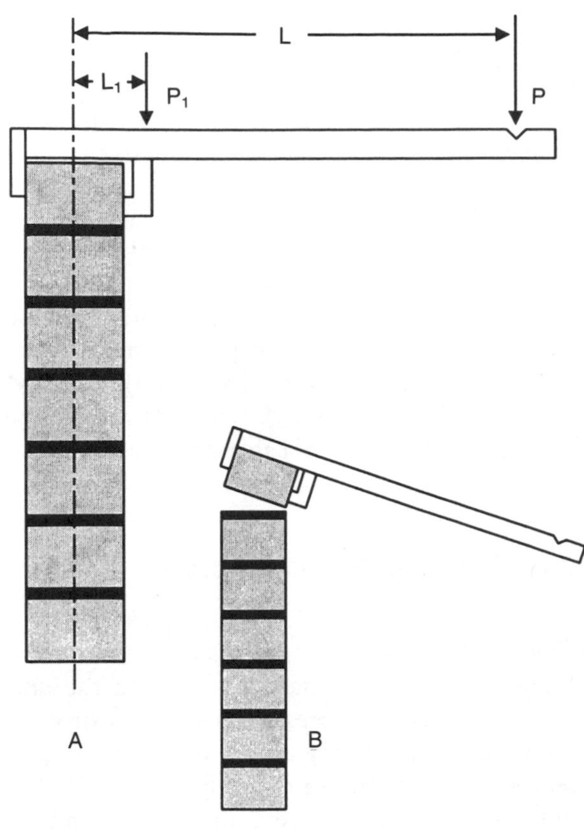

FIGURE 23.2 Bond wrench A before and B after test.

tionally measured by the parallel wallette test. In this test a small wall is built and tested in the vertical attitude by a four point bend test using articulated loading arms and supports, to prevent the application of any twisting moments, and resilient bolsters to prevent uneven loading. The standard specimens for UK bricks and 100 mm thick 440 × 215 mm blocks are shown in Figure 25.14.

The bond wrench (ASTM C1072-86) has been introduced and specified in some codes and standards as a simpler way to measure bond although it may give slightly higher values than the wallette test. This device measures the moment required to detach a single unit from the top of a wall or stack-bonded prism using a lever clamped to the unit as in Figure 23.2. The load may be applied in a variety of ways, commonly by filling a container with lead shot. An electronically gauged version (BRE Digest 359, 1991) exists where the load is applied via a load cell transducer. Its main advantage is that it can be used on site for quality control and diagnosis of problems and failures as well as a laboratory tool.

Table 23.5 gives the common formulations of

TABLE 23.5 Strength ranges for mortar at 28 days

Mortar designation	*Proportions by volume of ingredients*			*Strength properties (ranges)*		
	Cement: lime: sand	*Masonry cement: sand*	*Cement: sand + plasticizer*	*Observed strength ranges at 28 days*		
				Compressive (N/mm^2)	*Flexural (N/mm^2)*	*Bond (N/mm^2)*
(i)	$1:0-\frac{1}{4}:3$	–	–	8–30	2.8–6.6	0.6–1.6
(ii)	$1:\frac{1}{2}:4\frac{1}{2}$	1:2.5–3.5	1:3–4	5–18	1.8–4.5	0.3–1.0
(iii)	1:1:5–6	1:4–5	1:5–6	2–12	0.7–3.7	0.2–1.1
(iv)	1:2:8–9	1:5.5–6.5	1:7–8	0.8–5.5	(0.7–1.7)	(0.36–0.5)
(v)	1:3:10–12	1:6.5–7	1:8	0.5–1.0	(0.7–0.9)	No data
(vi)*	0:1:2–3	–	–	0.5–1.0	No data	No data
(vii)†	0:1:2–3	–	–	0.5–1.0	No data	No data

* Hydraulic lime mortars.
† Pure lime mortars.
Items in parentheses denote limited data range.

mortars used today and also lime mortars for restoration works. The table estimates the performance of the mortars in terms of the range of compressive, flexural and bond strength. A 'designation' is a term used for a group of prescribed mortars giving approximately similar performance.

It is clear from the table that a very wide range of strengths is possible for any nominal mix ratio and that parameters other than just the binder type and content influence the strength, including water/cement ratio, sand grading and air content. A further factor which only affects the properties of the mortar in the bed (and not, of course, mortar specimens cast in impervious moulds) is the amount of dewatering and compaction by the units. Where dewatering occurs it generally increases the intrinsic strength and density of the mortar but may reduce the bond by also causing shrinkage and local microcracking.

Other key parameters are: density, porosity (indicative of permeability), Young's modulus and drying shrinkage. Density (ρ) is measured by dividing the weight of a prism or cube by its volume. The volume may be obtained by measuring all the dimensions or by weighing the prism/cube submerged in water and calculating:

$$\rho = m/b \cdot d \cdot L \text{ or } = m/(m - m_s) \tag{23.5}$$

where m = mass derived from a weighing, b is the width of the prism/cube, d is the depth of the prism/cube, L is the length of the prism/cube and m_s is the mass submerged. The density will vary with moisture content and W is measured as saturated or oven dry. Typical densities for mortars are usually in the range 1500–2000 kg/m^3. The water porosity is obtained by measuring the water absorption by evacuating the weighed dry specimen then immersing it in water at atmospheric pressure and weighing. The gain in weight of water can be converted to volume and then divided by the volume of the specimen to give the percentage of porosity. The Young's modulus may be derived from the flexural strength test provided deflection is measured. Drying shrinkage is measured by attaching precision reference points to the ends of a damp or saturated prism and then measuring the length with a micrometer screw gauge or other precision length measuring device. After a drying regime the length is again measured and the change is expressed as a percentage of the overall length. Various drying regimes have been used (BRE Digest 35 (1963), RILEM (1975) and CEN (1991)). Some data on these properties are given in Table 25.4.

23.4 Fired clay bricks and blocks

23.4.1 Introduction

Fired clay units are made by forming the unit from moist clay by pressing, extrusion or casting followed by drying and firing (burning) to a temperature usually in the range 850–1300°C. During the firing process there are complex chemical changes and the clay and other particles that go to make up the brick are bonded together by sintering (transfer of ions between particles at points where they touch) or by partial melting to a glass. During the drying and the firing process the units generally shrink by several per cent from their first made size and this has to be allowed for in the process. Some clays contain organic compounds, particularly the coal measure shales and the Oxford clay used to make Fletton bricks. Some clays are deliberately compounded with waste or by-product organic compounds since their oxidation during firing contributes to the heating process and thus saves fuel. The burning out of the organic material leaves a more open, lower density structure. The ultimate example of this is 'Poroton' which is made by incorporating fine polystyrene beads in the clay. Wood and coal dust can be used to achieve a similar effect in some products.

23.4.2 Forming and firing

Soft mud process

The clay is dug, crushed and ground then blended with water using mixers to make a relatively sloppy mud. A water content of 25–30% is required for this process. In some plants other additives may be incorporated such as a proportion of already fired clay from crushed reject bricks (grog), lime, pfa, crushed furnace clinker and organic matter to act as fuel. In the well-known yellow or London Stock brick, ground chalk and ground refuse are added. The mud is formed into lumps of the size of one brick and the lump is dipped in sand to reduce the stickiness of the surface. In the traditional technique the lump is thrown by hand into a mould and the excess is cut off with a wire. This gives rise to the characteristic 'folded' appearance of the faces of the brick caused by the dragging of the clay against the mould sides as it flows. Nowadays most production is by machine which mimics the handmaking process. These bricks usually have a small frog (depression) formed by a raised central area on the bottom face of the mould. Because of the high drying shrinkage of such wet mixes and the plasticity of the green brick the size and shape of such units are fairly variable. This variability adds to their 'character' but means that precision brickwork with thin mortar beds is not feasible. The finished brick is also fairly porous which improves its insulation properties, and paradoxically its effectiveness as a rain screen, but limits the strength.

Stiff plastic process

The clay is dug, crushed and ground then blended with water using mixers to make a very stiff but plastic compound with a water content of 10–15%. This is then extruded from the mixer and cut into roughly brick-shaped pieces and allowed to dry for a short period before being pressed in a die. The clay is very stiff so when ejected straight from the mould it retains very precisely the shape of the die. The low moisture content means that the shrinkage is low and therefore the size is easier to control and the drying time is relatively short. Another advantage is that the unfired brick is strong enough to be stacked in the kiln or on kiln cars without further drying. This type of unit will usually have at least one shallow frog and may have frogs in both bed faces. The process is used to produce engineering bricks, facing bricks, bricks with very accurate dimensions and pavers.

Wire cut process

Clay of softer consistency than the stiff plastic process is used with a moisture content of 20–25% and the clay is extruded from a rectangular die with the dimensions of the length and breadth of the finished unit. The ribbon of clay, the 'column', is then cut into bricks by wires set apart by the height of the unit plus the allowance for process shrinkage. The cutting machines are usually arranged such that the group of cutting wires can travel along at the same speed as the column while the cut is made. This means that the process is fully continuous and the cut is perpendicular to the face and ends of the unit. A plain die produces a solid column with just the characteristic wire cut finish and these bricks will have no depressions in their bed faces. In this process it is easy, however, to include holes or perforations along the length of the column by placing hole-shaped blockages in the die face. This has the following advantages.

1. Reduction in the weight of clay required per unit so transport costs at every stage of the

production and use of the units and all clay preparation costs, i.e. for shredding, grinding, mixing, etc. are also reduced.
2. A reduction in the environmental impact by reducing the rate of use of clay deposits and therefore the frequency of opening up new deposits.
3. Reduction in the mass and opening up of the structure of the units thus speeding up drying and firing, cutting the fuel cost for these processes and reducing the capital cost of the plant per unit produced.
4. The oxidation of organic matter in the clay is facilitated by increasing the surface area to volume ratio and reducing the chance of blackhearting.
5. The thermal insulation is improved. This has a modest effect for UK-Standard size bricks but the improvement can be substantial for large clay blocks.
6. The units are less tiring to lay because of the lower weight.

Because of these factors and the very large proportion of the production cost spent on fuel, most clay units are perforated at least to the extent of 10–25% by volume. It should be stressed that there is a penalty in that the clay must be very well ground and uniform in consistence for successful production of perforated units. Any lumps or extraneous air pockets can ruin the column. To improve consistence the mixers are commonly heated and the front of the extruder is de-aired (evacuated) to prevent air bubbles. Figure 23.3 illustrates the production of a typical three-hole perforated brick by stiff plastic extrusion and wirecutting.

Semi-dry pressing

This is one of the simplest processes of forming bricks. In the UK only Lower Oxford clay (or shale) is used which comes from the Vale of Aylesbury and runs in a band towards the east coast. This clay contains about 7% natural shale oil which reduces the cost of firing but gives rise to some pollution problems. It is dug and then milled and ground to go through a 2.4 mm or 1.2 mm sieve without altering the water content markedly from that as-dug (8–15%). The coarser size is used for common bricks and the finer for facings. The powdered clay is then fed into very powerful automated presses which form a deep frogged, standard

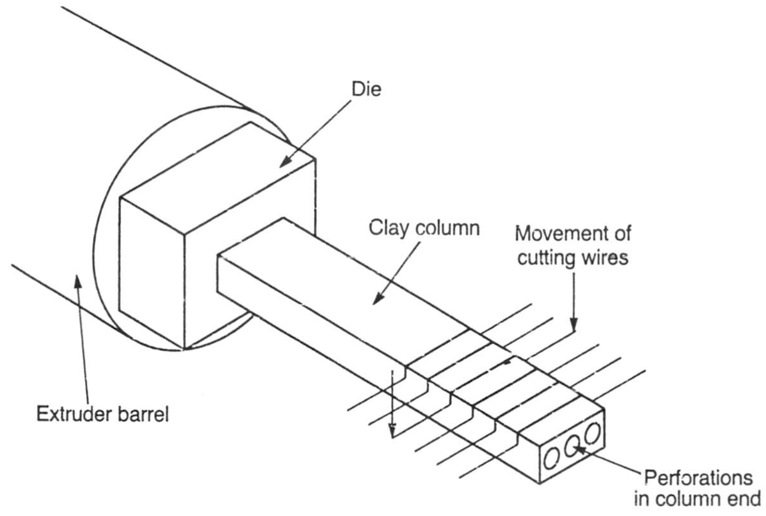

FIGURE 23.3 Stiff plastic extrusion of perforated clay bricks.

size brick known as a Fletton (named after one of the early manufacturers). Unmodified Flettons are limited to a single barred pink/cream colour. All facing Flettons are either mechanically deformed to give a patterned surface (rusticated) or an applied surface layer, such as coloured sand, is fired on.

Hoffman kilns firing

The Hoffman kiln is a multichamber kiln in which the bricks remain stationary and the fire moves. It is mainly used for manufacture of Flettons. In the classic form it consists of a row of chambers built of firebricks in the form of short tunnels or arches. In the most efficient form the tunnels form a circle or oval shape and are connected together and to a large central chimney by a complex arrangement of ducts. A single 'fire' runs round the circle and at any one time one chamber will be being loaded or 'set' ahead of the fire and one will be being unloaded behind the fire. The bricks are stacked in the kiln in groups of pillars termed 'blades', which leaves lots of spaces between units to enable the gases to circulate freely. Chambers immediately in front of the fire will be heating up using the exhaust gases from the hottest chamber and those further ahead will be being dried or warmed by gases from chambers behind the fire which are cooling down.

Figure 23.4 illustrates the broad principles of the system showing only the ducts actually in use for the fire in one position. In practice the ducts are positioned to ensure a flow through from the inlets to the outlets. The whole process is very efficient particularly as a large proportion of the fuel is provided by the oil in the

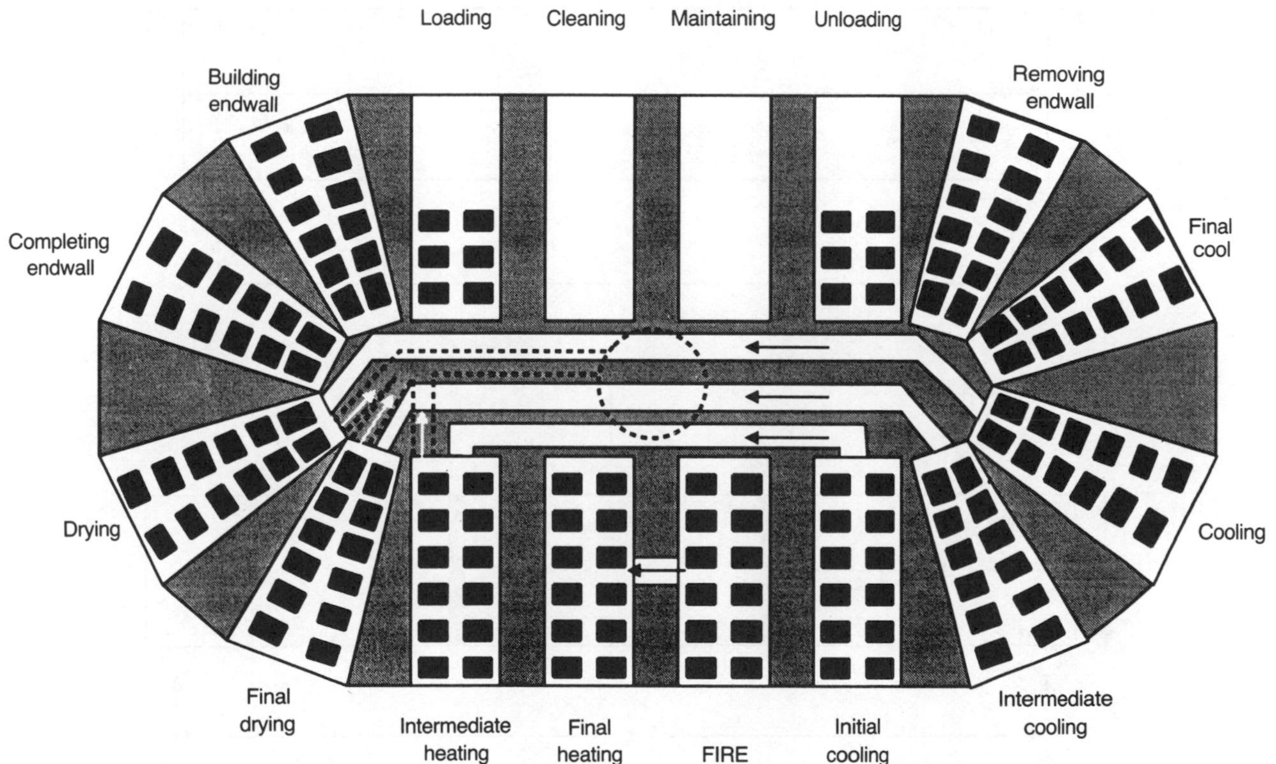

FIGURE 23.4 Principles of the Hoffman kiln.

bricks themselves. Because of the organic content of the bricks the firing has to be done under oxidizing conditions during the last phases in order to burn out the oil. If this is not done the bricks have a dark unreduced central volume, known as a blackheart, which can give rise to deleterious soluble salts. During this phase some fuel is added to keep the temperature up. This is essentially a batch process and the average properties of the contents will vary a little from chamber to chamber. Additionally, the temperature and oxidizing condition will vary with position in the chamber and thus some selection is necessary to maintain the consistency of the product.

Tunnel kilns

Tunnel kilns are the complement of Hoffman kilns in that the fire is stationary and the bricks move through the kiln as stacks on a continuous train of cars. In practice a long insulated tunnel is heated in such a way that temperature rises along its length, reaches a maximum in the centre and falls off again on the other side. To maximize efficiency only the firing zone is fuelled and hot gases are recycled from the cooling bricks and used to heat the drying and heating-up zones of the kiln. Most extruded wirecuts and stiff plastic bricks are now fired in such kilns which are continuous in operation. Stocks and other mud bricks may also be fired

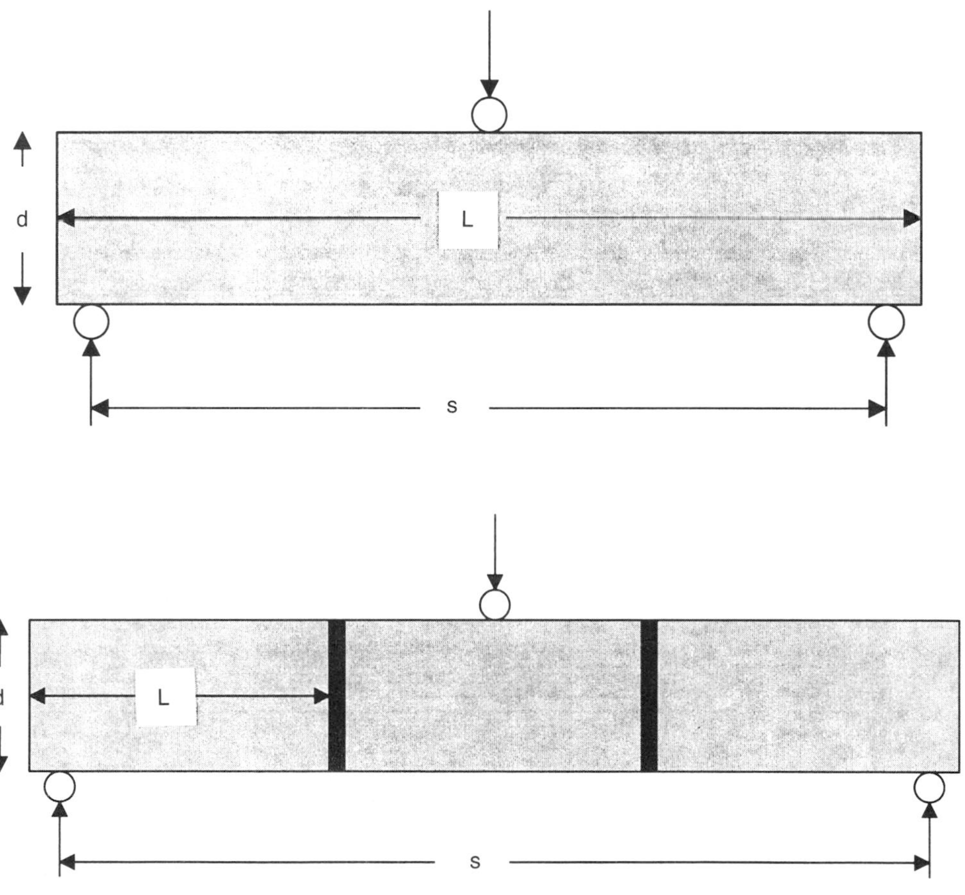

FIGURE 23.5 Specimens for flexural strength test of units (a) where L > 4d, (b) where L < 4d.

this way after a predrying phase to make them strong enough to withstand the stacking forces.

Clamps

Clamps are the traditional batch kilns comprising a simple insulated refractory beehive-shaped space with air inlets at the base and a chimney from the top.

Intermittent kilns

These are the modern version of the clamp where the units are fired in batch settings using oil or gas as a fuel. They are now only used for production of small runs of specially shaped brick 'specials'.

23.4.3 Properties

Clay bricks probably have the widest range of strengths of any of the masonry materials with the compressive strength ranging from $10\,N/mm^2$ for an underfired soft mud brick to as much as $200\,N/mm^2$ for a solid engineering brick. The compressive strength is measured by a crushing test on whole units with the stress applied in the same direction as the unit would be loaded in a wall. Solid and perforated units are tested as supplied, but frogs are normally filled with mortar as they would be in a wall. Thin plywood sheet packing is used (BS 3921: 1985) to try to reduce the effect of high spots and unevenness of the faces. Alternatively mortar capping or face grinding can be used to achieve even loading. The quoted strength is the average of six to ten determinations of stress based on the load divided by the area of the bed face. The flexural strength is not normally a designated test parameter in unit standards but is becoming important as a means of calculating the flexural strength of masonry. A standard three-point bending method is available (BS 4551: 1980). Units having a span to depth ratio in the test geometry exceeding 4 (Figure 23.5(a)) may be tested without any further preparation provided they are sufficiently flat and true to allow even loading. Units which are not flat or true may need to be made true by applying a layer of rapid setting mortar or plaster to the bearing area.

Units having a span/depth ratio less than 4 have too low an aspect ratio to give true bending. The span/depth ratio may be increased by gluing three units together in a line, as shown in Figure 23.5(b), and testing the central unit. The formula used is:

$$S = M/Z \tag{23.6}$$

where

M = the bending moment at failure, in Newton millimetres = $P \cdot l/4$,

Z = section modulus of test specimen in cubic millimetres = $b \cdot d^2/6$,

P = maximum load applied to the prism, in Newtons,

l = distance between the axes of the support rollers, mm,

b = the mean width of prism at the line of fracture, mm = $(b_1 + b_2)/2$,

d = the mean height of prism at the line of fracture, mm = $(d_1 + d_2)/2$.

Other important properties are the dimensions, water absorption (and porosity), suction rate, density and soluble salts content. The dimensions are commonly measured by laying 12 units in a line and dividing the overall length by 12, i.e. it is an averaging process and gives no data on individual variability. The process is repeated for each dimension with the units in the appropriate attitude. Water absorption and density are measured in the same way as for mortar (see Section 23.3.2), except that the preferred saturation technique is to boil the units in water for 5 hours. The initial rate of absorption (IRA, suction rate) is measured to give some idea of the effect of the unit on the mortar. Units with high suction rates need very plastic, high water/cement ratio mortars while units with low suction rates need stiff mortars. The parameter is measured by standing the unit in 10 mm depth of water and measuring

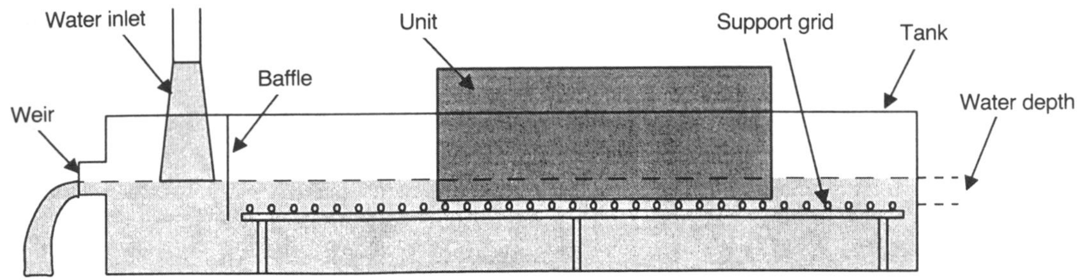

FIGURE 23.6 Apparatus for wetting units in a suction rate test.

the uptake of water in 60 seconds. A typical apparatus is depicted in Figure 23.6.

The IRA is calculated:

$$w_i = \frac{m_2 - m_1}{L \cdot b} \tag{23.7}$$

where

w_i = initial rate of absorption,
m_1 = initial mass of the unit/specimen,
m_2 = mass after 60 seconds of water absorption,
L = length of the bed (mortar) face in service to an accuracy of 0.5%,
b = width of the bed (mortar) face in service to an accuracy of 0.5%.

The measurements should be in SI units and the result quoted as kg/m^2/min.

The content of soluble salts is measured by standard wet chemical analysis techniques or by modern instrumental techniques such as flame photometry. The elements and compounds of concern are sulphates, sodium, potassium, calcium and magnesium. Table 23.6 gives typical values/ranges for some of the key properties of clay bricks.

In most brickwork, bricks are loaded across their normal bed face but often they are loaded on edge or on end. Typical examples are headers

TABLE 23.6 Properties of clay bricks (ranges given for generic types)

Brick type	*Compressive strength* (N/mm²)*	*Water absorption (weight %)*	*Water porosity (volume %)*	*Suction rate (IRA) (kg/m²/min)*	*Bulk density‡ (kg/m³)*	*Flexural strength† (N/mm²)*
Handmade facing	10–60	9–28	19–42	1.0–2.0	–	–
London Stock	5–20	22–37	36–50	–	1390	1.60
Gault wirecut	15–20	22–28	38–44	–	1720	–
Keuper marl wirecut	30–45	12–21	24–37	1.0–2.0	2030	–
Coal measure shale	35–100	1–16	2–30	–	2070	–
Fletton	15–30	17–25	30–40	1.5–2.5	1630	2.80
Perforated wirecut	72.4	3.3	5.8	–	–	7.00
Solid wirecut	109.9	4.2	10.0	0.28	2370	6.50
Solid wirecut	55.5	8.9	17.5	1.46	2110	–
Solid wirecut	21.3	21.2	35.2	1.87	1710	–

* Tested on bed.
† Tested as per RILEM method, Figure 23.5(b).
‡ Of solid body.

TABLE 23.7 Strengths of bricks in various orientations

Type and reference	*Perforations (%)*	*Compressive strength*			*Water absorption (weight %)*	*Suction rate (IRA) (kg/m²/min)*	*Bulk density (kg/m³)*
		On bed (N/mm²)	*On end (N/mm²)*	*On edge (N/mm²)*			
23 hole (a)	?	65.5	7.5	18.9	6.9	0.6	1648
14 hole (b)	21.3	74.3	10.4	26.2	3.9	–	–
14 hole (c)	?	44.8	5.0	13.0	4.7	1.8	1690
10 hole (d)	23.1	70.2	21.7	29.5	5.4	–	–
3 hole (e)	12.2	82.0	40.2	53.2	4.2	–	–
3 hole (f)	?	57.8	14.6	20.9	8.5	1.5	1900
5 cross slots (g)	20.0	64.1	13.8	51.8	3.4	–	–
16 hole (A)	20.1	64.7	8.6	20.2	5.5	0.35	–
Frog (B)	15.1	25.4	9.1	10.5	21.7	2.86	–
Frog (C)	6.2	33.7	17.1	16.6	14.4	1.06	–
Frog (D)	8.6	31.7	15.9	29.1	11.9	0.54	–
Solid (E)	0.0	43.5	28.1	29.0	22.8	3.31	–

Note: The reference given links this table to the masonry strengths given in Table 25.1.

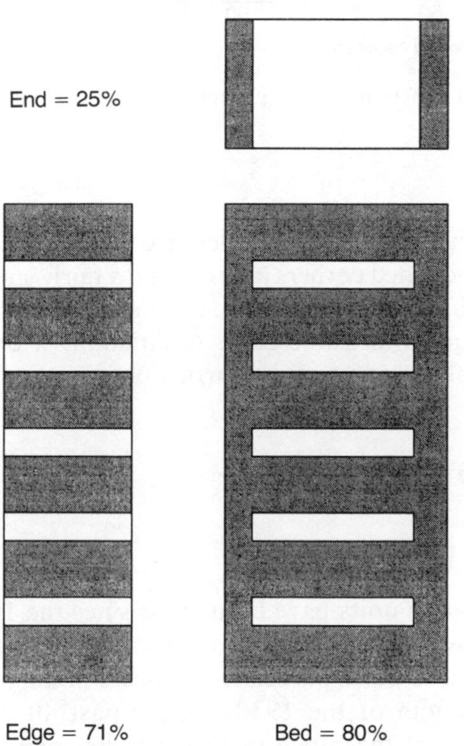

FIGURE 23.7 Area of 5-slot brick resisting load in the three orientations.

and soldiers in normal walls, stretchers in arches and reinforced beams and headers in reinforced beams. While solid bricks show a small variation in strength for loading in different directions, due to the change in aspect ratio (height/thickness), perforated, hollow or frogged units may show marked differences as illustrated in Table 23.7 from data in Lenczner (1977), Davies and Hodgkinson (1988) and Sinha and de Vekey (1990).

Taking the simplest geometry as an example it can be seen from Figure 23.7 that the minimum cross-sectional area of the 5-slot unit resisting the load will be 80% on bed but 71% on edge and 25% on end. The ratios of the strengths in Table 23.7 follow approximately the ratios of the areas. Other factors such as the slenderness of the load-bearing sections and the effect of high local stresses at rectangular slot ends complicate the behaviour and may explain the variations between different types. It can also be shown that porosity in the form of vertical perforations results in a smaller reduction of the strength of a material than does generally distributed porosity and is the more efficient

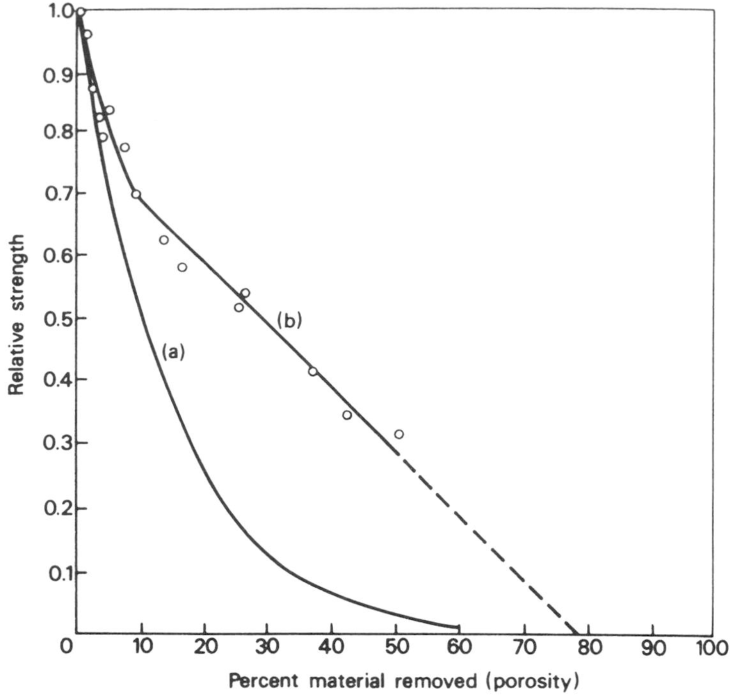

FIGURE 23.8 Compressive strength of ceramic bodies as a function of: (a) general porosity; (b) vertically aligned perforations of constant diameter.

way of reducing the weight. This is illustrated in Figure 23.8.

23.5 Calcium silicate units

These are manufactured from mixtures of lime, silica sand and water. Aggregates such as crushed rocks or flints may be incorporated to alter the performance and appearance and pigments may be used to vary the colour. Common colours are whites, blacks, buffs and grey-blues. Reds are produced but they seldom have the richness of fired clay units. There is only one basic process, in which the mixture is pressed to high pressures in a die in a static press, ejected, set on cars and then placed in autoclaves and cured in high-pressure steam for several hours. The mix is invariably fully compacted and makes a very precisely shaped, low tolerance unit with sharp, well-defined corners (arrises) and a fairly smooth finish. The properties commonly measured are given in Table 23.8. Additionally a drying shrinkage test may be carried out.

23.6 Concrete units

23.6.1 Introduction

Concrete units have been made since the 1920s and were widely used, in the form of the 'breeze' block, to build partitions in houses in the building boom of the 1930s. In the past 40 years, however, the range of products has expanded enormously to cover facing bricks and blocks, high-strength units, simulated stone units, thermally insulating blocks and pavers. Chapters

TABLE 23.8 Property ranges of calcium silicate bricks (West *et al.*, 1979)

Brick type	*Compressive strength (N/mm^2)*	*Water absorption (weight %)*	*Initial rate of suction ($kg/m^2/min$)*	*Bulk density (kg/m^3)*	*Frog volume (%)*
Solid	20–50	8–22	0.25–2.0	1750–2000	0
Frogged	20–55	13–20	0.5–1.2	1650–1950	4–7

15 and 16 should be referred to for background data on the performance and behaviour of concrete. Most aggregate concrete units are produced by pressing specially designed mixes. Some of the processes used and the resulting products, e.g. autoclaved aerated concrete (AAC), are wholly different from normal concrete; thus a full description is given.

23.6.2 Production processes

Casting concrete

Concrete blocks can be manufactured by pouring or vibrating a concrete mix into a mould and demoulding when set. While this method is used, particularly for some types of reconstituted stone or faced blocks, it is not favoured because of its slowness and labour demands.

Pressing of concrete

This is a widely used method for producing solid and hollow bricks and blocks either in dense concrete or as a porous open structure by using gap-graded aggregates and not compacting fully. The machine is basically a static mould (or die), which is filled automatically from a mixer and hopper system, and a dynamic presshead which compacts the concrete into the die. After each production cycle the green block is ejected on to a conveyor system and taken away to cure either in air or often in steam. The presshead may have multiple dies. A variation of the method is the 'egg layer'. This performs the same basic function as a static press but ejects the product straight on to the surface on which it is standing and then moves itself to a new position for the next production cycle.

Curing

All aggregate concrete products may either be cured at ambient or elevated temperature. The elevated temperatures are usually achieved by the use of steam chambers and allow the manufacturer to decrease the curing period or increase the strength or both. Products cured externally should not be made when the temperature is near or below 0°C since they will be damaged by freezing while in the green state.

Autoclaved aerated concrete (AAC) manufacture

AAC is made by a process, developed originally in Scandinavia, to produce solid microcellular units which are light and have good insulating properties. The method involves pouring a slurry containing a fine siliceous base material, a binder, some lime and a raising agent into a mould maintained in warm surroundings. As the raising agent gives off gas the slurry rises like baker's dough and sets to a weak 'cake'. The cake is then cured for several hours at elevated temperature, demoulded, trimmed to a set height and cut with two orthogonal sets of oscillating parallel wires to the unit size required using automatic machinery. The cut units are then usually set, as cut, on to cars which are run on rails into large autoclaves. The calcium silicate binder forms by reaction under the influence of high-pressure steam. Additional curing after autoclaving is not necessary and the units can be incorporated in work as soon as they have cooled down.

The binder reaction is conventional as given in Section 23.1. The cellular structure, which gives the product good thermal properties and a high strength/density ratio, is produced by reaction between the alkaline lime/opc component and added aluminium powder to give bubbles of hydrogen.

$$Ca(OH)_2 + 2Al + 2H_2O \rightarrow CaAl_2O_4 + 3H_2 \quad (23.8)$$

This produces a structure of small closed cells surrounded by cell walls composed of a fine siliceous aggregate bound together by calcium silicate hydrates. The nature of the principal siliceous material is identifiable from the colour: ground sand produces a white material and pulverized fuel ash a grey material.

23.6.3 Products

Dense aggregate concrete blocks and concrete bricks

These are generally made from well-graded natural aggregates, sands, pigments, and ordinary or white Portland cement by static pressing to a well-compacted state. Figure 23.9(a) illustrates the principle of such materials where the voids between large particles are filled with smaller particles. They are strong, dense products and are often made with a good surface finish suitable for external facing masonry. They are also suitable for engineering applications. Bricks are produced mainly as the standard size (215 × 102 × 65 mm) in the UK but in a wide range of sizes in continental Europe. Blocks are produced either solid or hollow by varying the quantity of mix and the shape of the press platen. In order to facilitate demoulding the hollows will always have a slight taper. The hollows in UK products are all designed to run vertically in the finished masonry as this gives the optimum strength to weight ratio. The

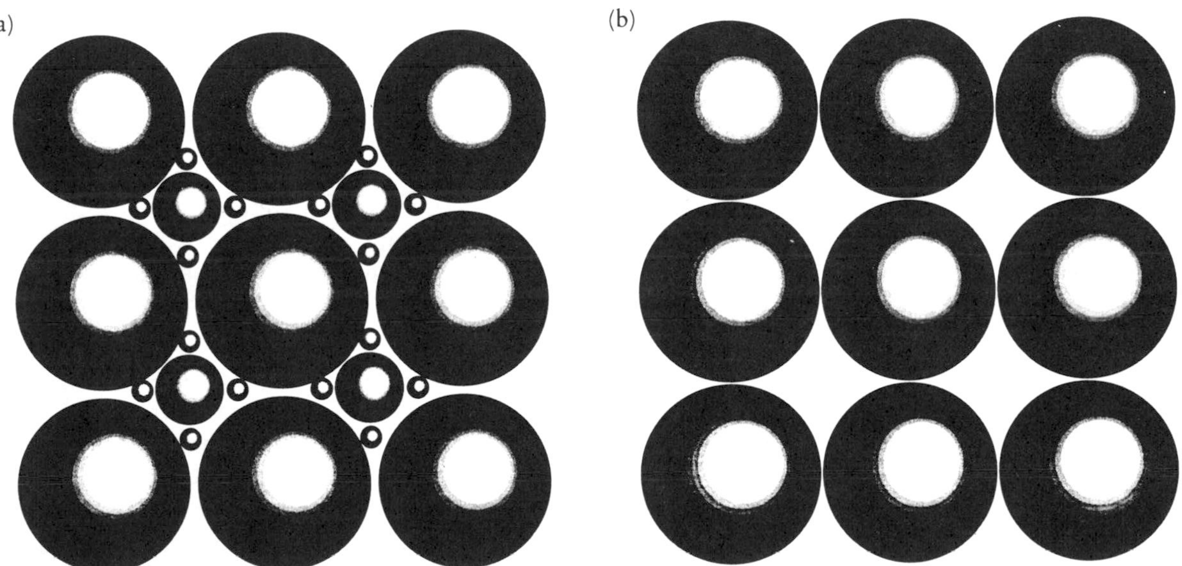

FIGURE 23.9 Type of aggregates: (a) well graded; (b) gap graded.

TABLE 23.9 Properties of aggregate concrete units

Type and size mm	*Void (%)*	*Bulk density (kg/m³)*	*Concrete density (kg/m³)*	*Compressive strength* (N/mm²)*	*Flexural strength† (N/mm²)*	*Young's modulus (kN/mm²)*	*Vacuum absorption (weight %)*
Brick 215 × 65 × 103	0	2160	2160	32.5	–	–	6.3
DA block 438 × 213 × 98	0	2140	2140	15.5	2.59	–	10.9
DA block 390 × 190 × 140	41.6	1350	2320	31.6	–	42.3	–
LWA block 390 × 190 × 140	22.1	1630	2090	21.5	–	32.8	–
LWA block 390 × 190 × 140	0	2170	2170	29.9	–	23.6	–
LWA block 390 × 190 × 90	0	2060	2060	21.6	–	17.5	–
LWA block 390 × 190 × 90	19.9	1100	1380	8.1	–	9.0	–
LWA block 439 × 215 × 98	0	2190	2190	6.6	0.5	–	35.0

Note: DA = dense aggregate and LWA = lightweight aggregate.
* Compressive strength tested wet and mortar capped in accordance with BS 6073 (1981) Appendix B. Similar values are obtained by testing between fibreboard at ex-factory water content.
† Flexural strength (MOR) measured in accordance with BS 6073 (1981) Appendix C.

TABLE 23.10 Properties of AAC

Type	*Dry density (kg/m³)*	*Typical compressive strength† (N/mm²)*	*Flexural strength† (N/mm²)*	*Values tensile‡ (N/mm²)*	*Young's modulus† (kN/mm²)*	*Thermal conductance at 3% moisture (W/mK)*
Low density	450	2.8 (3.2)	0.65	0.41	1.60	0.12
	525	3.5 (4.0)	0.75*	0.52	2.00*	0.14
Standard	600	4.0 (4.5)	0.85	0.64	2.40	0.16
	675	5.8 (6.3)	1.00*	0.76	2.55	0.18
High density	750	7.0 (7.5)	1.25	0.88	2.70	0.20

† Tests carried out in accordance with BS 6073 (1981). Nominal values of compressive strength are given together with values typical of modern production plants in brackets.
‡ Linear extrapolation of a limited range of splitting tests (Grimer and Brewer, 1965).
* Interpolated value.

face size of UK units is generally 440 mm long by 215 mm high but the thickness may vary from 50 mm to 300 mm. Some of the important properties are summarized in Table 23.9.

Reconstructed stone masonry units

These have essentially the same specification as dense-aggregate concrete blocks except that the main aggregate will be a crushed natural rock such as limestone or basalt and the other materials will be chosen such that the finished unit mimics the colour and texture of the natural stone.

Lightweight aggregate concrete blocks

These are generally produced as load-bearing building blocks for housing, small industrial buildings, in-fill for frames and partition walling. High strength is rarely a prime consideration but handling weight, thermal properties and economy are important. Inherently low-density aggregates are used and are often deliberately gap-graded, as illustrated by Figure 23.9(b), and only partly compacted to keep the density down. They will frequently be made hollow as well to reduce the weight still further. The aggregates used are sintered pfa nodules, expanded clay, furnace clinker, furnace bottom ash, pumice or foamed slag together with sand and binder. Breeze is a traditional term for a lightweight block made from furnace clinker. Often low-density fillers or aggregates such as sawdust, ground bark or polystyrene beads are incorporated to further reduce the density. They are produced either by static pressing or in egg-layer plants. Some of the important properties are summarized in Table 23.8. The properties commonly measured include the compressive strength by the method used for clay bricks for brick-sized units but capped with mortar to achieve flat parallel test faces for blocks. The flexural strength has also been used to evaluate partition blocks which bear lateral loads but only self-weight compressive loads. It is a simple, three point bend test of the type described in Section 23.4.3 for clay units with an aspect ratio greater than 4. Other properties measured include dimensions, water absorption by the method of vacuum absorption, density and drying shrinkage.

Autoclaved aerated concrete (AAC)

Fine sand or pulverized fuel ash or mixtures thereof is used as the main ingredient. The binder is a mixture of ordinary Portland cement (opc), to give the initial set to allow cutting, and lime which reacts with the silica during the autoclaving to produce calcium silicate hydrates and gives the block sufficient strength for normal building purposes. Some of the key properties are summarized in Table 23.10.

23.7 References

ASTM C1072-86 *Standard method for measurement of masonry flexural bond.*

BRE Digest 35 (1963) *Shrinkage of natural aggregates in concrete*, Building Research Establishment, Watford (revised 1968).

BRE Digest 273 (1983) *Perforated clay bricks*, Building Research Establishment, Watford.

BRE Digest 359 (1991) *Repairing brick and block masonry*, Building Research Establishment, Watford.

BS 1200: 1976 (amended in 1984): *Sands from natural sources: sands for mortar for plain and reinforced brickwork, blockwork and stone masonry.*

BS 4551: 1980: *Methods of testing mortars, screeds and plasters.*

BS 6073: Part 1: 1981: *Precast concrete masonry units. Part 1: Specification for precast concrete masonry units.*

BS 6100: Part 5.3: 1984: *Glossary of building and civil engineering terms. Part 5: Masonry.*

BS 3921: 1985: *Specification for clay bricks.*

BS 4729: 1990: *Specifications for dimensions of bricks of special shapes and sizes.*

CEN prEN 772-12 (1991) Methods of test for masonry units, Part 12: Determination of length change during moisture movement in autoclaved aerated concrete units, Part 14: Determination of moisture movement of aggregate concrete units.

Central Electricity Generating Board (1972) *PFA Utilization.*

Davies, S. and Hodgkinson, H.R. (1988) *The stress–strain relationships of brickwork when stressed in directions other than normal to the bed face: Part 2, RP755*, British Ceramic Research Establishment, Stoke on Trent.

Grimer, F.J. and Brewer, R.S. (1965) The within cake variation of autoclaved aerated concrete. *Proceedings of symposium on Autoclaved Calcium Silicate Building Products*, Society of Chemical Industry, May 1965, pp. 163–70.

ISO DIS 9652: Part 4: 1991: *Masonry – methods of test.*

Lenczner, D. (1977) *Strength of bricks and brickwork prisms in three directions*, Report No. 1, University of Wales Institute of Science and Technology, Cardiff.

RILEM (1975) Recommendations for testing methods of aerated concrete, *Materials and Structures*, **8**, No. 45, 211.

RILEM (1978) Recommendations for the testing of mortars and renderings, *Materials and Structures*, **11**, No. 63, 207.

Sinha, B.P. and de Vekey, R.C. (1990) A study of the compressive strength in three orthogonal directions of brickwork prisms built with perforated bricks, *Masonry International*, **3**, No. 3, 105–10.

Southern, J.R. (1989) *BREMORTEST: A rapid method of testing fresh mortars for cement content*, BRE Information Paper IP8/89, Building Research Establishment, Watford.

Task group of ASTM Subcommittee section C09.03.08.05. Pigments for integrally coloured concrete, *Cement, Concrete and Aggregates*, CCAGDP, **2**, No. 2, Winter 1980, pp. 74–7.

de Vekey, R.C. (1975) The properties of polymer-modified cement pastes, *Proceedings of the First International Polymer Congress*, London.

de Vekey, R.C. and Majumdar, A.J. (1977) Durability of cement pastes modified by polymer dispersions, *Materials and Structures*, **8**, No. 46, 315–21.

West, H.W.H., Hodgkinson, H.R., Goodwin, J.F. and Haseltine, B.A. (1979) *The resistance to lateral loads of walls built of calcium silicate bricks*, BCRL, Technical Note 288.

WRC Information and Guidance Note IGN 4–10–01, *Bricks and Mortar*, Water Research Council, Oct. 1986.

Chapter twenty-four

Masonry construction and forms

24.1 Introduction
24.2 Mortar
24.3 Walls and other masonry forms
24.4 Bond
24.5 Specials
24.6 Joint style
24.7 Workmanship and accuracy
24.8 Appearance
24.9 References

24.1 Introduction

This chapter is concerned with how masonry is built and the architectural forms used. Appearance is a very important aspect; the basic structural form of many types of masonry is expressed on the surface of the buildings and other structures and can be a very attractive and reassuring aspect of these structures. Appearance is a synthesis of the size, shape and colour of the units, the bond pattern, the mortar colour and finish, the masonry elements – walls, piers, columns, corbels, arches, etc. – and the scale and proportion of the whole structure. Other key aspects are the workmanship, the accuracy, the detailing in relation to other features and the use of specially shaped units.

The basic method of construction has hardly changed for several thousand years: units are laid one on top of another in such a way that they form an interlocking mass in at least the two horizontal dimensions. It is not practical to achieve interlocking in a third dimension with normal rectangular prismatic units. Most practical masonry employs a mortar interlayer to allow for small inaccuracies of size between units and to make walls watertight, airtight and soundproof.

24.2 Mortar

Mortar must be mixed thoroughly and its proportions kept constant. It should not be overmixed as this will introduce too much air and reduce the durability. Portland cement mortars have a pot life of about one hour and they should be discarded after the time limit or if they become unworkable. Traditional lime mortars and retarded opc mortars have a much longer pot life which makes them easier to use. For optimum bond and ease of laying, the mortar should always be matched to the units being laid. As a general rule dense low absorption units need a fairly firm dry mortar (e.g. with a dropping ball consistence of around 10 or less) while high absorption units need a sloppy wet mortar with a dropping ball consistence of 13–15. Alternative techniques for improving usability are the use of agents in the mortar which hold water in (water retentivity aids) or wetting the units to reduce their suction.

24.3 Walls and other masonry forms

Walls are built by laying out a plan at foundation level and bringing the masonry up layer by layer. To maximize the strength and attractiveness it is important to make sure that all the foundation levels are horizontal, are accurate to the plan and allow multiples of whole units to fit most runs between returns, openings, etc. It is also essential to maintain the verticality (plumb),

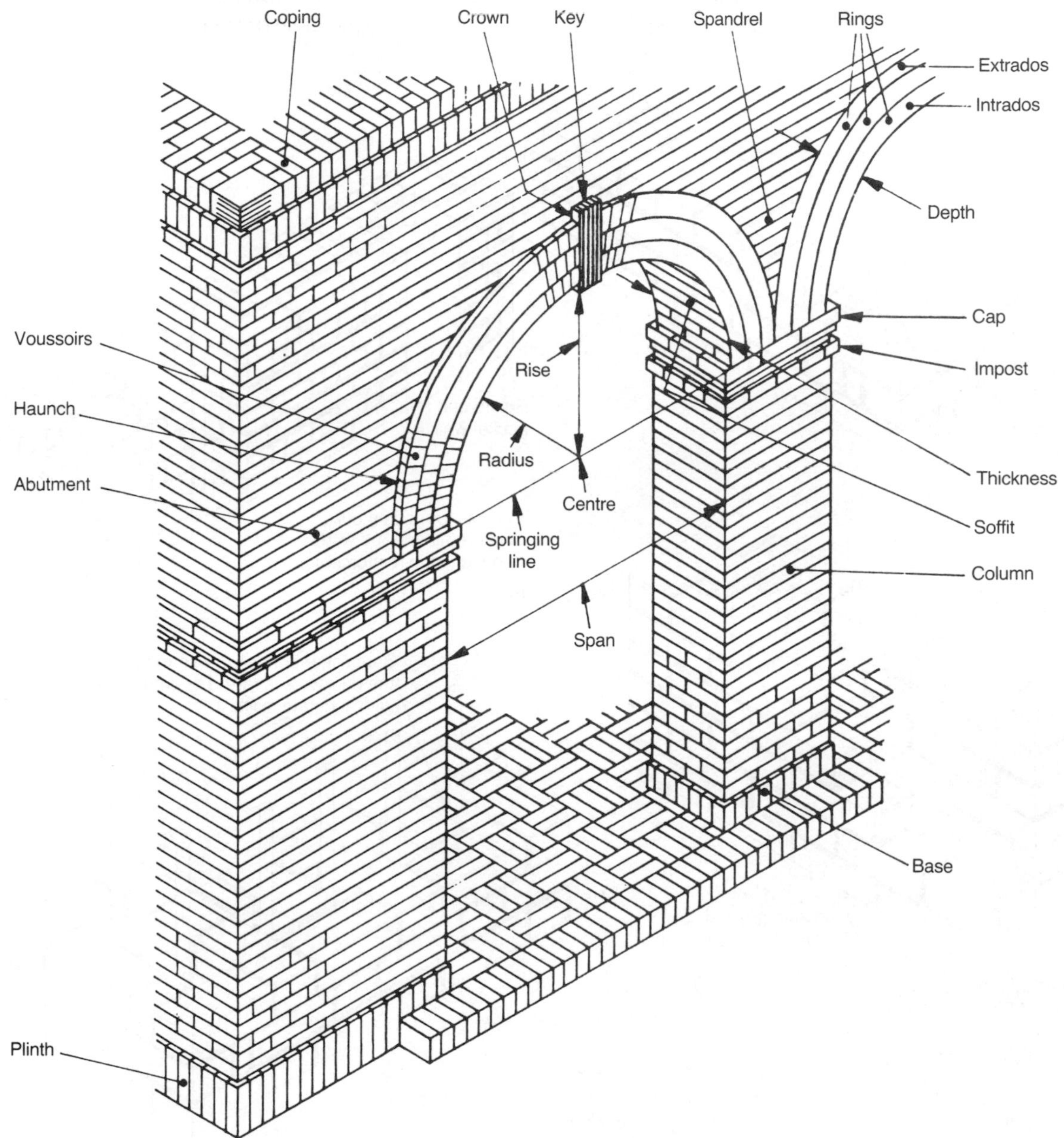

FIGURE 24.1 Structural elements and terminology of arches.

the level of bed joints and the straightness of the masonry within reasonable limits. The thickness of the mortar joints must be kept constant within a small range, otherwise the masonry will look untidy. The standard technique used is to generate reference points by building the corners (quoins) accurately using a plumb bob and line, a builder's level, a straight edge and a rule. Any openings are then filled with either a temporary or permanent frame placed accurately in the plan position. Lines are stretched between the reference points and the intervening runs of masonry are built up to the same levels.

Columns, piers and chimneys are built in the same way but need plumbing in two dimensions and more care because of their small dimensions.

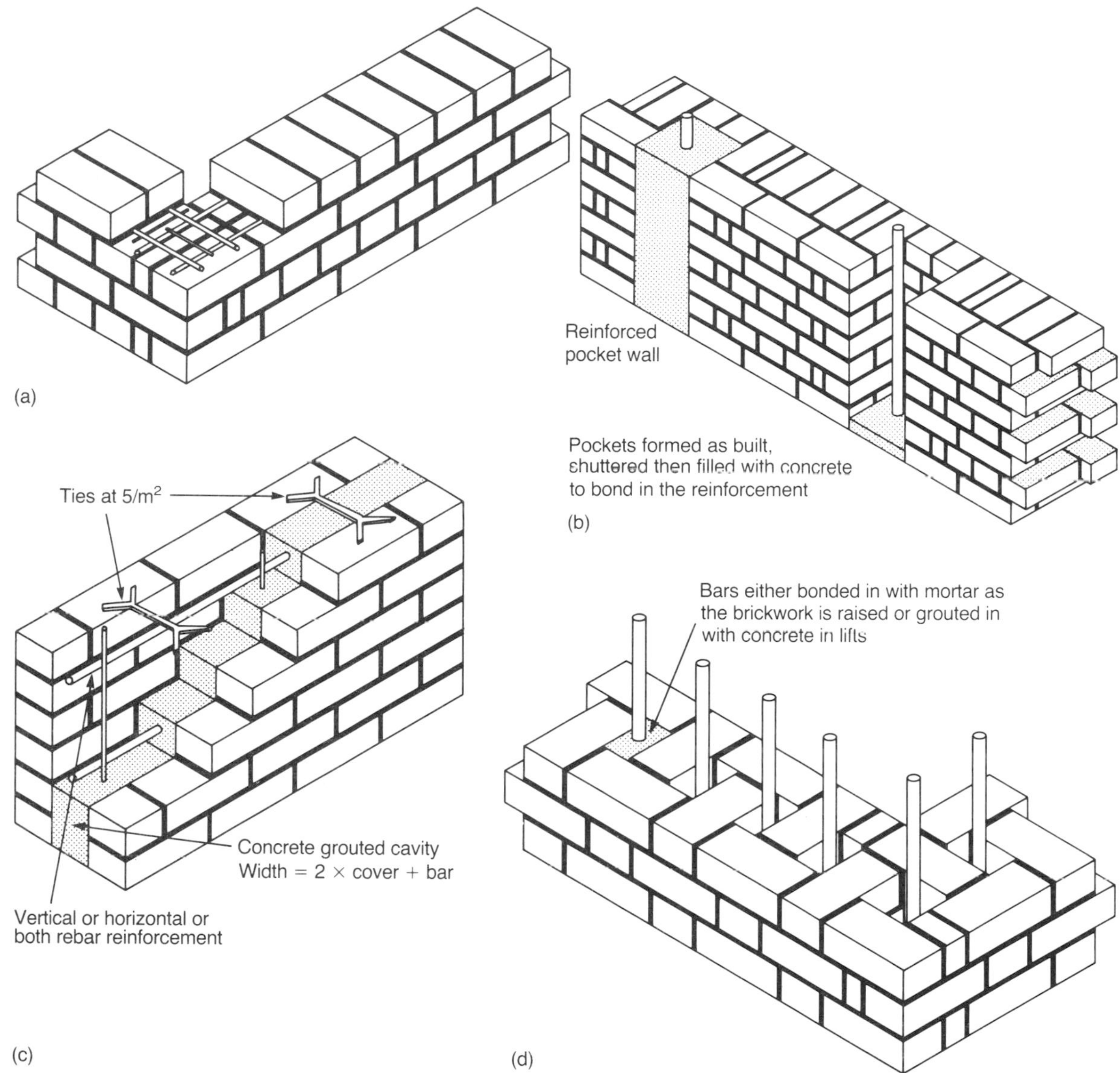

FIGURE 24.2 Reinforced and post-stressed masonry forms: (a) bed joint reinforced; (b) reinforced pocket walls; (c) grouted cavity; (d) quetta bond.

Arches and tunnels must follow a curved shape defined by the architect or engineer and are traditionally built on timber formwork. Adjustable reusable metal formwork systems are also available. Some arches use special tapered units called voussoirs but large radius or shallow arches may be built with standard units. Figure 24.1 illustrates the main elements of arches and the special vocabulary for them.

Reinforced and post-tensioned masonry are used to a limited extent in the UK mainly for civil engineering structures, high single-storey halls, retaining walls and lintels within walls. Masonry lintels may sometimes be constructed by laying special bed joint reinforcement in the mortar. This acts as a tension reinforcement for a masonry beam. Most other reinforced masonry is formed by building masonry boxes in the form of hollow piers, walls with cavities or walls with slots in them, and then locking the reinforcing elements into the voids using a concrete grout. Post-tensioned masonry may be built in the same way but the reinforcement is then passed through the cavities and stressed against end plates which removes any necessity to fill with grout. Figure 24.2 shows some typical reinforced masonry forms.

24.4 Bond

Most modern masonry is the thickness of a single unit breadth and is built by overlapping

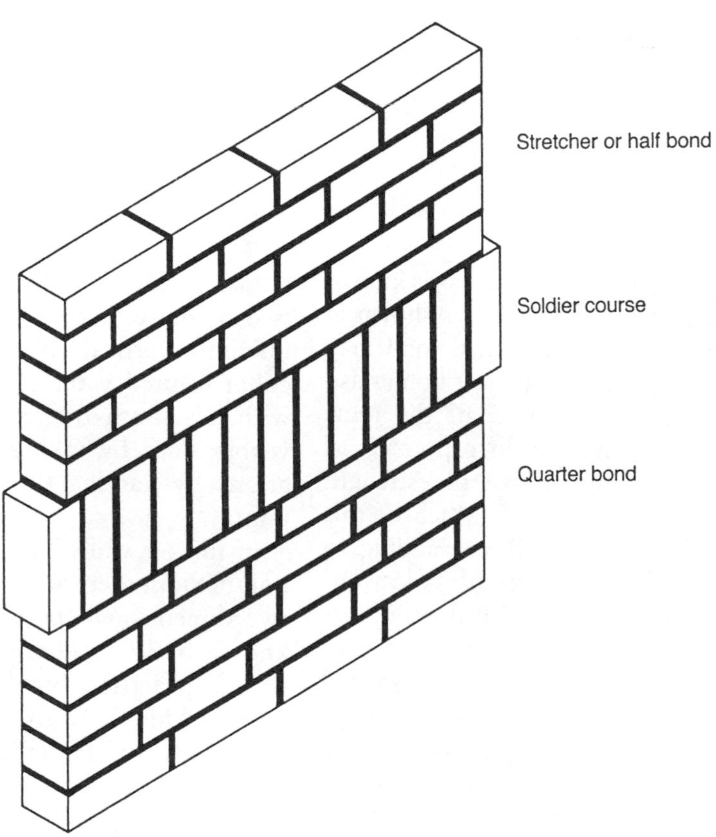

FIGURE 24.3 Half-brick bonds.

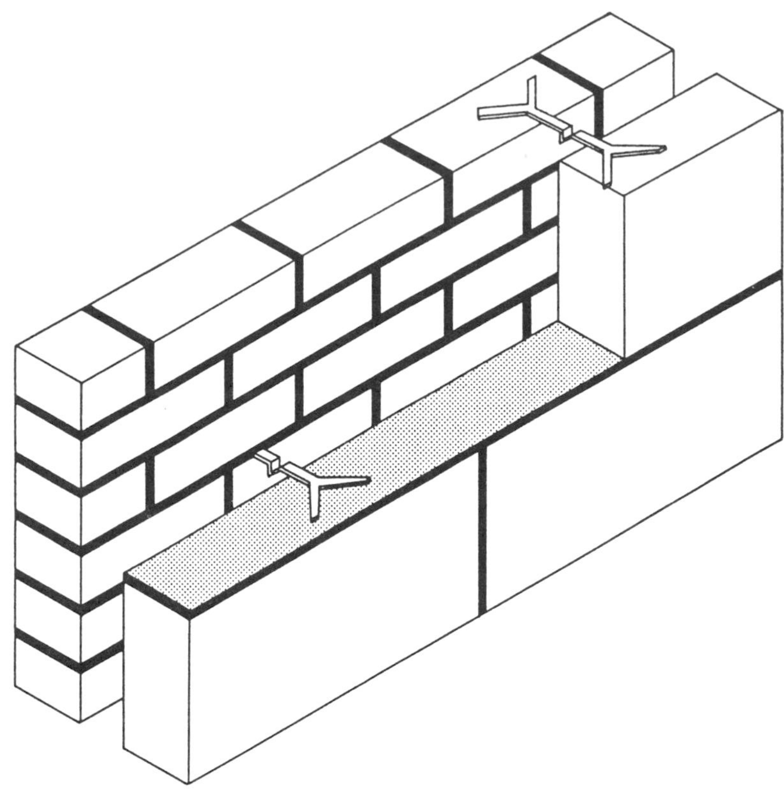

FIGURE 24.4 Typical block/brick cavity wall.

half the length with the next unit. This is known as stretcher bond or half bond and is shown in Figure 24.3. Variations of stretcher bond may be achieved by using third or quarter bond (also shown). Soldier courses, where all the units stand on their ends, may be incorporated as a decorative feature but reduce the strength and robustness of the masonry. Much of this stretcher bonded work is used as cladding to frame structures where the strength is less important because of the presence of the supporting structure. In occupied structures it is widely used in the form of the cavity wall, as illustrated in Figure 24.4, which comprises two such walls joined with flexible metal ties across a space which serves principally to keep out rain and keep the inner wall dry. Blockwork is almost universally built with this bond and broader units are used to achieve thicker walls. Stretcher bonded walls may be built thicker by linking two or more layers with strong metal ties and filling the vertical 'collar' joint with mortar. The collar jointed wall, Figure 24.5, may be built with a smooth true face ('fair face') on both visible sides by taking up any thickness variations by varying the thickness of the collar joint.

In thicker walls built in multiples of a single unit breadth there are a large number of possible two-dimensional bonding patterns available known by the traditional names. A few of the widely practised bonds are shown in Figure 24.6 and more are given in BS 5628. Part 3 and Handisyde and Haseltine (1980).

24.5 Specials

It has always been possible to make structures

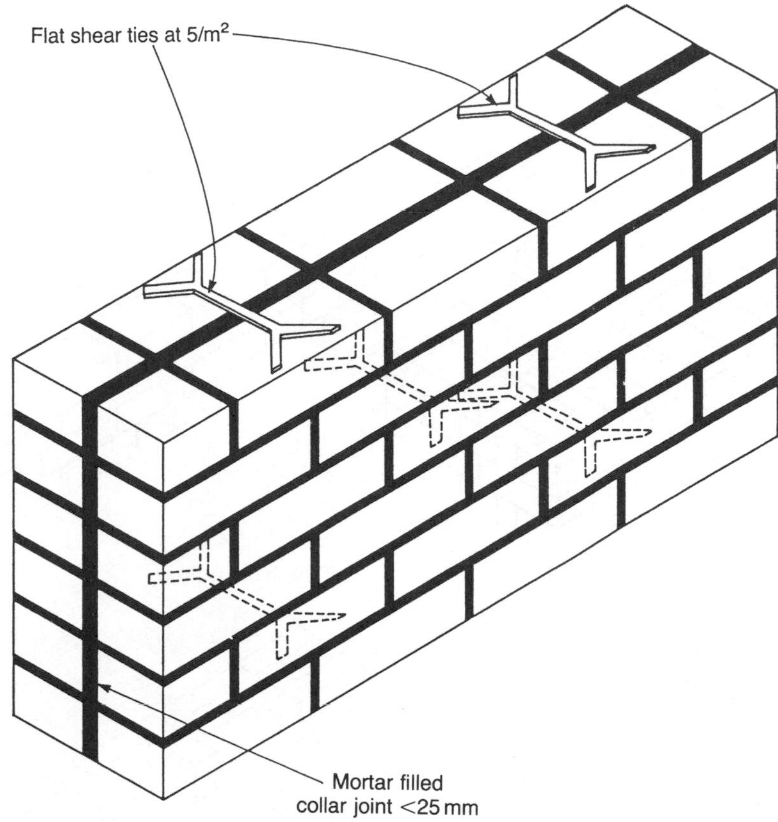

FIGURE 24.5 Collar jointed wall.

more interesting by using specially shaped units to vary angles from 90°, to generate tapers, plinths, curves, etc. In recent years such features have, if anything, become more popular. A very large range of shapes is available on a regular basis and are known as 'standard specials'. Additionally, it is possible to get almost any shape manufactured to order although it is inevitably quite expensive for small quantities. Some of the typical varieties are illustrated in Figure 24.7.

24.6 Joint style

It is often not realized how much the joint colour and shape influence the appearance and performance of masonry. Obviously the colour contrast between the mortar and the units must have a profound effect on the appearance but so does the shape of the finished joint. The common joint styles are shown in Figure 24.8. Recessed and weathered joints cast shadows and increase the contrast between mortars and lighter bricks.

24.7 Workmanship and accuracy

Standards of good workmanship in terms of how to lay out work and avoid weather problems by protection of new work against rain, wind and frost are covered in BS 5628 (1985). Realistic tolerances for position on plan, straightness, level, height and plumb are given in BS 5606 (1978) and tighter tolerances are specified in SP 56 (1980) for structural quality masonry.

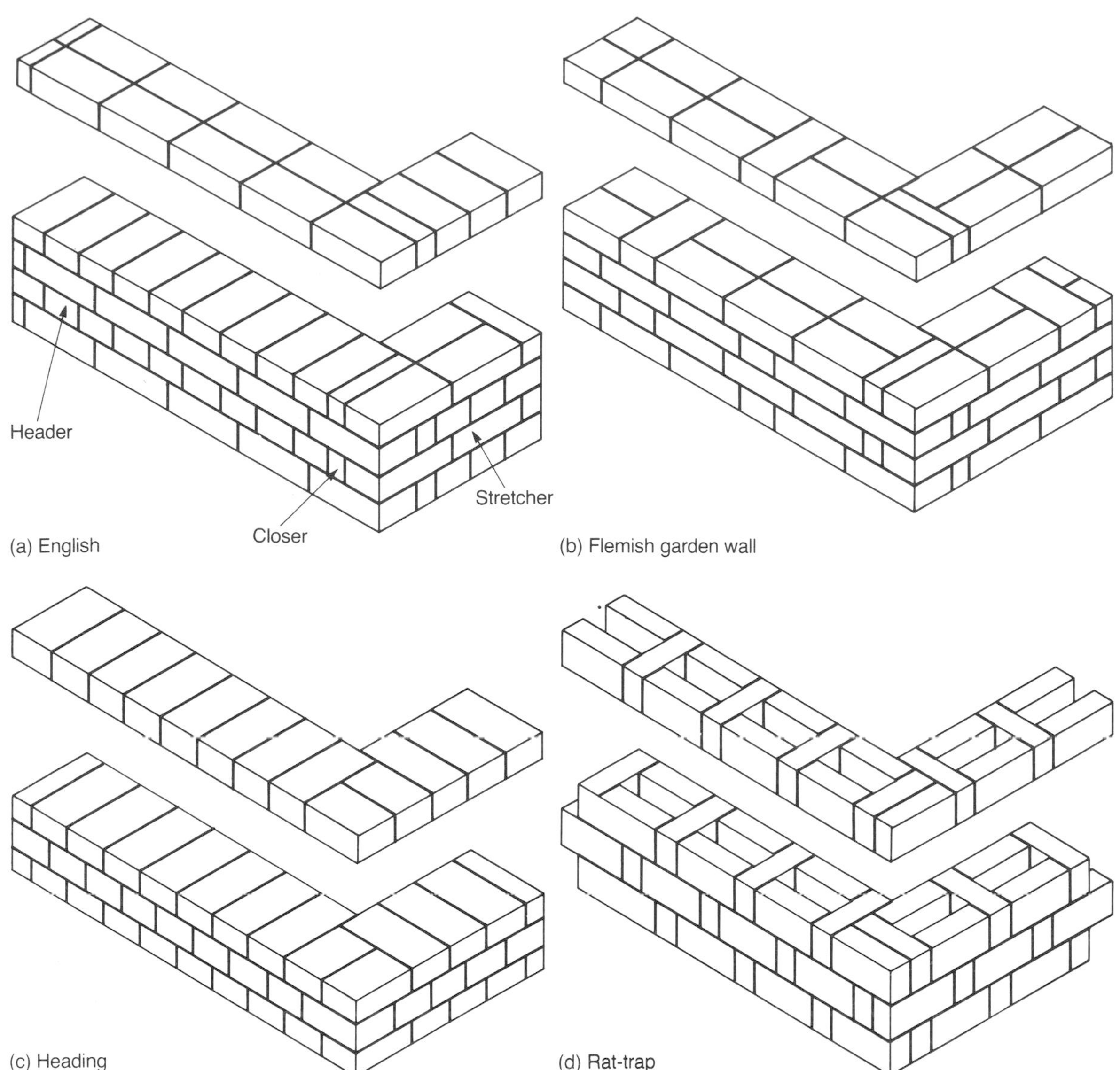

FIGURE 24.6 Bonded wall types: (a) English bonded wall. (b) Flemish garden wall. (c) Heading bond. (d) Rat-trap bond.

24.8 Appearance

This is very much a matter of taste and expectation but there are some general rules to follow. Precisely shaped bricks with sharp arrises demand accurate layout with perpends lined up vertically and evenly sized mortar joints throughout, otherwise they tend to look untidy. Less accurate uneven bricks will tolerate some variation in joint size and position without looking ugly. Except with very accurate bricks, walls can only be made fair faced on one side while the

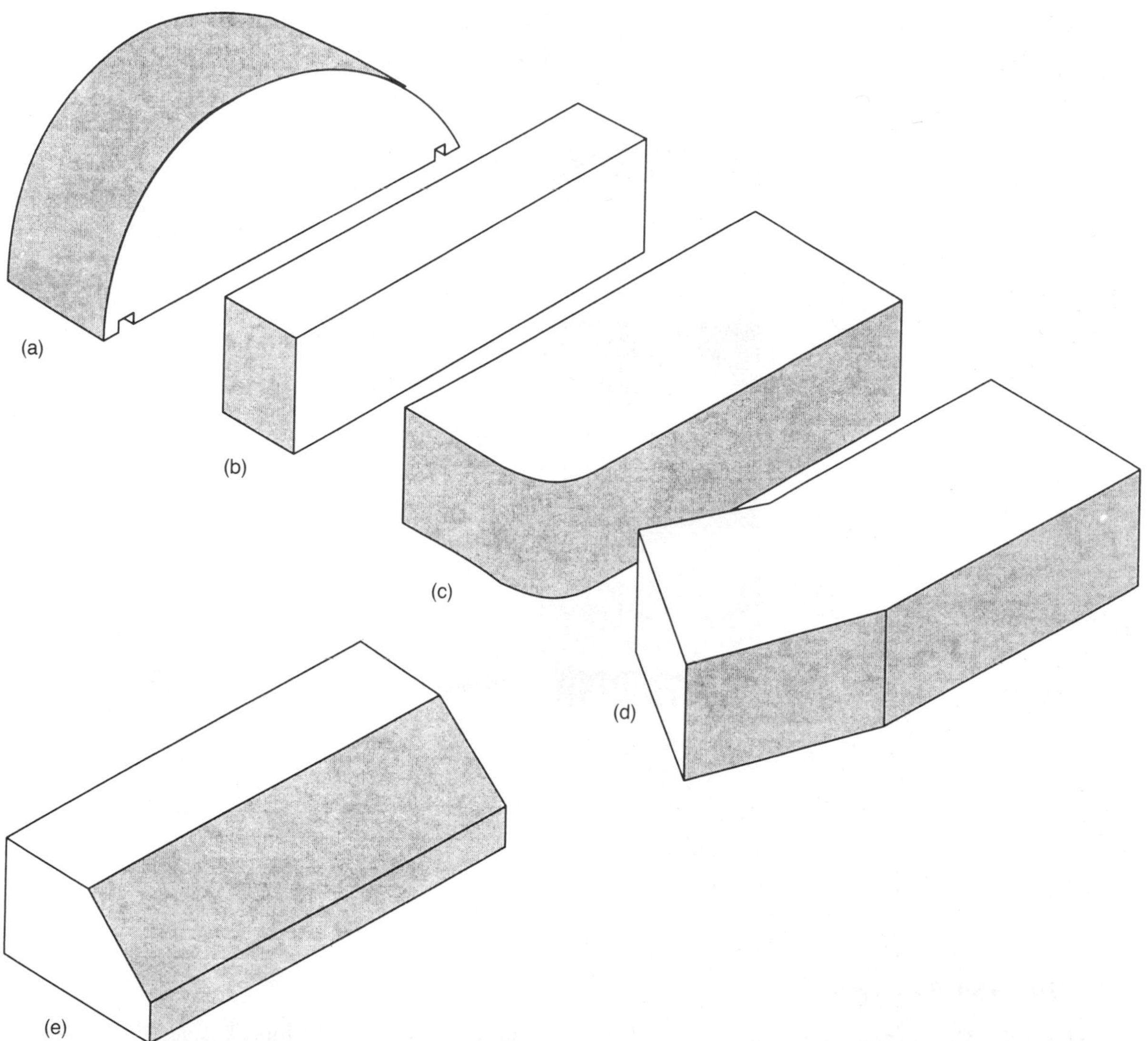

FIGURE 24.7 Typical specials (a) Coping (b) Queen closer (c) Single bullnose (d) External angle (e) Plinth.

other side has to suffer from any variability in thickness of the units. If a solid 220 mm thick wall is required to have two fair faces it should be built as a collar jointed wall. If an internal half-brick wall is exposed on both faces it is probably best to use a joint which is tolerant of some inaccuracy such as a recessed joint.

Exposed external walls should be protected as much as possible from run-off of rain. Any detail which causes large amounts of rain water to course down the wall in one spot or leach out through mortar joints at damp-proof membranes will eventually lead to discolouration due to staining by lichen, lime or silica.

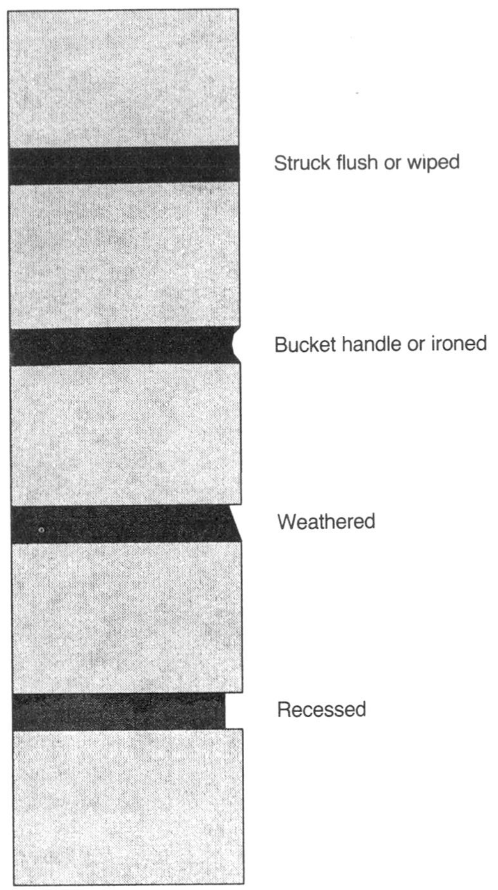

FIGURE 24.8 Joint styles.

24.9 References

BS 5606: 1978: *Code of practice for accuracy in building.*

BS 5628: 1985: *Code of practice for the use of masonry. Part 1: Structural use of unreinforced masonry; Part 2: Structural use of reinforced and prestressed masonry; Part 3: Materials and components, design and workmanship.*

Handisyde, C.C. and Haseltine, B.A. (1980) *Bricks and Brickwork*, Brick Development Association.

SP 56: 1980: *Model specification for clay and calcium silicate structural brickwork*, British Ceramic Research Establishment, Stoke on Trent.

Chapter twenty-five

Structural behaviour and movement of masonry

25.1 Introduction
25.2 Compressive loading
25.3 Shear load in the bed plane
25.4 Flexure (bending)
25.5 Tension
25.6 Elastic modulus
25.7 Movement and creep of masonry materials
25.8 References

25.1 Introduction

Like any structural material, masonry must resist loads or forces due to a variety of external influences (actions) and in various planes. Figure 25.1 from BRE Digest 246 (1981) illustrates the various forces that can arise and the likely actions. Like plain concrete, unreinforced masonry is good at resisting compression forces, moderate to bad at resisting shear but very poor when subjected to direct tension. Masonry structures which are required to resist significant tensile forces should be reinforced by adding steel or other tension components. Unlike concrete, however, masonry is highly anisotropic because of its layer structure and this must always be borne in mind in design.

Masonry is quite effective at resisting bending forces when spanning horizontally between vertical supports but it is somewhat less effective at resisting bending forces when spanning vertically or cantilevering from a support (Figure 25.2) because the resistance of a lightly loaded wall in that direction is dependent solely on the mass and the adhesion of the units to the mortar. Much of the resistance to bending and collapse, especially of simple cantilever masonry structures, is simply due to self-weight. Masonry is a heavy material, usually with a density in the range 500–2500 kg/m^3, i.e. between 0.5 and 2.5 tonnes per cubic metre. In relatively squat structures such as some chimneys, parapets or low or thick boundary walls the force needed to rotate the wall to a point of instability is sufficient to resist normal wind forces and minor impacts. Any masonry under compressive stress also resists bending since the compressive prestress in the wall must be overcome before any tensile strain can occur.

There is much empirical knowledge about how masonry works and many small structures are still designed using experience-based rules. The Limit State Code of Practice in the UK (BS 5628: 1985) gives a calculated design procedure but much of this code is based on empirical data such as given by Davey (1952), Simms (1965),

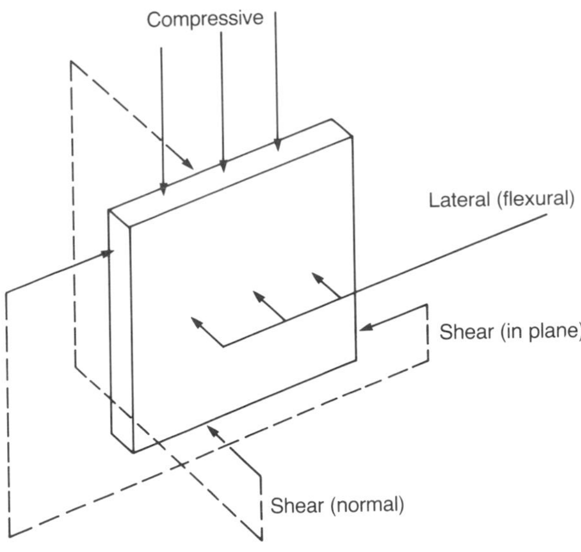

FIGURE 25.1 Forces on walls.

de Vekey *et al.* (1986; 1990), West *et al.* (1977; 1986). Broadly, it predicts the characteristic strength of masonry elements, such as walls, from data on the characteristic strength or other characteristics of the materials using various engineering models for the different loading conditions. A check is then made that the predicted strength is greater than the expected worse loading derived from data about wind, dead loads, snow loads and occupancy loads. To allow for statistical uncertainty in loading data a safety factor γ_f is applied and to allow for uncertainty about the strength of the masonry a further factor γ_m is used. The combination of these partial factors of safety (FOS) gives an overall safety factor against failure of the structure which is usually in the range 3.5–5. This relatively high FOS is used because of the high variability of masonry properties and the brittle failure mode which gives very little warning of failure.

25.2 Compressive loading

Masonry is most effective when resisting axial compressive loads normal to the bedding plane (Figure 25.1). This is, clearly, the way in which most load-bearing walls function but also the way that arches and tunnels resist load since an inward force on the outside surface of a curved plate structure or tube will tend to put the material into compression as in Figure 25.3. If a load or force is put on a wall at a point, it would logically spread outward from the point of application in a stretcher bonded wall since each unit is supported by the two units below it. This mechanism, shown diagrammatically in Figure 25.4 by representing the magnitude of the force by the width of the arrows, leads to some stress being spread at 45° in a half-bond wall but the stress still remains higher near the axis of the load for 2 m or more. Such a compressive force causes elastic shortening (strain) of the masonry. As a result of Poisson's ratio effects, a tension strain and hence a stress is generated normal to the applied stress. In bonded masonry the overlapping of the units restrains the propagation of cracks which are generated in the vertical joints by the tension until the stress exceeds the tensile strength of the units.

The compressive strength of masonry is measured by subjecting small walls or prisms or larger walls of storey height (2–3 m) to a force in a compression test machine. Loading is usually axial but may be made eccentric by offsetting the wall and loading only part of the thickness.

Masonry is not so good at resisting compression forces parallel to the bedding plane because there is no overlapping and the bed joints fail easily under the resultant tensile forces. Additionally, most bricks with either frogs, perforations or slots are weaker when loaded on end than on bed because the area of material resisting the load is reduced and the stress distribution is distorted by the perforations. Data on bricks are given in Table 23.6. The equivalent data in Table 25.1 for prisms show that the strength does vary with loading direction although not to the same extent as for units because the aspect ratios of the masonry specimens are all similar.

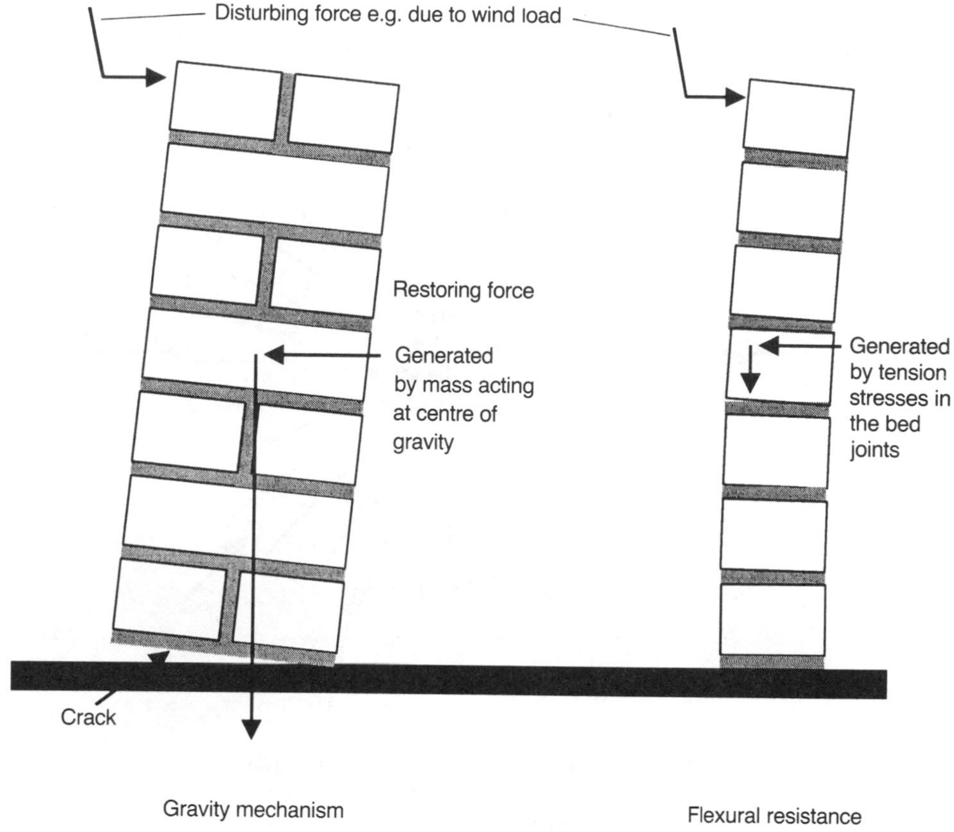

FIGURE 25.2 Mechanisms for resisting bending forces in masonry cantilevers.

The axial strength of masonry might be expected to depend on the strength of the units and of the mortar and, to a first approximation, the contribution of each to the overall strength should be related in some way to the volume proportion of each. This gives a reasonable model for behaviour of squat structures. A complication is that most masonry comprises units much stronger than the mortar and the three-dimensional confining restraint increases the effective strength of the thin mortar beds. Figure 25.5 shows the minor effect of mortar strength on the compressive strength of masonry made with medium strength clay bricks. Figure 25.6 shows the influence of the masonry unit strength for the normal range of mortar strengths.

This broad principle has been expressed using formulae of the type:

$$f_k = K \cdot f_b^{\alpha} \cdot f_m^{\beta} \qquad (25.1)$$

Where f_k, f_b and f_m are the strength of the masonry, the units and the mortar respectively, K is a factor which may vary to take into account the shape or type of the units, α is a fractional power of the order of 0.7–0.8, and β is a fractional power of the order 0.2–0.3.

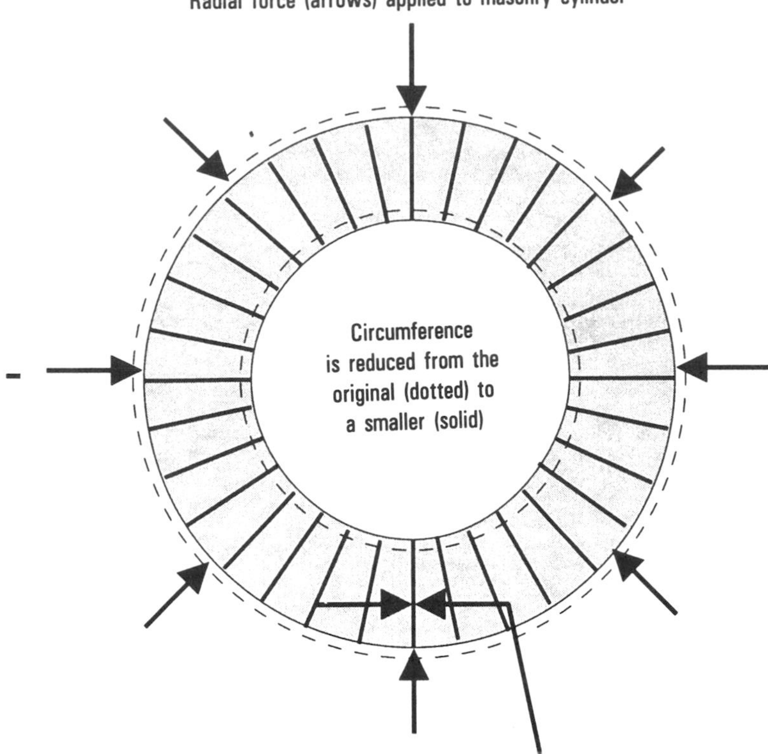

FIGURE 25.3 Forces on masonry cylinders, e.g. arches, tunnels and sewers.

25.2.1 Stability: slender structures and eccentricity

If a structure in the form of a wall or column is squat, so that the ratio of height to thickness (slenderness ratio) is small, then the strength will depend largely on the strength of the constituent materials. In real structures the material will be stiffer on one side than the other, the load will not be central and other out-of-plane forces may occur. This means that if the slenderness ratio is increased, at some point the failure mechanism will become one of instability and the structure will buckle and not crush.

Loads on walls, typically from floors and roofs, are commonly from one side and thus stress the wall eccentrically. Figure 25.7 illustrates, in an exaggerated form, the effect of an eccentric load in reducing the effective cross-section bearing the load and putting part of the wall into tension.

This is recognized in practice and usually a formula is used to reduce the design load capacity of structures in which the reduction is a function of the slenderness ratio and the net eccentricity of all the applied loads. A standard formula is given in BS 5628 (1985).

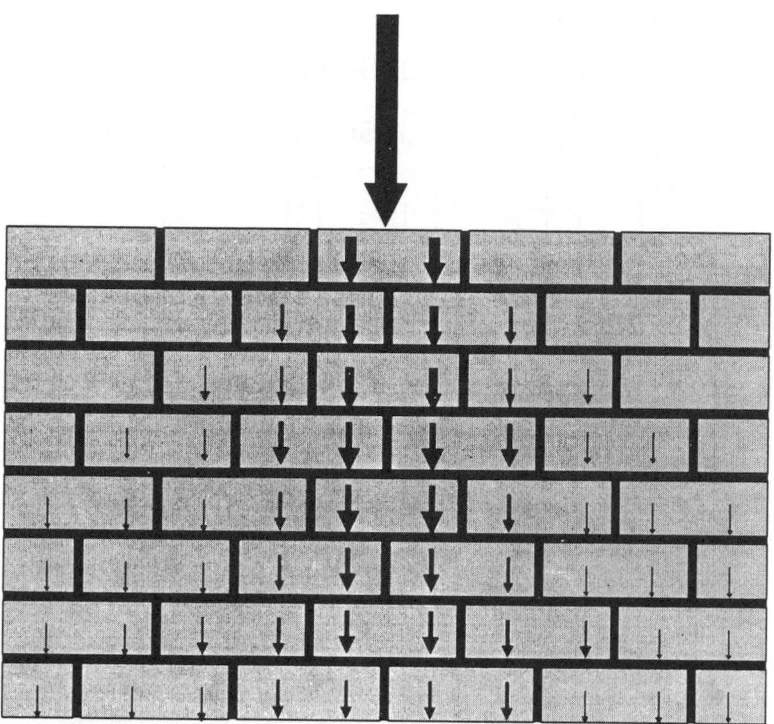

FIGURE 25.4 Load spreading in stretcher bonded walls.

TABLE 25.1 Masonry prism strengths with bricks loaded in various directions

*Type and reference**	*Mortar* Mix	*Mortar* Strength (N/mm²)	*Compressive strength of prism* On bed (N/mm²)	On end (N/mm²)	On edge (N/mm²)
23 hole perf. (a)	$1:\frac{1}{4}:3$	23.1	22.4	10.7	15.8
14 hole perf. (b)	$1:\frac{1}{4}:3$	26.6	28.9	14.6	8.5
14 hole perf. (c)	$1:\frac{1}{4}:3$	23.1	19.9	11.3	11.5
10 hole perf. (d)	$1:\frac{1}{4}:3$	26.6	22.0	20.0	15.0
3 hole perf. (e)	$1:\frac{1}{4}:3$	26.6	37.6	21.8	30.5
3 hole perf. (f)	$1:\frac{1}{4}:3$	23.1	23.2	6.8	14.1
5 cross slots (g)	$1:\frac{1}{4}:3$	26.6	34.1	13.9	29.0
16 hole (A)	$1:\frac{1}{4}:3$	–	26.0	7.5	5.2
Frog (B)	$1:\frac{1}{4}:3$	–	9.7	5.3	5.3
Frog (C)	$1:\frac{1}{4}:3$	–	10.8	13.2	14.4
Frog (D)	$1:\frac{1}{4}:3$	–	19.2	16.6	17.8
Solid (E)	$1:\frac{1}{4}:3$	–	16.0	10.2	11.7

* The reference letters relate the data in this table to those in Table 23.7.

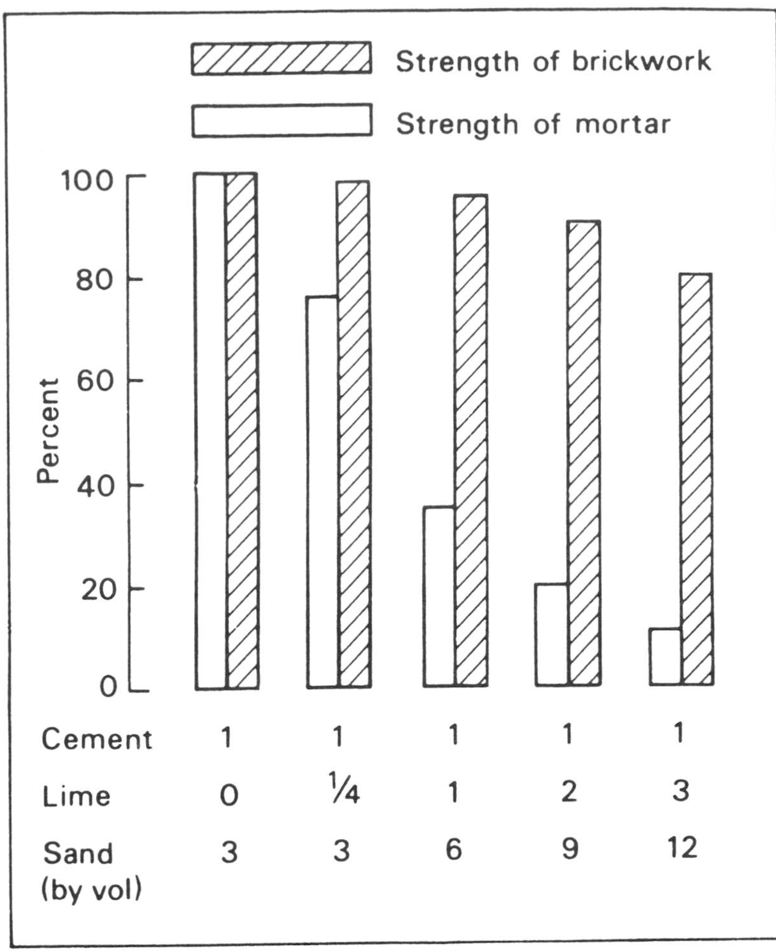

FIGURE 25.5 Effect of mortar strength on the compressive strength of masonry.

25.2.2 Concentrated load

Many loads are fairly uniform in nature being derived from the weight of the structure above or more locally to floors. There will always be, however, some point loads, termed concentrated loads, in structures at the ends of beams, lintels, arches, etc. In general the masonry must be capable of withstanding the local stresses resulting from the concentrated loads but the designer may assume that the load will spread out in the manner of Figure 25.4 so that it is only critical in the first metre or so below the load. Additionally, because the area loaded is restrained by adjacent unloaded areas, some local enhancement can be assumed.

Figure 25.8(a) shows the condition for a small isolated load applied via a pad where there is restraint from four sides and Figures 25.8(b), (c) and (d) show further conditions with reducing restraint. The local load capacity of the masonry in the patches compared to the average load capacity (the enhancement factor) can vary from 0.8 for case (d) to as much as 4 for case (a) (Ali and Page (1986), Arora (1988) and Malek and Hendry (1988)). The enhancement factor

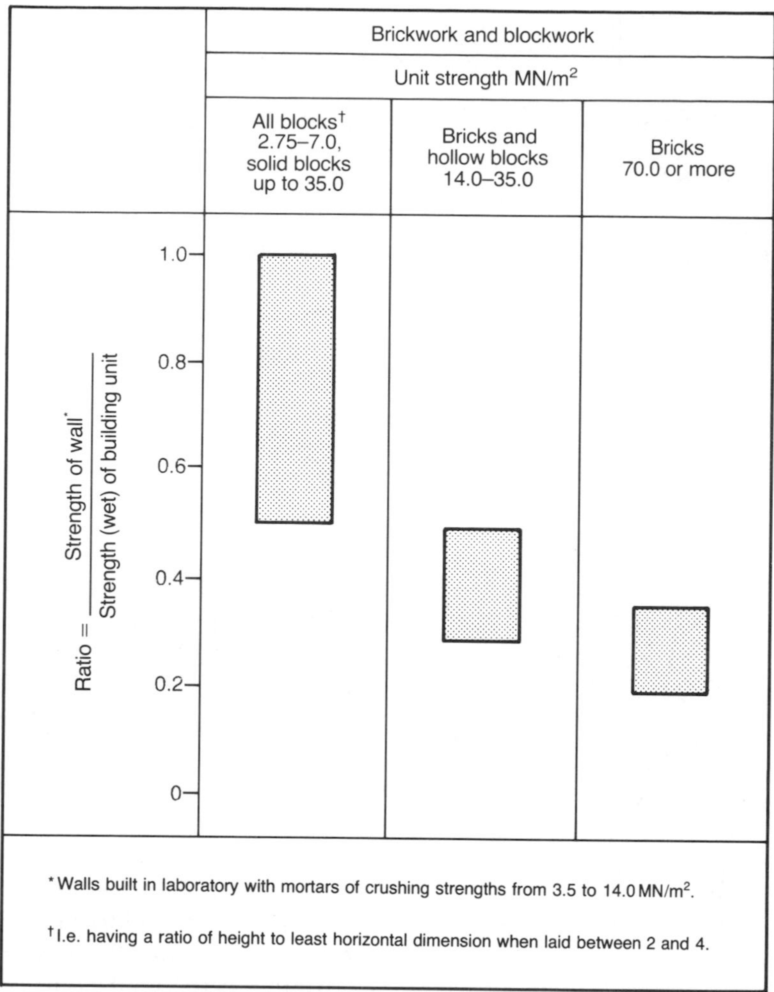

FIGURE 25.6 Effect of unit strength on the compressive strength of masonry.

decreases as the ratio of the area of the load to the area of the wall increases, as the load moves nearer the end of a wall and as the load becomes more eccentric. Formulae describing this behaviour are proposed in many of the references in Section 25.8.

25.2.3 Cavity walls in compression

If a compression load is shared equally by the two leaves of a cavity wall then the combined resistance is the sum of the two resistances provided their elastic moduli are approximately the same. If one leaf is very much less stiff than the other, the stress is all likely to predominate in the stiffer wall and be applied eccentrically and then the combined wall may have less capacity than the single stiff wall loaded axially. It is common practice to put all the load on the inner leaf and use the outer leaf as a rain screen. In this load condition more stress is allowed on the loaded wall because it is propped by the

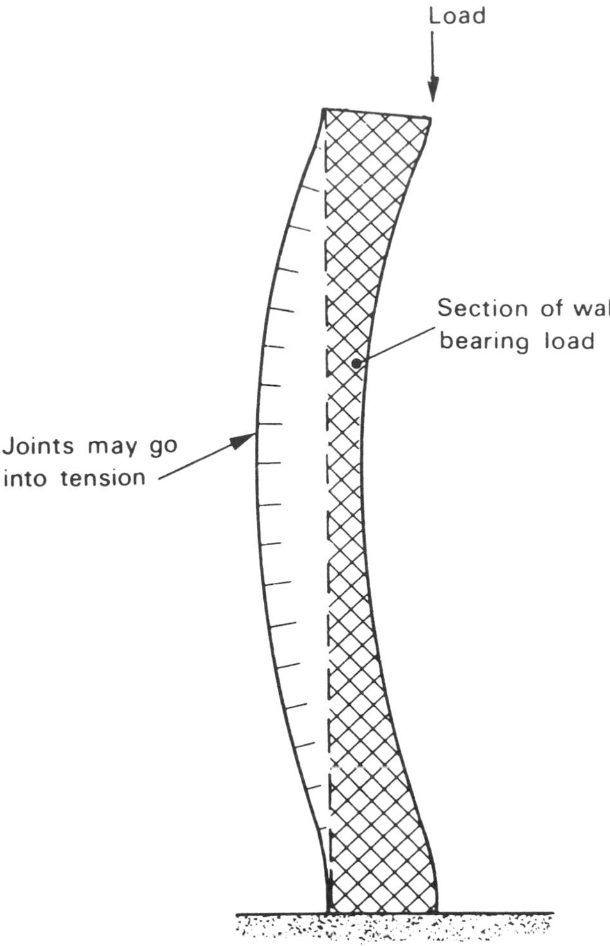

FIGURE 25.7 Effect of eccentric load on masonry (exaggerated).

outer leaf. This is achieved mathematically by increasing the effective thickness of the loaded wall used for slenderness calculations.

25.3 Shear load in the bed plane

If a wall is loaded by out-of-plane forces, e.g. by wind, impact, or seismic (earthquake) actions, the force will act to try to slide the wall sideways (like a piston in a tube). In practice the action can be at any angle in the 360° plane although it is most common parallel or normal to the wall face. This is a very complex loading condition and the result is rarely a pure shearing failure. For small test pieces measured in an idealized test, the shear strength f_v can be shown to follow a friction law with a static threshold 'adhesion' f_{v0} and a dynamic friction term K dependent on the force normal to the shearing plane σ_a. The formula is simply:

$$f_v = f_{v0} + \sigma_a K. \tag{25.2}$$

Measurement of pure shear is very difficult because of the tendency to induce rotation in virtually any physical test arrangement. The simple double shear test of the type shown in Figure 25.9 is suitable for measuring shear resistance of damp-proof course (dpc) materials but is unsatisfactory for mortar joints where a much shorter specimen is preferred. Table 25.2 gives some typical shear data derived from Hodgkinson and West (1981).

In the example sketched in Figure 25.10 the ends are supported so the wall tends to adopt a curved shape. In this case it is shown as failing by shear at the line of the dpc. If a wall is loaded by lateral forces acting on the end as in Figure 25.11 (which can arise from wind load on a flank wall at right angles) the force will initially tend to distort the wall to a parallelogram shape as in Figure 25.11(a). If the wall fails it may be by crushing at the load point or at the 'toe' of the wall as in Figure 25.11(a), by sliding shear failure along the dpc, by 'shear' failure, i.e. actual diagonal tensile failure, or by rotation as in Figure 25.11(b).

A further important shear condition occurs between masonry elements bonded together, i.e. where piers or buttressing walls join other walls, as in Figure 25.11(a), or in box structures at the corners. If the composite is loaded to generate flexure there is a vertical shear force at the interface which is resisted by the punching shear resistance of the units crossing the junction. In standard bond, units cross the shear plane for 50% of the height of the structure and the shear strength will be, at best, the sum of these

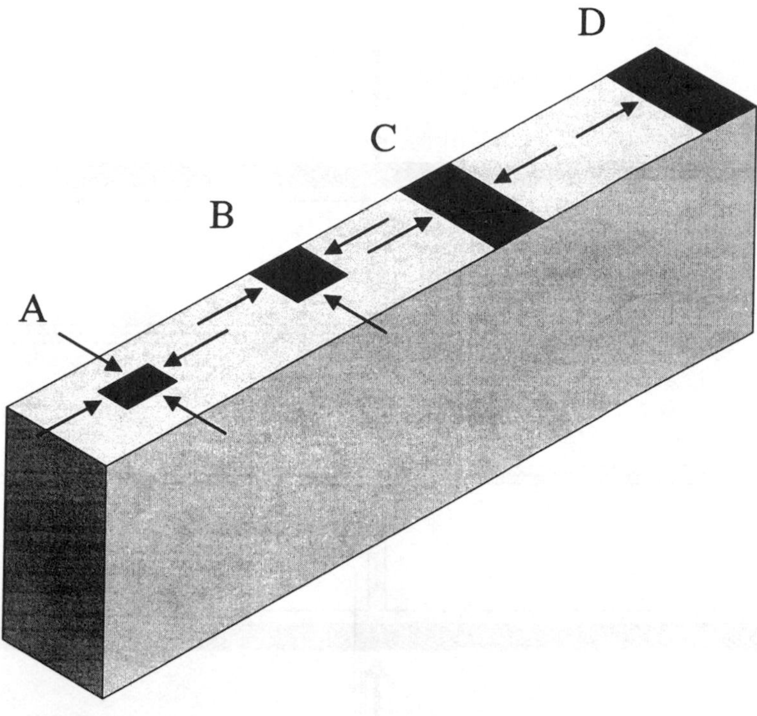

FIGURE 25.8 Concentrated loads on masonry (restraint indicated by arrows).

TABLE 25.2 Shear data for two mortars and some damp-proof course (dpc) materials (Hodgkinson and West, 1981)

Brick	*dpc*	*1:¼:3 Mortar*		*1:1:6 Mortar*	
		σ_a	*K*	σ_a	*K*
16 hole wire-cut	Blue brick[1]	0.72	0.82	0.44	1.14
	Bituminous	0.4	0.80	0.31	0.91
	Permagrip[2]	0.8	0.58	0.43	0.61
	Hyload[3]	0.21	0.80	0.17	0.58
	Vulcathene[4]	0.06	0.47	0.04	0.54
Frogged semi-dry pressed	Blue brick[1]	0.73	0.95	0.36	1.57
	Bituminous	0.45	0.84	0.36	0.72
	Permagrip[2]	0.55	0.93	0.41	0.72
	Hyload[3]	0.17	0.82	0.18	0.79
	Vulcathene[4]	0.09	0.52	0.06	0.49

[1] Where blue engineering bricks are used for the dpc the shear strength is limited effectively by the mortar.
[2] Permagrip is a trade name for a reinforced bitumen product with a coarse sand surface.
[3] Hyload is a pitch/polymer system.
[4] Vulcathene is a trade name for a polyethylene-based dpc.

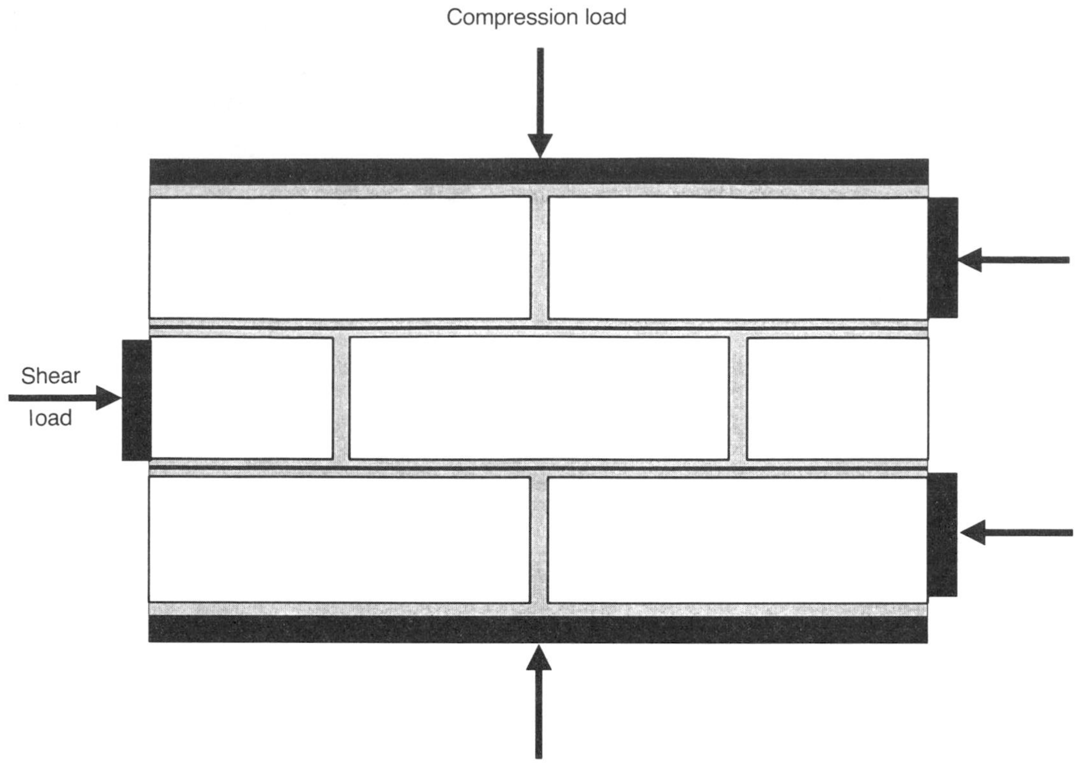

FIGURE 25.9 Specimen for measuring shear resistance of dpc materials etc.

resistances plus a small contribution from the mortar.

25.4 Flexure (bending)

Traditionally, masonry was made massive or made into shapes which resisted compression forces. Such structures do not depend to any great extent on the bond of mortar to units. Much of the masonry built in the last few decades has, however, been in the form of thin walls for which the critical load condition will result from lateral forces, e.g. wind loads. This phenomenon was largely made possible by the use of opc mortars which give a positive bond to most units and allow the masonry to behave as an elastic plate. There are two distinct principal modes of flexure about the two main orthogonal planes: (1) the vertically spanning direction shown in Figure 25.2 which is commonly termed the parallel (or p) direction because the stress is applied about the plane parallel to the bed joints; and (2) the horizontally spanning direction, shown in Figure 25.12, which is commonly termed the normal (or n) direction because the stress is applied about the plane normal to the bed joints. Clearly the strength is likely to be highly anisotropic since the stress in the parallel direction is only resisted by the adhesion of the units to the mortar while the stress in the normal direction is resisted (a) by the shear resistance of the mortar beds, (b) by the elastic resistance of the head joints to the rotation of the units, (c) by the adhesion of the head joints and (d) by the flexural resistance of the units themselves. Generally the limiting flexural

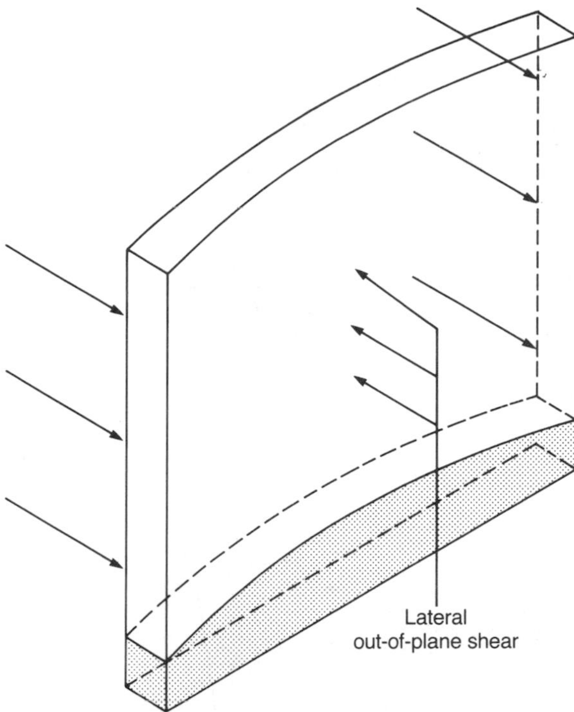

FIGURE 25.10 Shear failure on dpc line of laterally loaded wall.

resistance will be the lesser of (a) + (b) or (c) + (d) giving two main modes of horizontal spanning failure – shearing and snapping, shown in Figure 25.12.

Using small walls (wallettes), shown in Figure 25.13, and tested in four point bending mode, the flexural strength of a large range of combinations of UK units and mortars has been measured for the two orthogonal directions and a typical range is given in Table 25.3; further data are given in West *et al.* (1986), de Vekey *et al.* (1986) and de Vekey *et al.* (1990).

The ratio of the strength in the two directions, expressed as p-direction divided by n-direction, is termed the orthogonal ratio and given the symbol μ. In cases where only the bond strength (p-direction) is required a simpler and cheaper test is the bond wrench discussed in Section 23.3.2.

The flexural strengths given in Table 25.3 are for simply supported pieces of masonry spanning in one direction. If the fixity of the masonry at the supports (the resistance to rotation) is increased the load resistance will increase in accordance with normal structural principles (Figure 25.14). Again, if one area of masonry spans in two directions the resistances in the two directions are additive. Seward (1982), Haseltine *et al.* (1977) and Lovegrove (1988) cover some aspects of the resistance of panels.

25.5 Tension

Masonry made with conventional mortars has a very limited resistance to pure tension forces and, for the purposes of design, the tensile strength is usually taken to be zero. In practice it does have some resistance in the horizontal direction and somewhat less in the vertical direction. In an attempt to make a viable prefabricated masonry panel product for use as a cladding material, polymer latex additives can be used to improve the tensile strength. Panels of storey height and a metre or more wide have been manufactured and could be lifted and transported without failure. Unfortunately the polymer used, PVDC, released some chloride ions and has caused early failure of steel support angles and ties.

Horizontal tensile strength is very rarely measured and no standard test or any significant data are available. Tensile bond strength is often measured, the most familiar test being the ASTM cross brick test (ASTM C952-76) illustrated in Figure 25.15. Data from this test indicate that the direct tensile strength across the bond is between one-third and two-thirds of the parallel flexural strength. Other tests have been developed along similar lines including one in which one unit is held in a centrifuge and the bond to another unit is stressed by centrifuging.

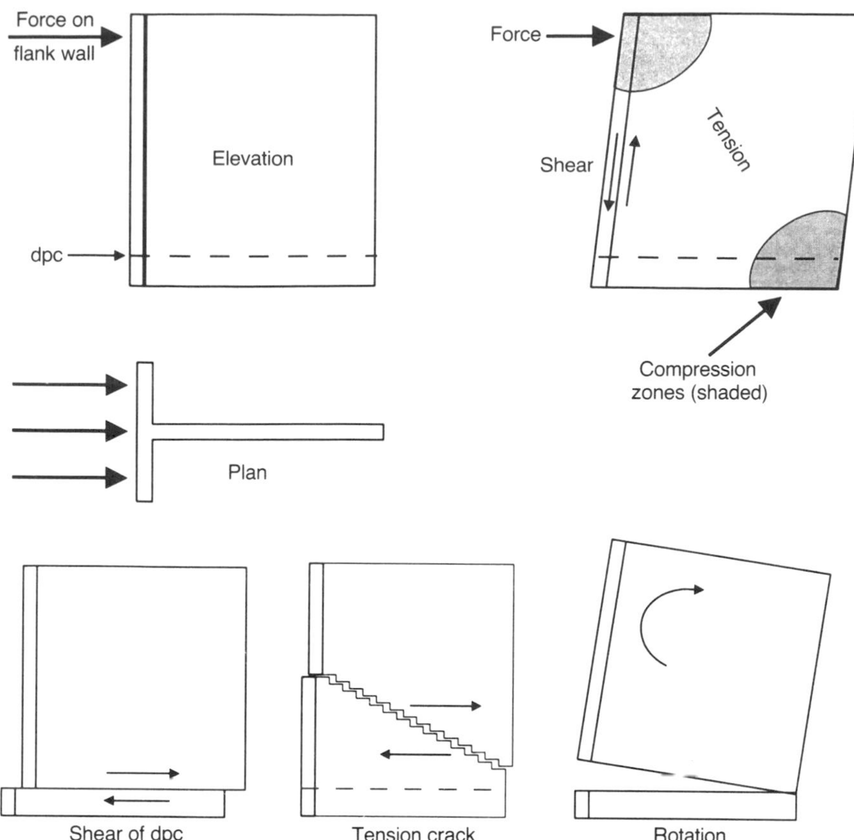

FIGURE 25.11 Stresses and strains resulting from an in-plane shear load. The wall may fail by crushing in the zones of higher compressive stress or by shear at the junction of the two walls at right angles, by horizontal shear at the dpc line, by tension splitting or by rotation.

25.6 Elastic modulus

The stiffness or elastic modulus of masonry is an important parameter required for calculations of stresses resulting from strains arising from loads, concentrated loads, constrained movement and also for calculating the required area of reinforcing and post-stressing bars.

The most commonly measured value is the Young's modulus (E) but the Poisson's ratio (ν) is also required for theoretical calculations using techniques such as finite element analysis. If required the bulk (K) and shear (G) moduli may be derived from the other parameters. Young's modulus is normally measured in a compression test by simultaneously measuring strain (ε_p) parallel to the applied stress (σ) whereupon:

$$E = \sigma/\varepsilon_p. \tag{25.3}$$

If the strain (ε_N) perpendicular to the applied stress is also measured, Poisson's ratio may be derived:

$$\nu = \varepsilon_N/\varepsilon_p. \tag{25.4}$$

Masonry is not an ideally elastic material because it is full of minor imperfections such as microcracks in the bond layers and because the differences between the unit and mortar stiff-

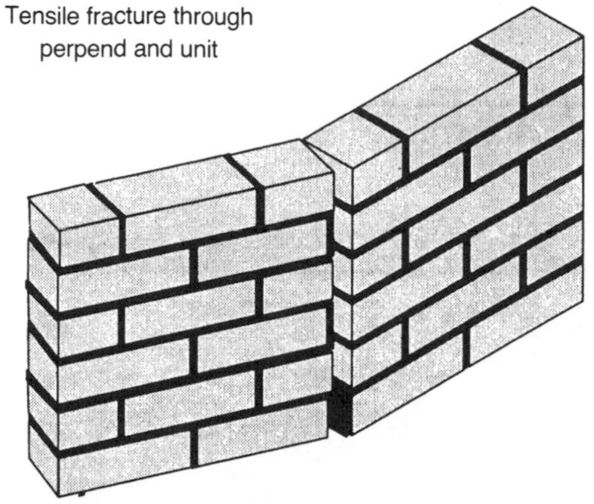

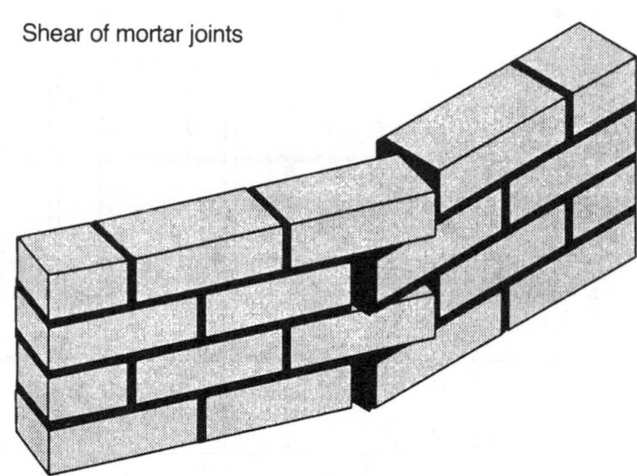

FIGURE 25.12 Modes of failure for laterally loaded masonry in the strong (n) direction.

nesses and Poisson's ratios produce high local strains at the interface which result in non-linear behaviour. This means that the stress–strain curve is typically of a broadly parabolic form with an early elastic region. The instantaneous Young's modulus is derived from the tangent to the curve at any point but for some calculations, such as creep loss of post-stressed masonry, the effective Young's modulus required is derived from the secant value. Figure 25.16 illustrates this behaviour. Data on elastic properties in compression are given in Davies and Hodgkinson (1988).

Elastic modulus is also important in estimating the deflections of walls out of plane due to lateral loads such as wind. In this case the modulus can be measured by using load deflection data for small walls tested in four point bending. In this case E is derived from:

$$E = \frac{8 \cdot W \cdot a(3L^2 - 4a^2)}{384 \cdot I \cdot \delta} \qquad (25.5)$$

where W is the applied force, L is the span of the supports, a is the distance from the supports to the loading points, I is the moment of inertia and δ is the deflection.

In compression tests the value of E has generally been found to be in the range 500–1000 times the compressive strength. For typical materials this is likely to be around 2 to 30 kN/mm^2.

TABLE 25.3 Flexural strength ranges for common materials

Material	*Mortar*	*Strong direction (n)*	*Weak direction (p)*
Clay brick 0–7% WA	(iii)	1.8 to 4.7	0.35 to 1.1
Clay brick 7–12% WA	(iii)	1.9 to 3.2	0.3 to 1.3
Clay brick >12% WA	(iii)	1.0 to 2.1	0.3 to 0.8
Concrete brick (25–40)	(iii)	1.9 to 2.4	0.5 to 0.9
Calcil brick (25–40)	(iii)	0.7 to 1.5	0.05 to 0.4
AAC block (100 mm)	(iii)	0.3 to 0.7	0.3 to 0.6
LWAC block (100 mm)	(iii)	0.7 to 1.3	0.3 to 0.5
DAC block (100 mm)	(iii)	0.7 to 1.7	0.2 to 0.7

Note: Ranges are only given for designation (iii) mortars (1:1:6 and equivalent strength). There is some dependence of masonry flexural strength on mortar strength. Thicker block units lead to reduced flexural strength. WA = water absorption; AAC = autoclaved aerated concrete; LWAC = lightweight aggregate concrete; DAC = dense aggregate concrete.

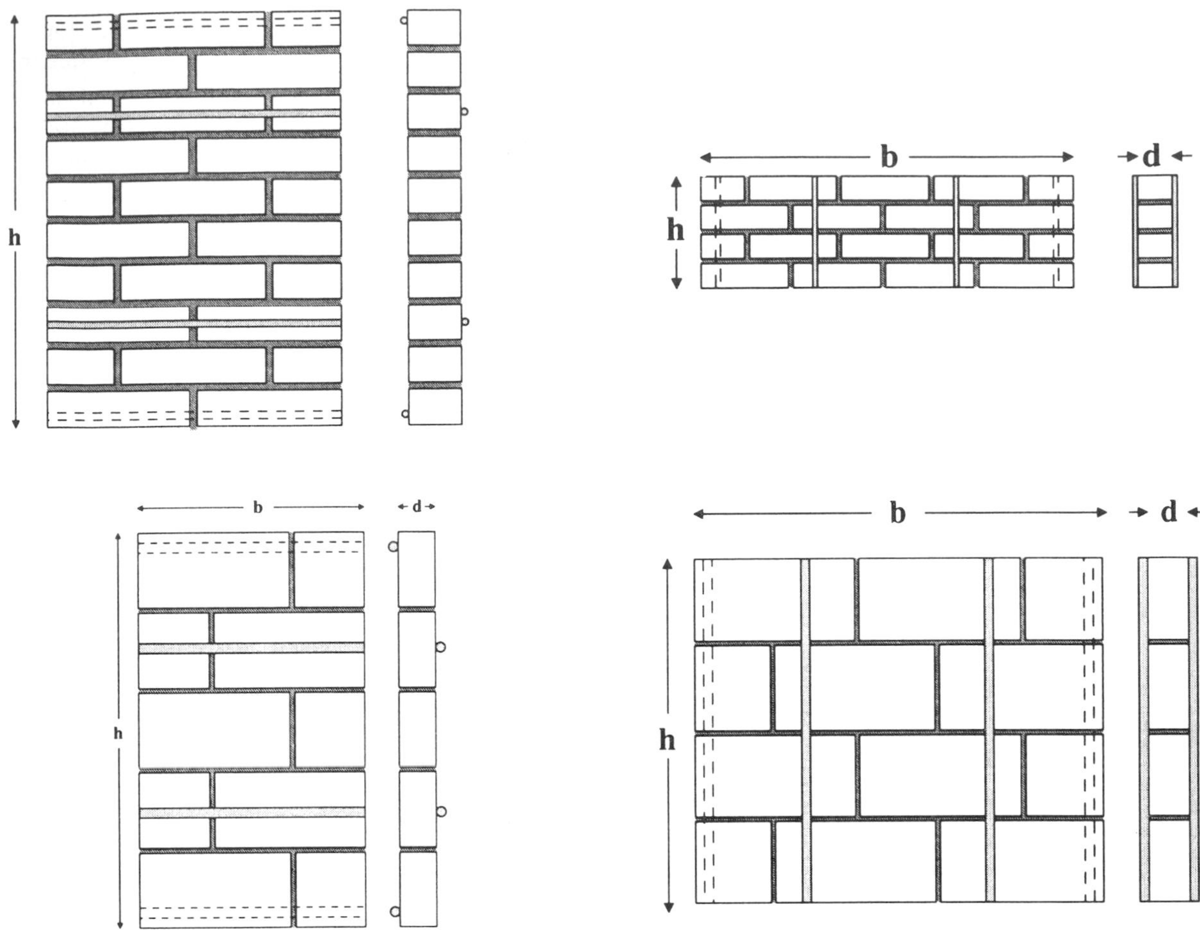

FIGURE 25.13 Wallette specimens for measuring flexural resistance of masonry.

In flexure the early tangent modulus has been found to be in the range 2–4 kN/mm^2 for tests in the strong (normal) direction and 1–2 kN/mm^2 for equivalent tests in the weak (parallel) direction. Some more data are given in Table 25.4.

25.7 Movement and creep of masonry materials

Unrestrained masonry is subject to cyclic movement due to moisture and temperature changes, permanent creep due to dead loads or post-stress loads, permanent shrinkage due to drying/carbonation of mortar, concrete and calcium silicate materials and expansion due to adsorption of moisture by fired clay materials. Table 25.4 contains some typical ranges for common masonry components.

In simple load-bearing masonry elements vertical movements are accommodated by the structure going up and down as required and are no problem. Problems can arise, however, where materials with different movement characteristics are joined or where thick elements have differential temperature/moisture gradients

TABLE 25.4 Movements and elastic moduli of masonry materials (BRE Digest 228, 1979)

Masonry component material	*Thermal expansion coefficient a (per °C × 10^{-6})*	*Reversible moisture movement (%)*	*Irreversible moisture movement (%)*	*Modulus of elasticity E (kN/mm²)*
Granite	8–10	–	–	20–60
Limestone	3–4	0.01	–	10–80
Marble	4–6	–	–	35
Sandstone	7–12	0.07	–	3–80
Slate	9–11	–	–	10–35
Mortar	10–13	0.02–0.06	−0.04–0.1	20–35
Dense concrete brick/blockwork	6–12	0.02–0.04	−0.02–0.06	10–25
LWAC blockwork	8–12	0.03–0.06	−0.02–0.06	4–16
AAC blockwork	8	0.02–0.03	−0.05–0.09	3–8
Calcil brickwork	8–14	0.01–0.05	−0.01–0.04	14–18
Clay brickwork	5–8	0.02	0.02–0.10	4–26

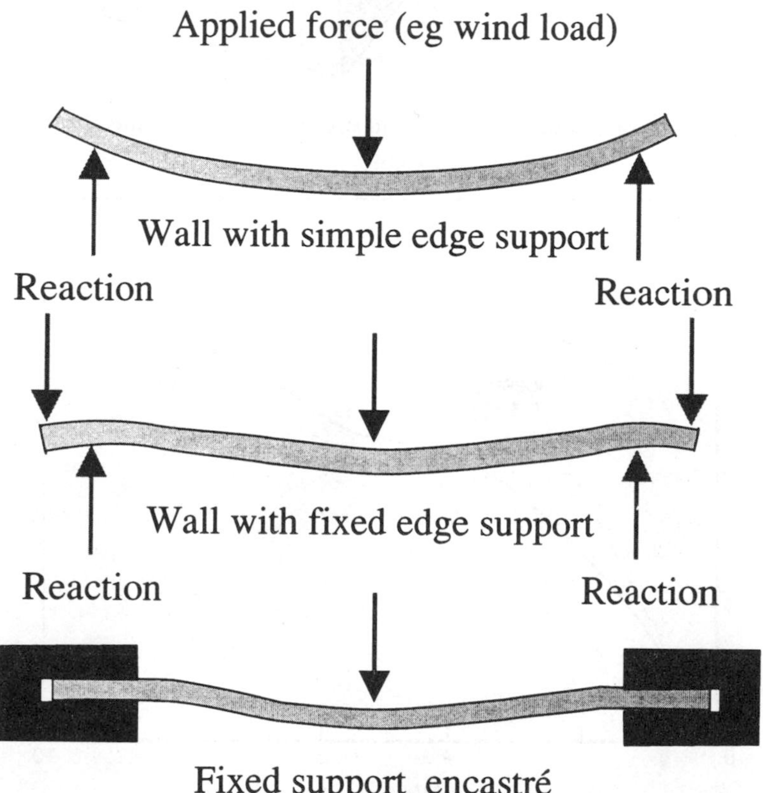

FIGURE 25.14 Effect of edge support conditions on the flexural behaviour of masonry.

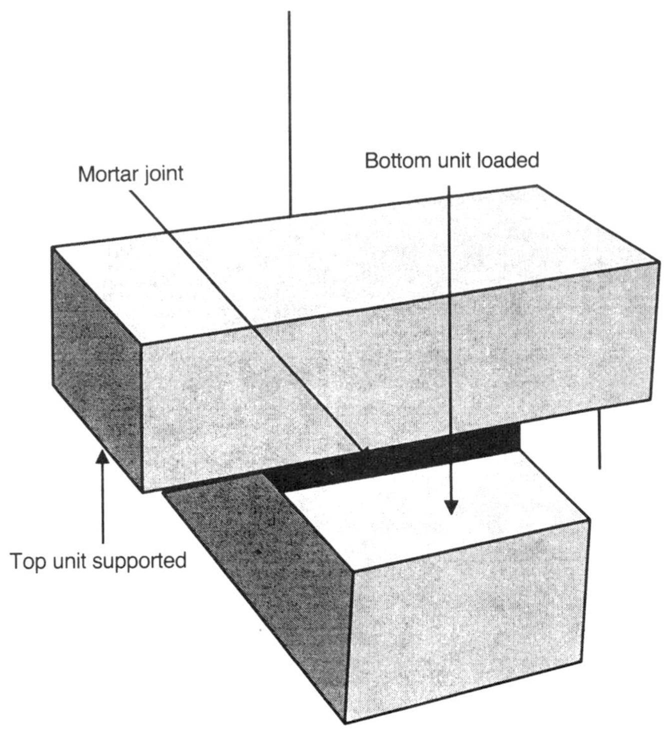

FIGURE 25.15 ASTM cross brick test for tensile bond strength of mortar joints.

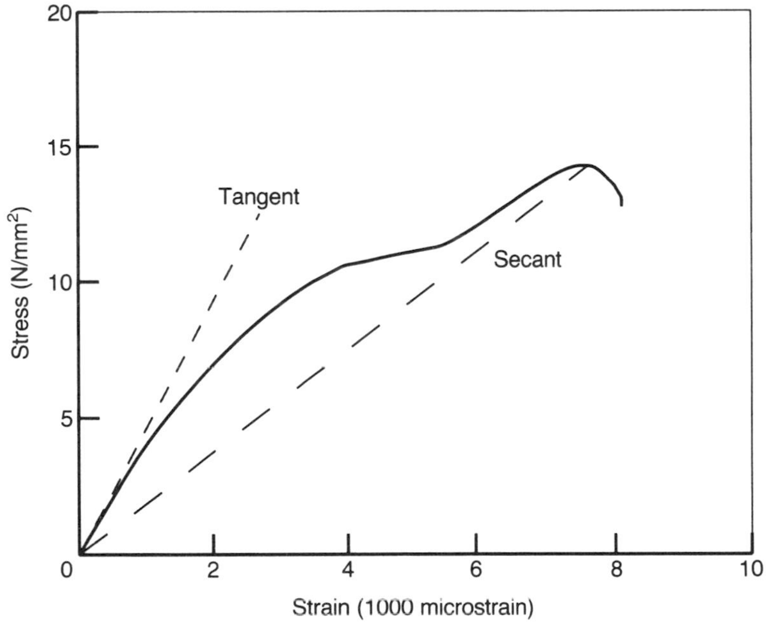

FIGURE 25.16 Load deflection curve for masonry.

through them. Elements with a vertical prestress much larger than the differential stresses will tolerate the movement, but lightly stressed and unrestrained elements will need a slip plane or soft joint between the elements to avoid problems. A classic case is (expanding) clay masonry on (shrinking) concrete frames where soft joints are used to stop stress transfer to the masonry.

Where restraint is present horizontal shrinkages will be converted into tensile forces and expansions into compressive forces. Since walls are probably two orders of magnitude weaker in tension than in compression the result is that restrained walls in tension usually crack while those in compression usually just build up stress. Where walls are unrestrained the reverse is usually the case: the shrinking wall simply contracts but the expanding wall interacts with flank walls (those at right angles) and causes cracking by generating rotation at the corner.

Because there is nearly always differential restraint the pure tensile or compressive forces will usually give rise to some associated shear forces.

25.8 References

Ali, S. and Page, A.W. (1986) An elastic analysis of concentrated loads on brickwork, *International Journal of Masonry Construction*, No. 6, Edinburgh, pp. 9–21.

Arora, S.K. (1988) Review of BRE research into performance of masonry walls under concentrated load, *Proceedings of the 8th International Brick/Block Masonry Conference*, Dublin, p. 446.

ASTM C952-76 (1976) *Standard test method for bond strength of mortar to masonry units.*

BRE Digest 228 (1979) *Estimation of thermal and moisture movements and stresses: Part 2*, Building Research Establishment, Watford (also Digests 227 and 229).

BRE Digest 246 (1981) *Strength of brickwork and blockwork walls: Design for vertical load*, Building Research Establishment, Watford.

BS 5606: 1978: *Code of practice for accuracy in building.*

BS 5628: 1985: *Code of practice for the use of masonry. Part 1: Structural use of unreinforced masonry; Part 2: Structural use of reinforced and prestressed masonry; Part 3: Materials and components, design and workmanship.*

Davey, N. (1952) Modern research on loadbearing brickwork, *The Brick Bulletin*, 1–16.

Davies, S. and Hodgkinson, H.R. (1988) *The stress–strain relationships of brickwork, Part 2*, BCRL research paper 755.

Haseltine, B.A., West, H.W.H. and Tutt, J.N. (1977) Design of walls to resist lateral loads, *The Structural Engineer*, **55**, No. 10, 422–30.

Hodgkinson, H.R. and West, H.W.H. (1981) *The shear resistance of some damp-proof course materials*, Technical Note 326, British Ceramic Research Ltd, Stoke on Trent.

Lovegrove, R. (1988) The effect of thickness and bond pattern upon the lateral strength of brickwork, *Proc. Brit. Masonry Soc.*, No. 2, 95–7.

Malek, M.H. and Hendry, A.W. (1988) Compressive strength of brickwork masonry under concentrated loading, *Proc. Brit. Masonry Soc.*, No. 2, 56–60.

Seward, D.W. (1982) A developed elastic analysis of lightly loaded brickwork walls with lateral loading, *International Journal of Masonry Construction*, **2**, No. 2, 129–34.

Simms, L.G. (1965) The strength of walls built in the laboratory with some types of clay bricks and blocks, *Proc. Brit. Ceram. Soc.*, July, 81–92.

SP 56: 1980: *Model specification for clay and calcium silicate structural brickwork*, British Ceramic Research Limited, Stoke on Trent.

de Vekey, R.C., Bright, N.J., Luckin, K.R. and Arora, S.K. (1986) Research results on autoclaved aerated concrete blockwork, *The Structural Engineer*, **64A**, No. 11, 332–40.

de Vekey, R.C., Edgell, G.J. and Dukes, R. (1990) The effect of sand grading on the performance and properties of masonry, *Proc. Brit. Masonry Soc.* No. 4, 152–9.

West, H.W.H., Hodgkinson, H.R. and Davenport, S.T.E. (1968) *The performance of walls built of wirecut bricks with and without perforations*, Special Publication No. 60, British Ceramic Research Ltd, Stoke on Trent.

West, H.W.H., Hodgkinson, H.R. and Haseltine, B.A. (1977) The resistance of brickwork to lateral loading, *The Structural Engineer*, **55**, No. 10, 411–21.

West, H.W.H., Hodgkinson, H.R., Haseltine, B.A. and de Vekey, R.C. (1986) Research results on brickwork and aggregate blockwork since 1977, *The Structural Engineer*, **64A**, No. 11, 320–31.

Chapter twenty-six

Durability and non-structural properties of masonry

26.1 Introduction
26.2 Durability
26.3 Chemical attack
26.4 Erosion
26.5 Thermal conductivity
26.6 Rain resistance
26.7 Sound transmission
26.8 Fire resistance
26.9 References

26.1 Introduction

The main non-structural function of masonry elements is as a cladding to buildings and the key function of such elements is to maintain habitable conditions within the building. It is thus paramount that the masonry be durable with respect to the external actions it is subjected to. It is also important to know how effective masonry is in controlling the temperature, preventing ingress of wind and rain, reducing noise transmission and limiting the spread of fire should it break out.

26.2 Durability

There are a large number of mechanisms by which masonry structures can deteriorate which can be categorized into:

1. chemical/biological attack on either the mortar or the units or both, due to water and waterborn acids, sulphates, pollution and chemicals released by growing plants;
2. corrosion of embedded metal (usually steel) components, particularly ties, straps, reinforcing rods, hangers, etc. which is a special case of chemical attack;
3. erosion of units or mortar by particles in flowing water and wind, by frost attack and by salt crystallization;
4. stress-related effects due to movement of foundations, movement/consolidation/wash-out of in-fill, vibration, overloading, moisture movement of bricks and blocks, thermal movement, growth of plants;
5. staining due to efflorescence, lime, silica, iron and vanadium.

Mortar is generally a less durable material than fired clay or dense concrete because it contains reactive and finely divided binders such as opc and it usually has a relatively high porosity and, comparatively, a lower hardness and abrasion resistance. The durability of natural stone is very variable ranging from the highest given by dense impermeable granites and marbles to quite poor performance of porous limestones and sandstones. Erosion processes such as wind and water scour attack both units and mortar but erode the softer of the two at a faster rate. Frost and salt crystallization are complex processes where the susceptibility is dependent as much on pore distribution as hardness and overall porosity. Stress effects normally cause cracking of varying types but the effect is on the masonry composite and not on the individual components. There are some problems related to faults in manufacture of the units, particularly under- or over-firing of clay bricks and the inclusion of foreign particles in bricks or other types of unit. A good range of coloured illustrations of problems is given in BRE Digest 361 (1991).

26.3 Chemical attack

Water and acid rain

Water percolating into masonry is always a potential source of damage and, where possible, the structure should be designed to channel water away or at least to allow it to escape via weepholes. Absolutely pure water will have no direct chemical effect but some of the constituents of mortar are very slightly soluble and will leach away very slowly. Rain water contains dissolved carbon dioxide which forms a very mild acid which dissolves calcium carbonate by formation of the soluble bicarbonate via the reaction:

$$CO_2 + H_2O \rightarrow H_2CO_3 + CaCO_3 \rightarrow Ca(HCO_3)_2. \qquad (26.1)$$

This means that lime mortars, weak opc : lime mortars, porous limestones and porous lime-bonded sandstones will eventually be destroyed by percolating rain water because calcium carbonate is their main binding agent. Strong opc mortars with well-graded sand and most concrete and sandlime units are less susceptible partly because the calcium silicate binder is less soluble but mainly because they are less permeable and so prevent free percolation. Typical visible effects of water leaching on mortar are loose sandy or friable joints, loss of mortar in the outside of the joints giving a raked joint appearance, and in serious cases the loss of bricks from the outer layer of masonry particularly from tunnel/arch heads. The process will sometimes be accompanied by staining due to reprecipitation of the dissolved materials. Stones lose their surface finish and may develop pits or rounded arrises.

Sulphur dioxide reacts with water to form initially sulphurous acid but can oxidize further in air to sulphuric acid:

$$2SO_2 + 2H_2O \rightarrow 2H_2SO_3 + O_2 \rightarrow 2H_2SO_4 \qquad (26.2)$$

There is no systematic evidence that rain acidified by sulphur dioxide from flue gases at the normal levels has a significant effect on mortar, but in special cases such as where there is a high level of gaseous pollution near industrial sites there may be a very significant increase in the deterioration rate of all forms of structure including mortar and limestones. Unlined chimneys are a particular case and can suffer severe sulphate attack in the exposed parts where rain saturation or condensation of fumes containing sulphur occurs.

Carbonation

Gaseous carbon dioxide (CO_2) at humidities between about 30% and 70% neutralizes any alkalis present. This process occurs for all lime and opc binders with the conversion of compounds such as sodium hydroxide (NaOH) and, most commonly, calcium hydroxide ($Ca(OH)_2$) to their respective carbonates. In lime mortars this process probably increases the strength and durability. In opc-based materials the key effect of the process is to reduce the pH from around 12–13 down to below 7, i.e. converting the material from highly alkaline to slightly acid. This can have a profound effect on the durability of buried steel components, see Section 17.4.2.

There is also some evidence that there is a slight associated shrinkage which may reduce the strength of very lightweight concrete units. Very dense concrete and calcium silicate units will carbonate slowly and may take 50–100 years or more to carbonate through.

Sulphate attack

Sulphate attack is the next most common problem which is due to the reaction between sulphate ions in water solution and the components of set Portland cement. Section 17.3.1 gives a detailed coverage of the physical/chemical mechanism.

The resulting expansion, which can be of the order of several per cent, causes both local disruption of mortar beds and stresses in the brickwork but only in wet or saturated conditions and where there is a source of water-soluble sulphate compound. It will never occur in dry or slightly damp masonry. The common sulphates found in masonry are the freely soluble sodium, potassium and magnesium salts and calcium sulphate which is less soluble but will leach in persistently wet conditions. The sulphates may be present in groundwaters and can affect masonry below the dpc, and masonry in contact with the ground such as retaining walls, bridges and tunnels. Sulphates are also present in some types of clay brick and will be transported to the mortar in wet conditions. Old types of solid brick with unoxidized centres ('blackhearts') often have large amounts of soluble sulphates as do some Scottish composition bricks, while semi-dry pressed bricks made from Oxford clay (Flettons) have high levels of calcium sulphate. Sulphates may attack lime mortars by conversion of the lime to gypsum. Sulphate resisting Portland cement is deliberately formulated to have a low C_3A content but may be attacked in very extreme conditions. Sulphate attack is more likely in porous mortars while rich, dense, impervious mortars are affected less despite their higher cement content.

Visible effects of such attack on mortar are expansion of the masonry where it is unrestrained and stress increases where it is restrained. Typically the mortar is affected more within the body of the wall than on the surface, so small horizontal cracks are sometimes visible in the centre of each bed joint as in Figure 26.1. In thick masonry, vertical cracks may appear on

FIGURE 26.1 Sulphate attack.

the external elevations due to the greater expansion in the centre of the wall which remains wetter for longer than the outside which can dry out by evaporation. Horizontal cracking may also occur but it is likely to be less obvious where there is a high vertical deadload stress. Rendered masonry exhibits a network of cracks termed 'map-cracking'. If walls also have a face to an internal space which is kept dry, then efflorescence (growth of crystals) may occur due to transport of the sulphates to the surface. These faults are most common where the water is leaking into the structure from faulty details, leaking roofs or from ground contact, especially with sulphate-bearing groundwaters.

Sulphates do not usually have a significant chemical effect on properly fired clay units although they are commonly the source of such compounds. Sulphate attack on concrete blocks and bricks can occur but is not a common problem. Certain precautions are advisable when building in ground containing sulphates or constructing flumes and tunnels to carry contaminated water (WRC, 1986).

A special type of 'engineering quality' concrete brick is now available which is designed to be stable in effluents containing sulphates and other harmful compounds. These units are manufactured to a high strength and low permeability with srpc as the binder. A limited test has been carried out on samples of three different 'engineering quality' concrete bricks using simulated industrial and commercial effluent solutions (Concrete, 1986).

Mundic concrete blocks made using tin-mine tailings as aggregate in south-west England have suffered attack from indigenous sulphates (see Section 17.3.1).

Acids

The effects of acids, e.g. rain run-off from peat moors or industrial or agricultural pollution, on cement-based products is covered in Section 17.3.1. Clay products are normally resistant.

Chlorides

Chlorides can have a weakening effect on calcium silicate units but have little effect on mortars, clay units or concrete masonry units.

Corrosion of buried metals

See Part Three (Concrete) for a detailed discussion. Refer to de Vekey (1990*a*) and de Vekey (1990*b*) for specific coverage of wall tie corrosion.

26.4 Erosion

Frost

Frost is the principal eroding agent of masonry exposed to normal exterior conditions. Quite clearly it will not affect masonry buried more than a few feet and so will not affect foundations, the insides of tunnels or buried culverts. It may affect any masonry exposed on the exterior of structures but is more likely to affect exposed components that become saturated. Typical problem areas are civil engineering structures such as bridges, earth-retaining walls and exposed culverts and parts of buildings such as parapets, chimneys, freestanding walls and masonry between the ground and the damp-proof course.

Frost attack is due to the stresses created by the expansion of water on freezing to ice in the pore systems of units and mortars and thus only occurs in water-saturated or near saturated masonry. Some clay bricks and natural stones are particularly susceptible, whereas most good quality clay engineering bricks, stock bricks and concrete and calcium silicate units are very resistant. Mortar is also subject to frost damage, particularly in combination with any of the other forms of chemical deterioration.

Typical effects are the spalling of small pieces of either the unit or the mortar or both forming a layer of detritus at the foot of the wall. Figure 26.2 shows typical damage. Clay bricks, particularly lightly fired examples of types made from some shales and marls, are especially

FIGURE 26.2 Erosion (frost).

susceptible and tend to laminate. Semi-dry pressed bricks made from the Oxford clay tend to break down into grains the same size as they were made from (e.g. around 7–14 mesh). Old types of solid clay brick with unoxidized centres tend to spall from the boundary between the heart and the outside of the brick. Some natural stones with a large proportion of fine pores are also susceptible. Modern perforated clay bricks are generally more frost-resistant because the more open structure allows more even drying and firing with less chance of shrinkage/firing cracks forming.

The susceptibility of building materials to frost attack can be very difficult to understand. Clearly materials such as glass, plastic and metals which are totally non-porous to water are not affected. Materials such as well-fired 'glassy' clay bricks, well-compacted concretes, low-porosity granites, marbles and slates are also affected very little by frost since the tiny amount of water that can penetrate will cause only a trivial level of stress on freezing. Materials with water absorptions ranging from about 4% to 50% tend to suffer frost damage but not invariably. As a general rule materials with a wide range of pore sizes from very large to fine tend to be resistant while those having a limited range of pore sizes, usually of the finer sizes, tend to fail. This is probably because it is difficult to saturate fully the mixed pore system, the water filling the fine but not the larger pores. Providing around 10% of the pore system is still air filled there is sufficient space for the ice crystals to expand into without damaging the structure.

This has given rise to tests of pore distribution being used to predict frost durability. For stone a test is used in which the stone is saturated with water then pressurized to a level at which the larger pores will be emptied. This gives a measure of the ratio between the volume of pores above and below a chosen critical size and some idea of durability.

Most of the older data on susceptibility to frost attack are based on experience but this is a very slow and inefficient way of evaluating new products. To try to speed up the process, accelerated freezing tests have been developed. A typical example is the panel test (West *et al.*, 1984).

The method is designed to test small panels of brickwork. The panel is first totally immersed in water for seven days, then one face is exposed to repeated cycles of freezing and thawing usually up to a limit of 100 cycles. The other face and the top and the sides of the panel are enclosed in a close-fitting jacket of 25 mm thick expanded polystyrene. Bricks showing no signs of failure after 100 cycles should be frost-resistant, those failing between 10 and 100 cycles would be expected to be durable under most conditions of exposure, but some failure could occur if they were used in a situation where repeated freeze–thaw cycling occurred when the bricks were saturated with water. Bricks which fail in less than 10 cycles are considered to be suitable for internal use only.

Efflorescence

This is simply a staining process caused by dissolution of soluble salts such as sodium, potassium, magnesium and calcium sulphates by rain or construction water from within brickwork which then crystallize on the surface as a white powder or encrustation. The surface may be any surface from which drying occurs. It is commonly the external facade but may be the interior of solid walls particularly those in contact with earth, e.g. cellar walls and ground floor walls in older structures without damp courses. The salts commonly derive from clay bricks, but may also come from groundwaters.

Crypto-efflorescence damage

This is basically the same process as efflorescence but at certain temperature/humidity conditions it occurs just below the surface of the masonry unit. The hydrated crystals of species such as calcium and sodium sulphates growing in the pore structure result in a tensile force on the surface layers in a way which is analogous to frost attack. In UK conditions it is more likely to affect natural stones than other units. It normally occurs in warm conditions where there is rapid drying of water from the face causing the salts to crystallize out. Additionally there needs to be a source of water or water containing salts.

Typical appearance is similar to that of frost damage but it will usually be associated with efflorescence crystals.

Abrasion

Abrasion by particles in wind and water probably acts more in concert with other processes than in isolation. Likely areas for such erosion are bridge columns founded in river beds and buildings near road surfaces where splash-up can occur from vehicles. All types of marine/hydraulic structures such as dams, culverts, lock walls, flumes, etc. where high-velocity flows can occur may suffer from localized abrasion damage known as 'scour'.

26.5 Thermal conductivity

The thermal conductivity determines the rate of heat flow through a given material. Generally metals have the higher and very porous materials (containing a lot of air or other gas) the lower conductivities. Masonry materials fall in a band between the two extremes. The property is important in that it affects the amount of heat loss from a building through the walls and thus the energy efficiency of the structure. Surprisingly, although it is often of lower density and quite porous, mortar is frequently a poorer insulator than many bricks and blocks. Figure 26.3 is a photograph taken with an infra-red scanning camera showing the higher heat loss from the 1 : 1 : 6 mortar than from the semi-dry pressed bricks. Because porosity is a key parameter the thermal conductivity is bound to be partially related to material density and general equations for dry solid porous building materials tend to be a function of density and give a regression expression of the form:

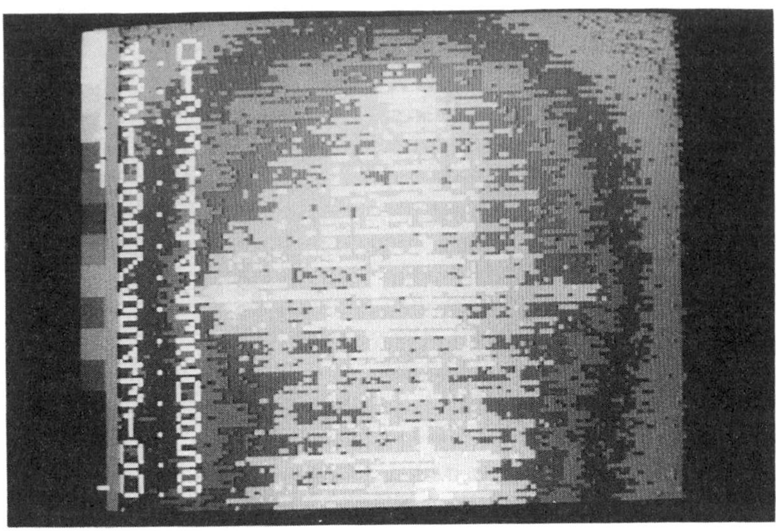

FIGURE 26.3 Infra-red photograph showing heat loss through joints.

$$k = 0.0536 + 0.000213\rho - 0.0000002\rho^2. \quad (26.3)$$

The presence of moisture increases the conductivity of porous materials because evaporation/condensation heat transfer mechanisms become possible.

Hollow and perforated products give some improvement over plain solid products although the potential gain from the trapped air pockets is compromised by the convection of the air within them. If the air is prevented from convecting by filling the hollows with foamed plastic materials such as urea-formaldehyde or polyurethane there is an immediate improvement. Clay bricks or blocks with many small perforations also perform better than solid units because the smaller size of the holes reduces convection and the smaller solid cross-section reduces conduction. There is also an improvement if the holes are staggered such that the direct conduction path through the solid material is as long as possible. Figure 26.4 illustrates the effects of different perforation patterns on thermal resistance.

The properties of walls used as thermal barriers are normally expressed in the form of the 'U value', the overall heat transfer coefficient which is a synthesis of the k value of the actual materials and the heat transfer coefficients at the hot and cold sides. More detail on thermal insulation is given in Diamant (1986), BRE Digest 108 (1975) and BRE Digest 273 (1983).

26.6 Rain resistance

From the earliest use of built housing it has been one of the primary requirements that the walls will keep the occupants dry and thus most masonry forming the perimeter walls of houses and other buildings is called upon to resist the ingress of rain. All masonry component materials are porous, however, and there are always some imperfections in the bond and seal of the mortar joints which will admit some water so no solid masonry wall is likely to be absolutely watertight.

Paradoxically, it is normally easier under UK conditions to make a rain-resistant wall from porous bricks. This is because some leakage always occurs at the joints which is mopped up by high absorption units but allowed free

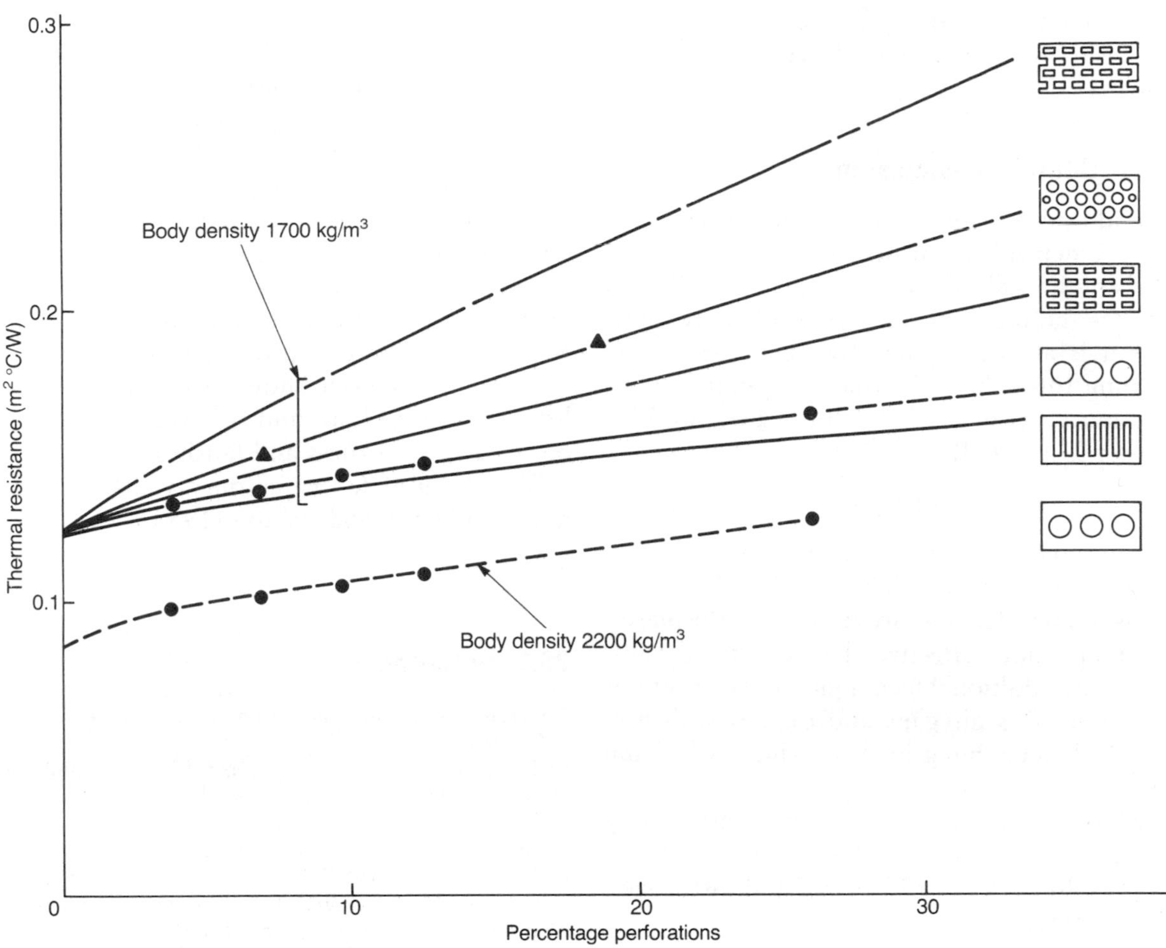

FIGURE 26.4 Effect of perforations on thermal resistance.

passage by low absorption units. Provided the rain does not persist until the units are saturated, they can dry out in the intervening dry spell and do not actually leak significant amounts of moisture to the inner face. Under similar conditions, some modern, low-absorption facings may leak quite seriously during a moderate storm. As would be expected resistance is greater for thicker walls or if a coating is applied to the wall which reduces the surface rate of absorption. Typical coatings are renders and paints or overcladding systems.

The commonest technique for avoiding rain penetration in the UK is the cavity wall. This is a twin layer wall with an enclosed air space between the two leaves. Some leakage through the outer layer (leaf) is anticipated and any such water is directed back out through weepholes before it reaches the inner leaf by use of damp-proof membranes and cavity trays. This is sometimes thought of as a very recent wall form but it was probably used in ancient Greece and has been in use in the damper parts of the UK for nearly 200 years. It has given remarkably good service and is quite tolerant of workmanship variations and the only significant problem has been the corrosion of the steel ties used to ensure shared structural action of the two leaves.

26.7 Sound transmission

Sound transmission is another parameter which is very dependent on density because it is the mass of the wall which is critical. Generally, the greater the mass, m, of a wall the more effective it is at attenuating (absorbing) the sound passing through it. A typical equation for the resistance, R, in decibels, dB, is given by BRE Digest 273 (1983).

$$R = 14.3 \log m + 11.4\text{dB} \qquad (26.4)$$

Any holes will short circuit the wall so that wet plastered walls where any minor perforations or imperfections are repaired by the plaster layer are more effective than dry-lined walls. There are additional techniques to try to cut out sound such as air gaps and cavities with fireproof blankets hung in them which will damp out some frequencies.

More details on principles and basic values are given in Diamant (1986), BRE Digest 337 (1988), BRE Digest 338 (1988) and BRE Digest 333 (1988).

26.8 Fire resistance

Fire resistance of masonry is an important characteristic since it has long been recognized that masonry is a very effective material for resisting and preventing the spread of fire. This is now enshrined in various building regulations dating from the Great Fire of London. Its effectiveness in this role is due to the following characteristics: (1) a relatively low thermal conductivity which prevents the fire spreading by inhibiting the rise in temperature of the side of a wall away from the fire; (2) a relatively high heat capacity which also inhibits the rise in temperature of the side of a wall away from the fire (this is especially true of concrete-based products which contain a lot of loosely bound water which absorbs heat while being boiled away); (3) zero flammability and surface spread of flame; (4) refractory properties which mean that it retains its strength and integrity up to very high temperatures approaching 1000°C in some cases. These properties mean that it does not catch fire itself, it inhibits spread of fire by conduction and radiation and it is not easily breached by the fire. Insulating finishes such as vermiculite plaster improve performance still further. It has been shown to resist fire for between half an hour and six hours depending on material, thickness and finishes.

The classic data on masonry walls are contained in Davey and Ashton (1953).

26.9 References

Concrete (1986) The concrete engineering quality brick, *Concrete*, April.

BRE Digest 108 (1975) *Standard U-values*, Building Research Establishment, Watford.

BRE Digest 273 (1983) *Perforated clay bricks*, Building Research Establishment, Watford.

BRE Digest 337 (1988) *Sound insulation: basic principles*, Building Research Establishment, Watford.

BRE Digest 333 (1988) *Sound insulation of separating walls and floors. Part 1: Walls*, Building Research Establishment, Watford.

BRE Digest 338 (1988) *Insulation against external noise*, Building Research Establishment, Watford.

BRE Digest 361 (1991) *Why do buildings crack?*, Building Research Establishment, Watford.

Davey, N. and Ashton, L.A. (1953) *Investigation of building fires. Part V. Fire tests on structural elements*, National Building Studies No. 12, HMSO, London.

Diamant, R.M.E. (1986) *Thermal and Acoustic Insulation*, Butterworth, London.

de Vekey, R.C. (1990*a*) *Corrosion of steel wall ties: background, history of occurrence and treatment*, BRE Information Paper IP12/90, Building Research Establishment, Watford.

de Vekey, R.C. (1990*b*) *Corrosion of steel wall ties: recognition and assessment*, BRE Information Paper IP13/90, Building Research Establishment, Watford.

West, H.W.H., Ford, R.W. and Peake, F.A. (1984) A panel freezing test for brickwork, *Proc. Brit. Ceram. Soc.*, 83, 112.

Further reading

British Standards

BS 3921: 1985: *Specification for clay bricks.*

BS 6073: 1981: *Precast concrete masonry units. Part 1: Specification for precast concrete masonry units; Part 2: Method for specifying precast concrete masonry units.*

BS 187: 1978: *Calcium silicate bricks.*

BS 6677: Part 1: 1985: *Specification for clay and calcium silicate pavers.*

BS 6717: Part 1: 1986: *Specification for precast concrete paving blocks.*

BS 1200: 1976: *Sands from natural sources: sands for mortar for plain and reinforced brickwork, blockwork and stone masonry.*

Codes of Practice

BS 5628: Part 1: 1978 covers normal unreinforced structural masonry such as walls, arches, tunnels, columns, etc. subject to compressive, lateral and shear loads.

BS 5628: Part 2: 1985 is the section for design of reinforced or prestressed brickwork, e.g. for earth-retaining walls, chamber covers, etc., and has a useful treatment of the use of corrosion-resistant reinforcement for service in harsh conditions such as foul drains.

BS 5628: Part 3: 1985 covers all non-structural aspects of brickwork design, particularly the specification of units and mortars for durability over a wide range of applications and also workmanship, detailing, bonding patterns, fire resistance and resistance to weather conditions.

BS 6100: Part 5.3: 1986 defines terms relevant to bricks and brickwork.

Building Research Establishment publications

Digest 157, *Calcium silicate (sandlime, flintlime) brickwork.*

Digest 164, *Clay brickwork: 1.*

Digest 165, *Clay brickwork: 2.*

Digest 240, *Low rise buildings on shrinkable clay soils: Part 1.*

Digest 246, *Strength of brickwork and blockwork walls: design for vertical load.*

Digest 250, *Concrete in sulphate bearing soils and groundwaters.*

Digest 273, *Perforated clay bricks.*

Digest 298, *The influence of trees on house foundations in clay soils.*

Digest 329, *Installing wall ties in existing construction.*

Digest 359, *Repairing brickwork.*

Digest 361, *Why do buildings crack?*

Digest 362, *Building mortar.*

Performance specifications for wall ties – BRE report.

BRE CP24/70, *Some results of exposure tests on durability of calcium silicate bricks.*

BRE CP23/77 (1977) Chemical resistance of concrete, *Concrete*, **11**, No. 5, 35–7.

Harrison, W.H. (1987) Durability of concrete in acidic soils and groundwaters, *Concrete*, **21**, No. 2.

Brick Development Association publications

Brick diaphragm walls in tall single storey buildings (and earth retaining walls).

BDA Design note 3, *Brickwork Dimensions Tables.*

BDA Design note 7, *Brickwork Durability.*

British Ceramic Research Limited publications

Technical Note 368, *The performance of calcium silicate brickwork in high sulphate environments.*

SP56: 1980: *Model specification for clay and calcium silicate structural brickwork* (in process of updating).

Supplement No. 1 to SP56, *Glossary of terms relating to the interaction of bricks and brickwork with water.*

SP108, *Design guide for reinforced clay brickwork pocket-type retaining walls.*

SP109, *Achieving the functional requirements of mortar.*

British Cement Association

Technical report TRA/145, *The effects of sulphates on Portland cement concretes and other products.*

Concrete Brick Manufacturers Association publications

CBMA Information Sheet 2, *Concrete bricks – product information.*

Miscellaneous publications

An Introduction to Load Bearing Brickwork Design, A.W. Hendry, B.B. Sinha and S.R. Davies, Ellis Horwood, Chichester.

Part Six

Fibre Composites

Section One: Polymers and polymer composites

L. Hollaway

Section Two: Fibre-reinforced Cements and Concretes

D. Hannant

Introduction

This part is divided into two sections to reflect the difference in the mechanics of the reinforcing process between fibre-reinforced polymers and cementitious materials. The first, on fibre-reinforced polymers, is mostly concerned with pre-cracking behaviour, and the second, on fibre-reinforced cement and concrete, is mainly concerned with post-cracking performance.

The history of fibre-reinforced composites as construction materials is more than 3000 years old. Well-known examples are the use of straw in clay bricks, mentioned in Exodus, and horsehair in plaster. Other natural fibres have been used over the ages to reinforce mud walls and give added toughness to rather brittle building materials.

In contrast with these ancient and relatively simple natural materials, the development of polymers as matrices and as fibres in the last 100 years stems from the growth of the oil industry. Since the 1930s oil has been our main source of organic chemicals, from which synthetic plastics, fibres, rubbers and adhesives are made. The by-products of the distillation of petroleum are called basic chemicals and they provide the building blocks from which many chemicals and products, including plastics, can be made. Pioneers in the development of plastics include Alexander Parkes in the UK in the 1860s and the US chemist Leo Baekeland, who developed 'Parkesine' and 'Bakelite' respectively.

A large variety of polymers, with a wide range of properties, has been developed commercially since 1955. Phenol formaldehyde (PF) is a hard thermosetting material, polystyrene is a hard, brittle thermoplastic; polythene and plasticized polyvinyl chloride (PVC) are soft tough thermoplastic materials. Plastics can also exist in various physical forms: bulk solids, rigid or flexible foams, or sheet or film.

These materials are relatively strong, but have low stiffness. They can be combined with fibres of high stiffness and strength to form composites with improved structural properties.

Fibre-reinforced composites can also be based on inorganic cements and binders. Most fibre-reinforced, cement-based composites differ from fibre-reinforced polymers in that most of the reinforcing effects of the fibres occur after the brittle matrix has cracked either at the microscopic level or with visible cracks through the composite. This is the result of the relatively low strain to failure of the cement matrix (~0.01–0.05%) compared with the high elongation of the fibres (~1–5%). The fibres in cement-based systems often have a lower modulus of elasticity than the cement matrix and hence little or no increase in cracking stress is expected from the fibre reinforcement.

The most notable exception to this division is asbestos cement which has been the most commercially successful fibre-reinforced composite this century, in terms of both tonnage and turnover, the latter having been in excess of £1 billion per annum worldwide for many years. Asbestos cement was invented in about 1900 by Hatschek and its high tensile cracking stress and failure strain (in excess of 0.1%) results in part from the suppression of cracks propagating from flaws (see Section 33.2).

Usage of asbestos fibres has been reduced since about 1980 due to their carcinogenic effects and this has stimulated the search for alternative fibre systems which will enable the traditional products to be safely marketed even if with considerably changed properties. There has also been a growing interest since the 1960s in modifying the properties of fresh and hardened concrete by the addition of fibres, and these materials are described in Section 2.

Section One

Polymers and polymer composites

L. Hollaway

Chapter twenty-seven

Polymer and fibre properties and manufacture

27.1 Polymeric materials
27.2 Fibres
27.3 Processing of thermoplastic polymers
27.4 Mechanical properties

27.1 Polymeric materials

Polymers are produced by combining a large number of small molecular units (monomers) by the chemical process known as polymerization to form long-chain molecules. There are two main types. Thermoplastics consist of a series of long-chain polymerized molecules. All the chains of the molecules are separate and can slide over one another. In thermosetting polymers the chains become cross-linked so that a solid material is produced which cannot be softened and which will not flow.

Polymers are usually made in one of two polymerization processes. In condensation-polymerization the linking of molecules creates by-products, usually water, nitrogen or hydrogen gas. In addition-polymerization no by-products are created. Both thermosetting and thermoplastic polymers can be manufactured by these processes.

27.1.1 Thermoplastic polymers

In a thermoplastic polymer the long-chain molecules are held together by relatively weak van der Waals forces, but the chemical bond along the chain is extremely strong, see Figure 27.1(a). When the material is heated, the intermolecular forces are weakened and the polymer becomes soft and flexible; at high temperatures it becomes a viscous melt. When it is allowed to cool again it solidifies. The cycle of softening by heating and hardening by cooling can be repeated almost indefinitely, but with each cycle the material tends to become more brittle.

Thermoplastic materials have a semi-crystalline ordered structure or an amorphous random structure. Polypropylene, Nylon 66 and polycarbonate are examples of amorphous thermoplastic polymers.

Recent developments in the field of engineering polymers include the introduction of high-performance polymers, such as polyethersulphone (PES), which is amorphous, and polyetheretherketone (PEEK), which is semicrystalline. These offer properties far superior to those of the normal thermoplastic polymers.

27.1.2 Thermosetting polymers

The principal thermosetting polymers which are used in composites in construction are polyesters, epoxies and phenolics. Thermosetting polymers are formed in a two-stage chemical reaction. Firstly, a substance consisting of a series of long-chain polymerized molecules,

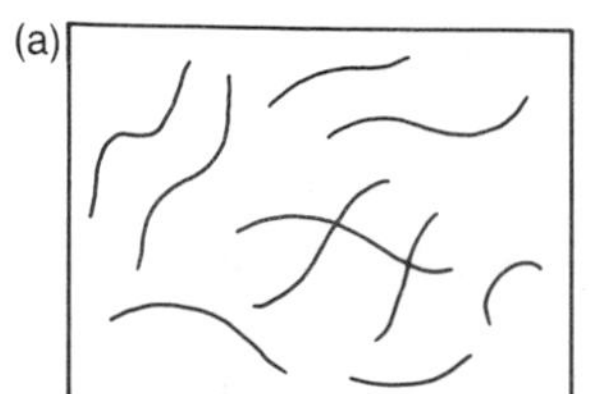

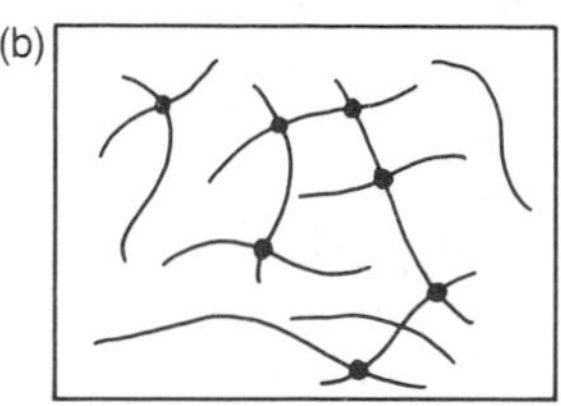

FIGURE 27.1 (a) Schematic representation of long-chain molecules of a thermoplastic polymer; (b) schematic representation of long-chain molecules of a thermosetting polymer illustrating the cross-linking.

similar to those in thermoplastics, is produced; then the chains become cross-linked. This reaction can take place either at room temperature or under the application of heat and pressure. As the cross-linking is by strong chemical bonds, thermosetting polymers are rigid materials and their mechanical properties are affected by heat. Figure 27.1(b) shows a schematic representation.

27.1.3 Foamed polymers

A rigid foam is a two-phase system of gas dispersed in solid polymer, and is produced by adding a blowing agent to molten resin. In the exothermic polymerization reaction, the gas is released and causes the polymer to expand, increasing its original volume many times by the formation of small gas cells. Like solid polymers, rigid foam polymers can be either thermoplastic or thermosetting and generally any polymer can be foamed.

27.1.4 Elastomers

Elastomers consist of long-chain polymer molecules. The chains are different from those in rigid polymers in that they are coiled and twisted randomly. The material is flexible and can undergo very large deformations, although uncured elastomers cannot recover completely from such deformations because the long chains slide past one another. To prevent this, the molecules are cross-linked by a curing process known as vulcanization; this process is similar to the one that takes place during the cross-linking of thermosetting polymers. It does not change the form of the coiled molecules so the elastomeric material will recover its original shape after the force which is causing the deformation is removed; whilst the material is under load the deformation will be large.

27.2 Fibres

When a load is applied to a fibre-reinforced composite consisting of a low-modulus matrix reinforced with high-strength, high-modulus fibres, the plastic flow of the matrix under stress transfers the load to the fibre; this results in a high-strength, high-modulus material which determines the stiffness and strength of the composite and is in the form of particles of high aspect ratio (i.e. fibres), is well dispersed and bonded by a weak secondary phase (i.e. matrix).

Many amorphous and crystalline fibres can be used, including glass, carbon and boron and fibres produced from synthetic polymers. Making a fibre involves aligning the molecules of the material and the high tensile strength is associated with improved intermolecular attraction resulting from this alignment. Polymeric fibres are made from those polymers whose chemical composition and geometry are basically crystalline and whose intermolecular forces are strong. As the extensibility of the material has already been utilized in the process of manufacture, fibres have a low elongation.

The following sections will discuss the manufacture and make-up of fibres which can be used to upgrade polymers, cements, mortars and concretes. The latter will be covered in greater detail in Chapter 32.

Glass, carbon and Kevlar fibres are used in conjunction with thermosetting polymers such as polyesters and epoxies.

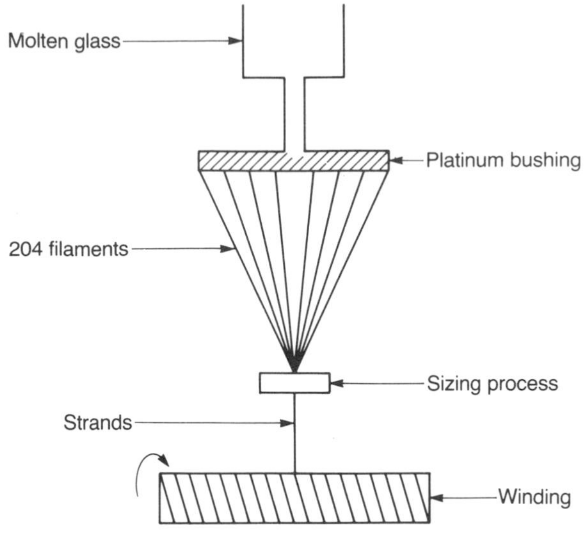

FIGURE 27.2 Schematic representation of the manufacture of glass fibre.

27.2.1 Glass fibres

Glass fibres are manufactured by drawing molten glass from an electric furnace through platinum bushings at high speed; see Figure 27.2. The filaments cool from the liquid state at about 1200°C to room temperature in 10^{-5} seconds. On emerging from the bushings the filaments are treated with a lubricant or size and 204 filaments are bundled together to form a strand. The lubricant

1. facilitates the manufacturing of the strands and moulding of the composite;
2. reduces damage to the fibres during mechanical handling;
3. reduces the abrasive effect of the filaments against one another.

The following four types of glass are used for fibres.

1. E-glass of low alkali content is the commonest glass on the market and is the major one used in composites in the construction industry. It was first used in 1942 with polyester resin and is now widely used with polyester and epoxy resin.
2. A-glass fibre of high alkali content was formerly used in the aircraft industry, but it is now little used.
3. Z-glass (zirconia glass) was developed for reinforcing cements, mortars and concretes because of its high resistance to alkali attack (see Chapter 34).
4. S2-glass fibre is used in extra-high-strength and high-modulus applications in aerospace.

Strands of glass fibre are combined to form thicker parallel bundles called rovings which, when twisted, can form several different types of yarn; rovings or yarns can be used individually or in the form of woven fabric.

Glass strands for reinforcing thermosetting polymers may be used in a number of different forms:

1. woven rovings, to provide high strength and stiffness characteristics in the direction of the fibres;
2. chopped fibres, to provide a randomly orientated dispersion of fibres in the composite;
3. chopped strand mat, to provide a quasi-isotropic reinforcement to the composite;
4. surface tissues, to provide a thin glass-fibre mat when a resin-rich surface of composite is required.

27.2.2 Carbon fibres

Carbon fibres are produced commercially as synthetic fibres similar to those used for making textiles, and from pitch, which is obtained by the destructive distillation of coal. However, carbon fibre production from pitch is not common and will not be discussed further.

The synthetic fibre polyacrylonitrile (known as PAN) is spun as a bundle of continuous filaments and concurrently is stretched so that the molecular chains are aligned parallel to the fibre axis. The PAN fibre is then heated under tension to 250°C in an oxygen environment where it absorbs energy and gains in strength. It eventually forms a black polymer containing nitrogen. Carbonization of the fibre commences when the polymer, unstressed, is heated in an inert atmosphere; the greater the heat energy given to the carbon filament, the higher is its stiffness. The mechanical properties may be modified by varying the process conditions. There are three grades of carbon fibre.

1. Type I is the stiffest and has the highest modulus of elasticity of the three. The heat treatment temperature is in excess of 2000°C.
2. Type II is the strongest and is heat treated at about 1500°C.
3. Type III is the least stiff of the three grades and has the lowest heat treatment temperature.

27.2.3 Kevlar fibres

A most successful commercial organic fibre is that developed by the Du Pont Company with the trade name Kevlar. The poly-para-benzamide fibres have a modulus of elasticity of 130 GN/m^2. There are two forms: Kevlar 29, with a high strength and intermediate modulus; and Kevlar 49, with a high modulus and the same strength as Kevlar 29. Table 27.2 gives the mechanical properties of the two fibres. Kevlar 49 is preferred for high-performance composite materials.

The fibre is produced by an extrusion and spinning process. A solution of the polymer in a suitable solvent at a temperature between −50°C and −80°C is extruded into a hot walled cylinder at 200°C; this causes the solvent to evaporate and the resulting fibre is wound on to a bobbin. The fibre then undergoes a stretching and drawing process to increase its strength and stiffness.

27.2.4 Other synthetic fibres

The most important fibres for upgrading cements and mortars or for use in reinforced earth situations are polypropylene, polyethylene, polyester and polyamide. The first two are utilized in the manufacture of cement/mortar composites and are discussed further in Chapter 34, but all four are used in geosynthetics, especially to form geotextiles and geogrids as described in Chapter 31. Synthetic fibres are the only ones which can be engineered chemically, physically and mechanically to suit particular geotechnical engineering applications. Natural fibres (e.g. cotton, jute) and the majority of regenerated fibres (e.g. cellulose, rayon) are seldom used to make geotextiles because they are biodegradable; however, geotextiles made from natural fibres and even paper (another fibrous product) may serve temporary functions where biodegradation is desirable (e.g. temporary erosion control).

Manufacture begins with the transformation of the raw polymer from solid to liquid either by dissolving or melting. Synthetic polymers such as acrylic, modacrylic, aramid and vinylad-polymers are dissolved into solution, whereas the polyolefin and polyester polymers are transformed into molten liquid; chlorofibre polymers can be transformed into a liquid by either means. A spinneret consisting of many holes is used to extend the liquid polymer which is then solidified into continuous filaments.

The filaments undergo further extension in their longitudinal axes; thus further increasing the orientation of the molecular chain within the filament structure, with a consequent improvement in the stress–strain characteristics. Different types of synthetic fibre or yarn may be produced, including monofilament fibres, heterofilament fibres, multifilament yarns, staple fibres, staple yarns, split-film tapes and fibrillated yarns.

27.3 Processing of thermoplastic polymers

Thermoplastic polymers may readily be processed into sheets or rods or complex shapes in one operation, which is often automated. Stages such as heating, shaping and cooling will ideally be a single event or a repeated cycle. The principal processing methods are extrusion, injection moulding, thermoforming and calendering.

The first is the most important method from the civil engineering viewpoint, and this is therefore outlined below. Powder or granules of thermoplastic polymer are fed from a hopper to a rotating screw inside a heated barrel; the screw depth is reduced along the barrel so that the material is compacted. At the end of the barrel the melt passes through a die to produce the desired finished article. Changing the die allows a wide range of products to be made, such as:

1. profile products;
2. film-blown plastic sheet;
3. blow-moulded hollow plastic articles;
4. co-extruded items;
5. highly orientated grid sheets.

Profile production

With different extrusion dies, many profiles can be manufactured, such as edging strips, pipes, window-frames, etc. However, success depends upon the correct design of the die.

Film-blown plastic sheet

Molten plastic from the extruder passes through an annular die to form a thin tube; a supply of air inside the tube prevents collapse and when the film is cooled it passes through collapsing guides and nip rolls and is stored on drums. Biaxial orientation of the molecules of the polymer can be achieved by varying the air pressure in the polymer tube, which in turn controls the circumferential orientation. Longitudinal orientation can be achieved by varying the relative speeds of the nip roll and the linear velocity of the bubble; this is known as draw-down.

Blow-moulded hollow plastic articles

A molten polymer tube, the Parison, is extruded through an annular die. A mould closes round the Parison and internal pressure forces the polymer against the sides of the mould. This method is used to form such articles as bottles and cold water storage tanks. The materials commonly used are polypropylene, polyethylene and PET.

Co-extrusion

A multilayered plastic composite is sometimes needed to withstand the end use requirements. Two or more polymers are combined in a single process by film blowing with an adhesive film between them. Reactive bonding processes to chemically cross-link the polymers are under development.

Highly orientated grid sheets

Polymer grids are used in civil engineering as the reinforcement to soil in reinforced earth. Continuous sheets of thermoplastic polymers, generally polypropylene or polyethylene, are extruded to very fine tolerances and with a controlled structure. A pattern of holes is stamped out in the sheet and the stampings are saved for re-use. The perforated sheet is stretched in the longitudinal and then in the transverse direction to give a highly orientated polymer in the two directions with a tensile strength similar to that of mild steel. The low original stiffness of the material can be increased ten-fold. The stiffness of unorientated high-density polyethylene (HDPE), for instance, is initially only 1 GPa and after forming into an orientated molecular structure it increases to 10 GPa. Chapter 31 discusses how these sheets are used in geosynthetics.

In injection moulding, softened thermoplastic polymer is forced through a nozzle into a clamped cold mould. When the plastic becomes cold, the mould is opened and the article is ejected; the operation is then repeated.

27.4 Mechanical properties

27.4.1 Polymer properties

The physical and mechanical properties of thermosetting resins, specifically polyesters and epoxies, can vary greatly. As mentioned in Section 27.1.2, thermosetting polymers are cross-linked and form a tightly bound three-dimensional network of polymer chains; the mechanical properties are highly dependent upon the network of molecular units and upon the lengths of cross-link chains. The characteristics of the network units are a function of the chemicals used and the length of the cross-linked chains is determined by the curing process. It is usual to cure composites by heating to achieve optimum cross-linking and hence to enable the mechanical properties to realize their potential. Shrinkage during curing does occur, particularly with polyesters, and contraction on cooling to ambient temperature can lead to stress build-up. This latter problem is due to the differences between the thermal expansion coefficients of the matrix and fibre, and it can have a major effect on the internal microstresses which are sometimes sufficient to produce micropacking, even in the absence of external loads.

Thermoplastic polymers which are not cross-linked derive their strength and stiffness from the properties of the monomer units and the high molecular weight. Consequently, in crystalline thermoplastic polymers there is a high degree of molecular order and alignment, and during any heating the crystalline phase will tend to melt and to form an amorphous viscous liquid. In amorphous thermoplastic polymers, there is a high degree of molecular entanglement so that they act like a cross-linked material. On heating, the molecules become disentangled and the polymer changes from a rigid solid to a viscous liquid.

Table 27.1 gives the most important mechanical properties of thermosetting and thermoplastic polymers.

27.4.2 Time-dependent characteristics

Polymer materials exhibit a time-dependent strain response to a constant applied stress; this behaviour is called creep. Conversely, if the stress on a polymer is removed it exhibits a strain recovery. Figure 27.3 illustrates the total creep curve for a polymer under a given uniaxial tensile stress at constant temperature; the graph can be divided into five regions. When a polymer is subjected to a constant tensile stress, its strain increases until the material fails. This failure point depends on the level of stress, and as the material approaches failure creep rupture occurs. The designer must be aware of this failure mode and realize that polymers, which

TABLE 27.1 Mechanical properties of common thermosetting and thermoplastic polymers

Material properties	*Specific weight*	*Ultimate tensile strength MPa*	*Modulus of elasticity in tension GPa*	*Coefficient of linear expansion 10^{-6}/°C*
Thermosetting				
Polyester	1.28	45–90	2.5–4.0	100–110
Epoxy	1.30	90–110	3.0–7.0	45–65
Phenolic (with filler)	1.35–1.75	45–59	5.5–8.3	30–45
Thermoplastics				
Polyvinyl chloride (PVC)	1.37	58.0	2.4–2.8	50
Acrylonitrile butadiene styrene (ABS)	1.05	17–62	0.69–2.82	60–130
Nylon	1.13–1.15	48–83	1.03–2.76	80–150
Polyethylene (high-density)	0.96	30–35	1.10–1.30	120

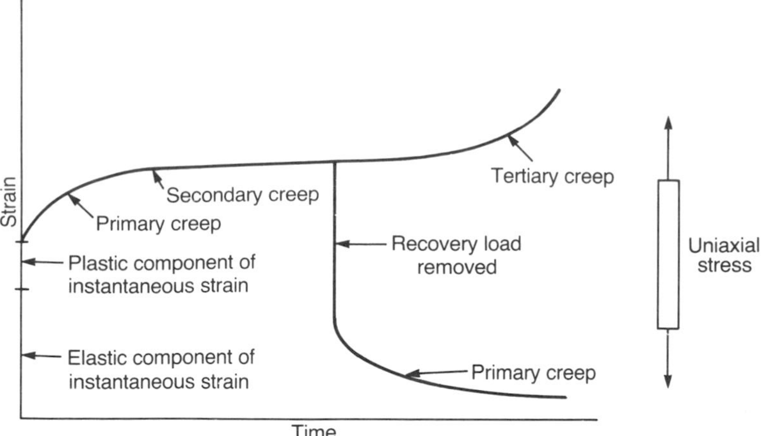

FIGURE 27.3 Total creep curve for a polymer under a given uniaxial stress state.

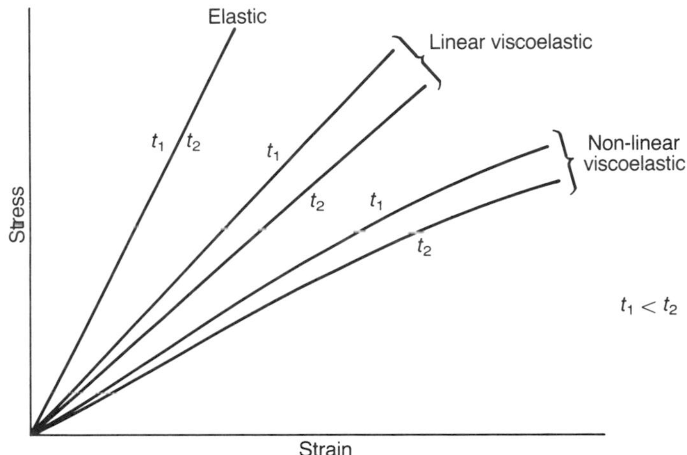

FIGURE 27.4 Stress–strain behaviour of elastic and viscoelastic materials at two values of time.

are tough under short static loads, may become embrittled under long-term loading.

A further important consequence of the time-dependent behaviour of polymers is that when they are subjected to a particular strain, the stress necessary to maintain this strain decreases with time.

Polymer materials have mechanical properties which lie somewhere between the ideal Hookean material, where stress is proportional to strain, and the Newtonian material, where stress is proportional to rate of strain. They are termed 'viscoelastic' materials and their stress is a function of strain and time, as described by the equation:

$$\sigma = f(\varepsilon, t).$$

This non-linear viscoelastic behaviour can be simplified for design purposes:

$$\sigma = \varepsilon . f(t).$$

This linear viscoelastic response indicates

that, under sustained tensile stress, after a particular time interval the stress is directly proportional to strain. Figure 27.4 describes the various types of response discussed above.

Short-term tensile tests are commonly used to characterize metals. However, they must be treated with caution when testing polymers. It is possible to obtain quite different results by changing, for instance, the rate of extension of the specimen under a tensile force. At high rates of strain an unplasticized PVC will show brittle characteristics and relatively high modulus and strength, whereas at low rates of strain the material will be ductile and have a lower modulus and strength. Consequently, the test conditions must be consistent with the service condition for which the material is being designed.

Creep tests are often used to measure the deformational behaviour of polymeric materials. The variation of strain with time, when the specimen is under constant load, is usually recorded on a logarithmic timescale so that the time dependence for long periods can be extrapolated if necessary. Figure 27.5 represents a typical relationship between strain and time; a family of curves may be obtained for different stress levels. Figure 27.6 shows the relationship drawn on a logarithmic timescale.

Figure 27.7(a) shows a family of strain–time graphs for a typical non-linear polymer. From

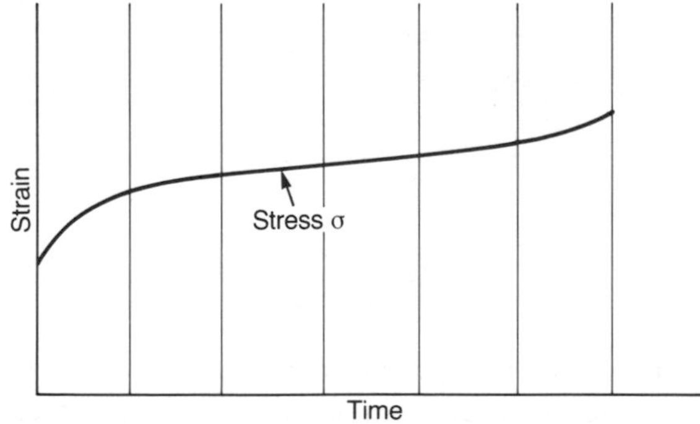

FIGURE 27.5 Typical relationship for a linear viscoelastic material.

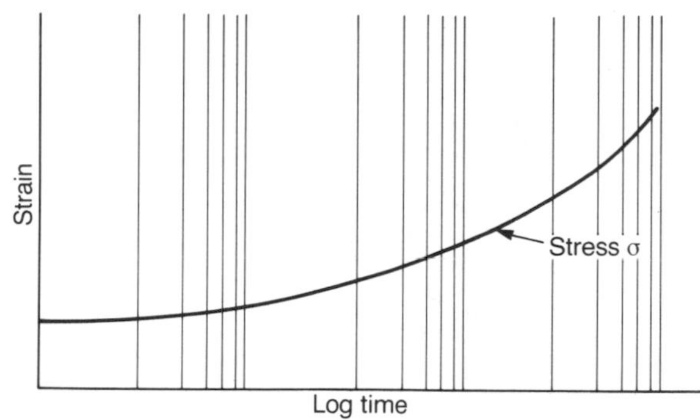

FIGURE 27.6 Typical relationship for a linear viscoelastic material drawn on a logarithmic timescale.

this, it is clear that the higher the stress applied to the polymer, the higher is the creep rate. Replotted as a stress–time relationship, Figure 27.7(b) represents the relaxation of stress in the polymer at constant strain; this is termed an isometric graph. If the stresses at a particular time *t* on the creep curve are divided by the respective strain values, then the modulus of elasticity–time curve is shown in Figure 27.7(c). Finally, if at time *t* the stress values are plotted against the respective strain values, an isochronous graph, Figure 27.7(d), results. Isochronous data are often represented on log–log scales; the graph will generally be a straight line and its slope will indicate the degree of nonlinearity of the polymer material; a slope of 45° represents a linear material, whereas a nonlinear material will have a slope less than 45°.

27.4.3 Fibre properties

The advantage of composite materials over conventional ones is that they have high specific strength and high specific stiffness, achieved by the use of low-density fibres with high strength and modulus values. The strength and stiffness values of carbon, glass and Kevlar fibres are given in Table 27.2.

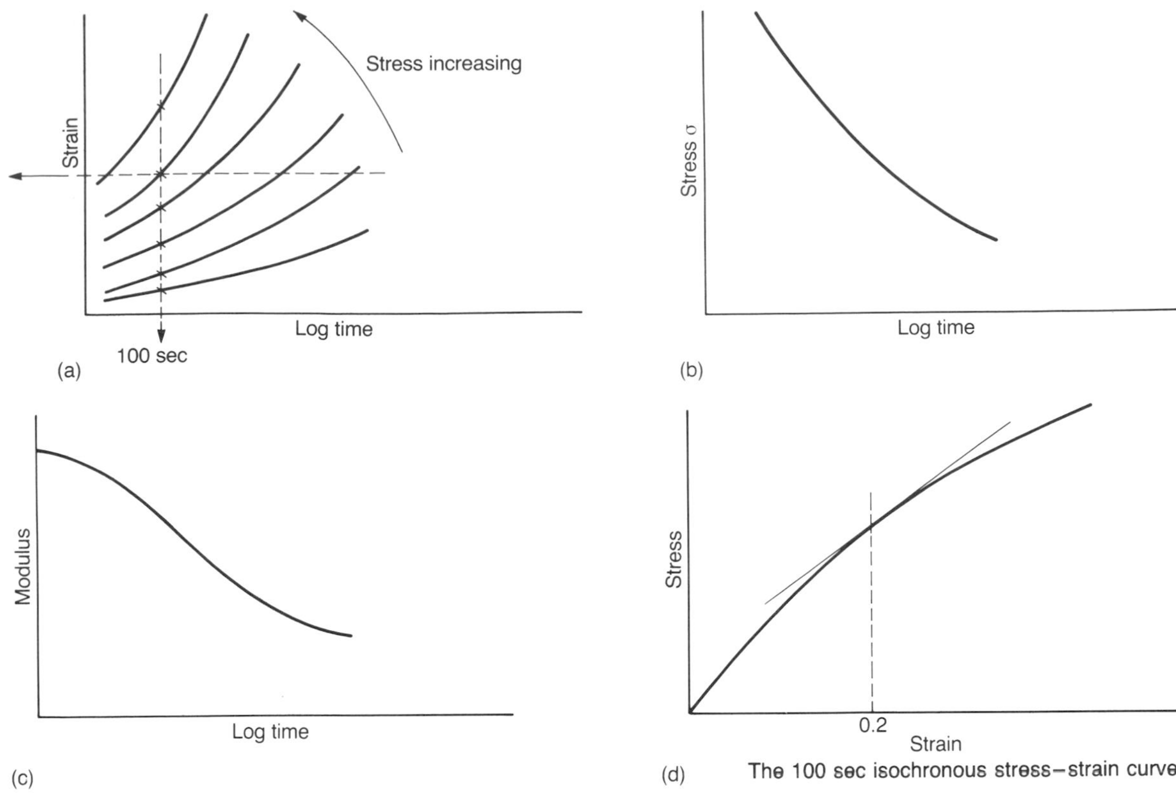

FIGURE 27.7 Typical creep curves for a non-linear viscoelastic material for varying stress values. Isometric and isochronous stress–strain curves.

TABLE 27.2 Mechanical properties of common fibres

Material properties	*Specific weight*	*Ultimate tensile strength (GPa)*	*Modulus of elasticity in tension (GPa)*
Carbon fibre			
Type I	1.92	2.00	345
Type II	1.75	2.41	241
Type III	1.70	2.21	200
E-glass fibre	2.55	2.4	72.4
S2-glass fibre	2.47	4.6	88.0
Kevlar fibres			
29	1.44	2.65	64
49	1.45	2.65	127

It has been stated that there are three types of carbon fibre: the high-modulus, the high-strength and the intermediate-modulus fibre. The degree of alignment of the small crystalline units in the fibres varies considerably with the manufacturing technique, which thus affects the stiffness of the fibre. The arrangement of the layer planes in the cross-section of the

TABLE 27.3 Typical mechanical properties for glass-reinforced polymer composites

Material	*Glass content (weight %)*	*Specific gravity*	*Tensile modulus (GPa)*	*Tensile strength (MPa)*
Unidirectional rovings (filament winding or pultrusion)	50–80	1.6–2.0	20–50	400–1250
Hand lay-up with chopped strand mat	25–45	1.4–1.6	6–11	60–180
Matched dye moulding with preform	25–50	1.4–1.6	6–12	60–200
Hand lay-up with woven rovings	45–62	1.5–1.8	12–24	200–350
DMC polyester (filled)	15–20	1.7–2.0	6–8	40–60
SMC	20–25	1.75–1.95	9–13	60–100

fibre is also important, because it affects the transverse and shear properties. Table 27.2 gives the principal mechanical properties of these fibres and illustrates this point.

The strength and modulus of elasticity of glass fibres are determined by the three-dimensional structure of the constituent oxides which can be of calcium, boron, sodium, iron or aluminium. The structure of the network and the strength of the individual bonds can be varied by the addition of other metal oxides and so it is possible to produce glass fibres with different chemical and physical properties. Unlike carbon fibres the properties of glass fibres are isotropic and the modulus of elasticity is the same along and across the fibre.

The main factors which determine the ultimate strength of glass fibres are the processing condition and the damage sustained during handling and processing. The mechanical properties of two types of glass fibre are given in Table 27.2.

The manufacturing processes for Kevlar fibres align the stiff polymer molecules parallel to the fibre axes, and the high modulus achieved indicates that a high degree of alignment is possible. Typical properties of Kevlar fibres are given in Table 27.2. When the fibres have been incorporated into a matrix material, composite action takes place and as discussed in the next chapter, a knowledge of the fibre alignment, fibre volume fraction and method of manufacture is necessary to obtain the mechanical characteristic of the material. To illustrate this, Table 27.3 gives the tensile characteristics of the different systems of GRP composites; the various methods of manufacture of the composites are given in Chapter 29.

Chapter twenty-eight

Polymer composites

28.1 Characterization and definition of composite materials
28.2 Elastic properties and continuous unidirectional laminae
28.3 Elastic properties of in-plane random long-fibre laminae
28.4 Macro-analysis of stress distribution in a fibre/matrix composite
28.5 Elastic properties of short-fibre composite materials
28.6 Laminate theory
28.7 Isotropic lamina
28.8 Orthotropic lamina
28.9 The strength characteristics and failure criteria of composite laminae
28.10 References

28.1 Characterization and definition of composite materials

The mechanical properties of polymcrs can be greatly enhanced by incorporating fillers and/or fibres into the resin formulations. Therefore, for structural application, such composite materials should:

1. consist of two or more phases, each with their own physical and mechanical characteristics;
2. be manufactured by combining the separate phases such that the dispersion of one material in the other achieves optimum properties of the resulting material;
3. have enhanced properties compared with those of the individual components.

In fibre-reinforced polymer materials, the primary phase (the fibre) uses the plastic flow of the secondary phase (the polymer) to transfer the load to the fibre; this results in a high-strength, high-modulus composite. Fibres generally have both high strength and high modulus but these properties are only associated with very fine fibres with diameters of the order of 7–15 μm; they tend to be brittle. Polymers, however, may be either ductile or brittle and will generally have low strength and stiffness. By combining the two components a bulk material is produced with a strength and stiffness dependent upon the fibre volume fraction and the fibre orientation.

The properties of fibre/matrix composite materials are highly dependent upon the microstructural parameters such as;

1. fibre diameter;
2. fibre length;
3. fibre volume fraction of the composite;
4. fibre orientation and packing arrangement.

It is important to characterize these parameters when considering the processing of the composite material and the efficient design and manufacture of the composite made from these materials.

The interface between the fibre and the matrix plays a major role in the physical and mechanical properties of the composite material. The transfer of stresses between fibre and fibre takes place through the interface and the matrix and in the analysis of composite materials a certain number of assumptions are made to enable solutions to mathematical models to be obtained:

1. the matrix and the fibre behave as elastic materials;
2. the bond between the fibre and the matrix is perfect and consequently there will be no strain discontinuity across the interface;
3. the material adjacent to the fibre has the same properties as the material in bulk form;
4. the fibres are arranged in a regular or repeating array.

The properties of the interface region are very important in understanding the stressed composite. The region is a dominant factor in the fracture toughness of the material and in its resistance to aqueous and corrosive environments. Composite materials which have weak interfaces have low strength and stiffness but high resistance to fracture, and those with strong interfaces have high strength and stiffness but are very brittle. This effect is a function of the ease of debonding and pull-out of the fibres from the matrix material during crack propagation.

Using the above assumptions, it is possible to calculate the distribution of stress and strain in a composite material in terms of the geometry of the component materials.

28.2 Elastic properties of continuous unidirectional laminae

Longitudinal stiffness

A basic laminate is shown in Figure 28.1 and it is assumed that the orthotropic layer has three mutually perpendicular planes of property symmetry; it is characterized elastically by four independent elastic constants (refer to Section 28.6 and to Section 28.8, Figure 28.5). They are:

E_{11} = modulus of elasticity along fibre direction

E_{22} = modulus of elasticity in the transverse direction

ν_{12} = Poisson's ratio, i.e. strains produced in direction 2 when specimen is loaded in direction 1

G_{12} = longitudinal shear modulus

ν_{21} = Poisson's ratio, i.e. obtained from the equation $E_{11}\nu_{21} = E_{22}\nu_{12}$

If the line of action of a tensile or compressive force is applied parallel to the fibres of a unidirectional lamina, the strain ε_m in the matrix will be equal to the strain ε_f in the fibre, provided the bond between the two components

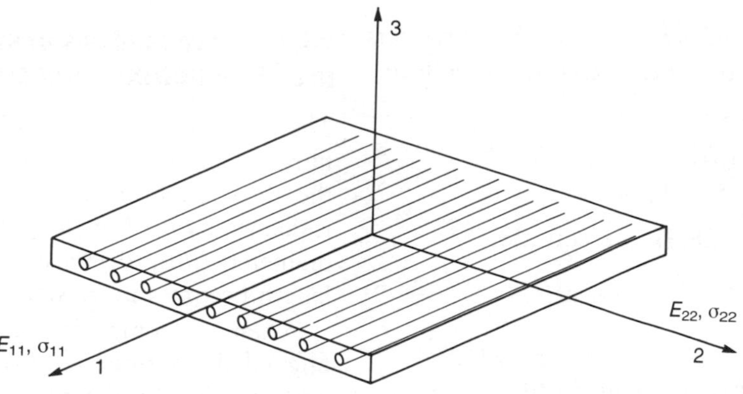

FIGURE 28.1 Basic laminate.

is perfect. As both fibre and matrix behave elastically then:

$$\sigma_f = E_f\varepsilon_f \text{ and } \sigma_m = E_m\varepsilon_m \text{ where } \varepsilon_f = \varepsilon_m.$$

As $E_f > E_m$ the stress in the fibre must be greater than the stress in the matrix and will therefore bear the major part of the applied load.

The composite load $P_c = P_m + P_f$ or

$$\sigma_c A_c = \sigma_m A_m + \sigma_f A_f$$
$$\sigma_c = \sigma_m V_m + \sigma_f V_f \quad (28.1)$$

where A = the area of the phase, V = the volume fraction of the phase with $V_c = 1$, V_c = the volume of composite.

As the bond is perfect

$$\varepsilon_c = \varepsilon_m = \varepsilon_f$$

from eqn (28.1)

$$E_c\varepsilon_c = E_m\varepsilon_c V_m + E_f\varepsilon_c V_f \quad (28.2)$$
$$E_c = E_m V_m + E_f V_f$$
$$E_c = E_{11} = E_m(1 - V_f) + E_f V_f. \quad (28.3)$$

This equation is often referred to as a law of mixtures equation.

Transverse stiffness

The same approach can be used to obtain the transverse modulus of a unidirectional lamina E_{22}.

The applied load transverse to the fibres acts equally on the fibre and matrix and therefore

$$\sigma_f = \sigma_m$$
$$\varepsilon_f = \sigma_{22}/E_f \text{ and } \varepsilon_m = \sigma_{22}/E_m \quad (28.4)$$
$$\varepsilon_{22} = V_f\varepsilon_f + V_m\varepsilon_m \quad (28.5)$$

Substituting eqn (28.4) into eqn (28.5)

$$\varepsilon_{22} = V_f\sigma_{22}/E_f + V_m\sigma_{22}/E_m \quad (28.6)$$

Substituting

$$\sigma_{22} = E_{22}\varepsilon_{22} \text{ into eqn (28.6)}$$
$$E_{22} = E_f E_m/[E_f(1 - V_f) + E_m V_f] \quad (28.7)$$

Equation (28.7) predicts E_{22} with reasonable agreement when compared with experimental results. The eqn (28.8) has been proposed and takes account of Poisson contraction effects.

$$E_{22} = E'_m E_f/[E_f(1 - V_f) + V_f E'_m] \quad (28.8)$$

where

$$E'_m = E_m/(1 - \nu_m^2).$$

28.3 Elastic properties of in-plane random long-fibre laminae

Laminae manufactured from long randomly orientated fibres in a polymer matrix are, on a microscopic scale, isotropic in the plane of the lamina. The general expression (the proof is given in Hollaway (1989)) for the elastic modulus of laminae consisting of long fibres is:

$$1/(E_\theta) = (1/E_{11})(\cos^4\theta) + (1/E_{22})(\sin^4\theta) + [(1/G_{12}) - (2\nu_{12}/E_{11})]\cos^2\theta\sin^2\theta \quad (28.9)$$

where θ = angle defining the direction of required stiffness. Figure 28.2 shows the relationship of E_θ when angle θ varies between 0° and 90°.

It can be seen then that laminae can be made with predetermined fibre orientation distribution so that elastic and other mechanical properties can be designed to meet specific needs.

28.4 Macro-analysis of stress distribution in a fibre/matrix composite

The behaviour of composites reinforced with fibres of finite length l cannot be described by the above equations. As the aspect ratio, which is defined by the fibre length divided by the fibre diameter (l/d), decreases, the effect of fibre length becomes more significant.

When a composite containing uniaxially aligned discontinuous fibres is stressed in tension parallel to the fibre direction there is a portion at the end of each finite fibre length, and

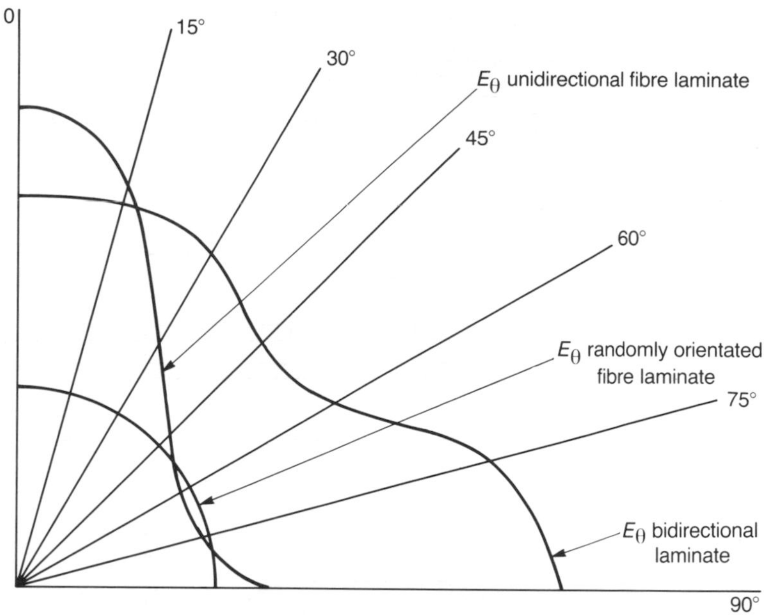

FIGURE 28.2 Orientation dependence of the modulus of elasticity of a fibre/matrix composite.

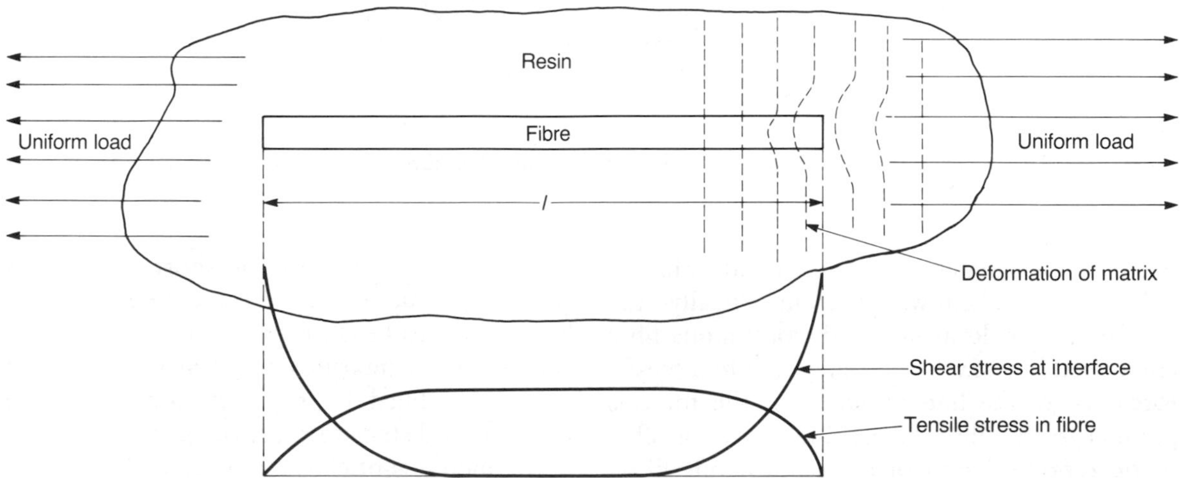

FIGURE 28.3 Diagrammatic representation of the deformation field around a discontinuous fibre embedded in a matrix.

in the surrounding matrix, where the stress and strain fields are modified by the discontinuity. The efficiency of the fibre to stiffen and to reinforce the matrix decreases as the fibre length decreases. The critical transfer length over which the fibre stress is decreased from the maximum value, under a given lamina load, to zero at the end of the fibre is referred to as half the critical length of the fibre. To achieve the maximum fibre stress, the fibre length must be

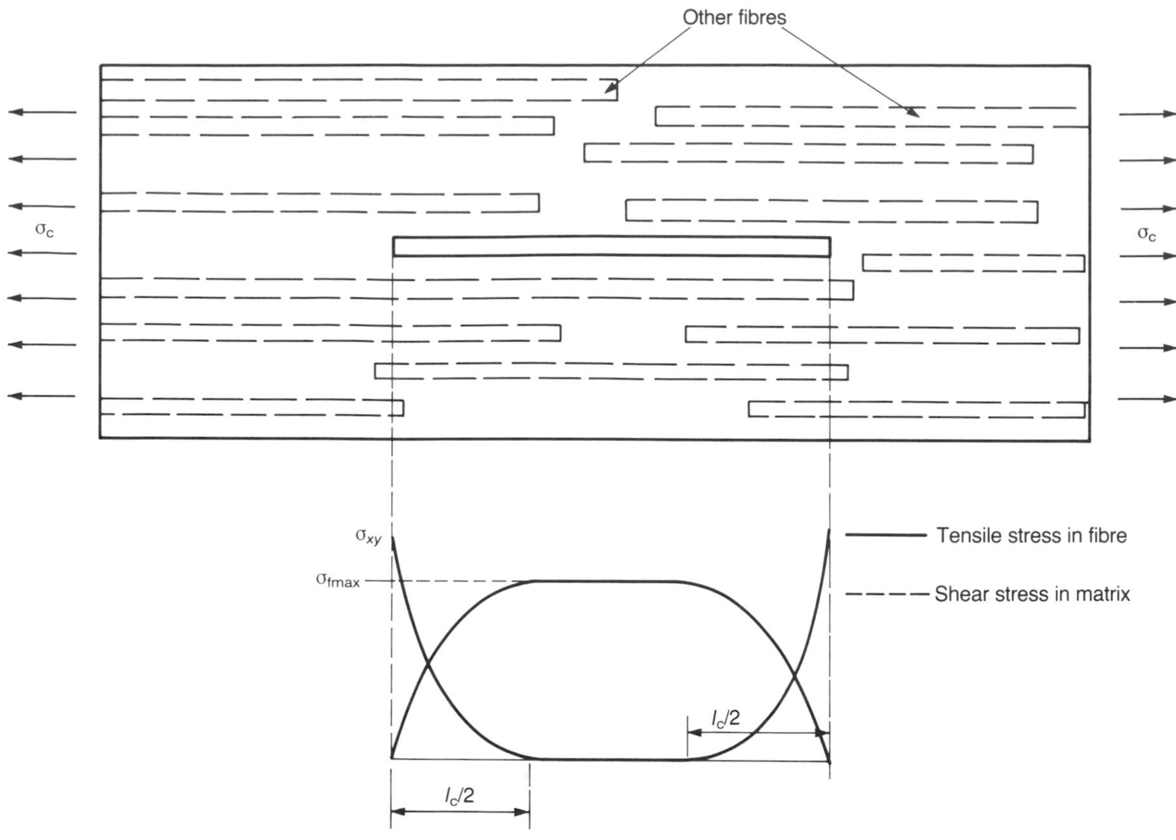

FIGURE 28.4 Schematic representation of an aligned, discontinuous fibre composite subjected to an axial stress; stress distribution at failure is shown.

equal to or greater than the critical value l_c.

Figure 28.3 shows diagrammatically the deformation field around a discontinuous fibre embedded in a matrix and subjected to a tensile force where the line of action of the force is parallel to the fibre. Figure 28.4 shows a schematic representation of a discontinuous fibre/matrix lamina subjected to an axial stress; the stress distributions of the tensile and shear components are shown.

28.5 Elastic properties of short-fibre composite materials

As discussed above the reinforcing efficiency of short fibres is less than that for long fibres. In addition the orientation of short fibres in a lamina is random and therefore the lamina can be assumed to be isotropic on a macro scale.

The rule of mixtures as given in eqn (28.3) can be modified by the inclusion of a fibre orientation distribution factor η, thus the composite modulus of elasticity is given by

$$E_c = E_{11} = \eta E_f V_f + E_m V_m. \quad (28.10)$$

Values of η have been calculated by Krenchel (1964) for different fibre orientations

η = 0.375 for a randomly orientated fibre array
 = 1.0 for unidirectional laminae when tested parallel to the fibre

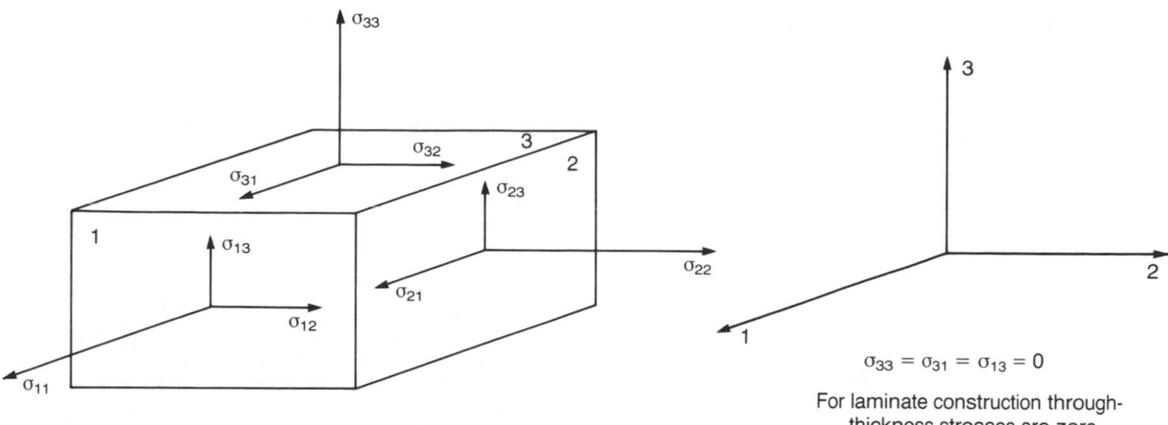

FIGURE 28.5 Components of stress acting on an elemental unit cube.

= 0 for unidirectional laminae when tested perpendicularly to the fibre
= 0.5 for a bidirectional fibre array.

The following sections within Chapter 28 are important for a complete understanding of composite theory and you may find that you have to go back to study them in more detail after the first reading.

28.6 Laminate theory

The Sections 28.2, 28.3, 28.4 and 28.5 discussed the individual lamina properties; this section concentrates upon laminates which are formed when two or more laminae are combined to produce a composite. It describes the methods used to calculate the elastic properties of the laminates, and briefly introduces the elasticity theory.

The stresses at a point in a body are generally represented by stress components acting on the surface of a cube; Figure 28.5 shows the three normal and the three shear stresses. The notation employed here is such that the first subscript refers to the plane upon which the stress acts and the second subscript is the coordinate direction in which the stress acts; the equivalent strains have the same notation. As laminae are assumed to be sufficiently thin the through-thickness stresses are zero. Thus $\sigma_{33} = \sigma_{31} = \sigma_{13} = 0$ and plane stress conditions hold.

28.7 Isotropic lamina

For homogeneous isotropic lamina the stress–strain relationship for a lamina and laminates is:

$$\begin{aligned}\sigma_{11} &= (E/(1-\nu^2))(\varepsilon_{11}+\nu\varepsilon_{22})\\ \sigma_{22} &= (E/(1-\nu^2))(\varepsilon_{22}+\nu\varepsilon_{11})\\ \sigma_{12} &= (E/2(1+\nu))(\varepsilon_{12}) \qquad (28.11a)\end{aligned}$$

or in matrix form

$$\begin{bmatrix}\sigma_{11}\\ \sigma_{22}\\ \sigma_{12}\end{bmatrix} = \begin{bmatrix}Q_{11} & Q_{12} & 0\\ Q_{21} & Q_{22} & 0\\ 0 & 0 & Q_{33}\end{bmatrix}\begin{bmatrix}\varepsilon_{11}\\ \varepsilon_{22}\\ \varepsilon_{12}\end{bmatrix}$$

$$[\sigma] = [Q][\varepsilon] \qquad (28.11b)$$

where

$$\begin{aligned}Q_{11} &= E/(1-\nu^2) = Q_{22}\\ Q_{12} &= \nu E/(1-\nu^2) = Q_{21}\\ Q_{33} &= E/2(1+\nu) = G.\end{aligned}$$

There are two independent constants in these equations; these are E and ν and this indicates isotropic material properties.

The corresponding set of equations to those

in eqn (28.11b), which relate strains to stresses, are:

$$\begin{bmatrix}\varepsilon_{11}\\ \varepsilon_{22}\\ \varepsilon_{12}\end{bmatrix} = \begin{bmatrix}S_{11} & S_{12} & 0\\ S_{21} & S_{22} & 0\\ 0 & 0 & S_{33}\end{bmatrix}\begin{bmatrix}\sigma_{11}\\ \sigma_{22}\\ \sigma_{12}\end{bmatrix} \quad (28.12a)$$

$$[\varepsilon] = [S][\sigma] \quad (28.12b)$$

where

$$S_{11} = 1/E = S_{22}$$
$$S_{33} = 1/G$$
$$S_{12} = -\nu/E$$

28.8 Orthotropic lamina

The orthotropic lamina can be assumed to be isotropic in plane 1, as shown in Figure 28.5 (i.e. the plane normal to the axis direction 1), as the properties are independent of direction in that plane. The stress–strain relationship for an orthotropic lamina is

$$\sigma_{11} = [E_{11}/(1 - \nu_{12}\nu_{21})][\varepsilon_{11} + \nu_{21}\varepsilon_{22}]$$
$$\sigma_{22} = [E_{22}/(1 - \nu_{12}\nu_{21})][\varepsilon_{22} + \nu_{12}\varepsilon_{11}]$$
$$\sigma_{12} = G_{12}\varepsilon_{12} \quad (28.13a)$$

or in matrix form

$$\begin{bmatrix}\sigma_{11}\\ \sigma_{22}\\ \sigma_{12}\end{bmatrix} = \begin{bmatrix}Q_{11} & Q_{12} & 0\\ Q_{21} & Q_{22} & 0\\ 0 & 0 & Q_{33}\end{bmatrix}\begin{bmatrix}\varepsilon_{11}\\ \varepsilon_{22}\\ \varepsilon_{12}\end{bmatrix}$$

$$[\sigma] = [Q][\varepsilon] \quad (28.13b)$$

where

$Q_{11} = E_{11}/(1 - \nu_{12}\nu_{21})$; $Q_{22} = E_{22}/(1 - \nu_{12}\nu_{21})$
$Q_{12} = \nu_{21}E_{11}/(1 - \nu_{12}\nu_{21})$; $Q_{21} = \nu_{12}E_{22}/(1 - \nu_{12}\nu_{21})$
$Q_{33} = G_{12}$.

As the Q matrix is symmetric we have $\nu_{21}E_{11} = \nu_{12}E_{22}$. The Poisson's ratio ν_{12} refers to the strains produced in direction 2 when the lamina is loaded in direction 1.

There are four independent constants in these equations; these are E_{11}, E_{22}, ν_{12} and ν_{21} and this indicates orthotropic material properties.

From the above equation it can be seen that the shear stress σ_{12} is independent of the elastic properties E_{11}, E_{22}, ν_{12}, ν_{21}, and therefore no coupling between tensile and shear strains takes place.

The corresponding set of equations to those in eqn (28.13b) which relate strains to stresses are:

$$\begin{bmatrix}\varepsilon_{11}\\ \varepsilon_{22}\\ \varepsilon_{12}\end{bmatrix} = \begin{bmatrix}S_{11} & S_{12} & 0\\ S_{21} & S_{22} & 0\\ 0 & 0 & S_{33}\end{bmatrix}\begin{bmatrix}\sigma_{11}\\ \sigma_{22}\\ \sigma_{12}\end{bmatrix} \quad (28.14a)$$

$$[\varepsilon] = [S][\sigma] \quad (28.14b)$$

where

$S_{11} = 1/E_{11}$; $S_{33} = 1/G_{12}$
$S_{22} = 1/E_{22}$; $S_{12} = -\nu_{21}/E_{22} = -\nu_{12}/E_{11}$.

If the line of application of the load is along some axis other than the principal one, then the lamina principal axes do not coincide with the reference axes x, y of the load and the former axes must be transformed to the reference axes. Figure 28.6 illustrates the orientation of the orthotropic lamina about the reference axis.

Hollaway (1989) shows that the stress–strain relationship in the (x, y) coordinate system at an angle θ to the principal material direction becomes:

$$\begin{bmatrix}\sigma_{xx}\\ \sigma_{yy}\\ \sigma_{xy}\end{bmatrix} = \begin{bmatrix}\bar{Q}_{11} & \bar{Q}_{12} & \bar{Q}_{13}\\ \bar{Q}_{21} & \bar{Q}_{22} & \bar{Q}_{23}\\ \bar{Q}_{31} & \bar{Q}_{32} & \bar{Q}_{33}\end{bmatrix}\begin{bmatrix}\varepsilon_{xx}\\ \varepsilon_{yy}\\ \varepsilon_{xy}\end{bmatrix} \quad (28.15a)$$

or

$$\begin{bmatrix}\sigma_{xx}\\ \sigma_{yy}\\ \sigma_{xy}\end{bmatrix} = [\bar{Q}]\begin{bmatrix}\varepsilon_{xx}\\ \varepsilon_{yy}\\ \varepsilon_{xy}\end{bmatrix} \quad (28.15b)$$

where

$$\bar{Q}_{11} = Q_{11}m^4 + Q_{22}n^4 + 2(Q_{12} + 2Q_{33})n^2m^2$$
$$\bar{Q}_{12} = \bar{Q}_{21} = (Q_{11} + Q_{22} - 4Q_{33})n^2m^2 + Q_{12}(n^4 + m^4)$$
$$\bar{Q}_{13} = \bar{Q}_{31} = (Q_{11} - Q_{12} - 2Q_{33})nm^3 + (Q_{12} - Q_{22} + 2Q_{33})n^3m$$

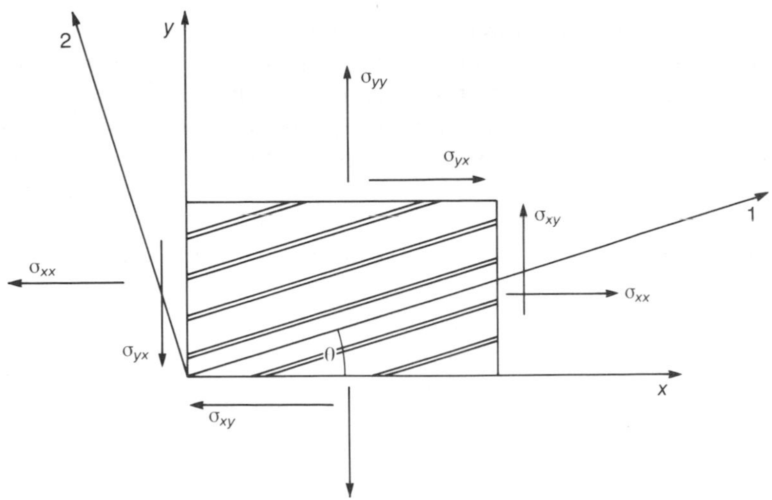

FIGURE 28.6 Orientation of orthotropic lamina about reference axis.

$$\bar{Q}_{22} = Q_{11}n^4 + Q_{22}m^4 + 2(Q_{12} + 2Q_{33})n^2m^2$$
$$\bar{Q}_{23} = \bar{Q}_{32} = (Q_{11} - Q_{12} - 2Q_{33})n^3m + (Q_{12} - Q_{22} + 2Q_{33})nm^3$$
$$\bar{Q}_{33} = (Q_{11} + Q_{22} - 2Q_{12} - 2Q_{33})n^2m^2 + Q_{33}(n^4 + m^4)$$

where Q_{11}, Q_{22}, Q_{12}, Q_{21} and Q_{33} have been defined in eqn (28.13b) and $m = \cos\theta$, $n = \sin\theta$ and the equivalent expression for strain components in the reference axis x, y in terms of the stress components in that axis become:

$$\begin{bmatrix} \varepsilon_{xx} \\ \varepsilon_{yy} \\ \varepsilon_{xy} \end{bmatrix} = [\bar{S}] \begin{bmatrix} \sigma_{xx} \\ \sigma_{yy} \\ \sigma_{xy} \end{bmatrix} \tag{28.16}$$

where $[\bar{S}]$ is a 3×3 compliance matrix where the components are:

$$\bar{S}_{11} = S_{11}m^4 + S_{22}n^4 + (2S_{12} + S_{33})n^2m^2$$
$$\bar{S}_{12} = \bar{S}_{21} = S_{12}(n^4 + m^4) + (S_{11} + S_{22} - S_{33})n^2m^2$$
$$\bar{S}_{13} = S_{31} = 2(S_{11} - 2S_{12} - S_{33})nm^3 - (2S_{22} - S_{12} - S_{33})n^3m$$
$$\bar{S}_{23} = S_{32} = (2S_{11} - 2S_{12} - S_{33})n^3m - (2S_{22} - 2S_{12} - S_{33})nm^3$$
$$\bar{S}_{22} = S_{11}n^4 + S_{22}m^4 + (2S_{12} + S_{33})n^2m^2$$
$$\bar{S}_{33} = 2(2S_{11} + 2S_{22} - 4S_{12} - S_{33})n^2m^2 + S_{33}(n^4 + m^4)$$

where S_{11}, S_{22}, S_{12}, S_{21} and S_{33} have been defined in eqn (28.14b).

28.9 The strength characteristics and failure criteria of composite laminae

In the two preceding sections, the stiffness relationships in terms of stress and strain were presented for isotropic and orthotropic materials. It is now necessary to have an understanding of the ultimate strengths of the laminae to enable a complete characterization of the composite material to be made. The stress–strain relationship stated in the previous sections described the actual stresses occurring at any point in a lamina, and the strength characteristics may be considered as describing the allowable stress at any point.

When the formulation of the stiffness characteristics of the lamina was developed, properties in both tension and compression were assumed. However, the ultimate strength behaviour of composite systems may be different in tension and compression and the characteristics of the failure mode will be highly dependent upon the component materials. Therefore, a systematic development of the strengths of these materials is not possible; consequently a series of failure criteria for composite materials will be given.

Strength theories for isotropic laminae

In isotropic materials both normal and shear failure can occur, but it is usual to equate the combined stress situation to the experimentally determined uniaxial tension or compression value. When a tensile load is applied to a specimen in a uniaxial test it is possible for failure in the specimen to be initiated by either an ultimate tensile stress or a shear stress, because a tensile stress of σ (the maximum principal stress in this type of test) on the specimen produces a maximum shear value of $\sigma/2$. Consequently the failure theories are related to the applied tensile or compressive stress that causes failure, irrespective of whether it was a normal or a shear stress failure.

Many theories and hypotheses have been developed to predict the failure surface for composite materials under tensile loads and probably the best known theories which have been used to predict failure and which are discussed in Holmes and Just (1983) are:

Maximum principal stress theory

$$\sigma_{xx} = \sigma_t^* \tag{28.17}$$

where

σ_{xx} = maximum principal stress
σ_t^* = failure stress in a uniaxial tensile test

or

$$\sigma_{zz} = \sigma_c^*$$

σ_{zz} = minimum principal stress
σ_c^* = failure stress in a uniaxial compressive test.

Figure 28.7 shows the principal stresses acting on an element of material.

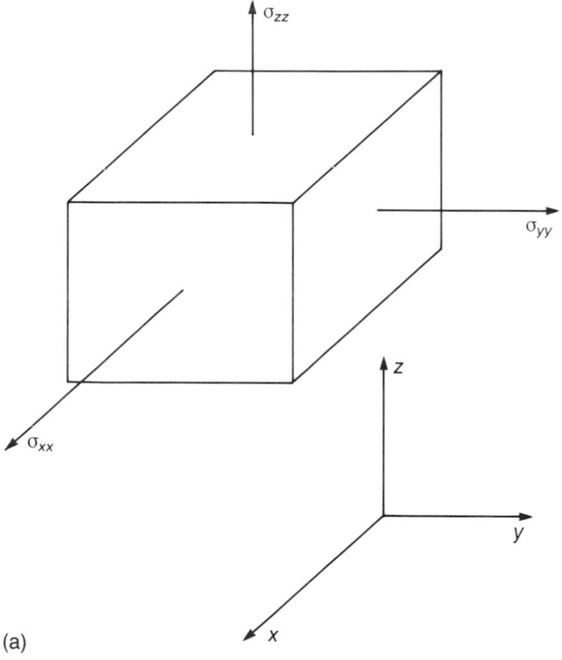

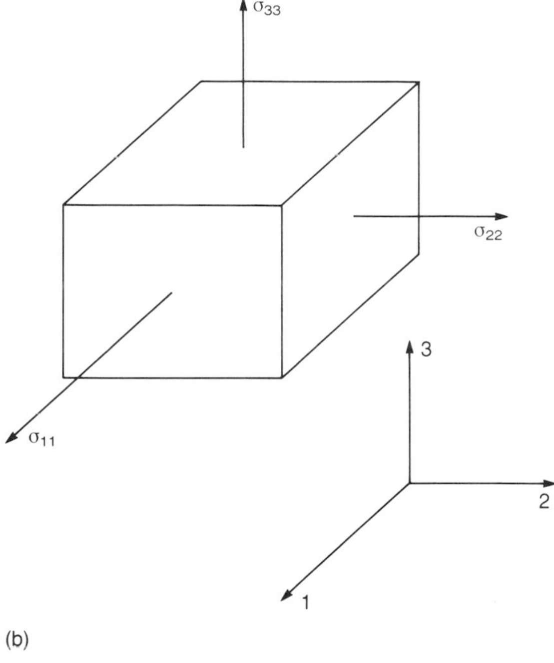

FIGURE 28.7 Isotropic and orthotropic materials under normal stress: (a) element under three principal stresses $\sigma_{xx} > \sigma_{yy} > \sigma_{zz}$; (b) orthotropic material under normal stress.

Maximum principal strain theory

$$\varepsilon_{xx} = \varepsilon_t^* \qquad (28.18)$$

where

ε_{xx} = maximum principal tensile strain
ε_t^* = tensile strain at failure

in terms of stress

$$(\sigma_{xx} - \nu\sigma_{yy} - \nu\sigma_{zz})/E = \sigma_t^*/E$$

or

$$(\sigma_{xx} - \nu\sigma_{yy} - \nu\sigma_{zz}) = \sigma_t^*$$

ν = Poisson's ratio.

Similarly

$$\varepsilon_{zz} = \varepsilon_c^*$$

ε_{zz} = minimum principal strain
ε_c^* = compression strain at failure

or $\quad \sigma_{zz} - \nu(\sigma_{xx} + \sigma_{yy}) = \sigma_c^*$.

Both the above theories assume failure to be due to normal stresses and ignore any shear stress present. Consequently the theories are relevant to the failure of brittle materials under tension.

The total strain energy theory
The above theories express the failure criterion as either limiting stress or limiting strain; the total strain energy theory attempts to combine the above two theories. The development of the theory, which is based upon strain energy principles, has been discussed in Hollaway (1989) and only the final solution will be given here.

The lamina theory gives the solution as:

$$\sigma^{*2} = \sigma_{xx}^2 + \sigma_{yy}^2 - 2\sigma_{xx}\sigma_{yy}\nu. \qquad (28.19)$$

The theory applies particularly to brittle materials where the ultimate tensile stress is less than the ultimate shear stress.

Deviation strain energy theory
This theory is known as the von Mises criterion and in it the principal stresses σ_{xx}, σ_{yy} and σ_{zz} can be expressed as the sum of two components, namely the hydrostatic stress which causes only a change in volume and the deviation stress which causes distortion of the body. The system is shown in Figure 28.8.

The hydrostatic stress components produce equal strains in magnitude and are consistent in the three directions and therefore produce equal strain in these directions. The system, therefore, undergoes change in volume but not change in shape. The stress deviation system will cause the body to undergo changes in shape but not in volume.

Again the theory has been developed in

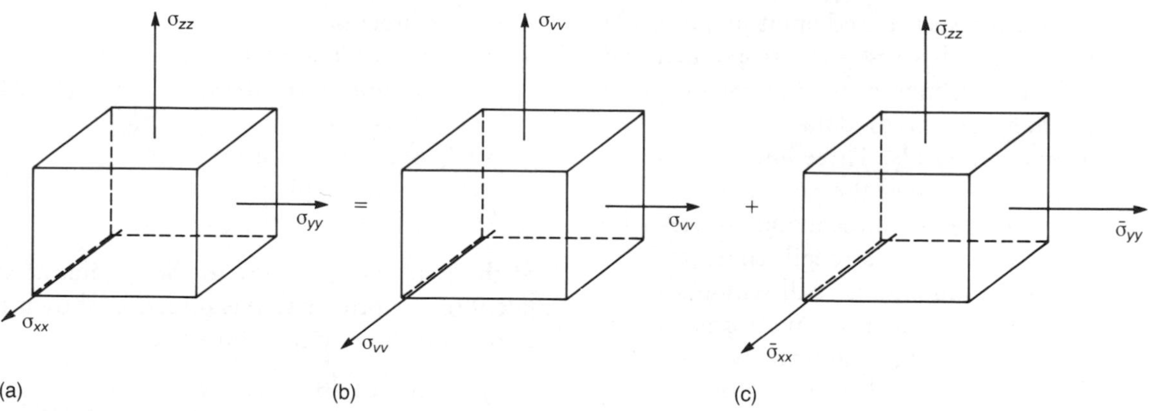

FIGURE 28.8 Volume and deviation stress system: (a) principal stress; (b) volume stress system; (c) stress deviation (or distortion) system.

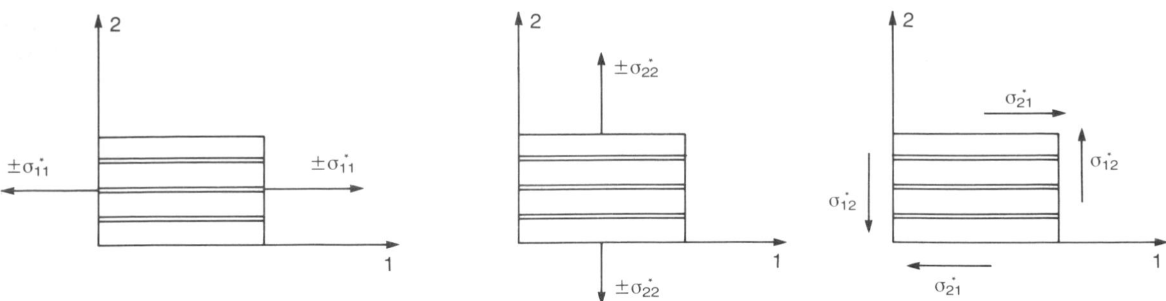

FIGURE 28.9 Critical stress values in the principal material axes.

Hollaway (1989) and will not be repeated here; the lamina theory gives the solution as:

$$\sigma_{xx}^2 + \sigma_{yy}^2 - \sigma_{xx}\sigma_{yy} = \sigma^{*2} \quad (28.20)$$

The above failure criterion is most relevant to ductile materials. It is not obvious which of the above failure criteria is most relevant to composites as the fibre volume fraction and orientation of the fibres in the polymer will influence their strength and ductility properties. However, the last theory has been applied to quasi-isotropic composites with some success.

Strength theories of orthotropic laminae

The theories based upon the strength characteristics of orthotropic materials are considerably more complicated than those for the isotropic ones. As with these latter materials the strength hypothesis is based upon simple fundamental tests, but because orthotropic materials have different strengths in different directions a more intensive set of data is required than for isotropic materials. Three uniaxial tests are required, one in each of the principal axis directions to determine the three moduli of elasticity, Poisson's ratio and the strength characteristics; tests in these directions will eliminate any coupling effects of shearing and normal strains which would occur if the laminate were tested in any other direction. The shearing strengths with respect to the principal directions must be determined from independent experiments.

Figure 28.9 shows schematically the critical stress values in the principal material axes.

For orthotropic materials the stress condition at a point is resolved into its normal and shearing components relative to the principal material axis at the point. Consequently the failure criteria in these materials become functions of the basic normal and shearing strengths described for isotropic materials.

Maximum stress theory

The maximum stress theory of failure assumes that failure occurs when the stresses in the principal material axes reach a critical value. The three possible modes of failure are:

$\sigma_{11} = \sigma_{11}^*$ the ultimate tensile or compressive stress in direction 1.

$\sigma_{22} = \sigma_{22}^*$ the ultimate tensile or compressive stress in direction 2. (28.21)

$\sigma_{12} = \sigma_{12}^*$ the ultimate shear stress acting in plane 1 in direction 2.

If the load were applied to the lamina at an angle θ to the principal axis direction shown in Figure 28.6 then by transformation

$$\begin{aligned} \sigma_{11} &= \sigma_{xx}\cos^2\theta = \sigma_\theta\cos^2\theta \\ \sigma_{22} &= \sigma_{xx}\sin^2\theta = \sigma_\theta\sin^2\theta \\ \sigma_{12} &= -\sigma_{xx}\sin\theta\cos\theta = -\sigma_\theta\sin\theta\cos\theta \end{aligned} \quad (28.22)$$

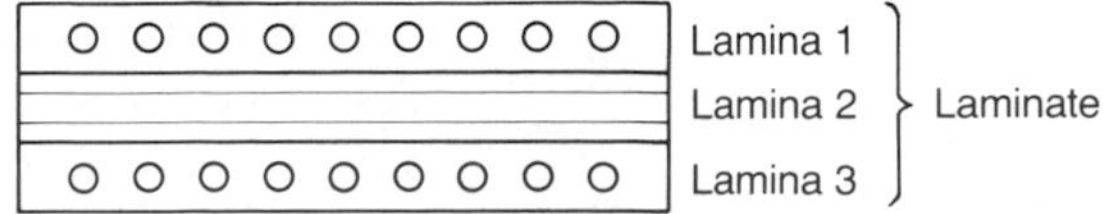

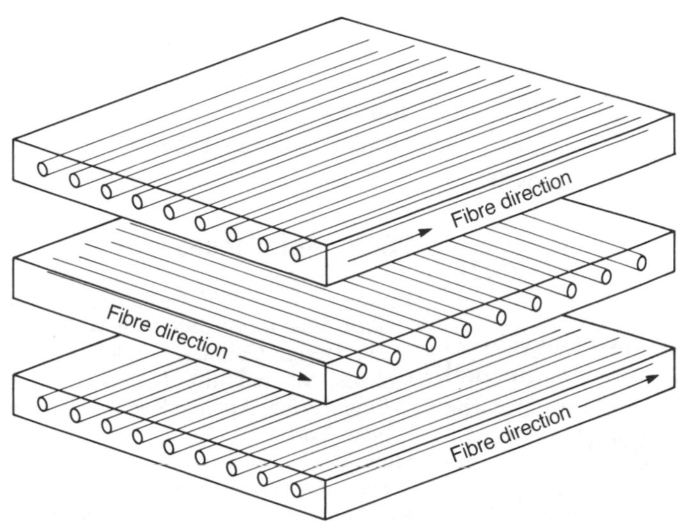

FIGURE 28.10 Laminate arrangements.

The failure strength produced by the maximum stress theory would depend upon the relative values of σ_{11}, σ_{22} and σ_{12} and would therefore be the smallest value of the following:

$$\begin{aligned} \sigma_\theta &= \sigma_{11}^*/\cos^2\theta \\ \sigma_\theta &= \sigma_{22}^*/\sin^2\theta \\ \sigma_\theta &= \sigma_{12}^*/\sin\theta\cos\theta \end{aligned} \qquad (28.23)$$

Maximum strain theory

The maximum strain theory of failure assumes that failure occurs when the strains in the principal material axes reach a critical value. Here again there are three possible modes of failure:

$$\begin{aligned} \varepsilon_{11} &= \varepsilon_{11}^* \\ \varepsilon_{22} &= \varepsilon_{22}^* \\ \varepsilon_{12} &= \varepsilon_{12}^* \end{aligned} \qquad (28.24)$$

Where ε_{11}^* is the maximum tensile or compressive strain in direction 1, ε_{22}^* is the maximum tensile or compressive strain in direction 2 and ε_{12}^* is the maximum shear strain on plane 1 in direction 2.

Tsai–Hill energy theory

The Tsai–Hill criterion is based upon the von Mises failure criterion which was originally applied to homogeneous isotropic bodies. It was then modified by Hill to suit anisotropic bodies, and finally applied to composite materials by Tsai.

Hollaway (1989) has discussed the derivation of the equation which describes the failure envelope and this may be expressed as:

$$\frac{\sigma_{11}^2}{\sigma_{11}^{*2}} - \frac{\sigma_{11}\sigma_{22}}{\sigma_{11}^{*2}} + \frac{\sigma_{22}^2}{\sigma_{22}^{*2}} + \frac{\sigma_{12}^2}{\sigma_{22}^{*2}} = 1. \qquad (28.25)$$

For most composite materials $\sigma_{11}^* \gg \sigma_{22}$; consequently, the second term of eqn (28.25) is negligible and this equation becomes:

$$\frac{\sigma_{11}^2}{\sigma_{11}^{*2}} + \frac{\sigma_{22}^2}{\sigma_{22}^{*2}} + \frac{\sigma_{12}^2}{\sigma_{22}^{*2}} = 1. \qquad (28.26)$$

The eqns (28.25) and (28.26) only apply to orthotropic laminae under in-plane stress conditions.

To enable a prediction to be made of the failure strength in direction θ to the principal axes (Figure 28.6) on unidirectional laminae, eqns (28.25) and (28.23) can be combined to give:

$$\sigma_{xx} = \sigma_\theta = \left[\frac{\cos^4\theta}{\sigma_{11}^{*2}} + \left(\frac{1}{\sigma_{12}^{*2}} - \frac{1}{\sigma_{11}^{*2}}\right)\sin^2\theta\cos^2\theta + \frac{\sin^4\theta}{\sigma_{22}^{*2}}\right]^{-1/2} \qquad (28.27)$$

Hull (1992) has stated that when eqn (28.27) has been fitted to the results of experimental tests on carbon fibre–epoxy resin laminates the predicted values are much better than for the maximum stress theory, eqn (28.21).

Finally, Figure 28.10 shows a laminate made from three lamina. Providing lamina 1 and 3 have the same thickness, the laminate would be described as symmetric; lamina 2 could have any value of thickness. If, however, the thickness of lamina 1 and 3 were different, the laminate would be described as non-symmetric. Under a thermal and mechanical load, coupling forces are introduced into a non-symmetric laminate because of the different mechanical properties of the individual lamina. For this reason it is common practice in many applications to use symmetric laminates which are not subjected to this type of coupling.

28.10 References

Hollaway, L. (1989) Design of composites. In *Design with Advanced Composite Materials* (ed. L. Phillips), The Design Council, London.

Holmes, M. and Just, D.J. (1983) *GRP in Structural Engineering*, Applied Science Publishers, London and New York.

Hull, D. (1992) *An Introduction to Composite Materials*, Cambridge University Press.

Krenchel, H. (1964) *Fibre Reinforcement*, Akademisk Forlag, Copenhagen.

Chapter twenty-nine

Manufacturing techniques for polymer composite materials

29.1 Manufacture of fibre-reinforced thermosetting composites
29.2 Manufacture of fibre-reinforced thermoplastic composites
29.3 References

The two parts of this chapter concentrate upon the manufacturing techniques for fibre-reinforced thermosetting and thermoplastic polymer composites respectively.

29.1 Manufacture of fibre-reinforced thermosetting composites

Fibre-reinforced thermosets are manufactured in three ways and examples of each are given here:

1. manually – hand lay-up, spray-up, pressure bag and autoclave moulding;
2. semi-automatically – cold pressing, compression moulding and resin injection;
3. automatically – pultrusion, filament winding and injecton moulding.

Processes which use only one mould are known as open-mould techniques; the surface of the product in contact with the mould is able to reproduce the surface of the mould completely. Processes in which the product is formed within a closed space by two moulds are known as closed-mould techniques. Figure 29.1 shows a schematic diagram of the various fabrication processes.

29.1.1 Open-mould processes (contact moulding)

The hand lay-up technique

This is the simplest and most common technique for producing fibre-reinforced polymer components (Figure 29.2(a)). It is ideally suited to the production of a small number of similar components such as fibre-reinforced polymer infill panels which could be used in civil engineering. Most materials are suitable for mould making, but the most common are glass-reinforced polymers (GRP). A master pattern is prepared from which GRP moulds may be made. A release agent is used to prevent bonding to the moulds during manufacture. It is necessary to protect fibres from exposure to the atmosphere to prevent fracture and this protection is achieved by applying a resin-rich area, known as a gel coat, on the exposed surface of the composite.

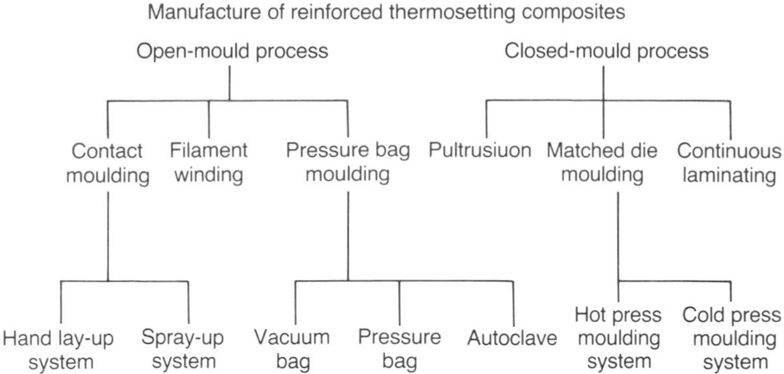

FIGURE 29.1 Schematic diagram of the fabrication processes for thermosetting polymer composites.

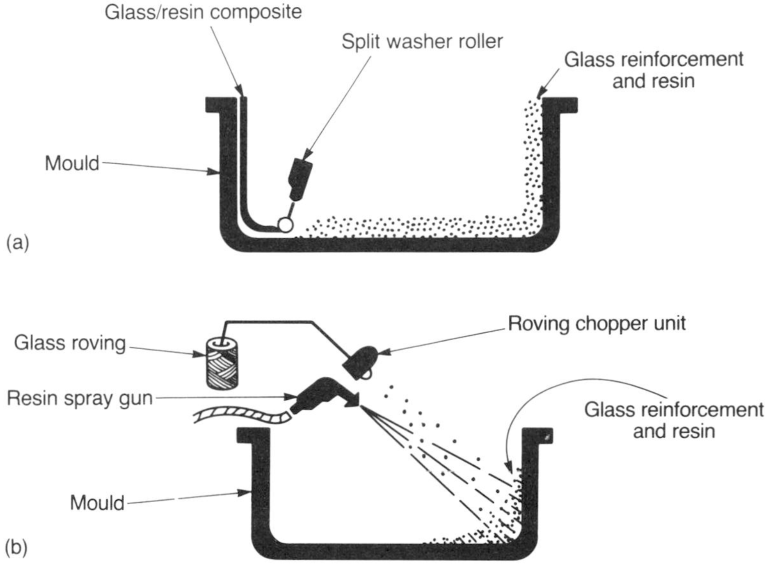

FIGURE 29.2 (a) Hand lay-up moulding method; (b) spray-up moulding technique.

The function of the gel coat is:

1. to protect fibres from external influences, especially moisture penetration to the interface of the fibre and matrix with consequent breakdown of the interface bond;
2. to provide a smooth finish and to reproduce precisely the surface texture of the mould.

The thickness of the gel coat is generally about 0.35 mm. Sometimes a surface tissue mat is used to reinforce the gel coat.

After the gel coat has become tacky but firm, a liberal coat of resin is brushed over it and the first layer of glass reinforcement is placed in position and consolidated with brush and roller. The glass fibre may be in the form of chopped strand mat or woven fabric, precut to the correct size. Layers of resin and reinforcement are then applied until the required thickness of composite is reached.

Spray-up technique

The spray-up technique, shown in Figure 29.2(b), is less labour intensive than the hand lay-up method. It involves the simultaneous deposition of chopped glass fibre roving and polymer on to the mould with a spray gun. The roving is fed through a chopping unit and projected into the resin stream. The glass resin mixture is then rolled by a split washer roller to remove any air.

The technique requires considerable operator skill to control the thickness of the composite and to maintain a consistent glass/polymer ratio. After the initial polymerization of the composite, and when it has been demoulded, the unit must be cured usually by heating for eight hours at 60°C.

As the tooling costs for the above two processes are low, the designer has considerable versatility from the point of view of shape and form.

Pressure bag techniques

Pressure is exerted on the open face of the moulding to enable:

1. a greater compaction of the composite (the voids are reduced to zero);
2. a higher fibre volume ratio;
3. a higher quality of surface finish on this face.

These techniques are ideal for the manufacture of low-cost open-mould products such as structural panels without sophisticated mechanization.

Vacuum bag

A contact moulding is produced by the hand lay-up method, but before curing commences a rubber membrane is placed over the composite component and all joints between the membrane and mould are sealed and a vacuum is applied between the bag and composite (Figure 29.3(a)). The pressure of about one atmosphere applied to the surface of the moulding, forces out air and excess polymer; glass/polymer weight ratios of up to 55% are possible. A protective sheet of cellophane is used between the rubber and composite.

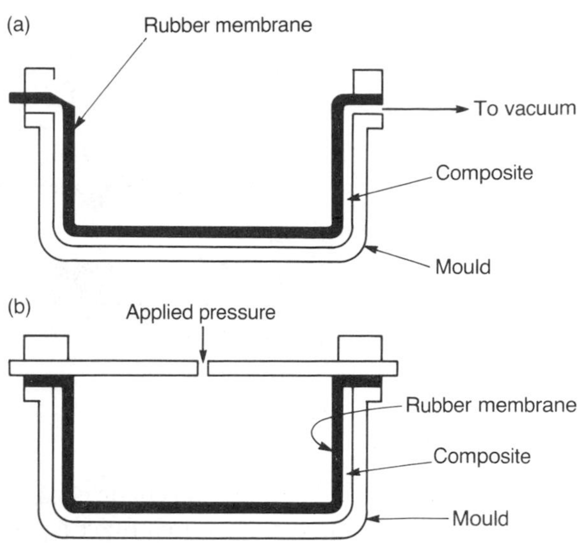

FIGURE 29.3 Pressure bag techniques.

Pressure bag

This technique is similar to the vacuum bag except that a pressure is applied to the open surface (Figure 29.3(b)). The contact moulding is produced and before curing commences a rubber bag with the cellophane sheet is sealed to the mould with a plate and pressurized up to about three atmospheres. Because of the higher pressure compared with that for the vacuum bag a greater fibre/matrix weight ratio is obtained. This value can be increased to about 65%. Superior composites can be manufactured by this technique but more equipment is required than for the vacuum bag, with a consequent increase in cost.

Autoclave

The autoclave is a modification of the pressure bag method; pressures of up to 6 atmospheres are developed within the autoclave and the system produces a high-quality composite with a fibre/matrix weight ratio of up to 70%. The cost of production also increases.

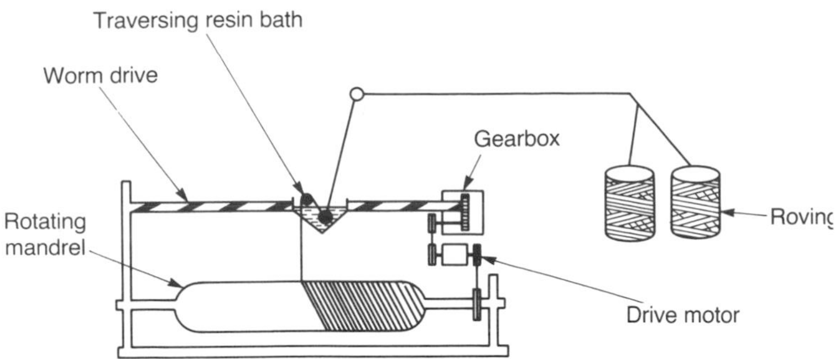

FIGURE 29.4 Filament winding technique.

Filament winding

Filament winding is a highly mechanized and sophisticated technique for the manufacture of pressure vessels, pipes and rocket casings when exceptionally high strengths are required. Continuous reinforcement, usually rovings, is fed through a traversing bath of activated resin and is then wound on to a rotating mandrel. If resin preimpregnated reinforcement is used, it is passed over a hot roller until tacky and is then wound on to the rotating mandrel. Figure 29.4 illustrates the process and it is evident that the angle of the helix is determined by the relative speeds of the traversing bath and the mandrel. After completion of the initial polymerization, the composite is removed from the mandrel and cured; the composite unit is then placed into an enclosure at 60°C for eight hours.

29.1.2 Closed-mould processes

The product is formed within a closed-mould system, utilizing pressure and sometimes heat rapidly to produce high-quality units. Because of the high capital equipment outlay, particularly for the manufacture of the metal moulds, it is essential that large production runs are performed. Because of the mechanization of the system only a small skilled workforce is required. There are two closed-mould processes:

1. matched die;
2. pultrusion and modified pull-winding.

Matched die

Cold press moulding
Pressure is applied to two unheated matched metal moulds to disperse resin throughout a prepared fibre fabric stack placed in the mould; a release agent and a gel coat would be applied to the mould surface before the fibre stack is placed in position. The activated polymer is poured on to the top of the mat and the mould is then closed; the polymer spreads throughout the fabric under the mould pressure. Pressures applied may be as low as 100 kPa and the heat generated during the exothermic polymerization process warms the tools; this helps in the curing process but additional curing after demoulding is essential.

Hot press moulding
Glass fibre reinforcement and a controlled quantity of hot curing catalysed resin are confined between heated, matched, polished metal dies brought together under pressure (Figure 29.5). The pressures vary depending upon the process but will normally be between 0.5 and 15 MPa and the mould temperatures will be between 120°C and 150°C. The heat ensures rapid curing and so no subsequent curing is required. Both preform moulding and premix moulding of the fibre and the polymer can be used in this process.

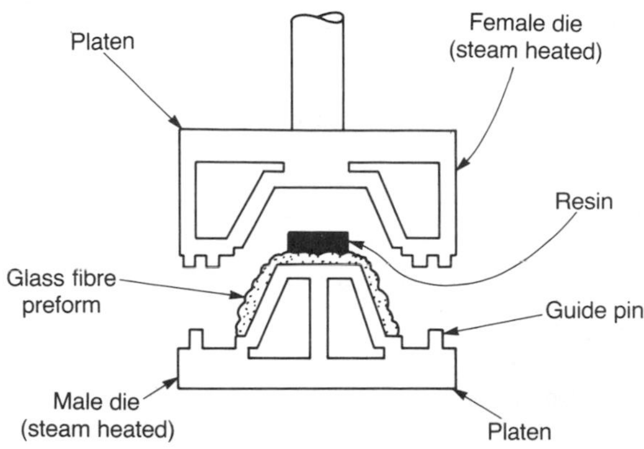

FIGURE 29.5 Hot press moulding technique.

In the preform moulding chopped rovings are projected on to a rotating fine metal mesh screen shaped to the required dimensions; the fibres are held on the screen by suction. The strands are bonded together by spraying the preform with a resinous binder in the form of a powder or an emulsion and the whole is transferred to an oven at 150°C for two to three minutes, after which time the preform is ready for the press.

Sheet moulding compound (or prepreg) is a polyester-resin-based moulding material which consists of a mixture of chopped strand mat or chopped fibre resin, fillers, catalyst and pigment. It is produced and supplied in the form of a continuous sheet wound into a roll and protected on both sides by sheets of polythene film which are removed before loading into the press. An advantage of this method is that no liquid resin is involved and the prepreg sheets can be prepared to the design size by cutting.

Dough moulding compound (or bulk moulding compound) contains a mixture of chopped strands (20% by weight) with resin, catalyst and pigment. As the compound flows readily it may be formed into shape by compression transfer or injection and the pressure required to produce a component is relatively low so that large mouldings can readily be produced. Curing takes about 2 minutes for moulding temperatures in the region of 120–160°C although this will depend upon the section thickness.

Resin injection

Resin injection is a cold mould process using low pressures of about 450 kN/m^2. The surfaces of the mould are prepared with release agents and gel coat before the glass fibre reinforcement is placed in position in the bottom mould and allowed to extend beyond the sides of the moulds. The upper mould is clamped in position to stops and the activated resin is injected under pressure into the mould cavity. Figure 29.6(a) shows the arrangement. It is possible to obtain a fibre/matrix ratio by weight of 65%.

Pultrusion and modified pull-winding

The pultrusion technique consists of impregnating continuous strands of a reinforcing material with a polymer and drawing them through a die as shown in Figure 29.6(b). Thermosetting polymers are used in this process although research is being undertaken currently to pultrude thermoplastic materials. Curing of the composite component is undertaken when the die is heated to about 135°C. A glass content of between 60 and 80% by weight can be achieved. Composites manufactured by this method tend to be reinforced mainly in the longitudinal direction with only a relatively small percentage of fibres in the transverse direction. A technique has been developed (Shaw-Stewart, 1988) to 'wind' fibres in the transverse direction simultaneously with the pultrusion operation. The process is known as pull-winding and gives the designer greater flexibility in the production of composites, particularly those of circular cross-section.

29.2 Manufacture of fibre-reinforced thermoplastic composites

Reinforced thermoplastic composites can be manufactured by most of the thermoplastic processing techniques such as extrusion, blow moulding and thermoforming of short-fibre-reinforced thermoplastics. However, the most important technique for industrial use is injection moulding. It is a similar technique to the manu-

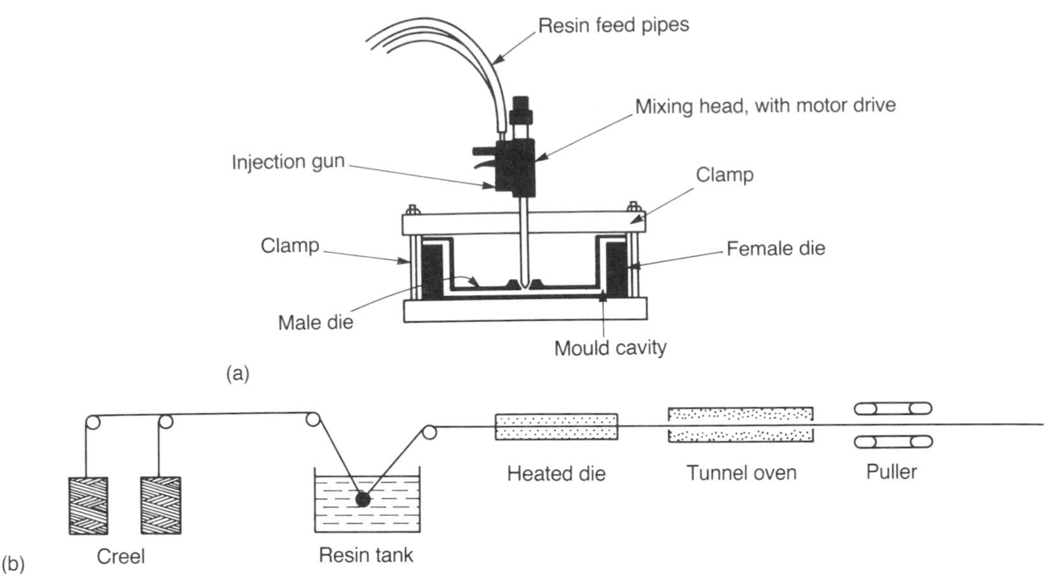

FIGURE 29.6 (a) Resin injection process; (b) pultrusion technique.

facture of unreinforced thermoplastics but the melt viscosity is higher in the reinforced polymer process and consequently the injection pressures are higher. With all the techniques, production difficulties can occur because the reinforced composite is stiffer than the unreinforced one. The cycle time is less but the increased stiffness can affect the ejection from the mould so the mould design has to be modified from that of the unreinforced polymer mould.

One of the problems of thermoplastic composites is that they use short fibres (typically 0.2–0.4 mm long) and consequently their full strength is not developed. Continuous fibre tapes and mats in the form of prepregs can help to overcome this. The best known examples of these systems are the aromatic polymer composites (APC) and the glass-mat-reinforced thermoplastic composites (GMT). The systems use unidirectional carbon fibre in a matrix of polyethersulphone (PES) or polyetheretherketone (PEEK). The material for the APC comes in prepreg form of unidirectional or 0°/90° fibre and for GMT in a tape prepreg form. The composite is manufactured by the film stacking process with the prepregs arranged in the desired directions.

The film stacking process

This is a relatively new method in which the prepreg is made from cloth reinforcement and has a polyethersulphone polymer content of about 15% by weight. The final volume fractions of fibre and resin are obtained by adding matrix in the form of film. The film stacking process, therefore, consists of alternating layers of fibre impregnated with insufficient matrix, with polymer films of complementary mass to bring the overall laminate to the correct fibre volume ratios. The required stacked sequence is placed into one part of a split mould; the two half moulds are brought together and heat and pressure are applied.

This technique is used mainly for high technology composites in the aerospace and space industries.

29.3 References

Shaw-Stewart, D. (1988) Pullwinding. *Proceedings of the Second International Conference on Automobile Composites 88*, Noordwijkerhout, The Netherlands.

Chapter thirty

Durability and design

30.1 Temperature
30.2 Fire
30.3 Moisture
30.4 Solution and solvent action
30.5 Weather
30.6 Design with composites
30.7 References

Polymer composites change with time and the most significant influencing factors are:

1. elevated temperatures;
2. fire;
3. moisture, particularly when immersed for long periods;
4. adverse chemical environments;
5. natural weathering particularly when exposed to the sun's ultra-violet radiation.

30.1 Temperature

Temperature plays an important part in the manufacture of GRP composites which are normally cured (and post-cured) with heat to a state of chemical and physical stability. A certain amount of shrinkage takes place during the curing process, due to the polymer chains being drawn together. On occasions post-curing of composites at elevated temperatures presents practical difficulties for large structural composites and a gradual change in physical and dimensional properties may be expected for a period if a laminate is imperfectly cured. However, this effect is not normally significant unless there is excessive undercure. This situation could occur if, for instance, immediately after manufacture the units were placed in the fabricator's yard because there was no room in the fabrication shop. In this situation only partial curing would have occurred before the unit was exposed to environmental conditions.

Constantly fluctuating temperatures have a greater deleterious effect on GRP. At a micro scale, the difference in the coefficients of thermal expansion of the glass and the resin may contribute to progressive debonding and weakening of the materials, although the extensibility of the resin system will usually accommodate differential movement.

When GRP composites are exposed to high temperatures a discolouration of the resin may occur; this is noticed by the composite becoming yellow. Both polyester and epoxy show this effect and the problem will be aggravated if flame retardants are added to the resin during manufacture of the composite. In addition, as a result of the exposure to high temperatures, the composite will become brittle.

30.2 Fire

When a composite material is specified, it must meet the appropriate standards of fire performance. It is usually possible to select a resin system which will achieve the standard laid down in British Standard Specification BS 476.

The Building Regulations require that, depending upon their use, building components or structures should conform to given standards of fire safety. The fire tests by which these are measured fall into two categories:

1. reaction to fire – tests on materials;
2. fire resistance – tests on structures.

The tests under these two headings are laid down in BS 476: Parts 4, 5, 6 and 7, and in BS 476: Parts 3–8 respectively.

Resins will probably contain fillers and colourants which may affect fire properties.

Some mineral fillers, such as specially treated calcium carbonate, can improve the mechanical properties of composites made from polyester and epoxies. No more than 25% of the filler should be used, although as an exposed aggregate in a decorative surface a greater proportion of the coarse particles may be used. To enable flame-retardant properties of the plastic to be improved, aluminium trihydrate and antimony trioxide may be used as fillers for both lamination and gel-coated resins, but the use of flame retardants can affect the colour retention of the polymer; the pigment would have been added to produce a particular colour in a structural component. Het-acid-based resins can be used where flame-retardant characteristics are required.

30.3 Moisture

Polymers which are cross-linked are not easily hydrolysed but they are sufficiently hydrophilic for water to be absorbed. The effect of this uptake of water is to reduce the modulus of elasticity and strength. Wet strength can be 25% lower than that of the dry specimen. The wet strength values are sometimes used in design to reflect the possible effects of water and weather. The long-term effects on these two properties seem to be greater for epoxy resins than for polyesters. The absorption of water by both the polyesters and epoxies leads to swelling of the laminate with an increase in thickness; the wet laminates can also warp if the structure is unbalanced.

Water can have a deleterious effect on glass fibre. The high strength of fibres is largely due to surface imperfections but a small amount of solution in the surface of the fibres can produce surface flaws which will reduce the overall strength of the laminate. The alkali-resistant glass fibre has a better resistance to water than the E-glass fibre which is generally used for the manufacture of GRP.

On a short-term basis water absorption is a surface effect and if the composite has a gel coat (see later in the section) this effect is of little consequence. On a long-term basis, however, immersion of the composite in water will allow penetration through the thickness of the coating and water-filled voids will occur at the fibre/polymer interface and may weaken the bond. High-quality materials and good control of the composite fabricating process can reduce the above effects to a minimum. The glass fibres, as mentioned earlier, are treated with a size to protect them after manufacture and when the in-service requirements demand it, a water-resistant size should be used to minimize blistering.

The ends of fibres will be exposed if GRP is cut during shaping of the component, and the fibres may suffer from a wicking action, but experience shows that only a narrow strip at the cut edge will be affected by water penetration. If, however, the composite fibre volume fraction is high the effect of water may be significant and should be investigated.

Work by the Building Research Establishment (1963) showed that wetting and drying of GRP composites, from natural exposure to environmental conditions, is much less severe than continuous exposure to water in producing changes at the glass/resin interface.

30.4 Solution and solvent action

A fully cured polyester resin exhibits good resistance to acidic and alkaline attack if selected and designed properly; resin manufacturers should be consulted when choosing a resin to be utilized for a specific corrosive environment.

30.5 Weather

Natural weathering does cause some deterioration of GRP composites; sunlight degrades both polyester and epoxy resins. The first sign of degradation is a discolouration of the material which develops into a breakdown of the surface of the composite. In addition there is a loss of light transmission in translucent sheeting. The UV component from the sun is largely responsible for this degradation; the short wavelength band at 330 nm has most effect on polyesters but longer wavelengths are also significant. To reduce this weathering problem with polyester resin, UV absorbers and stabilizers are added to the resin formulations during fabrication of the composite. There is, however, little improvement in the stability of epoxy resins when UV stabilizers are added.

When pigments are placed in polyester resin infra-red and visible radiation can accelerate the rate of degradation of the polymer by raising its temperature; a rise of 10°C approximately doubles chemical reaction and hence degradation. Consequently, resin degradation proceeds more rapidly in hot than in more temperate climates. The rate of degradation of epoxy resins is similar to that of polyesters.

Weathering can affect the mechanical properties of GRP composites; surface debonding of fibres as a result of degradation of the resin will reduce the load-bearing capacity. The deterioration could be caused by solar effects or by water on the surface of the composite. Because weathering is largely a surface effect, the thickness of the composite has a significant influence upon the mechanical properties and it has been shown (Scholz, 1978) that a 3 mm thick GRP laminate has a reduction in flexural strength of between 12% and 20% after 15 years' exposure to natural weathering, whereas it has been estimated that for a 10 mm laminate a reduction of no more than 3% would take place after 50 years' exposure.

The above discussion has assumed a general-purpose resin without any surface protection. If a polyester resin has been specifically designed by the manufacturer to resist weathering, degradation would not be so severe.

The three principal types of polyester used as a laminating resin are orthophthalic, isophthalic and het acid resins. The orthophthalic type is a general-purpose resin, the isophthalic one has superior weathering and chemical resistance properties and the het acid resin is used for flame-retardant purposes. Fillers and pigments may be used in resins, the former principally to improve mechanical properties and the latter for appearance and protective action. Fillers such as aluminium trihydrate may be used to improve flame-retardant characteristics, but it is important that the correct amount of the fillers should be incorporated; if too high a proportion is employed, adverse effects on weathering properties may result. This is only applicable for composites exposed to the weather and internal applications; where water or chemicals are not in contact with the polymer, the composites are not affected. Ultraviolet stabilizers can be incorporated into the resin at the time of fabrication and a gel coat surface coating can be applied to the composite for increased weather protection.

It is clear that the durability of a GRP laminate depends upon the quality of the exposed surface and a good in-service performance is most commonly achieved by the use of a surface coat or gel coat of pigmented resin. This protects the glass fibre reinforcement from the action of moisture and the laminating resin from harmful radiation and from moisture. The polymer that is used for this purpose has been formulated to provide good weathering or chemical resistance properties. The gel coat is generally applied in a uniform thickness of 0.5 mm to the mould surface and can be pigmented to give the required colour. A surface tissue of glass fibre is often incorporated into the gel coat to reinforce it and to enhance its appearance, whilst maintaining the resin-rich surface.

It is important that, for the satisfactory design of composites, the resin system, the reinforcement and the structure of the laminate should be assessed properly. This may involve an evaluation programme to assess the design and manufacture of the system to ensure that the product gives and maintains satisfactory performance throughout its service life. As an aid, the British Plastics Federation has produced guidance notes on the construction of glass-reinforced plastics cladding panels, dealing mainly with the in-service requirements.

30.6 Design with composites

Designing with composites is an interactive process between the designer and the production engineer responsible for the manufacturing technique. It is essential that a design methodology is selected and rigorously used, because many different materials are on the market and they can be affected by quality, the environment and the manufacturing process. It is also important that the designer recognizes the product cost, because the constituents of composite materials (the fibre and the matrix) can vary significantly in price and the manufacturing process can range from simple compact moulded units cured at room temperature to sophisticated high temperature and pressure cured composites.

The design process can be divided into five main phases. These phases are:

1. the design brief and an estimation of cost;
2. the structural, mechanical and in-service details;
3. the manufacturing processes and cost details;
4. the material testing and specification information;
5. the quality control and structural testing information.

The solution of design factors of safety is an important aspect of the work; these factors are likely to be covered in the relevant code of practice. If the design is unique, it may be necessary for the designer/analyst to select specific factors of safety, bearing in mind the exactness of the calculations, the manufacturing processes, the in-service environment, the life of the product and the loading. The selection of these design factors follows the pattern for other materials but, with the variation in properties, due to the anisotropic nature and the different manufacturing techniques of the composites, a more involved calculation and a greater reliance upon the design factors will result.

Polymer composite structures can be manufactured from thin plate and shell laminated plies to form continuum systems or from pultruded or filament wound tubes to form skeletal structures. The properties of these thin laminated plate or tube elements may be calculated in terms of laminate structures and ply thicknesses and properties by using laminate theory or by commercially available microcomputer programs such as Engineering Science Data Unit (1991) and Think Composites Software (1987).

30.7 References

BS 476: British Standards Institution, London.

Building Research Establishment (1963) Internal records, Building Research Establishment, Garston, UK.

Engineering Science Data Unit (1987*a*) *Stiffnesses and properties of laminated plates*, ESDU 20–22, ESDU International, London.

Engineering Science Data Unit (1987*b*) *Failure of composite laminates*, ESDU 20–33, ESDU International, London.

Scholz, D. (1978) *Kunststoffe*, **68**, 556.

Think Composites Software (1987) MIC-MAC, Think Composites Software, Dayton.

Chapter thirty-one

The end use of polymers and polymer composites

31.1 References

The use of polymers and polymer composites in the construction industry falls into three categories. These are:

1. non-load-bearing;
2. semi-load-bearing;
3. load-bearing.

Unreinforced polymers are used in non-load-bearing and semi-load-bearing applications, whilst fibre-reinforced polymers are used in load-bearing applications. Thermoplastic materials can be drawn into fibres which are then used in geotextiles.

Polymers and fibre-reinforced polymers offer many advantages over other materials, but the most appropriate resin must be selected for the particular end use since every material does not possess all the following characteristics:

1. high light transmission for glazing and lighting fixtures;
2. infinite texture possibilities;
3. minimum maintenance requirements;
4. infinite design possibilities;
5. resistance to water and corrosion;
6. high specific strength;
7. high impact resistance.

The disadvantages that have impeded the utilization of polymers in construction are as follows.

1. The cost of the materials is relatively high, although when their low density is considered and the structure as a whole has been designed as a composite system (e.g. the reduced foundation size compared with what would be required for conventional material), then polymers are competitive.
2. The stiffness and strength of the polymer or the composite is less than that of competitor materials and therefore they must be used in conjunction with the latter.
3. The scratch resistance is poor.
4. UV light can attack the material unless stabilizers are incorporated into the resin formulations.
5. Organic materials will burn, but fire-retardant additives can be used with the polymers to retard or eliminate burning.

The non-load-bearing thermoplastic polymers such as polyethylene have been used to manufacture pipes for the transportation of water, gas and oil and it is now accepted for the cold water systems in houses.

The materials used in a soil (geo) environment are the thermoplastic polymers known as geosynthetics. They can be divided into five categories:

1. geotextiles;
2. geomembranes;
3. geo-linear elements;
4. geogrids;
5. geocomposites.

Geotextiles

Geotextiles are usually classified by their method of manufacture and are made in two stages; the manufacture of the linear elements, such as fibres, tapes, etc. and the fabrication of those linear elements into geotextiles. The fibres are the basic load-bearing elements in the material and the forming technique determines the structure and hence the physical and mechanical characteristics of the system. The main fibres used in geotextiles are the synthetic ones such as polyethylene, polypropylene, polyester and polyamide.

Geomembranes

Geomembranes are synthetic materials manufactured in impermeable sheet form from thermoplastic polymers or bituminous materials. Both materials can be reinforced or unreinforced; the former is manufactured on a production line and the latter can be produced on a production line or in situ. The matrix can be reinforced by textiles.

Geo-linear elements

Geo-linear elements are long, slender strips or bars consisting of a unidirectional filament fibre core which is made from a polyester, aramid or glass fibre in a polymer sheath of a low-density polyethylene or a resin. The components of the system form a composite, in that the fibre provides the strength and extension characteristics and the matrix protects the fibre from internal influences and provides the bonding characteristics with the soil.

Geogrids

Geogrids are often grid-like structures of thermoplastic polymer material, and in conjunction with the soil form a quasi-composite system, where the grid structure is the fibre and the soil is assumed to be the 'matrix' and forms an efficient bond with the fibre. Geogrids are of two forms:

1. cross-laid strips; and
2. punched thermoplastic polymer sheets.

The manufacturing techniques have been discussed in Chapter 27 and Hollaway (1993).

Geocomposites

Geocomposites consist of two or more different types of thermoplastic polymer systems combined into a hybrid material. Their main function is to form a drainage passage along the side of the water course, with a polymer core as the drainage channel and the geotextile skin as the filter.

There are many examples of structural applications of polymer composites, and whilst some of those mentioned below are outside the construction field, they are particularly noteworthy because they demonstrate how fibre-reinforced polymer composites have offered unique solutions to a range of product demands.

Marine applications

Polymer composites are now the dominant materials for pleasure craft. These materials have been particularly effective in replacing wood because of the following factors.

1. Design: the moulds to obtain the hydrodynamic and aesthetic forms of the craft can be readily manufactured.
2. Manufacture: the operations of cutting, fitting, assembly and finishing are reduced

or eliminated in composite constructions compared with those required for a wood construction.
3. Structure: continuous stiff and strong shell forms can be produced in a composite construction.

The Sandown Class Single Role Minehunter has been built for the Royal Navy by Vosper Thorneycroft and features an advanced glass-reinforced plastic hull structure.

Truck and automobile systems
Polymer composites are used in the manufacture of certain sports-car bodies and truck cabs. Strength, stiffness, toughness, corrosion resistance and the high-quality finishes are the physical and mechanical properties that must be satisfied, but economics is the crucial consideration governing the choice of composites over conventional materials.

Aircraft and space applications
The high technology composites are increasingly being used for components in the aircraft industry. The fin of the European Airbus is a component made from a sandwich construction with carbon fibre/epoxy resin face material. The Westland helicopter rotor blades are made from carbon fibre composite material. In space, the solid-fuel rocket-motor cases house the propellant for many missiles. These cases are fabricated in the form of a cylinder, having dome ends made by the filament winding process.

Pipes and tanks for chemicals
The chemical industry uses polymer composite pipes and tanks for storage. Whilst the critical consideration is the corrosive resistance under extreme environmental conditions, the ease of fabrication of complex tank shapes and the simplicity of connections makes the composite material cost-effective.

Civil engineering structures
Two sophisticated GRP structures have played a major role in the development of polymer composite materials for construction; these are the

FIGURE 31.1 Mondial House.

dome structure erected in 1968 in Benghazi, Libya, and the roof structure at Dubai Airport, built in 1972. The composite units for the latter were designed and manufactured in the United Kingdom and shipped to Dubai.

During the 1970s and early 1980s, prestigious buildings were erected in this country, notably Morpeth School, Mondial House (the GPO Headquarters in London), Covent Garden Flower Market and the American Express Building in Brighton. Figure 31.1 shows a photograph of Mondial House situated on the bank of the Thames. Because of the relatively low modulus of elasticity of the material, these buildings were erected as a composite system, with either steel or reinforced concrete units as the main structural elements and the GRP composite as the load-bearing infill panels.

In the mid 1970s, Lancashire County Council manufactured a classroom system, using only GRP, by folding flat plates into a folded plate system so that the structural shape provided the stiffness to the building. In the late 1980s, more ambitious structural elements were produced; two examples are the Manchester City Football Club grandstand, in which the construction is a barrel vault system using glass-reinforced polyester composite, and the dome at Sharjah Airport, where the dome is manufactured in the form of curved panels which in the erected position drain to composite channels concealed under the panels.

Hollaway (1993) has given further examples of the use of polymers and polymer composites in construction.

31.1 References

Hollaway, L. (1993) *Polymer and Polymer Composites for Civil and Structural Engineering*, Blackie Academic and Professional, Glasgow.

Section Two

Fibre-reinforced cements and concretes

D. Hannant

Chapter thirty-two

Properties of fibres and of matrices

32.1 Structure of fibre–matrix interface

The performance of a fibre-reinforced composite is controlled mainly by the volume of the fibres, the physical properties of the fibres and the matrix, and the bond between the two. Values for bond strength rarely exceed 4 MPa and may be much less for some polymer fibres. The bond strengths will also change with time and with storage conditions which may permit densification of the interface region due to continuing hydration. Typical ranges for other physical properties of fibres and matrices are shown in Table 32.1.

It is apparent from this table that the elongations at break of all the fibres are two or three orders of magnitude greater than the strain at failure of the matrix and hence the matrix will usually crack long before the fibre strength is approached. This fact is the reason for the emphasis on post-cracking performance in the theoretical treatment in Chapter 33.

On the other hand, the modulus of elasticity of the fibre is generally less than five times that of the matrix and this, combined with the low fibre volume fraction, means that the modulus of the composite is not greatly different from that of the matrix.

Low-modulus organic fibres are generally subject to relatively high creep which means that if they are used to support permanent high stresses in a cracked composite, considerable elongations or deflections may occur over a period of time. They are therefore more likely to be used in situations where the matrix is expected to be uncracked, but where transitory overloads such as handling stresses, impacts or wind loads are significant.

Another problem with the low-modulus fibres of circular cross-section is that they generally have large values of Poisson's ratio and this, combined with their low moduli, means that if stretched along their axis they contract laterally much more than the other fibres. This leads to a high lateral tensile stress at the fibre–matrix interface which for smooth circular section fibres is likely to cause a short aligned fibre to debond and pull out. Devices such as woven meshes or networks of fibrillated fibres may therefore be necessary to give efficient composites.

Even the high-modulus short fibres may require mechanical bonding to avoid pull-out unless the specific surface area is very large. Thus steel fibres are commonly produced with varying cross-sections or bent ends to provide anchorage and glass fibre bundles may be

TABLE 32.1 Typical properties of cement-based matrices and fibres

Material or fibre	*Relative density*	*Diameter or thickness (microns)*	*Length (mm)*	*Elastic modulus (GPa)*	*Tensile strength (MPa)*	*Failure strain (%)*	*Volume in composite (%)*
Mortar matrix	1.8–2.0	300–5000	–	10–30	1–10	0.01–0.05	85–97
Concrete matrix	1.8–2.4	10 000–20 000	–	20–40	1–4	0.01–0.02	97–99.5
Aromatic polyamides (aramids)	1.45	10–15	5–continuous	70–130	2900	2–4	1–5
Asbestos	2.55	0.02–30	5–40	164	200–1800	2–3	5–15
Carbon	1.16–1.95	7–18	3–continuous	30–390	600–2700	0.5–2.4	3–5
Cellulose	1.5	20–120	0.5–5.0	10–50	300–1000	20	5–15
Glass	2.7	12.5	10–50	70	600–2500	3.6	3–7
Polyacrylonitrile (PAN)	1.16	13–104	6	17–20	900–1000	8–11	2–10
Polyethylene							
Pulp	0.91–0.97	1–20	1	–	–	–	3–7
HDPE filament	0.96	900	3–5	5	200	–	2–4
High modulus	0.96	20–50	Continuous	10–30	>400	>4	5–10
Polypropylene							
Monofilament	0.91	20–100	5–20	4	–	–	0.1–0.2
Chopped film	0.91	20–100	5–50	5	300–500	10	0.1–1.0
Continuous nets	0.91–0.93	20–100	Continuous	5–15	300–500	10	5–10
Polyvinyl alcohol (PVA, PVOH)	1–3	3–8	2–6	12–40	700–1500	–	2–3
Steel	7.86	100–600	10–60	200	700–2000	3–5	0.5–2.0

penetrated with cement hydration products to give a more effective mechanical bond after a period of time.

The mortar and concrete matrices in Table 32.1 are differentiated mainly by particle size and strain to failure. The maximum particle size of the matrix is important because it affects the fibre distribution and the quantity of fibres which can be included in the composite. The average particle size of cement paste before hydration is between 10 and 30 microns, whereas mortar contains aggregate particles up to 5 mm maximum size. Concrete which is intended to be used in conjunction with fibres should not have particles greater than 20 mm and preferably not greater than 10 mm otherwise uniform fibre distribution becomes difficult to achieve.

In order to avoid shrinkage and surface crazing problems in finished products it is advisable to use at least 50% by volume of inert mineral filler, which may be aggregate or could include pulverized fuel ash, or limestone dust. However, if the inert filler consists of a large volume of coarse aggregates the volume of fibres which can be included will be limited which will in turn limit the tensile strength and ductility of the composite.

Strength of the matrix is mainly affected by the free water/cement ratio and this parameter also has a considerable though lesser effect on the modulus so that the properties of the matrices can vary widely.

32.1 Structure of fibre–matrix interface

The strength, deformation and failure characteristics of the whole range of fibre-reinforced cementitious materials is critically dependent on the bond between fibre and cement, which itself depends on the microstructure of the interface. The interface consists of an initially water-filled transition zone which does not develop the dense microstructure typical of the bulk matrix and contains a large volume of calcium hydroxide crystals which deposit in large cavities. Three layers are commonly observed in this zone, a thin (less than one micron) calcium-hydroxide-rich rather discontinuous layer directly in contact with the fibre, a massive calcium hydroxide layer and a porous zone up to 40 microns from the surface consisting of calcium silicate hydrate and some ettringite. The porosity of these layers is affected by w/c ratio, age and whether or not microsilica is used in the mixture. Further information on the constituents of cement and concrete is given in Chapters 13–17.

When a force is applied to the composite, high shear stresses exist at the fibre–cement interface but failure may be initiated in the porous layer rather than at the interface itself. It is partly the changing nature with continuing hydration of this rather weak interfacial zone which is used to explain the embrittlement of some fibre cements with time.

When considering the microstructure in the interfacial zone, a distinction should be made between discrete monofilaments such as steel and elements of polypropylene nets and bundled filaments such as glass or asbestos. With monofilaments the entire surface of the fibre can be in direct contact with the matrix and the perimeter (P_f) carrying the shear forces is known. With bundled filaments only the external fibres initially have direct contact with the matrix and the perimeter transferring shear stress can only be estimated. As time goes on the vacant spaces between filaments in a strand may slowly become filled with hydration products.

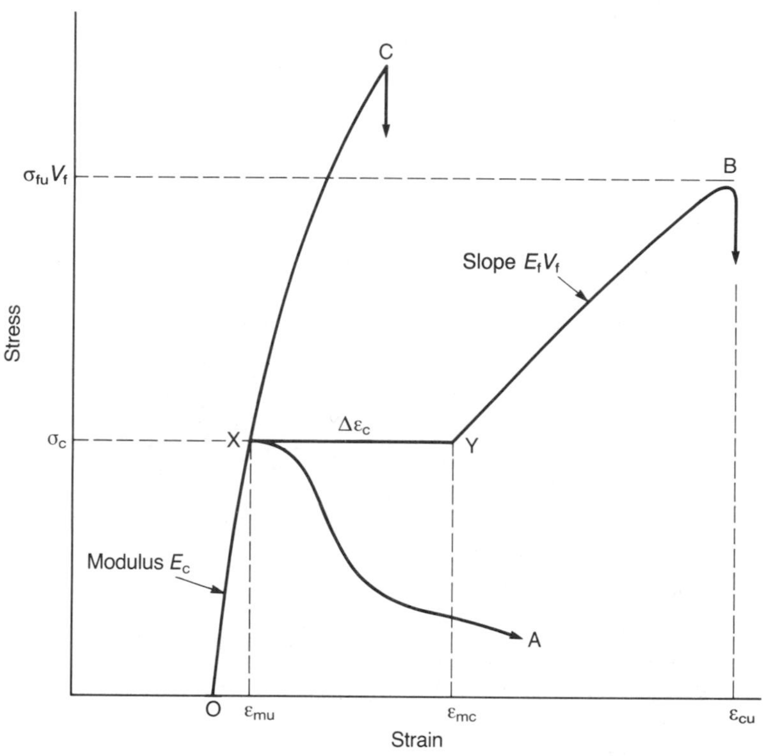

FIGURE 32.1 Theoretical tensile stress–strain curves for different fibre composites.

At an intermediate stage some central fibres in a bundle are free to slide while the outside fibres are rigidly locked into the matrix. The final stage is complete penetration of the bundle which may then show brittle fracture.

Thus the accurate calculation of bond stress (τ), which relies on a knowledge of the perimeter in contact with cement, is not possible with fibre bundles because this area is unknown and changes with time. Fortunately, the specific value of τ does not affect the shape of the stress–strain curve OXYB in Figure 32.1, nor the length of the multiple crack region ($\Delta\varepsilon_c$) nor the failure strain ε_{cu}. Bond strength does, however, affect crack spacing and crack width which are significant parameters affecting the performance of the composites in practical situations.

Chapter thirty-three

Structure and post-cracking composite theory

33.1 Theoretical stress–strain curves in uniaxial tension
33.2 Uniaxial tension – fracture mechanics approach
33.3 Principles of fibre reinforcement in flexure
33.4 References

As discussed in Chapter 27, the main benefits of including fibres in hardened cement-based products occur in the post-cracking state, where the fibres bridging the cracks contribute to the increase in strength, failure strain and toughness of the composite. This type of reinforcing mechanism requires a different theoretical approach from that described in Chapter 28 although the principles covered there adequately describe the pre-cracking behaviour.

Another significant difference from fibre-reinforced polymers is that the fibre volume in fine grained cement-based products rarely exceeds 15% and is more commonly less than 10%. In concrete the fibre volume is usually less than 2%, often with low-modulus fibres being included, and it is for these reasons, together with the relatively stiff matrix, that little emphasis is placed on increasing the elastic modulus of the composite by the inclusion of fibres.

33.1 Theoretical stress–strain curves in uniaxial tension

33.1.1 Characteristic shapes of stress–strain curves

Fibre-reinforced cements and concretes are generally considered to be most useful when carrying bending or impact loads but unfortunately a theoretical analysis of the mechanics of reinforcement in these systems is very complex. A more fundamental and more easily understood stress system is that of direct tension and a sound knowledge of the behaviour of fibres in such a system provides a good background by which the potential merits of a fibre cement composite can be judged for a given end use.

The three basic types of tensile stress–strain properties are shown in the curves in Figure 32.1. Curves B and C are based on the assumption that the stress in the composite is increased at a constant rate.

For all three curves, the portion OX defines the elastic modulus of the uncracked composite

(E_c). Curves A and C are for composites in which there are insufficient fibres to carry the load in the composite after continuous cracks in the matrix propagate completely across the component. In curve A, after the cracks have formed at X, the fibres slowly pull out and absorb energy leading to a tough but rather weak composite typified by steel fibre concrete or short random fibre polypropylene concrete. In curve C, which is representative of asbestos cement and of some cellulose-fibre-based composites when dry, the relatively high crack propagation stress leads to a sudden large release of energy and to an almost instantaneous fibre fracture or fibre pull-out at C. However, stable microcracks may exist well before point C is reached. The mechanism of the reinforcement of cement by asbestos fibre is very complex and leads to the special case of a rather brittle composite with high tensile strength. A full understanding of the fracture process has not yet been achieved but it appears to require a combination of the reinforcing theory described for curve B with a knowledge of fracture mechanics as outlined in Section 33.2.

Curve B is typical of a composite in which there are sufficient fibres to maintain the load on the composite when the matrix cracks. The horizontal portion XY is a result of multiple cracking at approximately constant stress and YB represents extension or pull-out of fibres up to separation of the component into two parts at point B. Curve OXYB is typified by fine grained materials such as glass-reinforced cement or some continuous fibre composites such as polypropylene-network-reinforced cement.

Apart from the special case of curve OXC it is unusual for fibres to significantly increase the cracking stress (σ_c) of the cement-based composite and therefore it is of value to consider the load-carrying ability of the fibres after matrix cracking has occurred. An important concept in this respect is the critical volume fraction of fibres.

33.1.2 Critical volume fraction (V_{fcrit}) in uniaxial tension

The critical fibre volume is the volume of fibres which, after matrix cracking, will carry the load which the composite maintained before cracking.

This definition needs to be used with a little care because material which has less than the critical volume of fibre in tension (curve OXA) may have considerably more than the critical fibre volume required for flexural strengthening. However, it is common practice to assume that the above definition of critical fibre volume refers only to uniaxial tensile stresses.

For the simplest case of fibres aligned in the stress direction with frictional bond, let:

ε_{mu} = matrix cracking strain
σ_c = composite cracking stress
V_{fcrit} = critical volume of fibres
σ_{fu} = fibre strength or average pull-out stress of fibre depending on whether fibres break or pull out at a crack.

Just before cracking

$$\sigma_c = E_c \varepsilon_{mu}. \tag{33.1}$$

After cracking, the whole stress is carried by the fibres. Assume that there are just sufficient fibres to support this stress, i.e. fibre volume = V_{fcrit}:

$$\sigma_c = \sigma_{fu} V_{fcrit} \tag{33.2}$$

From (33.1) and (33.2)

$$V_{fcrit} = \frac{E_c \varepsilon_{mu}}{\sigma_{fu}} \tag{33.3}$$

From (33.2)

$$V_{fcrit} = \frac{\sigma_c}{\sigma_{fu}}. \tag{33.4}$$

There are important points to note about eqns (33.3) and (33.4).

1. E_c, ε_{mu} and hence σ_c may vary with time and E_c and σ_c will generally increase if the

cement continues to hydrate. This implies that a composite which has just sufficient fibre volume to exceed V_{fcrit} at early ages may, after some years, have less fibre than V_{fcrit} at that age and hence may suffer brittle fracture.
2. V_{fcrit} can be decreased by decreasing σ_c.
3. Poor bond may reduce σ_{fu} by allowing fibre pull-out at a fraction of the fibre strength. Additionally the orientation of the fibres will have a large effect on V_{fcrit} because random fibre orientation will reduce the number of fibres across a crack surface compared with the aligned case.

In the common practical case of short, randomly orientated fibres where the fibres pull out at a crack rather than break, the stress in the fibre causing pull-out may be substantially less than σ_{fu} and hence V_{fcrit} for such composites may be up to 10 times that required for continuous aligned fibres. In the equations in Section 33.1.3 it is assumed that the fibre orientation and stress efficiency factors are 1.0 and hence V_f and σ_{fu} for the wide variety of composites in current use must be modified by the use of efficiency factors to allow for the effective volume of fibres in the direction of stress. The effect of short random fibres on V_{fcrit} may be calculated using the equations in Section 33.1.6.

33.1.3 Stress–strain curve, multiple cracking and ultimate strength

If the critical fibre volume for strengthening has been reached then it is possible to achieve multiple cracking of the matrix. This is a desirable situation because it changes a basically brittle material with a single fracture surface and low energy requirement to fracture into a pseudo-ductile material which can absorb transient minor overloads and shocks with little visible damage. The aim of the materials engineer is often therefore to produce a large number of cracks at as close a spacing as possible so that the crack widths are very small (say, <0.1 mm). These cracks are almost invisible to the naked eye in a rough concrete surface and the small width reduces the rate at which aggressive materials can penetrate the matrix when compared with commonly allowable widths in reinforced concrete of up to 0.3 mm.

High bond strength helps to give a close crack spacing but it is also essential that the fibres debond sufficiently adjacent to the crack to give the ductility which will absorb impacts.

The principles behind the calculation of the complete stress–strain curve, the crack spacing and the crack width for long aligned fibres for the simplified case where the bond between the fibres and matrix is purely frictional and the matrix has a well-defined single value breaking stress have been given by Aveston *et al.* (1971) and Aveston *et al.* (1974). The following has been simplified from these publications.

Long fibres with frictional bond

The idealized stress–strain curve for a fibre-reinforced brittle matrix composite is OXYB in Figure 32.1. If the fibre diameter is not too small, the matrix will fail at its normal failure strain (ε_{mu}) and the subsequent behaviour will depend on whether the fibres can withstand the additional load without breaking, i.e. whether

$$\sigma_{fu} V_f > \sigma_c.$$

If they can take this additional load, it will be transferred back into the matrix over a transfer length χ' (Figure 33.1) and the matrix will eventually be broken down into a series of blocks of length between χ' and $2\chi'$ with an average spacing (C) of $1.364\chi'$.

We can calculate χ' from a simple balance of the load $\sigma_{mu} V_m$ needed to break a unit area of the matrix and the load carried by N fibres of individual cross-sectional area A_f and perimeter P_f across the same area after cracking. This load is transferred over a distance χ' by the limiting maximum shear stress τ, i.e.

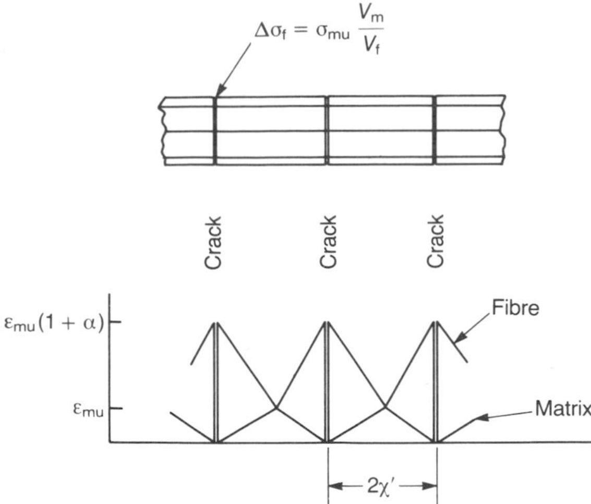

FIGURE 33.1 Strain distribution after cracking of an aligned brittle matrix composite (Aveston *et al.*, 1971). (Crown copyright reserved.)

$$N = V_f/A_f \tag{33.5}$$

$$P_f N\tau\chi' = \sigma_{mu} V_m \tag{33.6}$$

or

$$\chi' = \frac{V_m}{V_f}\frac{\sigma_{mu}}{\tau}\frac{A_f}{P_f}. \tag{33.7}$$

This strain distribution in the fibres and matrix (crack spacing $2\chi'$) will then be as shown in Figure 33.1.

The additional stress ($\Delta\sigma_f$) on the fibres due to cracking of the matrix varies between $\sigma_{mu}V_m/V_f$ at the crack and zero at distance χ' from the crack so that the average additional strain in the fibres, which is equal to the extension per unit length of composite at constant stress σ_c, is given by

$$\Delta\varepsilon_c = \frac{1}{2}\sigma_{mu}\frac{V_m}{V_f}\frac{1}{E_f}, \tag{33.8}$$

i.e.

$$\Delta\varepsilon_c = \frac{\varepsilon_{mu}E_m V_m}{2E_f V_f} = \frac{\alpha\varepsilon_{mu}}{2} \tag{33.9}$$

where

$$\alpha = E_m V_m/E_f V_f \tag{33.10}$$

and the crack width (ω), bearing in mind that the matrix strain relaxes from ε_{mu} to $\varepsilon_{mu}/2$ will be given by

$$\omega = 2\chi'\left(\frac{\alpha\varepsilon_{mu}}{2} + \frac{\varepsilon_{mu}}{2}\right) \tag{33.11}$$

or

$$\omega = \varepsilon_{mu}(1+\alpha)\chi'. \tag{33.12}$$

For practical composites, the factor α may range from about 2 for asbestos cement to over 100 for some polymer fibre composites, thus making a very wide range of properties available.

At the completion of cracking the blocks of matrix will all be less than the length ($2\chi'$) required to transfer their breaking load ($\sigma_{mu}V_m$) and so further increase in load on the composite results in the fibres sliding relative to the matrix, and the tangent modulus becomes $E_f V_f$ (see Figure 32.1).

In this condition, the load is supported entirely by the fibres and the ultimate strength (σ_{cu}) is given by

$$\sigma_{cu} = \sigma_{fu}V_f \tag{33.13}$$

If the average crack spacing $C = 1.364\chi'$ is used in the calculations instead of the $2\chi'$ crack spacing then parameters associated with curve OXYB in Figure 32.1 are:

Average crack spacing,

$$C = 1.364\frac{V_m}{V_f}\frac{\sigma_{mu}}{\tau}\frac{A_f}{P_f}. \tag{33.14}$$

Length XY,

$$\Delta\varepsilon_c = 0.659\,\alpha\varepsilon_{mu}. \tag{33.15}$$

Average crack width between X and Y,

$$W = \varepsilon_{mu}\cdot 0.9(1+\alpha)\chi'. \tag{33.16}$$

Composite failure strain

$$\varepsilon_{cu} = \varepsilon_{fu} - 0.341\alpha\varepsilon_{mu}. \tag{33.17}$$

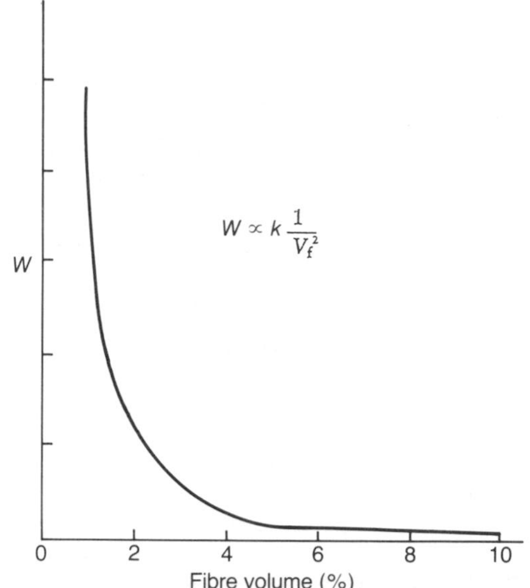

FIGURE 33.2 Relationship between crack width (W) at the end of multiple cracking and fibre volume (V_f) for the case in which α is much greater than unity.

The relationship between the average crack width W at the end of multiple cracking and fibre volume is shown in Figure 33.2 for the case in which α is much greater than unity. It is apparent that, even using the most optimistic assumption, large variations in crack width are likely to occur for small variations in fibre volumes at less than 2% by volume of fibre and volumes above 5% are desirable if a uniformly and invisibly cracked composite is to be achieved. Hence the fabrication techniques must be adjusted to produce a uniformly dispersed fibre and preferably a high (5–10%) fibre volume if invisible cracking is required in the product.

33.1.4 Efficiency of fibre reinforcement

The efficiency of fibre reinforcement depends on fibre length and orientation. Different efficiency factors are required for pre-cracking performance, as described in Chapter 28, and post-cracking performance. Allowance also has to be made for static frictional resistance prior to sliding and dynamic frictional resistance during sliding. A detailed treatment of efficiency factors is beyond the scope of this section but may be found in Aveston *et al.* (1974), Laws (1971), Hannant (1978) and Bentur and Mindess (1990). A simplified approach for specific cases is given in Section 33.1.6.

33.1.5 Application of theory to real composites

Typical stress–strain curves for real composites may be obtained using the theory in the previous sections and four such curves for different fibre types are shown in Figure 33.3 in which V_f' is the effective volume of fibre in the direction of stress calculated from the total V_f using the appropriate efficiency factors.

The values for α shown in Figure 33.3 have been calculated from eqn (33.10), and, when substituted in eqn (33.15) they give an indication of the possible range for real composites of the horizontal part $\Delta\varepsilon_c$ of Figure 32.1.

Figure 33.3(b) shows that it is possible for glass-reinforced cement to have a typical extension due to multiple cracking alone of about 12 times the matrix cracking strain, whereas asbestos cement (Figure 33.3(a)) can only extend by about 1 times the matrix cracking strain before the fibres take over completely. Likewise, a similar effective volume of continuous polypropylene fibre to that of asbestos fibre (Figure 33.3(c)) could increase the strain due to multiple cracking alone by 51 times the matrix cracking strain even under fairly rapid loading. This would probably be exceeded for extended loading periods because the modulus of polypropylene is time-dependent.

The lack of a horizontal portion in Figure 33.3(a) is a serious deficiency in that it results in the material having limited capability to absorb shock and accidental overstrains. It is possible that the asbestos fibres have such a small diameter (0.02–20 μm) that matrix cracking is

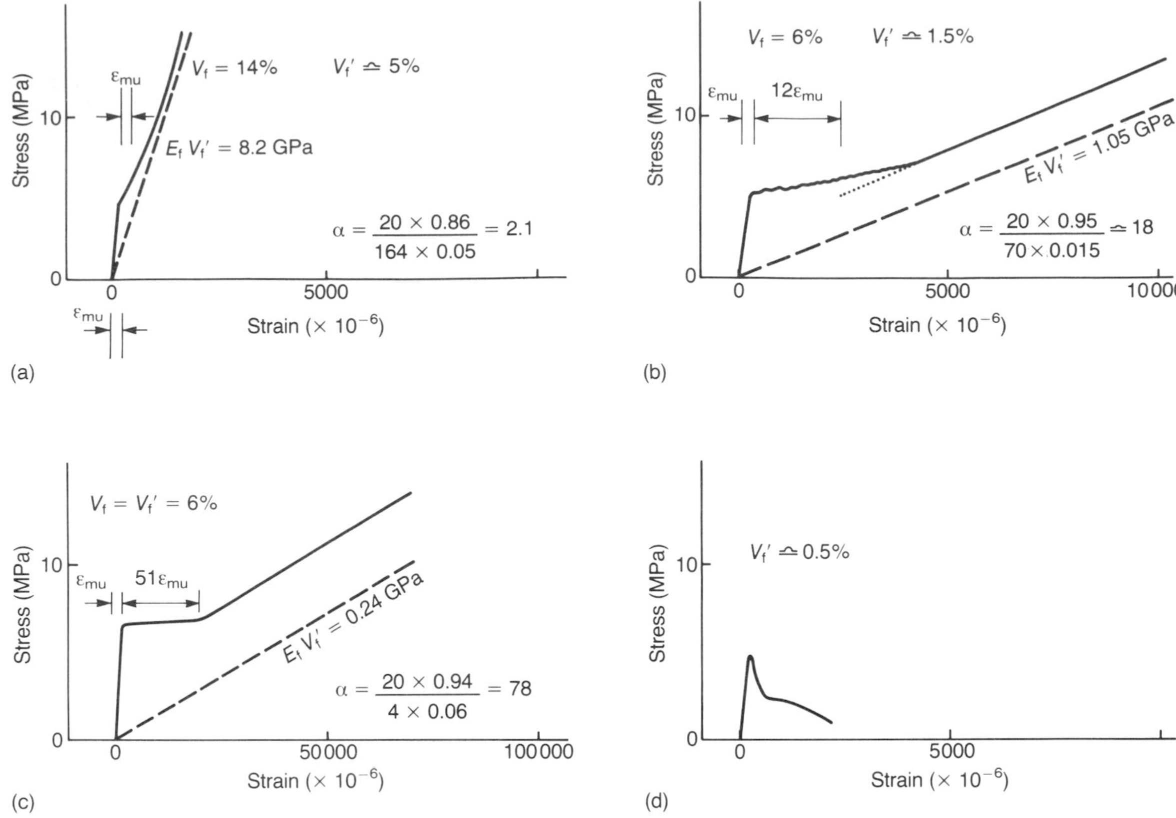

FIGURE 33.3 Typical stress–strain curves for real composites: (a) asbestos fibres in cement paste; (b) two-dimensional random glass fibres in cement paste; (c) continuous aligned polypropylene fibres in cement paste; (d) short, random, chopped steel or polypropylene fibres in concrete.

suppressed until successively higher strains are reached as described in Section 33.2 and final failure is by single fracture with some pull-out.

The strain to failure for the polypropylene continuous fibre composite in Figure 33.3(c) is an order of magnitude greater than for the other composites and hence the energy absorbing capability under overload conditions, which depends on the area under the stress–strain curve, is likely to be higher. However, the ultimate strain may never be reached in practice due to excessive deformation.

Figure 33.3(d) is typical of concretes containing less than the critical volume of short chopped fibres, generally steel or polypropylene in random three-dimensional orientation. The fibres in these circumstances are generally sufficiently short to pull out, rather than break, when cracks occur in the matrix and the ultimate load on the composite is then controlled by the number of fibres across a crack, the length/diameter ratio of the fibres and the bond strength. The stress in the fibre at pull-out is often less than half the strength of the fibre and hence higher bond strength, rather than high fibre strength, may be the most important requirement for this type of composite.

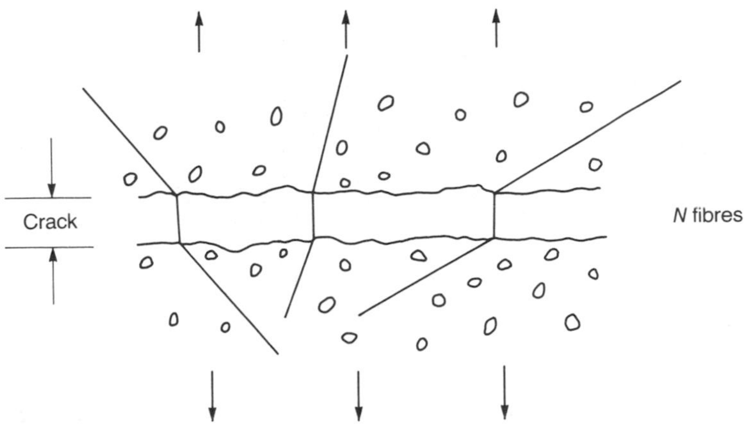

FIGURE 33.4 Change in fibre orientation at a crack. (Reprinted by permission of John Wiley & Sons Ltd, from D.J. Hannant (1978).)

33.1.6 Short random round fibres which pull out rather than break

Factors affecting a realistic estimate of V_{fcrit} and post-cracking strength are:

1. number of fibres across a crack;
2. bond strength and fibre pull-out load.

Number of fibres across a crack

The situation in a cracked composite may be represented by Figure 33.4. For short random fibres, such as steel or chopped fibrillated polypropylene, which are generally shorter than the critical length for fibre breakage, the fibres mostly pull out across a crack. A realistic estimate of the load carried after cracking can therefore be obtained by multiplying the number of fibres crossing a unit area of crack by the average pull-out force per fibre. For fibres which break before pulling out, the situation is more complicated.

The appropriate number of fibres, N per unit area, can be calculated as follows:

A_f = cross-sectional area of a single fibre

For fibres aligned in one direction

$$N = \frac{V_f}{A_f} \tag{33.18}$$

For fibres random in two dimensions

$$N = \frac{2}{\pi}\frac{V_f}{A_f} \tag{33.19}$$

For fibres random in three dimensions

$$N = \frac{1}{2}\frac{V_f}{A_f} \tag{33.20}$$

Bond strength and fibre pull-out force

If the composite failure is by fibre pull-out it has been shown that the mean fibre pull-out length is $l/4$ (see Figure 33.5).

Provided that the average sliding friction bond strength (τ) is known and assuming that it does not vary with the angle of the fibre to the crack then the average pull-out force per fibre (F) is given by:

$$F = \tau P_f l/4 \tag{33.21}$$

where P_f = the individual fibre perimeter in contact with the cement.

The ultimate stress (σ_{cu}) sustained by a unit area of composite after cracking is therefore given by N times F, i.e.

$$\sigma_{cu} = \frac{N\tau P_f l}{4} \tag{33.22}$$

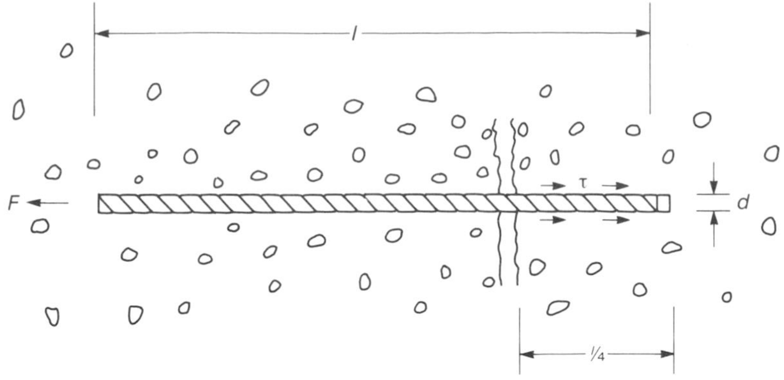

FIGURE 33.5 Average pull-out force per fibre. (Reprinted by permission of John Wiley & Sons Ltd, from D.J. Hannant (1978).)

and the average fibre stress at pull-out (σ_f) is,

$$\sigma_f = \frac{P_f}{A_f}\frac{l}{4} \qquad (33.23)$$

which for round fibres reduces to

$$\sigma_f = \tau\frac{l}{d}.$$

Substituting for N from eqns (33.18), (33.19) and (33.20) in eqn (33.22) gives:

Aligned fibres in one direction

$$\sigma_{cu} = V_f\tau\frac{l}{4}\cdot\frac{P_f}{A_f} \qquad (33.24)$$

Random two-dimensional

$$\sigma_{cu} = \frac{2}{\pi}V_f\tau\frac{l}{4}\cdot\frac{P_f}{A_f} \qquad (33.25)$$

Random three-dimensional

$$\sigma_{cu} = \frac{1}{2}V_f\tau\frac{l}{4}\cdot\frac{P_f}{A_f} \qquad (33.26)$$

Thus, the three-dimensional random fibre concrete should have about half the post-crack strength of the aligned composite.

The critical fibre volume for short random fibres can be obtained by rearranging eqns (33.24), (33.25) and (33.26) to give V_f on the left-hand side of the equation.

In contrast to the use of the above equations for short chopped polypropylene fibre or steel fibre concrete the glass-reinforced cement industry has sometimes used empirical efficiency factors. Thus, for a commonly used two-dimensional random chopped glass fibre cement composite the effectiveness of the fibre at the end of the multiple cracking zone has been shown to be between 0.16 and 0.27 depending on the direction of stress to the spray-up direction.

33.1.7 Toughness in uniaxial tension

One of the major attributes of fibre cement composites is their increased toughness in comparison with plain concrete. However, the theoretical prediction of the increased toughness and its measurement in practice are both fraught with problems. Commercial tests tend to rely on empirical comparisons between composites with and without fibres, tested with drop weights until 'no rebound' or with beams deflected to specific values. These tests do not determine basic material parameters and are often highly dependent on support conditions or on specimen and machine dimensions and stiffnesses.

A more fundamental approach is to calculate the very large increase in area of the tensile stress–strain curve resulting from the presence of the fibres. This increase, which may be several orders of magnitude, is indicative of greatly enhanced toughness and ductility, properties often loosely associated with impact strength or impact resistance. The theory outlined in Section 33.1.3 can therefore be used as the basis of toughness predictions.

In fibre cements and concretes there are essentially two modes of failure, one mainly involving fibre pull-out after single fracture and the other involving multiple fracture of the matrix followed by fibre pull-out or fracture. In the former case, which is typical of steel fibre concrete, the energy U to pull out N fibres per unit area of composite cross-section is proportional to the frictional fibre matrix bond strength, τ, and to the square of the fibre length (l) as in eqn (33.27) (Hibbert and Hannant, 1982).

$$U = \frac{N \cdot P_f \cdot \tau l^2}{24} \qquad (33.27)$$

In the case where failure occurs by multiple cracking followed by fibre fracture rather than fibre pull-out the energy is absorbed throughout the volume of material and may be calculated from the area under the tensile stress–strain curve OXYB in Figure 32.1. The resulting energy is that absorbed per unit volume of composite, i.e.

$$U = 0.5\sigma_{fu}\varepsilon_{fu}V_f + 0.159\alpha E_c\varepsilon_{mu}^2 \qquad (33.28)$$

where the first term represents the fibre strain energy and the second term the contribution from multiple cracking of the matrix.

For practical situations, we really require to know the energy which can be absorbed by the product before it breaks into two pieces or before it is rendered unserviceable. The amount of energy which can be absorbed before reaching an acceptable amount of damage in terms of visible cracking depends very much on whether fracture occurs mainly by a single crack opening or by multiple cracking. Thus a careful decision has to be made as to whether the energy should be predicted from a material parameter related to unit *area* of fracture surface (J/m^2) for the case of a single crack or from a parameter for energy absorbed per unit *volume* of material (J/m^3) for multiple cracks.

An additional complexity is that because the composite modulus (E_c) and the matrix failure strain (ε_{mu}) may increase with time in external environments, then V_{fcrit} calculated from eqn (33.3) may increase above the original value required to ensure multiple cracking. Thus a composite which is tough and ductile at early ages may suffer single fracture after some years with an energy to failure defined by the area under the curve OX in Figure 32.1 (eqn (33.29)).

$$U = 0.5E_c\varepsilon_{mu}^2. \qquad (33.29)$$

Although E_c and ε_{mu} may have increased with ageing, the energy calculated from eqn (33.29) is very much less than the energy given by eqn (33.28).

Some typical toughness values for real composites calculated from the area under the tensile stress–strain curves are shown in Table 33.1.

33.2 Uniaxial tension – fracture mechanics approach

It has been observed that asbestos cement has a strain to failure or to first visible crack often in

TABLE 33.1 Typical toughness values for real composites

Material		*Energy to failure (kJ/m^3)*
Asbestos cement		5.5
Glass-reinforced cement	(dry)	120
	(wet)	3
Continuous polypropylene networks in cement		1000
Kevlar in cement		150

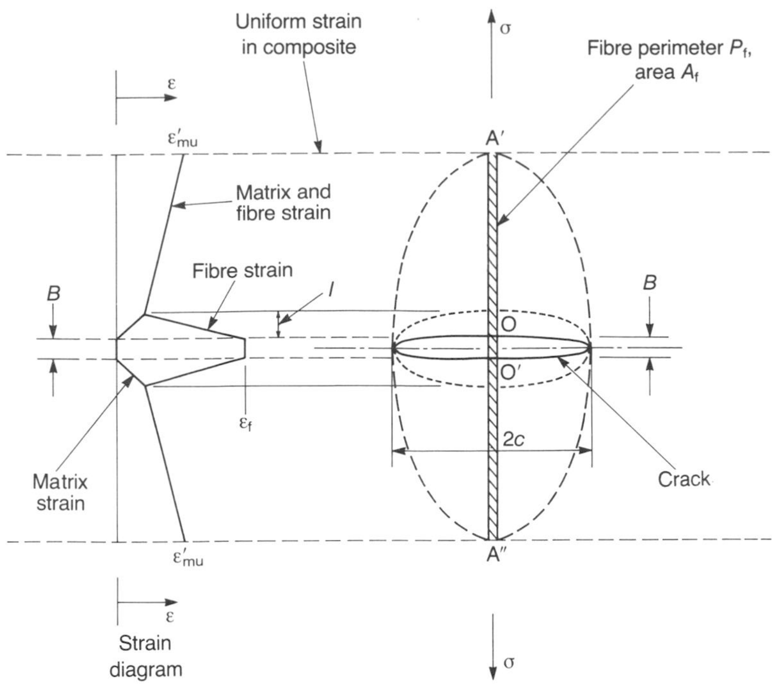

FIGURE 33.6 Possible zone of relaxation of strain around a crack under stress that is traversed by a single fibre. The left side of the figure illustrates the variation in strain within the fibre and matrix along the line A′A″ (Hannant *et al.*, 1983).

excess of 1000×10^{-6} and sometimes up to 2000×10^{-6}. This implies that the cracking strain of the matrix has been increased by the presence of fibres since the cracking strain of the cement paste from which the composite is made is usually less than 400×10^{-6}. The composite materials approach outlined in Section 33.1 is not adequate to explain this observation.

The implication is that microcrack propagation from pre-existing flaws in the matrix has been suppressed by the very high volume (~12%) of very small diameter, high modulus of elasticity fibres and the concepts of fracture mechanics are required to quantify the possible improvements in performance.

It has been shown that typical pre-existing flaws in the matrix may be 3 mm long with a critical opening of about 1 micron. For asbestos cement and some other fibre composites the flaws will be crossed by many fibres but, to demonstrate the principle of the argument, Figure 33.6 shows a flaw traversed by a single fibre (Hannant *et al.*, 1983).

If the strain in the specimen is increased from zero with the crack initially closed the fibre will be stressed by the crack opening to width B and this stress will be transferred back into the matrix as shown in the strain diagram in Figure 33.6. The matrix will slide back over the fibres by a distance l producing a difference in strain between fibre and matrix at the crack face of ε_f.

$$\therefore\ E_f\varepsilon_f = \frac{P_f\tau l}{A_f}. \qquad (33.30)$$

Also, the crack opening B is obtained from the integrated difference in strain between reinforcing fibres and matrix, i.e.

$$l = \frac{B}{\varepsilon_f}. \qquad (33.31)$$

So, by eliminating l the stress in the fibre σ_f is given by

$$\sigma_f = \left(\frac{P_f}{A_f}\tau E_f B\right)^{1/2}. \qquad (33.32)$$

The fibres therefore exert a closing force on the crack and reduce its opening. If there are N fibres crossing a crack, the total closing force F reducing the crack opening is

$$F \sim N\sigma_{fmax}A_f. \qquad (33.33)$$

Using typical values for bond, modulus and specific surface area for glass fibres indicates stresses in the fibres of ~300 MPa before the pre-existing cracks reach sufficient width to propagate. The flaws will propagate catastrophically as soon as the rate of energy release becomes greater than the rate of energy absorption. The calculation is made using a computer iterative process which shows, in accord with experiment, that the ultimate failure strain of asbestos fibres in asbestos cement at $V_f = 5\%$ and 10% is reached before the crack becomes unstable. We therefore could expect breaking of the specimen and first cracking of the matrix to occur simultaneously at a strain of 860×10^{-6} for $V_f = 5\%$ and at 1200×10^{-6} for $V_f = 10\%$.

Although similar effects should exist in all fibre cements where the fibre spacing is less than the flaw size, it is only where composites contain very high volumes of high-modulus small-diameter fibres with high surface area and good bonding characteristics that the effects of increased matrix cracking strain become sufficiently significant to be observable in practice.

33.3 Principles of fibre reinforcement in flexure

33.3.1 Necessity for the theory

In many of their major applications, cement-bound fibre composites are likely to be subjected to flexural stresses in addition to direct stresses, and hence an understanding of the mechanism of strengthening in flexure may be of equal importance to the analysis of direct stress.

The need for a special theoretical treatment for flexure arises because of the large differences which are observed experimentally between the flexural strength and the direct tensile strengths, both in glass-reinforced cement and in steel-fibre concrete. In both of these materials the so-called flexural strength can be up to three times the direct tensile strength even though, according to elastic theory, they are nominally a measure of the same value. The same situation occurs to a lesser degree with plain concrete.

The main reason for the discrepancy in fibre cement composites is that the post-cracking stress–strain curves XA and XYB in Figure 32.1 on the tensile side of a fibre cement or fibre concrete beam are very different from those in compression and, as a result, conventional beam theory is inadequate. The flexural strengthening mechanism is mainly due to this quasi-plastic behaviour of fibre composites in tension as a result of fibre pull-out or elastic extension of the fibres after matrix cracking.

Figures 33.7(a) and (b) show a cracked fibre-reinforced beam with a linear strain distribution and the neutral axis moved towards the compression surface. At a crack the fibres effectively provide point forces holding the section together (Figure 33.7(c)). However, the exact stresses in the fibres are generally ignored in flexural calculations and an equivalent composite stress block such as in Figure 33.7(d) is assumed based on Figure 32.1. The shape of this stress block depends on fibre volume, bond strength, orientation and length efficiency factors. An accurate analysis of such a system presents formidable problems but a simplified treatment which is satisfactory for many practical situations is given below.

33.3.2 Analysis using a rectangular stress block in the tensile zone of a beam

The analysis which follows is based on a simplified assumption regarding the shape of the

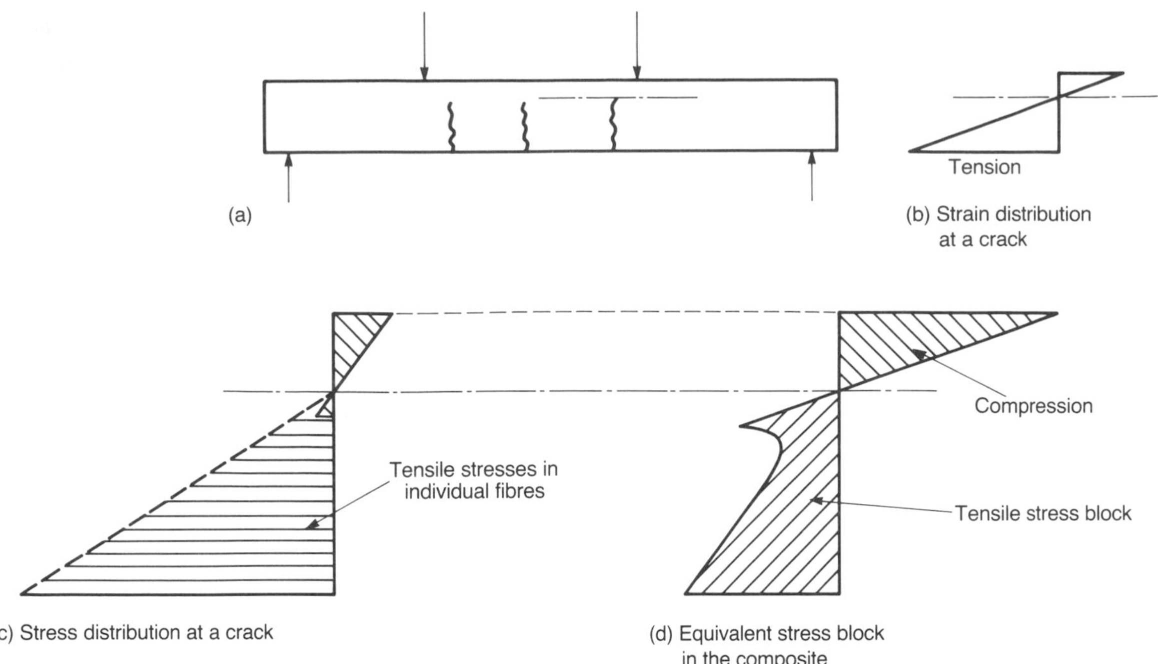

FIGURE 33.7 Strain and stress distributions in a cracked fibre-reinforced concrete beam. (Note: scales of (c) and (d) are different.)

stress block in the tensile zone after cracking.

The stress block for an elastic material in bending is shown in Figure 33.8(a) and this is usually used to calculate the flexural strength (σ_{fl}) even though it is known to be grossly inaccurate for quasi-ductile fibre composites.

Figure 33.8(b) shows a simplified stress block in bending for the type of tensile stress–strain curve OXY in Figure 32.1. This is typical of a fibre concrete composite after cracking, where the fibres are extending or are pulling out at constant load across a crack throughout the tensile section. The ultimate post-cracking tensile strength of the composite is σ_{cu} and σ_{comp} is the compressive stress on the outer face of the beam. Figure 33.8(b) approximates to the stresses in steel fibre concrete where the crack widths are small (<0.3 mm) compared with the fibre length, and possibly to glass-reinforced cement at early ages when the fibres are poorly bonded and extend before fracture or pull out after fracture at roughly constant load. It also simulates composites with $>V_{fcrit}$ of continuous polypropylene nets.

A conservative estimate for the distance of the neutral axis from the compressive surface is $\frac{1}{4}D$ and using this assumption the moments of resistance of the two stress blocks can be compared:

$$\text{moment of resistance} = \frac{1}{6}\sigma_{fl}D^2 \text{ for Figure 33.8(a)} \quad (33.34)$$

$$\text{moment of resistance} = \frac{13}{32}\sigma_{cu}D^2 \text{ for Figure 33.8(b)} \quad (33.35)$$

In order that the two beams represented in Figure 33.8 can carry the same load, their moments of resistance should be equal, i.e.

$$\frac{1}{6}\sigma_{fl}D^2 = \frac{13}{32}\sigma_{cu}D^2. \quad (33.36)$$

Therefore

$$\sigma_{fl} = 2.44\sigma_{cu}. \quad (33.37)$$

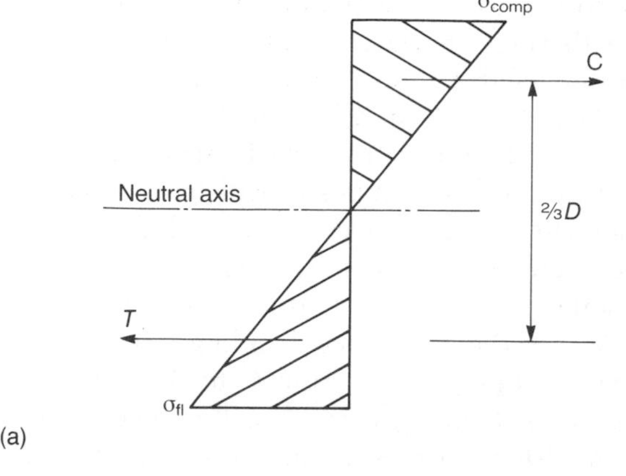

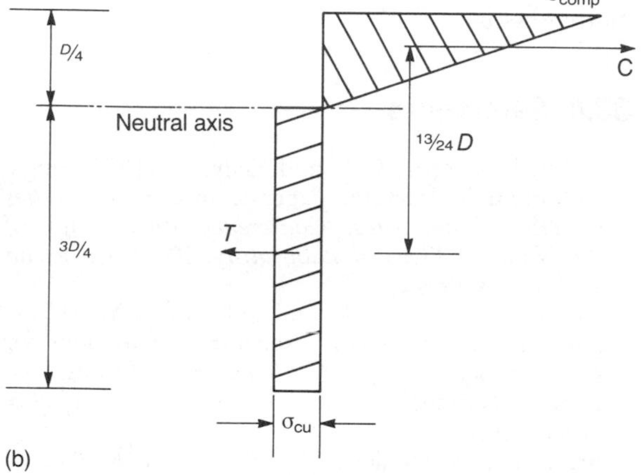

FIGURE 33.8 Stress blocks in flexure. (a) Elastic material; moment of resistance = $(1/6)\,\sigma_{fl}D^2$. (b) Elastic in compression, plastic in tension; moment of resistance = $13/32\,\sigma_{cu}D^2$.

Equation (33.37) implies that if the critical fibre volume in uniaxial tension has just been achieved as shown in Figure 33.9(b) then the flexural tensile strength will appear to be about 2.44 times the composite cracking stress. Conversely, a material with less than half the critical fibre volume in tension which has the uniaxial tensile stress–strain curve shown in Figure 33.9(a) will not exhibit a decrease in flexural load capacity after cracking implying that the critical fibre volume in flexure has been achieved.

The limiting condition in Figure 33.8(b) is when the neutral axis reaches the compressive surface of the beam while maintaining the maximum tensile strength (σ_{cu}) throughout the section. In this case

$$\frac{1}{2}\sigma_{cu}D^2 = \frac{1}{6}\sigma_{fl}D^2, \quad \text{i.e. } \sigma_{fl} = 3\sigma_{cu}. \tag{33.38}$$

This type of simplified analysis explains why the flexural strength for fibre cements and fibre concretes is often quoted to be between 2 and 3 times the tensile strength. Because the flexural strengths calculated using the normal 'elastic theory' approach often imply unrealistically high tensile strengths it is unwise to use such strengths in the design of fibre-reinforced cement or concrete components. For the same reason it is preferable to avoid flexural tests wherever possible when the tensile strengths of fibre-reinforced cement-based composites are required.

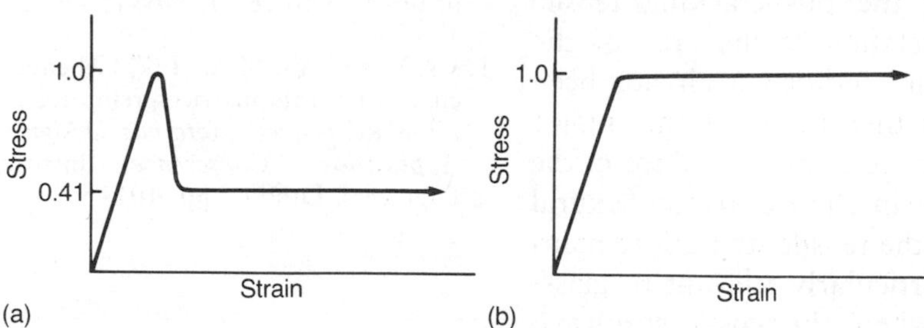

FIGURE 33.9 Stress–strain curves in uniaxial tension: (a) no decrease in flexural load capacity after cracking; (b) load capacity after cracking = 2.44 times the cracking load for compressive strength/tensile strength ⩾ 6.

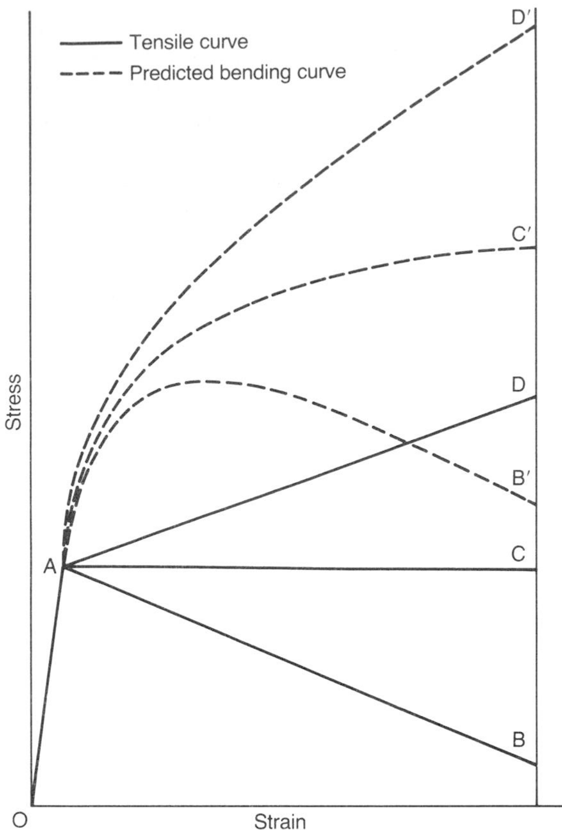

FIGURE 33.10 Apparent bending flexural strength curves predicted for assumed direct tensile curves (Laws and Ali, 1977). (By permission of the Institution of Civil Engineers.)

33.3.3 Effect of loss of ductility in tension on the flexural strength

The importance of the post-cracking tensile strain capacity in relation to the area of the tensile stress block in bending has already been demonstrated. A further result of this major factor is that changes in strain to failure in the composite can result in changes in the flexural strength even when the tensile strength remains constant. This is particularly relevant to glass-reinforced cement where the tensile strain capacity can reduce by an order of magnitude (1 to 0.1%) over a period of years of natural weathering or water curing. The movement of the neutral axis towards the compressive surface depends on a high post-cracking strain in tension and if this tensile strain decreases sufficiently, the composite will have a reduced moment of resistance (Laws and Ali, 1977). This effect is shown in Figure 33.10. For instance, OAC is a tensile strain curve and OAC′ is the associated bending curve. If the tensile strain reduces from C to A at constant stress, the bending strength will reduce from C′ to A with an increasing rate of reduction as A is approached and the material becomes essentially elastic.

33.4 References

Aveston, J., Cooper, G.A. and Kelly, A. (1971) Single and multiple fracture. Paper 2 in *The Properties of Fibre Composites, Conference Proceedings of the National Physical Laboratory*. IPC Science and Technology Press.

Aveston, J., Mercer, T.A. and Sillwood, J.M. (1974) Fibre-reinforced cement – scientific foundations for specifications. *Composites Standards, Testing and Design*. National Physical Laboratory Conference Proceedings.

Bentur, A. and Mindess, S. (1990) *Fibre Reinforced Cementitious Composites*. Elsevier Applied Science.

Hannant, D.J. (1978) *Fibre Cements and Fibre Concretes*. Wiley.

Hannant, D.J., Hughes, D.C. and Kelly, A. (1983) Toughening of cement and other brittle solids with fibres. *Phil. Trans. R. Soc. Lond. A*, **310**, 175–90.

Hibbert, A.P. and Hannant, D.J. (1982) Toughness of fibre-cement composites. *Composites*, pp. 105–11.

Laws, V. (1971) The efficiency of fibrous reinforcement of brittle matrices. *J. Physics D: Applied Physics*, **4**, 1737–46.

Laws, V. and Ali, M.A. (1977) The tensile stress–strain curve of brittle matrices reinforced with glass fibre. *Fibre Reinforced Materials Design and Engineering Applications Conference*. Institution of Civil Engineers, London, pp. 101–9.

Chapter thirty-four

Composites: Fibres in a cement matrix

34.1 Asbestos cement
34.2 Glass-reinforced cement
34.3 Polymer-fibre-reinforced cement
34.3.1 Polypropylene
34.3.2 Polyvinyl alcohol (PVA) fibres
34.3.3 Polyethylene pulp
34.3.4 Continuous networks of high-modulus polyethylene fibres
34.4 Natural fibres in cement
34.5 References

34.1 Asbestos cement

Asbestos cement is familiar as the ubiquitous very low cost roofing and cladding material which has had excellent durability during the past 80 years. A reason for its success is the great durability of asbestos fibres as shown in Figure 34.1. The fibres shown in this micrograph have been exposed to weathering for more than 10 years but the sub-micron fibres within the fibre bundle show no sign of deterioration. Other studies have shown that the strengths of the fibre bundles vary between 400 MPa and 1400 MPa irrespective of exposure up to seven years.

The proportion by weight of asbestos fibre is normally between 9 and 12% for flat or corrugated sheet, 11 to 14% for pressure pipes and 20 to 30% for fire-resistant boards, and the binder is normally a Portland cement. Fillers such as finely ground silica at about 40% by weight may also be included in autoclaved processes where the temperature may reach 180°C. Fibre volume, stress direction and product density all have an effect on properties and hence the properties depend to a certain extent on the manufacturer.

Asbestos cement is the only fibre composite for which there are international standards requirements for certain properties. These are generally expressed in terms of minimum bending strength, density, impermeability and frost resistance. For instance, the minimum bending strength generally varies between 15 and 23 MPa when tested under defined conditions and depending whether the sheet is semi- or fully compressed. Also, various loading requirements are defined for corrugated sheets such as snow loads up to 1.5 kPa, and point loads to simulate men working on a roof. Water absorption should not exceed 20 to 30% of the dry weight depending on the type of product.

A typical tensile stress–strain curve for a commercial product is shown in Figure 34.2 where the failure strain is about 2000×10^{-6}. No cracks were visible before failure which may be controlled by crack suppression as described in Section 33.2. A modulus of elasticity of about 20 GPa in tension and compression and a modulus of rupture well in excess of 30 MPa have combined to provide probably the

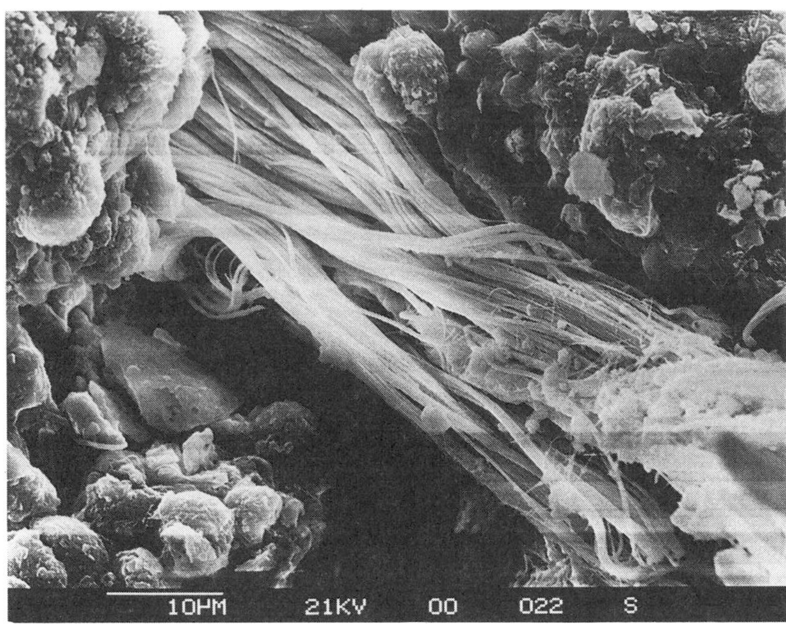

FIGURE 34.1 Asbestos fibre bundle in cement paste after natural weathering for more than 10 years.

most successful example of all time of a fibre-reinforced composite both in terms of tonnage and profitability.

However, statistics have shown a rapid decrease since 1980 in the UK in sales of asbestos cement sheeting products partly due to the well-publicized health hazards associated with asbestos fibres. Safety precautions are now essential to prevent inhalation of dust during cutting and drilling such sheets on site.

Another significant problem is that the material is brittle and the impact strength is notoriously low so that there are a number of deaths every year as a result of people falling through roofs when not using the required crawling boards.

34.2 Glass-reinforced cement (GRC)

Glass-reinforced cement is normally made with alkali-resistant glass-fibre bundles combined with a matrix consisting of ordinary Portland cement plus inorganic fillers. E-glass fibres have been used with a polymer modified cement matrix to protect the glass against attack by the alkalis in the cement. The material described in this section relates to zirconia-based alkali-resistant fibres which are normally produced in the form of strands consisting of 204 filaments each of between 13 and 20 microns in diameter. Several strands may be wound together as a roving which is cut during the making of GRC into strands 12 mm to 38 mm long. A photograph of a strand embedded in cement is shown in Figure 34.3.

The presence of zirconia (ZrO_2) in the glass imparts resistance to the alkalis in the cement because the Zr–O bonds, in contrast to the Si–O bonds, are only slightly attacked by the OH^- ions thus improving the stability of the glass network.

The mechanical properties of GRC depend on the matrix type as shown in Figure 34.4. Fibre length and volume also affect the performance of the composite at 28 days in uniaxial tension

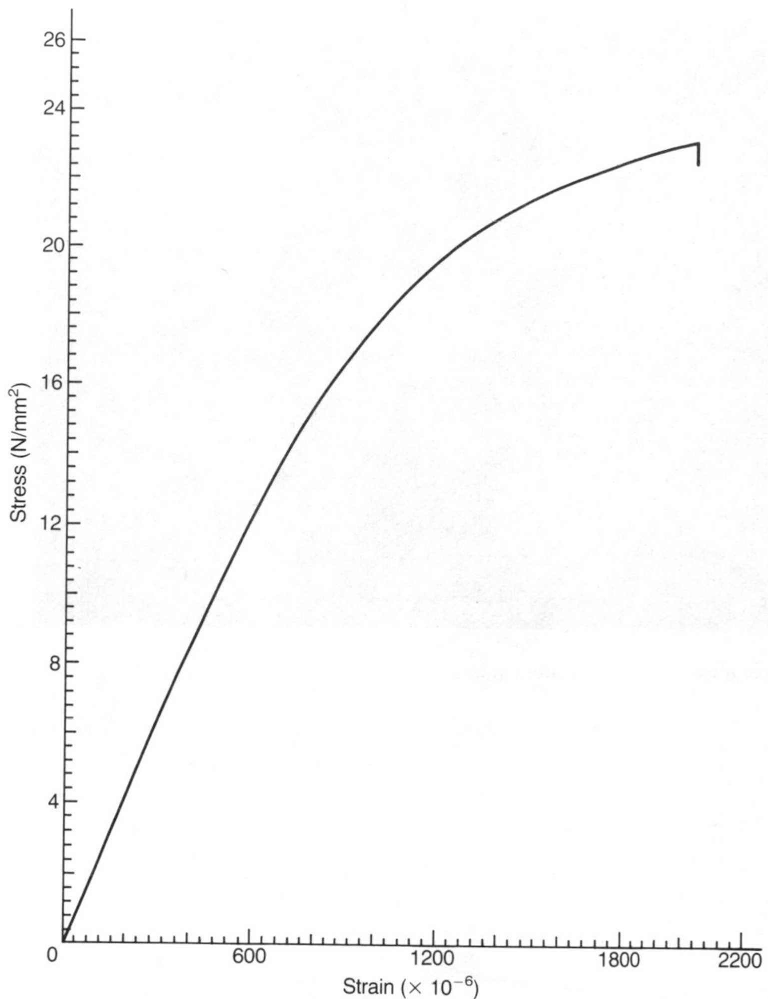

FIGURE 34.2 Tensile stress–strain curve for asbestos cement.

(Ali *et al.*, 1975). The shape of the curves is approximated by the theoretical approach described in Section 33.1 and it has been shown that strength and strain to failure are both increased by increases in fibre length and volume. Nominal flexural tensile strengths may vary between 15 MPa and 50 MPa.

However, although the mechanical properties are good at early ages, the strength and toughness of GRC may change with time and hence design stresses are conservative. Typical design stresses quoted from trade literature are shown in Table 34.1.

34.3 Polymer-fibre-reinforced cement

The inclusion of polymer fibres into cement-based products is potentially a very large world-wide market. For instance, about 90 countries produce asbestos cement for cladding, roofing or pipes and about 3.5 million tonnes of asbestos fibre are used annually in the asbestos cement

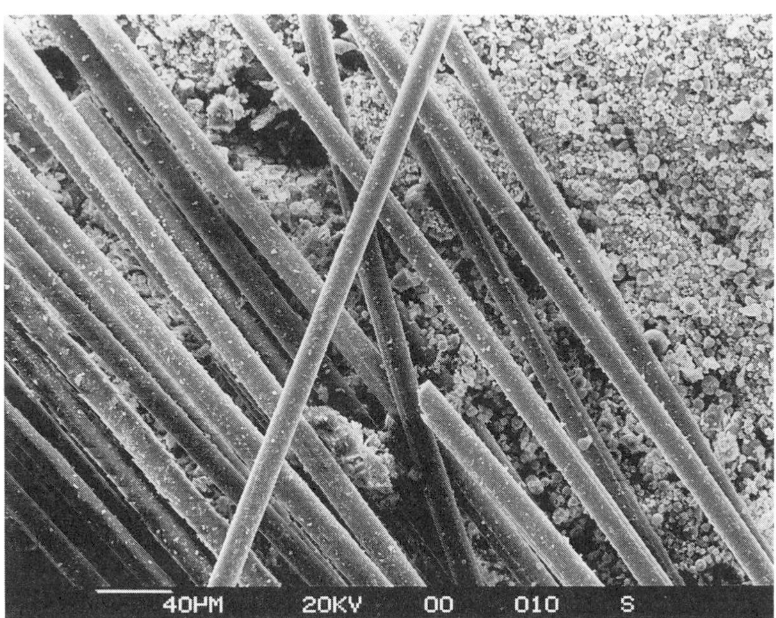

FIGURE 34.3 Glass fibre strand in cement paste.

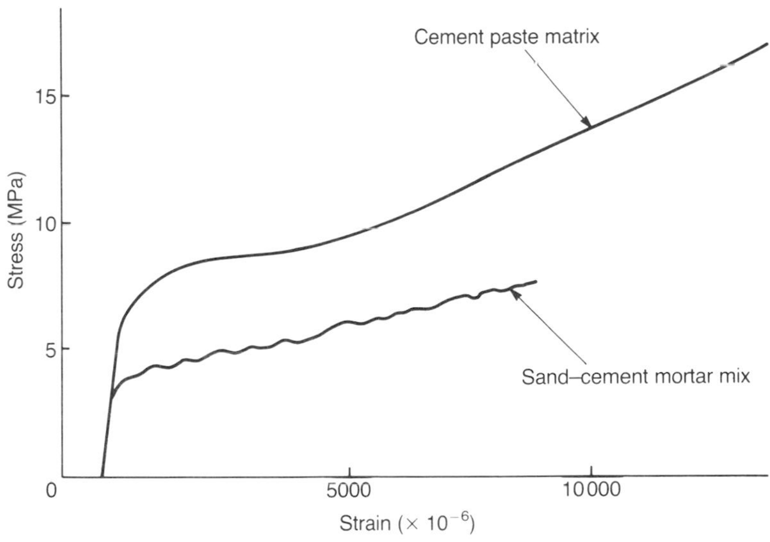

FIGURE 34.4 Tensile stress–strain curves of spray dewatered glass-reinforced cement (Oakley and Proctor, 1975).

and building products industries giving about 28 million tonnes of products. Most of this fibre will eventually be substituted by man-made fibres to avoid the health problems associated with asbestos fibres. It is clear therefore that there is a potential market and considerable inroads have been made since the early 1980s by polymer fibres into this industry.

TABLE 34.1 Typical design stresses used for Cem-FIL GRC (trade literature)

Design value	*Loading example*	*Unit*	*Hand or machine spray*	*Premix*
Compression	Compressive	N/mm^2	12	12
Tension	Cylinder hoop stress. Bending sandwich panels	N/mm^2	3	2
Tensile/bending	Bending box sections or channels	N/mm^2	4	2.5
Bending	Bending solid beams or plates	N/mm^2	6	4
Shear stress	Shear loading	N/mm^2	1	1

Note: These design values may be varied in certain product areas, e.g. formwork. Limit state methods are also used.

Although a wide variety of polymers have been used on a trial basis in cement-based materials, only a few have been commercially successful. Polypropylene and polyvinyl alcohol have been the most used although polyethylene pulp is also used in some thin sheet products.

34.3.1 Polypropylene

Chopped polypropylene films

Chopped polypropylene films have been used at fibre volumes of 3% to 5% to produce alternative products to asbestos cement with some modifications being required to the traditional machinery. The polypropylene in this case was specially stretched and heat treated to give elastic moduli of 9 to 18 GPa with tensile strengths from 500 to 700 MPa and ultimate strain of 5 to 8%. Various surface treatments to improve wetting of the films and increase their bond were carried out before splitting the film and chopping into lengths between 6 and 24 mm to give fibres with a basically rectangular cross-section but with frayed edges.

Continuous opened polypropylene networks

Layers of networks of continuous polypropylene films as shown in Figure 34.5 with similar properties to the chopped films have been used in fine-grained cement materials to produce alternative products to asbestos cement. The advantage of this system is that the full fibre strength is used because there is no pull-out and excellent mechanical bonding is achieved by virtue of the uneven micro- and macro-slits in the films and the many fine hairs produced in the production process. Bending strengths in excess of 40 MPa and tensile strengths above 25 MPa have been measured at aligned film volumes of about 9%. A total fibre volume of 6.5% with 4% in the main stress direction and 2.5% orthogonal is sufficient to give adequate two-dimensional strength to replace asbestos cement in most of its roofing applications. Typical tensile stress–strain curves for two fibre volumes are shown in Figure 34.6 in which the shape of the curve follows that predicted by the general theory in Section 33.1 for greater than the critical fibre volumes for curve OXYB in Figure 32.1. An uncracked region of high stiffness is followed by increasing strain at approximately constant stress as multiple cracking occurs. Finally the fibres extend at increasing stress until failure occurs. Toughness values of 1000 kJ/m^3 are possible and the failure strain remains in excess of 5% even after weathering provided that the critical fibre volume is exceeded at the appropriate age.

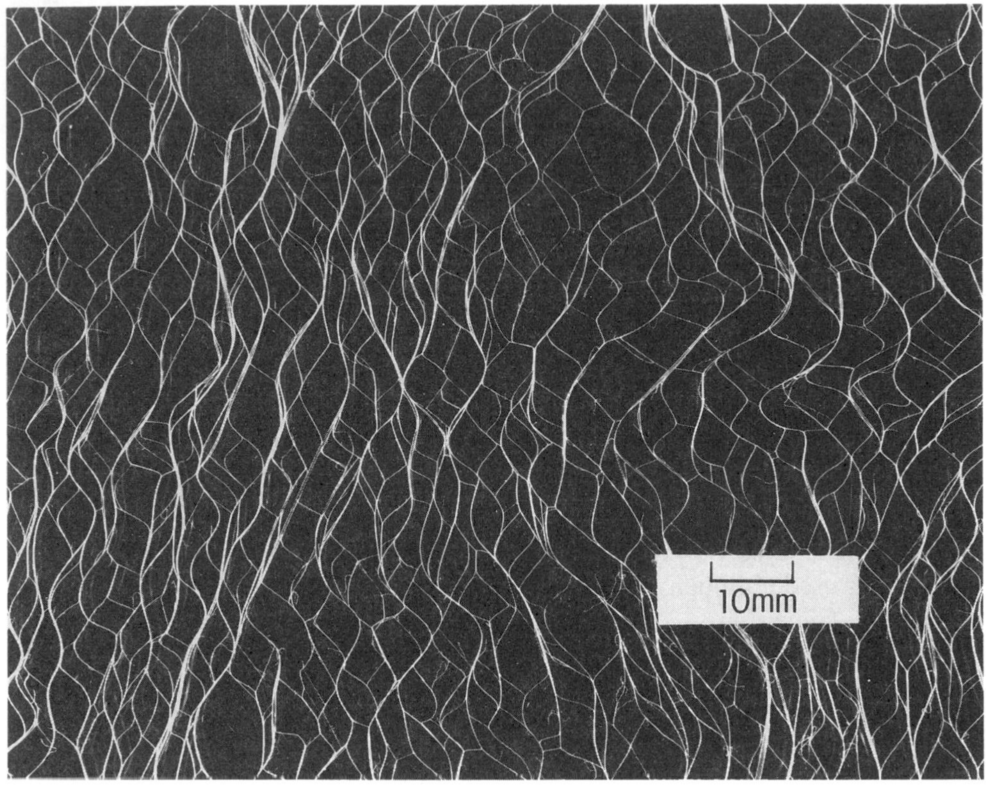

FIGURE 34.5 Polypropylene networks.

34.3.2 Polyvinyl alcohol (PVA) fibres

High strength and stiffness PVA fibres are used widely as an asbestos replacement in asbestos cement products. However, taken by themselves in a cement slurry, they retain little of the cement grains and hence must be used in conjunction with cellulose pulp to keep the cement in the system as water is sucked out by vacuum. The fibres are treated on the surface to enhance their compatibility with the matrix, the quantity of fibres being typically 3% by volume. Flexural strengths of the sheeting are adequate to meet the requirements of the appropriate European standards. Alkali resistance has been stated by the manufacturers to be excellent and the fibres can survive exposure to temperatures of 150°C without loss in strength.

34.3.3 Polyethylene pulp

Polyethylene pulp made from short fibres has mainly been used as a cement retention and drainage aid as a substitute for asbestos fibres in a Hatschek-type process for the manufacture of thin sheet products. Up to 12% by volume has been used and at this level improvements in flexural strength and ductility have also been observed. Because the fibres do not swell in the presence of water, the durability of the products is said to be improved in comparison with similar systems using cellulose fibres.

34.3.4 Continuous networks of high-modulus polyethylene fibres

Highly orientated polyethylene fibres may be

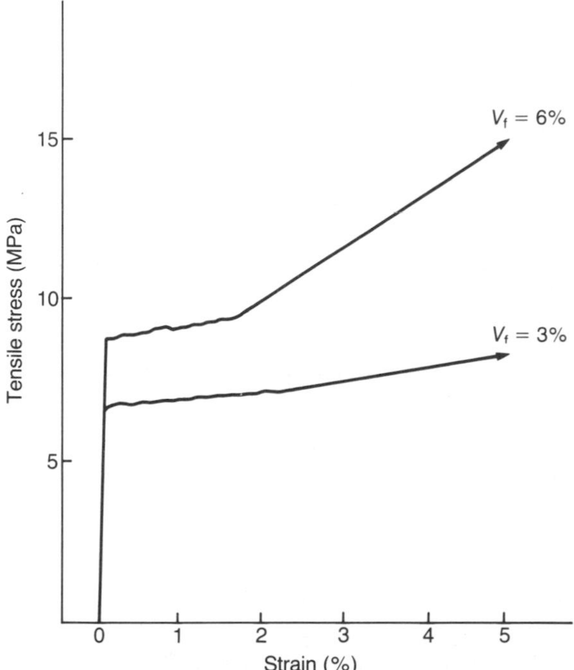

FIGURE 34.6 Tensile stress–strain curves for cement sheet reinforced with polypropylene networks at two fibre volumes.

produced by gel spinning or high stretch ratios and fibres have been produced with the elastic modulus of glass and the strength of steel. Commercial fibrillated tapes with initial elastic moduli of about 30 GPa have been used in thin cement sheets in a similar fashion to polypropylene nets. These improved composites in terms of stiffer post-cracking performance and smaller crack widths have behaved as predicted by the theory in Section 33.1. Durability in the alkaline cement matrix is expected to be good but the films which have been available have suffered from high creep strain in comparison with polypropylene.

34.4 Natural fibres in cement

The use of natural cellulose or vegetable fibres in cement or mortar products is common in both developed and developing countries and the subject has been reviewed in detail by Swamy (1988) and Bentur and Mindess (1990).

34.4.1 Wood fibres

In developed countries the bulk usage is for wood cellulose fibres from trees. The wood is mechanically and chemically pulped to separate the individual fibres which may be between 1 mm and 3 mm long and up to 45 microns in width. Hardwoods and softwoods are used and the elastic modulus of individual fibres may vary between 18 GPa and 80 GPa with strengths between 350 MPa and 1000 MPa depending on the angle of cellulose chains in the cell wall. Cellulose fibres produced from timber have several advantages when used in thin cement or autoclaved calcium silicate sheets. The fibres are cheap compared with most man-made fibres, they are a renewable resource, there is considerable experience in the use of such fibres in existing plant for asbestos cement, and they have an adequate tensile strength for cement reinforcement. However, cellulose is sensitive to humidity changes and the elastic modulus of the fibres reduces when wet so the properties of the composite may vary considerably from dry to wet.

When suitably pretreated by refining, wood fibres used in conjunction with polyvinyl alcohol in a matrix of Portland cement and fillers can provide a tough and durable fibre cement. This composite is suitable for the commercial production of corrugated sheeting and pressed tiles on traditional slurry dewatered systems such as the Hatschek machine (Section 37.1.1). The variation in composite properties wet to dry and pressed to unpressed is shown in typical tensile stress–strain curves for commercial composite in Figure 34.7.

In Australia, cellulose fibres have completely replaced asbestos fibres in flat sheeting products made from an autoclaved calcium silicate. Autoclaved systems are said to have the advantage

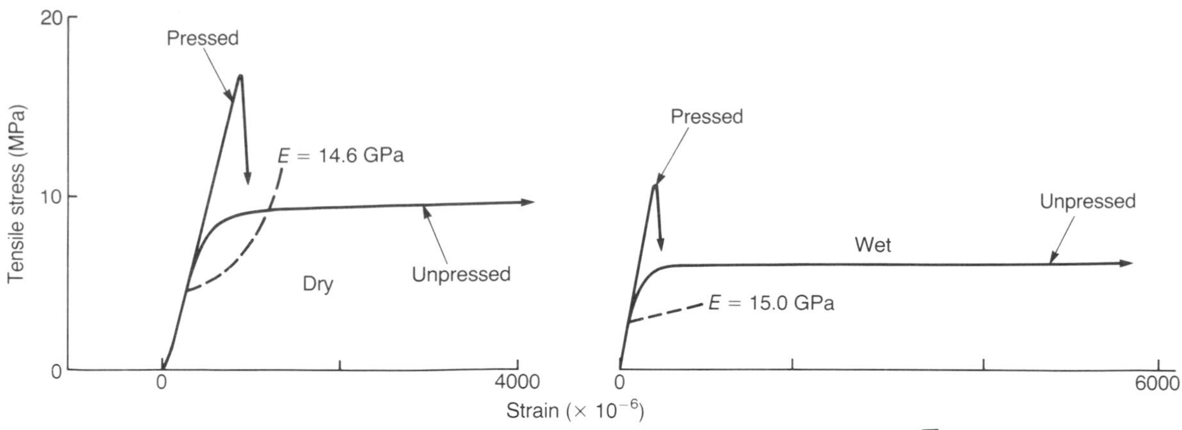

FIGURE 34.7 Effect of moisture condition on the tensile properties of a cement composite containing cellulose fibres and artificial organic fibres – pressed, unpressed.

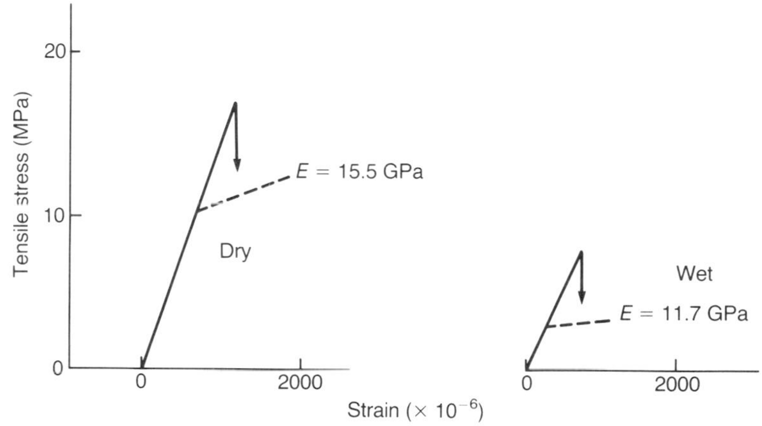

FIGURE 34.8 Effect of moisture condition on tensile properties of autoclaved calcium silicate containing cellulose fibres.

over air-cured hydrated cement binders in that there is greater dimensional stability in relation to moisture and temperature movements. Also, because of the absence of free alkalinity, the boards can be more easily decorated. In the UK, flat sheet for internal and external applications has been available for a number of years produced from cellulose fibres in an autoclaved calcium silicate matrix. A wide range of properties is available in cellulose fibre boards, typical values being an elastic modulus of 12 GPa with the tensile strength varying between 6 MPa and 20 MPa and the modulus of rupture between 15 MPa and 30 MPa depending on whether the composite is wet or dry and on the fibre volume. Typical tensile stress–strain curves in the dry and wet states for these materials are shown in Figure 34.8.

Wood cellulose fibres are not suitable for use in bulk concrete applications because of difficulties in mixing and compaction and their use is therefore limited to automated factory processes. In some of these processes wood chips or flakes at up to 20% by weight are mixed with cement and fine sand to make a variety of compressed wood chipboards or particleboards. These are generally used internally and have low flexural tensile strength, often below 1 MPa. They are not strictly fibre-reinforced cements.

34.4.2 Vegetable fibres

The use of vegetable stem fibres in developing countries is generally aimed at producing cheap but labour-intensive locally constructed cement-based roof sheeting often of corrugated or folded plate design. Long fibres which are indigenous to the locality are used such as akwara, banana, bamboo, coir, elephant grass, flax, henequen, jute, malva, musamba, palm, plantan, pineapple leaf, sisal, sugar cane and water reed. Lengths of fibres may be up to 1 m or more and are hand placed in a matrix of sand and cement. Corrugated sheets of up to 2 m by 1 m in size of 6–10 mm thickness and tiles may be produced with fibres in preferential directions.

The cracking stress and strength of the composites are not greatly increased compared with the unreinforced matrix but the fibres enable the sheets to be formed in the fresh state and handled and transported in the hardened state. Considerable toughness is achieved in the short term although embrittlement can occur in the long term.

Bamboo, when split into strips and woven into meshes, has been used as reinforcement for a variety of uses from roads and structures to water tanks. Tensile strengths of the fibre are commonly in excess of 100 MPa with elastic moduli between 10 and 25 GPa. Toughening and post-cracking performance are the most important characteristics and optimum fibre volumes between 1.5% and 3% have been quoted.

34.5 References

Ali, M.A., Majumdar, A.J. and Singh, B. (1975) Properties of glass fibre cement – the effect of fibre length and content. *J. Material Science*, 10, 1732–40.

Bentur, A. and Mindess, S. (1990) *Fibre Reinforced Cementitious Composites*. Elsevier Applied Science.

Oakley, D.R. and Proctor, B.A. (1975) Tensile stress-strain behaviour of glass fibre reinforced cement composites. In *Fibre Reinforced Cement and Concrete*, Construction Press Ltd, Lancaster, UK, pp. 347–59.

Swamy, R.N. (ed.) (1988) *Natural Fibre Reinforced Cement and Concrete*, Vol. 5, Concrete Technology and Design. Blackie, Glasgow.

Chapter thirty-five

Fibre-reinforced concrete

35.1 Steel-fibre concrete
35.2 Polymer-fibre-reinforced concrete
35.3 Glass-reinforced concrete

35.1 Steel-fibre concrete

Concrete reinforced with steel fibres in volumes generally less than 1% has a tensile stress–strain curve of the type OXA shown in Figure 32.1. The reason for this is that it is physically very difficult to include sufficient fibres in the mix to exceed the critical fibre volume which typically may be more than 3%. This is because concrete contains about 70% by volume of aggregate particles which obviously cannot be penetrated by fibres. Also, the fibres tend to end up in a three-dimensional random distribution when mixed in a rotary mixer which, together with their short length, makes them very inefficient as reinforcement in any given direction of tensile stress. Nevertheless, useful properties in the composite have been achieved by many practical systems.

A great variety of fibre shapes and lengths are available depending on the manufacturing process. Cross-sectional shapes include: circular (from drawn fibres); rectangular (from slit sheet); sickle-shaped (from the melt extract process); and mechanically deformed in various ways to improve the bond strength. Fibre lengths range from 10 to 60 mm with equivalent diameters between 0.1 and 0.6 mm. Mild steel and stainless steel fibres are available.

Sketches of some of these fibre types are shown in Figure 35.1. It should be realized that the average fibre pull-out length is $l/4$, which for 60 mm fibres is only 15 mm. This length is insufficient to allow efficient use to be made of the high tensile strength of drawn wire.

One of the main benefits of steel-fibre concrete is in flexural situations where the flexural strength may be increased by about 50% of the matrix strength at 1% to 1.5% by volume of fibres although the tensile strength may be effectively unchanged (Figure 35.2). The increase in flexural strength results from the increased area of the tensile part of the stress block shown in Figure 33.8b. Other major benefits are obtained from increased toughness under impact or abrasion loads. This is shown by the increased area under the load–deflection curve in flexure (Figure 35.3). A variety of toughness indices have been proposed in the literature depending on the deflection which is chosen to represent a typical serviceability limit.

35.2 Polymer-fibre-reinforced concrete

The major polymer fibre in concrete is polypropylene which has been used commercially in many forms since 1970 to modify some properties of fresh and hardened concrete. Fibre additions have ranged from very low concentrations (~0.1%) of 5 mm long round monofilaments, through similar volumes of 5–25 mm long split fibres, to about 0.4% by volume of

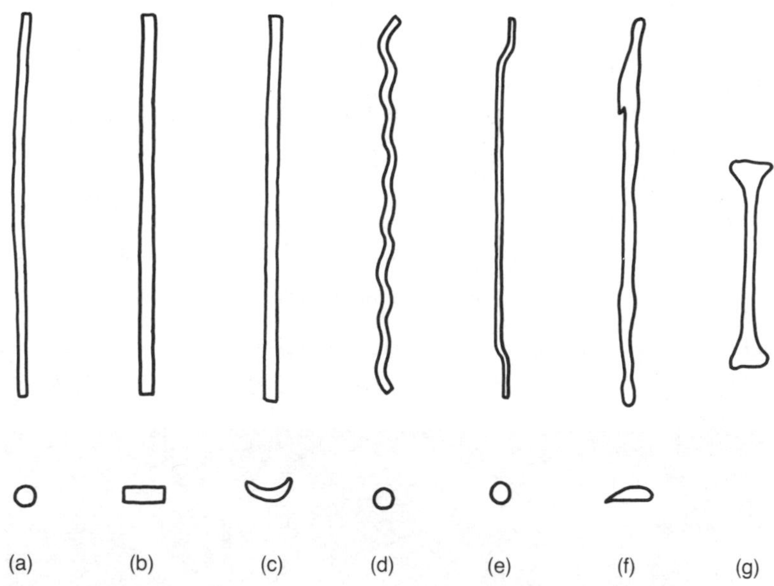

FIGURE 35.1 Wire types showing deformations to improve bond: (a) round; (b) rectangular; (c) milled; (d) crimped; (e) hooked ends; (f) melt extract; (g) pressed ends.

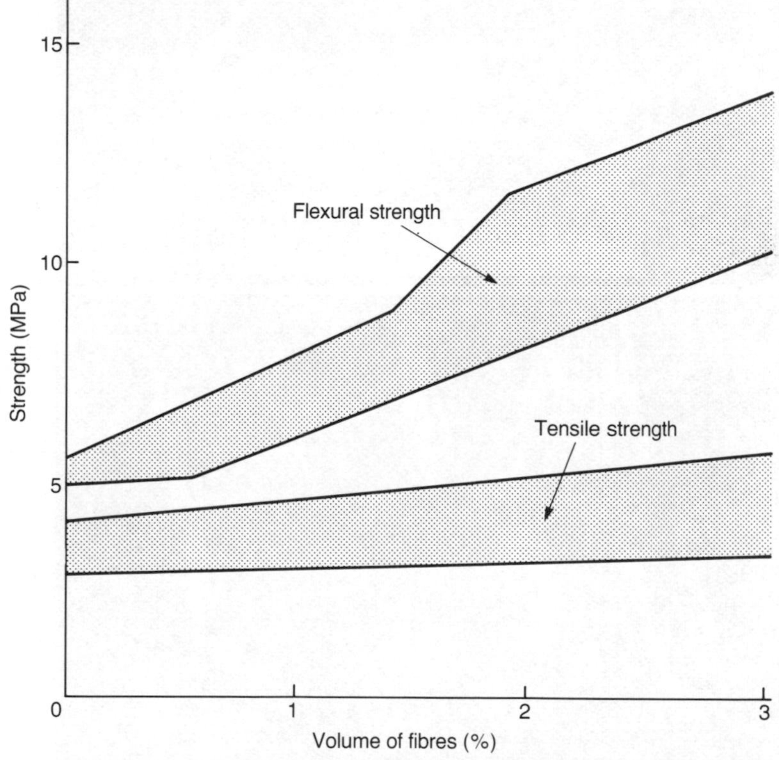

FIGURE 35.2 Typical direct tensile and flexural strengths of steel-fibre-reinforced concrete and mortar (Edgington, 1973).

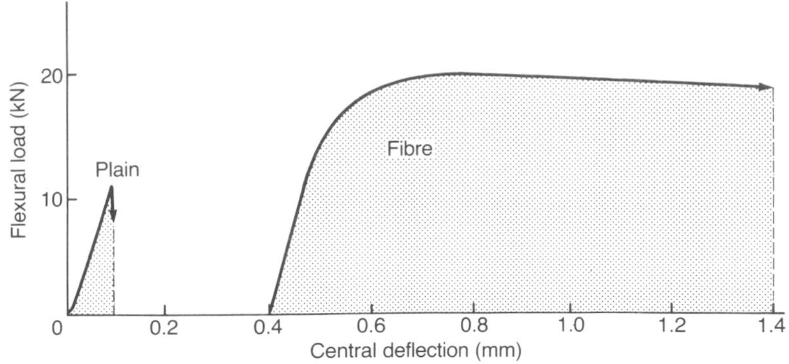

FIGURE 35.3 Load–deflection curves for plain concrete and steel-fibre concrete. 1.5% by volume of fibres of *l*/*d* ratio = 100.

(a)

(b)

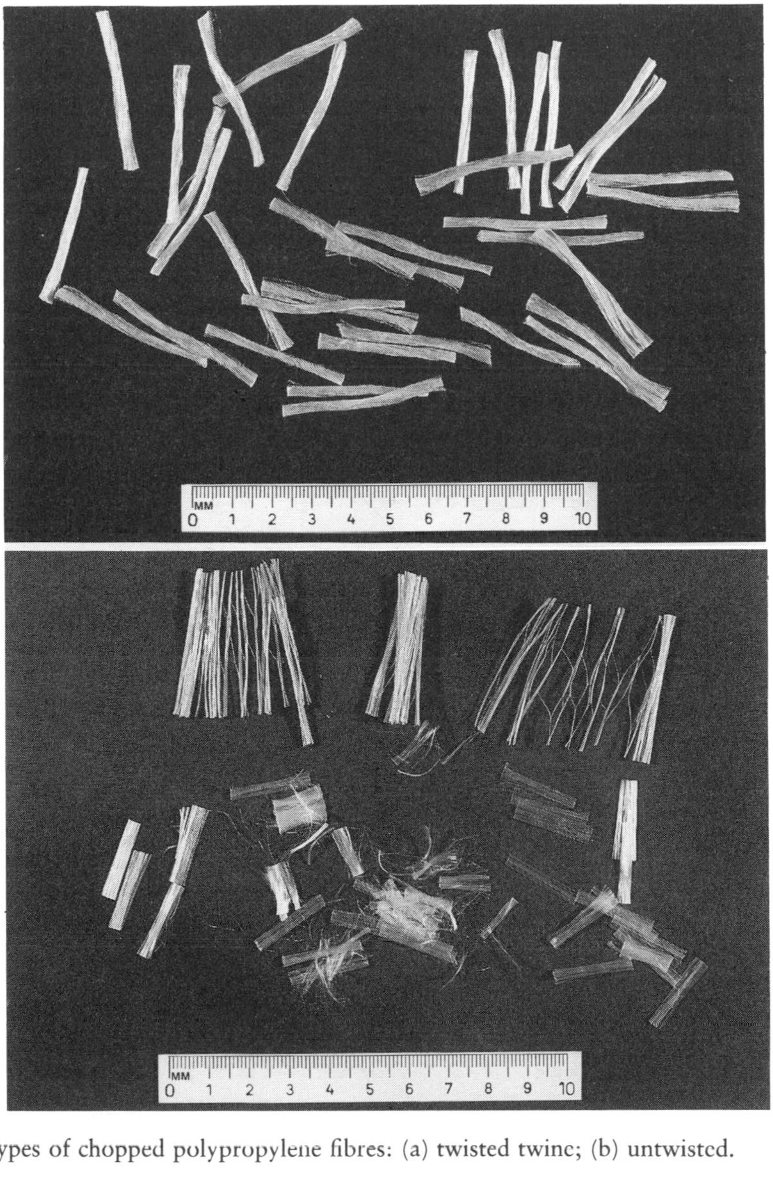

FIGURE 35.4 Types of chopped polypropylene fibres: (a) twisted twine; (b) untwisted.

40 mm twisted twine. Twisted and untwisted split films are shown in Figure 35.4.

The main benefit endowed on the concrete by the polypropylene twine at 0.44% by volume is additional impact strength, the tensile and bending strengths being virtually unchanged. For the system containing 0.1% by volume of film fibres there may be reduced bleeding and plastic shrinkage cracking. It can easily be shown theoretically that at 0.1% by volume the fibre will have no measurable effect on the tensile or flexural strength of hardened concrete and that it cannot be considered as a primary reinforcement. However, even though the fibre volumes are very small, there is some evidence which indicates a reduction in total crack widths in accelerated plastic shrinkage tests.

35.3 Glass-reinforced concrete

There are few uses for glass fibre reinforcement in bulk concrete because the cost of including even a small percentage of random glass fibre would not be cost-effective. However, one application which has had limited success is the use of glass fibre in concrete pipes. These have been produced mainly of unreinforced concrete but with glass fibre in the form of continuous strands concentrated at the inner and outer surfaces. Among advantages claimed for the pipe are that it has a lower weight and an in-wall joint rather than a conventional bell end.

Another use for low fibre volumes of between 0.1% and 0.4% is to inhibit bleeding in in-situ slabs in a similar way to 0.1% volume of polypropylene fibre in concrete.

Chapter thirty-six

Durability

36.1 Durability of asbestos cement
36.2 Durability of glass-fibre-reinforced cement
36.3 Durability of polymer-fibre-reinforced cement and concrete
36.4 Durability of natural-fibre-reinforced concrete
36.5 Durability of steel-fibre concrete
36.6 References

The durability of fibre cement composites is highly dependent on the type and volume of fibre and each composite is therefore described independently.

36.1 Durability of asbestos cement

Asbestos cement is known to be very durable under natural weathering conditions and little deterioration in flexural properties takes place due to weathering although the material becomes progressively more brittle.

However, it has been shown that asbestos fibres in cement sheets at ages of 2, 16, and 58 years do suffer a certain amount of corrosion which is compensated for, in terms of composite strength, by an increase in bond between the fibre and the cement. The corrosion of the fibre is promoted by the penetration of airborne carbon dioxide which causes carbonation at the surface of the fibre. Also, certain magnesium hydroxides and magnesium carbonates may be formed as reaction products.

Attempts have been made to measure the strength of fibre bundles extracted from the asbestos cement boards stored under various exposure conditions but it is apparent that the variability in strength, both in the pristine condition and when extracted from boards, is so large that it masks any small variations in strength which may occur because of weathering.

36.2 Durability of glass-fibre-reinforced cement

The durability of glass-reinforced cement is strongly affected by the environment in which it is used (Building Research Establishment, 1979). For instance, in dry air there is little change in flexural or tensile strength during a 10-year period, whereas under water or in natural weathering there may be a decrease in strength of the composite of more than 50%. The decrease in impact strength is even more severe, reducing by an order of magnitude. The changes are due to a combination of factors including a loss in fibre strength due to alkali attack, an increase in matrix cracking stress due to continuing cement hydration and the filling of the voids in the fibre bundle which decreases fibre pull-out. The net result of these changes is to reduce the composite strain to failure, in some cases down to the matrix failure strain, thus reducing the once ductile material to a brittle material.

An example of the way in which the increase in matrix strength and reduction in composite strain to failure can affect the critical fibre volume and toughness of the composite is shown below.

For glass-reinforced cement, the following values have been published (Building Research Establishment, 1979): 28 days, $E_c = 22.5$ GPa with a bend-over point at 9.5 MPa, which gives $\varepsilon_{mu} = 422 \times 10^{-6}$, $\sigma_{fu} = 1000$ MPa; 10 years,

E_c = 28.5 GPa, no accurate value for the bend-over point is given. If we assume no change in ε_{mu} and take σ_{fu} equal to 600 MPa after 10 years, eqn (33.3) gives an increase in V_{fcrit} from 1% at 28 days to 2% at 10 years for aligned fibres.

Most glass-reinforced cement is sprayed with short fibres in a random two-dimensional (2-D) orientation. To take account of the non-alignment, we multiply the value of σ_{fu} by 0.27 (the efficiency factor for stress) and find that a total fibre volume fraction of more than 3.5% at 28 days and more than 7.4% at 10 years is required to maintain ductility. Typical total fibre volumes are about 4% and it is known that the energy absorbed to failure, found from the area under the measured stress–strain curve, reduces from about 120 kJ/m^3 at 28 days to less than 5 kJ/m^3 at five years. This change may therefore be explained by the increase in critical fibre volume fraction with time and the effect is shown graphically in Figure 36.1.

Glass-reinforced cement systems with improved durability are being developed by the use of polymer additions to the matrix, surface treatments to the fibres and modifications to the Portland cement matrix with pozzolanic fillers such as pulverized fuel ash and silica fume which reduce the alkalinity of the matrix. Most of these developments rely on the reduced deposition of calcium hydroxide crystals within the fibre bundle to provide an improvement in strain to failure.

36.3 Durability of polymer-fibre-reinforced cement and concrete

The durability of polymer-fibre composites will vary depending on the sensitivity to alkaline environments of the individual polymers. Polymer types with potential for cement reinforcement are included in this section even if no previous mention has been made.

The resistance to alkalis of aramids is not

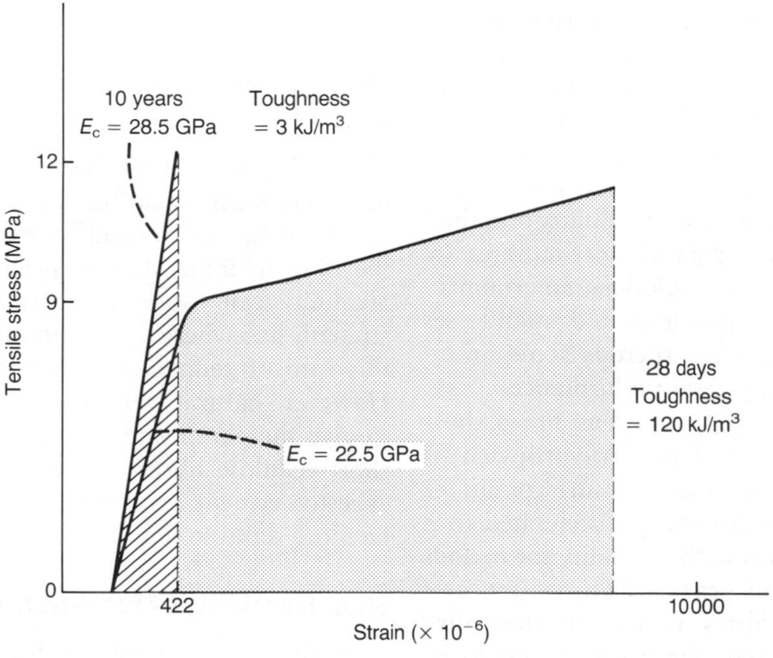

FIGURE 36.1 Effect of natural weathering on the toughness of glass-reinforced cement.

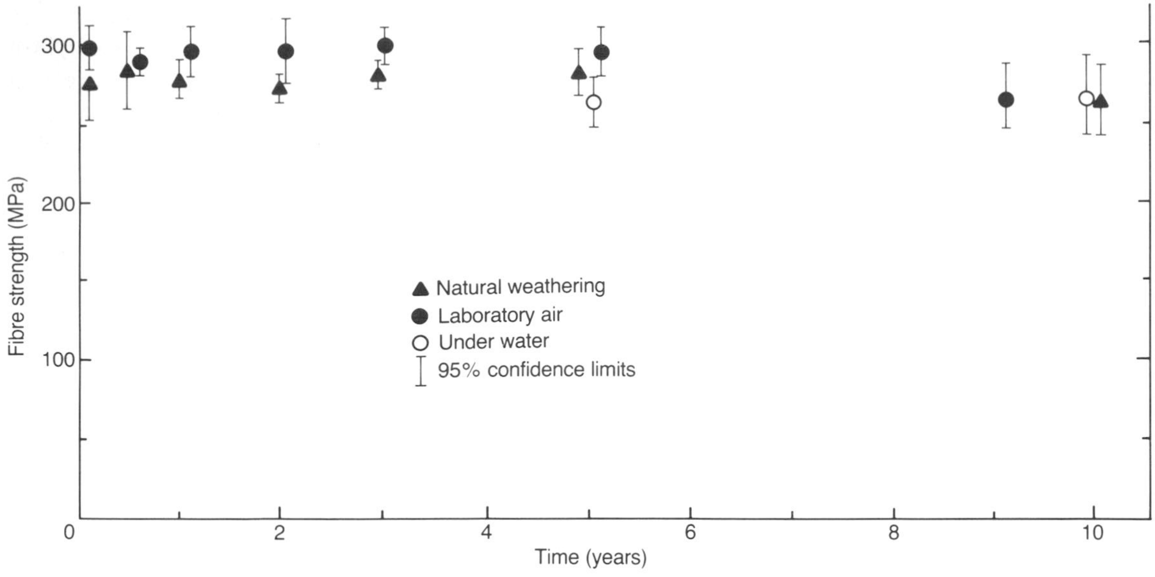

FIGURE 36.2 Durability of polypropylene networks in cement.

entirely clear but the 20-year performance of the uncoated fibres in a cement matrix is thought to be satisfactory. However, in order to avoid damage and also to give protection against alkalis, continuous fibre bundles used in prestressing applications may be impregnated with epoxy resin or coated with a polymer sheath. Aramids avoid corrosion problems associated with steel tendons and show considerable potential for the future. Long-term durability of carbon fibres is expected to be good. Acrylic fibres are relatively stable in an alkaline environment although some tests have indicated small losses in strength and therefore there is some uncertainty about the long-term performance.

Polyethylene and polypropylene fibres show excellent resistance to alkalis. Polypropylene is very durable in a variety of exposure conditions up to 10 years (Figure 36.2). Accelerated tests indicate no problems with durability for periods well in excess of 30 years. Alkali resistance of polyvinyl alcohol fibres used as an alternative to asbestos fibres has also been shown to be excellent.

The general conclusion is that the polymers which are most commonly used in cementitious matrices are likely to provide durable composites for periods of at least 30 years.

36.4 Durability of natural-fibre-reinforced concrete

The high alkalinity of the pore water prevents microbiological decay in the fibres but, to set against this, the calcium hydroxide penetrates the fibre to mineralize or petrify it. The high alkalinity can cause severe reduction in fibre strength but where carbonation has penetrated this rate of reduction in strength is reduced. However, natural stem fibres are not expected to give the composite a long lifetime although short cellulose fibres as used in alternatives to asbestos cement products have been shown to be more durable than natural stem fibres.

36.5 Durability of steel-fibre concrete

Steel fibres are generally well protected in uncracked concrete where the high alkalinity provides a passive layer on the fibre surface. Even when the fibres are near the surface in a carbonated zone, serious corrosion takes many years to occur and surface spalling is rare. It may be that the short fibre length results in a more or less uniform potential adjacent to the fibre which limits the setting up of corrosion cells.

In cracked concrete, however, the fibres may corrode relatively rapidly if chlorides are present (Hannant, 1978) and it would be appropriate, if cracking is expected, to use stainless steel fibres. If these are not used, the mode of failure in cracked concrete subject to water and chlorides will eventually change from ductile with fibre pull-out to brittle with fibre fracture and this change will not be predictable by extrapolation of real-time data from durability experiments.

36.6 References

Building Research Establishment (1979) Properties of GRC: Ten year results. Information Paper IP36/79, Building Research Establishment, Garston.

Edgington, J. (1973) Steel reinforced fibre reinforced concrete. Ph.D. thesis, University of Surrey.

Hannant, D.J. (1978) *Fibre Cements and Fibre Concretes*. Wiley.

Chapter thirty-seven

Manufacture and uses

37.1 Asbestos cement
37.2 Glass-reinforced cement
37.3 Polymer-fibre-reinforced cement and concrete
37.4 Natural-fibre-reinforced cement
37.5 Steel-fibre concrete
37.6 References

37.1 Asbestos cement

37.1.1 Manufacture

The most widely used method of manufacture of asbestos cement was developed from paper-making principles in about 1900 and is known as the Hatschek process. A slurry or suspension of asbestos fibre and cement in water at about 6% by weight of solids is continuously agitated and allowed to filter out on a fine screen cylinder. The filtration rate is critical and coarser cement than normal (typically with a specific surface area of 280 m^2/kg, compared with the normal value of 320 m^2/kg) is used to minimize filtration losses.

Other types of fibre such as cellulose derived from wood pulp or newsprint have also been added to the slurry to produce different effects in the wet or hardened sheet.

Referring to Figure 37.1, in very much simplified terms the Hatschek machine operates as follows. A dilute slurry pours into the vat and drains through a porous sieve cylinder depositing the solid contents as a layer on the surface of the sieve. The water passes through the sieve surface and into the cylinder, and then pours out of the open ends of the cylinder to the backwater return circuit. The sieve cylinder rotates and the layer rises out of the vat. A continuous felt runs in a loop from the sieve cylinder to an accumulation roll. Surface tension forces the layer to transfer from the top of the sieve cylinder to the underside of the felt. The movement of the felt transfers the layer from the sieve to the accumulation roll. On the way, it is vacuum dewatered.

Typical outputs are one tonne per hour per metre width of vat. Felt speeds range from 40 to 70 metres per minute. A typical three-vat machine will make a 6 mm thick sheet in six to nine revolutions and will make one sheet every 20 seconds. Manufacturing costs (other than materials) are therefore very low. The physical properties of the composite are to a certain extent dependent on this type of fabrication technique because the dispersion of the fibres is essentially in two directions due to the process of forming each thin layer, and the layers themselves are laminated to give the required thickness to the product. Also, because of the rotation of the sieve cylinder there is a predominant alignment of the fibres in the direction of rotation.

Curing of the products is often by stacking on pallets and is accelerated by the heat which is built up by the exothermic reaction between cement and water. Temperatures in excess of 60°C may be reached in this process but auto-

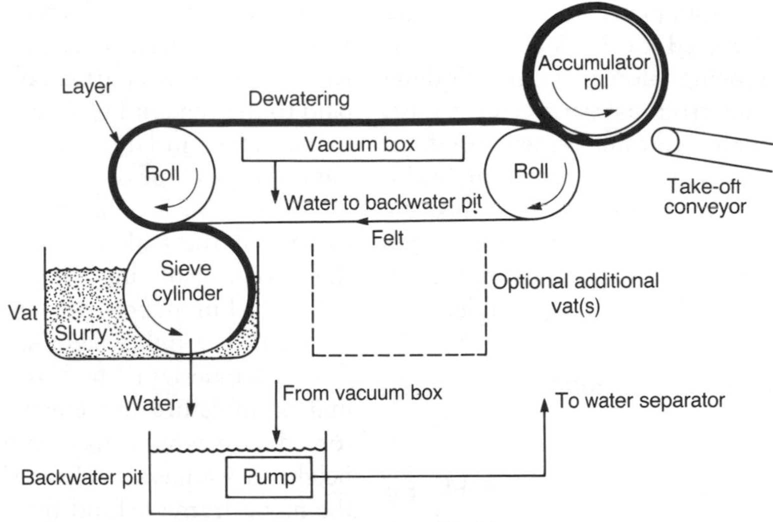

FIGURE 37.1 Hatschek manufacturing process for asbestos-cement sheeting.

claving may also be used in some countries to accelerate or alter the characteristics of the reaction compounds and increase the rate of turnover of the products. Also, pressure may be applied to flat sheets to increase the density and strength of the composite.

37.1.2 Uses

Corrugated roofing and cladding for agricultural and industrial buildings forms by far the largest application, and the ability to be moulded into complex shapes has enabled a wide range of accessories such as ridge pieces, cappings, eaves fillers, and flashings to be produced for roofing applications. Flat sheet is used for slates or diagonal tiles for light roof coverings with a weight of about 20 kg/m^2 and, with colouring pigments, they have been used to replace natural slate. Fully compressed sheet has a number of additional minor uses such as infill panels, shelving, bath panels, shuttering, dropping boards for poultry houses, bench tops, pig-pen partitions, and weatherboard strips. Water-based and chlorinated-rubber-based paints can be applied without a primer but gloss paints require an alkali-resistant primer.

Asbestos-cement pressure pipes have been used for many years for conveying mains water, sewage, gas, sea water, slurries, and industrial liquors. Diameters range from 50 mm to 900 mm with working pressures from 0.75 MN/m^2 to 1.25 MN/m^2. The crushing loads on buried pipes can be quite severe. An advantage of asbestos-cement pipes is that their smooth uniform bore inhibits the formation of internal deposits so the hydraulic resistance is low. Also, non-pressure fluid containers and pipes such as rainwater goods, conduits, troughs, tanks, and flue pipes account for a large proportion of the minor applications of asbestos cement.

There is a general trend in the USA, Europe and Australia to ban any products containing asbestos fibres due to their carcinogenic properties. There is no current ban in the UK but the factory inspectorate have recommended that basic precautions be taken during certain cutting operations, in particular that the inhalation of dust from cutting, turning, or drilling asbestos cement be avoided. Preferably the cutting area should be dampened and waste should be buried or disposed of in such a way as to prevent dust being blown about. Clothing should be kept free from asbestos-cement dust.

In addition, many asbestos-cement products will be required to carry a government health warning. Alternative products have become available for most uses except pressure pipes and on health and safety grounds the alternatives should be used wherever possible.

37.2 Glass-reinforced cement

37.2.1 Manufacture

Many production processes are available for glass-reinforced cement including pre-mixing combined with gravity moulding, pressing, injection moulding and extrusion. One of the most common techniques is spray-up with or without the removal of water by suction and automated systems are available. In the normal spraying process, cement/sand mortar paste is sprayed simultaneously with chopped glass fibre from a dual-head spray gun which may be either hand-held or mechanized. The slurry mortar is typically 1:1 cement:sand ratio often with an acrylic polymer to improve air curing, moisture movement and durability. Glass-fibre roving is fed to a chopper/feeder unit which cuts the fibre into predetermined lengths and compressed air is used to inject them into the slurry stream. Roller compaction or vacuum dewatering may be used.

Winding and lay-up processes have also been used and blockwork walls can be built by dry-stacking the blocks and applying a rendering of pre-bagged glass-fibre cement. Special developments have included the use of continuous glass filaments concentrated at the inner and outer surfaces of concrete pipes to give maximum fibre efficiency.

37.2.2 Uses

Cladding panels have been a major field of application of glass-reinforced cement since 1970. Due to cracking caused by restrained warping in early applications particular attention should be paid to thermal and moisture movements and to fixing details in large double-skinned sandwich panels of this type of construction. Light colouring of the panels is preferred because this helps to reduce thermal stresses particularly where there is an insulating core.

Single-skin panels are also commonly used attached to a lightweight steel stud frame. The fixings are designed to allow unrestrained thermal or moisture movements of the glass-reinforced skin which may be 6 m long by storey height. A stainless steel rainshield is attached to the metal frame behind the decorative skin.

An important use where the early age strength and toughness are beneficial is in permanent formwork for bridge decks. Long spans may also incorporate a stainless steel mesh, the advantages being that no temporary support works are required and a dense high-quality cover is provided on the concrete surface.

The greater efficiency ensured by using continuous glass-fibre rovings in the main stress direction has been utilized in a process for producing corrugated sheeting. The corrugated sheets start as a continuous flat sheet made from two layers each 3.25 mm thick. Short strands as cross reinforcement are immersed in the matrix on the upper/underside and this leads to an ideal sandwich structure. The lengthwise reinforcement is mostly made up of one-directional inlaid glass-fibre rovings, which are sandwiched between the two layers that make up the sheet. The flat sheets are then corrugated before curing on corrugated formers.

There are many other uses such as pipes, ducting, agricultural uses, sewer linings, culverts, tanks, drainage systems, ceiling units and mortar renders for dry block wall construction. Some trials have been made using glass-fibre tendons protected with polyester resin as prestressing tendons in concrete structures.

37.3 Polymer-fibre-reinforced cement and concrete

37.3.1 Manufacture of polymer-fibre-reinforced cement

Short chopped fibres are used in combination with cellulose fibres in Hatschek-type machinery for producing roofing products.

A separate major development in recent years has been the use of continuous fibrillated nets of polypropylene supplied in reels containing nets laid up in two directions in 12-layer pads.

Three or four packs are fed simultaneously to a machine which impregnates them with cement slurry in sequence producing a wet, flat sheet with good two-dimensional strength. This is then corrugated in a vacuum corrugator. Other fibres such as glass may be included in the process in both continuous and chopped forms in order to give complex composites with a range of stiffness and strength. Because there is no mixing of fibres and cement, high fibre volumes can be used and the fibre orientation can be controlled to suit the intended application.

37.3.2 Uses of polymer-fibre-reinforced cement

This material is mainly used for flat or corrugated sheeting for roofing and cladding applications. Tiles and sheets up to 2.5 m long are produced and they have many uses in the building and construction industries as direct alternatives to asbestos cement.

37.3.3 Manufacture of polymer-fibre-reinforced concrete

For low fibre volumes (~0.1%) the polymer fibres are tipped from a pre-weighed bag directly into the mixer or the ready-mixed concrete truck. After 4–5 minutes mixing the fibres are sufficiently well dispersed for the concrete to be discharged.

For chopped polypropylene twine at about 0.4% by volume a variety of mixes has been used in practice, some requiring an adjustment to the existing equipment, some none at all. Additional equipment has been installed in some plants to chop and/or to facilitate proportioning the fibres. The type of short fibre chosen is mostly based on film, e.g. a twine of 1400 m/kg, chopped to 50 mm staple length. As the fibres cannot be wetted, the mixing need only achieve a homogeneous dispersion and therefore they are often added shortly before the end of mixing the normal ingredients. A long residence time in any mixer leads to undesirable shredding of the fibres and should be avoided. Occasional alterations to the angle of the scraper blades may be all that is required to facilitate mixing in some pan mixes.

The mix of polypropylene concrete will take account of the fibre size and the fibre length that will best suit the aggregate, the workability required and the equipment to be used in making the product. For instance, a thin-walled product would not accommodate the fairly stiff fibres of 700 m/kg because some would lie across the wall and would tend to break out on demoulding. The more flexible twine of 1400 m/kg would therefore be chosen, and would be cut to a shorter staple length. A heavy precast pile, on the other hand, would accept coarse fibres which would give a higher workability for the same fibre content.

37.3.4 Uses of polymer-fibre-reinforced concrete

Concrete containing low fibre volumes (~0.1%) is commonly used for ground floor slabs such as driveways or factory floors.

The chopped twine at 0.4% by volume has been successfully used for many years in precast concrete shell piles, flotation units for marinas and marine defence units. All these applications require increased toughness and impact resistance and under marine conditions the chemical stability of the fibres is an advantage. A number of these applications have allowed the replacement of steel mesh reinforcement by the polymer fibres thus avoiding the need for extra thickness to provide cover to the steel.

37.4 Natural-fibre-reinforced cement

37.4.1 Manufacture and uses

The use of natural cellulose fibres is split into two distinct areas. In one case short cellulose fibres have been used for many years in the asbestos-cement industry and are also used at volumes of up to 10% in conjunction with polymer fibres in asbestos-free products. Manufacturing procedures are very similar to the Hatschek process already described for asbestos cement.

In the other case cellulose stem fibres are used in simple hand lay-up processes for making cementitious composites of various shapes, which are potentially suitable for low-cost housing applications. In these applications the fibre content is usually less than 5% when applying mixing technologies, but may be greater when using technologies of hand lay-up of long fibre rovings. The long fibres can be obtained by tying together or by spinning of twines. Hand laying involves the application of a thin mortar layer on a mould, followed by alternate layers of fibres and mortar matrix. The fibres can be rolled into the matrix or worked into it manually, and the process may involve some vibration. In the mixing technique, there is a limit to the content and length of fibres that can be incorporated, since as with any other fibres workability is reduced. However, many of the natural fibre composites are intended for the production of thin components such as corrugated sheets and shingles, and for these applications there is a requirement for both plasticity and green strength that will permit the shaping of the product. In these components, which have a typical thickness of about 10 mm, the matrix is a cement mortar, and the mix with fibres, or with hand-laid fibres, is spread on a mould surface and then shaped. Corrugation can be achieved by pressing between two corrugated sheets.

37.5 Steel-fibre concrete

37.5.1 Manufacture

Steel fibres of a length : diameter ratio of less than 100 may be mixed with concrete using conventional rotary mixers. Special attention has to be paid to the mix design to avoid 'balling' or collecting together of the fibres and a high proportion of fines with a maximum aggregate size of 10 mm is preferable if an effective fibre volume is to be included.

Typical mixes for pavement applications may include 0.3 to 1% by volume of 0.5 mm diameter by 50 mm long fibres.

A rough guide to the quantity of fibre which can be included using normal site mixing and compaction procedures is given by the following equation:

$$W_f < \frac{600(1 - A)}{l/d} \qquad (37.1)$$

where

W_f = weight of fibres, as a percentage of the concrete matrix, which can be compacted with normal site techniques

$$A = \frac{\text{weight of aggregate greater than 5 mm}}{\text{total weight of concrete}}$$

$$\frac{l}{d} = \frac{\text{length}}{\text{diameter}} \text{ of fibre.}$$

It can be seen that the amount of fibres available for reinforcement is inversely proportional to the l/d ratio, whereas the post-cracking tensile strength of the composite is directly proportional to the l/d ratio, i.e. tensile strength is proportional to $2\,kV_f\tau l/d$,

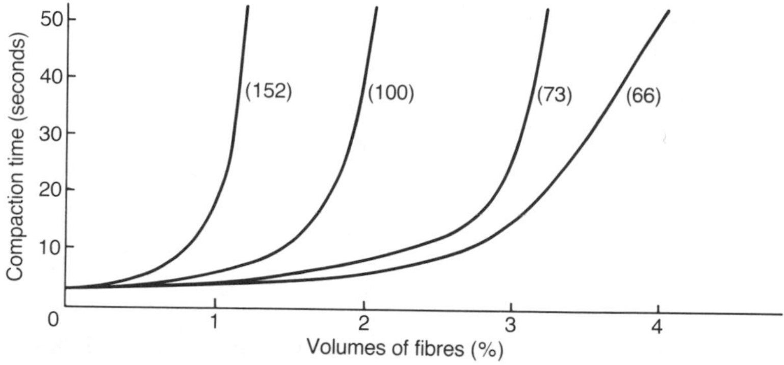

FIGURE 37.2 Effect of length/diameter ratio ( ) of the fibre on compaction time of steel-fibre-reinforced mortar as measured in the VB consistometer (Edgington, 1973).

where
k = a constant depending on fibre orientation
V_f = fibre volume
τ = bond strength.

Therefore the requirements of reinforcement and workability act against each other and a compromise must be reached usually at *l*/*d* ratios between 40 and 100.

An indication of the effects which *l*/*d* ratio and aggregate size have on workability as assessed by VB time (time measured using the VB consistometer) is shown in Figures 37.2 and 37.3 (Edgington, 1973). These figures show that if the VB time is to be less than about 10 seconds and 1% by volume (about 3.3% by weight) of fibres is to be included then the *l*/*d* ratio should be less than 100 and aggregate size less than 10 mm.

The problems of mixing steel fibres into concrete can be overcome by guniting and this is a widely used and an effective technique for a variety of uses, including stabilization of rock slopes and new rock tunnels, and repair of deteriorating sewers and tunnel linings. A higher volume (~2%) of fibres can be included in the guniting process either sprayed with or independently of the matrix. The higher fibre volumes which are possible with guniting without mixing are because of the avoidance of problems associated with rotary mixers and vibrators.

In another procedure for including a high fibre volume without mixing, the fibres are preplaced into the mould or construction and then infiltrated with a fine-grained cement-based slurry. Twenty-eight-day flexural strength up to 60 MPa and tensile strengths up to 16 MPa are said to be possible with this system.

37.5.2 Uses

Uses for mild steel fibres with conventional mixing and compaction techniques have included hydraulic structures such as spillways and sluices, highway and airfield pavements and precast components.

A major use of steel-fibre concrete is in industrial floors in which the quantity of fibres is typically 30 kg/m^3 (~0.4% by volume) which is too low to increase the tensile or flexural strength of the concrete. Use is therefore made of post-cracking load capacity and toughness to provide floors with a thickness of generally between 120 mm and 200 mm depending on loading conditions. Joints should be sawn at an early age between 6 m and 10 m spacing.

Overlays to both concrete and bituminous pavements including airfields have also been successful at between 100 mm and 120 mm

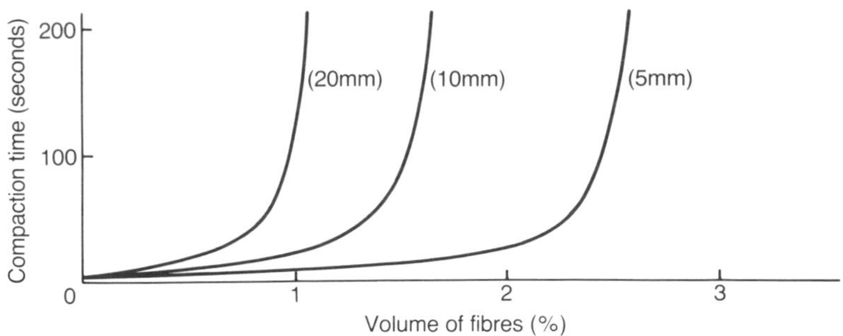

FIGURE 37.3 Effect of maximum aggregate size ( ) on compaction time of steel-fibre-reinforced concrete for fibres of length/diameter ratio of 100 (Edgington, 1973).

thickness with up to 60 kg/m^3 (~0.8% by volume) of fibre. Even when overlaying concrete roads, an isolating layer of 30 mm of asphalt has been found to be important and bonding the new and old work together is a critical part of the operation. Joints between 10 m and 15 m are essential and reflected cracks must be expected. However, performance has been shown to be very good when properly designed and constructed.

Another major application for steel-fibre concrete is tunnel lining and rock slope stabilization using the 'gunite' or sprayed concrete technique, and the use of steel mesh in these situations is being steadily replaced, which results in savings in labour costs.

Steel fibres have been used in hydraulic structures such as spillways and stilling basins where toughness and resistance to cavitation are important. The experience in dams such as Tarbela has been generally satisfactory although there have been one or two failures in other large dams due to inadequate construction techniques. The use of very high strength silica fume concrete has also been very encouraging in such situations.

One of the most successful uses of stainless steel fibres produced by the melt extract process has been in castable refractory concretes for use at temperatures up to 1600°C. In these products, initial cost is not the prime consideration, a more important result being increase in product life, which in many cases may be more than doubled.

37.6 References

Edgington, J. (1973) Steel fibre reinforced concrete. Ph.D. thesis, University of Surrey.

Further reading

General texts

Ashbee, K. (1989) *Fibre Reinforced Composites*. Technomic Publishing Co. Ltd, Lancaster, Pennsylvania; Basel.

Bentur, A. and Mindess, A. (1990) *Fibre Reinforced Cementitious Composites*. Elsevier Applied Science.

Fordyce, M.W. and Wodehouse, R.G. (1983) *GRC and Buildings*. Butterworth.

Hannant, D.J. (1978) *Fibre Cements and Fibre Concretes*. Wiley.

Hollaway, L. (ed.) (1990) *Polymers and Polymer Composites in Construction*. Thomas Telford, London.

Majumdar, A.J. and Laws, V. (1991) *Glass Fibre Reinforced Cement*. Blackwell Scientific Publications.

Swamy, R.N. (ed.) (1988) *Natural Fibre Reinforced Cement and Concrete*. Blackie.

Weatherhead, R.C. (1980) *FRP Technology: Fibre Reinforced Resin Systems*. Applied Science Publishers, London.

Part Seven

Timber

J.M. Dinwoodie

Introduction

From the early part of the industrial era the UK has been a large importer of timber and timber products. In 1989 (the last year for which figures are available) the value of timber and timber products (but excluding pulp and paper) imported into the UK was £2320 million and, as such, constituted about 2.2% of all our imports. Home production is small in comparison to the volume of imports: only about 10% of timber requirements are met by home production, while all plywood requirements have to be imported. It is only in the case of fibreboard and chipboard that UK production goes some way to meeting UK consumption – 30% in the case of fibreboard, and 55% in the case of chipboard.

In the UK, timber and timber products are consumed by a large range of industries, but the bulk of the material (60–65%) continues to be used in construction, either structurally, such as roof trusses, floor joists, and flooring, or wall framing, or non-structurally, such as doors, window frames, skirting boards, external cladding, and built-in furniture such as kitchen units.

Timber is cut and machined from trees, themselves the product of nature and time. The structure of the timber of trees has evolved through millions of years to provide a most efficient system which will support the crown, conduct mineral solutions and store food material. Since there are approximately 30 000 different species of tree it is not surprising to find that timber is an extremely variable material. A quick mental comparison of the colour, texture and density of a piece of balsa and a piece of lignum vitae, previously used to make bowling balls, will illustrate the wide range that occurs. Nevertheless, people have found timber to be a cheap and effective material and, as we have seen, continue to use it in vast quantities. However, we must never forget that the methods by which we utilize this product are quite different from the purpose that nature intended and many of the criticisms levelled at timber as a material are a consequence of our use or misuse of nature's product. Unlike so many other materials, especially those used in the construction industry, timber cannot be manufactured to a particular specification. Instead the best use has to be made of the material already produced, though it is possible from the wide range available to select timbers with the most desirable range of properties. Timber as a material can be defined as a low-density, cellular, polymeric composite, and as such does not conveniently fall into any one class of material, rather tending to overlap a number of classes. In terms of its high-strength performance and low cost timber remains the world's most successful fibre composite.

Four orders of structural variation can be recognized – macroscopic, microscopic, ultrastructural and molecular – and in subsequent chapters the various physical and mechanical properties of timber will be related to these four levels of structure. In seeking correlations between performance and structure it is tempting to describe the latter in terms of smaller and smaller structural units. Whilst this desire for refinement is to be encouraged, a cautionary note must be recorded for it is all too easy to overlook the significance of the gross features. This is particularly so where large sections of timber are being used under practical conditions; in these situations gross features such as knots and grain angle are highly significant factors.

Chapter thirty-eight

Structure of timber

38.1 Structure at the macroscopic level
38.2 Structure at the microscopic level
38.3 Molecular structure and ultrastructure
38.4 Variability in structure
38.5 Appearance of timber in relation to its structure
38.6 Mass–volume relationships
38.7 Moisture in timber
38.8 References

38.1 Structure at the macroscopic level

The trunk of a tree has three physical functions to perform; firstly, it must support the crown, a region responsible for the production not only of food but also of seed; secondly, it must conduct the mineral solutions absorbed by the roots upwards to the crown; and thirdly it must store manufactured food (carbohydrates) until required. As will be described in detail later, these tasks are performed by different types of cell.

Whereas the entire cross-section of the trunk fulfils the function of support, and increasing crown diameter is matched with increasing diameter of the trunk, conduction and storage are restricted to the outer region of the trunk. This zone is known as **sapwood**, while the region in which the cells no longer fulfil these tasks is termed the **heartwood**. The width of sapwood varies with species and with age of the tree, but it is seldom greater, and is usually much less than, one third of the total radius (Figures 38.1 and 38.2). The advancement of the heartwood to include former sapwood cells results in a number of cell changes, primarily chemical. The acidity of the cells increases slightly, though certain timbers have heartwood of very high acidity. Substances, collectively called **extractives**, are formed in small quantities and these impart not only colouration to the heartwood but also resistance to both fungal and insect attack. Different substances are found in different species of wood and some timbers are devoid of them altogether: this explains the very wide range in the natural durability of wood about which more will be said later. Many timbers develop gums and resins in the heartwood while the moisture content of the heartwood of most timbers is appreciably lower than that of the sapwood in the freshly felled state.

With increasing radial growth of the trunk commensurate increases in crown size occur, resulting in the enlargement of existing branches and the production of new ones; crown development is not only outwards but upwards. Radial growth of the trunk must accommodate the existing branches and this is achieved by the structure that we know as the **knot**. If the cambium of the branch is still alive at the point where it fuses with the cambium of the trunk, continuity in growth will arise even though there will be a change in orientation of the cells. The structure so formed is termed a **green** or **live** knot (Figure 38.3). If, however, the cambium of the branch is dead, and this frequently happens to the lower branches, there will be an absence

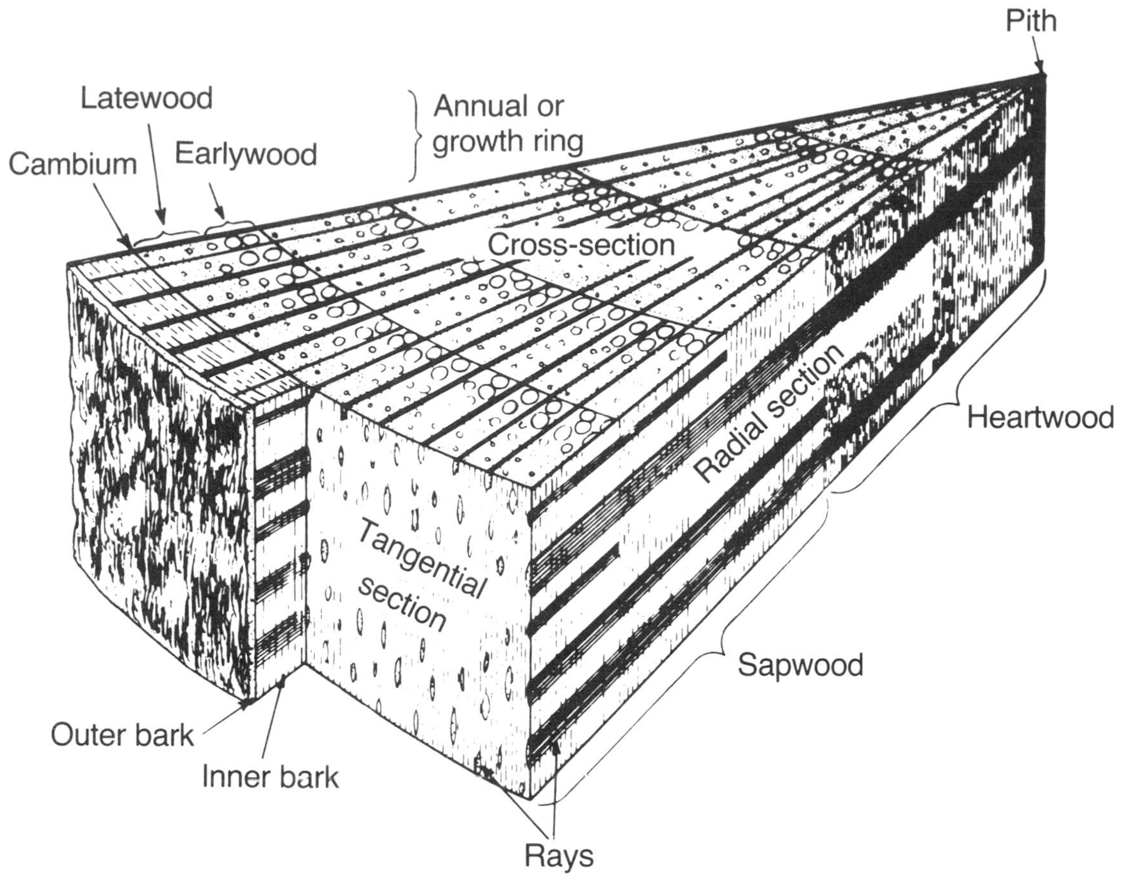

FIGURE 38.1 Diagrammatic illustration of a wedge-shaped segment cut from a five-year-old hardwood tree, showing the principal structural features (Building Research Establishment © Crown copyright).

of continuity, the trunk growing round the dead branch often complete with its bark. Such a knot is termed a **black** or **dead** knot (Figure 38.4), frequently dropping out of planks on sawing. The grain direction in the vicinity of knots is frequently distorted and in a later section the loss of strength due to different types of knots will be discussed.

38.2 Structure at the microscopic level

The cellular structure of wood is illustrated in Figures 38.5 and 38.6. These three-dimensional blocks are produced from micrographs of samples of wood 0.8 × 0.5 × 0.5 cm in size removed from a coniferous tree (Figure 38.5) – known technically as a **softwood** – and a broadleaved tree (Figure 38.6) – a **hardwood.** In both samples it will be observed that 90–95% of cells are aligned in the vertical axis, while the remaining percentage is present in bands (rays) aligned in one of the two horizontal planes known as the radial plane or quarter-sawn plane (Figure 38.1). This means that there is a different distribution of cells on the three principal axes and this is one of the two principal reasons for the high degree of anisotropy present in timber.

It is popularly believed that the cells of wood are living cells: this is certainly not the case. Wood cells are produced by division of the

FIGURE 38.2 Cross-section through the trunk of a Douglas fir tree. The annual growth rings, the darker heartwood and the lighter sapwood can all be clearly seen (Building Research Establishment © Crown copyright).

cambium, a zone of living cells which lies between the bark and the woody part of the trunk and branches (Figure 38.1). During the growing season these cells undergo radial subdivision to produce what are known as daughter cells and some of these will remain as cambial cells while others, to the outside of the zone, will develop into bark or, if on the inside, will change into wood.

To accommodate the increasing diameter of the tree the cambial zone must increase circumferentially and this is achieved by the periodic tangential division of the cambial cells. In this case the new wall is sloping and subsequent elongation of each half of the cell results in cell overlap, often frequently at shallow angles to the vertical axis, giving rise to spiral grain formation in the timber. The rate at which the cambium divides tangentially has a significant effect on the average cell length of the timber produced.

The daughter cells produced radially from the cambium undergo a series of changes extended over a period of about three weeks; this process is known as differentiation. Changes in cell shape are paralleled with the formation of the secondary wall, the final stages of which are associated with the death of the cell; the degenerated cell contents are frequently to be found lining the cell cavity. It is during the process of differentiation that the standard daughter cell is transformed into one of four

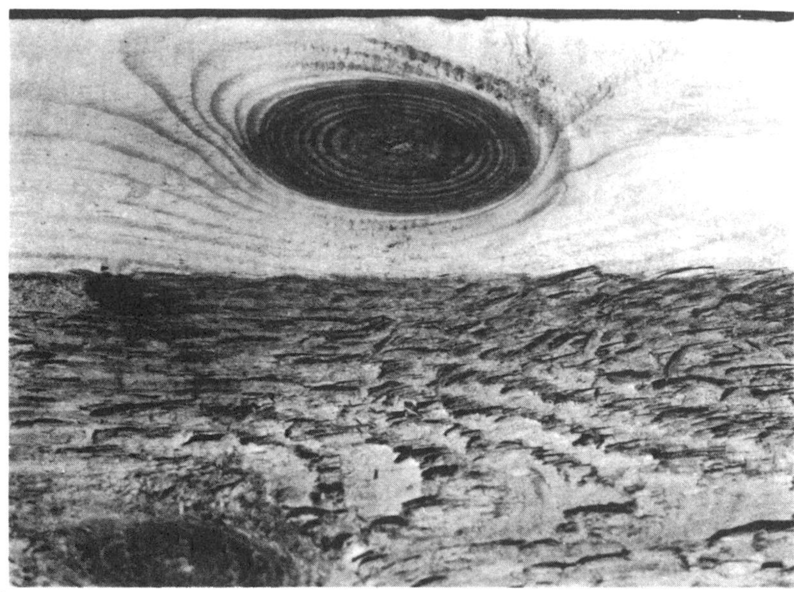

FIGURE 38.3 Green or live knot showing continuity in structure between the branch and tree trunk (Building Research Establishment © Crown copyright).

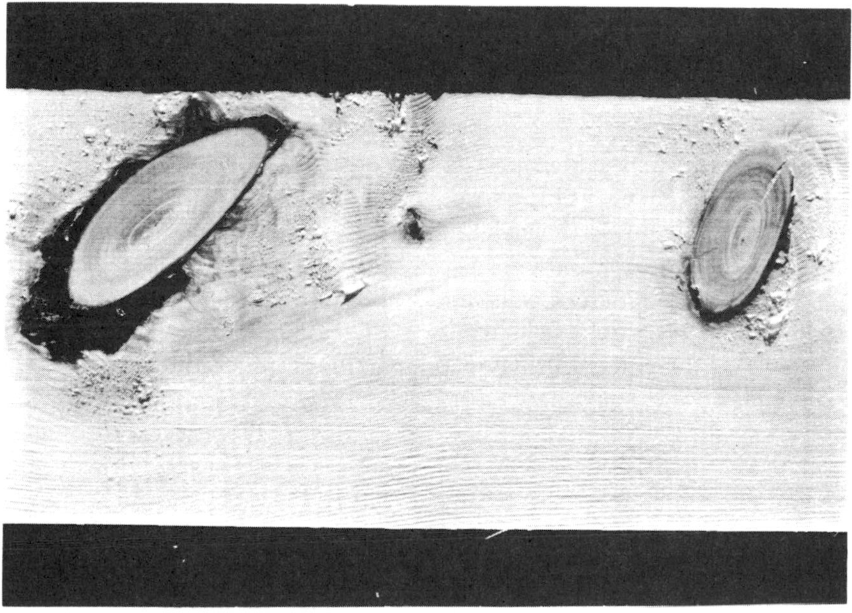

FIGURE 38.4 Black or dead knot surrounded by the bark of the branch and hence showing discontinuity between branch and tree trunk (Building Research Establishment © Crown copyright).

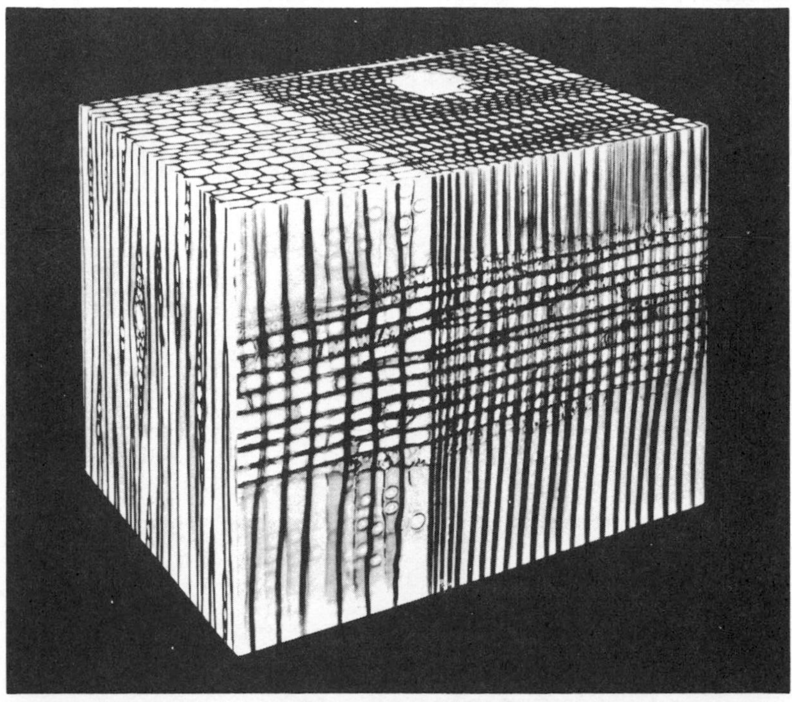

FIGURE 38.5 Cellular arrangement in a softwood (*Pinus sylvestris* – Scots pine, redwood) (Building Research Establishment © Crown copyright).

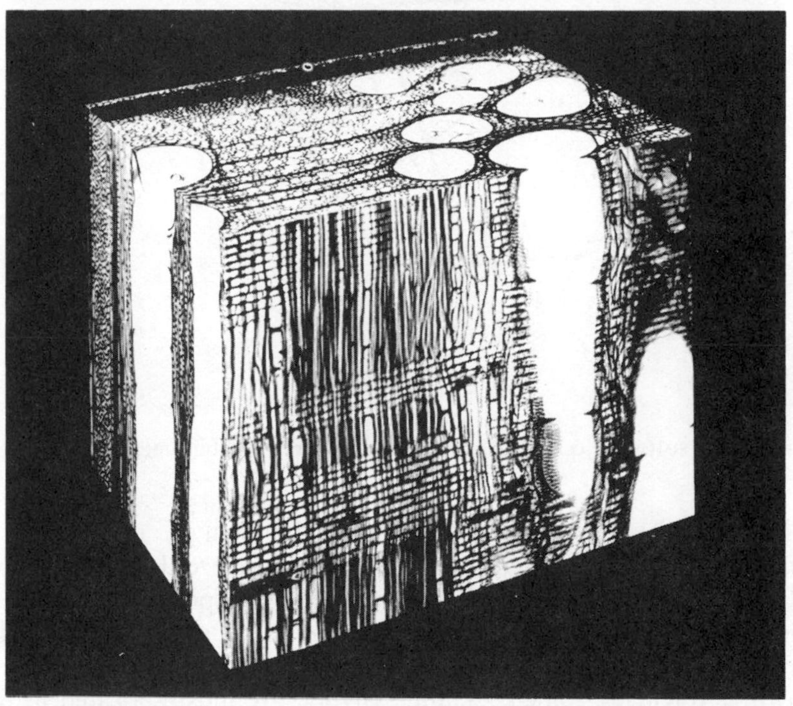

FIGURE 38.6 Cellular arrangement in a ring-porous hardwood (*Quercus robur* – European oak) (Building Research Establishment © Crown copyright).

TABLE 38.1 The functions and wall thicknesses of the various types of cell found in softwoods and hardwoods

Cells	*Softwood*	*Hardwood*	*Function*	*Wall thickness*
Parenchyma	+	+	Storage	
Tracheids	+	+	Support Conduction	
Fibres		+	Support	
Vessels (pores)		+	Conduction	

FIGURE 38.7 Individual softwood cells (×20) (Building Research Establishment © Crown copyright).

basic cell types (Table 38.1). Chemical dissolution of the lignin–pectin complex cementing together the cells will result in their separation. In the softwood (Figure 38.7) two types of cell can be observed. Those present in greater number are known as **tracheids**, some 2–4 mm in length with an aspect ratio (L/D) of about 100:1. These cells, which lie vertically in the trunk, are responsible for both the supporting and conducting roles. The small block-like cells some 200 × 30 μm in size, known as **parenchyma**, are mostly located in the rays and are

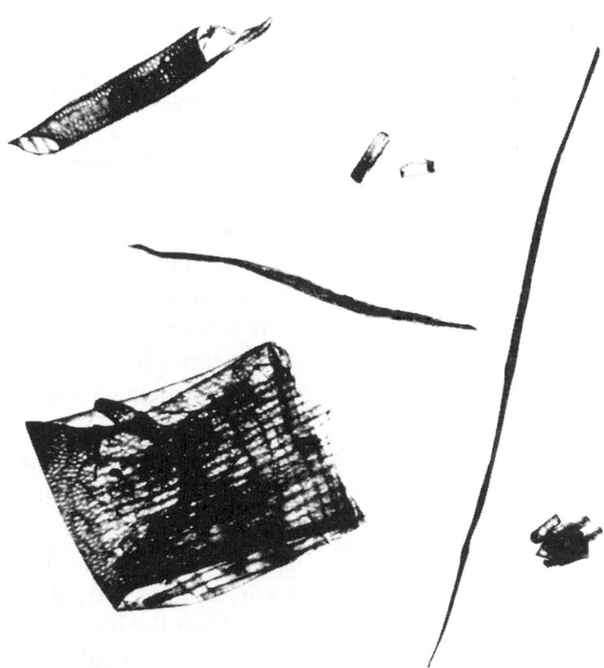

FIGURE 38.8 Individual cells from a ring-porous hardwood (×50) (Building Research Establishment © Crown copyright).

responsible for the storage of food material.

In contrast, in the hardwoods (Figure 38.8), four types of cell are present albeit that one, the tracheid, is present in small amounts. The role of storage is again primarily taken by the parenchyma, which can be present horizontally in the form of a ray, or vertically, either scattered or in distinct zones. Support is effected by long thin cells with very tapered ends, known as **fibres**; these are usually about 1–2 mm in length with an aspect ratio of about 100:1. Conduction is carried out in cells whose end walls have been dissolved away either completely or in part. These cells, known as **vessels** or **pores**, are usually short (0.2–1.2 mm) and relatively wide (up to 0.5 mm) and when situated above one another form an efficient conducting tube. It can be seen, therefore, that while in the softwoods the three functions are performed by two types of cell, in the hardwoods each function is performed by a single cell type (Table 38.1).

Although all cell types develop a secondary wall this varies in thickness, being related to the function that the cell will perform. Thus the wall thickness of fibres is several times that of the vessel (Table 38.1). Consequently, the density of the wood, and hence many of the strength properties as will be discussed later, will be related to the relative proportions of the various types of cell. Density, of course, will also be related to the absolute wall thickness of any one type of cell, for it is possible to obtain fibres of one species of wood several times thicker than those of another. The range in density of timber is from 120 to 1200 kg/m^3 corresponding to pore volumes of 92% to 18%.

Growth may be continuous throughout the year in certain parts of the world and the wood formed tends to be uniform in structure. In the temperate and subarctic regions and in parts of the tropics growth is seasonal, resulting in the formation of **growth rings**; in this country where there is a single growth period each year these rings are referred to as **annual rings** (Figure 38.1).

When seasonal growth commences, the dominant function appears to be conduction, while in the latter part of the year the dominant factor is support. This change in emphasis manifests itself in the softwoods with the presence of thin-walled tracheids (about 2 μm) in the early part of the season (the wood being known as **early-wood**) and thick-walled (up to 10 μm) and slightly longer (10%) in the latter part of the season (the **latewood**) (Figure 38.1).

In some of the hardwoods, but certainly not all of them, the earlywood is characterized by the presence of large-diameter vessels surrounded primarily by parenchyma and tracheids; only a few fibres are present. In the latewood, the vessel diameter is considerably smaller (about 20%) and the bulk of the tissue comprises fibres. It is not surprising to find, therefore, that the technical properties of the earlywood and latewood are quite different from one another. Timbers with this characteristic two-phase system are referred to as having a **ring-porous** structure (Figure 38.6).

The majority of hardwoods, whether of temperate or tropical origin, show little differentiation between earlywood and latewood. Uniformity across the growth ring occurs not only in cell size, but also in the distribution of the different types of cells (Figure 38.9): these timbers are said to be **diffuse-porous**.

In addition to determining many of the technical properties of wood, the distribution of cell types and their sizes is used as a means of timber identification.

Interconnection by means of pits occurs between cells to permit the passage of mineral solutions and food in both longitudinal and horizontal planes. Three basic types of pit occur. **Simple pits**, generally small in diameter and taking the form of straight-sided holes with a transverse membrane, occur between parenchyma and parenchyma, and also between fibre and fibre. Between tracheids a complex struc-

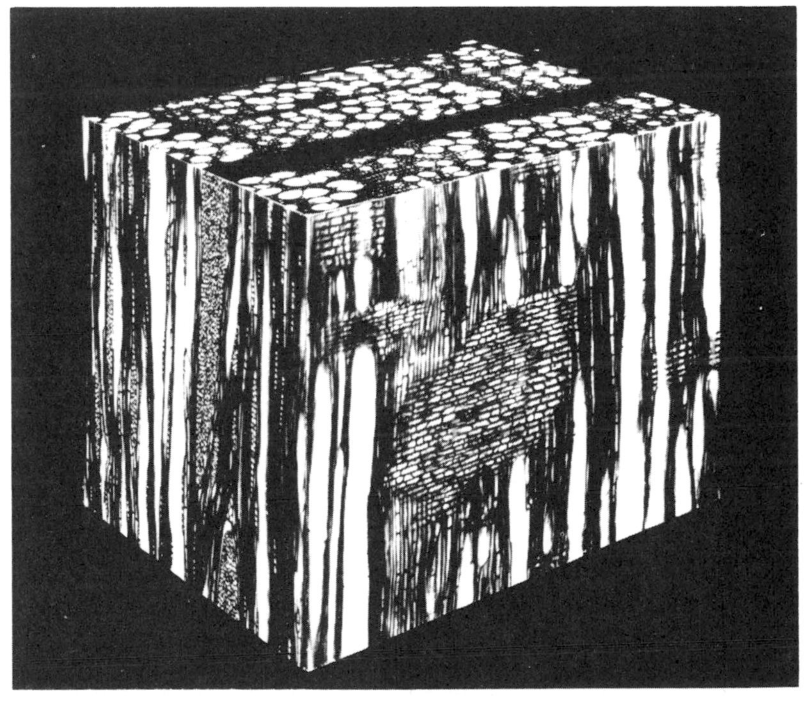

FIGURE 38.9 Cellular arrangement in a diffuse porous hardwood (*Fagus sylvatica* – beech) (Building Research Establishment © Crown copyright).

FIGURE 38.10 Electron micrograph of the softwood bordered pit showing the margo strands supporting the diaphragm (torus), which overlaps the aperture (×3600) (Building Research Establishment © Crown copyright).

ture known as the **bordered pit** occurs (Figure 38.10; see also Figure 40.4(a) for sectional view). The entrance to the pit is domed and the internal chamber is characterized by the presence of a diaphragm (the **torus**) which is suspended by thin strands (the **margo**). Differential pressure between adjacent tracheids will cause the torus to move against the pit aperture, effectively stopping flow. As will be discussed later, these pits have a profound influence on the degree of artificial preservation of the timber. Similar structures are to be found interconnecting vessels in a horizontal plane. Between parenchyma cells and tracheids or vessels there occur **semi-bordered** pits, often referred to as ray pits. These are characterized by the presence of a dome on the tracheid or vessel wall and the absence of such on the parenchyma wall: a pit membrane is present, but the torus is absent. Differences in the shape and size of these pits is an important diagnostic feature in the softwoods.

38.3 Molecular structure and ultrastructure

38.3.1 Chemical constituents

Chemical analysis reveals the existence of four constituents and provides data on their relative proportions. This information may be summarized as in Table 38.2: proportions are for timber in general and slight variations in these can occur between timber of different species, or among the different parts of a single tree.

Cellulose

Cellulose $(C_6H_{10}O_5)_n$ occurs in the form of long slender filaments or chains, these having been built up within the cell wall from the glucose

TABLE 38.2 Chemical composition of timber

	Percentage weight	*Polymeric state*	*Molecular derivatives*	*Function*
Cellulose	40–50	Crystalline, highly oriented large molecule	Glucose	'Fibre'
Hemicelluloses	20–25	Semi-crystalline, smaller molecule	Galactose Mannose Xylose	'Matrix'
Lignin	25–30	Amorphous, large 3-D molecule	Phenyl propane	
Extractives	0–10	Some polymeric	e.g. Terpenes Polyphenols	Extraneous

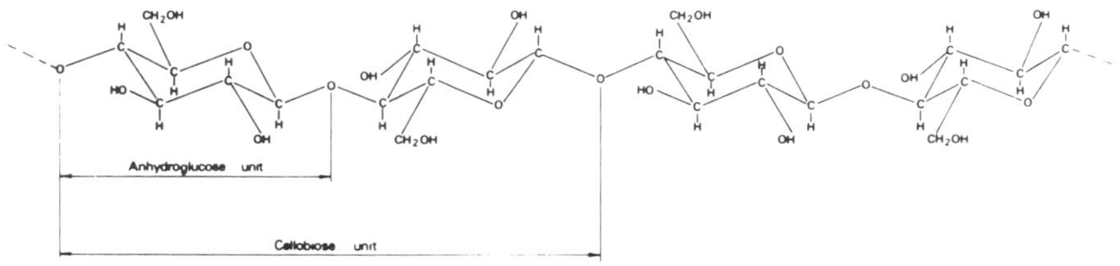

FIGURE 38.11 Structural formula for the cellulose molecule (Building Research Establishment © Crown copyright).

monomer ($C_6H_{12}O_6$). Whilst the number of units per cellulose molecule (the degree of polymerization) can vary considerably even within one cell wall it is thought that a value of 8000–10 000 is a realistic average. The anhydroglucose unit $C_6H_{10}O_5$, which is not quite flat, is in the form of a six-sided ring consisting of five carbon atoms and one oxygen atom (Figure 38.11); the side groups play an important part in intermolecular bonding as will be noted later. Successive glucose units are covalently linked in the 1,4 positions giving rise to a potentially straight and extended chain; i.e. moving in a clockwise direction around the ring it is the first and fourth carbon atoms after the oxygen atom that combine with adjacent glucose units to form the long-chain molecule. Glucose, however, can be present in one of two forms dependent on the position of the OH group attached to carbon 1. When this group lies below the ring, the unit is known as β-glucose, and on combining with adjacent units by a condensation reaction a molecule of cellulose is produced in which alternative glucose units are rotated through 180°: it is this product which is the principal wall-building constituent.

Cellulose chains may crystallize in many ways, but one form, namely cellulose I, is characteristic of natural cellulosic materials. Over the years there have been various attempts to model the structure of cellulose I. One of the more recent, and one which has gained wide acceptance, is that proposed by Gardner and Blackwell (1974). Using X-ray fibre diffraction methods these authors, working on the cellulose of the alga *Valonia*, proposed an eight-chain unit cell with all the chains running in the same direction. Forty-one reflections were observed in

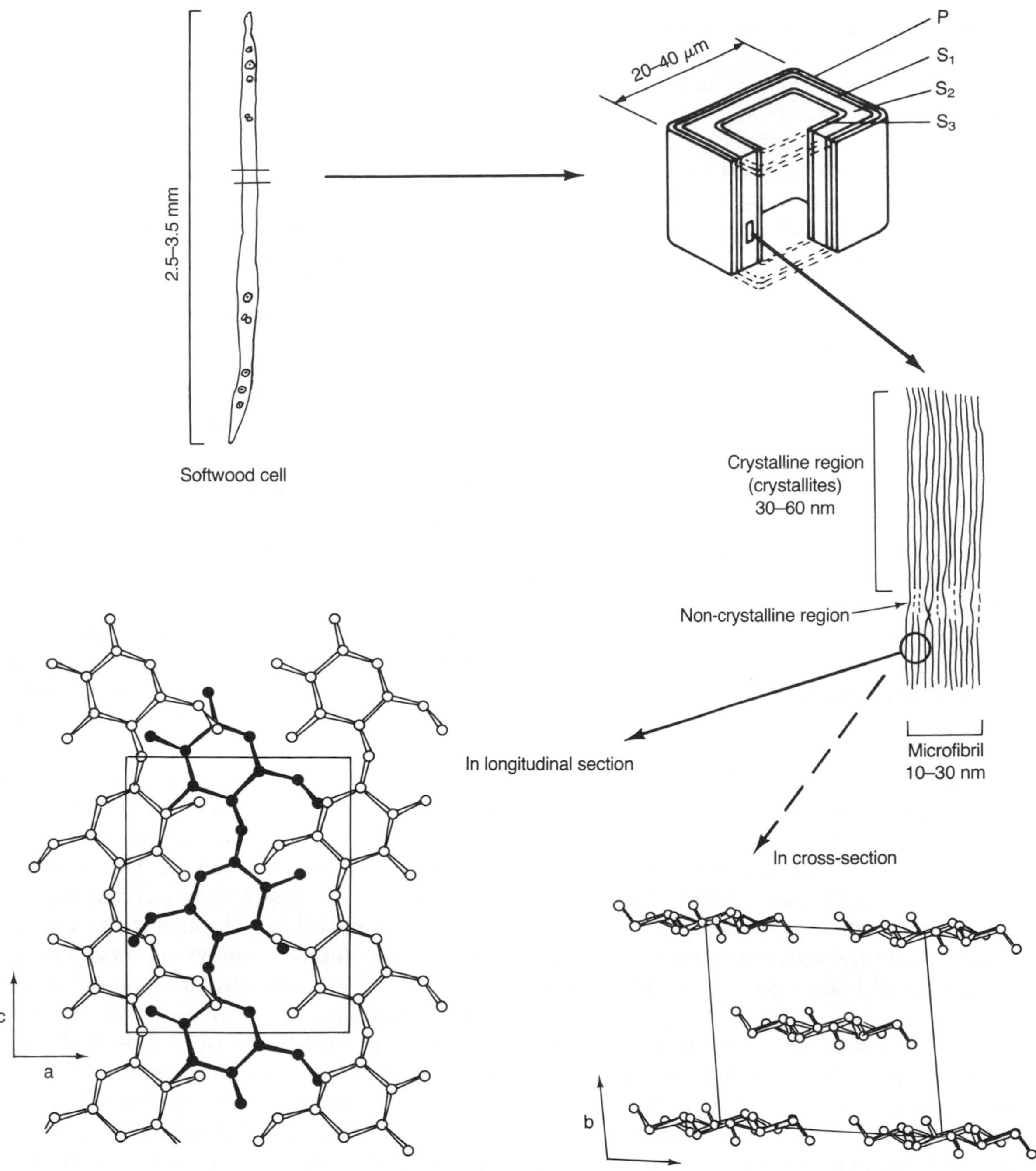

FIGURE 38.12 Relationship between the structures of timber at different levels of magnitude. The lower two diagrams are projections of the Gardener and Blackwell two-chain cell used as an approximation to the eight-chain unit cell of the real structure. On the left is the projection viewed perpendicular to the *ac* plane; on the right the projection viewed perpendicular to the *ab* plane (i.e. along the cell axis). Planes are character- ized according to North American rather than European terminology. (The lower two diagrams from K.H. Gardener and J. Blackwell (1974) by permission of John Wiley and Sons; the upper three diagrams adapted from J.F. Siau (1971), reproduced by permission of Syracuse University Press.)

their X-ray diffractions and these were indexed using a monoclinic unit cell having dimensions $a = 1.634$ nm, $b = 1.572$ nm and $c = 1.038$ nm (the fibre axis) with $\beta = 97°$; the unit cell therefore comprises a number of whole chains or parts of chains totalling eight in number.

All but three of the reflections can be indexed by a two-chain unit cell almost identical to that of Meyer and Misch (1937) though this latter model had adjacent chains running in opposite directions. These three reflections are reported as being very weak, which means that the differences between the four Meyer and Misch unit cells making up the eight-chain cell must be small. Gardner and Blackwell therefore take a two-chain unit cell ($a = 0.817$ nm, $b = 0.786$ nm and $c = 1.038$ nm) as an adequate approximation to the real structure. Their proposed model for cellulose I is shown in Figure 38.12, which shows the chains lying in a parallel configuration, the centre chain staggered by $0.266 \times c$ (= 0.276 nm).

Although these results have not been confirmed for the structure of crystalline cellulose in timber, it is difficult to see why the structure of cellulose in timber should vary from that in *Valonia*; it is widely accepted now that the Gardner and Blackwell model applies to cellulose in timber.

Cellulose which has regenerated from a solution displays a different crystalline structure and is known as cellulose II: in this case there is complete agreement that the unit cell possesses an anti-parallel arrangement of the cellulose molecule.

Within the structure of cellulose I both primary and secondary bonding are represented and many of the technical properties of wood can be related to the variety of bonding present. Covalent bonding both within the glucose rings and linking together the rings to form the molecular chain contributes to the high axial tensile strength of timber. There is no evidence of primary bonding laterally between the chains: rather this seems to be a complex mixture of the fairly strong hydrogen bonds and the weak van der Waals forces. The same OH groups that give rise to this hydrogen bonding are highly attractive to water molecules and explain the affinity of cellulose for water. Gardner and Blackwell (1974) on cellulose from *Valonia* identify the existence of both intermolecular and intramolecular hydrogen bonds all of which, however, are interpreted as lying only on the *ac* plane; they consider the structure of cellulose as an array of hydrogen-bonded sheets held together by van der Waals forces across the *cb* plane.

The degree of crystallinity is usually assessed by X-ray and electron diffraction techniques and has been shown to be at least 67%, though some workers have assessed cellulose as up to 90% crystalline. This range is due in a large extent to the fact that wood is composed not just of the crystalline and non-crystalline constituents but rather a series of substances of varying crystallinity. Regions of complete crystallinity and regions with a total absence of crystalline structure (amorphous zones) can be recognized, but the transition from one state to the other is gradual.

The length of the cellulose molecule is about 5000 nm (0.005 mm), whereas the average size of each crystalline region determined by X-ray analysis is only 60 nm in length, 5 nm in width and 3 nm in thickness. This means that any cellulose molecule will pass through several regions of high crystallinity – known as crystallites or micelles – with intermediate non-crystalline or low-crystalline zones in which the cellulose chains are in only loose association with each other (Figure 38.12). Thus the majority of chains emerging from one crystallite will pass to the next creating a high degree of longitudinal coordination (Figure 38.12); this collective unit is termed a **microfibril** and has infinite length; it is clothed with chains of cellulose mixed with chains of sugar units other than glucose (see below) which lie parallel, but are not regularly spaced. This brings the microfibril in timber to about 10 nm in breadth. The degree of crystallinity will therefore vary along its length and it has been proposed that this could be periodic.

Hemicelluloses and lignin

In Table 38.2 reference was made to the other constituents of wood additional to cellulose. Two of these, the hemicelluloses and lignin, are regarded as cementing material contributing to the structural integrity of wood and also to its high stiffness. The hemicelluloses, like cellulose itself, are carbohydrates and differ in composition depending on whether the wood is from a conifer or a broadleaved tree. Both the degree of crystallization and the degree of polymerization are low, the molecule containing less than 150 units; in these respects and also in their lack of resistance to alkaline solutions the hemicelluloses are quite different from true cellulose.

Lignin, present in about equal proportions to the hemicelluloses, is chemically dissimilar to these and to cellulose. Lignin is a complex aromatic compound composed of phenyl groups, but the detailed structure has still not been established. It is non-crystalline and the structure varies between wood from a conifer and from a broadleaved tree. About 25% of the total lignin in timber is to be found in the middle lamella, an intercellular layer composed of lignin and pectin. Since the middle lamella is very thin, the concentration of lignin is correspondingly high (about 70%).

The bulk of the lignin (about 75%) is present within the cell wall, having been deposited following completion of the cellulosic framework; the termination of the lignification process towards the end of the period of differentiation coincides with the death of the cell. Most cellulosic plants do not contain lignin and it is the inclusion of this substance within the framework of wood that is largely responsible for the high stiffness of wood.

38.3.2 The cell wall as a fibre composite

In the introductory remarks, wood was defined as a natural composite and the most successful model used to interpret the ultrastructure of wood from the various chemical and X-ray analyses ascribes the role of 'fibre' to the cellulosic microfibrils while the lignin and hemicelluloses are considered as separate components of the 'matrix'. The cellulosic microfibril is interpreted therefore as conferring high tensile strength to the composite owing to the presence of covalent bonding both within and between the anhydroglucose units. Experimentally it has been shown that reduction in chain length following gamma irradiation markedly reduces the tensile strength of timber (Ifju, 1964); the significance of chain length in determining strength has been confirmed in studies of wood with inherently low degrees of polymerization. While Ifju considered slippage between the cellulose chains to be an important contributor to the development of ultimate tensile strength, this is thought to be unlikely due to the forces involved in fracturing large numbers of hydrogen bonds.

Preston (1964) has shown that the hemicelluloses are usually intimately associated with the cellulose, effectively binding the microfibrils together. Bundles of cellulose chains are therefore seen as having a polycrystalline sheath of hemicellulose material and consequently the resulting high degree of hydrogen bonding would make chain slippage unlikely: rather it would appear that stressing results in fracture of the C–O–C linkage.

The deposition of lignin is variable in different parts of the cell wall, but it is obvious that its prime function is to protect the hydrophilic (water-seeking) cellulose and hemicelluloses which are mechanically weak when wet. Experimentally, it has been demonstrated that removal of the lignin markedly reduces the strength of wood in the wet state, though its reduction results in an increase in its strength in the dry state calculated on a net cell wall area basis.

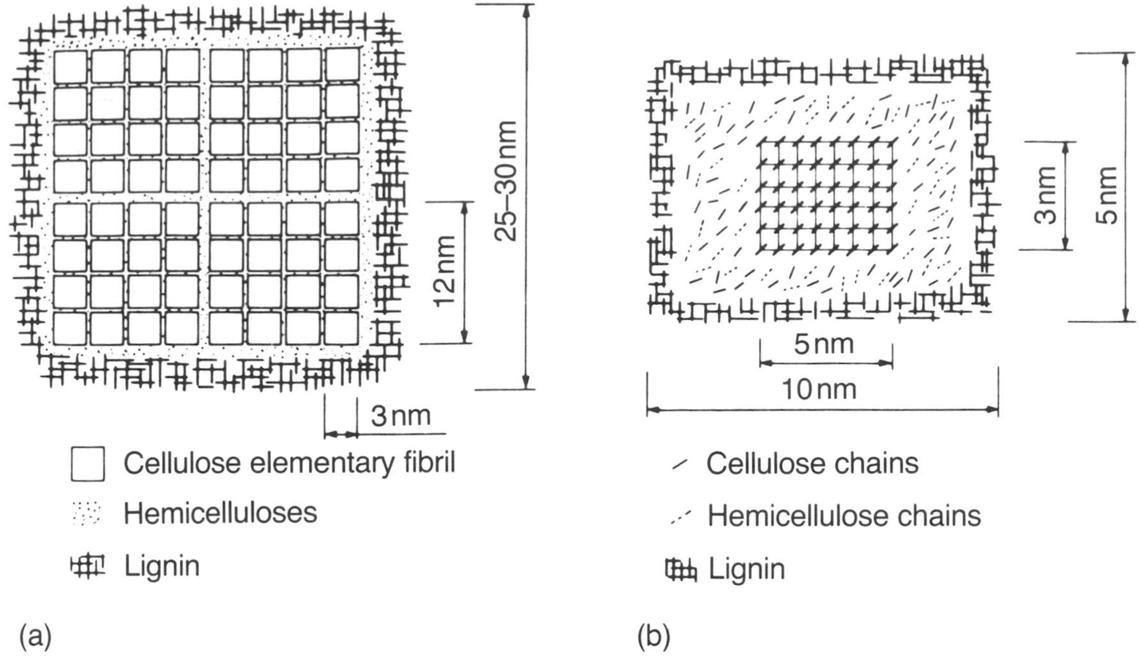

FIGURE 38.13 Models of the cross-section of a microfibril. In (a) the crystalline core has been subdivided into elementary fibrils, while in (b) the core is regarded as being homogeneous. ((a) adapted from D. Fengel (1970) © TAPPI, with permission; (b) adapted from R.D. Preston (1974) with permission from Chapman and Hall.)

Consequently, the lignin is regarded as lying to the outside of the fibril forming a protective sheath.

Since the lignin is located only on the exterior it must be responsible for cementing together the fibrils and in imparting shear resistance in the transference of stress throughout the composite. The role of lignin in contributing towards the stiffness of timber has already been mentioned.

Two schools of thought exist on the possible location within the microfibril of these two components of the matrix. These are illustrated in Figure 38.13. The model that was more widely held some 10 to 15 years ago is depicted on the left where cellulosic subunits some 3 nm in diameter are thought to exist. These units, comprising some 40 cellulose chains, are known as elementary fibrils or protofibrils. Gaps (1 nm) between these units are filled with hemicellulose while more hemicellulose and lignin form the sheath. This subdivision of the microfibril is in dispute and it has been suggested that the evidence to support such a subdivision has been produced by artefacts in sample preparation for electron microscopy. In the alternative model (Figure 38.13(b)) the crystalline core is considered to be about 5 nm × 3 nm containing about 48 chains in either four- or eight-chain unit cells; the latter configuration is now receiving much wider acceptance. Both models are in agreement, however, in that passing outwards from the core of the microfibril the highly crystalline cellulose gives way first to the partly crystalline layer containing mainly hemicellulose but also some cellulose, and then to the amorphous lignin: this gradual transition of crystallinity from fibre to matrix results in high interlaminar shear strength which contributes considerably to the high tensile strength and toughness of wood.

38.3.3 Cell wall layers

When a cambial cell divides to form two daughter cells a new wall is formed comprising the middle lamella and two primary cell walls, one to each daughter cell. These new cells undergo changes within about three days of their formation and one of these developments will be the formation of a secondary wall. The thickness of this wall will depend on the function the cell will perform, as described earlier, but its basic construction will be similar in all cells.

Early studies on the anatomy of the cell wall used polarization microscopy, which revealed the direction of orientation of the crystalline regions. These studies indicated that the secondary wall could be subdivided into three layers and measurements of the extinction position were indicative of the angle at which the microfibrils were orientated. Subsequent studies with transmission electron microscopy confirmed these findings and provided some addi-

TABLE 38.3 Microfibrillar orientation and percentage thickness of the cell wall layers in spruce timber (*Picea abies*)

Wall layer	*% thickness*	*Angle to longitudinal axis*
P	5	Random
S_1	9	50°–70°
S_2	85	10°–30°
S_3	1	60°–90°

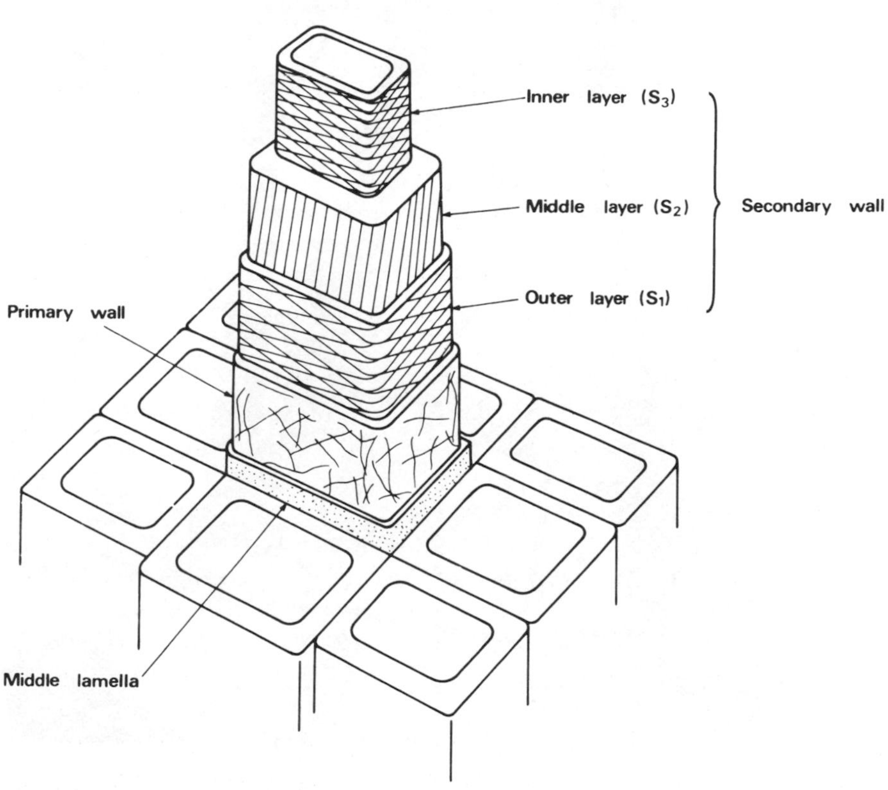

FIGURE 38.14 Simplified structure of the cell wall showing orientation of microfibrils in each of the major wall layers (Building Research Establishment © Crown copyright).

tional information with particular reference to wall texture and variability of angle. The relative thicknesses and mean microfibrillar angles of these layers in a sample of spruce timber are illustrated in Table 38.3.

The middle lamella, a lignin–pectin complex, is devoid of cellulosic microfibrils while in the primary wall (P) the microfibrils are loosely packed and interweave at random (Figure 38.14); no lamellation is present. In the secondary wall layers the microfibrils are closely packed and parallel to each other. The outer layer of this wall, the S_1, is again thin and is characterized by having from four to six lamellae, the microfibrils of each alternating between a left- and right-hand spiral both with a pitch to the longitudinal axis of from 50° to 70° depending on the species of timber.

The middle layer of the secondary wall (S_2) is thick and is composed of 30–150 lamellae, the

FIGURE 38.15 Electron micrograph of the cell wall in Norway spruce timber (*Picea abies*) showing the parallel and almost vertical microfibrils of an exposed portion of the S_2 layer (Building Research Establishment © Crown copyright).

microfibrils of which all exhibit a similar orientation in a right-hand spiral with a pitch of 10–30° to the longitudinal axis as illustrated in Figures 38.14 and 38.15. Since over three quarters of the cell wall is composed of the S_2 layer it follows that the ultrastructure of this layer will have a very marked influence on the behaviour of the timber. In later sections, anisotropic behaviour, shrinkage, tensile strength, stiffness (Cowdrey and Preston, 1966), and failure morphology will all be related to the microfibrillar angle in the S_2 layer.

The S_3 layer, which may be absent in certain timbers, is very thin with only a few lamellae; it is characterized, as in the S_1 layer, by alternate lamellae possessing microfibrils orientated in opposite spirals with a pitch of 60–90° (Figure 38.14). Generally this wall layer has a looser texture than the S_1 and S_2 layers and is frequently encrusted with extraneous material. The layer is also characterized by a relatively high proportion of lignin.

Further investigations have indicated that the values of microfibrillar angle quoted above are only average for the layers and that systematic variation in angle occurs within each layer. The inner lamellae of the S_1 tend to have a smaller angle, and the outer lamellae a larger angle than the average for each layer: a similar but opposite situation occurs in the S_3 layers. Electron microscopy has also revealed the presence of a thin warty layer overlaying the S_3 layer in certain timbers.

Microfibrillar angle appears to vary systematically along the length of the cell as well as across the wall thickness. Thus the angle of the S_2 layer has been shown to decrease towards the ends of the cells, while the average S_2 angle appears to be related to the length of the cell, itself a function of rate of growth of the tree. Systematic differences in microfibrillar angle have also been found between radial and tangential walls. Openings occur in the walls of cells and many of these pit openings are characterized by localized deformations of the microfibrillar structure.

Before leaving the chemical composition of wood, mention must be made of the presence of extractives (Table 38.2). This is a collective name for a series of highly complex organic compounds which are present in certain timbers in relatively small amounts. Some, like waxes, fats and sugars, have little economic significance, but others, for example rubber and resin, from which turpentine is distilled, are of considerable importance. The heartwood of timber, as described previously, generally contains extractives which, in addition to imparting colouration to the wood, bestow on it its natural durability, since most of these compounds are toxic to both fungi and insects.

38.4 Variability in structure

Variability in performance of wood is one of its characteristic deficiencies as a material. It will be discussed later how differences in mechanical properties occur between timbers of different species and how these are manifestations of differences in wall thickness and distribution of cell types. However, superimposed on this genetic source of variation is both a systematic and an environmental one.

There are distinct patterns of variation in many features within a single tree. Length of the cells, thickness of the cell wall, angle at which the cells are lying with respect to the vertical axis (spiral grain), angle at which the microfibrils of the S_2 layer of the cell wall are located with respect to the vertical axis, all show systematic trends outwards from the centre of the tree to the bark and upwards from the base to the top of the tree. This pattern results in the formation of a core of wood in the tree with many undesirable properties including low strength and high shrinkage. This zone, usually some ten growth rings in width, is known as the **core** wood or **juvenile** wood as opposed to the **mature** wood occurring outside this area.

Environmental factors have considerable influence on the structure of the wood and any environmental influence, including silviculture, which changes the tree's rate of growth will affect the technical properties of the wood. However, the relationship is a complex one; in softwoods, increasing growth rate generally results in a decrease in density and mechanical properties. In diffuse-porous hardwoods increasing growth rate, provided it is not excessive, has little effect on density, while in ring-porous hardwoods, increasing rate of growth, again provided it is not excessive, results in an increase in density and strength.

There is a whole series of factors which may cause defects in the structure of wood and consequent lowering of its strength. Perhaps the most important defect with regard to its utilization is the formation of **reaction wood**. When trees are inclined to the vertical axis, usually as a result of wind action or growing on sloping ground, the distribution of growth-promoting hormones is disturbed, resulting in the formation of an abnormal type of tissue. In the softwoods, this reaction tissue grows on the compression side of the trunk and is characterized by having a higher than normal lignin content, a higher microfibrillar angle in the S_2 layer resulting in increased longitudinal shrinkage, and a generally darker appearance (Figure 38.16): this abnormal timber, known as **compression wood**, is also considerably more brittle than normal wood. In the hardwoods, reaction wood forms on the tension side of trunks and large branches and is therefore called **tension wood**. It is characterized by a higher than normal cellulose content which imparts a rubbery characteristic to the fibres resulting in difficulties in sawing and machining.

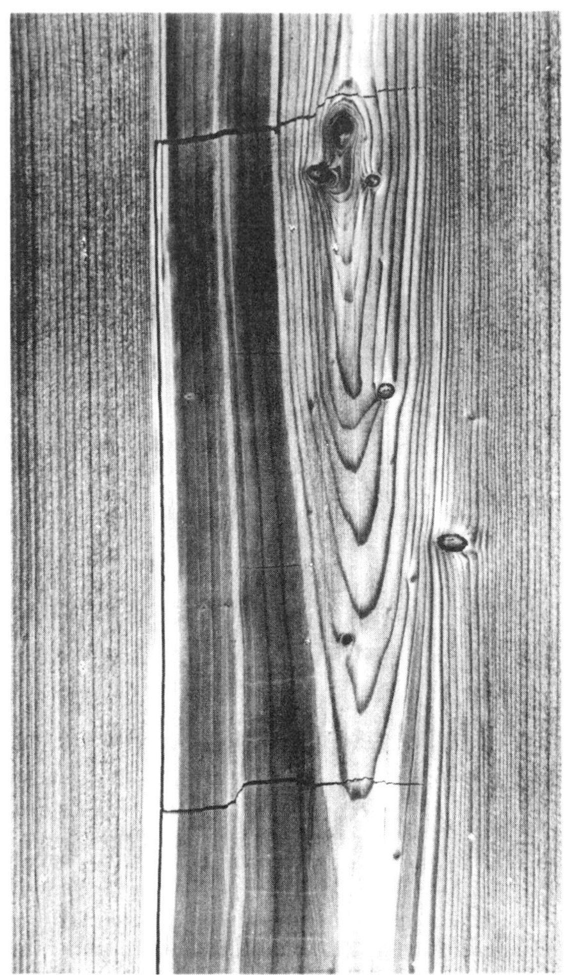

FIGURE 38.16 A band of compression wood (centre left) in a Norway spruce plank, illustrating the darker appearance and higher longitudinal shrinkage of the reaction wood compared with the adjacent normal wood (Building Research Establishment © Crown copyright).

One other defect of considerable technical significance is **brittleheart**, which is found in many low-density tropical hardwoods. Due to the slight shrinkage of cells after their formation, the outside layers of the tree are in a state of longitudinal tension resulting in the cumulative increase of compression stress in the core. A time is reached in the growth of the tree when the compression stresses due to growth are greater than the natural compression strength of the wood. Yield occurs with the formation of shear lines through the cell wall and throughout the wood. Compression failure will be discussed in greater detail in a later chapter.

38.5 Appearance of timber in relation to its structure

Most readers will agree that many timbers are aesthetically pleasing and the various and continuing attempts to simulate the appearance of timber in the surface of synthetic materials bear testament to the very attractive appearance of most timbers. Although a very large proportion of the timber consumed in the UK is used within the construction industry, where the natural appearance of timber is of little consequence, excepting the use of hardwoods for flush doors, internal panelling and wood-block floors, a considerable quantity of timber is still utilized purely on account of its attractive appearance particularly for furniture. The decorative appearance of many timbers is due to the texture or to the figure or to the colour of the material and, in many instances, to combinations of these.

38.5.1 Texture

The texture of timber depends on the size of the cells and on their arrangement. A timber such as boxwood in which the cells have a very small diameter is said to be **fine-textured**, while a **coarse-textured** timber such as keruing has a considerable percentage of large-diameter cells. Where the distribution of the cell types or sizes across the growth ring is uniform, as in beech, or where the thickness of the cell wall remains fairly constant across the ring, as in some of the softwoods, e.g. yellow pine, the timber is described as being **even-textured**: conversely, where variation occurs across the growth ring, either in distribution of cells as in teak or in thickness of the cell walls as in larch or Douglas fir, the timber is said to have an **uneven texture**.

38.5.2 Figure

Figure is defined as the 'ornamental markings seen on the cut surface of timber, formed by the structural features of the wood', but the term is also frequently applied to the effect of marked variations in colour. The four most important structural features inducing figure are grain, growth rings, rays and knots.

Grain

Grain refers to the general arrangement of the vertically aligned cells. It is convenient when examining timber at a general level to regard these cells as lying truly vertical; however, in practice these cells may deviate from the vertical axis in a number of different patterns.

Where the direction of the deviation is consistent, the direction of the cells assumes a distinct spiral mode which may be either left- or right-handed. In young trees the helix angle is frequently of the order of 4°, though considerable variability occurs both within a species and also between different species of timber. As the trees grow, so the helix angle in the outer rings decreases to zero and quite frequently in very large trees the angle in the outer rings subsequently increases but the spiral has changed hand. Although spiral grain does not produce any figure effect, it has very significant technical implications: strength is lowered, while the degree of twisting on drying and amount of pick-up on machining increase as the degree of spirality of the grain increases.

In certain hardwood timbers, and the mahoganies are perhaps the best example, the direction of the helix alternates from left to right hand at very frequent intervals along the radial direction; grain of this type is said to be **interlocked.** Tangential faces of machined timber will be normal, but the radial face will be characterized by the presence of alternating light and dark longitudinal bands produced by the reflection of light from the tapered cuts of fibres inclined in different directions. This type of figure is referred to as **ribbon** or **stripe** and is desirous in timber for furniture manufacture.

If instead of alternating in a longitudinal radial plane the helix alternates in a longitudinal tangential plane, a wavy type of grain is pro-

FIGURE 38.17 'Fiddleback' figure due to wavy grain (Building Research Establishment © Crown copyright).

duced. This is very conspicuous in machined tangential faces where it shows up clearly as alternating light and dark horizontal bands (Figure 38.17); this type of figure is described as **fiddleback**, since timber with this distinctive type of figure has been used traditionally for the manufacture of the backs of violins: it is to be found also on the panels and sides of wardrobes and bookcases.

Growth rings

Where variability occurs across the growth ring, either in the distribution of the various cell types or in the thickness of the cell walls, distinct patterns will appear on the machined faces of the timber. Such patterns, however, will not be regular like many of the artificial imitations, but will vary according to changes in width of the growth ring and in the relative proportions of early and latewood.

On the radial face the growth rings will be vertical and parallel to one another, but on the tangential face a most pleasing series of concentric arcs is produced as successive growth layers are intersected. In the centre part of the plank of elm timber illustrated in Figure 38.18 the growth rings are cut tangentially forming these attractive arcs, while the edge of the board with parallel and vertical growth rings reflects timber cut radially: in the case of elm it is the presence of the large earlywood vessels which makes the growth ring so conspicuous, while in timbers like Douglas fir or pitch pine the striking effect of the growth ring can be ascribed to the very thick walls of the latewood cells.

Rays

Another structural feature which may add to the attractive appearance of timber is the ray, especially where, as in the case of oak, the rays are both deep and wide. When the surface of the plank coincides with the longitudinal radial plane these rays can be seen as sinuous light-coloured ribbons running across the grain.

Knots

Knots, though troublesome from the mechanical aspects of timber utilization, can be regarded as a decorative feature; the fashion of knotty-pine furniture and wall panelling in the early 1970s is a very good example of the decorative feature of knots. However, as a decorative feature, knots do not possess the subtlety of variation in grain and colour that arises from the other structural features described above.

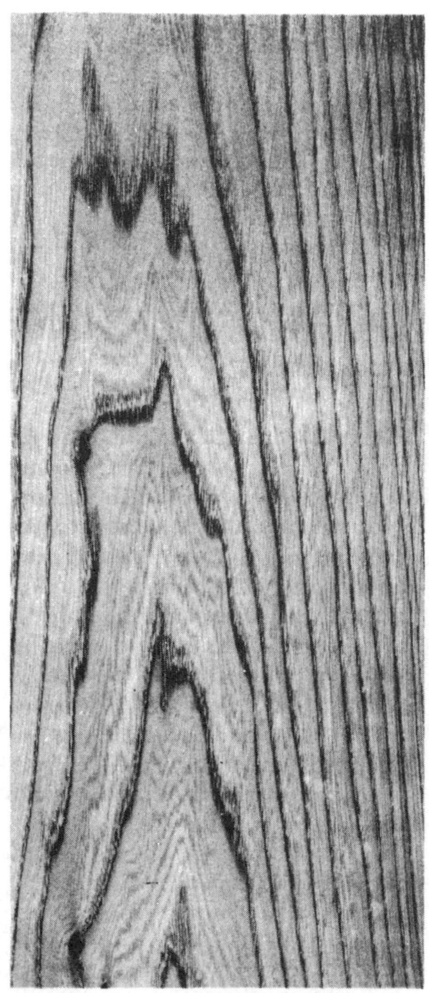

FIGURE 38.18 The effect of growth rings on figure in elm (*Ulmus* sp.) (Building Research Establishment © Crown copyright).

Exceptionally, trees produce a cluster of small shoots at some point on the trunk and the timber subsequently formed in this region contains a multitude of small knots. Timber from these **burrs** is highly prized for decorative work, especially if walnut or yew.

38.5.3 Colour

In the absence of extractives, timber tends to be a rather pale straw colour which is characteristic of the sapwood of almost all timbers. The onset of heartwood formation in many timbers is associated with the deposition of extractives, most of which are coloured, thereby imparting colouration to the heartwood zone. In passing, it should be recalled that although a physiological heartwood is always formed in older trees extractives are not always produced; thus the heartwood of timbers such as ash and spruce is colourless.

Where colouration of the heartwood occurs, a whole spectrum of colour exists among the different species. The heartwood may be yellow, e.g. boxwood; orange, e.g. opepe; red, e.g. mahogany; purple, e.g. purpleheart; brown, e.g. African walnut; green, e.g. greenheart; or black, e.g. ebony. In some timbers the colour is fairly evenly distributed throughout the heartwood, while in other species considerable variation in the intensity of the colour occurs. In zebrano distinct dark brown and white stripes occur, while in olive wood patches of yellow merge into zones of brown. Dark gum-veins, as present in African walnut, contribute to the pleasing alternations in colour. Variations in colour such as these are regarded as contributing to the 'figure' of the timber.

It is interesting to note in passing that the non-coloured sapwood is frequently coloured artificially to match the heartwood, thereby adding to the amount of timber converted from the log. In a few rare cases, the presence of certain fungi in timber in the growing tree can result in the formation of very dark coloured heartwood: the activity of the fungus is terminated when the timber is dried. Both **brown oak** and **green oak**, produced by different fungi, have always been prized for decorative work.

38.6 Mass–volume relationships

38.6.1 Density of timber

The density of a piece of timber is determined not only by the amount of wood substance present, but also by the presence of both extractives and moisture. In a few timbers extractives are completely absent, while in many they are present, but only in small amounts and usually less than 3% of the dry weight of the timber. In some exceptional cases the extractive content may be as high as 10% and in these cases it is necessary to remove the extractives prior to the determination of density.

The presence of moisture in timber not only increases the weight of the timber, but also results in swelling of the timber, and hence both weight and volume are affected. Thus in the determination of density where

$$\rho = \frac{m}{v} \tag{38.1}$$

both the mass (m) and volume (v) must be determined at the same moisture content. Generally, these two parameters are determined at zero moisture content but, as density is frequently quoted at moisture contents of 12% since this level is frequently experienced in timber in use, the value of density at zero moisture content is corrected for 12% if volumetric expansion figures are known, or else the density determination is carried out on timber at 12% moisture content.

Thus if

$$m_x = m_0(1 + 0.01\,\mu) \tag{38.2}$$

where m_x is the mass of timber at moisture content x, m_0 is the mass of timber at zero moisture content, and μ is the moisture content percentage; and

$$v_x = v_0(1 + 0.01\,s_v) \tag{38.3}$$

where v_x is the volume of timber at moisture content x, v_0 is the volume of timber at zero moisture content, and s_v is the volumetric shrinkage/expansion percentage, it is possible to obtain the density of timber at any moisture content in terms of the density at zero moisture content thus:

$$\rho_x = \frac{m_x}{v_x} = \frac{m_0(1 + 0.01\,\mu)}{v_0(1 + 0.01\,s_v)} = \rho_0\left(\frac{1 + 0.01\,\mu}{1 + 0.01\,s_v}\right). \tag{38.4}$$

As a very approximate rule of thumb the density of timber increases by approximately 0.5% for each 1.0% increase in moisture content up to 30%. However, at moisture contents above 30%, density will increase rapidly with increasing moisture content, since, as will be explained later in this chapter, the volume remains constant above this value, whilst the mass increases.

In Section 38.2 timber was shown to possess different types of cell which could be characterized by different values of the ratio of cell wall thickness to total cell diameter. Since this ratio can be regarded as an index of density, it follows that density of the timber will be related to the relative proportions of the various types of cells. Density, however, will also reflect the absolute wall thickness of any one type of cell, since it is possible to obtain fibres of one species of timber the cell wall thickness of which can be several times greater than that of fibres of another species.

Density, like many other properties of timber, is extremely variable: within timber it can vary by a factor of ten ranging from an average value at a moisture content of 12% of 176 kg/m^3 for balsa to about 1230 kg/m^3 for lignum vitae. Balsa then has a density similar to that of cork, while lignum vitae has a density slightly less than half that of concrete or aluminium. The values of density quoted for different timbers, however, are merely average values: each timber will have a range of densities reflecting differences between early and latewood, between the pith and outer rings, and between trees on the same site. Thus, the density of balsa can vary from 40 to 320 kg/m^3.

38.6.2 Specific gravity

The traditional definition of specific gravity (G) can be expressed as:

$$G = \frac{\rho_t}{\rho_w} \qquad (38.5)$$

where ρ_t is the density of timber, and ρ_w is the density of water at 4°C = 1.0000 gm/ml. G will therefore vary with moisture content and consequently the specific gravity of timber is usually based on the oven-dry mass and volume at some specified moisture content. This is frequently taken as zero though, for convenience, green or other moisture conditions are sometimes used when the terms **basic specific gravity** and **nominal specific gravity** are applied respectively. Hence:

$$G_\mu = \frac{\text{Oven-dry mass of timber}}{\text{Mass of displaced volume of water}} = \frac{m_0}{V_\mu \rho_w} \qquad (38.6)$$

where m_0 is the oven-dry mass of timber, V_μ is the volume of timber at moisture content μ; ρ_w is the density of water, and G_μ is the specific gravity at moisture content μ.

At low moisture contents specific gravity decreases slightly with increasing moisture content up to 30%, thereafter remaining constant. In research activities specific gravity is defined usually in terms of oven-dry mass and volume. However, for engineering applications specific gravity is frequently presented as the ratio of oven-dry mass to volume of timber at 12% moisture content; this can be derived from the oven-dry specific gravity, thus:

$$G_{12} = \frac{G_0}{1 + 0.01\,\mu G_0/G_{s12}} \qquad (38.7)$$

where G_{12} is the specific gravity of timber at 12% moisture content, G_0 is the specific gravity of timber at zero moisture content, μ is the moisture content percentage, and G_{s12} is the specific gravity of bound water at 12% moisture content. The relationship between density and specific gravity can be expressed as:

$$\rho = G(1 + 0.01\,\mu)\rho_w \qquad (38.8)$$

where ρ is the density at moisture content μ, G is the specific gravity at moisture content μ, and ρ_w is the density of water. Eqn (38.8) is valid for all moisture contents. When $\mu = 0$ the equation reduces to

$$\rho = G_0$$

i.e. density and specific gravity are numerically equal.

38.6.3 Density of the dry cell wall

Although the density of timber may vary considerably, as already discussed, the density of the actual cell wall material remains constant for all timbers with a value of approximately 1500 kg/m^3 (1.5 gm/ml) when measured by volume-displacement methods.

38.7 Moisture in timber

In the living tree, water is to be found not only in the cell cavity but also within the cell wall. Consequently the moisture content of green wood (newly felled) is high, usually varying from about 60% to nearly 200% depending on the location of the timber in the tree and the season of the year. However, seasonal variation is slight compared to the differences that can occur within a tree between the sapwood and heartwood regions. This degree of variation is illustrated for a number of softwoods and hardwoods in Table 38.4: within the former group the sapwood may contain twice the percentage of moisture to be found in the corresponding heartwood, while in the hardwoods this difference is appreciably smaller or even absent. Nevertheless, in general terms, the mass of water present in newly felled timber is approximately equal to the mass of cell wall material of the timber.

Green timber will yield moisture to the atmosphere with consequent changes in its dimensions: at moisture contents above 20% many timbers, especially their sapwood, are susceptible

TABLE 38.4 Average green moisture contents of the sapwood and heartwood

Botanical name	*Commercial name*	*Moisture content (%)*	
		Heartwood	*Sapwood*
Hardwoods			
Betula lutea	Yellow birch	64	68
Fagus grandifolia	American beech	58	79
Ulmus americana	American elm	92	84
Softwoods			
Pseudotsuga menziesii	Douglas fir	40	116
Tsuga heterophylla	Western hemlock	93	167
Picea sitchensis	Sitka spruce	50	131

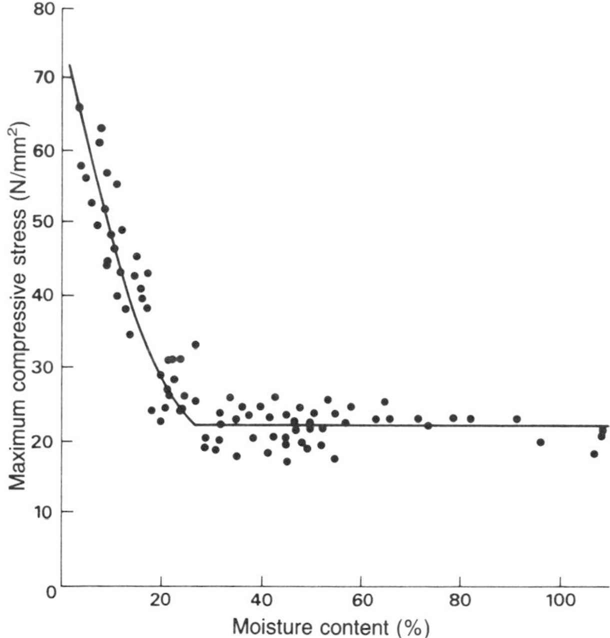

FIGURE 38.19 Relationship between longitudinal compressive strength and moisture content (Building Research Establishment © Crown copyright).

to attack by fungi: the strength and stiffness of green wood is considerably lower than for the same timber when dry. For all these reasons it is necessary to dry or **season** timber following felling of the tree and prior to its use in service.

Drying or seasoning of timber can be carried out in the open, preferably with a top cover. However, it will be appreciated from the previous discussion on equilibrium moisture contents that the minimum moisture content that can be achieved is determined by the lowest relative humidity of the summer period. In this country it is seldom possible to achieve moisture contents less than 16% by air-seasoning. The planks of timber are separated in rows by stickers which permit air currents to pass through the pile; nevertheless it may take from two to ten years to air-season timber.

The process of seasoning may be accelerated artificially by placing the stacked timber in a drying kiln, basically a large chamber in which the temperature and humidity can be controlled and altered throughout the drying process: the control may be carried out manually or programmed automatically. Humidification is sometimes required in order to keep the humidity of the surrounding air at a desired level when insufficient moisture is coming out of the timber; it is frequently required towards the end of the drying run and is achieved either by the admission of small quantities of live steam or by the use of water atomizers or low-pressure steam evaporators. Various designs of kilns are used and these are reviewed in detail by Pratt (1974).

Drying of timber in a kiln can be accomplished in two to five days, the optimum rate of drying varying widely from one timber to the next. Following many years of experimentation kiln schedules have been published representing a compromise between time on the one hand and degree of degrade, splitting and twisting on the other (Pratt, 1974). Most timber is now seasoned by kilning: little air drying is carried out.

As previously mentioned, water in green or freshly felled timber is present both in the cell cavity and within the cell wall. During the seasoning process, irrespective of whether this is by air or within a kiln, water is first removed from within the cell cavity: this holds true down to moisture contents of about 27–30%. Since the water in the cell cavities is free, not being chemically bonded to any part of the timber, it can readily be appreciated that its removal will have no effect on the strength or dimensions of the timber. The lack of variation of the former parameter over the moisture content range of 110–27% is illustrated in Figure 38.19.

However, at moisture contents below 27–30% water is no longer present in the cell cavity but is restricted to the cell wall where it is chemically bonded (hydrogen bonding) to the matrix constituents, to the hydroxyl groups of the cellulose molecules in the non-crystalline regions and to the surface of the crystallites. The uptake of water by the lignin component is considerably lower than that by either the hemicellulose or the amorphous cellulose: water may be present as a monomolecular layer though frequently up to six layers can be present. Water cannot penetrate the crystalline cellulose since the hygroscopic hydroxyl groups are mutually satisfied by the formulation of both intra- and intermolecular bonds within the crystalline region as previously described. This view is confirmed from X-ray analyses which indicate no change of state as the timber gains or loses moisture.

However, the percentage of non-crystalline material in the cell wall varies between 8 and 33% and the influence of this fraction of cell wall material as it changes moisture content on the behaviour of the total cell wall is very significant. The removal of water from these areas within the cell wall results first in increased strength and secondly in marked shrinkage. Both changes can be accounted for in terms of drying out of the water-reactive matrix, thereby causing the microfibrils to come into closer proximity, with a commensurate increase in interfibrillar bonding and decrease in overall dimensions. Such changes are reversible, or almost completely so.

Fibre saturation point

The increase in strength on drying is clearly indicated in Figure 38.19 from which it will be noted that there is a threefold increase in strength as the moisture content of the timber is reduced from about 27% to zero. The moisture content corresponding to the inflexion in the graph is termed the **fibre saturation point**, where in theory there is no free water in the cell cavities while the walls are holding the maximum amount of bound water. In practice this rarely exists; a little free water may still exist while bound water is removed from the cell wall. Consequently, the fibre saturation 'point', while a convenient concept, should really be regarded as a 'range' in moisture contents over which the transition occurs.

The fibre saturation point therefore corresponds to the moisture content of the timber when placed in a relative humidity of 100% and it is generally found that the moisture contents of hardwoods at this level are from 1 to 2% higher than for softwoods.

Below the fibre saturation point timber is hygroscopic, that is it will absorb moisture from the atmosphere if it is dry and correspondingly yield moisture to the atmosphere when wet, thereby attaining a moisture content which is in equilibrium with the water vapour conditions of the surrounding atmosphere. Thus for any combination of relative humidity and temperature of the atmosphere there is a corresponding moisture content of the timber such that there will be no inward or outward diffusion of water

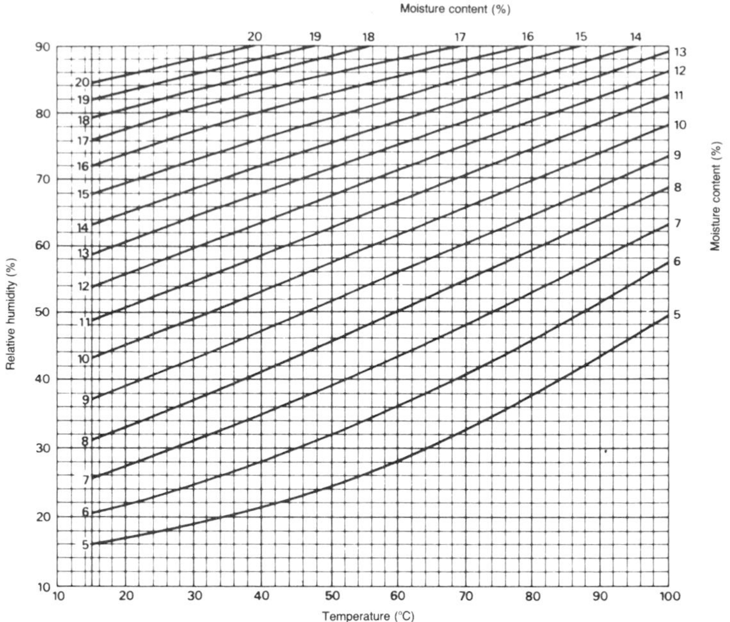

FIGURE 38.20 Chart showing the relationship between the moisture content of wood and the temperature and relative humidity of the surrounding air; approximate curves based on values obtained during drying from green condition (Building Research Establishment © Crown copyright).

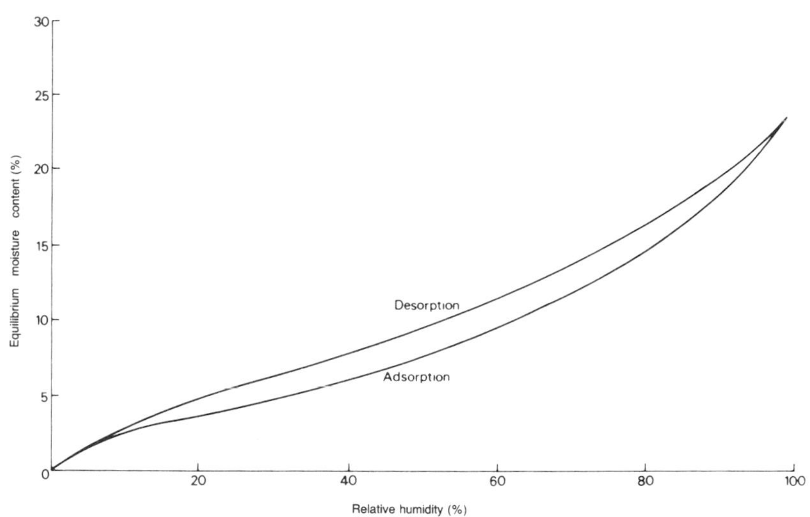

FIGURE 38.21 Hysteresis loop resulting from the average adsorption and desorption isotherms for six species of timber at 40°C (Building Research Establishment © Crown copyright).

vapour: this moisture content is referred to as the **equilibrium moisture content.**

The fundamental relationships between moisture content and atmospheric conditions have been determined experimentally and the average equilibrium moisture content values are shown graphically in Figure 38.20. A timber in an atmosphere of 20°C and 22% relative humidity will have a moisture content of 6%, while the same timber if moved to an atmosphere of 40°C and 64% relative humidity will double its moisture content. It should be emphasized that the curves in Figure 38.20 are average values and that slight variations in moisture content will occur due to differences between timbers or to the previous moisture history of the timber.

Sorption and diffusion

Timber, as already noted, assumes with the passage of time a moisture content which is in equilibrium with the relative vapour pressure of the atmosphere. This process of water sorption is typical of solids with a complex capillary structure and this phenomenon has also been observed in concrete. The similarity in behaviour between timber and concrete with regard to moisture relationships is further illustrated by the presence of S-shaped isotherms when moisture content is plotted against relative vapour pressure. Both materials have isotherms which differ according to whether the moisture content is reducing (desorption) or increasing (adsorption) thereby producing a hysteresis loop (Figure 38.21).

38.7.1 Moisture content

It is customary to express the moisture content of timber in terms of its oven-dry mass using the equation

$$\mu = 100\frac{m_w - m_0}{m_0} \qquad (38.9)$$

where m_w is the mass of wet timber, m_0 is the mass of timber after oven drying at 105°C and μ is the moisture content (%).

The expression of moisture content of timber on a dry mass basis is in contrast to the procedure adopted for other materials where moisture content is expressed in terms of the wet mass of the material.

Determination of moisture content in timber is usually carried out using the basic gravimetric technique, though it should be noted that at least a dozen different methods have been recorded in the literature. Suffice it here to mention only two of these alternatives. First, where the timber contains volatile extractives which would normally be lost during oven drying, thereby resulting in erroneous moisture content values, it is customary to use a distillation process, heating the timber in the presence of a water-immiscible liquid such as toluene, and collecting the condensed water vapour in a calibrated trap. Second, where ease and speed of operation are preferred to extreme accuracy, moisture contents are assessed using electric moisture meters: these may be either DC in operation, measuring the change in resistivity of wet timber compared with dry, or AC in operation, determining the increase in dielectric constant and loss tangent that occurs with higher moisture contents. These meters require calibrating and different scales are present for different groups of timbers.

38.8 References

Cowdrey, D.R. and Preston, R.D. (1966) Elasticity and microfibrillar angle in the wood of Sitka spruce. *Proceedings of the Royal Society*, **B166**, 245–72.

Fengel, D. (1970) *The Physics and Chemistry of Wood Pulp Fibres*. TAPPI, New York.

Gardner, K.H. and Blackwell, J. (1974) The structure of native cellulose. *Biopolymers*, **13**, 1975–2001.

Ifju, G. (1964) Tensile strength behaviour as a function of cellulose in wood. *Forest Products Journal*, **14**, 366–72.

Meyer, K.H. and Misch, L. (1937) Position des atomes dans le nouveau modèle spatial de la cellulose. *Helvetica Chimica Acta*, **20**, 232–44.

Pratt, G.H. (1974) *Timber Drying Manual*. HMSO.
Preston, R.D. (1964) Structural and mechanical aspects of plant cell walls. In *The Formation of Wood in Forest Trees* (ed. H.M. Zimmermann). Academic Press, New York.
Preston, R.D. (1974) *The Physical Biology of Plant Cell Walls*. Chapman and Hall, London.
Siau, J.F. (1971) *Flow in Wood*. Syracuse University Press, Syracuse, NY.

Chapter thirty-nine

Strength and failure in timber

39.1 Introduction
39.2 Sample size
39.3 Strength values
39.4 Variability in strength values
39.5 Interrelationships among the strength properties
39.6 Factors affecting strength
39.7 Strength, failure and fracture morphology
39.8 Working (grade) stresses for timber
39.9 References

39.1 Introduction

While it is easy to appreciate the concept of deformation primarily because it is something that can be observed, it is much more difficult to define in simple terms what is meant by the strength of a material. Perhaps one of the simpler definitions of strength is that it is a measure of the resistance to failure, providing of course that we are clear in our minds what is meant by failure.

Let us start therefore by defining failure. In those modes of stressing where a distinct break occurs with the formation of two fracture surfaces failure is synonymous with rupture of the specimen. However, in certain modes of stressing, fracture does not occur and failure must be defined in some arbitrary way such as the maximum stress that the sample will endure or, in exceptional circumstances such as compression strength perpendicular to the grain, the stress at the limit of proportionality.

Having defined our end point it is now easier to appreciate our definition of strength as the natural resistance of a material to failure. But how do we quantify this resistance? This may be done by calculating either the stress necessary to produce failure or the amount of energy consumed in producing failure. Under certain modes of testing it is more convenient to use the former method of quantification while the latter tends to be more limited in application.

39.2 Sample size

There are two approaches to the measurement of strength in timber. The first, and until about 1975 the principal approach is to assess strength on small, knot-free, straight-grained samples either 2 × 2 inches or 20 × 20 mm in cross-section; because of a small effect of specimen size on strength, these two sizes will give slightly different results. The methods are set out in BS 373: 1957 *Methods of testing small clear specimens of timber*, and an example of test data obtained by using the 20 × 20 mm cross-section size of samples is given in Table 39.1. It must be appreciated that data of this type represent the ultimate strength that can be obtained from absolutely perfect wood, and they afford the means of making direct comparisons between different species of wood. For practical purposes the data must be reduced because of the presence of knots, sloping grain and other defects: the derivation of grade stresses from these data is explained later in the chapter.

TABLE 39.1 Average and standard deviation of various mechanical properties of small, clear samples of selected timbers at 12% moisture content

	Density	Static bending*				Impact	Compression	Hardness	Shear	Cleavage	
	Dry kg/m³	*Modulus of rupture N/mm²*	*Modulus of elasticity N/mm²*	*Energy to max load mmN/mm²*	*Energy to fracture mmN/mm²*	*Drop of hammer m*	*Parallel to grain N/mm²*	*On side grain N*	*Parallel to grain N/mm²*	*Radial plane N/mm width*	*Tangential plane N/mm width*
HARDWOODS											
Balsa	176	23 7.3	3200 1060	0.018 0.007	0.035 0.017	–	15.5 4.43	–	2.4 0.62	–	–
Obeche	368	54 6.5	5500 620	0.058 0.010	0.095 0.015	0.48 0.072	28.2 3.00	1910 268	7.7 0.67	9.3 1.82	8.4 1.58
Mahogany (*Khaya ivorensis*)	497	78 15.0	9000 1520	0.070 0.026	0.128 0.044	0.58 0.149	46.4 8.45	3690 816	11.8 2.56	10.0 2.08	14.0 2.90
Sycamore	561	99 11.0	9400 1160	0.121 0.028	0.163 0.049	0.84 0.136	48.2 4.83	4850 639	17.1 2.32	16.8 2.95	27.3 3.91
Ash	689	116 16.6	11 900 2170	0.182 0.045	0.281 0.097	1.07 0.216	53.3 7.73	6140 1158	16.6 2.52	–	–
Oak	689	97 16.8	10 100 1960	0.093 0.026	0.167 0.051	0.84 0.209	51.6 7.98	5470 911	13.7 2.38	14.5 2.86	20.1 2.08
Afzelia	817	125 26.6	13 100 1760	0.100 0.043	0.203 0.087	0.79 0.215	79.2 12.02	7870 914	16.6 2.28	10.5 2.00	13.3 2.49
Greenheart	977	181 20.9	21 000 1990	0.213 0.047	0.395 0.088	1.35 0.207	89.9 8.49	10 450 1531	20.5 3.06	17.5 4.79	22.2 4.97
SOFTWOODS											
Norway spruce (European spruce)	417	72 10.2	10 200 2010	0.086 0.022	0.116 0.040	0.58 0.116	36.5 5.26	2140 353	9.8 1.44	8.4 1.07	9.1 1.20
Yellow pine (Canada)	433	80 10.9	8300 1440	0.089 0.015	0.097 0.019	0.56 0.100	42.1 6.14	2050 473	9.3 1.61	8.2 1.57	11.6 1.77
Douglas fir (UK)	497	91 16.9	10 500 2160	0.097 0.038	0.172 0.081	0.69 0.200	48.3 8.03	3420 865	11.6 2.29	9.5 1.90	11.4 2.17
Scots pine (UK)	513	89 16.9	10 000 2130	0.103 0.032	0.134 0.053	0.71 0.167	47.4 9.25	2980 697	12.7 2.45	10.3 1.82	13.0 2.47
Caribbean Pitch pine	769	107 14.5	12 600 1800	0.126 0.042	0.253 0.060	0.91 0.196	56.1 7.76	4980 1324	14.3 2.81	12.1 1.23	13.3 1.58

* In three point loading.

The alternative approach, and one that has gained favour more recently, is to measure strength on actual structural-size pieces of wood, thereby eliminating the need to apply rather crude correction factors for knots and other defects. However, this method requires much more timber and heavier testing equipment.

39.3 Strength values

For a range of strength properties determined on small clear specimens, but excluding tensile strength parallel to the grain, the mean values and standard deviations are presented in Table 39.1 for a selection of timbers covering the range in densities to be found in the hardwoods and softwoods. All values relate to a moisture content which is in equilibrium with a relative humidity of 65% at 20°C; these are of the order of 12% and the timber is referred to as 'dry'. Modulus of elasticity has also been included in the table. The upper line for each species provides the estimated average value while the lower line contains the standard deviation.

In Table 39.2 tensile strength parallel to the grain is listed for certain timbers and it is in this mode that timber is at its strongest. Comparison of these values with those for compression parallel to the grain in Table 39.1 will indicate that, unlike many other materials, the compression strength is only about one-third that of tensile strength along the grain.

TABLE 39.2 Tensile strength parallel to the grain of certain timbers

Timber		*Moisture content* %	*Tensile strength* N/mm^2
Hardwoods			
Ash	(Home grown)	13	136
Beech	(Home grown)	12.6	180
Yellow poplar	(Imported)	15	114
Softwoods			
Scots pine	(Home grown)	16	92
Scots pine	(Imported)	15	110
Sitka spruce	(Imported)	15	139
Western hemlock	(Imported)	15	137

39.4 Variability in strength values

In Chapter 38 attention was drawn to the fact that timber is a very variable material and that for many of its parameters, e.g. density, cell length and microfibrillar angle of the S_2 layer, distinct patterns of variation could be established within a growth ring, outwards from the pith towards the bark, upwards in the tree, and from tree to tree. The effects of this variation in structure are all too apparent when mechanical tests are performed.

Test data are usually found to follow a normal distribution and, as described earlier, an efficient estimator of the variability which occurs in any one property is the **sample standard deviation**, denoted by s. It is the square root of the variance and is derived from the formula:

$$s = \sqrt{\frac{\Sigma x^2 - \frac{(\Sigma x)^2}{n}}{n - 1}} \qquad (39.1)$$

where x stands for every item successively and n is the number of items in the sample.

39.5 Interrelationships among the strength properties

39.5.1 Modulus of rupture and modulus of elasticity

Although a high correlation exists between the moduli of rupture and elasticity for a particular species, it is doubtful whether this correlation represents any causal relationship; rather it is more probable that the correlation arises as a result of the strong correlation that exists between density and each modulus. Whether it is a causal relationship or not, it is nevertheless put to good advantage for it forms the basis of the stress grading of timber by machine. The stiffness of a piece of timber is measured as it is deflected between rollers and this is used to predict its strength. Further reference to stress grading will be made later in this chapter.

39.5.2 Impact bending and total work

Good correlations have been established between the height of drop in the impact bending test and both **work** to **maximum load** and **total work**: generally the correlation is higher with the latter property.

39.5.3 Hardness and compression perpendicular to the grain

Correlation coefficients of 0.902 and 0.907 have been established between hardness and compression strength perpendicular to the grain of timber of 12% moisture content and timber in the green state respectively. It is general practice to predict the compression strength from the hardness result using the following equations:

$$Y_{12} = 0.00147x_{12} + 1.103 \qquad (39.2)$$

$$Y_g = 0.00137x_g - 0.207 \qquad (39.3)$$

where Y_g and Y_{12} are compression perpendicular to the grain in N/mm^2 for green timber and timber at 12% moisture content respectively, and x_g and x_{12} are hardness in Newtons.

39.6 Factors affecting strength

Many of the variables noted in the previous chapter as influencing stiffness also influence the various strength properties of timber. Once again, these can be regarded as being either material-dependent or manifestations of the environment.

39.6.1 Anisotropy and grain angle

The marked difference between the longitudinal and transverse planes in both shrinkage and stiffness has already been discussed. Strength likewise is directionally dependent and the degree of anisotropy present in both tension and compression is presented for Douglas fir in Table 39.3. Irrespective of moisture content the highest degree of anisotropy is in tension (48 : 1): this reflects the fact that the highest strength of timber is in tension along the grain while the lowest is in tension perpendicular. A similar degree of anisotropy is present in the tensile stressing of both glass-reinforced plastics and carbon-fibre-reinforced plastics when the fibre is laid up in parallel strands.

Table 39.3 also demonstrates that the degree of anisotropy in compression is an order of magnitude less than in tension. Whilst the compression strengths are markedly affected by moisture content, tensile strength is relatively insensitive, reflecting the exclusion of moisture from the crystalline core of the microfibril (Chapter 38): it is this crystalline core which imparts the high tensile strength. The comparison of tension and compression strengths along the grain in Table 39.3 reveals that timber, unlike most other materials, has a tensile strength considerably greater than the compression strength.

Anisotropy in strength is due in part to the

TABLE 39.3 Anisotropy in strength

Timber	*Moisture content %*	*Tension*			*Compression*		
		Along grain N/mm²	*Across grain N/mm²*	*Along / Across*	*Along grain N/mm²*	*Across grain N/mm²*	*Along / Across*
Douglas fir	>25	131	2.69	48.7	24.1	4.14	5.82
	12	138	2.90	47.6	49.6	6.90	7.19

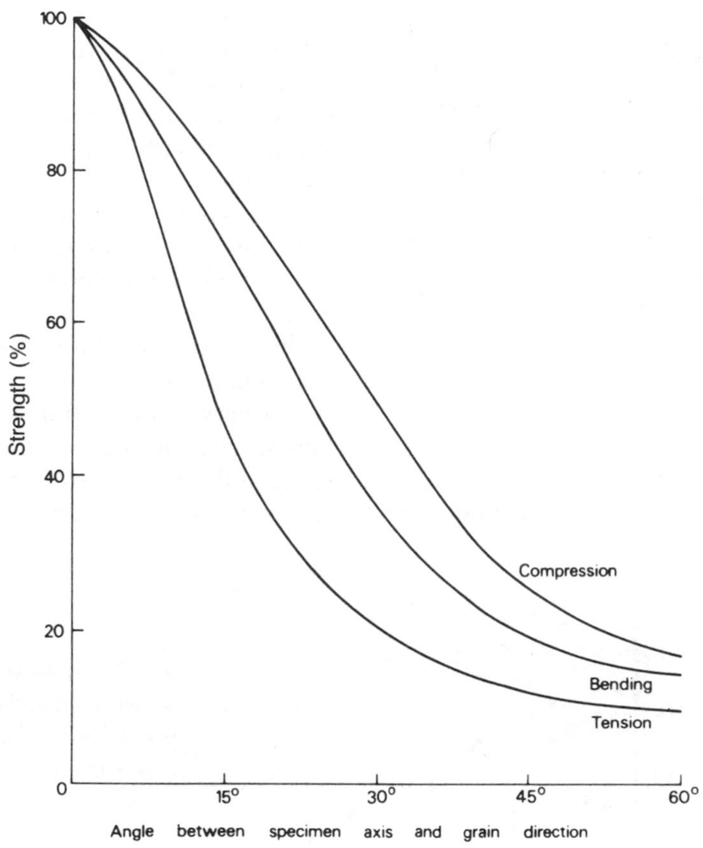

FIGURE 39.1 Effect of grain angle on the tensile, bending and compression strength of timber (after Baumann, 1922).

cellular nature of timber and in part to the structure and orientation of the microfibrils in the wall layers. Bonding along the direction of the microfibrils is covalent whilst bonding between microfibrils is by hydrogen bonds. Consequently, since the majority of the microfibrils are aligned at only a small angle to the longitudinal axis, it will be easier to rupture the cell wall if the load is applied perpendicularly than if applied parallel to the fibre axis.

Since timber is an anisotropic material it follows that the angle at which stress is applied relative to the longitudinal axis of the cells will determine the ultimate strength of the timber. Figure 39.1 illustrates that tensile strength is much more sensitive to grain angle than is compression strength. However, at angles as high as 60° to the longitudinal both tension and compression strengths have fallen to only about 10% of their value in straight-grained timber. The sensitivity of strength to grain angle in timber is identical with that for fibre orientation in both glass- and carbon-fibre-reinforced plastics.

It is possible to obtain an approximate value of strength at any angle to the grain from knowledge of the corresponding values both parallel and perpendicular to the grain using the following formula, which, in its original form, was credited to Hankinson:

$$\sigma_\theta = \frac{\sigma_p \sigma_q}{\sigma_p \sin^n \theta + \sigma_q \cos^n \theta} \quad (39.4)$$

where σ_θ is the strength property at angle θ from the fibre direction, σ_p is the strength parallel to the grain, σ_q is the strength perpendicular to the grain, and n is an empirically determined constant. In tension $n = 1.5-2$; in compression $n = 2-2.5$. The equation has also been used for stiffness where a value of 2 for n has been adopted.

39.6.2 Knots

Knots are associated with distortion of the grain and since even slight deviations in grain angle reduce the strength of the timber appreciably it follows that knots will have a marked influence on strength. The significance of knots, however, will depend on their size and distribution both along the length of a piece of timber and across its section.

Thus knots in clusters are more important than knots of a similar size which are evenly distributed, while knots on the top or bottom edge of a beam are more significant than those in the centre; large knots are much more critical than small knots.

It is very difficult to quantify the influence of knots; one of the parameters that has been successfully used is the **knot area ratio**, which relates the sum of the cross-sectional area of the

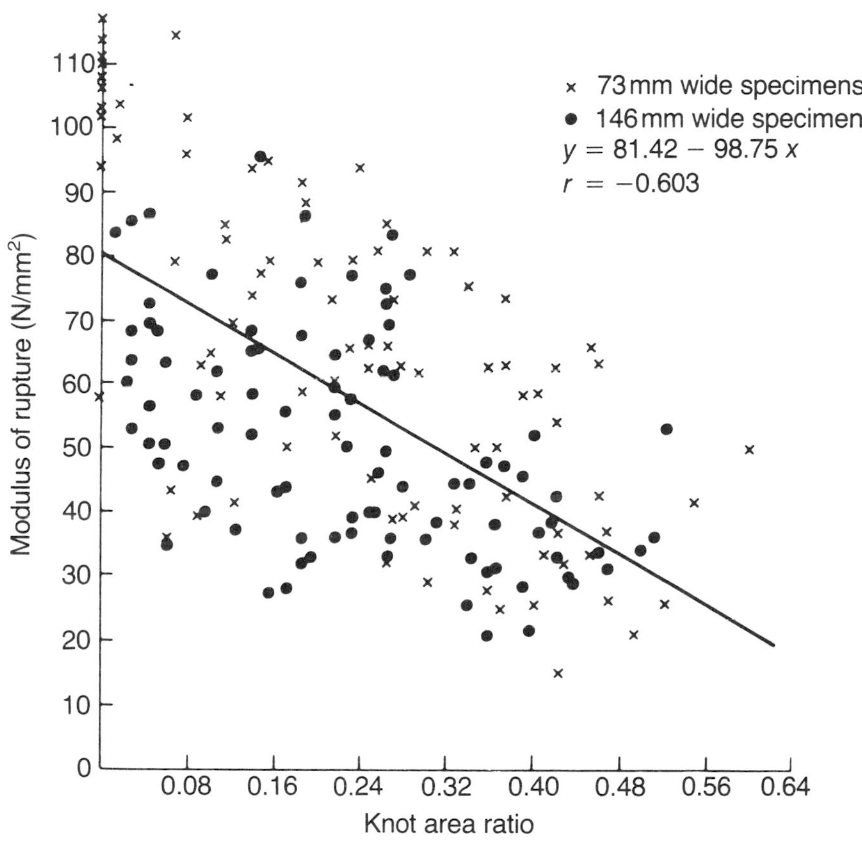

FIGURE 39.2 Effect of knot area ratio on the strength of timber (Building Research Establishment © Crown copyright).

knots at a cross-section to the cross-sectional area of the piece. The loss in bending strength that occurred with increasing knot area ratio in 200 home-grown Douglas fir boards is illustrated in Figure 39.2.

39.6.3 Density

In Chapter 38 density was shown to be a function of cell wall thickness and therefore dependent on the relative proportions of the various cell components and also on the level of cell wall development of any one component. However, variation in density is not restricted to different species, but can occur to a considerable extent within any one species and even within a single tree. Some measure of the interspecific variation that occurs can be obtained from the limited amount of data in Table 39.1. It will be observed that as density increases so the various strength properties increase. Density continues to be the best prediction of timber strength since high correlations between strength and density are a common feature in timber studies.

Most of the relations that have been established throughout the world between the various

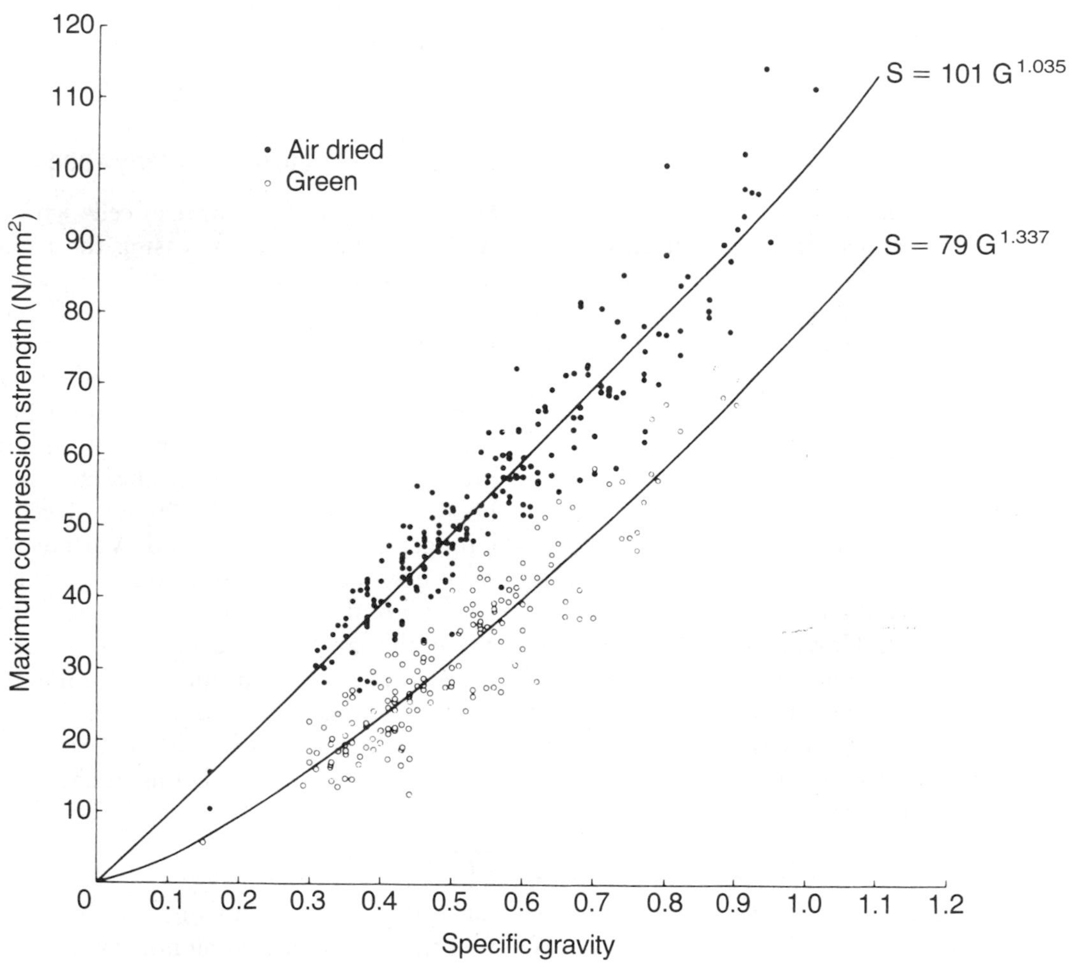

FIGURE 39.3 The relation of maximum compression strength to specific gravity for 200 species tested in the green and dry states (Building Research Establishment © Crown copyright).

strength properties and timber density take the form of

$$S = kG^n \qquad (39.5)$$

where S is any strength property, G is the specific gravity, k is a proportionality constant differing for each strength property, and n is an exponent that defines the shape of the curve. An example of the use of this expression on the results of over 200 species tested in compression parallel to the grain is presented in Figure 39.3: the correlation coefficient between compression strength and density of the timber at 12% moisture content was 0.902.

Similar relationships have been found to hold for other strength properties though in some the degree of correlation is considerably lower. This is the case in tension parallel to the grain where the ultrastructure probably plays a more significant role.

Over the range of density of most of the timbers used commercially the relationship between density and strength can safely be assumed to be linear with the possible exception of shear and cleavage; similarly, within a single species the range is low and the relationship can again be treated as linear.

39.6.4 Ring width

Since density is influenced by the rate of growth of the tree it follows that variations in ring width will change the density of the timber and hence the strength. However, the relationship is considerably more complex than it appears at first. In the ring-porous timbers such as oak and ash (see Chapter 38) increasing rate of growth (ring width) results in an increase in the percentage of the latewood which contains most of the thick-walled fibres; consequently, density will increase and so will strength. However, there is an upper limit to ring width beyond which density begins to fall owing to the inability of the tree to produce the requisite thickness of wall in every cell.

In the diffuse-porous timbers such as beech, birch and khaya, where there is uniformity in structure across the growth ring, increasing rate of growth (ring width) has no effect on density unless, as before, the rate of growth is excessive. In the softwoods, however, increasing rate of growth results in an increased percentage of the low-density earlywood and consequently both density and strength decrease as ring width increases. Exceptionally, it is found that very narrow rings can also have very low density: this is characteristic of softwoods from the very northern latitudes where latewood development is restricted by the short summer period. Hence ring width of itself does not affect the strength of the timber: nevertheless, it has a most important indirect effect working through density.

39.6.5 Ratio of latewood to earlywood

Since the latewood comprises cells with thicker walls it follows that increasing the percentage of latewood will increase the density and therefore the strength of the timber. Differences in strength of 150–300% between the late and earlywood are generally explained in terms of the thicker cell walls of the former: however, some workers maintain that when the strengths are expressed in terms of the cross-sectional area of the cell wall the latewood cell is still stronger than the earlywood. Various theories have been advanced to account for the higher strength of the latewood wall material; the more acceptable are couched in terms of the differences in microfibrillar angle in the middle layer of the secondary wall, differences in degree of crystallinity and, lastly, differences in the proportions of the chemical constituents.

39.6.6 Cell length

Since the cells overlap one another it follows that there must be a minimum cell length below which there is insufficient overlap to permit the transfer of stress without failure in shear occur-

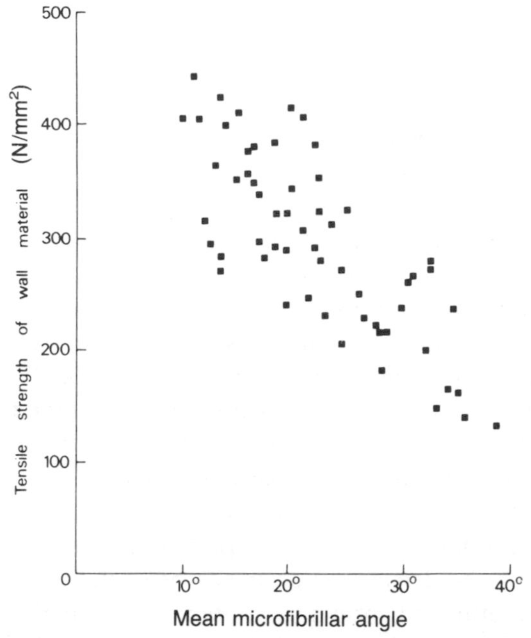

FIGURE 39.4 Effect of microfibrillar angle on the tensile strength of *Pinus radiata* blocks (Cave (1969) by permission of Springer-Verlag).

ring. Some investigators have gone further and have argued that there must be a high degree of correlation between the length of the cell and the strength of cell wall material, since a fibre with high strength per unit of cross-sectional area would require a larger area of overlap in order to keep constant the overall efficiency of the system.

39.6.7 Microfibrillar angle

The angle of the microfibrils in the S_2 layer has a most significant effect in determining the strength of wood. Figure 39.4 illustrates the marked reduction in tensile strength that occurs with increasing angle of the microfibrils: the effect on strength closely parallels that with changing grain angle.

39.6.8 Chemical composition

In Chapter 38 the structure of the cellulose molecule was described and emphasis was placed on the existence in the longitudinal plane of covalent bonds both within the glucose units and also linking them together to form filaments containing from 5000 to 10 000 units. There is little doubt that the high tensile strength of timber owes much to the existence of this covalent bonding. Certainly experiments in which many of the inter-unit bonds have been ruptured by gamma irradiation resulting in a decrease in the number of units in the molecule from over 5000 to about 200 have resulted in a most marked reduction in tensile strength; it has also been shown that timber with inherently low molecular lengths, e.g. compression wood, has a lower than normal tensile strength.

Until recently it has been assumed that the hemicelluloses which constitute about half of the matrix material play little or no part in determining the strength of timber. However, it has recently been demonstrated that some of the hemicelluloses are orientated within the cell wall and it is now thought that these will be load-bearing.

It is known that lignin is less hydrophilic than either the cellulose or hemicelluloses and, as indicated earlier, at least part of its function is to protect the more hydrophilic substances from the ingress of water and consequent reduction in strength. Apart from this indirect effect on strength, lignin is thought to make a not too insignificant direct contribution. Much of the lignin in the cell wall is located in the primary wall and in the middle lamella. Since the tensile strength of a composite with fibres of a definite length will depend on the efficiency of the transfer of stress by shear from one fibre to the next, it will be appreciated that in timber the lignin is playing a most important role: compression strength along the grain has been shown to be affected by the degree of lignification not between the cells but rather within the cell wall, when all the other variables have been held constant.

It would appear, therefore, that both the fibre and the matrix components of the timber composite are contributing to its strength as in fact they do in most composites: the relative significance of the fibre and matrix roles will vary with the mode of stressing.

39.6.9 Reaction wood

Compression wood

The chemical and anatomical properties of this abnormal wood, which is found only in the softwoods, were described in Chapter 38. When stressed, it is found that the tensile strength and toughness are lower and the compressive strength higher than that of normal timber. Such differences can be explained in terms of the changes in fine structure and chemical composition.

Tension wood

This second form of abnormal wood, which is found only in the hardwoods, has tensile strengths higher and compression strengths lower than normal wood: again these can be related to changes in fine structure and chemical composition.

39.6.10 Moisture content

The marked increase in strength on drying from the fibre saturation point to oven-dry conditions was described in detail in Chapter 38 and illustrated in Figure 38.19. Confirmatory evidence of this relationship is forthcoming from Figure 39.3 in which the regression line for over 200 species of compression strength of green timber against density is less steep than that for timber at 12% moisture content; strength data for timber are generally presented for these two levels of moisture content (Lavers, 1969).

Within certain limits the regression of strength, expressed on a logarithmic basis, and moisture content can be plotted as a straight line. The relationship can be expressed mathematically as:

$$\log_{10}\sigma = \log_{10}\sigma_f + k(\mu_f - \mu) \quad (39.6)$$

where σ is the strength at moisture content μ, σ_f is the strength at fibre saturation point, μ_f is the moisture content at fibre saturation point, and k is a constant. It is possible therefore to calculate the strength at any moisture content below the fibre saturation point, assuming σ_f to be the strength of the green timber and μ_f to be 27%. This formula can also be used to determine the strength changes that occur for a 1% increase in moisture content over certain ranges.

This relation between moisture content and strength may not always apply when the timber contains defects. Thus it has been shown that the effect of moisture content on strength diminishes as the sizes of knots increase. The relation, even for knot-free timber, does not always hold for the impact resistance of timber. In some timbers, though certainly not all, impact resistance or toughness of green timber is considerably higher than it is in the dry state; the impact resistances of green ash, cricket bat willow and teak are approximately 10%, 30% and 50% higher respectively than the values at 12% moisture content.

39.6.11 Temperature

At temperatures within the range +200°C to −200°C and at constant moisture content strength properties are linearly (or almost linearly) related to temperature, decreasing with increasing temperature. However, a distinction must be made between short- and long-term effects.

When timber is exposed for short periods of time to temperatures below 95°C the changes in strength with temperature are reversible. These reversible effects can be explained in terms of the increased molecular motions and greater lattice spacing at higher temperatures.

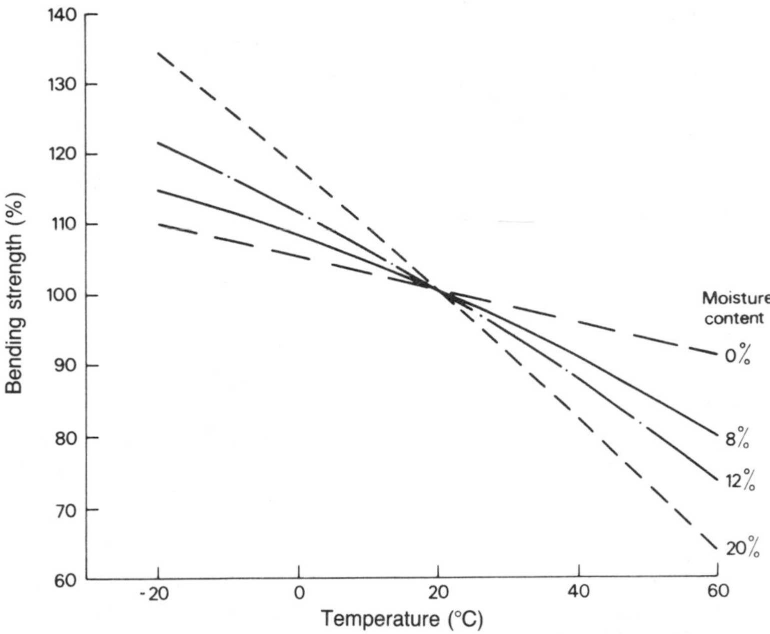

FIGURE 39.5 The effect of temperature on the bending strength of *Pinus radiata* timber at different moisture contents.

At temperatures above 95°C or at temperatures above 65°C for very long periods of time there is an irreversible effect of temperature due to thermal degradation of the wood substance, generally taking the form of a marked shortening of the length of the cellulose molecules and chemical changes within the hemicelluloses. All strength properties show a marked reduction with temperature, but toughness is particularly sensitive to thermal degrade. Repeated exposure to elevated temperature has a cumulative effect and usually the reduction is greater in the hardwoods than in the softwoods.

The effect of temperature is very dependent on moisture content, sensitivity of strength to temperature increasing appreciably as moisture content increases (Figure 39.5), as occurs also with stiffness (Figure 41.9). The relationship between strength, moisture content and temperature appears to be linear over the range 6–20% and −20°C to 60°C, thereby allowing transformation of results. However, in the case of toughness, while at low moisture content it is found that toughness decreases with increasing temperature, at high moisture contents toughness actually increases with increasing temperature.

39.6.12 Time

In Chapter 41 timber is described as a viscoelastic material and as such its mechanical behaviour is time-dependent. Such dependence is apparent in terms of its sensitivity to both rate of loading and duration of loading.

Rate of loading

Increase in the rate of load application results in increased strength values, the increase in 'green' timber being some 50% greater than that of timber at 12% moisture content; strain to failure, however, actually decreases. A variety of explanations have been presented to account for this phenomenon, most of which are based

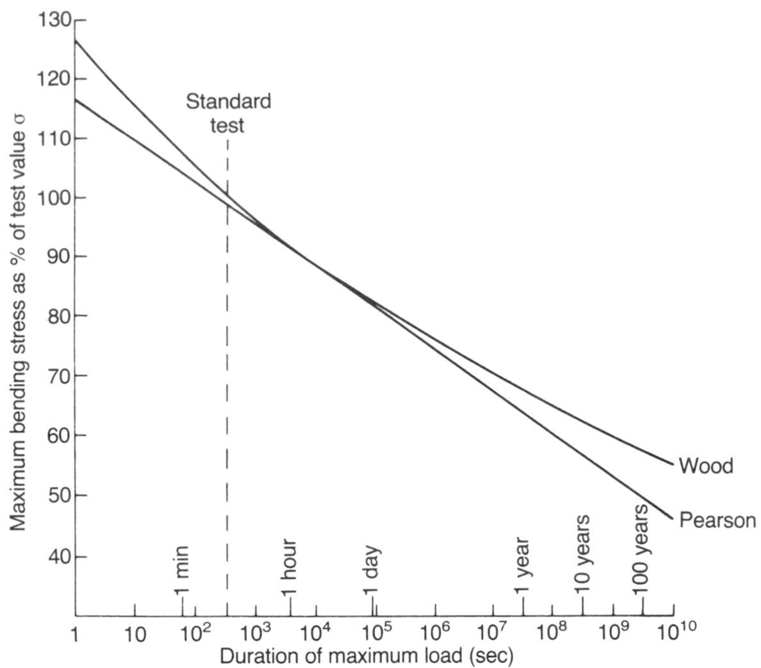

FIGURE 39.6 The effect of duration of load on the bending strength of timber (Wood (1951) and Pearson (1972)).

on the theory that timber fails when a critical strain has been reached and consequently at lower rates of loading viscous flow or creep is able to occur resulting in failure at lower loads.

The various standard testing procedures adopted throughout the world set tight limits on the speed of loading in the various tests: unfortunately, such recommended speeds vary throughout the world, thereby introducing errors in the comparison of results from different laboratories.

Duration of load

In terms of the practical use of timber the duration of time over which the load is applied is perhaps the single most important variable. Many investigators have worked in this field and each has recorded a direct relationship between the length of time over which a load can be supported at constant temperature and moisture content and the magnitude of the load. This relation appears to hold true for all forms of stress but is especially important for bending strength.

The modulus of rupture (maximum bending strength) will decrease in proportion, or nearly in proportion, to the logarithm of the time over which the load is applied; failure in this particular time-dependent mode is termed **creep rupture** or **static fatigue.** Wood (1951) indicated that the relation is slightly curvilinear and that there is a distinct levelling off at loads approaching 20% of the ultimate short-term strength such that a critical load or stress level occurs below which failure is unlikely to occur; the hyperbolic curve that fitted Wood's data best for both rapid and sustained loading is indicated in Figure 39.6.

Other workers have reported a linear relation, though a tendency to non-linear behaviour at very high stress levels has been recorded by some of them. Pearson (1972), in reviewing previous work in the field of duration of load and bending strength, plotted on a single graph the results obtained over the last 30 years and found that despite differences in species, specimen size, moisture content, or whether the timber was solid or laminated, the results showed remarkably little scatter from a straight line described by the regression:

$$\sigma = 91.5 - 7 \log_{10} t \qquad (39.7)$$

where σ is the stress level (%), and t is the effective duration of maximum load (h). This regression is also plotted in Figure 39.6 for comparison with the curvilinear line. Pearson's findings certainly throw doubt on the existence of a critical stress level below which creep rupture does not occur. These regressions indicate that timber beams which have to withstand a dead load for 50 years can be stressed to only 50% of their ultimate short-term strength.

Recent studies, however, have tended to indicate that the creep rupture response of timber beams differs considerably from the classic case for small clear specimens described above; for high stress ratios these recent findings indicate that the duration of load effect is less severe for large-sized timber than would be predicted from small clear tests (Madsen and Barrett (1976) and Madsen (1979)). Two approaches are being employed in the study of the duration of load effect in large-sized timber. The first approach is phenomenological, being based on the concept of material damage in which the rate of damage accumulation is taken to be a function of the current stress level (Barrett and Foschi, 1978). The second approach employs fracture mechanics concepts to study the process of slow crack growth (see Section 39.7.2).

The reduction in strength with time can be accelerated if instead of steady-state conditions cyclic changes in moisture content occur. This effect is described in Chapter 41 and illustrated in Figure 41.15: a beam loaded to only 37.5% of its short-term ultimate strength, but subjected to repeated wetting and complete drying, failed in a very short period of time. This work has been confirmed on a number of species and it appears that the significant factor is the range in moisture contents through which the samples were cycled rather than the actual values of moisture content obtained.

Variations in moisture content do occur in beams under service conditions, but, since the cross-section of the beams is usually considerable, the effect of daily changes in moisture content appear to be restricted to only the outer layers. Certain seasonal changes, however, will have an effect and will contribute to an increase in deflection and decrease in time to creep rupture; it should be appreciated that these contributions will be small since the range in moisture content change will be very much lower than the range used in the experiments described above.

In Chapter 41 attention is drawn to the fact that viscoelastic behaviour could manifest itself not only as creep (deformation under load increasing with time at constant stress) but also as stress relaxation (stress decreasing with time at constant strain). Very few experiments on stress relaxation have been conducted on timber, but in one of these, samples of Douglas fir at 8% moisture content and 22°C were strained to 90% of the estimated ultimate strain before allowing the samples to stress relax; over 50% failed within a period of seven days (Bach, 1967).

39.7 Strength, failure and fracture morphology

There are two fundamentally different approaches to the concept of strength and failure. The first is the classical strength of materials approach, attempting to understand strength and failure of timber in terms of the strength and arrangement of the molecules, the fibrils, and the cells by thinking in terms of a theoretical strength and attempting to identify the reasons why the theory is never satisfied.

The second approach is much more practical in concept since it considers timber in its present state, ignoring its theoretical strength and its microstructure and stating that its performance will be determined solely by the presence of some defect, however small, which will initiate on stressing a small crack; the ultimate strength of the material will depend on the propagation of this crack.

Both approaches have been applied to timber though the second to a lesser degree than the first primarily because it is fairly recent in concept and the theories require considerable modification for the different fracture modes in an anisotropic material; both approaches are discussed below for the more important modes of stressing.

39.7.1 Classical approach

Tensile strength parallel to the grain

Over the years a number of models have been employed in an attempt to quantify the theoretical tensile strength of timber. In these models it is assumed that the lignin and hemicelluloses make no contribution to the strength of the timber; in the light of recent investigations, however, this may be no longer valid for some of the hemicelluloses. One of the earliest attempts modelled timber as comprising a series of endless chain molecules, and strengths of the order of 8000 N/mm^2 were obtained. More recent modelling has taken into account the finite length of the cellulose molecules and the presence of amorphous regions. Calculations have shown that the stress to cause chain slippage is generally considerably greater than that to cause chain scission irrespective of whether the latter is calculated on the basis of a potential energy function or intrachain bond energies; preferential breakage of the cellulose chain is thought to occur at the C–O–C linkage. These important findings have led to the derivation of minimum tensile stresses of the order of 1000–7000 N/mm^2 (Mark, 1967).

The ultimate tensile strength of timber is of the order of 100 N/mm^2, though this varies considerably between species. This figure corresponds to a value between 10% and 1.5% of the theoretical strength of the cellulose fraction. Since this accounts for only half the weight of the timber (Table 38.1) and since it is assumed, perhaps incorrectly, that the matrix does not contribute to the strength, it can be said that the actual strength of timber lies between 20% and 3% of its theoretical strength.

In attempting to integrate these views of molecular strength with the overall concept of failure it is necessary to examine strength at the next order of magnitude, namely the individual cells. It is possible to separate these by dissolution of the lignin–pectin complex cementing them together (Chapter 38, Figures 38.7 and 38.8). Using specially developed techniques of mounting and stressing, it is possible to determine their tensile strengths: much of this work has been done on softwood tracheids, and mean strengths of the order of 500 N/mm^2 have been recorded by a number of investigators. The strengths of the latewood cells can be up to three times that of the corresponding earlywood cells.

Individual tracheid strength is therefore approximately five times greater than that for solid timber. Softwood timber also contains parenchyma cells which are found principally in the rays, and lining the resin canals, and which are inherently weak; many of the tracheids tend to be imperfectly aligned and there are numerous discontinuities along the cell; consequently it is to be expected that the strength of timber is lower than that of the individual tracheids. Nevertheless, the difference is certainly substantial and it seems doubtful if the features listed above can account for the total loss in strength especially when it is realized that the cells rupture on stressing and do not slip past one another.

FIGURE 39.7 Tensile failure in spruce (*Picea abies*) showing mainly transverse cross-wall failure of the earlywood (left) and longitudinal intrawall shear failure of the latewood cells (right) (×90, polarized light) (Building Research Establishment © Crown copyright).

When timber is stressed in tension along the grain, failure occurs catastrophically with little or no plastic deformation (Figure 41.3) at strains of about 1%. Visual examination of the sample usually reveals an interlocking type of fracture which can be confirmed by optical microscopy. However, as illustrated in Figure 39.7, the degree of interlocking is considerably greater in the latewood than in the earlywood; whereas in the former the fracture plane is essentially vertical, in the latter the fracture plane follows a series of shallow zig-zags in a general transverse plane; it is now thought that these thin-walled cells contribute very little to the tensile strength of the timber. Thus failure in the stronger latewood region is by shear, while in the earlywood, though there is some evidence of shear failure, most of the rupture appears to be in straight tension.

Examination of the fracture surfaces by electron microscopy reveals that the plane of fracture occurs either within the S_1 layer or, as is more common, between the S_1 and S_2 layers. Since shear strengths are lower than tensile strengths these observations are in accord with comments made previously on the relative superiority of the tensile strengths of individual fibres compared with the tensile strength of timber. By failing in shear this implies that the shear strength of the wall layers is lower than the shear strength of the lignin–pectin material cementing together the individual cells.

Confirmation of these views is forthcoming from the work of Mark (1967) who has calculated the theoretical strengths of the various cell wall layers and has shown that the direction and level of shear stress in the various wall layers was such as to initiate failure between the S_1 and S_2 layers. Mark's treatise has received a certain amount of criticism on the grounds that he has treated one cell in isolation, opening it up longitudinally in his model to treat it as a two-dimensional structure; nevertheless, the work marked the beginning of a new phase of investigation into elasticity and fracture and the approach has been modified and subsequently developed. The extension of the work has explained the initiation of failure at the S_1–S_2 boundary, or within the S_1 layer, in terms of either buckling instability of the microfibrils, or the formation of ruptures in the matrix or framework giving rise to a redistribution of stress.

Thus, both the microscopic observations and the developed theories appear to agree that failure of timber under longitudinal tensile stressing is basically by shear. However, under certain conditions the pattern of tensile failure

FIGURE 39.8 Formation of kinks in the cell walls of spruce timber (*Picea abies*) during longitudinal compression stressing. The angle, θ, lying between the plane of shear and the middle lamella, varies systematically between timbers and is influenced by temperature (×1300, polarized light) (Building Research Establishment © Crown copyright).

may be abnormal. At temperatures in excess of 100°C the lignin component is softened and its shear strength is reduced. Consequently, on stressing, failure will occur within the cementing material rather than within the cell wall.

Secondly, in timber that has been stressed in compression before being pulled in tension, it will be found that tensile rupture will occur along the line of compression damage which, as will be explained below, runs transversely. Consequently, the tensile fracture will be horizontal giving rise to a brittle-type fracture.

In the literature is recorded a wide range of tensile failure criteria, the most commonly applied being some critical strain parameter, an approach which is supported by a considerable volume of evidence, though its lack of universal application has been pointed out by several workers.

Compression strength parallel to the grain

Compression failure is a slow yielding process in which there is a progressive development of structural change. The initial stage of this

FIGURE 39.9 Failure under longitudinal compression at the macroscopic level. On the longitudinal radial plane the crease (shear line) runs horizontally, while on the longitudinal tangential plane the crease is inclined at 65° to the vertical axis (Building Research Establishment © Crown copyright).

sequence appears to occur at a stress less than 25% of the ultimate failing stress (Dinwoodie, 1968) though Keith (1971) considers that these early stages do not develop until about 60% of the ultimate. There is certainly a very marked increase in the amount of structural change above 60% which is reflected by the marked departure from linearity of the stress–strain diagram illustrated in Figure 41.3. The former author maintains that linearity here is an artefact resulting from insensitive testing equipment and that some plastic flow has occurred at levels well below 60% of the ultimate stress. Compression deformation assumes the form of a small kink in the microfibrillar structure, and because of the presence of crystalline regions in the cell wall it is possible to observe this feature using polarization microscopy (Figure 39.8). The sequence of irreversible anatomical changes leading to failure originates in the tracheid or fibre wall at that point where the longitudinal cell is displaced vertically to accommodate the horizontally running ray. As stress and strain increase these kinks become more prominent and increase numerically, generally in a preferred lateral direction, horizontally on the radial plane (Figure 39.9) and at an angle to the vertical axis of from 45° to 60° on the tangential plane. These lines of deformation, generally called creases and comprising numerous kinks, continue to develop in width and length; at failure, defined in terms of maximum stress, these creases can be observed by eye on the face of the block of timber. At this stage there is considerable buckling of the cell wall and delamination within it, usually between the S_1 and S_2 layers. Models have been produced to simulate buckling behaviour and calculated crease angles for instability agree well with observed angles (Grossman and Wold, 1971).

At a lower order of magnification, Dinwoodie (1974) has shown that the angle at which the kink traverses the cell wall varies systematically between earlywood and latewood, between different species, and with temperature. Almost 72% of the variation in the kink angle could be accounted for by a combination of the angle of the microfibrils in the S_2 layer and the ratio of cell wall stiffness in longitudinal and horizontal planes.

Attempts have been made to relate the size and number of kinks to the amount of elastic strain or the degree of viscous deformation. Under conditions of prolonged loading, total strain and the ratio of creep strain to elastic strain (the creep function) appear to provide the most sensitive guide to the formation of cell wall deformation; the gross creases appear to be associated with strains of 0.33% (Keith, 1972).

The number and distribution of kinks are dependent on temperature and moisture content: increasing moisture content, though resulting in a lower strain to failure, results in the production of more kinks, although each smaller in size than its 'dry' counterpart; these are to be found in a more even distribution than they are in dry timber. Increasing temperature results in a similar wider distribution of the kinks.

Static bending

In the bending mode timber is subjected to compression stresses on the upper part of the beam and tensile on the lower part. Since the strength of clear timber in compression is only about one-third that in tension, failure will occur on the compression side of the beam long before it will do so on the tension side. In knotty timber, however, the compressive strength is often equal to and can actually exceed the tensile strength. As recorded in the previous section, failure in compression is progressive and starts at low levels of stressing: consequently the first stages of failure in bending will frequently be associated with compression failure and as both the bending stress and consequently the degree of compression failure increase so the neutral axis will move progressively downwards from its original central position in the beam (assuming uniform cross-section), thereby allowing the increased compression load to be carried over a greater cross-section. Fracture occurs when the stress on the tensile surface reaches the ultimate strength in bending.

Toughness

Timber is a tough material, and in possessing moderate to high stiffness and strength in addition to its toughness it is favoured with a unique combination of mechanical properties emulated only by bone, which, like timber, is a natural composite.

Toughness is generally defined as the resistance of a material to the propagation of cracks. In the comparison of materials it is usual to express toughness in terms of **work of fracture**, which is a measure of the energy necessary to propagate a crack thereby producing new surfaces.

In timber the work of fracture involved in the production of cracks at right angles to the grain is about $10^4\,J/m^2$; this value is an order of magnitude less than that for ductile metals, but

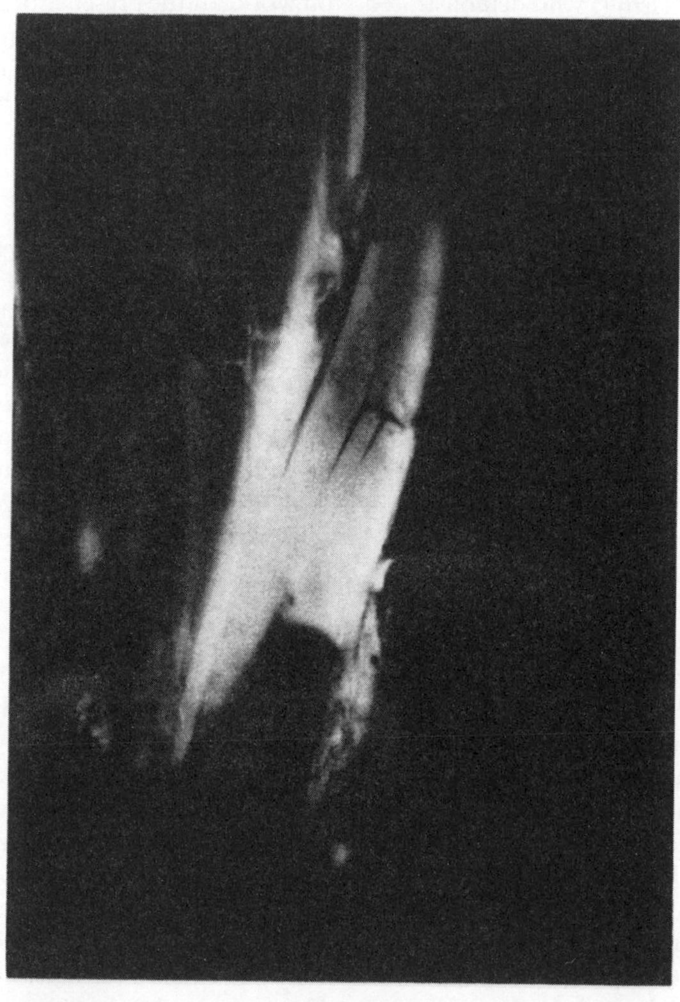

FIGURE 39.10 Crack-stopping in a fractured rotor blade. The orientation of the secondary cracks corresponds to the microfibrillar orientation of the middle layer of the cell wall (×800, polarized light) (Building Research Establishment © Crown copyright).

is comparable with that for the artificial composites. Now the energy required to break all the chemical bonds in a plane cross-section is of the order of $1-2\,J/m^2$; that is, four orders of magnitude lower than the experimental values. Since pull-out of the microfibrils does not appear to happen to any great extent it is not possible to account for the high work of fracture in this way (Gordon and Jeronimidis (1974) and Jeronimidis (1980)).

One of the earlier theories to account for the high toughness in timber was based on the work of Cook and Gordon (1964) who demonstrated that toughness in fibre-reinforced materials is associated with the arrest of cracks made possible by the presence of numerous interfaces. As these interfaces open, so secondary cracks are initiated at right angles to the primary thereby dissipating its energy. This theory is applicable to timber as Figure 39.10 illustrates, but it is doubtful whether the total discrepancy in energy between experiment and theory can be explained in this way.

Some recent and interesting results have contributed to a better understanding of the problem (Gordon and Jeronimidis (1974) and Jeronimidis (1980)). Prior to fracture it would appear that the cells separate in the fracture area; on further stressing these individual and unrestrained cells buckle inwards, generally assuming a triangular shape. In this form they are capable of extending up to 20% before final rupture thereby absorbing a large quantity of energy. Inward buckling of helically wound cells under tensile stresses is possible only because the microfibrils of the S_2 layer are wound in a single direction. Observations and calculations on timber have been supported by glass-fibre models and it is considered that the high work of fracture can be accounted for by this unusual mode of failure. It appears that increased toughness is possibly achieved at the expense of some stiffness, since increased stiffness would have resulted from contra-winding of the microfibrils in the S_2.

So far, we have discussed toughness in terms of only clear timber. Should knots or defects be present timber will no longer be tough and the comments made earlier as to viewpoint are particularly relevant here. The material scientist sees timber as a tough material: the structural engineer will view it as a brittle material because of its inherent defects and this theme will be developed in the following section.

Loss in toughness, however, can arise not only on account of the presence of defects and knots, but also through the effects of acid, prolonged elevated temperatures or fungal attack on wood, or the presence of compression damage resulting from overstressing within the living tree or in the handling or utilization of timber after conversion. Under these abnormal conditions the timber is said to be **brash** and failure occurs in a **brittle** mode.

39.7.2 Engineering approach to strength and fracture

The second approach to the concept of strength and failure is a more practical one and is based on the premise that all materials contain flaws or minute cracks, and that performance is determined solely by the propagation of cracks arising from these defects. The largest flaw will become self-propagating when the rate of release of strain energy exceeds the rate of increase of surface energy of the propagating crack.

The development of this concept has become known as fracture mechanics: its application to timber did not take place until as late as 1961. Part of the reason is due to the modelling of wood as an orthotropic material, and consequently there are six values of 'fracture toughness' (a material parameter, also known as the critical stress intensity factor, K_c) for each of the three principal modes of crack propagation.

However, the value of K_c is dependent not only on orientation and crack opening mode, but also on the density, moisture content and thickness of the specimen, as well as crack speed.

Fracture mechanics has been successfully applied to various aspects of wood behaviour and failure, such as the presence of knots and splits in timber beams, or joints in the laminae of glue-laminated beams. Treating these features as cracks, the calculation of beam strength using fracture mechanics agreed well with actual test data (see Dinwoodie, 1989).

39.8 Working (grade) stresses for timber

Timber, like many other materials, is graded according to its anticipated performance in service; because of its inherent variability, distinct grades of material must be recognized and the derived stresses for these are usually referred to as **grade stresses.**

Up until the mid-1970s, grade stresses of structural timber were derived from the strength values obtained from the small, clear specimens described earlier in this chapter. For each species and each strength parameter, it was necessary to calculate the statistical minimum by assuming that the range of strength values obtained due to variability conformed to a natural distribution curve, and that the chance of getting a lower value than the estimated minimum once in 100 times was not taking too high a risk. Thus the statistical minimum is the arithmetic mean value less 2.33 times the standard deviation. It was also necessary to reduce the resulting value by a safety factor to cover the effects of specimen size and shape, rate of loading, and duration of loading. The value of this factor varied from 1.0 to 2.25 among the different properties. The 'basic stresses' were obtained, therefore, by dividing the statistical minimum by the appropriate safety factor.

Earlier in this chapter the various factors that affect strength were described and sets of grading rules have been devised which were used to assess the strength of timber visually in terms of the size and distribution of knots, slope of grain, rate of growth, and presence of fissures, wane, resin pockets and distortion. The timber was assigned a numerical grade, e.g. 40, 50, 65 and 75 which was really the strength ratio of the piece of wood being graded relative to that of a perfect, straight-grained, clear piece. The grade stresses were therefore the basic stresses reduced by the strength ratios.

Both 'dry (grade) stresses' for wood with a moisture content less than 18%, and 'wet (grade) stresses' for wood with above 18% moisture content, were set out in the British Code of Practice CP 112, Part 2, 1971, *The structural use of timber*.

The Code also demonstrated how the **permissible stresses** used in structural design in timber are calculated from the product of the grade stresses and a series of modification factors which cover aspects such as load sharing between members, duration of load, slenderness ratio and bearing area.

Since 1971 there have been many changes in the grading and the derivation of 'grade stresses'. This resulted in the issue in 1984 of a new Code of Practice; BS 5268: *Structural use of timber*, Part 2, in which the new grade stresses were derived from structural sized pieces of wood and not from small, clear, straight-grained samples. This new, more direct approach necessitated the testing of vast quantities of wood of different qualities, a process which had to be repeated for each species of structural softwood.

39.8.1 Grading of timber

When cut for structural use wood must first be graded; this can be carried out either visually or mechanically in accordance with BS 4978.

Visual grading

The basis on which visual grading is now performed is similar to that already described for the early assessment of grade stresses. One major change, however, was the assessment of the significance of knots which is now quantified in terms of the **knot area ratio**; this is defined as the sum of the projected cross-sectional areas of

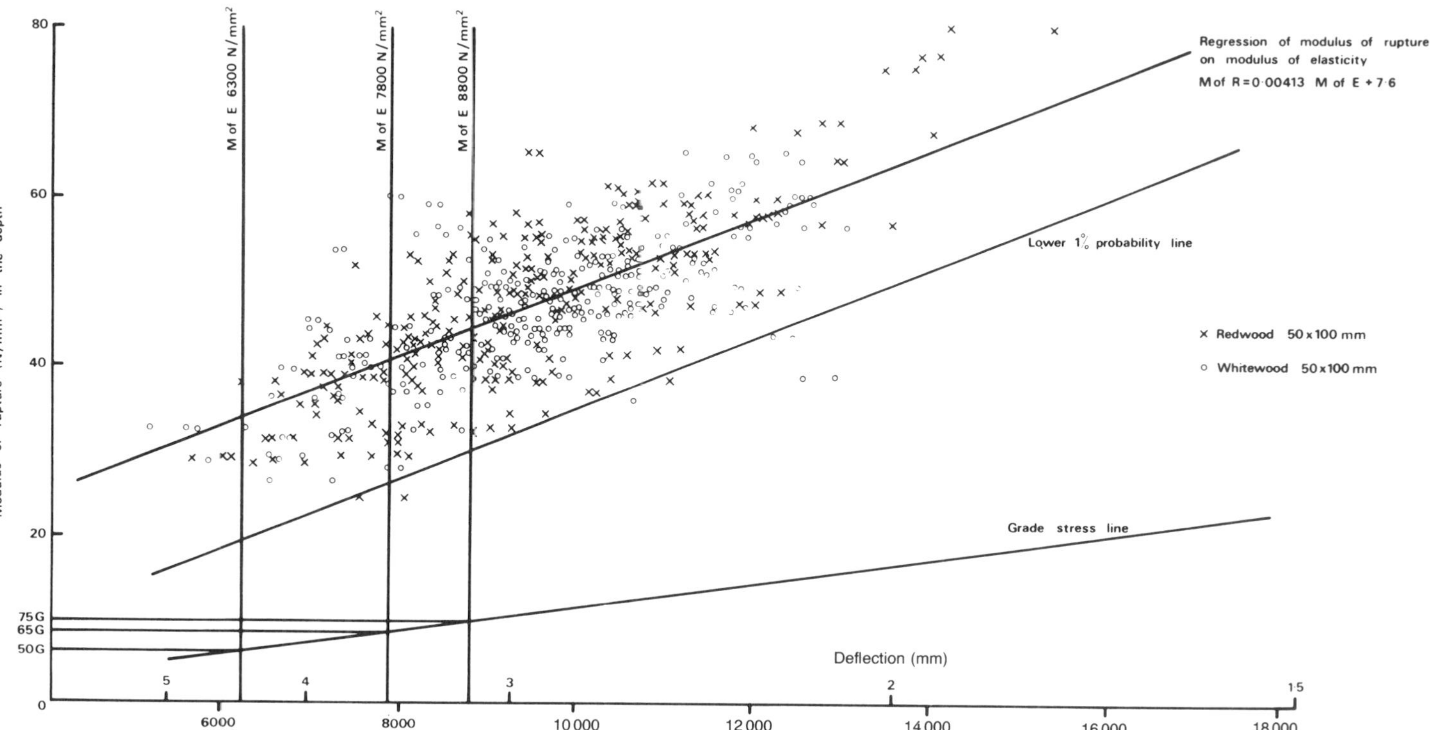

FIGURE 39.11 The relationship between modulus of rupture and modulus of elasticity for both redwood (*Pinus sylvestris*) and whitewood (principally *Picea abies*) (Building Research Establishment © Crown copyright).

all the knots at a cross-section in terms of the cross-sectional area of the piece. Other factors, such as grain angle, ring width, and the presence of splits, are estimated and have the same significance as previously. Two visual grades are defined: SS, special structural; and GS, general structural, the lower of the two grades. For example, for a rectangular section to qualify for SS grade, in addition to satisfying requirements for slope of grain, distortion, rate of growth and wane, the total knot area ratio at any cross-section in the timber sample must not exceed one-third, or, where more than half of the cross-section of either margin (the outer quarters of the depth of the cross-section) is occupied by knots, the total knot area ratio must not exceed one-fifth; the corresponding total knot area ratios for GS grade are one-half and one-third. Full information on the visual grading of wood is provided in BS 4978, *Timber grades for structural use.*

Courses are run to train people as stress graders, and certificates awarded. Wood graded visually by these operators is stamped with the grade class and with confirmation that it has been visually graded.

Mechanical grading

Visual grading is a laborious process since all four faces of the timber should be examined. Furthermore, it does not separate naturally weak from naturally strong timber and hence it has to be assumed that pieces of the same size and species containing identical defects have the same strength: such an assumption is invalid and leads to a most conservative estimate of strength.

Many of the disadvantages of visual grading can be removed by mechanical grading, a process which was introduced commercially in the early 1970s. The principle underlying the process is the high correlation that has been found to exist between the moduli of elasticity and rupture for any one species, or groups of two or three closely related species. An example of this relationship is illustrated in Figure 39.11. It has been proven that this relation provides a more accurate measure of strength than can be obtained by visual inspection.

In Figure 39.11 it will be noted that the relation for two species can be represented by a single regression line below which is drawn the lower confidence limit at a vertical distance of 2.33 × standard error of the estimate of the modulus of rupture: approximately 99% of the results lie above this line. When mechanical grading was still in its infancy the magnitude of the safety factor was set as 3: however, as more experience was gained in the method, the factor was reduced to near its original level. When applied to the lower confidence limit, as indicated in Figure 39.11, a grade stress line is produced and when deflection limits are imposed, different grade stresses can be read off from this grade stress line.

Having established the relation for each species, a stress-grading machine can then be set up to automatically grade the timber. Depending on the type of machine, as each length of timber passes through it is either placed under constant load and deflection is measured, or subjected to constant deflection and load is measured: a small computer then ascribes (strength) grade stresses to the measured stiffness for each species and these are indicated along the length of the plank by splashes of dye. A final colour stripe indicates the lowest grade stress that was present in the plank.

Machine grades are designated with the prefix M, e.g. MSS and MGS which correspond directly with the visual SS and GS grades. Two further machine grades for softwoods, M50 and M75, are included in BS 4978; tropical hardwood grades are contained in BS 5756.

The stress-grading machine must be reset for different species since the correlation between strength and modulus is species-dependent. In spite of this limitation, mechanical stress grading, even for small quantities of wood, is considerably faster than visual grading; equally important is the fact that output of a particular grade is much higher by mechanical stress grading than by the visual method, due to the very conservative approach that has to be adopted in the latter case.

Knowing the stress grade of his timber, the designer or structural engineer can then obtain his grade stresses from BS 5268, Part 2, either in the form of strength classes or for individual species and grades as described in the previous section. In order to allow substitution of one species for another, this Standard sets out a number of strength classes. For example, in strength Class 2, a GS (general structural) grade of home-grown Douglas fir is equivalent to an SS (special structural) grade of home-grown Norway spruce, and the corresponding stress for Class 2 applies whichever species is selected.

39.9 References

Bach, L. (1967) Static fatigue of wood under constant strain. *FPL* (Vancouver) *Info Rpt* VP-X-24.

Barrett, J.D. and Foschi, R.O. (1978) Duration of load and failure probability in wood, Part 1: Modelling creep rupture. *Canadian Journal of Civil Engineering*, 5, No. 4, 505–14.

Baumann, R. (1922) Die bisherigen Ergebnisse der Holzprüfungen in der Materialprüfungsanstalt an der Tech Hochschule Stuttgart. *Forsch. Gebiete. Ingenieurw.*, H231, Berlin.

Cave, I.D. (1969) The longitudinal Young's modulus of *Pinus radiata*. *Wood Science and Technology*, 3, 40–8.

Cook, J. and Gordon, J.E. (1964) A mechanism for the control of crack propagation in all brittle systems. *Proceedings of the Royal Society*, **A282**, 508.

Dinwoodie, J.M. (1968) Failure in timber, Part 1: Microscopic changes in cell wall structure associated with compression failure. *Journal of the Institute of Wood Science*, **21**, 37–53.

Dinwoodie, J.M. (1974) Failure in wood, Part 2: The angle of shear through the cell wall during longitudinal compression stressing. *Wood Science and Technology*, **8**, 56–67.

Dinwoodie, J.M. (1989) *Wood – Nature's Cellular, Polymeric, Fibre Composite*. The Institute of Metals, London.

Gordon, J.E. and Jeronimidis, G. (1974) Work of fracture of natural cellulose. *Nature* (London), **252**, 116.

Grossman, P.U.A. and Wold, M.B. (1971) Compression fracture of wood parallel to the grain. *Wood Science and Technology*, **5**, 147–56.

Jeronimidis, G. (1980) The fracture behaviour of wood and the relations between toughness and morphology. *Proceedings of the Royal Society*, **B208**, 447–60.

Keith, C.T. (1971) The anatomy of compression failure in relation to creep-inducing stress. *Wood Science*, **4**, No. 2, 71–82.

Keith, C.T. (1972) The mechanical behaviour of wood in longitudinal compression. *Wood Science*, **4**, No. 4, 234–44.

Lavers, G.M. (1969) The strength properties of timber. *Bulletin 50, Forest Products Res. Lab.*, 2nd edn. HMSO.

Madsen, B. (1979) Time-strength relationship for lumber. In *Proceedings of the First International Conference on Wood Fracture*, Banff, Alberta, 1978 (ed. J.D. Barrett and R.O. Foschi), Forintek Canada Corp., 111–28.

Madsen, B. and Barrett, J.D. (1976) Time-strength relationships for lumber. Structural Research Series, Report No. 13, University of British Columbia, Dept of Civil Engineering.

Mark, R.E. (1967) *Cell Wall Mechanics of Tracheids*. Yale University Press, New Haven.

Pearson, R.G. (1972) The effect of duration of load on the bending strength of wood. *Holzforschung*, **26**, No. 4, 153–8.

Wood, L.W. (1951) Relation of strength of wood to duration of load. *Forest Products Laboratory* (Madison), Report No. 1916.

Chapter forty

Durability of timber

40.1 The physical, chemical and biological agencies
40.2 Natural durability
40.3 Performance of timber in fire
40.4 Flow in timber
40.5 Thermal conductivity
40.6 References

40.1 The physical, chemical and biological agencies

Durability is a term which has different concepts for many people: it is defined here in the broadest possible sense to embrace the resistance of timber to attack from a whole series of agencies whether physical, chemical or biological in origin.

By far the most important are the biological agencies, the fungi and the insects, both of which can cause tremendous havoc given the right conditions. In the absence of fire, fungal or insect attack, timber is really remarkably resistant and timber structures will survive, indeed have survived, incredibly long periods of time, especially when it is appreciated that it is a natural organic material with which we are dealing. Examples of well-preserved timber items now over 2000 years old are to be seen in the Egyptian tombs.

The effects of hydrolytic, oxidative and photochemical reactions are usually of secondary importance in determining durability. On exposure to sunlight the colouration of the heartwood of most timbers will lighten, e.g. mahogany, afrormosia, oak, though a few timbers will actually darken, e.g. Douglas fir and Rhodesian teak. Indoors the action of sunlight will be slow and the process will take several years; however, outdoors the change in colour is very rapid, taking place in a matter of months, and is generally regarded as an initial and very transient stage in the whole process of **weathering.**

In weathering the action not only of light, but also of rain and wind renders the timber silvery-grey in appearance: part of the process embraces degradation of the cellulose by ultraviolet light, which erodes the cell wall and in particular the pit aperture and torus. However, the same cell walls that are attacked act as an efficient filter for those of the cells below and the rate of erosion from the combined effects of UV, light and rain is very slow indeed; in the absence of fungi and insects the rate of removal of the surface by weathering is of the order of only 1 mm in every 20 years. Nevertheless, because of the continual threat of biological attack, it is unwise to leave most timbers completely unprotected from the weather; it should be appreciated that during weathering the integrity of the surface layers is markedly reduced, thereby adversely affecting the performance of an applied surface coating. In order to effect good adhesion the weathered layers must first be removed (see Section 42.4).

As a general rule, timber is highly resistant to a large number of chemicals and its continued use for various types of tanks and containers, even in the face of competition from stainless steel, indicates that its resistance, certainly in terms of cost, is most attractive. Timber is far superior to cast iron and ordinary steel in its resistance to mild acids and for very many years timber was used for the separators in lead–acid batteries. However, in its resistance to alkalis timber is inferior to iron and steel: dissolution of both the lignin and the hemicelluloses occurs under the action of even mild alkalis.

Iron salts are frequently very acidic and in the presence of moisture result in hydrolytic degradation of the timber; the softening and darkish-blue discolouration of timber in the vicinity of iron nails and bolts is due to this effect.

Generally when durability of timber is discussed reference is being made explicitly to the resistance of the timber to both fungal and insect attack. This resistance is termed **natural durability**, but as the former agent of attack has a much higher significance the term natural durability is frequently and inaccurately applied to the natural resistance of timber to only fungal attack at ground contact.

The natural durability of wood can be enhanced by treating the wood with chemicals which are toxic to fungi and insects. This process is known as preservation and is described in a later chapter: such treatment is dependent on the laws of diffusion and flow, and their applicability as far as wood is concerned is set out later in this chapter.

40.2 Natural durability

Recalling that timber is an organic product it is surprising at first to find that it can withstand attack from fungi and insects for very long periods of time, certainly much greater than its herbaceous counterparts. This resistance can be explained in part on the basic constituents of the cell wall, and in part on the deposition of extractives (Sections 38.1 and 38.3.3; Table 38.2).

The presence of lignin which surrounds and protects the crystalline cellulose appears to offer a slight degree of resistance to fungal attack: certainly the resistance of sapwood is higher than that of herbaceous plants. Fungal attack can commence only in the presence of moisture and the threshold value of 20% for timber is about twice as high as the corresponding value for non-lignified plants.

Timber has a low nitrogen content being of the order of 0.03–0.1% by weight and, since this element is a prerequisite for fungal growth, its presence only in such a small quantity contributes to the natural resistance of timber.

The principal factor conferring resistance to biological attack is undoubtedly the presence of extractives in the heartwood. The far higher durability of the heartwood of certain species compared with the sapwood is attributable primarily to the presence in the former of toxic substances, many of which are phenolic in origin. Other factors such as a decreased moisture content, reduced rate of diffusion, density and deposition of gums and resins also play a role in determining the higher durability of the heartwood.

Considerable variation in durability can occur within the heartwood zone: in a number of timbers the outer band of the heartwood has a higher resistance than the inner region, owing, it is thought, to the progressive degradation of toxic substances by enzymatic or microbial action.

Durability of the heartwood varies considerably among the different species, being related to the type and quantity of the extractive present: the heartwood of timbers devoid of extractives has a very low durability. Sapwood of all timbers is susceptible to attack owing not only to the absence of extractives, but also to the presence in the ray cells of stored starch which constitutes a ready source of food for the invading fungus.

In the UK, timbers have been classified into five durability groups which are defined in terms of the performance of the heartwood when

TABLE 40.1 Durability classification (resistance of heartwood to fungi in ground contact) for the more common timbers*

Durability class	*Perishable*	*Non-durable*	*Moderately durable*	*Durable*	*Very durable*
Approximate life in contact with ground (years)	<5	5–10	10–15	15–25	>25
Hardwoods	Alder Ash, European Balsa Beech, European Birch, European Horse chestnut Poplar, black Sycamore Willow	Afara Elm, English Oak, American red Obeche Poplar, grey Seraya, white	Avodire Keruing Mahogany, African Oak, Turkish Sapele Seraya, dark red Walnut, European Walnut, African	Agba Chestnut, sweet Idigbo Mahogany, American Oak, European Utile	Afrormosia Afzelia Ekki Greenheart Iroko Jarrah Kapur Makore Opepe Purpleheart Teak
Softwoods		Hemlock, western 'Parana pine' Pine, Scots (redwood) Pine, yellow Podo Spruce, European (whitewood) Spruce, Sitka	Douglas fir Larch Pine, maritime	Pine, pitch Western red cedar Yew	

* Note that the sapwood of all timber is perishable.

buried in the ground. Examples of the more common timbers are presented in Table 40.1. Such an arbitrary classification is informative only in relative terms though these results on 2 inch × 2 inch ground stakes can be projected linearly for increased thicknesses. Timber used externally, but not in contact with the ground, will generally have a much longer life, though quantification of this is impossible.

40.2.1 Nature of fungal decay

In timber some fungi, e.g. the moulds, are present only on the surface and although they may cause staining they have no effect on the strength properties. A second group of fungi, the sap-stain fungi, live on the sugars present in the ray cells and the presence of their hyphae in the sapwood imparts a distinctive colouration to that region of the timber. One of the best examples of sap stain is that found in recently felled Scots pine logs. In temperate countries the presence of this type of fungus results in only inappreciable losses in bending strength, though several staining fungi in the tropical countries cause considerable reductions in strength.

By far the most important groups of fungi are those that cause decay of the timber by chemical decomposition; this is achieved by the digesting action of enzymes secreted by the fungal hyphae. Two main groups of timber-decaying fungi can be distinguished.

1. The **brown rots**, which consume the cellulose and hemicelluloses but attack the lignin only slightly. During attack the wood usually

darkens and in an advanced stage of attack tends to break up into cubes and crumbles under pressure. One of the best known fungi of this group is *Serpula lacrymans* which causes dry rot. Contrary to what its name suggests, the fungus requires an adequate supply of moisture for development.
2. The **white rots**, which attack all the chemical constituents of the cell wall. Although the timber may darken initially, it becomes very much lighter than normal at advanced stages of attack. Unlike attack from the brown rots, timber with white rot does not crumble under pressure, but separates into a fibrous mass.

In very general terms, the brown rots are usually to be found in constructional timbers, whereas the white rots are frequently responsible for the decay of exterior joinery.

Decay, of course, results in a loss of strength, but it is important to note that considerable strength reductions may arise in the very early stages of attack; toughness is particularly sensitive to the presence of fungal attack. Loss in weight of the timber is also characteristic of attack and decayed timber can lose up to 80% of its air-dry weight.

40.2.2 Nature of insect attack

Although all timbers are susceptible to attack by at least one species of insect, in practice only a small proportion of the timber in service actually becomes infested. Some timbers are more susceptible to attack than others and generally the heartwood is much more resistant than the sapwood: nevertheless the heartwood can be attacked by certain species.

Insect attack can take one of two forms. In certain insects the timber is consumed by the adult form and the best known example of this mode of attack is the termites. Few timbers are immune to attack by these voracious eaters and it is indeed fortunate that these insects cannot survive the cooler weather of this country. They are to be found principally in the tropics but certain species are present in the Mediterranean region including southern France.

In this country insect attack is always by the second form of attack, namely by the grub or larval stage of certain beetles. The adult beetle lays its eggs on the surface of the timber, frequently in surface cracks, or in the cut ends of cells; these eggs hatch to produce grubs which tunnel their way into the timber, remaining there for periods of up to three years. The size and shape of the tunnel and the type of detritus left behind in the tunnel (frass) are characteristic of the species of beetle. Well-known examples of beetle larvae attacking timber in this country are the **furniture** and **death watch** beetles, but considerable damage also occurs from the **powder-post** and **longhorn** beetles.

40.2.3 Marine borers

Timber used in salt water is subjected to attack by marine-boring animals such as the shipworm (*Teredo* sp.) and the gribble (*Limnoria* sp.). Marine borers are particularly active in tropical waters; nevertheless around the coast of Great Britain *Limnoria* is fairly active and *Teredo*, though spasmodic, has still to be considered a potential hazard. The degree of hazard will vary considerably with local conditions and there are relatively few timbers which are recognized as having heartwood resistant under all conditions: the list includes ekki, greenheart, okan, opepe and pyinkado.

The sapwood and heartwood of many species of timber can have their natural durabilities increased by impregnation with toxic chemicals; the preservative treatment of timber is considered in Chapter 42 which is concerned with the mechanical and chemical processing of timber.

40.3 Performance of timber in fire

The performance of materials in fire is an aspect of durability which has attracted much attention in recent years, not so much from the research scientist, but rather from the material user who has to conform with recent legislation on safety and who is influenced by the weight of public opinion on the use of only 'safe' materials. While various tests have been devised to assess the performance of materials in fire there is a fair degree of agreement in the unsatisfactory nature of many of these tests, and an awareness that certain materials can perform better in practice than is indicated by these tests.

Thus, while no one would doubt that timber is a combustible material showing up rather poorly in both the 'spread of flame' and 'heat release' tests, nevertheless in at least one aspect of performance, namely the maintenance of strength with increasing temperature and time, wood performs better than steel.

There is a critical surface temperature below which timber will not ignite. As the surface temperature increases above 100°C volatile gases begin to be emitted as thermal degradation slowly commences; however, it is not until the temperature is in excess of 250°C that there is a sufficient build-up in these gases to cause ignition of the timber in the presence of a pilot flame. Where this is absent the surface temperature can rise to about 500°C before the gases become self-igniting. Ignition, however, is related not only to the absolute temperature but also to the time of exposure at that temperature, since ignition is primarily a function of heat flux.

Thermal degrade certainly occurs at temperatures down to 120°C and it has been suggested that degrade can occur at temperatures as low as 66°C when timber is exposed for long periods of time.

The performance of timber at temperatures above ignition level is very similar to that of certain reinforced thermosetting resins which have been used as sacrificial protective coatings on space-return capsules. Both timber and these ablative polymers undergo thermal decomposition with subsequent removal of mass, leaving behind enough material to preserve structural integrity.

The onset of pyrolysis in timber is marked by

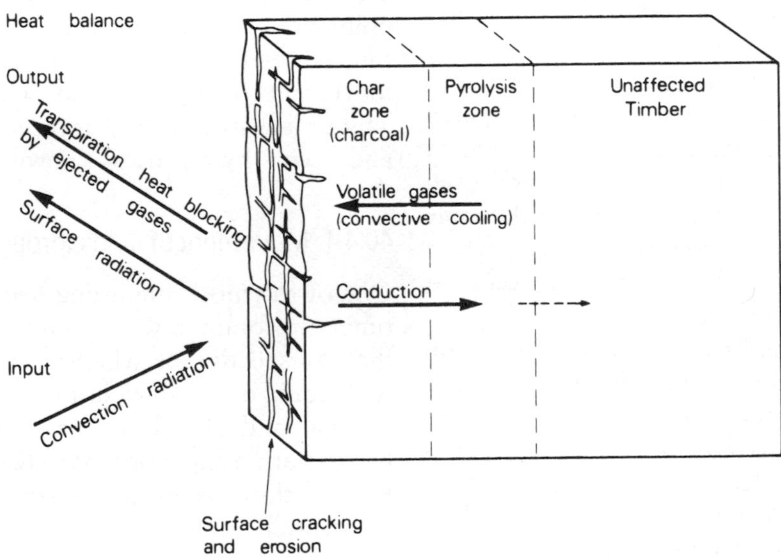

FIGURE 40.1 Diagrammatic representation of the thermal decomposition of timber (Building Research Establishment © Crown copyright).

a darkening of the timber and the commencement of emission of volatile gases; the reaction becomes exothermic and the timber reverts to a carbonized char popularly known as charcoal (Figure 40.1). The volatiles, in moving to the surface, cool the char and are subsequently ejected into the boundary layer where they block the incoming convective heat: this most important phenomenon is known as **transpirational cooling.** High surface temperatures are reached and some heat is rejected by thermal radiation: the heat balance is indicated in Figure 40.1. The surface layers crack badly both along and across the grain and surface material is continually but slowly being lost.

A quasi-steady state is reached, therefore, with a balance between the rate of loss of surface and the rate of recession of the undamaged wood. For most softwoods and medium-density hardwoods the rate at which the front recedes is about 0.64 mm/min: for high-density hardwoods the value is about 0.5 mm/min (Hall and Jackman, 1975).

The formation of the char, therefore, protects the unburnt timber which may be only a few millimetres from the surface. Failure of the beam or strut will occur only when the cross-sectional area of the unburnt core becomes too small to support the load. By increasing the dimensions of the timber above those required for structural consideration, it is possible to guarantee structural integrity in a fire for a given period of time. This is a much more desirable situation than that presented by steel, where total collapse of the beam or strut occurs at some critical temperature.

Four parts of the British Standard BS 476 on fire tests on building materials and structures are particularly important in the evaluation of the performance in fire of timber and board materials: Part 4: *Non-combustibility*; Part 5: *Ignitability*; Part 6: *Fire propagation*; and Part 7: *Surface spread of flame*. Unfortunately, in three out of these four tests timber and board products do not fare at all well. None of the four tests demonstrates the predictability of the performance of timber in fire, nor do they indicate the guaranteed structural integrity of the material for a calculable period of time. The performance of timber in the widest sense is certainly superior to that indicated by the present set of standard tests.

40.4 Flow in timber

The movement of liquids and gases through wood is important not only in the controlled drying of timber, but also in its treatment with chemicals in order to impart greater durability, higher flame retardancy, or improved dimensional stability in changing environmental conditions.

Taking water as an example, moisture in timber is present in three ways: (1) as **free** liquid water in the cell cavities above the fibre saturation point (Chapter 38); (2) as **bound** water within the cell walls both below and above the fibre saturation point; and (3) as water **vapour** both above and below the fibre saturation point.

Flow of both liquid water and water vapour can therefore occur above the fibre saturation point both along the cell cavities and through the cell wall. Below the fibre saturation point, movement of both bound water and water vapour is restricted to that through the cell wall and occurs by a process known as **diffusion.**

40.4.1 Movement of fluids through timber

One of the most interesting features of flow in timber in common with many other materials is that irrespective of whether one is concerned with liquid or gas flow, diffusion of moisture, or thermal and electrical conductivity, the same basic relationship holds, namely that the flux, or rate of flow, is proportional to the pressure gradient:

$$\frac{\text{Flux}}{\text{Gradient}} = K \qquad (40.1)$$

where flux is the rate of flow per unit cross-sectional area, gradient is the difference in pressure, concentration, or moisture content causing flow per unit length, and K is a constant, dependent on form of flow, e.g. permeability, diffusion or conductivity.

40.4.2 Flow of fluids through the cell cavities (permeability)

By far the most important aspect of flow in terms of wood utilization is that which occurs through the cell cavities, the bulk of which takes place as **laminar** flow.

Flow in porous materials such as timber is quantified in terms of permeability, and the process of laminar flow can be described by Darcy's law:

$$K_p = -\frac{F\eta}{\Delta P} \qquad (40.2)$$

where K_p is the liquid viscous permeability constant, F is the flux (V/tA). ΔP is the pressure gradient and η is the viscosity of the liquid. This expression can be rewritten in terms of volume flow per unit time (Q) as

$$Q = \frac{K_p A \Delta P}{\eta l} \qquad (40.3)$$

where A is the cross-sectional area of the capillary. It may be shown theoretically that this law remains applicable for a number of capillaries in

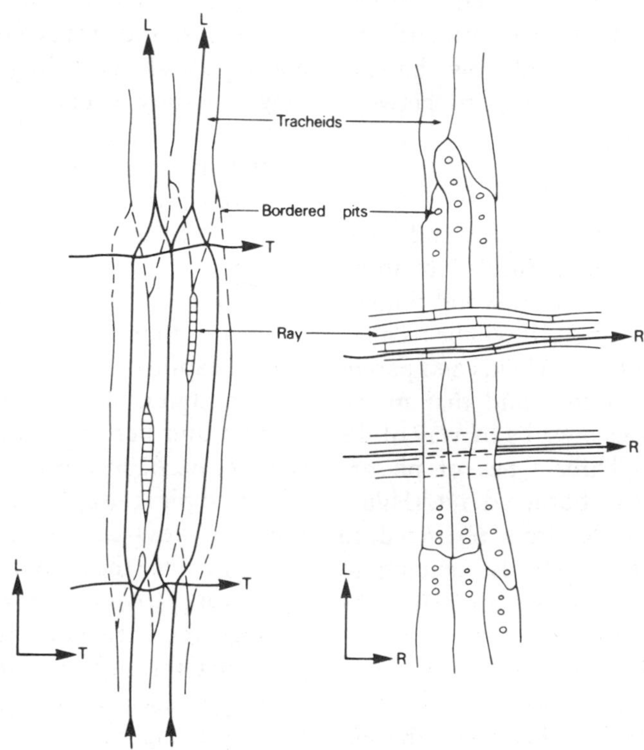

FIGURE 40.2 On the left, a representation of the cellular structure of a softwood in a longitudinal–tangential plane illustrating the significance of the bordered pits in both longitudinal and tangential flow; on the right, softwood timber in the longitudinal–radial plane, indicating the role of the ray cells in defining the principal pathway for radial flow (Building Research Establishment © Crown copyright).

parallel, or even for a heterogeneous porous medium in which different types of capillary are combined in series, providing that A is then taken as the area of the medium normal to flow.

Due to the compressible nature of gases, eqn (40.3) for gas flow becomes

$$Q = \frac{K_{pg} A \Delta P}{\eta l} \frac{\overline{P}}{P} \quad (40.4)$$

where $\overline{P}$ is the mean pressure in the specimen, P is the pressure at which Q is measured, K_{pg} is the gas viscous permeability constant and η is the viscosity of the gas.

40.4.3 Flow paths in timber

Turning specifically to the question of impregnation of timber with preservatives in order to improve its natural durability, the effectiveness of such a treatment is determined primarily by the natural pathways for liquid flow that are present in timber. These differ slightly between softwoods and hardwoods.

Softwoods

Because of their simpler structure and their greater economic significance much more attention has been paid to flow in softwood timbers than in the hardwood timbers. It will be recalled from Chapter 38 that both tracheids and parenchyma cells have closed ends and that movement of liquids and gases must be by way of the pits in the cell wall. Three types of pit are present. The first is the bordered pit (Figure 38.10) which is almost entirely restricted to the radial walls of the tracheids, tending to be located towards the ends of the cells. The second type of pit is the ray or semi-bordered pit which interconnects the vertical tracheid with the horizontal ray parenchyma cell, while the third type is the simple pit between adjacent parenchyma cells.

For very many years it was firmly believed that the bordered pits would be the limiting factor controlling longitudinal flow. However, it has now been demonstrated that much of the total resistance to longitudinal flow in sapwood that has been specially dried to ensure that the torus remains in its natural position, can be accounted for by the resistance of the cell cavity (Petty and Puritch, 1970).

Both longitudinal and tangential flowpaths in softwoods are predominantly by way of the bordered pits as illustrated in Figure 40.2, while the horizontally aligned ray cells constitute the principal pathway for radial flow, though it has been suggested that very fine capillaries within the cell wall may contribute slightly to radial flow. The rates of radial flow are found to vary very widely between species.

It is not surprising to find that the different pathways to flow in the three principal axes result in anisotropy in permeability. Thus for most timbers longitudinal permeability is about 10^4 times the transverse permeability and mathematical modelling of longitudinal and tangential flow supports a degree of anisotropy of this order. Since both longitudinal and tangential flow in softwoods are associated with bordered pits, a good correlation is to be expected between them; radial permeability is only poorly correlated with that in either of the other two directions and is frequently found to be greater than tangential permeability.

Permeability is not only directionally dependent, but is also found to vary with moisture content and between earlywood and latewood (Figure 40.3). In green timber the torus of the bordered pit is usually located in a central position and flow can be at a maximum (Figure 40.4(a)). Since the earlywood cells possess larger and more frequent bordered pits, the flow through the earlywood is considerably greater than that through the latewood. However, on drying, the torus of the earlywood cells becomes aspirated (Figures 38.10, 40.4(b)), owing, it is thought, to the tension stresses set up by the retreating water meniscus (Hart and Thomas, 1967): in this process the margo strands obviously undergo very considerable extension

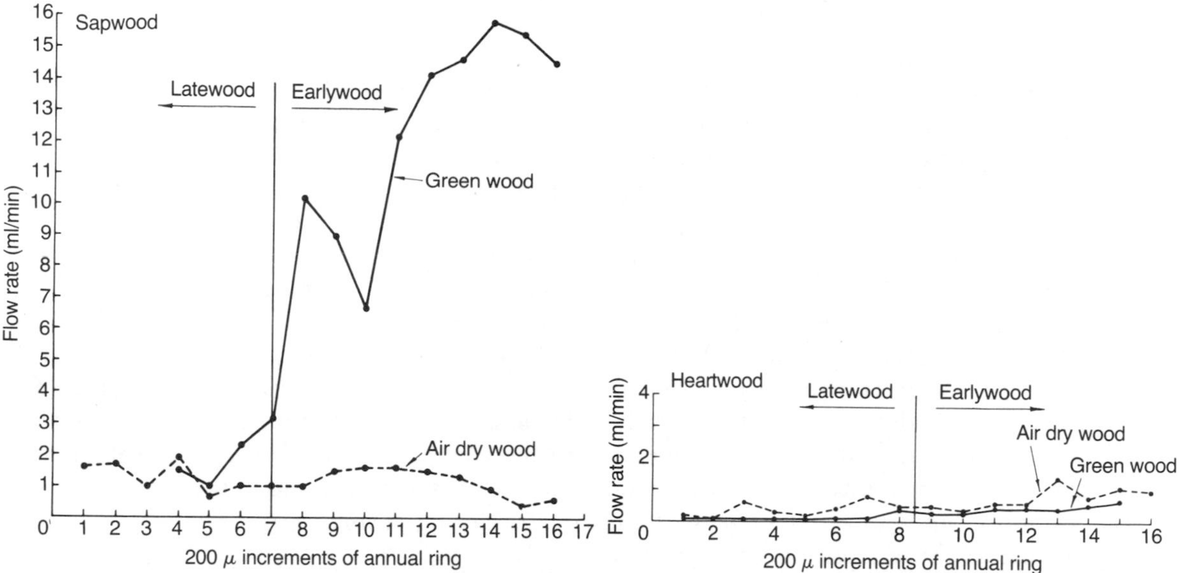

FIGURE 40.3 The variation in rate of longitudinal flow through samples of green and dry earlywood and latewood of Scots pine sapwood and heartwood (Banks (1968) © Crown copyright).

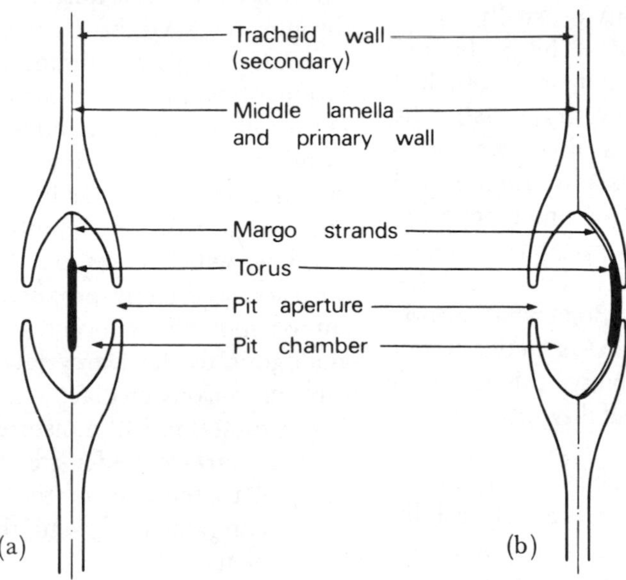

FIGURE 40.4 Cross-section of a bordered pit in the sapwood of a softwood timber: (a) in timber in the green condition with the torus in the 'normal' position; and (b) in timber in the dried state with the torus in an aspirated position (Building Research Establishment © Crown copyright).

and the torus is rigidly held in a displaced position by strong hydrogen bonding.

This displacement of the torus effectively seals the pit and reduces the level of permeability of dry earlywood to a value similar to that of green latewood. In the latewood, only about half the pits become aspirated and consequently the percentage reduction in permeability with drying is much lower than in the earlywood. Rewetting of the timber causes only a partial reduction in the number of aspirated pits and it appears that aspiration is mainly irreversible.

Quite apart from the fact that many earlywood pits are aspirated in the heartwood of softwoods, the permeability of the heartwood is usually appreciably lower than that of the sapwood due to the deposition of encrusting materials over the torus and margo strands and also within the ray cells (Figure 40.3).

Hardwoods

The longitudinal permeability is usually high in the sapwood of hardwoods. This is because these timbers possess vessels, the ends of which have been either completely or partially dissolved away. Radial flow is again by way of the rays, while tangential flow is more complicated, relying on the presence of pits interconnecting adjacent vessels, fibres and vertical parenchyma. Transverse flow rates are usually much lower than in the softwoods, but somewhat surprisingly a good correlation exists between tangential and radial permeability; this is due in part to the very low permeability of the rays in hardwoods.

Since the effects of bordered pit aspiration, so dominant in controlling the permeability of softwoods, are absent in hardwoods, the influence of drying on the level of permeability in hardwoods is very much less than is the case with softwoods.

Permeability is highest in the outer sapwood, decreasing inwards and reducing markedly with the onset of heartwood formation as the cells become blocked either by the deposition of gums or resins or, as happens in certain timbers, by the ingrowth into the vessels of the cell wall material of neighbouring cells, a process known as the formation of **tyloses**.

Of all the numerous physical and mechanical properties of timber, permeability is by far the most variable; when differences between timbers and differences between the principal directions within a timber are taken into consideration the range is of the order of 10^7.

Not only is it important in the impregnation of artificial preservatives, fire retardants and stabilizing chemicals, but it is also significant in the chemical removal of lignin in the manufacture of wood pulp and in the removal of **free** water during drying.

40.4.4 Moisture diffusion

Flow of water below the fibre saturation point embraces both the diffusion of water vapour through the void structure comprising the cell cavities and pit membrane pores and the diffusion of bound water through the cell walls. Diffusion is another manifestation of flow, conforming with the general relationship between flux and pressure. Thus it is possible to express diffusion of moisture in timber in terms of Fick's first law, which states that the flux of moisture diffusion is directly proportional to the gradient of moisture concentration; as such, it is analogous to the Darcy law on flow of fluids through porous media.

The total flux F of moisture diffusion through a plane surface under steady-state conditions is equal to the sum of the flux of the bound water component F_b and that of the vapour component F_v:

$$F = F_b + F_v. \tag{40.5}$$

The flux of the bound water can be written in terms of Fick's first law, thus:

$$F_b = \frac{dm}{dt} = -K_b \frac{du}{dx} \tag{40.6}$$

where dm/dt ($=m/tA$) is the flux (rate of mass transfer), du/dx is the moisture concentration gradient in the x-direction, and K_b is the bound water moisture conductivity coefficient.

Similarly the flux of the vapour movement can be expressed as

$$F_v = \frac{dm}{dt} = -\frac{K_v}{u}\frac{dh}{dx} \quad (40.7)$$

where dh/dx is the vapour pressure gradient in the x-direction, K_v is the moisture conductivity of the water vapour and

$$u = \frac{\text{Resistance of gross wood to vapour movement}}{\text{Resistance offered by still air of same dimensions}}$$

The vapour component of the total flux is usually much less than that for the bound water. The rate of diffusion of water vapour through timber at moisture contents below the fibre saturation point has been shown to yield coefficients similar to those for the diffusion of carbon dioxide, provided corrections are made for differences in molecular weight between the gases. This means that water vapour must follow the same pathway through timber as does carbon dioxide and implies that diffusion of water vapour through the cell walls is negligible in comparison to that through the cell cavities and pits.

40.5 Thermal conductivity

The passage through timber and wood-based panels of thermal energy complies with the general laws of flow. The capacity of the material to allow the passage of this form of energy is quantified in terms of its thermal conductivity which is therefore yet another material constant.

The basic law for flow of thermal energy is ascribed to Fourier and when described mathematically as

$$K_h = \frac{Hl}{tA\Delta T} \quad , \quad (40.8)$$

where K_h is the thermal conductivity, H is the quantity of heat, t is time, A is the cross-sectional area, l is the length and ΔT is the temperature differential, is analogous to that of Darcy (eqn (40.3)) for fluid flow.

Thermal conductivity increases slightly with increased moisture content, especially when calculated on a volume-fraction-of-cell-wall basis; however, it appears that conductivity of the cell wall substance is independent of moisture content. Conductivity is influenced considerably by the density of the timber, i.e. by the volume-fraction-of-cell-wall substance, and various empirical and linear relations between conductivity and density have been established. Conductivity will also vary with timber orientation due to its anisotropic structure: the longitudinal thermal conductivity is about 2.5 times the transverse conductivity, the mean value of which for a number of timbers is 0.15 W/m/K.

Compared with the metals the thermal conductivity of timber is extremely low, though it is generally about three to eight times higher than that of insulating materials. The transverse value for timber is about one-quarter that for brick, thereby explaining the lower heating requirements of timber houses compared with the traditional brick house.

40.6 References

Banks, W.B. (1968) A technique for measuring the lateral permeability of wood. *Journal of the Institute of Wood Science*, 4, No. 2, 35–41.

Hall, G.S. and Jackman, P.E. (1975) Performance of timber in fire. *Timber Trades Journal*, 15 Nov. 1975, 38–40.

Hart, C.A. and Thomas, R.J. (1967) Mechanism of bordered pit aspiration as caused by capillarity. *Forest Products Journal*, 17, No. 11, 61–8.

Petty, J.A. and Puritch, G.S. (1970) The effects of drying on the structure and permeability of the wood of *Abies grandis*. *Wood Science and Technology*, 4, No. 2, 140–54.

Chapter forty-one

Deformation in timber

41.1 Introduction
41.2 Dimensional change due to moisture
41.3 Thermal movement
41.4 Deformation under stress
41.5 References

41.1 Introduction

Timber may undergo dimensional changes solely on account of variations in climatic factors; on the other hand, deformation may be due solely to the effects of applied stress. Frequently stress and climate interact to produce enhanced levels of deformation.

This chapter commences by examining the dimensional changes that occur in timber following variations in its moisture content and/or temperature. The magnitude and consequently the significance of such changes in the dimensions of timber are much greater in the case of alterations in moisture content compared with temperature. Consequently, the greater emphasis in this first section is placed on the influence of changing moisture content. Later in the chapter the effect of stress on deformation will be examined in detail.

41.2 Dimensional change due to moisture

In timber it is customary to distinguish between those changes that occur when green timber is dried to very low moisture contents, and those that arise in timber of low moisture content due to seasonal or daily changes in the relative humidity of the surrounding atmosphere. The former changes are called **shrinkage** while the latter are known as **movement.**

41.2.1 Shrinkage

As explained in Chapter 38, removal of water from timber below the fibre saturation point occurs within the amorphous region of the cell wall and manifests itself by reductions in strength and stiffness, as well as inducing dimensional shrinkage of the material.

Anisotropy in shrinkage

The reduction in dimensions of the timber, technically known as **shrinkage**, can be considerable but, owing to the complex structure of the material, the degree of shrinkage is different on the three principal axes: in other words timber is anisotropic in its water relationships. The variation in degree of shrinkage that occurs between different timbers and, more important, the variation among the different axes are illustrated in Table 41.1. It should be noted that the values quoted in the table represent shrinkage on drying from the green state (i.e. >27%) to 12% moisture content, a level which is of considerable practical significance since at 12% moisture content timber is in equilibrium with an atmosphere having a relative humidity of 60% and a temperature of 20°C; these con-

TABLE 41.1 Shrinkage (%) on drying from green to 12% moisture content

Botanical name	*Commercial name*	*Transverse*		*Longitudinal*
		Tangential	*Radial*	
Chlorophora excelsa	Iroko	2.0	1.5	<0.1
Tectona grandis	Teak	2.5	1.5	<0.1
Pinus strobus	Yellow pine	3.5	1.5	<0.1
Picea abies	Whitewood	4.0	2.0	<0.1
Pinus sylvestris	Redwood	4.5	3.0	<0.1
Tsuga heterophylla	Western hemlock	5.0	3.0	<0.1
Quercus robur	European oak	7.5	4.0	<0.1
Fagus sylvatica	European beech	9.5	4.5	<0.1

ditions would be found in buildings having regular but intermittent heating.

From Table 41.1 it will be observed that shrinkage ranges from 0.1% to 10%, i.e. a 100-fold range. Longitudinal shrinkage, it will be noted, is always an order of magnitude less than transverse, while in the transverse plane radial shrinkage is usually some 60–70% of the corresponding tangential figure.

The anisotropy between longitudinal and transverse shrinkage amounting to 40:1 is due in part to the arrangement of cells in timber and in part to the particular orientation of the microfibrils in the middle layer of the secondary cell wall (S_2). Thus, since the microfibrils of the S_2 layer of the cell wall are inclined at an angle of about 15° to the vertical, the removal of water from the matrix and the consequent movement closer together of the microfibrils will result in a horizontal component of the movement considerably greater than the corresponding longitudinal component.

Various models have been used to account for shrinkage in terms of microfibrillar angles. These generally consider the cell wall to consist of an amorphous hygroscopic matrix in which are embedded parallel crystalline microfibrils which restrain swelling or shrinking of the matrix. Early models considered part of the wall as a flat sheet consisting only of an S_2 layer in which microfibrillar angle has a constant value. Later models have treated the cell wall as two equal-thickness layers having microfibrillar angles of equal and opposite sense, and these two-ply models have been developed extensively over the years to take into account the layered structure of the cell wall, differences in structure between radial and tangential walls, and variations in wall thickness. Although models such as these are still relatively crude in simulating the anatomical and chemical properties of wood, the degree of agreement between calculated and experimental values is usually very good.

The influence of microfibrillar angle on degree of longitudinal and transverse shrinkage described for normal wood is supported by evidence derived from experimental work on **compression wood**, one of the forms of reaction wood described in Chapter 38. Compression wood is characterized by possessing a middle layer to the cell wall, the microfibrillar angle of which can be as high as 45° though 20–30° is more usual. The longitudinal shrinkage is much higher and the transverse shrinkage correspondingly lower than in normal wood and it has been demonstrated that the values for compression wood can be accommodated on the shrinkage/angle curve for normal wood.

Differences in the degree of transverse shrinkage between tangential and radial planes (Table 41.1) can be explained in terms of: first, the restricting effect of the rays on the radial plane; second, the increased thickness of the middle lamella on the tangential plane compared with the radial; third, the difference in degree of lignification between the radial and tangential cell walls; fourth, the small difference in micro-fibrillar angle between the two walls; and fifth, the alternation of earlywood and latewood in the radial plane, which, because of the greater shrinkage of latewood, induces the weaker early-wood to shrink more tangentially than it would do if isolated. Considerable controversy reigns as to whether all five factors are actually involved and their relative significance.

Volumetric shrinkage, s_v, is slightly less than the sum of the three directional components and is given by:

$$s_v = 100[1 - (1 - 0.01s_l)(1 - 0.01s_r)(1 - 0.01s_t)] \qquad (41.1)$$

where the shrinkages are in percentages. This simplifies to

$$s_v = s_l + s_r + s_t - 0.01s_r s_t$$

and subsequently to

$$s_v = s_r + s_t \qquad (41.2)$$

as greater approximations become acceptable.

Practical significance

In order to avoid shrinkage of timber after fabrication, it is essential that it is dried down to a moisture content which is in equilibrium with the relative humidity of the atmosphere in which the article is to be located. A certain latitude can be tolerated in the case of timber frames and roof trusses, but in the production of furniture, window frames, flooring and sports goods it is essential that the timber is seasoned to the expected equilibrium conditions, namely 12% for regular intermittent heating and 10% in buildings with central heating, otherwise shrinkage in service will occur with loosening of joints, crazing of paint films, and buckling and delamination of laminates. An indication of the moisture content of timber used in different environments is presented in Figure 41.1.

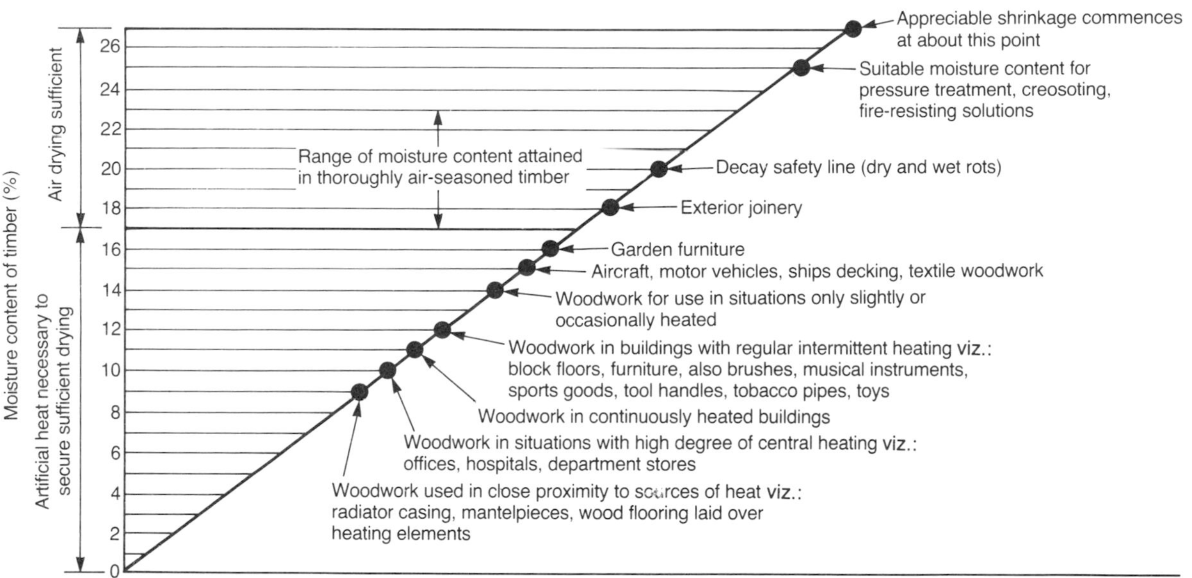

FIGURE 41.1 Equilibrium moisture content of timber in various environments. The figures for different species vary, and the chart shows only average values (Building Research Establishment © Crown copyright).

41.2.2 Movement

So far only those dimensional changes associated with the initial reduction in moisture content have been considered. However, dimensional changes, albeit smaller in extent, can also occur in seasoned or dried wood due to changes in the relative humidity of the atmosphere. Such changes certainly occur on a seasonal basis and frequently also on a daily basis. Since these changes in humidity are usually fairly small, inducing only slight changes in the moisture content of the timber, and since a considerable delay occurs in the diffusion of water vapour into the centre of a piece of timber it follows that these dimensional changes in seasoned timber are small, considerably smaller than those for shrinkage.

To quantify such movements for different timbers, dimensional changes are recorded over an arbitrary range of relative humidities. In the UK the standard procedure is to condition the timber in a chamber at 90% relative humidity and 25°C, to measure its dimensions and to transfer it to a chamber at 60% relative humidity, allowing it to come to equilibrium before remeasuring it; the corresponding change in moisture content is from 21% to 12%. Movement values in the tangential and radial planes for those timbers listed in Table 41.1 are presented in Table 41.2. The timbers are recorded in the same order, thus illustrating that although a broad relationship holds between values of shrinkage and movement, individual timbers can behave differently over the reduced range of moisture contents associated with movement. Since movement in the longitudinal plane is so small, it is generally ignored. Anisotropy within the transverse plane can be accounted for by the same set of variables that influence shrinkage.

Where timber is subjected to wide fluctuations in relative humidity care must be exercised in the selection of a species which has low movement values.

Moisture in timber has a very pronounced effect not only on its strength (Figure 38.19) but also on its stiffness, toughness and fracture morphology; these aspects are discussed in Chapter 39 and also later in this chapter.

41.3 Thermal movement

Timber, like other materials, undergoes dimensional changes commensurate with increasing temperature. This is attributed to the increasing distances between the molecules as they increase the magnitude of their oscillations with increasing temperature. Such movement is usually quantified for practical purposes as the coefficient of linear thermal expansion and values for certain timbers are listed in Table 41.3. Although differences occur between species these appear to be smaller than those occurring for shrinkage and movement. The coefficient for transverse

TABLE 41.2 Movement (%) on transferring timber from 90% relative humidity to 60%

Botanical name	*Commercial name*	*Tangential*	*Radial*
Chlorophora excelsa	Iroko	1.0	0.5
Tectona grandis	Teak	1.2	0.7
Pinus strobus	Yellow pine	1.8	0.9
Picea abies	Whitewood	1.5	0.7
Pinus sylvestris	Redwood	2.2	1.0
Tsuga heterophylla	Western hemlock	1.9	0.9
Quercus robur	European oak	2.5	1.5
Fagus sylvatica	European beech	3.2	1.7

TABLE 41.3 Coefficients of linear thermal expansion of various woods and board materials per degree kelvin

		Coefficient of thermal expansion × 10^{-6}/K	
		Longitudinal	*Transverse*
Picea abies	Whitewood	5.41	34.1
Pinus strobus	Yellow pine	4.00	72.7
Quercus robur	European oak	4.92	54.4
Plywood: five-ply birch			
In plane of board		7.6	
Through board		50.8	
Chipboard, in plane of board		10	

expansion is an order of magnitude greater than that in the longitudinal direction. This degree of anisotropy (10 : 1) can be related to the ratio of length to breadth dimensions of the crystalline regions within the cell wall. Anisotropy is absent in the board materials.

The expansion of timber with increasing temperature appears to be linear over a wide temperature range: the slight differences in expansion which occur between the radial and tangential planes are usually ignored and the coefficients are averaged to give a transverse value as recorded in Table 41.3.

The dimensional changes of timber caused by differences in temperature are small when compared to changes in dimensions resulting from the uptake or loss of moisture. Thus for timber with a moisture content greater than about 3%, the shrinkage due to moisture loss on heating will be greater than the thermal expansion, with the effect that the net dimensional change on heating will be negative. For most practical purposes thermal expansion or contraction can be safely ignored over the range of temperatures in which timber is generally employed.

41.4 Deformation under stress

This section is concerned with the type and magnitude of the deformation that results from the application of external stress. As in the case of both concrete and high polymers the stress–strain relationship is exceedingly complex, resulting from the facts that:

1. timber does not behave in a truly elastic mode, rather its behaviour is time-dependent; and
2. the magnitude of the strain is influenced by a wide range of factors; some of these are property-dependent, such as density of the timber, angle of the grain relative to the direction of load application, angle of the microfibrils within the cell wall; others are environmentally dependent, such as temperature and relative humidity.

Under service conditions timber has to withstand an imposed load for many years, perhaps even centuries. When loaded, timber will deform and a generalized interpretation of the variation of deformation with time together with the various components of this deformation is illustrated in Figure 41.2. On the application of a load at time zero an instantaneous (and reversible) deformation occurs which represents elastic behaviour. On maintaining the load to time t_1 the deformation increases, though the rate of increase is continually decreasing; this increase in deformation with time is termed **creep**. On removal of the load at time t_1 an instantaneous reduction in deformation occurs

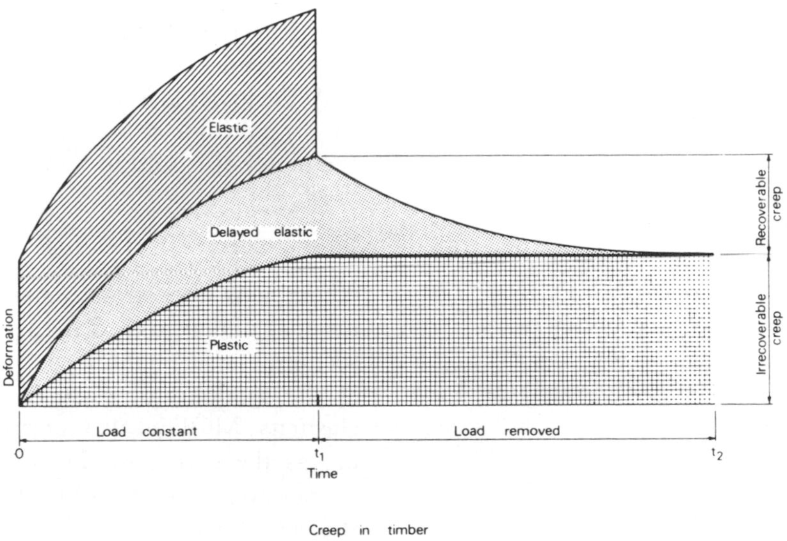

FIGURE 41.2 The various elastic and plastic components of the deformation of timber under constant load (Building Research Establishment © Crown copyright).

which is approximately equal in magnitude to the initial elastic deformation. With time, the remaining deformation will decrease at an ever-decreasing rate until at time t_2 no further reduction occurs. The creep that has occurred during stressing can be conveniently subdivided into a **reversible** component, which disappears with time and which can be regarded as **delayed elastic** behaviour, and an **irreversible** component which results from **plastic** or **viscous** flow. Therefore, timber on loading possesses three forms of deformation behaviour – elastic, delayed elastic and viscous. Like so many other materials timber can be treated neither as a truly elastic material where, by Hooke's law, stress is proportional to strain but independent of the rate of strain, nor as a truly viscous liquid where, according to Newton's law, stress is proportional to rate of strain but independent of strain itself. Where combinations of behaviour are encountered the material is said to be viscoelastic and timber, like many high polymers, is a viscoelastic material.

It has already been discussed how part of the deformation can be described as elastic and the section below will indicate how at low levels of stressing and short periods of time there is considerable justification for treating the material as such. Perhaps the greatest incentive to this viewpoint is the fact that classical elasticity theory is well established and when applied to timber has been shown to work very well. The question of time in any stress analysis can be accommodated by the use of safety factors in design calculations.

Consequently, this section will deal first with elastic deformation as representing a very good approximation of what happens, while the second part will deal with viscoelastic deformation, which embraces both delayed elastic and irreversible deformation.

41.4.1 Elastic deformation

When a sample of timber is loaded in tension, compression or bending the deformations obtained with increasing load are approximately proportional to the values of the applied

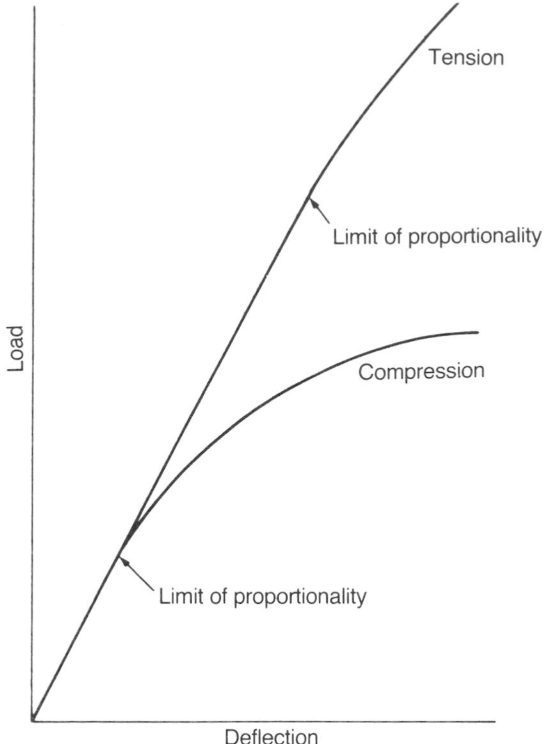

FIGURE 41.3 Load–deflection graphs for timber stressed in tension and compression parallel to the grain. The assumed limit of proportionality for each graph is indicated (Building Research Establishment © Crown copyright).

load. Figure 41.3 illustrates that this approximation is certainly truer of the experimental evidence in longitudinal tensile loading than in the case of longitudinal compression. In both modes of loading, the approximation appears to become a reality at the lower levels of loading. Thus it has become convenient to recognize a point of inflection on the load–deflection curve known as the **limit of proportionality**, below which the relationship between load and deformation is linear, and above which non-linearity occurs. Generally the limit of proportionality in longitudinal tension is found to occur at about 60% of the ultimate load to failure while in longitudinal compression the limit is considerably lower, varying from 30% to 50% of the failure value.

At the lower levels of loading, therefore, where the straight-line relationship appears to be valid the material is said to be linearly elastic. Hence

$$\varepsilon = \frac{\sigma}{E} \qquad (41.3)$$

where ε is the strain (change in dimension/original dimension), σ is the stress (load/cross-sectional area), and E is a constant, known as the modulus of elasticity. The modulus of elasticity, MOE, is also referred to in the literature as the elastic modulus, Young's modulus, or simply, though somewhat incorrectly, as stiffness.

The apparent linearity at the lower levels of

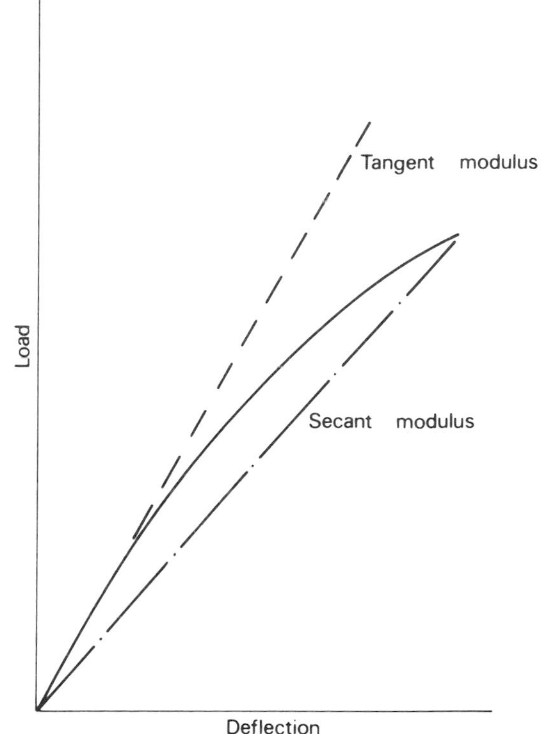

FIGURE 41.4 The approximation of a curvilinear load–deflection curve, for timber stressed at low loading rates, by linear tangent or secant regressions (Building Research Establishment © Crown copyright).

loading is really an artefact introduced by the rate of testing and the lack of precision: it is found not only in timber but in many other fibre composites. It is true that at fast rates of loading, or testing on insensitive equipment, a very good approximation to a straight line occurs, but as the rate of loading decreases, or the testing equipment sensitivity increases, the load–deflection line assumes a curvilinear shape (Figure 41.4). Such curves can be treated as linear by introducing a straight-line approximation, which can take the form of either a tangent or secant. Traditionally for timber and wood fibre composites tangent lines have been used as linear approximations of load–deflection curves.

Thus, while in theory it should be possible to obtain a true elastic response, in practice this is rarely the case, though the degree of divergence is frequently very low. It should be appreciated in passing that a curvilinear load–deflection curve must not be interpreted as an absence of true elastic behaviour. The material may still behave elastically, though not linearly elastically: the prime criterion for elastic behaviour is that the load–deflection curve is truly reversible, i.e. that no permanent deformation has occurred on release of the load.

The elastic behaviour of a material can be characterized by three types of elastic constants, the first of which, the modulus of elasticity, has been described above. The second type of constant is the modulus of rigidity, G. Within the elastic range, shearing stress is proportional to shearing strain. Thus

$$G = \frac{\tau}{\gamma} \tag{41.4}$$

where τ is the shearing stress and γ is the shearing strain.

The third type of constant is Poisson's ratio. Generally, when a body is subjected to a stress in one direction, the body will undergo a change in dimensions at right angles to the direction of stressing. The ratio of the contraction or extension to the applied strain is known as Poisson's ratio and for isotropic bodies is given as

$$\nu = -\frac{\varepsilon_y}{\varepsilon_x} \tag{41.5}$$

where ε_x and ε_y are strains in the x- and y-directions resulting from an applied stress in the x-direction. (The minus sign indicates that, when ε_x is a tensile positive strain, ε_y is a compressive negative strain.) In timber, because of its anisotropic behaviour and its treatment as a rhombic system, six Poisson's ratios occur.

Orthotropic elasticity and timber

In applying the elements of orthotropic elasticity to wood, and board materials made from wood, the assumption is made that the three principal elasticity directions coincide with the longitudinal, radial and tangential directions in the tree. The assumption implies that the tangential faces are straight and not curved, and that the radial faces are parallel and not diverging. However, by dealing with small pieces of timber removed at some distance from the centre of the tree, the approximation of rhombic symmetry for a system possessing circular symmetry becomes more and more acceptable.

The nine independent constants required to specify the elastic behaviour of timber are the three moduli of elasticity, one in each of the L, R and T directions; the three moduli of rigidity, one in each of the principal planes LT, LR and TR; and three Poisson's ratios, namely ν_{RT}, ν_{LR}, ν_{TL}. These constants, together with the three dependent Poisson's ratios ν_{RL}, ν_{TR}, ν_{LT} are presented in Table 41.4 for a selection of hardwoods and softwoods.

The table illustrates the high degree of anisotropy present in timber. Comparison of E_L with either E_R or E_T, and G_{TR} with G_{LT} or G_{LR} will indicate a degree of anisotropy which can be as high as 60:1. Note should be taken that the values of ν_{TR} are frequently greater than 0.5.

TABLE 41.4 Elastic constants of certain timbers (from Hearmon (1948), but with different notation for Poisson's ratios)

Species	*Density (kg/m^3)*	*Moisture content (%)*	E_L	E_R	E_T	υ_{TR}	υ_{LR}	υ_{RT}	υ_{LT}	υ_{RL}	υ_{TL}	G_{LT}	G_{LR}	G_{TR}
Hardwoods														
Balsa	200	9	6 300	300	106	0.66	0.018	0.24	0.009	0.23	0.49	203	312	33
Khaya	440	11	10 200	1130	510	0.60	0.033	0.26	0.032	0.30	0.64	600	900	210
Walnut	590	11	11 200	1190	630	0.72	0.052	0.37	0.036	0.49	0.63	700	960	230
Birch	620	9	16 300	1110	620	0.78	0.034	0.38	0.018	0.49	0.43	910	1180	190
Ash	670	9	15 800	1510	800	0.71	0.051	0.36	0.030	0.46	0.51	890	1340	270
Beech	750	11	13 700	2240	1140	0.75	0.073	0.36	0.044	0.45	0.51	1060	1610	460
Softwoods														
Norway spruce	390	12	10 700	710	430	0.51	0.030	0.31	0.025	0.38	0.51	620	500	23
Sitka spruce	390	12	11 600	900	500	0.43	0.029	0.25	0.020	0.37	0.47	720	750	39
Scots pine	550	10	16 300	1100	570	0.68	0.038	0.31	0.015	0.42	0.51	680	1160	66
Douglas fir*	590	9	16 400	1300	900	0.63	0.028	0.40	0.024	0.43	0.37	910	1180	79

* Also known as Oregon pine.
E is the modulus of elasticity in a direction indicated by the subscript (in N/mm^2).
G is the modulus of rigidity in a plane indicated by the subscript (in N/mm^2).

v_{ij} is Poisson's ratio for an extensional stress in the j direction $= \dfrac{\text{compressive strain in } i \text{ direction}}{\text{extensional strain in } j \text{ direction}}$.

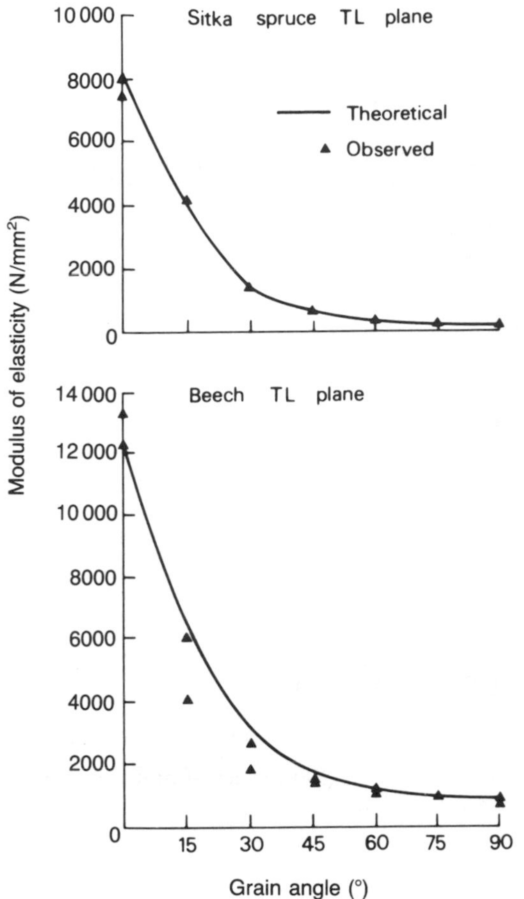

FIGURE 41.5 Effect of grain angle on the modulus of elasticity. The theoretical line has been calculated by transformation of the stresses and strains from the rotated to the principal axes (Building Research Establishment © Crown copyright).

Factors influencing the elastic modulus

The stiffness of timber is influenced by many factors, some of them properties of the material while others are components of the environment.

Grain angle

The angle at which the cells in the block of wood lie with respect to the direction of principal stress has a most marked influence on the magnitude of the elastic properties. This effect is illustrated for modulus of elasticity in Figure 41.5: for both a softwood and a hardwood, modulus decreased very rapidly with increasing angle up to an angle of 30° after which the rate of decline slowed down. The loss in modulus at an angle of only 15° is about 50%.

Density

Stiffness is related to density of the timber, a relationship which was apparent in Table 41.4 and which is confirmed by the plot of over 200 species of timber (Figure 41.6); the correlation coefficient is 0.88 for timber at 12% moisture content, and 0.81 for green timber and the relation is curvilinear. A high correlation is to be expected, since density is a function of the ratio of cell wall thickness to cell diameter: consequently increasing density will result in increasing stiffness of the cell.

Owing to the variability in structure that exists between different timbers the relation between density and stiffness will be higher where only a single species is under investigation. Because of the reduced range in density the regression is usually linear.

Similar relations with density have been recorded for the modulus of rigidity in certain species: in others, however, for example spruce, both the longitudinal–tangential and longitudinal–radial shear moduli have been found to be independent of density. Most investigators agree, however, that the Poisson's ratios are independent of density.

Knots

Since timber is anisotropic in behaviour, and since knots are characterized by the occurrence of distorted grain, it is not surprising to find that the presence of knots in timber results in a reduction in the stiffness. The relation is difficult to quantify since the effect of the knots will depend not only on their number and size but also on their distribution both along the length of the sample and across the faces. Dead knots, especially where the knot has fallen out, will

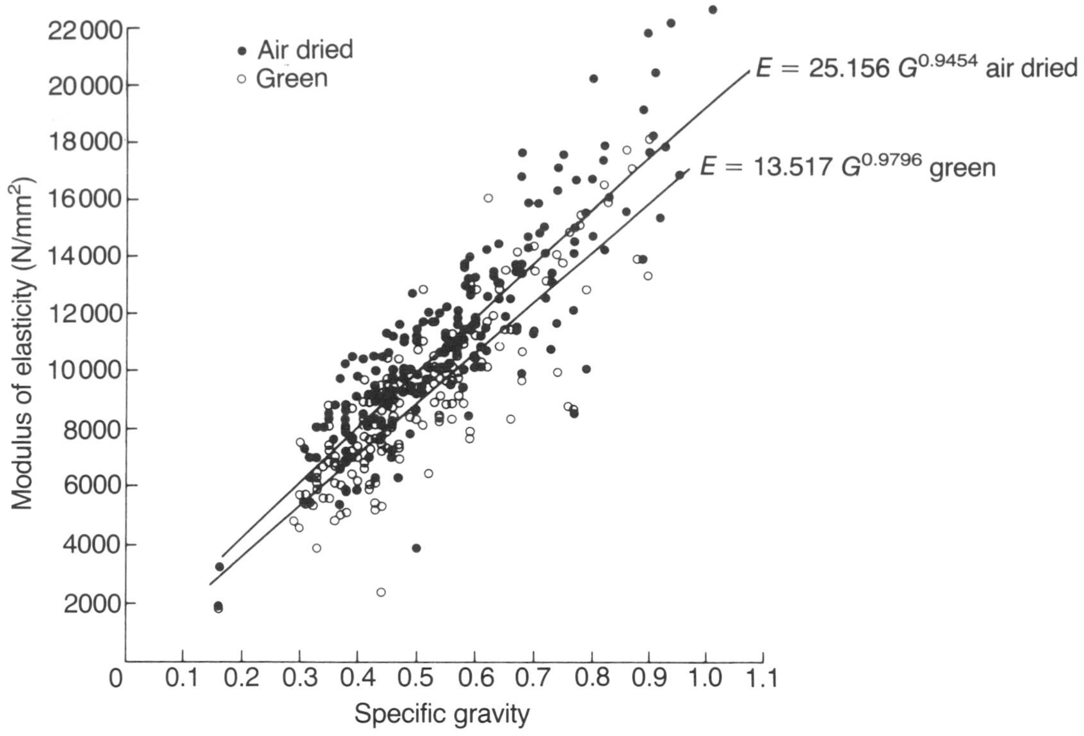

FIGURE 41.6 Effect of specific gravity on the modulus of elasticity for over 200 species of timber tested in the green and dry states (Building Research Establishment © Crown copyright).

result in larger reductions in stiffness than will green knots (see Chapter 38).

Ultrastructure

Two components of the fine or chemical structure have a profound influence on both the elastic and rigidity moduli. The first relates to the existence of a matrix material with particular emphasis on the presence of lignin. In those plants devoid of lignin, e.g. the grasses, or in wood fibres which have been delignified, the stiffness of the cells is low and it would appear that lignin, apart from its hydrophilic protective role for the cellulosic crystallites, is responsible to a considerable extent for the high stiffness found in timber.

The significance of lignin in determining stiffness is not to imply that the cellulose fraction plays no part: on the contrary it has been shown that the angle at which the microfibrils are lying in the middle layer of the secondary cell wall, S_2, also plays a significant role in controlling stiffness (Figure 41.7).

A considerable number of mathematical models have been devised to relate stiffness to microfibrillar angle. The early ones were two-dimensional in approach, treating the cell wall as a planar slab of material, but over the years the models have become much more sophisticated, taking into account the existence of cell wall layers other than the S_2, the variation in microfibrillar angle between the radial and tangential walls and consequently the probability that they undergo different strains, and, lastly, the possibility of complete shear restraint within the cell wall. These three-dimensional

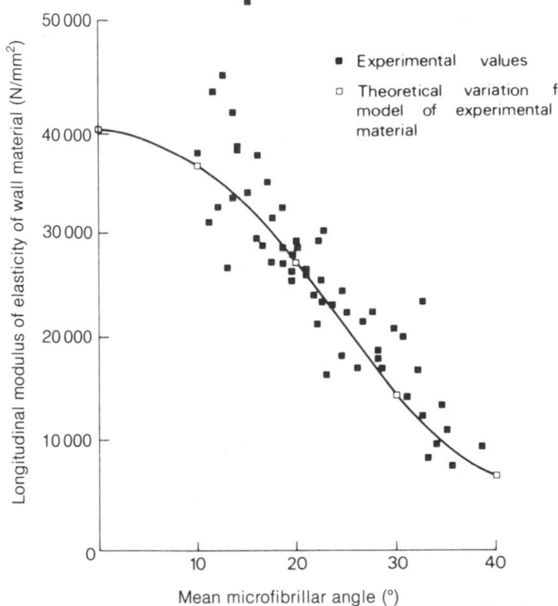

FIGURE 41.7 Effect of the mean microfibrillar angle of the cell wall on the longitudinal modulus of elasticity of the wall material in *Pinus radiata*. Calculated values from a mathematical model are also included (Cave (1968) by permission of Springer-Verlag).

models are frequently analysed using finite element techniques.

Recent modelling of timber behaviour in terms of structure uses the concept of an elastic fibre composite consisting of an inert fibre phase embedded in a water-reactive matrix. The constitutive relation is related to the overall stiffness of the composite, the volume fraction, stiffness and sorption characteristics of the matrix, and unlike previous models the equation can be applied not only to elasticity but also to shrinkage and even moisture induced creep (Cave, 1975).

Stiffness of a material is very dependent on the type and degree of chemical bonding within its structure and the abundance of covalent bonding in the longitudinal plane and hydrogen bonding in the transverse planes contribute considerably to the moderately high levels of stiffness characteristic of timber.

Moisture content

The influence of moisture content on stiffness is similar to though not quite so sensitive as that for strength as illustrated in Figure 38.19. Early experiments by Carrington (1922), in which stiffness was measured on a specimen of Sitka spruce as it took up moisture from the dry state, clearly indicated a linear loss in stiffness as the moisture content increased to about 30%, corresponding to the fibre saturation point as discussed in Chapter 38; further increase in moisture content has no influence on stiffness.

Carrington's results for the variation in longitudinal moduli have been confirmed using simple

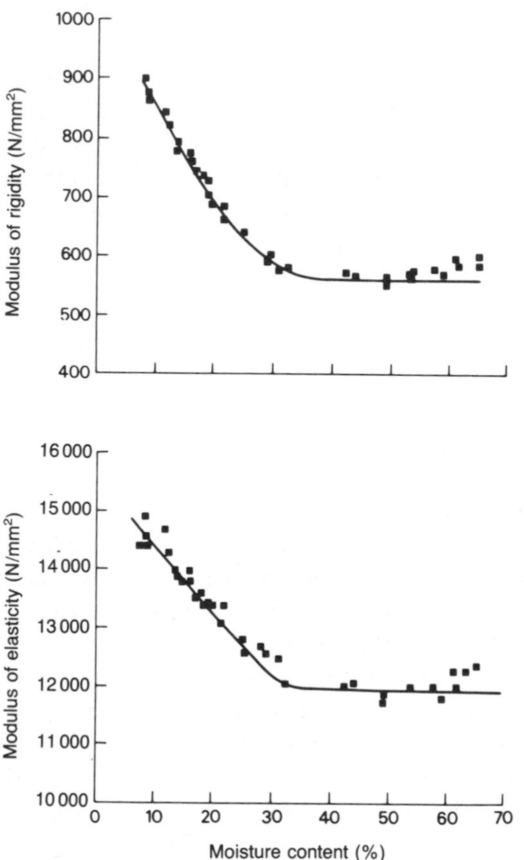

FIGURE 41.8 Effect of moisture content on the moduli of elasticity and rigidity in Sitka spruce. Both moduli were determined dynamically (Building Research Establishment © Crown copyright).

dynamic methods. Measurement of the frequency of vibration was carried out at regular intervals as samples of Sitka spruce were dried from 70% to zero moisture content (Figure 41.8).

Confirmation of the reduction in modulus of elasticity with increasing moisture content is forthcoming from Figure 41.6, in which the regression lines of elasticity against density for over 200 species of timber at 12% moisture content and in the green state are presented.

When timber is stressed in compression at constant relative humidity it will give up water to the atmosphere, and conversely under tensile stressing it will absorb moisture (Barkas, 1945). The equilibrium strain, therefore, will be the sum of that produced elastically and that caused by moisture loss or gain. It is therefore necessary to distinguish between the elastic constants at constant humidity (E_h) and those measured at constant moisture content (E_m). The ratio of E_h/E_m is 0.92 in the tangential direction, 0.95 in the radial direction and 1.0 in the longitudinal direction when spruce is stressed at 90% relative humidity. At 40% the ratio increases to 0.98 and 0.99 in the tangential and radial directions respectively (Hearmon, 1948).

Temperature

In timber, like most other materials, increasing temperature results in greater oscillatory movement of the molecules and an enlargement of the crystal lattice. These in turn affect the mechanical properties and the stiffness and strength of the material decrease.

Although the relationship between stiffness and temperature has been shown experimentally to be curvilinear, the degree of curvature is usually slight at low moisture contents and the relation is frequently treated as linear thus:

$$E_T = E_t[1 - a(T - t)] \qquad (41.6)$$

where E is the elastic modulus, T is a higher temperature, t is a lower temperature, and a is the temperature coefficient. The value a for longitudinal modulus has been shown to lie between 0.001 and 0.007 for low moisture contents.

At higher moisture contents the relationship of stiffness and temperature is markedly curvilinear and the interaction of moisture content and temperature in influencing stiffness is clearly shown in Figure 41.9, which summarizes the extensive work of Sulzberger (1947). At zero moisture content the reduction in stiffness between −20°C and +60°C is only 6%: at 20% moisture content the reduction is 40%.

41.4.2 Viscoelastic deformation

In the introduction to the deformation of timber under stress (Section 41.4) timber was described as being neither truly elastic in its behaviour nor truly viscous, but rather a combination of both states; such behaviour is usually described as viscoelastic and, in addition to timber, materials such as concrete, bitumen and the thermoplastics are also viscoelastic in their response to stress.

Viscoelasticity implies that the behaviour of the material is time-dependent; at any instant in time under load its performance will be a function of its past history. If the time factor under load is reduced to zero, a state which we can picture in concept but never attain in practice, the material will behave truly elastically. However, where stresses are applied for a period of time, viscoelastic behaviour will be experienced and, while it is possible to apply elasticity theory with a factor covering the increase in deformation with time, this procedure is at best only a first approximation.

In a material such as timber time-dependent behaviour manifests itself in a number of ways of which the more common are **creep, relaxation, damping capacity**, and the dependence of strength on **duration of load**. When the load on a sample of timber is held constant for a period of time the increase in deformation over the initial instantaneous elastic deformation is called creep and Figure 41.2 illustrates not only the

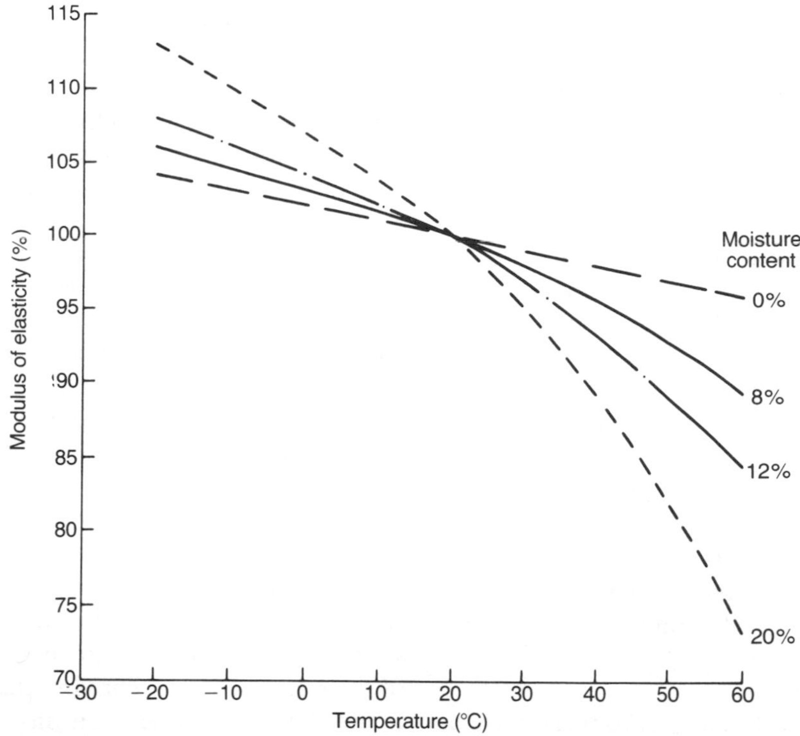

FIGURE 41.9 The interaction of temperature and moisture content on the modulus of elasticity. Results are averaged for six species of timber and the modulus at 20°C and 0% moisture content is taken as unity (Building Research Establishment © Crown copyright).

increase in creep with time but also the subdivision of creep into a reversible and an irreversible component of which more will be said in a later section.

Most timber structures carry a considerable dead load and the component members of these will undergo creep; the dip towards the centre of the ridge of the roof of very old buildings bears testament to the fact that timber does creep. However, compared to thermoplastics and bitumen the amount of creep in timber is appreciably lower.

Viscoelastic behaviour is also apparent in the form of relaxation where the load necessary to maintain a constant deformation decreases with time; in timber utilization this has limited practical significance and the area has attracted very little research. Damping capacity is a measure of the fractional energy converted to heat compared with that stored per cycle under the influence of mechanical vibrations; this ratio is time-dependent. A further manifestation of viscoelastic behaviour is the apparent loss in strength of timber with increasing duration of load; this feature is discussed in detail in Chapter 39 and illustrated in Figure 39.6.

Creep

Creep parameters

It is possible to quantify creep by a number of time-dependent parameters of which the two most common are **creep compliance** (known also as **specific creep**) and **relative creep** (known also as the **creep coefficient** or **creep factor**);

both parameters are a function of temperature.

Creep compliance is the ratio of increasing strain with time to the applied constant stress, i.e.

$$c_c(t, T) = \frac{\text{(varying) strain}}{\text{applied constant stress}} \quad (41.7)$$

while relative creep is defined as either the deflection or the increase in deflection at time t expressed in terms of the initial elastic deflection, i.e.

$$c_r(t, T) = \frac{\varepsilon_t}{\varepsilon_0} \quad \text{or} \quad \frac{\varepsilon_t - \varepsilon_0}{\varepsilon_0} \quad (41.8)$$

where ε_t is the deflection at time t, and ε_0 is the initial deflection.

Relative creep has also been defined as the change in compliance during the test expressed in terms of the original compliance.

Creep relationships

In both timber and timber products such as plywood or chipboard the rate of deflection or creep slows down progressively with time (Figure 41.10); the creep is frequently plotted against log time and the graph assumes an exponential shape. Results of creep tests can also be plotted as relative creep against log time or as creep compliance against stress as a percentage of the ultimate short-term stress.

In Section 41.4.1 it was shown that the degree of elasticity varied considerably between the horizontal and longitudinal planes. Creep, as one particular manifestation of viscoelastic behaviour, is also directionally dependent. In tensile stressing of longitudinal sections produced with the grain running at different angles it was found that relative creep was greater in the direction perpendicular to the grain than it was parallel to the grain.

When creep compliance is plotted against stress as a percentage of the ultimate short-term stress, the relation is linear over the lower half of the range in stress. For viscoelastic behaviour to be defined as linear the instantaneous, recoverable and non-recoverable components of

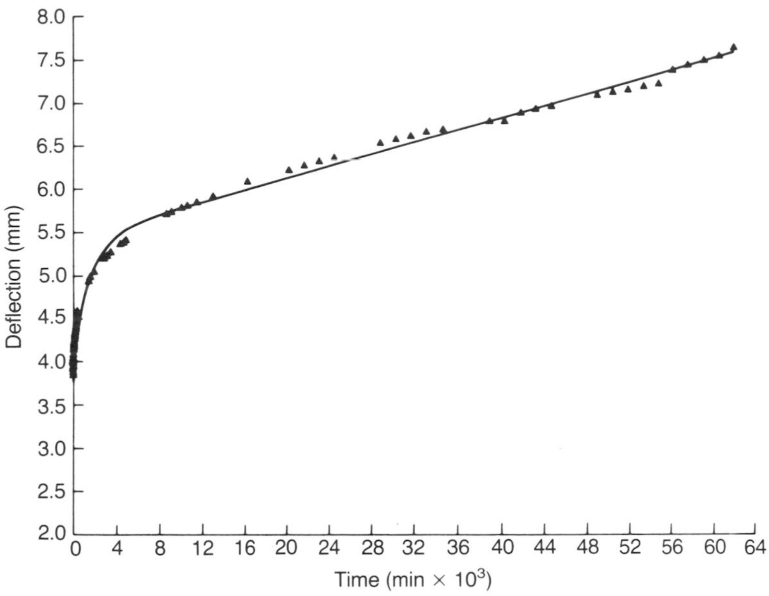

FIGURE 41.10 The increase in deformation with time of urea-formaldehyde-bonded chipboard; the regression line has been fitted to the experimental values using eqn (41.12) (Building Research Establishment © Crown copyright).

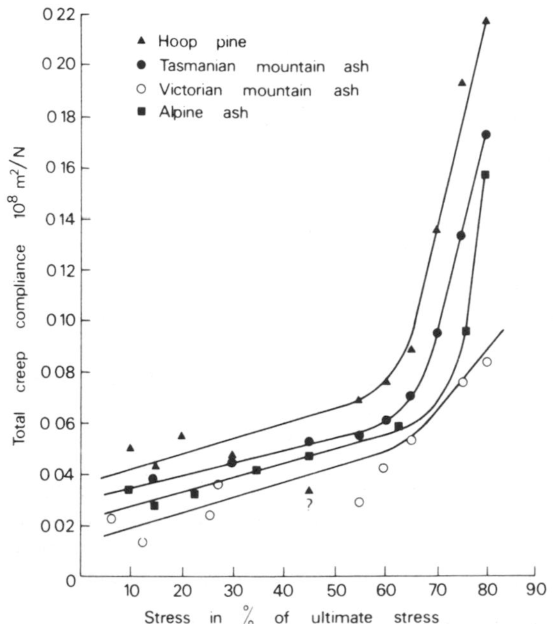

FIGURE 41.11 The relation of total creep compliance to stress as a percentage of the ultimate for four Australian species loaded in bending for 20 hours (Kingston and Budgen (1972) by permission of Springer-Verlag).

the deformation must vary directly with the applied stress. An alternative definition is that the ratio of stress to strain is a function of time (or frequency) alone and not of stress magnitude; such a relation appears as a straight isochronous graph.

The linear limit for the relation between creep and applied stress varies with mode of testing, with species of timber (Figure 41.11), and with both temperature and moisture content. In tension parallel to the grain at constant temperature and moisture content timber has been found to behave as a linear viscoelastic material up to about 75% of the ultimate tensile strength, though some workers have found considerable variability and have indicated a range from 36% to 84%. In compression parallel to the grain the onset of non-linearity appears to occur at about 70%, though the level of actual stress will be much lower than in the case of tensile strength since the ultimate compression strength is only one-third that of the tensile strength. In bending, non-linearity seems to develop very much earlier at about 56–60% (Figure 41.11); the actual stress levels will be very similar to those for compression.

In both compression and bending the divergence from linearity is usually greater than in the case of tensile stressing; much of the increased deformation occurs in the non-recoverable component of creep and is associated with progressive structural changes including the development of incipient failure (Section 39.7.1).

Increase not only in stress level, but also in temperature to a limited extent, and moisture content to a considerable degree, results in an earlier onset of non-linearity and a more marked departure from it. For most practical situations, however, working stresses are only a small percentage of the ultimate, rarely approaching even 50%, and it can be safely assumed that timber, like concrete, will behave as a linear viscoelastic material.

Principle of superposition

Since timber behaves as a linear viscoelastic material under conditions of normal temperature and humidity and at low to moderate levels of stressing, it is possible to apply Boltzmann's principle of superposition to predict the response of timber to complex or extended loading sequences. This principle states that the creep occurring under a sequence of stress increments is taken as the superposed sum of the responses to the individual increments. This can be expressed mathematically in a number of forms, one of which for linear materials is:

$$\varepsilon_c(t) = \sum_{1}^{n} \Delta\sigma_i c_{ci} \qquad (41.9)$$

where n is the number of load increments, $\Delta\sigma_i$ is the stress increment, c_{ci} is the creep compliance for the individual stress increments applied for differing times, $t - \tau_1, t - \tau_2, \ldots, t - \tau_n$, and

$\varepsilon_c(t)$ is the total creep at time t; or in integrated form

$$\varepsilon_c(t) = \int_{\tau_1}^{t} c_c(t - \tau)\frac{d\sigma}{d\tau}(\tau)\, d\tau. \quad (41.10)$$

In experiments on timber the superposition principle was found to be applicable even to high stresses in both shear and tension of dry samples. However, at high moisture contents the limits of linear behaviour appear to be considerably lower and it has been shown that superposition is no longer applicable at stresses somewhat below half the failing stress.

Mathematical expressions of creep

The relationship between creep and time has been expressed mathematically using a wide range of equations. It should be appreciated that such expressions are purely empirical, none of them possessing any sound theoretical basis. Their relative merits depend on how easily their constants can be determined and how well they fit the experimental results.

The most successful mathematical description for timber appears to be of the type

$$\varepsilon(t) = \varepsilon_0 + at^m \quad (41.11)$$

where $\varepsilon(t)$ is the time-dependent strain, ε_0 is the initial elastic deformation, a and m are constants ($m = 0.33$ for timber), and t is the elapsed time.

Creep behaviour in timber, like that of many other high polymers, has been interpreted with the aid of mechanical models comprising different combinations of springs and dashpots; the springs act as a mechanical analogue of the elastic component of deformation, while the dashpot simulates the viscous or flow component. When more than a single member of each type is used, these components can be combined in a wide variety of ways, though only one or two will be able to describe adequately the creep and relaxation behaviour of the material.

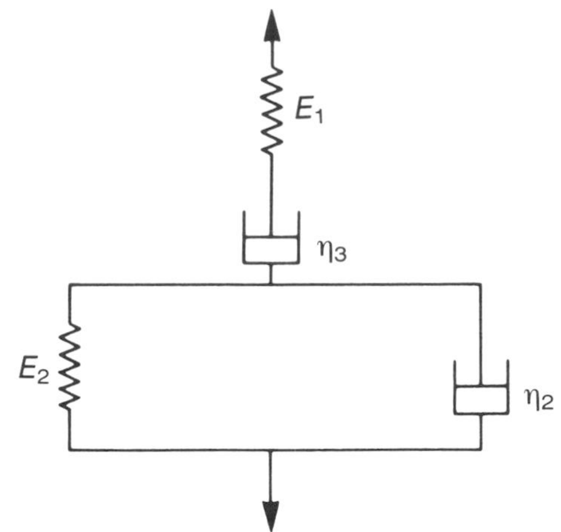

FIGURE 41.12 Mechanical analogue of the components of creep: the springs simulate elastic deformation and the dashpots viscous flow. The model corresponds to eqn (41.12) (Building Research Establishment © Crown copyright).

The simplest linear model which goes a long way to simulate the time-dependent behaviour of timber is the four element model illustrated in Figure 41.12; the lower part of the model will be recognized as a Kelvin element. To this unit has been added in series a second spring and dashpot. The strain at any time t under a constant load is given by the mathematical model

$$\varepsilon(t) = \frac{\sigma}{E_1} + \frac{\sigma}{E_2}(1 - e^{-t/\tau_2}) + \frac{\sigma t}{\eta_3} \quad (41.12)$$

where $\varepsilon(t)$ is the strain at time t, E_1 is the elasticity of spring 1, E_2 is the elasticity of spring 2, σ is the stress applied, η_3 is the viscosity of dashpot 3, and $\tau_2 = \eta_2/E_2$ = viscosity of dashpot 2/elasticity of spring 2.

The first term on the right-hand side represents the instantaneous deformation, while the second term describes the delayed elasticity and the third term the plastic flow component. Thus the first term describes the elastic behaviour while the combination of the second and third terms accounts for the viscoelastic or creep behaviour. The response of this particular model will be linear and it will obey the Boltzmann superposition principle. The degree of fit of the mathematically derived line and the experimentally derived values can be exceedingly good, as illustrated in Figure 41.10 for creep in bending of urea-formaldehyde-bonded chipboard.

A more demanding test of any model is the prediction of long-term performance from short-term data. For timber and the various board materials it has been found necessary to make the viscous term non-linear in these models where accurate predictions of creep (±10%) are required for long periods of time (>10 years) from short-term data (6–9 months). Consequently, while it is possible to treat timber and board materials at low levels of stress and short periods of time as linear viscoelastic materials, at high levels of stressing or when stressed at low levels for long periods of time, both timber and the board materials must be treated as non-linear viscoelastic materials.

Reversible and irreversible components of creep
In timber and many of the high polymers creep under load can be subdivided into reversible and irreversible components: passing reference to this was made in Section 41.4 and the generalized relationship with time was depicted in Figure 41.2. The relative proportions of these two components of total creep appear to be

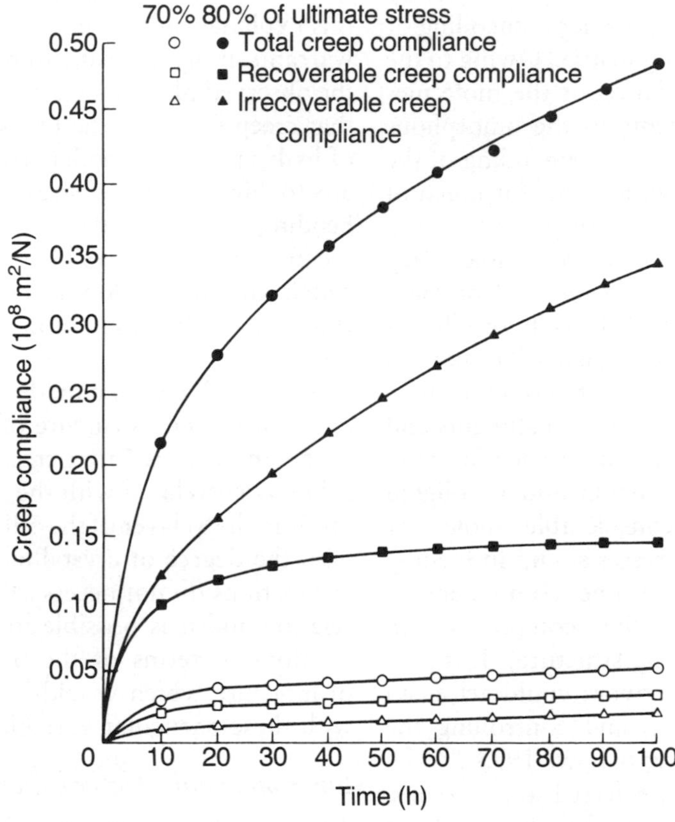

FIGURE 41.13 The relative proportions of the recoverable and irrecoverable creep compliance in samples of hoop pine (*Araucaria cunninghamii*) stressed in bending (Kingston and Budgen (1972) by permission of Springer-Verlag).

related to stress level and to prevailing conditions of temperature and moisture content.

The influence of level of stress is clearly illustrated in Figure 41.13, where the total compliance at 70% and 80% of the ultimate stress for hoop pine in compression is subdivided into the separate components: at 70% the irreversible creep compliance accounts for about 45% of the total creep compliance, while at 80% of the ultimate the irreversible creep compliance has increased appreciably to 70% of the total creep compliance at the longer periods of time, though not at the shorter durations. Increased moisture content and increased temperature will also result in an enlargement of the irreversible component of total creep.

Reversible creep is frequently referred to in the literature as delayed elastic or primary creep and is ascribed to either polymeric uncoiling or the existence of a creeping matrix. Owing to the close longitudinal association of the molecules of the various components in the amorphous regions it appears unlikely that uncoiling of the polymers under stress can account for much of the reversible component of creep.

The second explanation of reversible creep utilizes the concept of time-dependent two-stage molecular motions of the cellulose, hemicellulose and the lignin constituents. The pattern of molecular motion for each component is dependent on that of the other constituents and it has been shown that the difference in directional movement of the lignin and non-lignin molecules results in considerable molecular interference such that stresses set up in loading can be transferred from one component (a creeping matrix) to another component (an attached, but non-creeping structure). It is postulated that the lignin network could act as an energy sink, maintaining and controlling the energy set up by stressing (Chow, 1973).

Irreversible creep, also referred to as viscous, plastic or secondary creep, has been related to either time-dependent changes in the active number of hydrogen bonds, or to the loosening and subsequent remaking of hydrogen bonds as moisture diffuses through timber with the passage of time. Such diffusion can result directly from stressing; thus it has been found that when timber was stressed in tension it gained in moisture content, and conversely when stressed in compression its moisture content was lowered (Barkas, 1945). It is argued, though certainly not proven, that the movement of moisture by diffusion occurs in a series of steps from one absorption site to the next, necessitating the rupture and subsequent reformation of hydrogen bonds. The process is viewed as resulting in loss of stiffness and/or strength, possibly through slippage at the molecular level. However, it has been demonstrated that moisture movement, while affecting creep, can account for only part of the total creep obtained, and this explanation of creep at the molecular level warrants more investigation; certainly not all the observed phenomena support the hypothesis that creep is due to the breaking and remaking of hydrogen bonds under stress bias. At moderate to high levels of stressing, particularly in bending and compression parallel to the grain, the amount of irreversible creep is closely associated with the development of incipient failures: this point is discussed in more detail in Section 39.7.1.

Attempts have been made to describe creep in terms of the fine structure of timber and it has been demonstrated that creep in the short term is highly correlated with the angle of the microfibrils in the S_2 layer of the cell wall, and inversely with the degree of crystallinity. However, such correlations do not necessarily prove any causal relation and it is possible to explain these correlations in terms of the presence or absence of moisture which would be closely associated with these particular variables.

Environmental effects on rate of creep

Temperature In common with many other materials, especially the high polymers, the effect of increasing temperature on timber under stress is

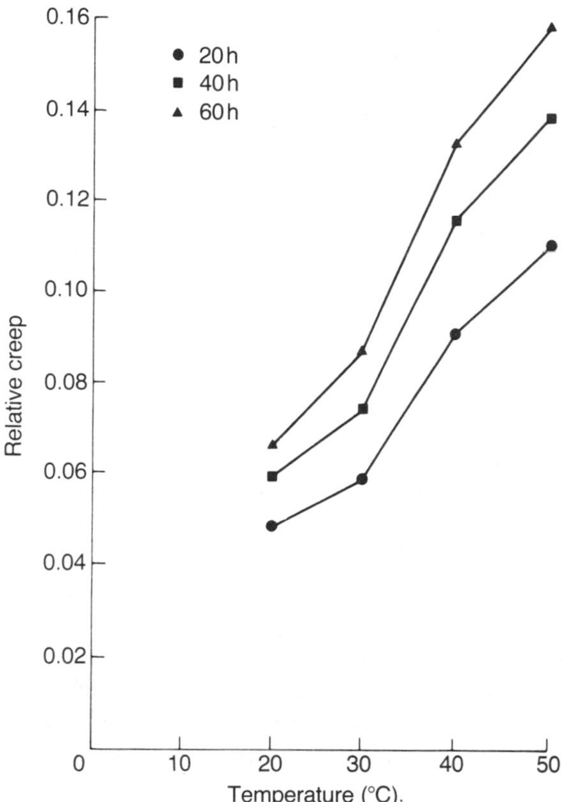

FIGURE 41.14 The effect of temperature on relative creep of samples of hoop pine (*Araucaria cunninghamii*) loaded in compression for 20, 40 and 60 hours (Kingston and Budgen (1972) by permission of Springer-Verlag).

to increase both the rate and the total amount of creep. Figure 41.14 illustrates a two-and-a-half-fold increase in the amount of creep as the temperature is raised from 20°C to 54°C; there is a marked increase in the irreversible component of creep at the higher temperatures. Cycling between low and high temperatures will induce in stressed timber a higher creep response than would occur if the temperature was held constant at the higher level.

Research has indicated that the principle of time–temperature superposition which is widely used in creep investigations on plastics is not applicable to creep in timber or timber-based board materials.

Moisture content The rate and amount of creep in timber of high moisture content is appreciably higher than that of dry timber. Moreover, if the moisture content of the timber under load is cycled from dry to wet and back to dry again the deformation will also follow a cyclic pattern; however, the recovery in each cycle is only partial and over a number of cycles the total amount of creep is very large: the greater the moisture differential in each cycle the higher the amount of creep (Hearmon and Paton, 1964). Figure 41.15 illustrates the deflection that occurs with time in matched samples loaded to $\frac{3}{8}$ ultimate short-term load where one is maintained in an atmosphere of 93% relative humidity, while the other is cycled between 0 and 93% relative humidity. After 14 complete cycles the latter sample had broken after increasing its initial deflection by 25 times; the former sample was still intact having increased in deflection by only twice its initial deflection. Failure of the first beam occurred, therefore, after only a short period of time and at a stress equivalent to only $\frac{3}{8}$ of its ultimate.

It should be appreciated that creep increased during the drying cycle and decreased during the wetting cycle with the exception of the initial wetting when creep increased. Unfortunately, the explanation of this phenomenon in terms of the microstructure of the timber is not yet forthcoming, though it must in some way be related to the diffusion of vapour through the cell wall and the rupture of the hydrogen bonds.

This complex behaviour of creep in timber when loaded under either cyclic or variable changes in relative humidity has been confirmed by a large number of research workers (e.g. Ranta-Mannus (1973) and Hunt (1982)). However, in board materials the effect appears to be either much reduced or absent.

Further work on timber has established that the amount of creep that occurs is related not to the rate of moisture change, but to the magnitude of the change; it is little affected by either its duration, or whether such change is brought

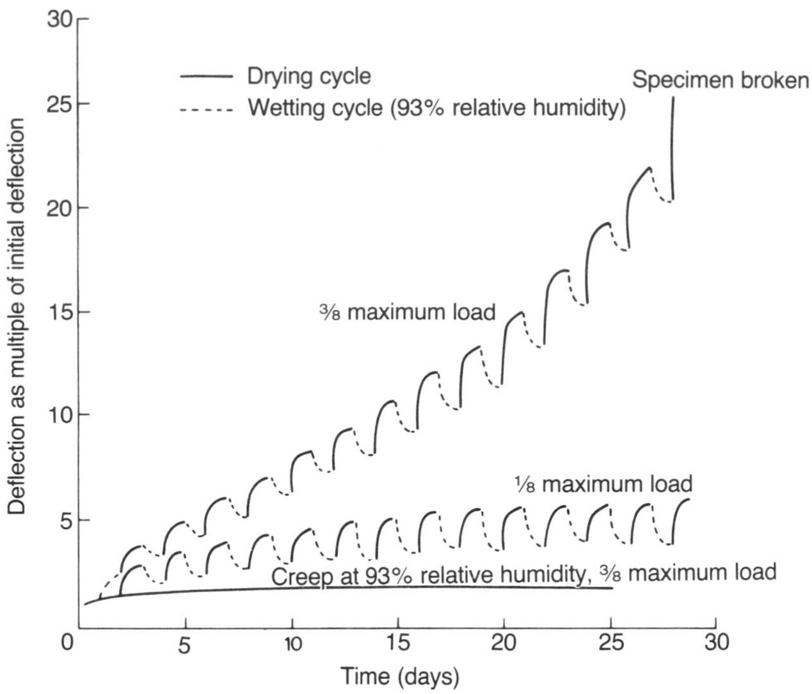

FIGURE 41.15 The effect of cyclic variations in moisture content on relative creep of samples of beech loaded to $\frac{1}{8}$ and $\frac{3}{8}$ of ultimate load (Building Research Establishment © Crown copyright).

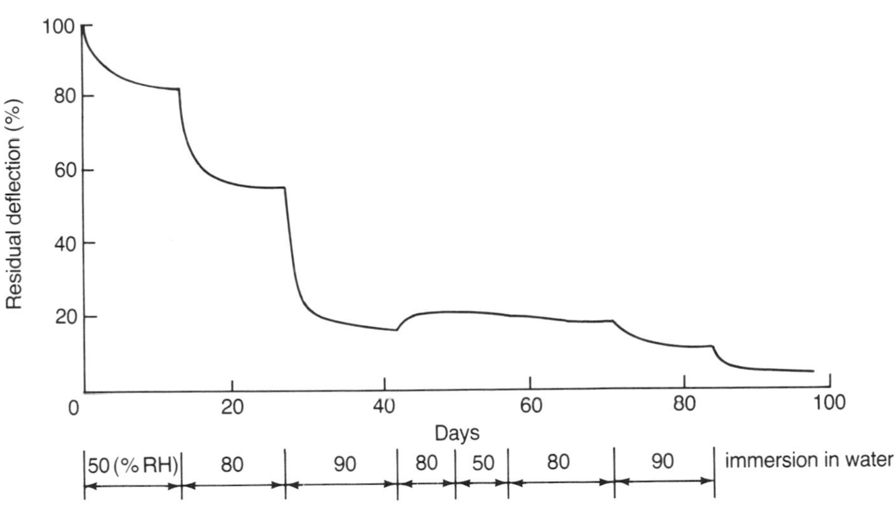

FIGURE 41.16 The amount of subsequent recovery of both viscoelastic and mechanosorptive deflection that occurred when prestressed dried beams were subjected to a sequence of humidity changes. Note that almost complete recovery was obtained (Arima and Grossman (1978) by permission of the Institute of Wood Science).

about in one or more steps, thereby casting doubts on whether this type of behaviour could be classified as creep.

Reinforcement of that doubt occurred with the publication of results of Arima and Grossman (1978). Small beams of *Pinus radiata* 680 × 15 × 15 mm were cut from green timber and stressed to about 25% of their short-term bending strength. While held in their deformed condition, the beams were allowed to dry for 15 days, after which the retaining clamps were removed and the initial recovery measured. The unstressed beams were then subjected to changes in relative humidity and Figure 41.16 shows the changes in recovery with changing humidity. Most important is the fact that total recovery was almost achieved; what was thought to have been viscous deformation in the post-drying and clamping stage turned out to be reversible.

These two phenomena – that creep is related to the magnitude of the moisture change, and that all deformation is reversible under moisture change – have cast very serious doubts on whether true creep actually occurs under changes in moisture content. Consequently, a term of convenience has been derived to describe this behaviour; namely **mechanosorptive** behaviour (Grossman, 1976).

So far, there is considerable disagreement in the form of the constitutive equations to describe mechanosorptive behaviour. Recent models have tended to include one or more diffusion terms for vapour movement.

41.5 References

Arima, T. and Grossman, P.U.A. (1978) Recovery of wood after mechanosorptive deformation. *Journal of the Institute of Wood Science*, **8**, No. 2, 47–52.

Barkas, W.W. (1945) Swelling stresses in gels. *Special Report on Forest Products Research, London*, No. 6.

Carrington, H. (1922) The elastic constants of spruce as affected by moisture content. *Aeronautical Journal*, **26**, 462.

Cave, I.D. (1975) Wood substance as a water-reactive fibre-reinforced composite. *Journal of Microscopy*, **104**, No. 1, 47–52.

Chow, S. (1973) Molecular rheology of coniferous wood tissues. *Transactions of the Society of Rheology*, **17**, 109–28.

Grossman, P.U.A. (1976) Requirements for a model that exhibits mechanosorptive behaviour. *Wood Science and Technology*, **10**, 163–8.

Hearmon, R.F.S. (1948) Elasticity of wood and plywood. *Special Report on Forest Products Research, London*, No. 7.

Hearmon, R.F.S. and Paton, J.M. (1964) Moisture content changes and creep in wood. *Forest Products Journal*, **14**, 357–9.

Hunt, D.G. (1982) Limited mechano-sorptive creep of beech wood. *J. Inst. Wood Sci.*, **9**, No. 3, 136–8.

Kingston, R.S.T. and Budgen, B. (1972) Some aspects of the rheological behaviour of wood, Part IV: Non-linear behaviour at high stresses in bending and compression. *Wood Science and Technology*, **6**, 230–8.

Ranta-Mannus, A. (1973) *A theory for the creep of wood with application to birch and spruce plywood.* Technical Research Centre of Finland, Building Technology and Community Development, Publication 4.

Sulzberger, P.H. (1947) *The effect of temperature on the strength of wood at various moisture contents in static bending*. Progress Report 7, Project TP 10-3, CSIRO (Aust.) Div. of Forest Products.

Chapter forty-two

Processing of timber

42.1 Introduction
42.2 Mechanical processing
42.3 Chemical processing
42.4 Finishes
42.5 References

42.1 Introduction

After felling, the tree has to be processed in order to render the timber suitable for use. Such processing may be basically mechanical or chemical in nature or even a combination of both. On the one hand timber may be sawn or chipped, while on the other it can be treated with chemicals which markedly affect its structure and its properties. In some of these processing operations the timber has to be dried. This technique has already been discussed in Chapter 38 and will not be referred to again in this chapter.

The many diverse mechanical and chemical processes for timber have been described in great detail in previous publications and it is certainly not the intention to repeat such description here: readers desirous of such information are referred to the excellent and authoritative texts listed in the References. In looking at processing in this chapter the emphasis is placed on the properties of the timber as they influence or restrict the type of processing. For convenience the processes are subdivided below into mechanical and chemical but frequently their boundaries overlap.

42.2 Mechanical processing

42.2.1 Solid timber

Sawing and planing

The basic requirement of these processes is quite simply to produce as efficiently as possible timber of the required dimensions having a quality of surface commensurate with the intended use. Such a requirement depends not only on the basic properties of the timber, but also on the design and condition of the cutting tool; many of the variables are interrelated and it is frequently necessary to compromise in the selection of processing variables.

In Chapter 38 the density of timber was shown to vary by a factor of 10 from about 120 to 1200 kg/m^3. As density increases so the time taken for the cutting edge to become blunt decreases: whereas it is possible to cut over 10 000 feet of Scots pine before it is necessary to resharpen, only one or two thousand feet of a dense hardwood such as jarrah can be cut. Density will also have a marked effect on the amount of power consumed in processing. When all the other factors affecting power consumption are held constant, this variable is highly correlated with timber density as illustrated in Figure 42.1.

Timber of high moisture content never machines as well as that at lower moisture levels. There is a tendency for the thin-walled cells to be deformed rather than cut because of

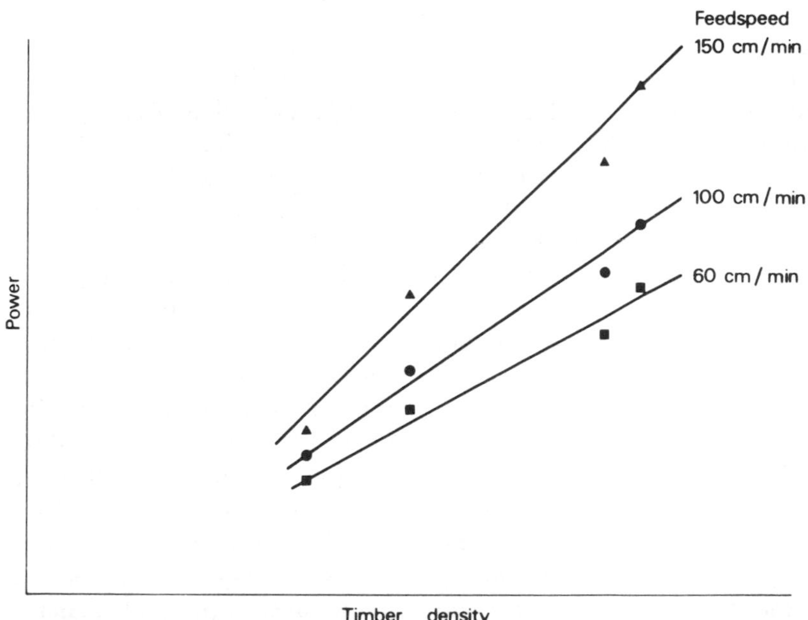

FIGURE 42.1 Effect of timber density and feedspeed on the consumption of power using a circular saw to cut along the grain (rip-sawing) (Building Research Establishment © Crown copyright).

their increased elasticity in the wet condition. After the cutters have passed over, these deformed areas slowly assume their previous shape resulting in an irregular appearance to the surface which is very noticeable when the timber is dried and painted; this induced defect is known as **raised grain.**

The cost of timber processing is determined primarily by the cost of tool maintenance, which in turn is related not only to properties of the timber, but also to the type and design of the saw or planer blade. In addition to the effect of timber density on tool life, the presence in certain timbers of gums and resins has an adverse effect because of the tendency for the gum to adhere to the tool thereby causing overheating; in saw blades this in turn leads to loss in tension resulting in saw instability and a reduction in sawing accuracy.

A certain number of tropical hardwood timbers contain mineral inclusions which develop during the growth of the tree. The most common is silica which is present usually in the form of small grains within the ray cells. The abrasive action of these inclusions can be considerable.

The cost of processing though determined primarily by tool life will be influenced also by the amount of power consumed. In addition to the effect of density of timber previously discussed, the amount of energy required will depend on the feedspeed (Figure 42.1), tool design and, above all, on tool sharpness.

Bending

Steam bending of certain timbers is a long-established process which was used extensively when it was fashionable to have furniture with rounded lines. The backs of chairs and wooden hat stands are two common examples from the past, but the process is still employed at the present time, albeit on a much reduced volume.

The handles for certain garden implements, walking sticks and various sports goods are all produced by steam bending.

The mechanics of bending involve a pre-steaming operation to soften the lignin, swell the timber, and render the timber less stiff. With the ends restrained, the timber is usually bent round a former, and after bending the timber must be held in the restrained mode until it dries out and the bend is set. In broad terms the deformation is irreversible, but over a long period of time, especially with marked alternations in humidity of the atmosphere, a certain degree of recovery will arise especially where the curve is unrestrained by some fixing. Although most timbers can be bent slightly, only certain species, principally the hardwood timbers of the temperate region, can be bent to sharp radii without cracking. When the timber is bent over a supporting but removable strap, the limiting radius of curvature is reduced appreciably. Thus it is possible to bend 25 mm thick ash to a radius of 64 mm and walnut to a radius of only 25 mm. The significance of the anatomy of the timber in determining the limiting radius of curvature is poorly understood.

42.2.2 Board materials

The total value of board materials used in the UK in 1990 was approximately £820 million, a value equivalent to about a third that of solid timber. Compared with the long history of timber utilization, the use and understanding of behaviour of board materials is still in its infancy.

As a material timber has a number of deficiencies.

1. It possesses a high degree of variability.
2. It is strongly anisotropic in both strength and moisture movement.
3. It is dimensionally unstable in the presence of changing humidity.
4. It is available in only limited widths.

Such material deficiencies can be lowered appreciably by reducing the timber to small units and subsequently reconstituting it, usually in the form of large flat sheets, though moulded items are also produced, e.g. trays, bowls, coffins, chair backs. The degree to which these boards assume a higher dimensional stability and a lower level of anisotropy than is the case with solid timber is dependent on the size and orientation of the component pieces of timber and the method by which they are bonded together. There are an infinite variety of board types though there are only three principal ones – plywood, chipboard and fibreboard: the production of these and their major properties are discussed in detail in subsequent sections.

Hence, in comparison with timber, board materials possess a lower degree of variability, lower anisotropy, and higher dimensional stability: they are also available in very large sizes. The reduction in variability is due quite simply to the random repositioning of variable components, the degree of reduction increasing as the size of the components decreases.

In Table 42.1 a comparison is made between the bending strength of timber and that of the three major types of board. When material of the same density is compared, the bending strength and stiffness of fibreboard and chipboard are considerably lower than those of plywood, which in turn are slightly lower than those for solid timber along the grain, though greater than for solid timber across the grain. Thus boards do not possess the high levels of anisotropy characteristic of timber: in both chipboard and fibreboard, anisotropy is almost absent and even in plywood with its higher strength and stiffness the degree of anisotropy is very much lower than for solid timber.

The dimensional stability in the plane of the board appears to be remarkably constant within a single board and even between boards of different types (Table 42.2); however, there is considerable difference in stability across the thickness of the board among the three types.

TABLE 42.1 Strength properties of timber and boards

	Thickness (mm)	*Density (kg/m^3)*	*Bending strength (N/mm^2)*		*E (N/mm^2)*	
			Parallel	*Perpendicular*	*Parallel*	*Perpendicular*
Solid timber – Douglas fir						
Small clear test pieces	20	500	80	2.2	12 700	800
Structural timber, SS grade	100	580	50	–	11 000	–
Plywood						
Douglas fir (three-ply)	4.8	520	73	16	12 090	890
Douglas fir (seven-ply)	19	600	60	33	10 750	3310
OSB (oriented strand board)	18	670	28	12.5	4 000	1500
Chipboard (BS 5669: 1989)						
Type C2	18	720	17		3000	
Type C5 (structural)	18	740	24		3750	
Fibreboard (BS 1142: 1989)						
Type SHA (standard hardboard)	3.2	900	45		–	
Type THE (tempered hardboard)	3.2	1000	54		4940	
Type MDF (medium density fibreboard)	18	790	30		2500	

The stability of all board types is poorer than that of timber along the grain, but vastly superior to that of timber across the grain; it is primarily for this latter reason that the various board materials are used so extensively where large widths are required, e.g. furniture, flooring and wall panelling.

Plywood

Logs, the denser of which are softened by boiling in water, are generally peeled by rotation against a slowly advancing knife to give a continuous strip of veneer. This is cut up into suitable lengths which are then fed through a large drying oven before being coated with adhesive. The plywood is laid up by hand with the grain directions in alternate layers (plies) running at right angles to each other. Plywood should contain an unequal number of plies, or an equal number with the central pair of plies similarly aligned: both systems confer a balanced structure about the centreline.

As the number of plies increases, so the degree of anisotropy in both strength and movement drops quickly from the value of 40 : 1 for timber in the solid state. With three-ply construction and using veneers of equal thickness the degree of anisotropy is reduced to 5 : 1, while for nine-ply this drops to 1.5 : 1. However, cost increases markedly with the number of plies and for most applications a three- or four-ply construction is regarded as a good compromise between isotropy and cost.

The mechanical and physical properties of the plywood will depend not only on the species of timber selected, but also on the type of adhesive used. Up to recent times more emphasis has been placed on characterizing the quality of plywood in terms of the property of the adhesive, but this situation has changed with the recognition of the significance of the timber as playing an equally important role in determining ultimate performance.

Both softwoods and hardwoods within a density range of 400–700 kg/m^3 are normally utilized. Plywood for internal use is produced from the non-durable species and urea-formaldehyde adhesive, while plywood for external use should be manufactured using phenol-formaldehyde resins and durable timbers, or

TABLE 42.2 Dimensional stability of timber and boards. Percentage change in dimensions from 65% to 85% relative humidity

	Direction to grain or board length		*Thickness (%)*
	Parallel	*Perpendicular*	
Solid timber			
Douglas fir	<0.1	0.8 (R)	1 (T)
Beech	<0.1	1.2 (R)	2 (T)
Plywood			
Douglas fir	0.15	0.15	2
OSB (oriented strand board)	0.2	0.2	15
Chipboard (BS 5669: Part 2: 1989)			
Type C2	0.25	0.25	7
Type C5 (structural)	0.20	0.20	4
Cement-bonded particleboard			
Type T2 (BS 5669: Part 4: 1989)	0.18	0.18	0.5
Fibreboard (BS 1142: 1989)			
Type SHA (standard hardboard)	0.15	0.15	3.5
Type THE (tempered hardboard)	0.15	0.15	3.5
Type MDF (medium density fibreboard)	0.20	0.20	3

Note: R = transverse radial direction; T = transverse tangential direction.

permeable non-durable timbers which have been preservative treated.

Plywood is the oldest of the timber sheet materials and for many years has enjoyed a high reputation as a structural sheet material. Its use in the Mosquito aircraft in the 1940s, and its subsequent performance for small boat construction, for sheathing in timber-frame housing, and in the construction of web and hollow-box beams, all bear testament to its suitability as a structural material.

It is not possible to talk about strength properties of plywood in general terms since not only are there different strength properties in different grain directions, but these are also affected by the configuration of the plywood in terms of number, thickness, orientation and quality of the veneers and by the type of adhesive used. The factors which affect the strength of plywood are the same as those set out previously for the strength of timber, though the effects are not necessarily the same. Thus the intrinsic factors, such as knots and density, play a less significant part than they do in the case of timber, but the effect of the extrinsic variables such as moisture content, temperature and time is very similar to that for timber.

In theory, any strength property of any plywood should be calculable from a detailed knowledge of the properties of the constituents, but in practice, because of the great range of variables affecting plywood strength, this is difficult to achieve and recourse is made to standard tests as set out in BS 4512.

In principle, the grade stresses for plywood are derived in a manner similar to that for solid timber prior to 1973. The basic stress for a particular property is first determined from the mean, standard deviation and a safety factor, and is subsequently reduced by a factor which allows for the occurrence of defects to give, at least in theory, the working stress. However, considerable difficulty occurs in ensuring that all the variables are in fact covered and it is fairly common practice, therefore, to carry out tests on structural sizes of plywood in order to obtain or to confirm the grade stress.

One approach to the calculation of grade stresses is to consider the plywood cross-section as homogeneous and to work out an equivalent stress for the complete cross-section – an approach which fails to provide the stress in each lamina, but one which allows the comparison of the thickness required for a particular application with that of other materials. Such an approach, however, requires the testing of all available types of plywood and can only be successful when a small number of types are standardized. Such an approach has been adopted in the current edition of the British Standard BS 5268: Part 2: 1991, to which reference has previously been made for solid wood.

Elasticity in plywood was examined in the early 1940s when it was shown that the values were property-dependent, unlike the case with solid timber. Working with veneers of the same thickness and same species, fairly simple generalized equations were derived, but as variation is built into the analysis the equations become complex.

Plywood possesses high strength and stiffness, especially when expressed in terms of specific gravity. It is unfortunate that it is now becoming a rather expensive material and is being replaced by other board materials in a number of applications.

Chipboard, OSB and cement-bonded particleboard

The chipboard industry dates from the mid-1940s and originated with the purpose of utilizing waste timber. After a long, slow start, when the quality of the board left much to be desired, the industry has grown tremendously, far exceeding the supplies of waste timber available and now relying to a very large measure on the use of small trees for its raw material. Such a marked expansion is due in no small part to the tighter control in processing and the ability to tailor-make boards with a known and reproducible performance.

Although the value of chipboard used in the UK (£400 million) is similar to that of plywood the volume of chipboard used is almost double. About 55% of our consumption is produced in the UK.

In the manufacture of chipboard the timber, which is principally softwood, is cut by a series of rotating knives to produce thin flakes which are dried and then sprayed with adhesive. Usually the flakes or chips are blown on to flat platens in such a way that the smaller chips end up on the surfaces of the board and the coarse chips in the centre. The fibre mat is first cut to length before passing into the press where it is held for 0.10–0.20 min per mm of board thickness at temperatures up to 200°C. The densities of boards produced range from 450 to 750 kg/m^3, depending on end-use classification, while the resin content varies from about 11% on the outer layers to 5% in the centre, averaging out for the board at about 8% on a dry weight basis.

Instead of using the batch platen process, chipboard can be made continuously using either the Mendé or an extrusion process. The former is applicable only in the manufacture of thin chipboard, i.e. 6 mm or less, and the process is analogous to that of paper manufacture in that the board is sufficiently flexible to pass between and over large heated rollers. In the extrusion process the chipboard mat is forced out through a heated die, but this results in the orientation of the chips at right angles to the plane of the board which reduces both the strength and stiffness of the material.

Direct comparison of the mechanical properties of chipboard and plywood are not available since their properties are assessed by different techniques set out in different international and national standards (BS 5669: 1989). However, it is fairly safe to say that in most strength properties chipboard is weaker than plywood of the same thickness. The strength of chipboard will increase with increasing length of chip for a given adhesive content, and the recent introduction of OSB (oriented strand board) in which the flakes are not only 30–50 mm in length but are orientated in three distinct layers, is an attempt to compete with plywood as a structural material.

The performance of chipboard, like that of plywood, is very dependent on the type of adhesive used. Most of the chipboard used in the UK contains urea-formaldehyde which, because of its sensitivity to moisture, renders this type of chipboard unsuitable for use where there is a risk of the material becoming wet, or even being subjected to marked alternations in relative humidity over a long period of time. More expensive boards possessing some resistance to the presence of moisture are manufactured using either melamine/urea-formaldehyde or phenol-formaldehyde adhesives: however, a true external-grade board has not yet been produced commercially.

Chipboard, like timber, is a viscoelastic material and an example of the deformation over an extended period of time has already been presented (Figure 41.10). However, the rate of creep in chipboard is higher than that in timber though it is possible to reduce it by increasing the amount of adhesive or by modifying the chemical composition of the adhesive. A structural grade of chipboard is specified in BS 5669: 1989, and grade stresses for its use in designed structures are set out in BS 5268: Part 2: 1991. The bulk of chipboard, however, continues to be used extensively in either semi-structural applications such as floor and roof decking, or in non-structural uses such as the manufacture of kitchen units and furniture.

Boards with a similar appearance to chipboard are produced from a wide variety of plant material and synthetic resin of which flaxboard and bagasse board are the best-known examples. These, along with chipboard, are collectively called particleboards in the UK, the term chipboard being restricted to the product produced from timber.

As noted earlier, there are distinct advantages in terms of strength in increasing chip size. In the 1970s there appeared on the market a product called 'waferboard' which was characterized by a random array of chips or flakes up to 50 mm in both length and width. More recently this product has been developed by aligning flakes of the same length, but up to only half the previous width. A three-layer board is produced in which the alignment of the core flakes is approximately at right angles to those of the two surface layers, a move intended to simulate the properties of plywood. While the bending strength and stiffness of this product (OSB, or oriented strand board) is greater than that of chipboard, these parameters still fall short of levels found in plywood. Nevertheless, OSB is making considerable inroads into the plywood market both in the UK and North America: in both places it is widely used for sheathing in timber frame construction, as well as for roof decking.

One of the limitations of both chipboard and OSB is their limited durability in the presence of prolonged wetting. One material not subject to such a limitation is cement-bonded particleboard, a product containing by weight about 65% of ordinary Portland cement. This confers high alkalinity and hence high durability against fungal attack. As well as having a very high modulus of elasticity, it also possesses good spread of flame resistance, good sound absorption, and good dimensional stability under changing relative humidity, as compared with resin-bonded particleboards including OSB. Such attributes are to some effect offset by a lower bending strength: nevertheless, the material is finding wide acceptance as an internal wall lining, especially in public buildings.

Fibreboard

Although much smaller quantities of fibreboard are used in the UK than either chipboard or plywood it is nevertheless a most important panel product, used extensively in the UK for sheathing in timber frame construction, insulation, the linings of doors, and furniture, and in Scandinavia as a cladding and roofing material.

The so-called process of manufacture is quite different from that of the other board materials in that the timber is first reduced to chips which are then steamed under very high pressure in order to soften the lignin which is thermoplastic in behaviour. The softened chips then pass to a defibrator which separates them into individual fibres or fibre bundles without inducing too much damage.

The fibrous mass is frequently mixed with hot water and formed into a mat which is cut into lengths and, like chipboard, pressed in a multiplaten hot press at a temperature of from 180°C to 210°C.

In the more modern dry-forming process the fibrous mass is conveyed in an air stream to the mat-forming station and, in order to obtain boards of adequate strength, small quantities of urea, or melamine/urea-formaldehyde resin, are added to supplement the bonding by the softened lignin. This process is used to produce MDF (medium density fibreboard).

By modifying the pressure applied in the final pressing, boards of a wide range of density are produced ranging from the insulation boards with a density of about 250 kg/m^3 to hardboard with a density of 950 kg/m^3. Fibreboard, like the other board products, is moisture sensitive, but a certain degree of resistance can be obtained by the passage of the material through a hot oil bath thereby imparting a high degree of water repellency: this material is referred to as tempered hardboard.

The assessment of the properties of the fibreboards is carried out according to BS 1142: once again, because of the lack of uniform testing methods, a direct comparison of properties with those of the other board materials is not possible; grade stresses for one type of fibreboard, namely oil-tempered hardboard, are included in BS 5268: Part 2: 1991.

42.2.3 Laminated timber

Where timber beams of a particular shape or excessive length are required these can be fabricated to order using a laminating process. Either urea-formaldehyde or resorcinol-formaldehyde adhesive is used depending whether the material is required for internal or external conditions.

In the process thin strips of timber are glued and laid parallel to one another in a jig, the whole assembly being clamped until the adhesive has set. Where the individual laminae are thin they are end-jointed using a scarf-joint, but where the laminae are thicker than 10 mm finger jointing techniques are usually employed (Figure 42.2).

Laminated construction is to be found in such diverse items as tennis racquets, skis, hulls of wooden ships and arched beams in halls and sports stadiums. Grade stresses for 'glu-lam' beams are set out in BS 5268: Part 2: 1991.

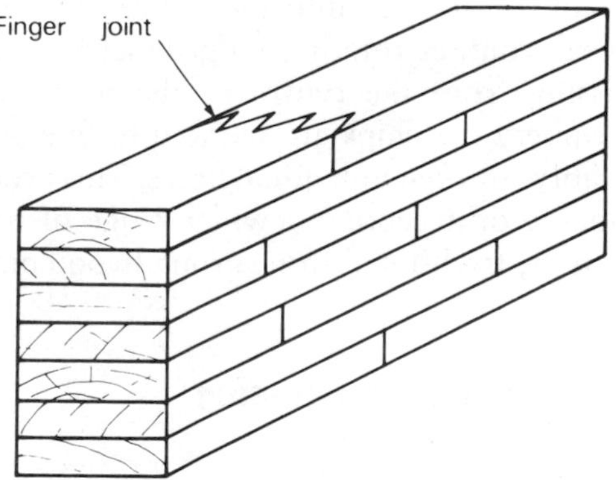

FIGURE 42.2 The construction of a laminated timber beam, the laminae of which are end-jointed using finger joints (Building Research Establishment © Crown copyright).

42.2.4 Mechanical pulping

The paper industry is the single largest consumer of wood. In the UK the value of pulp and paper imports for 1989 was £4912 million, compared with £2320 million for timber and timber products; pulp and paper account for about 4.1% of the total UK imports.

Pulp may be produced by either mechanical or chemical processes and discussion on the latter is postponed until later in this chapter. In the original process for producing mechanical pulp, logs with a high moisture content are fed against a grinding wheel which is continuously sprayed with water in order to keep it cool and free it of the fibrous mass produced. The pulp so formed, known as stone groundwood, is coarse in texture, comprising bundles of cells rather than individual cells, and is mainly used as newsprint.

To avoid the necessity to adopt a costly bleaching process, only light-coloured timbers are accepted. Furthermore, because the power consumed on grinding is a linear function of the timber density, only the low-density timbers with no or only small quantities of resin are used.

Developments in mechanical pulping have centered on disc-refining. Wood chips, softened in hot water, by steaming, or by chemical pretreatment, are fed into the centre of two high-speed, counter-rotating, ridged metal plates; on passing from the centre of the plates to the periphery the chips are reduced to fine bundles of fibres or even individual fibres. This process is capable of accepting a wider range of timbers than the traditional stone groundwood method.

42.3 Chemical processing

42.3.1 Impregnation

Although impregnation embraces both mechanical and chemical aspects of processing, it is included within this section on chemical processing purely for convenience.

The degree of impregnation of timber by chemical solutions is related directly to the permeability of timber which was discussed in an earlier chapter; the pathways of flow were described and it will be recalled that permeability was shown to be a function not only of moisture content and temperature, but also of grain direction, sapwood/heartwood, earlywood/latewood and species. Longitudinal permeability is usually about $10^4 \times$ transverse permeability owing principally to the orientation of the cells in the longitudinal direction. Heartwood, owing to the deposition of both gums and encrusting materials, is much less permeable than the sapwood, and earlywood in the dry condition also has a lower permeability than the latewood owing to aspiration of the bordered pits.

Perhaps the greatest variability in impregnation occurs between species. Within the softwoods this can be related to the number and distribution of the bordered pits and to the efficiency of the residual flow paths which utilize both the latewood bordered pits and the semi-bordered ray pits. Within the hardwoods variability in impregnation is related to the size and distribution of the vessels and to the degree of dissolution of the end walls of the vessel members.

Four arbitrary classes of impregnation are recognized, the timbers being apportioned to these according to the depth of penetration of the solution after a fixed period of time at a particular pressure. These classes are **permeable, moderately resistant, resistant** and **extremely resistant**. Whilst this classification is used more frequently with reference to the impregnation of artificial preservatives it is equally applicable to impregnation by flame retardants, or dimensional stabilizers for, although differences in viscosity will influence degree of penetration, the species will remain in the same relative order.

Artificial preservatives

Except where the heartwood of a naturally durable timber is being used, timber, provided it is permeable, should always be preservative treated if there is any significant risk that its moisture content will rise in excess of 20%; non-durable timber resistant to impregnation should not be used in these conditions. In theory, it should not be necessary to protect internal woodwork which should remain dry, but, because of water spillage, and leakage from pipes or from the roof, the moisture content of internal woodwork can also rise above this critical level.

Short-term dipping and surface treatments by brush or spray are the least effective ways of applying a preservative because of the small loading and poor penetration achieved. In these treatments only the surface layers are penetrated and there is a risk of deep splits occurring in service, thereby exposing untreated timber. Such treatments are not suitable for timber that is to be in ground contact, but they are used for window and door joinery.

The most effective treatment of timber is by pressure impregnation, which ensures deeper penetration and much higher loadings. Two variants of the process are available and the choice is usually determined by the preservative selected. In the first, the timber is placed in a sealed tank; the preservative is then allowed to enter the tank and pressures of up to $1.25\,N/mm^2$ are applied for periods of time varying from 0.5–3 hours depending on the species of wood being treated. This 'pressure' treatment is used for the waterborne preservatives and for creosote.

The second variant of the preservation process employs an initial vacuum treatment to the wood in the sealed container of up to $-0.08\,N/mm^2$ followed by the inlet of preservative and the application of pressures of up to $0.2\,N/mm^2$ for 0.25 hour. A final vacuum is applied in order to remove excess preservative from the wood. This 'double vacuum' treatment is used to apply organic solvent preservatives.

Four types of preservatives are available.

1. Waterborne preservatives, such as copper/chromium/arsenic compositions are used in the most hazardous situations; the preservative becomes fixed in the wood and does not leach out in wet conditions. The timber therefore does not have to be painted. The composition and method of use of this group of preservatives are given in BS 4072.
2. Organic solvent preservatives; the most commonly used are organotin, organocopper and organozinc fungicides, with water-repellents and insecticides where appropriate. Accurately machined components can be treated with these preservatives before assembly, but treated timber should be painted when exposed to the weather. These preservatives are defined in BS 5707.
3. Coal-tar creosotes; these must not be used inside buildings because of their strong smell. Creosoted timber is not painted unless it has been well weathered. The creosotes are specified and their methods of use described in BS 144: Parts 1 and 2.
4. Water-soluble borax-based preservatives; these are also used, but to a much lesser extent. They are applied by a diffusion process into green timber and remain soluble after the impregnation process. Treated timber must be painted when exposed to wetting.

In those timbers which can be impregnated, it is likely that the durability of the sapwood after pressure impregnation will be greater than the natural durability of the heartwood, and it is not unknown to find telegraph and transmission poles the heartwood of which is decayed while the treated sapwood is perfectly sound.

Mention has been made already of the difficulty of painting timber which has been treated with creosote. This disadvantage is not common to the other preservatives and not only is one able to paint the treated timber, but it is also possible to glue together treated components.

The British Standards BS 5589 *Code of practice for preservation of timber* and BS 5268 *Structural use of timber. Part 5: Code of practice for the preservative treatment of structural timber* should be consulted before specifying the use of timber where biological hazards are present.

Flame retardants

Flame-retardant chemicals may be applied as surface coatings or by vacuum-pressure impregnation, thereby rendering the timber less easily ignitable and reducing the rate of flame spread. Intumescent coatings will be discussed later and this section is devoted to the application of fire retardants by impregnation.

The salts most commonly employed in the UK for the vacuum-pressure impregnation process are monoammonium phosphate, diammonium phosphate, ammonium sulphate, boric acid and borax. These chemicals vary considerably in solubility, hygroscopicity and effectiveness against fire. Most proprietary flame retardants are mixtures of such chemicals formulated to give the best performance at reasonable cost. Since these chemicals are applied in an aqueous solution it means that a combined waterborne preservative and fire-retardant solution can be used which has distinct economic considerations. Quite frequently, corrosion inhibitors are incorporated where the timber is to be joined by metal connectors.

Considerable caution has to be exercised in determining the level of heating to be used in drying the timber following impregnation. The ammonium phosphates and sulphate tend to break down on heating giving off ammonia and leaving an acidic residue which can result in degradation of the wood substance. Thus it has been found that drying at 65°C following impregnation by solutions of these salts results in a loss of bending strength of from 10% to 30%. Drying at 90°C, which is adopted in certain kiln schedules, results in a loss of 50% of the strength and even higher losses are recorded for the impact resistance or toughness of the timber. It is essential, therefore, to dry the timber at as low a temperature as possible and also to ensure that the timber in service is never subjected to elevated temperatures which would initiate or continue the process of acidic degradation. Most certainly, timber which has to withstand suddenly applied loads should not be treated with this type of fire retardant, and care must also be exercised in the selection of glues for construction. The best overall performance from timber treated with this type of flame retardant is obtained when the component is installed and maintained under cool and dry conditions.

Conscious of the limitations of those flame retardants based on ammonium salts, a number of companies have developed retardants of markedly different composition which appear to display much reduced or even zero degradation of the timber at normal drying temperatures: such products, however, tend to be more expensive than their ammonium-based counterparts (TRADA, 1991).

Dimensional stabilizers

In Section 41.2.2 on movement, timber, because of its hygroscopic nature, was shown to change in dimensions as its moisture content varied in order to come into equilibrium with the vapour pressure of the atmosphere. Because of the composite nature of timber such movement will differ in extent in the three principal axes.

Movement is the result of water adsorption or desorption by the hydroxyl groups present in all the matrix constituents. Thus it should be possible to reduce movement (i.e. increase the dimensional stability) by eliminating or at least reducing the accessibility of these groups to water. This can be achieved by either chemical changes or by the introduction of physical bulking agents (Rowell and Youngs, 1981).

Various attempts have been made to substitute the hydroxyl groups chemically by less polar groups and the most successful has been by acetylation. In this process acetic anhydride is used as a source of acetyl groups. A very marked improvement in dimensional stability is achieved with only a marginal loss in strength.

Good stabilization can also be achieved by reacting the wood with formaldehyde which then forms methylene bridges between adjacent hydroxyl groups. However, the acid catalyst necessary for the process causes acidic degradation of the timber.

Most of the successful stabilizing processes involve the impregnation of the cell wall by chemicals which hold the timber in a swollen condition even after water is removed, thus minimizing dimensional movement. In the mid-1940s some solid timber, but more usually wood veneers, were impregnated with solutions of phenol-formaldehyde. The veneers were stacked, heated and compressed to form a high-density material with good dimensional stability which found wide usage as insulation in the electrical industry prior to the era of plastics.

Considerable success has also been achieved using polyethylene glycol (PEG), a wax-like solid which is soluble in water. Under controlled conditions, it is possible to replace all the water in timber by PEG by a diffusion process, thereby maintaining it in a swollen condition. The technique has found application among other things in the preservation of waterlogged objects of archaeological interest, the best example of which is the Swedish wooden warship *Wasa*, which was raised from the depths of Stockholm harbour in 1961 having foundered in 1628. From 1961 the timber was sprayed continuously for over a decade with an aqueous solution of PEG which diffused into the wet timber gradually replacing the bound water in the cell wall without causing any dimensional changes.

PEG may also be applied to dry timber by standard vacuum impregnation using solution strengths of from 5 to 30%. Frequently, preservative and/or fire-retardant chemicals are incorporated in the impregnating solution. It will be noted from Figure 42.3 that the amount of swelling has been reduced to one-third following impregnation.

42.3.2 Chemical pulping

The magnitude of the pulping industry has already been discussed as has also the produc-

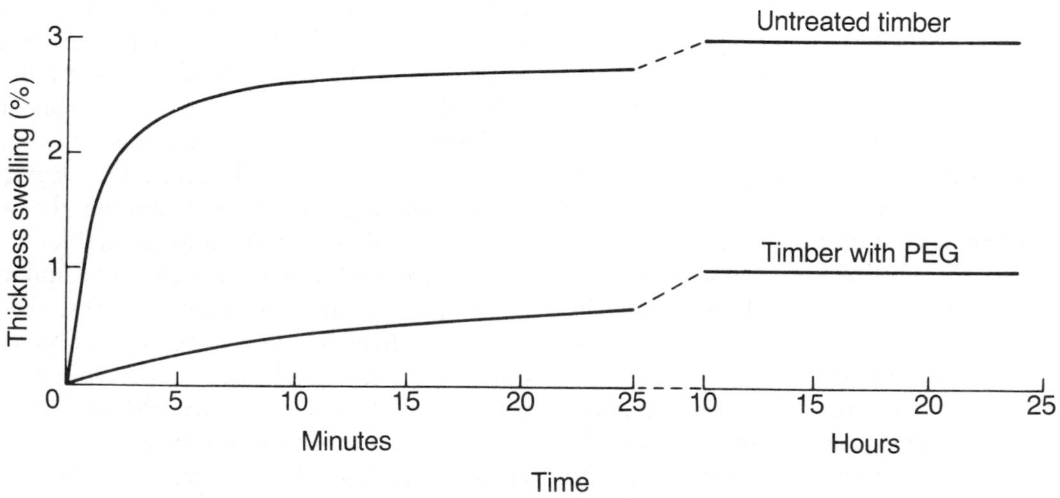

FIGURE 42.3 The comparative rates of swelling in water of untreated pine timber and timber impregnated with a 50% (by weight) solution of PEG (polyethylene glycol); this is equivalent to 22% loading on a dry wood basis (adapted from Morén (1964)).

tion of mechanical pulp. Where paper of a higher quality than newsprint or corrugated paper is required a pulp must be produced consisting of individual cells rather than fibre bundles. To obtain this type of pulp the middle lamella has to be removed and this can be achieved only by chemical means.

There are a number of chemical processes all of which are concerned with the removal of lignin, which is the principal constituent of the middle lamella. However, during the pulping process lignin will be removed from within the cell wall as well as from between the cells: this is both acceptable and desirable since lignin imparts a greyish colouration to the pulp which is unacceptable for the production of white paper.

It is not possible to remove all the lignin without also dissolving most of the hemicelluloses which not only add to the weight of pulp produced but also impart a measure of adhesion between the fibres. Thus a compromise has to be reached in determining how far to progress with the chemical reaction and the decision is dependent on the requirements of the end product. Frequently, though not always, the initial pulping process is terminated when a quarter to a half of the lignin still remains and this is then removed in a subsequent operation known as bleaching, which, though expensive, has relatively little effect on the hemicelluloses. The yield of chemical pulp will vary considerably depending on the conditions employed, but it will usually be within the range of 40–50% of the dry weight of the original timber.

The yield of pulp can be increased to 55–80% by semi-chemical pulping. Only part of the lignin is removed in an initial chemical treatment designed to soften the wood chips: subsequent mechanical treatment separates the fibres without undue damage. These high-yield pulps usually find their way into card and board-liner which are extensively used for packaging where ultimate whiteness is not a prerequisite.

42.3.3 Other chemical processes

Brief mention must be made of the destructive distillation of timber, a process which is carried out either for the production of charcoal alone or for the additional recovery of the volatile by-products such as methanol, acetic acid, acetone and wood-tar. The timber is heated initially to 250°C, after which the process is exothermic: distillation must be carried out either in the complete absence of air, or with controlled small amounts.

Timber can be softened in the presence of ammonia vapour as a result of plasticization of the lignin. Timber can therefore be bent or moulded using this process, but, because of the harmful effects of the vapour, the process has never been adopted commercially.

42.4 Finishes

Finishes have a combined decorative and protective function. Indoors they are employed primarily for aesthetic reasons though their role in resisting soiling and abrasion is also important; outdoors, however, their protective function is vital. In Section 40.1, the natural weathering process of timber was described in terms of the attack of the cell wall constituents by ultra-violet light and the subsequent removal of breakdown products by rain; the application of finishes is to slow down this weathering process to an acceptable level, the degree of success varying considerably among the wide range of finishes commercially available.

In Chapter 38 the complex chemical and morphological structure of timber was described as well as the hygroscopic nature of this fibre composite and its significance in determining the movement of timber. The combined effects of structure and moisture movement have a most profound effect on the performance of coatings. For example, in the softwoods the presence of distinct bands of early and latewood with their differential degrees of permeability results not only in a difference in sheen or reflectance of the coating between these zones, but also in marked differences in adhesion; in Douglas fir, where the latewood is most conspicuous, flaking of paint from the latewood is a most common occurrence. In addition the radial movement of the latewood has been shown to be as high as six times that of the earlywood and consequently the ingress of water to the surface layers results in differential movement and considerable stressing of the coatings. In those hardwoods characterized by the presence of large vessels the coating tends to sag across the vessel and it is therefore essential to apply a paste filler to the surface prior to paint; even with this, the life of a paint film on a timber such as oak (see Figure 38.6) is very short. The presence of extractives in certain timbers (see Section 38.3.3 and Table 38.2) results in the inhibition in drying of finishes; with iroko and Rhodesian teak clear varnish may never dry.

Contrary to general belief, deep penetration of the timber is not necessary for good adhesion, but it is absolutely essential that the weathered cells on the surface are removed prior to re-painting. Good adhesion appears to be achieved by molecular attraction rather than by mechanical keying into the cell structure.

Although aesthetically most pleasing, fully exposed varnish, irrespective of chemical composition, has a life of only a very few years, principally because of the tendency of most types to become brittle on exposure, thereby cracking and disintegrating because of the stresses imposed by the movement of the timber under changes in moisture content. Ultra-violet light can readily pass through the majority of varnish films, degrading the timber at the interface and causing adhesion failure of the coating.

A second type of natural finish which overcomes certain of the drawbacks of clear varnish are the exterior wood stains. There are many types available, but all consist of resin solutions of low viscosity and low to medium solids content: these solutions are readily absorbed into the surface layers of the timber. Their protective action is due in part to the effectiveness of water-repellent resins in preventing water ingress, and in part from the presence of finely dispersed pigments which protect against photochemical attack. The higher the concentration of pigments the greater the protection, but this is achieved at the expense of loss in transparency of the finish. Easy to apply and maintain these thin films, however, offer little resistance to the transmission of water vapour into and out of the timber. Compared with a paint or varnish, the exterior wood stain will allow the timber to wet up and dry out at a much faster rate, which of course could result in widely fluctuating moisture contents and dimensional instability in the wood. The stains also require more frequent maintenance, but nevertheless have become well established for the treatment of cladding and joinery.

By far the most widely used finish, especially for external softwood joinery, is the traditional opaque alkyd gloss system embracing appropriate undercoats and primers; a three-coat system is usually recommended. Multiple coats of oil-based paint are effective barriers to the movement of liquid and vapour water; however, breaks in the continuity of the film after relatively short exposure constitute a ready means of entry after which the film will act as a barrier to moisture escape, thereby increasing the likelihood of fungal attack.

Recent concerns over the poor performance of the traditional paint system have resulted in the introduction of paint coatings specifically designed for use on exterior timber. These are often based on alkyd resins, but waterborne resins are also used; the performance of these exterior paints can be exceptionally good.

With all these coatings the need for preservative pre-treatment of non-durable species of timber is essential. The use of water-repellent preservatives generally results in improved coating performance.

One specialized group of finishes for timber

and timber products is that of the flame-retardant coatings. These coatings must be applied fairly thickly and must neither be damaged in subsequent installation and usage of the material nor their effect negated by the application of unsuitable coverings. They generally intumesce on heating and the resulting foam forms a protective layer of resistant char (TRADA, 1991).

42.5 References

BS 144: *Wood preservation using coal tar adhesives. Part 1. Specification for preservative. Part 2. Methods for timber treatmemt.*

BS 1142: 1989: *Specification for fibre building boards.*

BS 4072: *Wood preservation by means of copper/chromium/arsenic compositions. Part 1. Specification for preservatives. Part 2. Method for timber treatment.*

BS 5268: 1991: *Structural use of timber. Part 2. Code of practice for permissible stress design, materials and workmanship. Part 5. Code of practice for the preservative treatment of structural timber.*

BS 5589: *Code of practice for preservation of timber.*

BS 5669: 1989: *Particleboard. Part 2. Specification for wood chipboard. Part 4. Specification for cement bonded particleboard.*

BS 5707: *Solutions of wood preservatives in organic solvents. Part 1. Specification for solutions for general purpose applications, including timber that is to be painted. Part 2. Specification for pentachlorophenol wood preservative solution for use on timber that is not required to be painted. Part 3. Methods of treatment.*

Morén, R.E. (1964) Some practical applications of polyethylene glycol for the stabilization and preservation of wood. Paper presented to the British Wood Preserving Association Annual Convention.

Rowell, K.M. and Youngs, R.L. (1981) *Dimensional stabilization of wood in use.* Research Note FPL-0243, Forest Products Laboratory, Madison.

TRADA (1991) Flame-retardant treatments for timber. *Wood Information*, Section 2/3, Sheet 3, Appendix March 1991.

Further reading

General texts

Barrett, J.D. and Foschi, R.O. (1979) *Proceedings of the First International Conference on Wood Fracture*, Banff, Alberta.

Bodig, J. and Jayne, B.A. (1982) *Mechanics of Wood and Wood Composites*, Van Nostrand Reinhold.

Building Research Establishment Digest 296 (1985) *Timbers: Their Natural Durability and Resistance to Preservative Treatment.*

Desch, H.W. (revised Dinwoodie, J.M. 1981) *Timber – Its Structure, Properties and Utilisation*, 6th edn. Macmillan, London.

Meyer, R.W. and Kellogg, R.M. (1982) *Structural Uses of Wood in Adverse Environments*, Van Nostrand Reinhold.

Wilson, K. and White, D.J.B. (1986) *The Anatomy of Wood: Its Diversity and Variability*. Stobart and Sons Ltd.

Index

AAC, *see* Autoclaved aerated concrete
Accelerators, cement 105–6, 263–4
Acid–silica reaction 181
Activation energy 14
Adhesives 35–7
Admixtures, concrete 103
  accelerators 105–6
  air entraining agents 107–8
  mineral 108
  plasticizers 104–5
  retarders 106–7
Adsorption 37–8
Ageing of aluminium alloys 82
Aggregates 112
  bituminous materials 209–10, 221
  classification 113–14
  in bricks and blockwork 259–60
  properties 114–15
  types 112
    heavyweight aggregates 113
    lightweight aggregates 112–13
    normal density aggregates 112
Air entrainment agents 107–8
Allotropy 56–7
Alloy steels 78
Alloys
  aluminium 81–3
  copper 83
Annealing 64
Annual rings, *see* Growth rings
APC, *see* Aromatic polymer composite
Aragonite 180
Aromatic polymer composite (APC) 350
Asbestos cement 379–80, 392
  manufacture 396–7
  uses 397–8
Asphalt 199, 240–1
Asphaltenes 204, 212
ASR, *see* Acid–silica reaction
Atomic structure
  covalent bonding 19–21
  ionic bonding 17–19
  metallic bonding 21–2
  metals 53–7
  Van der Waals bonds 22–4, 37
Austenitic stainless steel 81
Autoclaved aerated concrete (AAC) 275–6, 277, 278

Binders, mortar
  hydraulic lime 260
  masonry cement 260
  ordinary Portland cement 260
  quicklime 260
  sandlime 260
Bingham constants 118
Bingham equation 31 2
Bitumen 64–5, 199
  ageing 231
    ageing index 232
    loss of volatiles 231
    oxidation 231
  chemistry and molecular structure 204–5
    asphaltenes 204
    carbenes 204
    maltenes 204
  manufacture 204
  sources
    natural asphalts 203
    refinery bitumen 204
  types
    cutbacks 206–7
    emulsions 208
    oxidized bitumens 206
    penetration grades 205–6
Bituminous materials 199–201
  adhesion 234
    mechanisms for loss of adhesion 236–9
    nature of aggregate 234–5
    nature of bitumen 236
  deformation
    resistance to deformation 218–19
    stiffness modulus 218
    see also Permanent deformation
  durability 231
    adhesion 234–9
    ageing 231
    permeability 233–3
  failure
    modes 223–6
  fatigue characteristics 226
    effect of mix variables 229–30
    strain criteria 227–9
    stress and strain conditions 226–7
  permanent deformation
    determination 219–20
    factors affecting 220–2
  permeability 233
    factors affecting 234
    measurement and voids analysis 233–4
  practice and processing
    asphalts 240–1
    macadams 241–4
    methods of production 248–9
    recipe and designed mixes 244–8
  production 248–9
  strength
    road structure 223
  structure
    aggregates 208–10
    bitumen 203–5
    constituents 203, 244–5
    types 205–8
  viscosity
    binders 212
    influence of temperature 215–18
    measurement 213–15
Blockwork, *see* Brickwork and

blockwork
Boltzmann's constant 15
Boltzmann's equation 15, 28
Boltzmann's superposition principle 30–1
Bonds, atomic
covalent bonding 19–21
ionic bonding 17–19
metallic bonding 21–2
van der Waals bonds 22–4, 37
Brasses 83
Brazing 69
Bricks and blocks, concrete 274
production processes
autoclaved aerated concrete (AAC) 275–6
casting concrete 275
curing 275
pressing 275
products
autoclaved aerated concrete 278
dense aggregate concrete blocks and bricks 276–7
lightweight aggregate blocks 278
reconstituted stone masonry units 277–8
Bricks and blocks, fired clay 266
forming and firing
clamps 271
Hoffman kilns firing 269–70
intermittent kilns 271
semi-dry pressing 268–9
soft mud process 267
stiff plastic process 267
tunnel kilns 270–1
wire cut process 267–8
properties 271–4
Brickwork and blockwork 253
durability and non-structural properties of masonry 306–7
chemical attack 307–9
erosion 309–11
fire resistance 314
rain resistance 312–14
sound transmission 314
thermal conductivity 311–12
masonry construction and forms
appearance 286–8
bond 283–4
joint style 285
mortar 280
specials 284–5
walls and other masonry forms 281–3
workmanship and accuracy 285
materials
calcium silicate units 274
concrete units 274–8
fired clay bricks and blocks 266–74
manufacture of units and mortars 257–61
mortar 263–6
other constituents and additives 261–3
structural behaviour of masonry 289–90
compressive loading 290–6
elastic modulus 300–2
flexure (bending) 298–9
movement and creep 302–5
shear load in bed plane 296–8
tension 299
terminology 254–6
Brittleheart 426
Bronzes 83

Calcite 96
Cambium 410, 415
Cantilever 83–4
Capillary action
pores 96
tension 132
Carbenes 204
Carbonation-induced corrosion 189–90
Carbonation shrinkage 137–9
Carbon steels 78
Castings 67
Cast iron 52, 76
grey 77
malleable 77
nodular (ductile) 77
white 76
Cathodic protection 75
Cells (electric)
concentration cell 73
Daniel 72
simple 70–1, 72–3
Cellulose 417–20, 422
Cement replacement materials
composition 109–10
hardened structure and strength 111
other properties 111
pozzolanic behaviour 108–9, 110–11
types 109
Cements
fibre-reinforced cements and concretes 360
durability 392–5
fibre-reinforced concrete 388–91, 396–403
fibres and matrices, properties 361–4
fibres in a cement matrix 379–87
manufacture and uses 396–404
structure and post-cracking composite theory 365–78
glass-reinforced cement (GRC) 380, 392
manufacture 398
uses 398
low heat 103
Portland cements 90, 91
composition 92–3
drying shrinkage 101–3
hydration 93–6
manufacture 91–2
strength of hardened cement paste 97–101
structure of hardened cement paste 96–7
types 103
water in hcp 101–3
sulphate resisting 103
thermal expansion 139–40
white 103
Charpy test 77, 79
Chemisorption 37–8
Chipboard 499–500
Clays 259
Cold working of metals 67
drawing 68
extrusion 68
rolling 68
Compression wood 426, 446
Concentration cell 73
Concrete 89–90
behaviour after placing 122
bleeding 122
plastic settlement 123
plastic shrinkage 123
reducing bleed and its effects 123–4
constituent materials
admixtures 103–8
aggregates 112–15
cement replacement materials

Concrete *cont'd.*
108–15
Portland cements 91–103
cracking and fracture
creep rupture 164
fracture mechanics approach 165
microcracking 163–4
creep 147–8
factors influencing creep 148–50
mechanisms 150–2
prediction of 152–3
deformation
carbonation shrinkage 137–9
creep 147–53
drying shrinkage 129–37
stress–strain behaviour 140–7
thermal expansion 139–40
degradation of concrete
acid attack 180–1
alkali–aggregate reaction 181–4
attack by sulphates and sea water 179–80
fire resistance 186–7
frost damage 184–6
durability
degradation of concrete 179–87
durability of steel in concrete 187–92
measurements of flow constants 172–9
recommendations for durability 192–4
transport mechanisms through concrete 169–72
elastic modulus 145–7
Poisson's ratio 147
factors influencing strength
age 161
aggregate properties, size and volume concentration 162–3
humidity 162
temperature 161–2
water/cement ratio 160–1
fibre-reinforced cements and concretes 360
durability 392–5
fibre-reinforced concrete 388–91
fibres and matrices, properties 361–4
fibres in a cement matrix 379–87
manufacture and uses 396–404
structure and post-cracking composite theory 365–78
flow constants
diffusivity 175–6
permeability 172–5
sorptivity 176–9
properties, fresh and early age
behaviour after placing 122–4
fresh properties 117–18
strength gain and temperature effects 124–8
stress-strain behaviour 140–7
workability measurements 118–22
shrinkage
carbonation 137–9
drying 129–37
strength and failure 155–6
cracking and fracture 163–5
factors influencing strength 160–3
multiaxial loading 165–7
strength tests 156–60
strength gain and temperature effects
effect of curing temperature 124–5
heat of hydration effects 125–8
maturity 125
strength tests
compressive strength 156–8
flexural test 158–9
relationship between strength measurements 159–60
splitting test 159
tensile testing 158–9
stress–strain behaviour 140–7
elastic modulus of concrete 145–7
models for concrete behaviour 142–4
observed behaviour of concrete 144–5
thermal expansion 140
workability measurements
Bingham constants 118
compacting factor test 120–1
single point tests 119–22
slump tests 120–1
two point tests 118–19
Vebe test 120–1
Condensed silica fume (csf) 109
Condon–Morse curves 26, 37
Conductivity 44–6
Copper alloys
brasses 83
bronzes 83
Corrosion
carbonation-induced 189–90
chloride-induced 190–2
control 73
dry oxidation 70
steel in concrete 187–9
wet corrosion 70
cells 72–3
electromotive series 71–2
Corrosion protection
cathodic protection 75
design factors 73–4
isolation 74–5
Covalent bonding 19–21
$8-N$ rule 20
Creep 29
Creep in concrete 147–8
factors influencing 148–50
mechanisms 150–2
delayed elastic strain 152
microcracking 151–2
moisture diffusion 150–1
structural adjustment 151
prediction of 152–3
Creep in masonry 302–4
Creep in timber 477
creep parameters 485–7
environmental effects on rate of creep 490–3
mathematical expressions of creep 488–9
principle of superposition 487–8
reversible and irreversible components of creep 489–90
Creep rupture 448
Critical fibre volume 366
Critical point 7
Crystal structure
close-packed 22, 55
face-centred cubic (fcc) 55
hexagonal close-packed (hcp) 55
CSF, *see* Condensed silica fume

Darcy's law 171, 172, 467
Defects
dislocation 62
hot shortness 77
line 63
Dendrite 53, 54
Density 9
Design, for minimum weight 83–4
Diffusion 5–6
Fick's first law 6
Diffusivity 171
concrete 175–6
Dislocation 62
Dislocation energy 63
Dispersion hardening 64
Drift velocity 44
Drying shrinkage
capillary tension 132–3
concrete
effect of aggregate 134–6
effect of cement type 137
effect of geometry 136–7
hardened cement paste 129–32
mechanisms of shrinkage and swelling 132
capillary tension 132–3
disjoining pressure 133
movement of interlayer water 133–4
surface tension or energy 133
prediction of shrinkage 137
surface tension or energy 133
Ductility 60–1
Dynamic viscosity, coefficient 5
Durability
fibre-cement composites 392–5
masonry 306–14
polymer composites 352–5
timber 461–71
Duralumin (dural) 82

Earlywood 410, 416
Einstein's equation 31
Elastic constants 8–9, 300
bulk modulus 9
dynamic modulus 145
Poisson's ratio 10, 147, 300
shear modulus 9
static modulus 145
tangent modulus 145
Young's modulus 9, 300
Elasticity
of brickwork 300–2
of concrete 145–7
of hardened cement paste 140–2
linear 25–8
long-range 27–8
of polymer composites 333–9
of timber 439–40
Elastic limit 59
Elastic modulus, *see* Modulus of elasticity
Elastic properties of polymer composites
continuous unidirectional laminae
longitudinal stiffness 333–4
transverse stiffness 334
in-plane long-fibre laminae 334
laminate theory
isotropic lamina 337–8
orthotropic lamina 338–9
short-fibre composite 336–7
Elastic properties of timber 439–40
creep 485–93
elastic deformation 477–9
factors influencing elastic modulus 481–4
orthotropic elasticity 479–81
viscoelastic deformation 484–5
Elastic resilience 9–10
Electrical conductivity 44
Electromotive series 71–2
standard electromotive potentials 71
Electron 17
Energy
activation energy 14
conservation 15
dislocation 63
entropy 15–16
free energy 16
internal energy 14
mixing 14–15
stored energy 9–10
surface energy 33–4
Entropy 15–16
configurational 28
Equilibrium moisture content 435
Ettringite 94, 95
Extraction metallurgy 51
Extractives 409, 418, 425

Ferritic stainless steel 81
Fibreboard 501
Fibre composites 317–20
polymers and polymer composites
durability and design 352–5
end use 356–9
manufacturing techniques for polymer composite materials 345–51
polymer and fibre properties and manufacture 322–31
polymer composites 332–44
Fibre-reinforced cements and concretes 360–403
durability
asbestos cement 392
glass-fibre-reinforced cement 392–3
natural-fibre-reinforced concrete 394
polymer-fibre-reinforced cement and concrete 393–4
steel-fibre concrete 394
fibre-reinforced concrete
glass-reinforced concrete 391
polymer-fibre-reinforced concrete 388–91
steel-fibre concrete 388
fibres and matrices, properties 361–2
fibre–matrix interface 362–4
fibres in a cement matrix
asbestos cement 379–80
glass-reinforced cement 380–1
natural fibres 385–7
polyethylene 385
polymer fibre-reinforced cement 381
polypropylene 383
polyvinyl alcohol fibres 384–5
manufacture and uses
asbestos cement 396–8
glass-reinforced cement 398
natural-fibre-reinforced cement 400
polymer-fibre-reinforced cement and concrete 399–400
steel-fibre concrete 400–3
structure and post-cracking composite theory
fibre reinforcement in flexure 375–8
theoretical stress–strain curves in uniaxial tension

Fibre-reinforced cements *cont'd.* 365–73
uniaxial tension–fracture mechanics approach 373–5
Fibres 323
carbon 324–5
glass 324
Kevlar 325
other synthetic fibres 325
properties 329–31
Fibre saturation point 433
Fick's law 6, 171
Fiddleback 428
Figure, timber
grain 427–8
growth rings 428
knots 428–9
rays 428
Finishes, timber 506–8
Fire resistance
concrete 186–7
masonry 314
Flame retardants 504
Flow constants, measurement for cement paste and concrete
diffusivity 175–6
permeability 172–5
sorptivity 176–9
Fluids 5–8
diffusion 5–6
Fracture
Griffith criterion 40–2
microcrack theory 39–40
theoretical strength 39
Fracture mechanics 42–3
Fracture strength 59
Fracture toughness 42, 43
Free energy 16
Fresh properties of concrete
general behaviour 117–18
workability measurements 118–22
Frost damage, concrete 184–6
Fully plastic moment 66

Gases 5
perfect gas law 6
P-V-T curves 7
van der Waals equation 7
Gels 11–13
pores 97
thixotropy 12–13
GGBS, *see* Ground granulated blast furnace slag
Gibbs free energy 16
Glasses 11
Glass mat reinforced thermoplastic composite (GMT) 350
Glass-reinforced cement (GRC) 380, 392
manufacture 398
uses 398
Glass-reinforced plastic (GRP) 345
GMT, *see* Glass mat reinforced thermoplastic composite
Grain boundaries 63
Grain structure 53
Grain, timber 427–8, 494
GRC, *see* Glass-reinforced cement
Griffith criterion 40–2
Growth rings (annual rings) 410, 415, 428
Ground granulated blast furnace slag (ggbs) 109
GRP, *see* Glass-reinforced plastic
Gunmetal 83
Gypsum 94–5

Hardened cement paste (hcp) 95
drying shrinkage 101–3, 129
elasticity 140–2
hydration 98–101
strength 97–101
structure 96–7
thermal expansion 139–40
water in 101–3
Hardwood 410, 470
HCP, *see* Hardened cement paste
Heartwood 409–10
Helmholtz free energy 16, 25
Hemicelluloses 418, 421, 422
High carbon steels 78
Hookean solid 29, 30
Hooke's law 8, 26, 27
Hot shortness 77
Hot working of metals 67
Hydrated cement paste 98–9
strength 100–1
water in 101–3
Hydration 91, 93–7
degree of 96
heat of 125–8

Inert gas 17
Initial Surface Absorption Test (ISAT) 178
Intermediate compound 58
Internal energy 14
Ion 17
Ionic bonding 17–19
Iron 51–2
cast irons 76–7
extraction 76
pig 76
ISAT, *see* Initial Surface Absorption Test
Izod test 77

Joining metals
brazing and soldering 69
pinning 69
welding 69

Kelvin model, *see* Voigt model
Kelvin's equation 132
Kevlar 323, 325, 330, 331

Laminated timber 501
Latewood 410, 416
Latex additives to cement 261
Lignin 418, 421, 422
Limit of proportionality 59, 478
Line defect 63
Liquids, Newtonian 5, 6
Low carbon steels 78

Macadams 199–201, 241–4
Maltenes 204–5
Marshall test 246–7
Marshall quotient 246
Martensite 80, 81
Martensitic stainless steel 81
Masonry 253
Masonry construction and forms
appearance 286–8
bond 283–4, 286
joint style 285
mortar 280
specials 284–5
walls and other masonry forms 281–3
workmanship and accuracy 285
Masonry, durability
chemical attack 307–9
acids 309
carbonation 307–8
chlorides 309
corrosion of buried metals 309
sulphate attack 308–9
water and acid rain 307
erosion 309–11
abrasion 311
crypto-efflorescence damage 311

efflorescence 311
frost 309–11
fire resistance 314
mechanisms of attack 306–7
rain resistance 312–14
sound transmission 314
thermal conductivity 311–12
Masonry materials
calcium silicate units 274
concrete units 274
production processes 275–6
products 276–8
fired clay bricks and blocks 266–7
forming and firing 267–71
properties 271–4
manufacture of units and mortars
aggregates 259–60
binders 260–1
clays 259
sands and fillers 257–9
mortar 263
properties of hardened mortar 264–6
properties of unset mortar 264
other constituents and additives 261–3
accelerators 262–3
latex additives 261
organic plasticizers 261
pigments 261–2
retarders 262
Masonry, structural behaviour 289–90
compressive loading 290–2
cavity walls in compression 295–6
concentrated load 294–5
stability, slender structures 292–3
elastic modulus 300–2
flexure (bending) 298–9
movement and creep 302–5
shear load in bed plane 296–8
tension 299
Masonry terminology
components 254
general 256
size and dimensions 255
Maturity, concrete 125
Maxwell model 29–30
Mechanical metallurgy 52
castings 67
cold working 67
hot working 67
joining 68
Medium carbon steels 78
Metallic bonding 21–2
Metallography 53
Metallurgy
extraction 51
mechanical 52
castings 67
cold working 67
hot working 67
joining 68
physical 52
atomic structure of metals 53–7
grain structure 53
solutions and compounds 58
Metals and alloys 49–85
aluminium 81–3
atomic structure of metals 53–8
copper 83
brasses 83
corrosion
electromotive series 71–2
cells 72–3
wet 70
crystal structure 54–7
free-electron theory 21–2
grain structure 53
iron 76
cast iron 76–7
extraction 76
steel 77–81
mechanical metallurgy
castings 67
cold working 67
hot working 67
joining 68
mechanical properties
dislocation energy 63
ductility 60–1
plasticity 62–3
strengthening 63–6
stress–strain behaviour 59
tensile strength 60
metal forming 68
oxidation
dry 70
wet 70
physical metallurgy
atomic structure of metals 53–7
grain structure 53
solutions and compounds 58
Microcrack theory 39–40
Griffith criterion 40
Mild steels 78
Modulus of elasticity
brickwork 300–2
concrete 145–7
timber 438–40, 478, 481–4
Modulus of rigidity 479
Modulus of rupture, timber 438–9
Moisture in timber 431–5
Molecular solids 11
Mortar 263, 280
additives
accelerators 262
latex 261
organic plasticizers 261
pigments 261–2
retarders 262
materials used in manufacture
sand 257–9
properties of hardened mortar 264–6
properties of unset mortar 264
Moulding of thermosetting polymer composites
closed-mould processes
matched die 348–9
pultrusion and modified pull-winding 349–50
open-mould processes (contact moulding)
filament winding 348
hand-lay technique 345–6
pressure bag techniques 347–8
spray-up techniques 347

Natural-fibre-reinforced cement
durability 394
manufacture and uses 400
Newtonian liquid 5, 6, 29, 31
stress and strain in 5, 6
Normal distribution xxi
Nylon 322

Octet 17
Ohm's law 44
OPC (ordinary Portland cement), *see* Portland cement
Oriented strand board (OSB) 498, 499
Orthotropic elasticity
timber 479–80
OSB, *see* Oriented strand board
Oxidation
dry 70
wet 70

PAN, *see* Polyacrylonitrile
Parenchyma 414
Pearlite 57, 78
PEEK, *see* Polyetheretherketone
PEG, *see* Polyethylene glycol
Penetration index (PI) 215–17, 218
Perfect gas law 6
Permanent deformation, bitumen
  determination 219–20
  factors affecting 220–2
Permeability 170
  coefficient of 171
  measurement for concrete 172
PES, *see* Polyethersulphone
PF, *see* Phenol formaldehyde
Pfa, *see* Pulverized fuel ash
Phase 58
Phases, cement 92
Phenol formaldehyde (PF) 319
Physical metallurgy 52
  atomic structure of metals 53–7
  grain structure 53
  solutions and compounds 58
PI, *see* Penetration index
Pig iron 76
Pinning metals 69
Plastic design 66
Plasticity 62–3
  fully plastic moment 66
  plastic collapse 66
Plasticizers, cement
  dispersing action 104–5
  in mortar 261
  organic 261
  types 104
Plywood 497–9
Poisson's ratio 10, 147, 300, 479
Polyacrylonitrile (PAN) 324, 362
Polycarbonate 322
Polyetheretherketone (PEEK) 322, 350
Polyethylene glycol (PEG) 505
Polyethersulphone (PES) 322, 350
Polyethylene 27, 394
Polymer composites
  characterization 332
  design with composites 355
  durability 393–4
    fire 352–3
    moisture 353–4
    solution and solvent action 354
    temperature 352
    weather 354–6
  elastic properties of continuous unidirectional laminae 333–4
  elastic properties of in-plane random long-fibre laminae 334
  elastic properties of short-fibre composite materials 336–7
  isotropic lamina 337–8
  laminate theory 337
  macro-analysis of stress distribution in a fibre matrix composite 334–6
  manufacturing techniques
    thermoplastic composites 350–1
    thermosetting composites 345–50
  orthotropic lamina 338–9
  strength characteristics and failure criteria of composite laminae 339–44
    strength theories for isotropic laminae 340–2
    strength theories of orthotropic laminae 342–4
  stress distribution in fibre matrix composite 334–6, 337–9
  structure and post-cracking composite theory 365–78
  uses of polymer composites
    aircraft and space 358
    automobile and truck 358
    construction 356, 358–9
    marine 357–8
    pipes and tanks 358
    soil environment 357
Polymer-fibre-reinforced cement and concrete
  durability 393–4
  manufacture 399
  uses 399–400
Polymers
  mechanical properties of polymers 326–7
    fibre properties 329–31
    time-dependent characteristics 327–9
  processing of thermoplastic polymers 325–6
    blow-moulded hollow plastic articles 326
    co-extrusion 326
    film-blown plastic sheet 326
    highly orientated grid sheets 326
    profile production 326
  types of polymer
    elastomers 323
    foamed 323
    thermoplastic 322, 327
    thermosetting 323, 327
Polymer fibres 323
  carbon 324–5
  glass 324
  Kevlar 325
  other synthetic fibres 325
  properties 329–31
Polymorphism 56–7
Polypropylene 322, 383, 385, 394
Polystyrene 319
Polythene 319
Polyvinyl alcohol (PVA) 384
Polyvinyl chloride (PVC) 319, 362
Porosity, in cement 101, 107
Portland cements 90, 91
  composition 92–3
  drying shrinkage 101–3
  hydration 93–6
  manufacture 91–2
  strength of hardened cement paste 97–101
  structure of hardened cement paste 96–7
  types 103
  water in hcp 101–3
Pozzolans 89
Pozzolanic behaviour 108–9, 190
Preservatives, timber 503–4
Proton 17
Pulverized fuel ash (pfa) 109, 258
PVA, *see* Polyvinyl alcohol
PVC, *see* Polyvinyl chloride

Quicklime 260–1

Rain resistance, masonry 312–14
Recovery 64
Recrystallization 64
Relaxation
  spectrum 30
  time 29–30
Resistivity 45
Retarders, cement 106–7
Roman cement 89–90
Rupture, modulus of 159

Sample standard deviation 439
Sapwood 409, 410

Saturation vapour pressure 7
Self-desiccation 100
Shrinkage
  concrete 123
  wood 472–4
Single point tests 119–22
Slump test of workability 120–1
Softwood 410, 468
Soldering 69
Solids
  amorphous 11
  crystalline 11
  elastic constants 8–9
  gels 11–13
  molecular solids 11
  stored energy 9–10
Solid solutions 58
Sorption 435
Sorptivity 171
  initial surface absorption test 178
  measurement for concrete 176–9
Sound transmission, masonry 314
Spalling 188, 189
Specific gravity, timber 430–1
Specific stiffness 9
Standard electromotive potentials 71
States of matter
  fluids 5–8
  gases 5
  intermediate behaviour 11–13
  solids 8–11
Static fatigue 448
Steel 77
  durability in concrete 187–92
  heat treated 79
  mechanical properties 79
  stainless 81
  structural 78
  terminology 78
Steel-fibre concrete
  durability 394–5
  manufacture 400–1
  uses 402–3
Stiffness xxii, 219, 300
  modulus, bitumen 218
Strain 8
Strain energy 9
Strain hardening 59, 63
Strength xxii
  tensile 42
  theoretical 39
Strength and failure in timber 437–60
Strength characteristics of polymer composites 339–40
  isotropic laminae
    maximum principal strain theory 341
    maximum principal stress theory 340
    total strain energy theory 341
  orthotropic laminae
    maximum strain theory 343
    maximum stress theory 342–3
    Tsai–Hill energy theory 343–4
Strengthening of metals 63–6
  dispersion hardening 64–6
  grain boundaries 63
  strain hardening 63–4
Strength of concrete, *see* Concrete
Stress 8–9
Stress intensity factor 43
Stress relaxation 29
Stress–strain behaviour
  concrete 140–7
    elastic modulus of concrete 145–7
    models for concrete behaviour 142–4
    observed behaviour of concrete 144–5
  polymer composites 334–6, 365–78
  metals 59, 65
Stress–strain curves
  aggregates 144
  asbestos cement 381
  cellulose reinforced cement 386
  cement paste 144
  concrete 144
  elastic–plastic solid 65
  fibre-reinforced cement and concrete 356–73
  glass-reinforced cement 382, 393
  polypropylene reinforced cement 385
Substitutional solid solution 58
Surfaces
  adhesives 35–7
  adsorption 37–8
  energy 33–34
  water of crystallization 34
  wetting 34–5
Surface tension 33, 36, 133
Tar 199
Tensile strength 42, 60
  wood 439, 450–4
Tension wood 426, 446
Thermal capacity 45, 46
Thermal conductivity 44–6
  masonry 311–2
  timber 471
Thermal expansion
  cement paste 139–40
  concrete 140
  timber 476
Thermodynamics
  entropy 15–16
  equation of state 25
  first law 3, 15, 25
  free energy 16
  second law 3, 16, 25
Thermoplastic polymer 12
Thermosetting polymer 12
Thixotropy 12–13
Timber 407–8
  appearance in relation to structure
    colour 429
    figure 427
    texture 427
  chemical processing 502
    artificial preservatives 503
    chemical pulping 505–6
    dimensional stabilizers 504–5
    flame retardants 504
    impregnation 502
    other chemical processes 506
  deformation
    deformation under stress 476–93
    dimensional change due to moisture 472–5
    movement 472, 475
    shrinkage 472–4
    thermal movement 475–6
  durability
    fire performance 464–6
    fungal decay 463–4
    insect attack 464
    marine borers 464
    natural durability 462–3
    physical, chemical and biological agencies 461–2
  elastic deformation 476–9
    elastic modulus 438–40, 478, 481–4
    factors influencing elastic modulus 481–4

Timber *cont'd.*
orthotropic elasticity 479–80
finishes 506–8
flow in timber 466–7
flow paths in timber 468–70
fluid flow through cell cavities (permeability) 467–8
moisture diffusion 470–1
grading of timber
mechanical grading 459–60
visual grading 457–9
mass–volume relationships
density 429–30
density of dry cell wall 431
specific gravity 430–1
mechanical processing, solid timber
bending 495–6
sawing and planing 494–5
mechanical processing, board materials 496
chipboard, OSB and cement-bonded particleboard 499–501
fibreboard 501
laminated timber 501
plywood 497–9
pulping 502
mechanical properties 438–9
moisture in timber 431–3
equilibrium moisture content 435
fibre saturation point 433–4
sorption and diffusion 435
shrinkage 472
anisotropy in shrinkage 472–4
volumetric shrinkage 474
strength and failure 437, 497
hardness and compression 440
interrelationships between strength properties 439–40
sample size 437–9
strength values 439
variability in strength values 439
strength, factors affecting
anisotropy and grain angle 440–2
cell length 444–5
chemical composition 445
density 443–4
duration of load 448
knots 442–3
microfibrillar angle 445
moisture content 446
rate of loading 447–8
ratio of latewood to earlywood 444
reaction wood 446
ring width 444
temperature 446
strength, failure and fracture morphology 449
compression strength parallel to grain 453
engineering approach to strength and fracture 456–7
static bending 454–5
tensile strength parallel to grain 450–3
toughness 455–6
structure
cell wall as fibre composite 421–2
cell wall layers 423–5
chemical constituents 417–21
macroscopic level 409–10
microscopic level 410–17
variability in structure 425–6
thermal conductivity 471
viscoelastic deformation 484
creep 477, 485–7
environmental effects of rate of creep 490–3
mathematical expressions of creep 488–9
principle of superposition 487–8
reversible and irreversible components of creep 489–90
working (grade) stresses 457
grading of timber 457–60
Toughness 42
cement composites 372–3
wood 455–6
Tracheids 413
Tsai–Hill energy theory 343–4
Two point tests 118–19

Ultimate tensile strength 60, 366

Valency 17
Van der Waals bonds 22–4, 37
Van der Waals equation 7
isothermals 7
Vapour–liquid transition 6–8
Vapour pressure 7
Variability xxi
Vebe test 120–1
Vegetable fibres in cement 387
Viscosity 5
bituminous materials 212–8, 220
coefficient of 214
dynamic viscosity 214
Viscoelasticity 28
Maxwell model 29–30
Voigt model 29–30
Voigt model 29–30

Water of crystallization 34
Water reducers, *see* Plasticizers
Welding 69
Wiedemann–Franz ratio 45
Wood fibres in cement 385–7
Work hardening 59
Workability 117
Workability aids, *see* Plasticizers
Workability measurements
Bingham constants 118
compacting factor test 120–1
single point tests 119–22
slump tests 120–1
two point tests 118–19
Vebe test 120–1
Wrought iron 52

Yield point 59
Yield strength 59
Yield stress 59
Young's modulus 9, 300–1, 478